Iustitia Dei
A History of the Christian Doctrine of Justification

D0840415

The Christian doctrine of justification is of immense interest to historians and theologians, and continues to be of major importance in modern ecumenical discussions. The present work appeared in its first edition in 1986, and rapidly became the leading reference work on the subject. Its many acclaimed features include a detailed assessment of the semantic background of the concept in the ancient Near East, a thorough examination of the doctrine of the medieval period, and an especially careful analysis of its development during the critical years of the sixteenth century. The third edition thoroughly updates the work, adding new material where necessary, and responding to the latest developments in scholarly literature. It will be an essential resource for all concerned with the development of Christian doctrine, the history of the Reformation debates on the identity of Christianity, and modern discussions between Protestants and Roman Catholics over the nature of salvation.

ALISTER E. MCGRATH is Professor of Historical Theology at the University of Oxford. His major academic works include *The Genesis of Doctrine* (1990) and *The Intellectual Origins of the Reformation* (1987). He is also editor of the *Blackwell Encyclopedia of Modern Christian Thought* (1995) and the author of a number of acclaimed student textbooks including *Christian Theology: An Introduction*, 3rd edition (2001).

Iustitia Dei

A History of the Christian Doctrine of Justification

Third Edition

Alister E. McGrath

CAMBRIDGE
UNIVERSITY PRESS

CAMBRIDGE UNIVERSITY PRESS
Cambridge, New York, Melbourne, Madrid, Cape Town, Singapore, São Paulo

Cambridge University Press
The Edinburgh Building, Cambridge CB2 2RU, UK

Published in the United States of America by Cambridge University Press, New York

www.cambridge.org
Information on this title: www.cambridge.org/9780521826488

First published in two volumes in 1986

Volume I
First paperback edition 1989
Reprinted 1993, 1997

Volume II
Reprinted 1991
First paperback edition 1993
Reprinted 1994, 1996

Second edition in one volume 1998, 2002
Third edition in one volume 2005

Printed in the United Kingdom at the University Press, Cambridge

A catalogue record for this book is available from the British Library

ISBN 13 978 0 521 82648 8 hardback
ISBN 10 0 521 82648 9 hardback
ISBN 13 978 0 521 53389 8 paperback
ISBN 10 978 0 521 53389 9 paperback

Contents

Preface

The present study is an extended exploration of the manner in which the western church developed the Pauline concept of 'justification' throughout two thousand years of reflection and debate, culminating in the sixteenth-century Protestant declaration that the doctrine of justification was 'the article by which the church stands or falls (*articulus stantis et cadentis ecclesiae*).[1] It reflects my own interest in a number of areas of scholarship, especially the intellectual origins of the European Reformation of the sixteenth century, and the nature of doctrinal development within the Christian tradition. It is both a celebration and a criticism of the pioneering work of Albrecht Benjamin Ritschl, *Die christliche Lehre von der Rechtfertigung und Versöhnung* (1870). Despite its many weaknesses, this earlier work remains a landmark of scholarship in the field.

Three reasons may be given for exploring the history of the doctrine of justification within the Christian tradition at such length. First, the historical study of the development of any Christian doctrine from its origins to the present day is inherently significant, in that it offers a means of identifying and evaluating the factors which have influenced the development of doctrine in general. The development of the doctrine of justification is thus a paradigm for the study of ideological interaction in the development of doctrine, illustrating how theological and secular concepts were related as theologians responded to the cultural situation of their period.

---

[1] For the sense and origins of this celebrated phrase, see F. Loofs, 'Der articulus stantis et cadentis ecclesiae'. It is necessary to challenge Loofs upon several points, particularly his suggestion that the phrase is first used in the eighteenth century by the Lutheran theologian Valentin Löscher in his famous anti-Pietist diatribe *Vollständiger Timotheus Verinus oder Darlegung der Wahrheit und des Friedens in denen bisherigen Pietistischen Streitigkeiten* (1718–21), and is restricted to the Lutheran constituency within Protestantism. This is clearly incorrect. The *Reformed* theologian Johann Heinrich Alsted uses the phrase a century earlier, opening his discussion of the justification of humanity *coram Deo* as follows: 'articulus iustificationis dicitur articulus stantis et cadentis ecclesiae' (*Theologia scholastica didacta* (Hanover, 1618), 711). Precursors of the phrase may, of course, be found in the writings of Luther himself – e.g., WA 40/3.352.3: 'quia isto articulo stante stat Ecclesia, ruente ruit Ecclesia'. For more recent reflection, see Schwarz, 'Luthers Rechtfertigungslehre als Eckstein der christlichen Theologie und Kirche'.

The study is also of intrinsic interest to systematic theology. It could be argued that the theological situation today demands at least a *restatement*, and quite possibly also a *reinstatement*, of the Christian doctrine of reconciliation.[2] The essential prerequisite of any attempt to interpret, reinterpret or restate that doctrine is a due appreciation of the historical origins and subsequent development of the concept. It is clearly somewhat pointless to attempt to develop or defend theories of justification, reconciliation or atonement which can be shown to rest upon some misunderstanding of a Hebrew root, which represent a recent distortion of an older and more considered doctrine, or which represent a conditioned response to a specific cultural situation that no longer pertains today (a theme which I explored in my 1990 Bampton Lectures at Oxford University).[3]

Justification is one of several concepts that have been used within Scripture and the Christian tradition to articulate the reconciliation effected by God with the world through Christ. As will become clear, at certain points during the development of Christian theology – especially during the sixteenth century – this concept came to assume a particularly significant role. At others, however, the concept plays a much less prominent part in theological reflection on the foundations of salvation, or on the shape of the Christian life. The present study is offered as a resource to stimulate and inform this theological reflection on the ongoing place of the concept of justification in the church's self-understanding of its identity and mission.

In the third place, the study may serve as a resource for the dialogue between Christians of different traditions, most notably those whose present identities have been shaped decisively by the European Reformation of the sixteenth century. The doctrine came to assume a major, possibly pivotal, role at that time, with debates over the issue contributing significantly to the emergence of divisions within western Christianity. As pressure grows for Christians to attempt to settle their differences (or at least to understand one another better), an informed understanding of the sixteenth-century debates over the doctrine of justification clearly has

[2] This was certainly Ritschl's intention in undertaking his massive historical analysis of the concept: see M. Werner, *Der protestantische Weg des Glaubens*, Bern: Haupt, 1955, 799–815. Few have chosen to follow his lead subsequently, however, with the notable exception of Martin Kähler's important essay *Zur Lehre von der Versöhnung* (1898); see Schäfer, 'Die Rechtfertigungslehre bei Ritschl und Kähler'. In recent times, the Lutheran theologian Robert Jenson (b. 1930) has made some intriguing suggestions for the systematic role of the doctrine; see Jenson, 'Justification as a Triune Event'; idem, 'Rechtfertigung und Ekklesiologie.' However, his recent *Systematic Theology* (2 vols., New York: Oxford University Press, 1997–9) does not develop these suggestions to the extent that might have been anticipated.
[3] A. E. McGrath, *The Genesis of Doctrine*, Oxford: Blackwell, 1990.

a major role to play. It is no accident that discussions over this doctrine have played a major role in ecumenical dialogues since about 1980.

The origin of the research contained in this volume goes back to the earliest stage of my period as a theologian, when I studied for the Final Honour School of Theology at Oxford University (1976–8). I chose to specialise in scholastic theology, and was introduced to the ideas of leading representatives of this period, from Peter Lombard to Gabriel Biel. A period spent researching at the University of Cambridge allowed me to develop these interests further. I chose to focus on the theological development of Martin Luther, seen against his late medieval background. This work was published in 1985 as *Luther's Theology of the Cross: Martin Luther's Theological Breakthrough*.

As is so often the case, the initial research project proved to be a launching pad for others. At one level, it led me to take an interest in the theological methodology of the Reformation period, and to trace back its antecedents into the late medieval and Renaissance periods. This work was published in 1987 as *The Intellectual Origins of the European Reformation*, and revised in 2003 in the light of important scholarly advances in the field. Although my research interests moved on to areas more properly understood as systematic, rather than historical, theology, I nevertheless kept up my reading in the field, noting new developments which suggested that revision and expansion of my original approach were required. In 2003, I published a second edition of this work, in the light of ongoing work in the field which necessitated expansion, and occasionally revision, of my original conclusions.

The second area in which my original research developed was to consider the development of the doctrine of justification throughout the entire period of theological history. Having researched the origins of Luther's doctrine of justification in its late medieval context, it was entirely reasonable to extend this to embrace the western theological tradition as a whole.

At that time, the only serious attempt to document this development was Ritschl's *Die christliche Lehre von der Rechtfertigung und Versöhnung* (1870). The value of that work was rather reduced by the moralist assumptions Ritschl brought to his task, and by his decision to limit his analysis from the eleventh to the nineteenth century, focussing particularly on German-language Protestant contributions to the discussion. The vast scholarly undertakings which have given the modern period the magnificent critical editions denied to Ritschl (such as the Weimar Luther edition) have also cast new light on the theology of the medieval period, calling into question many of Ritschl's conclusions. One of the more troubling aspects of my investigation was the realisation that most of Ritschl's conclusions, particularly his very unsatisfactory account of Luther's theological formation, could no longer be sustained. *Iustitia Dei* was published in two volumes in 1986, and rapidly established itself as a benchmark for discussion of the doctrine, especially in the ecumenical dialogues of that era. In 1998, it was reissued in a new format, merging the two original volumes without revisions, and adding some new material relating to some developments in the twentieth century. Although designated a 'second edition', its new format did not allow for a detailed revision of the work. By this stage, it was, however, clear that such a review was needed.

This third edition represents a complete revision of the original work in the light of scholarly developments since the publication of the first edition in 1986. The new edition is based on a complete reappraisal of every aspect of the first edition, including its structure and format, as well as the positions I defended at that stage. My continuing engagement with both primary and secondary sources convinced me of the need to rewrite the work, retaining what was clearly sound and reliable, and correcting or modifying whatever was open to justified criticism. At points, I have had to make inevitable adjudications concerning intensely contested issues in the scholarly literature relating to the development of the doctrine, and have done so on the basis of the best evidence currently available.

The most obvious changes have to do with the presentation of the material. In response to many requests, I now cite primary sources in English translation (although retaining key phrases in the original languages where these are appropriate). I have introduced a substantial new section early in the work, exploring aspects of Paul's views on justification, noting especially the issues which would dominate subsequent theological debate.

The first edition made use of many scholarly studies published in the first half of the twentieth century, which often made landmark contributions to scholarship in the field. As time has passed, other studies have appeared, confirming some aspects of their work, and revising others. I have made every effort to base this new edition of the work on the best recent scholarship. However, it is still an uncomfortable fact that some of the most reliable and original scholarship on certain key matters dates from a previous generation. For this reason, certain older works continue to feature in the notes and scholarly apparatus, despite the appearance of more recent studies.

Those hoping for a definitive pronouncement on what the word 'justification' means will be disappointed. This is a work of historical analysis, not of theological prescription. It does not attempt to define the concept of justification, but sets out to offer an account of the various ways in

which the western theological tradition has understood the notion, both
as a resource and as a challenge to those who wish to provide such a
definition. It is a resource, in that it provides a detailed account of how
this notion has been conceived over two thousand years of theological
reflection. Yet it is also a challenge, in that the failure of that tradition of
reflection to agree on the meaning of the term must raise certain awkward
questions for those who believe that such a definition may be offered. The
evidence offered in this volume suggests that such definitions are dependent on certain implicit semantic, metaphysical and juristic assumptions
which were questioned, criticised, replaced, and occasionally retrieved,
as the development of Christian theology proceeded.

Finally, I must thank all those who have made this new edition possible, especially those who have read and commented on earlier versions
of the work. In particular, I wish to thank M. D. Chenu OP, Fergus
Kerr OP, Oliver O'Donovan, Cassian Reel OFMCap, E. G. Rupp, Beryl
Smalley, Peter Southwell, N. T. Wright, E. J Yarnold SJ, and Adolar
Zumkeller OESA, for their comments and suggestions over many years.
I owe particular thanks to Cambridge University Press for being all that
a good publisher should be, and to Elizabeth McGrath for her editorial
assistance. As always, I take full responsibility for any errors of fact or
judgement that remain.

Oxford, July 2004   ALISTER McGRATH

Abbreviations

Bibliographical abbreviations follow the guidelines provided by S. Schwertner, *Internationales Abkurzungsverzeichnis für Theologie und Grenzgebiete*, Berlin: de Gruyter, 1974.

ARG	*Archiv für Reformationsgeschichte*
AnAug	*Analecta Augustiniana*
AthA	*Année théologique augustinienne*
Augustinus	*Augustinus: Revista tremestral publicada por los Padres Agustinos Recoletos*
BHR	*Bibliothèque d'humanisme et Renaissance*
BIOSCS	*Bulletin of the International Organization for Septuagint and Cognate Studies*
BJRL	*Bulletin of the John Rylands Library*
BSLK	*Bekenntnisschriften der evangelisch-lutherischen Kirche*
BSRK	*Bekenntnisschriften der reformierten Kirche*
CBQ	*Catholic Biblical Quarterly*
CChr	Corpus Christianorum Series Latina
CFr	*Collectanea Franciscana*
ChH	*Church History*
CR	Corpus Reformatorum
CSEL	Corpus Scriptorum Ecclesiasticorum Latinorum
CT	Concilium Tridentinum: diariorum, actorum, epistolarum, tractatuum nova collectio
D	*Enchiridion Symbolorum Definitionum et Declarationum de Rebus Fidei et Morum*
DR	*Downside Review*
DThC	*Dictionnaire de théologie catholique*
EE	*Estudios eclesiásticos*
EETS	Early English Text Society
EThL	*Ephemerides Theologicae Lovanienses*
EvTh	*Evangelische Theologie*
FS	*Franziskanische Studien*

FrS	*Franciscan Studies*
HThR	*Harvard Theological Review*
JBL	*Journal of Biblical Literature*
JEH	*Journal of Ecclesiastical History*
JHI	*Journal of the History of Ideas*
JSNT	*Journal for the Study of the New Testament*
JThS	*Journal of Theological Studies*
KuD	*Kerygma und Dogma*
MF	*Miscellanea Franciscana*
MGH.Ep	*Monumenta Germaniae historica: Epistolae*
MGH.SRG	*Monumenta Germaniae historica: Scriptores rerum Germanicarum*
MoTh	*Modern Theology*
NRTh	*Nouvelle revue théologique*
NTS	*New Testament Studies*
NZSTh	*Neue Zeitschrift für Systematische Theologie*
OS	*Calvini opera selecta*
PG	Patrologiae cursus completus, Series Graeca
PL	Patrologiae cursus completus, Series Latina
REAug	*Revue des études augustiniennes*
RechAug	*Recherches augustiniennes*
RelSt	*Religious Studies*
RET	*Revista española de teología*
RMAL	*Revue du moyen âge latin*
RSPhTh	*Revue des sciences philosophiques et théologiques*
RSR	*Revue des sciences religieuses*
RThom	*Revue thomiste*
RThAM	*Recherches de théologie ancienne et médiévale*
SCJ	*Sixteenth Century Journal*
SJTh	*Scottish Journal of Theology*
StA	*Melanchthons Werke in Auswahl: Studienausgabe*
StB	*Studia Biblica*
StTh	*Studia Theologica*
ThLZ	*Theologische Literaturzeitung*
ThPh	*Theologie und Philosophie*
ThQ	*Theologische Quartalschrift*
ThRev	*Theological Review*
ThStKr	*Theologische Studien und Kritiken*
ThZ	*Theologische Zeitschrift*
VCaro	*Verbum Caro*
VT	*Vetus Testamentum*
VyV	*Verdad y Vida*

WA	D. Martin Luthers Werke: Kritische Gesamtausgabe
ZAW	*Zeitschrift für die alttestamentliche Wissenschaft*
ZKG	*Zeitschrift für Kirchengeschichte*
ZKTh	*Zeitschrift für katholische Theologie*
ZNW	*Zeitschrift für die neutestamentliche Wissenschaft*
ZSTh	*Zeitschrift für Systematische Theologie*
ZThK	*Zeitschrift für Theologie und Kirche*

1 Justification: the emergence of a concept

The Protestant Reformation of the sixteenth century brought about many significant changes within the life and thought of the western churches. This volume concerns one of those – the reconceptualisation and reformulation of the traditional Christian vocabulary of salvation using the Pauline image of justification.[1] Up to this point, the western theological tradition had chosen to develop its thinking about how humanity is reconciled to God in terms of 'salvation by grace' (Ephesians 2:8). One of the defining characteristics of the Protestant Reformation is a decisive shift, in both the conceptualities and the vocabulary, of the Christian theological tradition. For a relatively short yet theologically significant period, the reconciliation of humanity would be discussed within the entire western theological tradition primarily in terms of 'justification by faith' (Romans 5:1).

As the Reformation and its attendant authority figures slowly receded into the past, the difficulties associated with this way of speaking became increasingly apparent. From the late nineteenth century onwards, growing doubts were expressed as to whether the New Testament, including the Pauline epistles, placed anything even approaching such an emphasis upon the concept of justification.[2] Influential New Testament scholars such as William Wrede and Albert Schweitzer argued that the origins of the concept were polemical, relating to the early tensions between Christianity and Judaism.[3] Wrede insisted that the heart of Paul's thought lay in the concept of redemption.[4] For Schweitzer, the real focus of Paul's positive thought lay elsewhere, in the mystical idea of 'being in Christ', not in this 'subsidiary crater'.[5] Although Catholic responses to the

---

[1] Subilia, *La giustificazione per fede*, 117–27.
[2] Söding, 'Der Skopos der paulinischen Rechtfertigungslehre'.
[3] See, for example, A. Schweitzer, *Geschichte der paulinischen Forschung von der Reformation bis auf die Gegenwart*, Tübingen: Mohr, 1954, 132; F. Flückiger, *Der Ursprung des christlichen Dogmas: Eine Auseinandersetzung mit Albert Schweitzer und Martin Werner*, Zurich: Evangelischer Verlag, 1955, 52.
[4] W. Wrede, *Paulus*, 2nd edn, Tübingen, 1907, 90–100.
[5] A. Schweitzer, *Die Mystik des Apostels Paulus*, 2nd edn, Tübingen: Mohr, 1954, 216–20.

Reformation, such as the Council of Trent, initially reflected its shift in vocabulary, the Catholic tradition gradually reverted to more traditional ways of speaking and thinking about the transformation of the human situation through the life, death and resurrection of Jesus Christ. The highly influential and authoritative *Catechism of the Catholic Church* (1992), for example, retains the notion, while preferring to emphasise other Pauline images in its discussion of human salvation.

The rise of the ecumenical movement in the aftermath of the Second World War saw a new interest in the doctrine of justification. This did not, however, result from a new perception of the positive importance of this way of speaking, still less from a sense that the theological renewal of the West depended on a recovery of the specific conceptualities of justification. Justification was a problem, a barrier to church unity, which needed to be resolved. It was, in the view of many – but by no means all – an unwelcome relic of the past, which inhibited ecumenical collaboration in the present and future. The reconciliation of the churches demanded that the Reformation agendas, which originally led to their fissure in the sixteenth century, needed to be re-examined.[6]

One of the most important outcomes of this process of reflection was a new spurt of scholarly interest in the origins and significance of the doctrine of justification by faith, and its impact upon sixteenth-century western Christianity. This new ecumenical interest in the doctrine appears to have seen justification primarily as a problem from the past – a difficulty in the path of the reunification of the western churches, which needed to be neutralised, rather than something which was to be celebrated and proclaimed. A growing body of literature emerged, particularly within Lutheran circles during the 1960s, raising serious concerns about whether the notion of 'justification by faith' means anything to modern western secular culture.

Alongside increasing anxiety about the 'secular meaning of the gospel' (at least, as articulated in the notion of justification), a new issue emerged after the Second World War – a growing concern that traditional Protestant teachings on justification misrepresented the place of the law in Jewish life and thought. The Jewish theologian Claude G. Montefiore (1858–1938) argued that rabbinic Judaism did not hold – as Paul seemed to suggest – that Jews were self-righteous people who believed that they could earn their way into heaven. Judaism affirmed the graciousness of God, not human merit, in determining the destiny of Israel.[7] Others

---

[6] See Pannenberg, 'Die Rechtfertigungslehre im ökumenische Gespräch'; Hövelmann, 'Die ökumenische Vereinbarung zur Rechtfertigungslehre'.

[7] C. G. Montefiore, 'Rabbinic Judaism and the Epistles of St Paul', *Jewish Quarterly Review* 13 (1900–1), 161–217.

began to take up this criticism. With the publication of W. D. Davies' *Paul and Rabbinic Judaism* (1948), a new challenge to the western reading of Paul emerged. 'The gospel for Paul was not the annulling of Judaism, but its completion, and as such it took up into itself the essential genius of Judaism.'[8] The emergence of this 'new perspective' on Paul was given a decisive new impetus in 1977 with the publication of E. P. Sanders' *Paul and Palestinian Judaism*. From this point onwards, the plausibility of traditional Protestant formulations of the doctrine of justification, especially those following Luther's antithesis of law and gospel, were regarded with growing scepticism by biblical scholars. The debate continues, and it is unclear where it will end.

The history of the doctrine of justification primarily concerns the western, Latin-based theological tradition. The Orthodox emphasis upon the economic condescension of the Son leading to humanity's participation in the divine being is generally expressed in the concept of deification (*theosis* or *theopoiesis*) rather than justification. This is not, of course, to say that the western church was ignorant of such notions, at least one of which plays a significant (though, until recently, neglected) role in Martin Luther's soteriology;[9] nor is it to suggest that Orthodoxy neglected the Pauline image of justification in its theological reflections. Still less does it exclude the possible integration of the notions within a suitably comprehensive theological anthropology.[10] The issue concerns where the emphasis is placed, and which soteriological image came to dominate. Given the early church's relative lack of interest in the concept of justification, it is the western church's emphasis on justification, rather than the eastern church's emphasis on deification, which requires to be explained.[11]

This volume seeks to tell the story of the rise and fall of this highly significant development in western Christian thought, and to explore its implications for an understanding of the development of Christian doctrine. How is this refocussing of vocabulary and conceptualities of the Christian tradition to be explained? What is its significance? To what extent is this development foreshadowed in earlier Christian thinking? The only way in which such questions can be answered is by rigorous scholarly investigation of the development of the doctrine of justification

---

[8] Davies, *Paul and Rabbinic Judaism*, 323.
[9] See S. Peura, *Luther und Theosis: Vergöttlichung als Thema der abendländischen Theologie*, Helsinki: Luther-Akademie Ratzeburg, 1990; R. Flogaus, *Theosis bei Palamas und Luther: Ein Beitrag zum ökumenischen Gespräch*, Göttingen: Vandenhoeck & Ruprecht, 1997.
[10] As pointed out by Hinlicky, 'Theological Anthropology'.
[11] For the role of the concept of deification in the two traditions, see A. N. Williams, *The Ground of Union: Deification in Aquinas and Palamas*, New York: Oxford University Press, 1999.

within the first two thousand years of the western theological tradition, without any apologetic agenda. It is such an investigation that this new edition of this work seeks to offer.

The consolidation of the concept of justification as a means of articulating Christian insights into the economy of salvation as a whole takes place during the Middle Ages, a period of remarkable theological creativity and systematisation. Although significant differences emerge within the theological traditions of this period, a number of commonalities can nevertheless be discerned, particularly the virtually universal consensus that the term 'justification' designates a process of being 'made righteous'. In part, this reflects the high esteem placed on the works of Augustine of Hippo, whose influence over the theological renaissance of the twelfth century and beyond was immense. By far the largest section of this volume is thus dedicated to the documentation and analysis of the development of the doctrine of justification during the Middle Ages. Particular attention is paid to exploring why the image of 'justification' was found so useful as a means of articulating the Christian vision of the reconciliation of humanity to God, without achieving the conceptual dominance that is associated with the theology of the Protestant Reformation.

The sixteenth and early seventeenth centuries may be regarded as the 'high noon' of the fortunes of this concept within western Christianity, including both the Protestant Reformation and the Catholic responses to this development. A major section of the work explores the emergence of the Protestant approach to the doctrine. This critically important section attempts to account for the new interest in the concept of justification, and especially for the manner in which Protestantism came to focus so heavily on this one Pauline image of salvation as a means of both articulating its own distinctive insights into the redemption of humanity and distinguishing itself from its ecclesiological rivals. The distinctive features of the Protestant conception of justification are noted, and the continuities and discontinuities with earlier ways of thinking identified.

This leads on to a consideration of the Catholic response to the Reformation, supremely the Council of Trent's celebrated 'decree on justification' (1547). This involves a detailed examination of the background to this debate, careful identification of the positions represented during the Tridentine debates on justification, and their apparent influence on the final document. There is no doubt that Trent's decision to use the imagery and language of 'justification' was a direct response to the challenge of Protestantism. In a sense, it was a forced rather than a natural development, which was of decisive importance in consolidating the conceptual dominance of justification within western Christianity in the second half of the sixteenth century. Yet this proved to be a temporary development; within a hundred years, Catholicism had generally reverted to more traditional ways of conceptualising the economy of salvation, with the concept of 'justification' gradually giving way to a retrieval of older patterns of thought, which had been temporarily suppressed on account of the tactical need to respond to the Reformation on – and in – its own theological terms. The retrieval of more traditional ways of articulating the economy of salvation is a telling sign of the growing theological confidence of Catholicism in the seventeenth century.

Yet within the intellectual culture of western Europe, a series of developments took place which began to erode the dominance of justification as the preferred mode of discourse concerning the acceptance and transformation of humanity through Christ. The growth of rationalism in late seventeenth-century England catalysed similar developments throughout western Europe, particularly in Germany and France, which led to many of the central features of the doctrine of justification being undermined. Alongside this, New Testament scholarship began to question whether Luther's reading of Paul was quite as reliable as many had thought. Although German Lutheran scholars tended to remain fiercely loyal to their distinguished forebear, elsewhere growing anxiety was expressed. Did Paul's theological emphasis *really* fall on justification? That might well have been Luther's personal judgement; yet it seemed curiously inattentive to other soteriological conceptualities within the Pauline corpus. Despite these concerns, the modern period also witnessed some important attempts to retrieve and restate the traditional doctrine, with the concerns and agendas of the modern world in mind. Although widely regarded as a period of decline of interest in the doctrine of justification, the last three hundred years have given rise to some highly significant reappropriations of the doctrine.

Yet although the story of the doctrine of justification really begins in the Middle Ages, the foundations for this development were laid much earlier. Our account opens by documenting the emergence of the concept of justification, and identifying the foundational resources that would be deployed during the great period of medieval synthesis. A close reading of the medieval discussions of justification leaves no doubt as to the two primary sources on which they drew: the Vulgate translation of the Bible, and the works of Augustine of Hippo.

Three points are of particular importance in relation to the dogmatic positioning of the concept of justification within medieval theology.

1. The remarkable growth in Pauline scholarship during the theological renaissance of the twelfth century, and particularly the use of Pauline commentaries as vehicles of theological speculation.

2. The generally high regard for classical jurisprudence within the western church.
3. The semantic relationship between the Latin terms *iustitia* and *iustificatio*, which allowed the theologians of the medieval period to find in the cognate concept of justification a means of rationalising the divine dispensation towards humankind in terms of justice.

In this opening chapter, we therefore turn to consider these fundamental elements of the Christian understanding of justification, and how they shaped the western tradition at this point.

1.1   Semantic aspects of the concept of justification

'I am not ashamed of the gospel, for it is the power of God for salvation to everyone who has faith . . . for in it the righteousness of God is revealed' (Romans 1:16–17). For Paul, the Christian gospel is in some sense constituted by the revelation of the righteousness of God.[12] But what is this tantalizing 'righteousness of God'? As the present study will make clear, the interpretation of the 'righteousness of God' within the western theological tradition has been accompanied by the most intractable exegetical difficulties. The concept of *justification* (Latin, *iustificatio*) is inextricably linked with that of *righteousness* (Latin, *iustitia*), both semantically and theologically.[13] Central to the Christian understanding of the economy of salvation is the conviction that God is righteous, and that he acts in accordance with that righteousness in the salvation of humanity. It is clear, however, that this conviction raises certain fundamental questions, not least that of which concept of 'righteousness' can be considered appropriate to a discussion of the divine dispensation towards humankind. The relationship between God and humanity, according to the Christian understanding, may be characterised in three propositions:
1. God is righteous.
2. Humanity is sinful.
3. God justifies humanity.

The quintessence of the Christian doctrine of justification is that these three propositions do not constitute an inconsistent triad. God, acting in righteousness, justifies the sinner. The proclamation of the actuality of such a justification to those outside the church has always been accompanied by speculation within the church as to how it is actually possible for God, being righteous, to justify sinners in the first place. It is therefore of

---

[12] The issues are regularly surveyed in the literature; see, for example, P. Stuhlmacher, *Gerechtigkeit Gottes bei Paulus*; H. Brunner, 'Die Gerechtigkeit Gottes', *Zeitschrift für Religions- und Geistgeschichte* 39 (1987), 269–79.
[13] See McGrath, 'Justice and Justification'.

great importance to consider the various understandings of the concept of 'righteousness' or 'justice' which have been employed in the articulation of the doctrine of justification.

Modern theological vocabularies contain a host of Hebrew, Greek and Latin words, most of which possess, in their original contexts, a richness and depth of meaning which cannot possibly be conveyed by the mere translation of the word into English. Such an enterprise involves, not merely the substitution of a modern word for the original, but the transference of the latter from its own proper conceptual framework to one in which its meaning is distorted.[14] This problem has long been recognised. Jesus ben Sirach, presumably in an attempt to divert attention from the absence of a Hebrew original, complained that 'things originally spoken in Hebrew do not have the same force when they are translated into another language . . . with the law, the prophets and the rest of the writings, it makes no small difference when they are read in their original language'.[15] The conceptual foundations of the Christian doctrine of justification may be sought in the Old Testament, in a milieu quite different from that of western Europe, where it received its systematic articulation. The transference of the concept from this Hebraic matrix to that of western Europe has significant consequences, which we shall explore in the present section.

The primary source for Christian theological speculation is Holy Scripture; indeed, Christian theology may be regarded as an extended commentary upon the biblical material.[16] It is therefore evident that Christian theology will contain a number of important concepts originating from a Hebraic context, and that the transference of these concepts from their original context may result in a shift in meaning with unacceptable theological consequences. In particular, it must be pointed out that the equation of Hebraic and western concepts of 'righteousness' is frequently implicit in theological works, so that western concepts of justice are employed in the articulation of the Christian doctrine of justification. A study of the classic western understandings of justice suggests that these are essentially *secular* and *practical*, and therefore potentially quite unsuited to a discussion of the 'righteousness of God'. The present section, dealing with the Hebrew, Greek and Latin understandings of 'righteousness', is therefore intended as a prolegomenon to the study of

---

[14] See W. Schwarz, *Principles and Problems of Biblical Translation: Some Reformation Controversies and Their Background*, Cambridge: Cambridge University Press, 1970.
[15] Sirach, prologue.
[16] This is true throughout the medieval period, despite the important debates of the era concerning the role of tradition: see H. Schüssler, *Der Primät der Heiligen Schrift als theologisches und kanonistisches Problem im Spätmittelalter*, Wiesbaden: Steiner Verlag, 1977.

the doctrine of justification. Although not strictly a part of the history of the doctrine itself, the question exercised such an influence over the subsequent discussion of justification that its omission at this stage is impossible.

The etymology of the two Hebrew terms *sedeq* and *sedaqa*, both of which are usually translated as 'righteousness', is generally accepted to be obscure, and it is quite possible that the original meaning of the grapheme *sdq* is lost beyond recovery. The fact that there are two Hebrew words usually translated as 'righteousness', the masculine *sedeq* and the feminine *sedaqa*, has been the subject of much speculation. Although it might be supposed that these two terms are synonymous, this has been called into question for two reasons.[17] First, it is philologically improbable that two different words should bear exactly the same meaning at the same time. Second, *sedeq* is used as a characterising genitive, especially for weights and measures, as in Leviticus 19:36. *Sedaqa*, however, is not used in this manner. It is difficult to know how much can be read into this distinction. It is certainly possible to argue that the feminine form tends to refer to a concrete entity, such as a righteous action or a vindicating judgement, whereas the masculine form tends to be associated with the more abstract idea of 'that which is morally right' or 'right order'. Yet it is unclear quite how this impacts on our investigation.

Recent theories of the historical background of the Hebrew language have tended to divide the Hamito-Semitic languages into two groups: the archaic southern Cushitic and Chadic languages, and the more progressive northern group of languages, including the Semitic languages, the Berber languages of north Africa, and ancient Egyptian and Coptic.[18] The triliteral root is a conspicuous feature common to all the languages of the northern group, and it is possible to argue that at every level – whether semantic, grammatical or phonological – features of these languages are theoretically derivable from a common source. When the etymology of the grapheme *sdq* is examined, using other ancient near-eastern languages as models, a spectrum of possible meanings emerges, of which the most fundamental appears to be that of *conformity to a norm*.[19] This observation is confirmed by the fact that the dominant sense of the

---

[17] A. Jepsen, 'sdq und sdqh im Alten Testament', in H. G. Reventloh (ed.), *Gottes Wort und Gottes Land*, Göttingen: Vandenhoeck & Ruprecht, 1965, 78–89.

[18] A. Saènz-Badillos, *A History of the Hebrew Language*, Cambridge: Cambridge University Press, 1993.

[19] For example, the use of the Canaanite term *saduk* in the Tel el-Amarna texts to indicate that the king had acted 'correctly' when dealing with the 'Kasi' (= Cushite?) people. See D. Hill, *Greek Words and Hebrew Meanings: Studies in the Semantics of Soteriological Terms*, Cambridge: Cambridge University Press, 1967, 82–98, especially 82–6. The following

terms *sedeq* and *sedaqa* appears to be that of 'right behaviour' or 'right disposition'.[20] The world is understood to be ordered in a certain way as a result of its divine creation; to act 'rightly' is thus to act in accordance with this patterning of structures and events. Emphasis has often been placed on the idea that the divine act of creation involves the imposition of order upon chaos;[21] such ideas can be found throughout the wisdom literature of the ancient Near East.

The validity of such an appeal to etymological considerations has been criticised by James Barr,[22] who illustrates the alleged inadequacy of the tool with reference to the English word 'nice'. The etymology of the word indicates that it derives from the Latin *nescius*, presumably via the Old French *nice*, thereby suggesting that its meaning should be 'silly' or 'ignorant' – which is clearly of little use in determining its usage today. Barr neglects, however, to point out that etymological considerations can give an indication of the early meaning of a term, despite the connotations it may develop later as a consequence of constant use. While the derivation of 'nice' from *nescius* does not allow its modern meaning to be established, it is perfectly adequate to allow its *sixteenth*-century meaning to be established, it then bearing the sense of 'silly' or 'ignorant'. As the enterprise in question is to establish the meaning of the term in texts of widely varying age, etymological arguments are perfectly acceptable in an attempt to establish its *early* meaning; the later meaning of the term, of course, cannot be determined by such considerations, as nuances not originally present make their appearance. Thus, in later Hebrew, *sedaqa* came to mean 'almsgiving', a meaning that cannot be derived from etymological considerations alone. Here, as elsewhere, the semantic connection between a grapheme and the meaning of a word appears to have eventually become so strained as to have almost snapped completely. However,

studies should also be consulted: H. Cazelles, 'A propos de quelques textes difficiles relatifs à la justice de Dieu dans l'Ancien Testament', *Revue Biblique* 58 (1951) 169–88; A. Dünner, *Die Gerechtigkeit nach dem Alten Testament*, Bonn: Bouvier, 1963; O. Kaiser, 'Dike und Sedaqa. Zur Frage nach der sittlichen Weltordnung: Ein theologische Präludium', *Neue Zeitschrift für systematische Theologie und Religionsphilosophie* 7 (1965) 251–75; H. H. Schmid, *Gerechtigkeit als Weltordnung: Hintergrund und Geschichte des alttestamentlichen Gerechtigkeitsbegriffs*, Tübingen: Mohr, 1968.

20 W. Eichrodt, *Theology of the Old Testament*, 2 vols., London: SCM Press, 1975, 1.239–49; Gerhard von Rad, *Old Testament Theology*, 2 vols., London: SCM Press, 1975, 1.370–83.

21 See, for example, R. Rendtorff, 'Die theologische Stellung des Schöpfungsglaubens bei Deuterjesaja', *ZThK* 51 (1954), 2–13; M. Bauks, '"Chaos" als Metapher für die Gefärdung der Weltordnung', in B. Janowski, B. Ego and A. Krüger (eds.), *Das biblische Weltbild und seine altorientalischen Kontexte*, Tübingen: Mohr Siebeck, 2001, 431–64.

22 J. Barr, *The Semantics of Biblical Language*, Oxford: Oxford University Press, 1961, 107–60.

as we shall indicate below, this later meaning of the word *sedaqa* can be understood on the basis of its etymology if its theological associations are given due weight.

The *oldest* meaning of *sedaqa*, as judged by its use in the Song of Deborah (Judges 5:1–31), appears to be 'victory'.[23] This meaning appears to be retained in some later texts, such as 1 Samuel 12:7 and Micah 6:5, although it is clear that the nuances associated with the term have altered. In this early passage, which contains many unusual grammatical forms and rare words, God is understood to have acted in 'righteousness' by defending Israel when its existence was threatened by an outside agency. This use of the term allows us to appreciate that the term 'righteousness' can possess both retributive and salvific aspects, without being reduced to, or exclusively identified with, either concept. Thus God's act of judgement is retributive with regard to Israel's enemies, but salvific with regard to God's covenant people.

Underlying this understanding of *iustitia Dei* is the conceptual framework of the covenant: when God and Israel mutually fulfil their covenant obligations to each other, a state of righteousness can be said to exist – that is, things are *saddiq*, 'as they should be'. There is no doubt that much of the Old Testament thinking about righteousness is linked with the notion of a covenant between God and Israel, demanding fidelity on the part of both parties if a state of 'righteousness' is to pertain.[24] The close connection between the themes of creation and covenant in the Old Testament points to a linking of the moral and salvific orders.[25]

Similar understandings of 'righteousness' were common elsewhere in the ancient world. For example, contemporary Assyrian documents suggest that the king was to be seen as the guardian of the world order, who ensured the regularity of the world through his cultic actions.[26] The kinship of these notions can also be seen from the close semantic association between the ideas of 'righteousness' and 'truth' in the Aryan *rtá*

---

[23] G. Wildeboer, 'Die älteste Bedeutung des Stammes *sdq*', *ZAW* 22 (1902) 167–9. For related use of the feminine plural, see 1 Samuel 12:7; Psalm 103:6, Isaiah 45:24; Daniel 9:16; Micah 6:5.

[24] See the study of R. C. Ortlund, *Whoredom: God's Unfaithful Wife in Biblical Theology*, Grand Rapids: Eerdmans, 1996. Note how the terms 'righteousness' and 'covenant' are linked at Nehemiah 9:32–3; Psalms 50:1–6; 111:1–10; Isaiah 42:6; 61:8–11; Hosea 2:16–20.

[25] As pointed out by B. W. Anderson, *From Creation to New Creation*, Minneapolis: Fortress Press, 1994, 146–64.

[26] S. M. Maul, 'Der assyrische König: Hüter der Weltordnung', in K. Watanabe (ed.), *Priests and Officials in the Ancient Near East*, Heidelberg: Universitätsverlag C. Winter, 1999, 201–14.

and Iranian *aša*.[27] Thus Israel's triumphant victories over her enemies were seen as proofs of the *sidqot 'adonay* (Judges 5:11) – the *iustitiae Dei* of the Vulgate. Even where the specific term 'righteousness' is not found, it seems that a clear connection is understood to exist between God's activity as a judge and Israel's victory over its neighbours (as at Judges 11:27, and possibly also 2 Samuel 18:31).[28]

At this stage in the history of Israel, the 'righteousness' of the covenant does not appear to have been considered to have been under threat from within Israel itself, but merely from external agencies. However, with the establishment of Israel came the rise of prophecy, and the threat posed to the covenant relationship from within Israel itself became increasingly apparent. The eighth-century prophets Amos and Hosea stressed the importance of righteousness on Israel's part if if were to remain in a covenant relationship with its righteous God.[29] This insight was expressed by the prophets in terms of the *conditional election* of Israel as the people of God, For the prophets, *sedaqa* was effectively that condition or state required of Israel if its relationship with its God was to continue.[30] Although there are many instances where *sedaqa* can be regarded as corresponding to the concept of *iustitia distributiva*, which has come to dominate western thinking on the nature of justice (despite the rival claims of *iustitia commutativa*), there remains a significant number which cannot.

A particularly significant illustration of this may be found in the Old Testament attitude to the poor, needy and destitute. As we have noted, *sedaqa* refers to the 'right order of affairs' which is violated, at least in part, by the very existence of such unfortunates. God's *sedaqa* is such that God must deliver them from their plight – and it is *this* aspect of the Hebrew concept of *sedaqa* which has proved so intractable to those who attempted to interpret it solely as *iustitia distributiva*. It is

---

[27] On *rtá*, see H. Lüders, *Varuna I: Varuna und die Wasser*, Göttingen: Vandenhoeck & Ruprecht, 1997, 13–27, especially 27 (on the relation between the Vedic *rtá* and the Avestic *aša*); idem, *Varuna II: Varuna und das Rta*, Göttingen: Vandenhoeck & Ruprecht, 1997, 402–654. The Caucasian term *äcäg*, deriving from the Iranian, should also be noted in this context: see H. Hommel, 'Wahrheit und Gerechtigkeit. Zur Geschichte und Deutung eines Begriffspaars', *Antike und Abendland* 15 (1969), 159–86; 182–3 n. 86.

[28] For some important issues that arise from this notion of God as 'judge', see A. Gamper, *Gott als Richter in Mesopotamien und im Alten Testament: Zum Verständnis einer Gebetsbitte*, Innsbruck: Universitätsverlag Wagner, 1966; P. Krawczack, *'Es gibt einen Gott, der Richter ist auf Erden!' (Ps 58, 12b): Ein exegetischer Beitrag zum Verständnis von Psalm 58*, Berlin: Philo, 2001.

[29] H. Gossai, *Justice, Righteousness and the Social Critique of the Eighth-Century Prophets*, New York: Peter Lang, 1993.

[30] Schmid, *Gerechtigkeit als Weltordnung*, 67; cf. von Rad, *Old Testament Theology* 1.370.

clear that this aspect of the Hebraic understanding of 'righteousness' cannot be understood in terms of an impartial judge who administers justice according to whichever party has broken a universally accepted law.

Hermann Cremer (1834–1903) argued that the only way of making sense of the Old Testament usage of *sedaqa* was to assume that, in its basic sense, the term refers to an actual relationship between two persons, and implies behaviour which corresponds to, or is consistent with, whatever claims may arise from or concerning either party to the relationship. The relationship in question is that presupposed by the covenant between God and Israel, which must be considered as the ultimate norm to which *sedaqa* must be referred. The Hebrew concept of *sedaqa* thus stands in a conceptual class of its own – a class which Cremer brilliantly characterised as *iustitia salutifera*.[31]

The strongly soteriological overtones of the term *sedaqa* can be illustrated from a number of passages in which 'righteousness' and 'salvation' are practically equated, particularly in many passages within Deutero-Isaiah:[32]

I will bring my *sedaqa* near, it is not far away, And my salvation will not be delayed. (Isaiah 46:13)

A similar theme recurs throughout many Psalms, which stress and proclaim 'the reliable, foundational event of the covenant and the continuous salvific faithfulness of Yahweh in history and worship'.[33] This is not, it must be emphasised, to say that 'righteousness' and 'salvation' are treated as being synonymous; rather, they are regarded as being inextricably linked on account of the covenant relationship between God and Israel.[34] Semantic and theological considerations combine to give the Old Testament concept of the 'righteousness of God' such strongly soteriological overtones, which the western concept of *iustitia distributiva* cannot convey.

The later meaning of *sedaqa* in post-biblical Hebrew ('almsgiving') can thus be seen as the development of a trend already evident in passages

---

[31] H. Cremer, *Die paulinische Rechtfertigungslehre im Zusammenhange ihrer geschichtlichen Voraussetzungen*, Gütersloh: Bertelsmann, 1899. The German term 'Gemeinschaftstreue' has subsequently become increasingly used as a translation of *sedaqa*.

[32] C. F. Whitley, 'Deutero-Isaiah's Interpretation of *sedeq*', *Vetus Testamentum* 22 (1972), 469–75. For a related pattern in 'Trito-Isaiah', see B. Rosendal, 'Guds og menneskers retfærdighed hos Tritojesaja', in B. Rosendal (ed.), *Studier i Jesajabogen*, Aarhus: Universitetsforlag, 1989, 94–116.

[33] H. J. Kraus, *Theology of the Psalms*, Minneapolis: Augsburg, 1986, 157–8.

[34] See, for example, R. Murray, *The Cosmic Covenant: Biblical Themes of Justice, Peace and the Integrity of Creation*, London: Sheed & Ward, 1992.

such as Psalm 112:9 and Daniel 4:27 (Aramaic, 4:24: although this section of the book of Daniel is written in Aramaic, rather than Hebrew, the same word is used in each language). The 'right (or intended) order of affairs' is violated by the existence of the poor and needy; it is therefore a requirement of *sedaqa* that this be remedied by the appropriate means. Thus the sense which *sedaqa* assumes in the Targums and Talmud ('benevolence' in general, or 'almsgiving' in particular) can be seen to represent a natural development of the soteriological nuances which had been associated with the term from the earliest of times, rather than the final rupture of the semantic connection between a word and its root.[35] The etymology of the term on its own is inadequate to explain this development; the soteriological context within which it is deployed, especially when linked with the motif of the covenant between God and Israel, enables this extended meaning to be understood without difficulty.

The problems attending the translation of the Old Testament into any second language, whether modern English or Hellenistic Greek, are well illustrated by the application of semantic field theory. The *semantic field* of a word includes not merely its synonyms, but also its antonyms, homonyms and homophones.[36] As such, it is much broader than the *lexical field*, which may be defined very precisely in terms of words which are closely associated with one another.[37] The enormous size of such semantic fields may be illustrated from the associative field of the French word *chat*, which is estimated to consist of some two thousand words.[38] The translation of a word into a different language inevitably involves a distortion of its original semantic field, so that certain nuances and associations present in the original cannot be conveyed properly in a translation, while new nuances and associations not already present make their appearance. The word chosen to translate the original will itself have a well-established semantic field, so that an alien set of associations will come to

[35] Thus J. F. A. Sawyer, *Semantics in Biblical Research: New Methods of Defining Hebrew Words for Salvation*, London: SCM Press, 1972, 50. For a penetrating criticism of Sawyer's work, see the review by P. Wernberg-Møller, *JThS* 24 (1973), 215–17.

[36] On which see S. Öhmann, 'Theories of the "Linguistic Field"', *Word* 9 (1953), 123–34; N. C. W. Spence, 'Linguistic Fields, Conceptual Spheres and the Weltbild', *Transactions of the Philological Society* (1961), 87–106; V. L. Strite, *Old English Semantic-Field Studies*, New York: Peter Lang, 1989.

[37] For some excellent studies, see L. M. Sylvester, *Studies in the Lexical Field of Expectation*, Amsterdam: Rodopi, 1994; J. R. Schwyter, *Old English Legal Language: The Lexical Field of Theft*, Odense: Odense University Press, 1996.

[38] See the seminal study of P. Guiraud, 'Les Champs morpho-sémantiques', *Bulletin de la Société Linguistique de Paris* 52 (1956) 265–88, which defines such a field as 'le complexe de relations de formes et de sens formé par un ensemble de mots'. See further P. Guiraud, *La Sémantique*, Paris: Presses universitaires de France, 1972.

be imposed upon the word in question as a result of the translation process itself.

This difficulty is well illustrated in the two non-contiguous semantic transitions of importance to our study. In each case, a Hebrew word is replaced by a Latin equivalent in the Vulgate translation of the Old Testament. The state of biblical scholarship during the Middle Ages was such that it was the Vulgate, rather than the Hebrew original, which became normative for medieval theology.[39] Most theologians of the period were unaware of the semantic issues involved, not having access to the Hebrew original (and probably, in any case, being unable to understand the older language). In each case, the transition from Hebrew to Latin involves an intermediate Greek term in the Septuagint (LXX) translation of the Hebrew text, which itself introduces new issues. The two transitions are:

'righteousness': *sedaqa* → *dikaiosyne* → *iustitia*;
'to justify': *hasdiq* → *dikaioun* → *iustificare*.

We shall consider these semantic transitions individually.

1.1.1   'Righteousness': sedaqa → dikaiosyne → iustitia

The considerable influence of Greek philosophy and culture upon Christian thought in its formative period has been well documented.[40] This influence is also mediated through the LXX, whose origins date from the beginning of the third century BC.[41] The term *dikaiosyne* had by then acquired a generally Aristotelian sense, so that by *dikaiosyne* we may understand something very similar to *iustitia distributiva* – the notion of 'giving persons their due'.[42] Aristotle's ethical thinking is to be set in the context of the political community, the *polis*, so that 'righteousness' is defined teleologically, in terms of the well-being which it brings to the

---

[39] For a survey of the knowledge of Hebrew in the Middle Ages, see B. Smalley, 'Andrew of St Victor, Abbot of Wigmore: A Twelfth Century Hebraist', *RThAM* 10 (1938), 358–74; idem, *The Study of the Bible in the Middle Ages*, 2nd edn, Notre Dame: University of Notre Dame Press, 1970, 112–95. For the manuscripts on which such studies are based, see C. Sirat, *Du Scribe au livre: les manuscrits hébreux au Moyen Age*, Paris: CNRS Editions, 1994.

[40] See, for example, H. Chadwick, *Early Christian Thought and the Classical Tradition*, Oxford: Clarendon Press, 1984.

[41] See S. Olofsson, *God is my Rock: A Study of Translation Technique and Theological Exegesis in the Septuagint*, Stockholm: Almqvist & Wiksell International, 1990.

[42] For a useful general survey, see E. A. Havelock, 'DIKAIOSUNE: An Essay in Greek Intellectual History', *Phoenix* 23 (1969), 49–70. The best study at present is B. Yack, *The Problems of a Political Animal: Community, Justice, and Conflict in Aristotelian Political Thought*, Berkeley: University of California Press, 1993.

political community as a whole.[43] Lower beings, such as the animals, and higher beings, such as the gods, were excluded from Aristotle's discussion of *dikaiosyne* precisely because they were not members of the contracting political community.[44] The sphere of *dikaiosyne* is defined as that of the *polis*, so that the concept of the 'righteousness of God' has no immediate practical significance. The contrast with the Old Testament notion of Israel as a covenant community will be evident; both Aristotle and the Old Testament presuppose a covenant community as the basis for an understanding of 'righteousness'; the 'covenants' in question are, however, quite distinct, not least in the manner in which they implicate – or fail to implicate – God in human affairs.[45]

It is evident that Aristotle's understanding of 'righteousness' is quite different from that signified by the Hebrew word *sedaqa*. In particular, *dikaiosyne* is now a fundamentally secular concept incapable of assuming the soteriological overtones associated with the Hebrew term. While the translators of the LXX appear to have attempted consistency in this translation of Hebrew terms,[46] they were unable to accommodate the meaning of *sedaqa* by the simple substitution of *dikaiosyne* in every case. Of particular interest is the translation of *sdq* in the construct form (e.g., at Leviticus 19:36, Deuteronomy 25:15 and Ezekiel 45:10). Here, the Hebrew clearly has the sense of 'accurate' – that is, in the case of Leviticus 19:36, the weights are 'as they are intended to be' – namely, accurate. The LXX, however, translates this phrase as the 'weights of righteousness.' This phrase could easily be misunderstood as possessing developed cultic or religious overtones, when it clearly denotes nothing more than accurate weights. Similarly, the LXX 'sacrifices of righteousness' (Deuteronomy 33:19; Psalms 4:6; 51.21) are essentially 'correct sacrifices' – that is, those which are 'in order' under the cultic prescriptions of the covenant, rather than sacrifices which are to be thought of as ethically 'righteous' in themselves.

The basic meaning of the *sdq* group as 'conformity to a requirement', illustrated by the use of *sdq* in the construct form, caused some difficulty

---

[43] Aristotle, *Politics* I, 1253a 2–3.

[44] For an older perspective, see H. Lloyd-Jones, *The Justice of Zeus*, 2nd edn, Berkeley: University of California Press, 1983.

[45] For some of the issues that second-century writers faced in dealing with such concerns, see E. Peretto, *La giustizia: Ricerca su gli autori cristiani del secondo secolo*, Rome: Edizioni Marianum, 1977.

[46] For the difficulties they faced, see S. Olofsson, *The LXX Version: A Guide to the Translation Technique of the Septuagint*, Stockholm: Almquist & Wiksell, 1990. Older studies of interest include H. S. Gehman, 'The Hebraic Character of LXX Greek', *VT* 1 (1951), 81–90; H. M. Orlinsky, 'The Treatment of Anthropomorphisms and Anthropopathisms in the Septuagint of Isaiah', *Hebrew Union College Annual* 27 (1956), 193–200.

for the LXX translators, in that there was no satisfactory Greek equivalent for this grammatical form. While the *dik* lexical group appears to have been considered capable of translating the *sdq* group in the majority of cases, the soteriological connotations of *sedaqa* were occasionally so strong that it could not be translated by *dikaiosyne*, the translators being forced to use *eleemosyne* – in other words, 'mercy'.[47] This would be expected to have at least one very significant consequence for Greek readers of the Old Testament, unfamiliar with its Hebrew original; here they might encounter a reference to God's *dikaiosyne*, there to God's *eleemosyne* – yet the same Hebrew word, *sedaqa*, lies behind both. A reader who was unaware that the same Hebrew word was being 'translated' in each case might thus conceivably set God's 'righteousness' and 'mercy' in opposition, where no such tension is warranted on the basis of the text itself.

For the first fifteen hundred years of its existence, the western church's theologians depended mainly upon Latin translations of the Bible, chiefly the Vulgate, for their theological deliberations. As most theologians of the period did not have access to the original Hebrew version of the Old Testament – if they knew any Hebrew in the first place – their interpretation of such Latin theological terms as *iustitia Dei* and *iustificare* would ultimately be based upon the Latin version of the Bible available to them.[48] It is therefore of importance to appreciate the difficulties attending the translation of essentially Hebraic concepts, such as 'justification', into a Latin linguistic and conceptual framework.[49]

By the second century AD, the Latin term *iustitia* had acquired well-established juristic connotations which were to exert considerable influence over future theological interpretation of such notions as *iustitia Dei* – the 'righteousness of God.' The Ciceronian definition of *iustitia* as *reddens unicuique quod suum est* ('giving someone their due') had become normative.[50] As van Zyl notes:[51]

---

[47] For example, Psalms 24:5; 33:5; 103:6. The problem is particularly evident in Deutero-Isaiah; see J. W. Olley, *'Righteousness' in the Septuagint of Isaiah: A Contextual Study*, Missoula: Scholars Press, 1979, 65–78.

[48] For the resurgence of Hebraic scholarship in the sixteenth century, see T. Willi, 'Der Beitrag des Hebräischen zum Werden der Reformation in Basel', *ThZ* 35 (1979), 139–54; H. P. Rüger, 'Karlstadt als Hebräist an der Universität Wittenberg', *ARG* 75 (1984), 297–309.

[49] For discussion of how Christian Latin – including that of the Vulgate – coped with the linguistic demands it faced, see V. Binder, *Sprachkontakt und Diglossie: Lateinische Wörter im griechischen als Quellen für die lateinische Sprachgeschichte und das Vulgärlatein*, Hamburg: Buske, 2000.

[50] Cicero, *Rhetoricum libro duo* II, 53: 'Iustitia virtus est, communi utilitate servata, suam cuique tribuens dignitatem.' Cf. Justinian, *Institutio* I, 1: 'Iustitia est constans et perpetua voluntas suum unicuique tribuens.' On Cicero's fundamental notion of *iustitia*, see D. H. van Zyl, *Justice and Equity in Cicero*, Pretoria: Academica Press, 1991.

[51] Van Zyl, *Justice and Equity in Cicero*, 34.

The golden thread running through all of Cicero's thought on moral philosophy is the need, and indeed the desire, of all persons to achieve 'the greatest good' (*summum bonum*). This is done by a leading a virtuous, moral, and ethically acceptable life in accordance with the 'cardinal virtues' of wisdom, justice, fortitude, and self-restraint. Its purpose is to bring man back to his true nature (*natura*), in conformity with reason, justice, and equity. In this regard, Cicero is essentially a moralist and an idealist, who links his moral philosophy inextricably with his approach to law and good government as prerequisites for a stable and harmonious society.

In effect, the Ciceronian definition encapsulates the western concept of *iustitia distributiva*, the 'due' of each person being established through the *iuris consensus*, and embodied in *ius*.[52] The tension between this concept of 'righteousness' and that of the Old Testament will be evident. There is no fundamental appeal to a covenant between God and humanity as determinative of ethical or legal norms or conventions.

The most important book of the Old Testament, as judged by its influence upon the development of the Christian doctrine of justification, is the Psalter, the subject of major commentaries by Augustine, Peter Lombard and Luther, to name but three. The Vulgate, as we know it, contains Jerome's translation of the Hebrew books of the Old Testament, with the exception of the Psalter. The Psalter found in the Vulgate is the *Psalterium Gallicum*, Jerome's second revision of the Old Latin Psalter, itself based upon Origen's recension of the LXX version.[53] His later *Psalterium iuxta hebraicam veritatem* never gained general acceptance. The difference between the two Psalters may be illustrated from their translations of Psalm 24:5 (Vulgate, 23:5):

Psalterium Gallicum:
. . . accipiet benedictionem a Domino et *misericordiam* a Deo salvatore suo.
Psalterium iuxta hebraicam veritatem:
. . . accipiet benedictionem a Domino et *iustitiam* a Deo salutari suo.

Here the Gallic Psalter follows the LXX, and the *Psalterium iuxta hebraicam veritatem* the original Hebrew. The *Psalterium Gallicum* appeals to God's mercy (*misericordia*) for salvation; the *Psalterium iuxta hebraicam veritatem* appeals to God's righteousness (*iustitia*). The theological implications of this could have been considerable, not to mention the confusion that could arise from such fundamental disagreements.

Although it is clear that considerable confusion could potentially have arisen through such translations, two important factors served to greatly reduce this possibility.

---

[52] F. Wieacker, *Römische Rechtsgeschichte: Quellenkunde, Rechtsbildung, Jurisprudenz und Rechtsliteratur*, Munich: Beck, 1988.
[53] For details of the two translations, see J. N. D. Kelly, *Jerome: His Life, Writings and Controversies*, London: Duckworth, 1975.

1. The Vulgate itself is not consistent in its translation of the LXX. Thus the LXX *eleemosyne*, translating *sedaqa*, is translated into Latin as *iustitia* at Psalm 35:24 and elsewhere. It is almost as if the translation of the Greek has been corrected in the light of the original Hebrew, even though there are no persuasive arguments for believing that any such comparison took place. The reasons for this inconsistency are not clear.

2. The two passages in the Psalter which appear to have exercised the greatest influence over western conceptions of *iustitia Dei* are Psalm 31:1 (Hebrew and Vulgate, 30:2) and 71:2 (Vulgate, 70:2).[54] In both these passages, the Psalmist appeals to God, acting according to righteousness, for deliverance:

> In you, O Lord, do I take refuge,
> Let me never be put to shame.
> *In your righteousness* deliver me and rescue me.

In both cases, the LXX translated *sedaqa* as *dikaiosyne*, and the Vulgate thence as *iustitia*. The strongly soteriological sense of the Hebrew root lying behind the Latin term *iustitia* in this specific context could thus be appreciated, as is borne out by the study of the exegesis of such passages in the early medieval period.

1.1.2   'To justify': hasdiq → dikaioun → iustificare

In turning to consider the Hebrew term *hasdiq*, usually translated 'to justify', it is essential to note that it never, at any point in the canonical books of the Old Testament, bears the negative sense 'to condemn' or 'to punish', its primary sense apparently being 'to vindicate', 'to acquit', or 'to declare to be in the right'.[55] The difficulty faced by the LXX translators was that the corresponding Greek verb *dikaioun* differed from *hasdiq* in two important respects.

1. In its classical usage, *dikaioun* with a *personal* object almost invariably seems to be applied to someone whose cause is *unjust*, and thus bears the meaning of 'to do justice to' – that is, 'to punish'. Although it is possible to adduce occasional classical references in which *dikaioun* may conceivably be interpreted as assuming a *positive* sense – that is, to 'right an injustice suffered'[56] – it must be emphasised that this is extremely rare. In general,

---

[54] See the study of H. Bornkamm, 'Iustitia Dei in der Scholastik und bei Luther', *ARG* 39 (1942), 1–46.

[55] See N. M. Watson, 'Some Observations Concerning the Use of *Dikaioo* in the Septuagint', *JBL* 79 (1960), 255–66.

[56] For example, Polybius III, xxxi, 9; cited in Olley, *'Righteousness' in the Septuagint of Isaiah*, 38.

the classical usage of *dikaioun* is such that it is highly unusual to find it applied, with a personal object, in the sense of 'to justify' – and yet it is this positive sense which constitutes the *norm* for the Septuagintal use of the verb. Indeed, there are no known occurrences of *dikaioun* in a negative sense in any part of the Septuagint for which there exists a Hebrew original.[57] It is therefore clear that the Septuagintal usage of the term represents a significant shift away from the classical meaning of the term towards that of the corresponding Hebrew term – a shift which might prove stultifying to a Greek reader of the Old Testament, not familiar with the Hebrew original. No example of the classical use of *dikaioun* can be found within the LXX, and the normal meaning it assumes in the LXX can be adduced only in a few isolated and controversial passages in classical Greek literature.

2. In classical Greek, *dikaioun* with a personal object *applied to a person whose cause is unjust* invariably assumes the negative meaning 'to punish'. The Septuagintal use of the verb in an identical context demands that it assume a *positive* meaning – that is, 'to justify', 'to declare to be in the right', or 'to acquit'. For example, Isaiah 5:22–3 (LXX) follows the wording of the Hebrew Massoretic text very closely. The substance of the complaint is that certain people are, for the sake of financial considerations, 'justifying the wicked'. This complaint does not make sense if the classical sense of *dikaioun* (e.g., as it is encountered at Sirach 42:2) is presumed to apply; if the unjust are punished – that is, have 'justice done to them' – there can be no cause for complaint. The complaint does, however, make sense if the term is presumed to have a Hebraic background, in that the substance of the complaint is then that certain people have been bribed to declare the guilty to be innocent. It is clear that the term *dikaioun*, although of classical Greek provenance, has assumed a Hebraic meaning as a consequence of its being used to translate the *sdq* words. The Greek reader of the Old Testament, unfamiliar with the Hebraic background to such material, would find passages such as the above highly perplexing.

The *locus classicus* for the secular Greek use of the verb is Book V of Aristotle's *Nicomachean Ethics*. If the classical Aristotelian understanding of the concept is applied to the Septuagintal translation of Isaiah 43:26, an apparent absurdity results. Israel is there invited to confess her sins, 'so that she may be justified'. It is not clear why this should move Israel to confess her sins, since, in the classical sense of the verb, her punishment

---

[57] In apocryphal works, the secular Greek sense of the term is usually encountered, as at Sirach 42:2. Here the Greek phrase 'justification of the ungodly', so subtly nuanced in its Pauline sense, merely assumes the commonsense meaning of 'the punishment of the wicked'.

will follow as a matter of course. Of course, if it is assumed that the Greek verb *dikaioun* has here taken on the meaning of *hasdiq*, rather than conforming to secular Greek usage, the meaning becomes clear and comprehensible: Israel is invited to confess her sins, in order that she may be acquitted of them. A similar conclusion must be drawn in the case of Micah 6:11 (LXX), in which it is clear that the rhetorical question expects an answer in the *negative* – in other words, assuming a Hebrew, rather than Greek, meaning of the term.

It is therefore clear that, under the influence of the Hebrew original, the Septuagintal verb *dikaioun* came to assume a meaning quite distinct from its secular Greek origins. Furthermore, such a meaning must have become widespread and accepted within Greek-speaking Judaism – otherwise, the LXX would have been incomprehensible at points. It is apparent that this inherent difficulty reflects the quite different semantic fields of the *sdq* and *dik* words.

A difficulty of a quite different nature arose in the translation of terms such as *hasdiq* or *dikaioun* into Latin. The verb *iustificare* ('to justify'), employed for this purpose, was post-classical, and thus required interpretation. The general tendency among Latin-speaking theologians was to follow Augustine of Hippo (see 1.4) in interpreting *iustificare* ('to justify') as *iustum facere* ('to make righteous'). Augustine's etymological speculations have been the object of derision for some considerable time – for example, his impossible derivation of the name *Mercurius* from *medius currens*.[58] His explanation of the origins of the term *iustificare* is, however, quite plausible, for it involves the acceptable assumption that *-ficare* is the unstressed form of *facere*. While this may be an acceptable interpretation of *iustificare* considered in isolation, it is not an acceptable interpretation of the verb considered as the Latin equivalent of *dikaioun*.

'Messieurs, l'Angleterre est une île.' The great French historian Jules Michelet prefaced his lectures on British history by pointing to a single geographical factor – that England was an island – which had such a decisive influence upon his subject, and was all too easily overlooked. As we begin our study of the development of the Christian doctrine of justification, it is necessary to observe that the early theologians of the western church were dependent upon Latin versions of the Bible, and approached their texts and their subject with a set of presuppositions which, it could be argued, owe at least as much to the specifics and peculiarities of Latin language and culture as to Christianity itself.[59]

---

[58] *De civitate Dei* VII, 14, CSEL 40.322.10–17.
[59] A further semantic transition which may be noted at this point has had a highly significant impact on a substantial section of the western Christian tradition since the sixteenth

The initial transference of a Hebrew concept to a Greek, and subsequently to a Latin, context points to a fundamental alteration in the concepts of 'justification' and 'righteousness' as the gospel spread from its Palestinian source to the western world.[60] The most significant such development, as we shall see, was the widespread assumption that the all-important theological notion of the 'righteousness of God' – which, for Paul, lay at the heart of the Christian gospel – was about God giving each person their due. And as Martin Luther would later point out, that meant condemning sinners such as him, and justifying those who were already righteous. What, he asked, was good news about that?

We have only touched on Paul's contribution to the development of the western doctrine of justification. We must now turn to consider the role of the Pauline epistles in much greater detail.

1.2   Paul and the shaping of the Christian tradition

From the earliest times, Christian theologians have forged their theology through an obedient yet creative interaction with Scripture, with the Pauline epistles playing a particularly significant role in determining the contours of the emerging doctrine of justification in the West. The reasons for this are not difficult to discern: chief among them is the simple fact that the language of 'justification' is especially associated with Paul, and concentrated in the letters to Rome and Galatia. In one sense, the debates over justification within the western church may be regarded as an attempt to come to terms with the Pauline heritage, and to extract a coherent understanding of the grounds and nature of justification from this source.[61]

It is, however, necessary to appreciate that the church's attempt to grasp Paul's concept of justification is as a ship still at sea, rather than one which has entered its intellectual harbour. What is presented in this section is simply an overview of some of the themes that have dominated

century – namely, the transition of terms derived from Hebrew, Greek and Latin into *English*. For historical reasons, English developed two roots capable of expressing the Latin concept *iustitia* – the term 'justice', deriving from the Latin via a French intermediary, and 'righteousness', deriving from Anglo-Saxon roots. Although arguably equivalent in some ways, the two terms have come to have quite different connotations. 'Justice' has primarily legal connotations, whereas 'righteousness' tends to be associated with personal morality.

[60] See further H. Thielicke, 'Ius divinum und ius humanum', in G. Kretschmar and B. Lohse (eds.), *Ecclesia und Res Publica*, Göttingen: Vandenhoeck & Ruprecht, 1961, 162–75.

[61] For an excellent summary of the debates, with good bibliographies, see J. Dunn, *The Theology of Paul the Apostle*, Grand Rapids: Eerdmans, 1998.

the western theological tradition as it sought to make sense of this fundamental resource. It can only be descriptive, and makes no pretence at being prescriptive. Biblical scholars are cited to illustrate the importance of the debates and their possible outcomes; in no way can these matters be considered to have been settled. The entire subject matter of this book can be regarded as an extended attempt to interpret Paul correctly, and to erect such theological superstructure as may be thought necessary upon its basis.

Paul's use of the concept of justification is focussed particularly on two letters – Romans and Galatians – in which it plays a critical and constructive role in clarifying the connections and distinctions between Christianity and Judaism, particularly with regard to the relation of the 'works of the law' and 'faith'.[62] To speak of Paul's concept of 'justification' is perhaps misleading; the idea is expressed as a noun (*diakaiosis*) only twice in the Pauline letters. For Paul, justification is a divine action, and is thus to be expressed as a verb (*dikaioun*).[63] The Pauline vocabulary relating to justification is grounded in the Old Testament, and seems to express the notion of 'rightness' or 'rectitude' rather than 'righteousness'.[64] The Old Testament prefers the verb, rather than the noun, presumably thereby indicating that justification results from an action of God, whereby an individual is set in a right relationship with God – that is, vindicated, or declared to be in the right. Paul echoes this emphasis, using the verb 'to justify' to designate God's powerful, cosmic and universal action in effecting a change in the situation between sinful humanity and God, by which God is able to acquit and vindicate believers, setting them in a right and faithful relation to him.[65]

It has, however, proved problematical to integrate Paul's statements on justification into a coherent theological system. While Heikki Räisänen's thesis that Paul was neither a systematic nor a consistent thinker[66] has

---

[62] This is best construed as apologetic, rather than polemical, in tone: see W. S. Campbell, 'The Romans Debate', *JSNT* 10 (1981), 9–28.

[63] The verb is found 23 times, 8 in Galatians and 15 in Romans. The noun is found only in Romans.

[64] This point is made by a number of commentators. B. F. Westcott, *St Paul and Justification*, London: Macmillan, 1913, 38, suggests that 'rightness' is the fundamental theme of Paul's view of the gospel. See further L. E. Keck, *Paul and His Letters*, 2nd edn, Philadelphia: Fortress Press, 1988, 110–20; R. K. Moore, *Rectification ('Justification') in Paul, in Historical Perspective, and in the English Bible*, Lewiston: Edwin Mellen Press, 2002.

[65] See D. A. Campbell, *The Rhetoric of Righteousness in Romans 3.21–26*, Sheffield: Sheffield Academic Press, 1992.

[66] H. Räisänen, *Paul and the Law*, 2nd edn, Tübingen: Mohr, 1987, xi. See the positive comments of A. J. M. Wedderburn, 'Paul and the Law', *SJTh* 38 (1985), 613–22.

met with considerable resistance,[67] it remains difficult to integrate Paul's statements on justification into a coherent whole without recourse to subtle nuancing, strategic emphasis or selective attention. For example, Karl Donfried has recently suggested that the key Pauline concepts of justification, sanctification and salvation may be accommodated within a rather neat past–present–future framework, as follows:[68]

justification: a past event, with present implications (sanctification);
sanctification: a present event, dependent upon a past event (justification), which has future implications (salvation);
salvation: a future event, already anticipated and partially experienced in the past event of justification and the present event of sanctification, and dependent upon them.

Despite its admirable neatness, this approach is clearly inadequate. For example, within the Pauline corpus, justification has future, as well as past, reference (Romans 2:13; 8:33; Galatians 5:4–5), and appears to relate to both the beginning of the Christian life and its final consummation. Similarly, sanctification can also refer to a past event (1 Corinthians 6:11), or a future event (1 Thessalonians 5:23). And salvation is an exceptionally complex idea, embracing not simply a future event, but something which has happened in the past (Romans 8:24; 1 Corinthians 15:2), or which is even taking place now (1 Corinthians 1:18).

Justification language appears in Paul with reference to both the inauguration of the life of faith, and also its final consummation. It is a complex and all-embracing notion, which anticipates the verdict of the final judgement (Romans 8:30–4), declaring in advance the verdict of ultimate acquittal. The believer's present justified Christian existence is thus an anticipation of and advance participation in deliverance from the wrath to come, and an assurance in the present of the final eschatological verdict of acquittal (Romans 5:9–10).

So is the concept of justification of central importance to Paul? The question of the precise role of the concept of justification to Paul's understanding of the gospel remains intensely controversial within modern Pauline scholarship. Martin Luther regarded it as central, not simply to the apostle's theology, but to the proclamation of the Christian gospel as a whole, a judgement which some leading Protestant theologians maintain to this day.[69] While some recent writers have endorsed Luther's position,

---

[67] Most notably, see T. E. van Spanje, *Inconsistency in Paul? A Critique of the Work of Heikki Räisänen*, Tübingen: Mohr Siebeck, 1999.
[68] Donfried, 'Justification and Last Judgement in Paul'. See also Cosgrove, 'Justification in Paul'; Seifrid, *Justification by Faith*.
[69] Most notably, Jüngel, *Das Evangelium von der Rechtfertigung des Gottlosen als Zentrum des christlichen Glaubens*.

others have been somewhat more critical of this traditional Lutheran stance, seeing the centre of gravity of Paul's thought as lying elsewhere. On their reading of Paul, it is actually quite difficult to identify *any* centre to his thought, not least because there is disagreement among scholars as to what the idea of a 'centre' actually means. A principle of coherence? A summarising principle? A criterion of authenticity?[70] These difficulties stand in the path of any attempt to reach agreement on the importance of justification to Paul's thought. Three broad positions may be discerned within recent scholarship on this question.[71]

1. Justification by faith is of central importance to Paul's conception of Christianity. As noted above, this position has strong historical associations with Martin Luther, and it is perhaps not totally surprising that it is echoed by many modern German Lutheran New Testament scholars. This school of thought tends to regard justification as the real theological centre of gravity within Paul's thought, and is critical of any attempt to treat it as being of lesser importance. Justification by faith is not simply concerned with clarifying the Christian gospel in relation to first-century Judaism; it addresses the fundamental question of how sinful human beings can find favour or acceptance in the sight of a righteous God.[72]

Nevertheless, differences can be discerned within this broad approach. For example, Bultmann adopts what is recognisably a Lutheran position, stressing the positive importance of faith, while at the same time interpreting Paul's 'justification' language in existentialist terms. On the other hand, C. E. B. Cranfield takes what appears to be a more Reformed position on this matter (although it must be noted that this appears to be the outcome rather than the presupposition of his reflections), noting the continuing importance of the law for Paul.[73]

2. Justification by faith is a 'subsidiary crater' (Albert Schweitzer) in Paul's overall presentation and understanding of the Christian gospel. The origins of this view may be traced back to the nineteenth century,

---

[70] For related problems in identifying a literary or theological 'centre' in other biblical writings, see G. Fohrer, 'Der Mittelpunkt einer Theologie des Alten Testaments', *ThZ* 24 (1968), 161–72; K. Backhaus, 'Die Vision vom ganz Anderen: Geschichtlicher Ort und theologische Mitte der Johannes-Offenbarung', in K. Kertelge (ed.), *Theologie als Vision: Studien zur Johannes-Offenbarung*, Stuttgart: Verlag Katholisches Bibelwerk, 2001, 10–53.

[71] See, for example, C. J. A. Hickling, 'Centre and Periphery in the Thought of St Paul', *StB* 3, Sheffield: Sheffield Academic Press, 1978, 199–214.

[72] See, for example, H. Bornkamm, *Paul*, New York: Harper & Row, 1971; E. Käsemann, '"The Righteousness of God" in Paul', in *New Testament Questions of Today*, London: SCM Press, 1969, 168–82; Kertelge, *'Rechtfertigung' bei Paulus*; C. Müller, *Gottesgerechtigkeit und Gottesvolk*, Göttingen: Vandenhoeck & Ruprecht, 1964.

[73] C. E. B. Cranfield, *The Epistle to the Romans*, 2 vols., Edinburgh: T. & T. Clark, 1975.

especially the writings of William Wrede. Wrede argued that justification by faith was simply a polemical doctrine, designed to neutralise the theological threat posed by Judaism. Having neutralised this threat, Paul was then able to develop the positive aspects of his own thought (which, for Wrede, centred on the idea of redemption in Christ). The real emphasis of Paul's thought thus lies elsewhere than justification. Among those who adopt this position, the following may be noted (along with their views on where the centre of Paul's thought really lies): Schweitzer (the rising and dying of the believer with Christ),[74] R. P. Martin (reconciliation with God),[75] and E. P. Sanders (believing participation in Christ).[76]

3. A third view may be regarded as a compromise between these two views. Justification by faith is regarded as one of a number of ways of conceptualising what God has achieved for believers in and through Christ.[77] The centre of Paul's thought does not lie with justification as such; rather it lies with the grace of God. But justification is one of a number of ways of describing this grace (in juridical terms of unconditional pardon and forgiveness). It is thus central in one sense (in that it is a way of expressing the core of the gospel), and not central in another (in that it is only one way, among others, of expressing this core).

We have already noted that there is a close semantic connection between terms such as 'justification' (*dikaiosis*) and 'righteousness' (*dikaiosyne*) in Paul's thought. The idea of the revelation of the righteousness of God is obviously of major importance to Christian reflection on the grounds and means of salvation. It is therefore entirely to be expected that there has been an extensive and complex history of interpretation of this term within the western Christian tradition. Augustine of Hippo argued that 'the righteousness of God' referred, not to the personal righteousness of God (in other words, the righteousness by which God is himself righteous), but to the righteousness which he bestows upon sinners, in order to justify them (in other words, the righteousness which comes from God).

This interpretation of the phrase seems to have dominated the western theological tradition until the fourteenth century, when writers such as Gabriel Biel began to reinterpret it in terms of 'the righteousness by

---

[74] Schweitzer, *Die Mystik des Apostels Paulus.*
[75] R. P. Martin, *Reconciliation: A Study of Paul's Theology*, Atlanta: John Knox Press, 1981.
[76] E. P. Sanders, *Paul and Palestinian Judaism*, London: SCM Press, 1977, 467–8.
[77] See, for example, J. Jeremias, *The Central Message of the New Testament*, New York: Charles Scribner's Sons, 1965. See also his earlier discussion of the conceptual equivalence of 'the righteousness of God' and 'the salvation of God': J. Jeremias, *Der Opfertod Jesu Christi*, Stuttgart: Calwer Verlag, 1963, 19.

which God is himself righteous' – an interpretation which led to Luther's sustained engagement with the issue around 1515. Such an understanding of the nature of the righteousness of God has continued to find service in the modern period, especially on the part of Lutheran interpreters of Paul. Two such interpreters may be considered in a little more detail – Rudolf Bultmann and Ernst Käsemann.

Bultmann, basing himself especially on Romans 10:3 and Philippians 3:9, argued that the 'righteousness of God' was not a moral, but a relational, term. The believer is counted as being righteous, on account of his or her faith. The term 'righteousness of God' represents a genitive of authorship. Whereas Judaism regarded the bestowal of this righteousness as part and parcel of the future eschatological hope, something which would happen at the end of history, Bultmann argues that Paul is declaring that this righteousness is imputed to believers in the present time, through faith.[78]

Käsemann subjected Bultmann's interpretation to a penetrating criticism, on a number of grounds. First, he argued that Bultmann had fallen into the trap of a radical individualism, based on his anthropocentric approach to theology. Bultmann was mainly concerned with questions of human existence; he ought, according to Käsemann, to have concentrated on the purpose of God. Furthermore, by interpreting 'the righteousness of God' as a genitive of authorship, Bultmann had managed to drive a wedge between the God who gives and the gift which is given. Bultmann's approach isolates the gift from the giver, and concentrates upon the gift itself, rather than upon God himself. Käsemann comments thus: 'The Gift can never be separated from the Giver; it participates in the power of God, since God steps on to the scene in the gift.'

This lack of balance could be recovered by understanding 'righteousness' as referring to God himself, rather than to that which he gives. Käsemann then argues that the 'righteousness of God' refers to God in action. It refers to both God's power and God's gift. (Strictly speaking, then, Käsemann is not treating the 'righteousness of God' as a statement about God's attributes, but as a reference to God in action.) A cluster of phrases may help convey the sort of things that Käsemann has in mind here: 'salvation-creating power'; 'a transformation of [our] existence'; 'the power-character of the Gift'; 'a change of Lordship'. The basic theme that recurs throughout Käsemann's discussion is that of God's saving power

---

[78] Stuhlmacher, *Gerechtigkeit Gottes bei Paulus*; see also J. Reumann, *Righteousness in the New Testament*, Philadelphia: Fortress Press, 1982; J. A. Ziesler, *The Meaning of Righteousness in Paul*, Cambridge: Cambridge University Press, 1972; Hempel, *Rechtfertigung als Wirklichkeit*.

and action, revealed eschatologically in Jesus Christ. It merges a number of central Pauline themes, including those of victory through Christ, God's faithfulness to his covenant, and his giving of himself in power and action.[79]

Käsemann's approach has been very influential in recent years, both positively and negatively. Basing himself on Käsemann, Peter Stuhlmacher argues that it is unacceptable to treat the 'righteousness of God' as if it were a purely theocentric notion or an exclusively anthropocentric idea. It brings together elements of both, as the embodiment of the saving action of God in Christ, which brings new life for believers in its wake. The righteousness of God is both demonstrated and seen in action in the redemptive event of Christ – both in terms of God's faithfulness to his covenant, and in terms of the salvific transformation of the believer.

Once more, an important debate is still under way, and has yet to be resolved. J. Reumann suggests that four main lines of interpretation of the 'righteousness of God' may be discerned, along with their respective modern champions, as follows:[80]

1. An objective genitive: 'a righteousness which is valid before God' (Luther).
2. A subjective genitive: 'righteousness as an attribute or quality of God' (Käsemann).
3. A genitive of authorship: 'a righteousness that goes forth from God' (Bultmann).
4. A genitive of origin: 'humanity's righteous status which is the result of God's action of justifying' (C. E. B. Cranfield).

So in what way, according to Paul, does the 'righteousness of God' entail the justification of humanity? In recent years, a considerable debate on the relation of Paul's views on justification to those of first-century Judaism has developed, centring upon the writings of E. P. Sanders, especially *Paul and Palestinian Judaism* (1977), which was followed several years later by the more important *Paul, the Law and the Jewish People* (1983). Sanders' work represents a demand for a complete reappraisal of existing understandings of Paul's relation to the Judaism of his time. Sanders noted that Paul has too often been read through Lutheran eyes.

According to Luther's interpretation of Paul (which, in marked contrast to the Reformed standpoint, linked with Bullinger and Calvin, stresses the divergence between the law and the gospel), Paul criticised a totally

---

[79] Käsemann, *New Testament Questions of Today*; idem, *Commentary on Romans*. See Zahl, *Die Rechtfertigungslehre Ernst Käsemanns*, 58–62. See also S. K. Williams, 'The "Righteousness of God" in Romans', *JBL* 99 (1980), 241–90.
[80] Reumann, *Righteousness in the New Testament*, passim.

misguided attempt on the part of Jewish legalists to find favour and acceptance in the sight of God, by earning righteousness through performing
works of the law. This view, Sanders argued, coloured the analysis of such
Lutheran writers as Käsemann and Bultmann. These scholars, perhaps
unwittingly, read Paul through Lutheran spectacles, and thus failed to
realise that Paul had to be read against his proper historical context in
first-century Judaism – a religion of grace, rather than of legalism.[81]

According to Sanders, Palestinian Judaism at the time of Paul could be
characterised as a form of 'covenantal nomism'. The law is to be regarded
as an expression of the covenant between God and Israel, and is intended
to spell out as clearly and precisely as possible what forms of human conduct are appropriate within the context of this covenant. Righteousness
is thus defined as behaviour or attitudes which are consistent with being
the historical covenant people of God.[82] 'Works of the law' are thus not
understood (as Luther suggested) as the means by which Jews believed
they could gain access to the covenant; for they already stood within it.
Rather, these works are an expression of the fact that the Jews already
belonged to the covenant people of God, and were living out their obligations to that covenant.

Sanders thus rejects the opinion that 'the righteousness which comes
from the law' is 'a meritorious achievement which allows one to demand
reward from God and is thus a denial of grace'. 'Works of the law' were
understood as the basis, not of entry to the covenant, but of maintaining
that covenant. As Sanders puts it, 'works are the condition of remaining
"in", but they do not earn salvation'. If Sanders is right, the basic features of Luther's interpretation of Paul are incorrect, and require radical
revision.

So what, then, is Paul's understanding of the difference between
Judaism and Christianity, according to Sanders? Having argued that Jews
never believed in salvation on account of works or unaided human effort,
what does Sanders see as providing the distinctive advantage of Christianity over and against Judaism? Having argued that it is not correct to
regard Judaism as a religion of merit and Christianity as a religion of
grace, Sanders argues that Judaism perceives the hope of the Jewish people for salvation as resting upon 'their status as God's covenant people
who possess the law', whereas Christians believe in 'a better righteousness
based solely upon believing participation in Christ'. Paul, like Judaism,
was concerned with the issue of entering into and remaining within the

---

[81] Sanders, *Paul and Palestinian Judaism*; idem, *Paul, the Law, and the Jewish People*. See
further Dunn, 'The New Perspective on Paul'; Westerholm, *Israel's Law and the Church's
Faith*; Wright, *The Climax of the Covenant*.
[82] For a related theme at Qumran, see Betz, 'Rechtfertigung in Qumran'.

covenant. The basic difference is Paul's declaration that the Jews have no national charter of privilege; membership of the covenant is open to all who have faith in Christ, and who thus stand in continuity with Abraham (Romans 4).

This approach is not without difficulties.[83] First, Sanders is rather vague about why Paul is convinced of the superiority of Christianity over Judaism. Judaism is presented as being wrong, simply because it is not Christianity. They are different dispensations of the same covenant. But, as Sanders' critics have noted, Paul seems to regard Christianity as far more than some kind of dispensational shift within Judaism; salvation-history does not account for all that Paul says, much less for the passion with which he says it.[84]

Second, Sanders suggests that both Paul and Judaism understand works as the principle of continuing in salvation through the covenant. Yet Paul appears to regard good works as evidential, rather than instrumental. In other words, they are demonstration of the fact that the believer stands within the covenant, rather than instrumental in maintaining him within that covenant. One enters within the sphere of the covenant through faith. There is a radical new element here, which does not fit as easily with existing Jewish ideas as Sanders seems to imply. Sanders may well be right in suggesting that good works are both a *condition for* and a *sign of* remaining within the covenant. Paul, however, sees *faith* as the necessary and sufficient condition for and sign of being in the covenant, with works as (at best) a sign of remaining within its bounds.

Third, Sanders tends to regard Paul's doctrine of justification in a slightly negative light, as posing a challenge to the notion of a national ethnic election. In other words, Paul's doctrine of justification is a subtle challenge to the notion that Israel has special religious rights on account of its national identity. However, N. T. Wright has argued that Paul's doctrine of justification should be viewed positively, as an attempt to redefine who comes within the ambit of the promises made by God to Abraham.[85] Paul's teaching on justification by faith is thus seen as Paul's redefinition of how the inheritance of Abraham genuinely embraces the Gentiles apart from the law.

This modern debate is of considerable importance, as it marks a significant shift in interpretation of Paul. Most earlier Christian writers in

---

[83] For some important comments, see F. Thielman, *From Plight to Solution: A Jewish Framework for Understanding Paul's View of the Law in Galatians and Romans*, Leiden: Brill, 1989.

[84] See Gundry, 'Grace, Works, and Staying Saved in Paul', 1–38.

[85] Wright, *The Climax of the Covenant*. For an evaluation of Wright's approach, see C. C. Newman (ed.), *Jesus and the Restoration of Israel: A Critical Assessment of N. T. Wright's "Jesus and the Victory of God"*, Downers Grove: InterVarsity Press, 1999.

the West did not explore Paul's relation with Judaism in exploring his doctrine of justification.[86] For most patristic and medieval writers, the idea of being justified by 'works of the law' was synonymous with the idea of achieving salvation by moral effort, or being accepted by God on account of one's religious or ethical achievements. The term 'works of the law' was not interpreted within a specifically Jewish context, but as a universalised category addressing the universal human tendency to self-justification and self-assertion.

A tradition of interpretation within Protestant Pauline scholarship, drawing its inspiration largely from Luther in the sixteenth century, argued for an absolute contradiction between justification by faith and human works in the Pauline corpus.[87] The phrase 'works of the law' is here understood to mean something like 'human achievement', losing its specific cultic meaning within its original Jewish context.[88] On this reading of Paul, 'faith' and 'works' are to be seen as mutually exclusive entities, designating two radically opposed ways of thinking about, and responding to, God. The way of works is seen as orientated towards human achievement, centred upon human righteousness, and based upon human merit. The way of faith is seen as radically opposed, orientated towards God's achievement in Christ, centred upon the righteousness of God, and based upon divine grace.

Yet many recent writers have suggested that this represents an inadequate understanding of a complex aspect of Paul's understanding of justification, which fails to do justice to the highly nuanced understanding of the relation of faith and works within Paul's thought, most notably expressed in the terse statement that 'not the hearers, but the doers of the law will be justified' (Romans 2:13). Some have sought to dismiss this as a vestige of Paul's Jewish phase, although this has failed to win general acceptance.

Perhaps the most important issue to emerge from recent Pauline interpretation in this area aims to clarify the relation between Paul's theme of 'justification by faith' and 'judgement by works'. There seems to be an apparent contradiction here, the resolution of which is made considerably more difficult by the fact that Paul can speak of this future judgement both negatively (as a warning against disobedience) and positively (as an encouragement for obedience). E. P. Sanders argues that Paul reproduces a characteristic first-century Jewish attitude, which could be summarised in the words: 'God judges according to their deeds those whom he saves

---

[86] See Roo, 'The Concept of "Works of the Law" in Jewish and Christian Literature'.
[87] See Kroeger, *Rechtfertigung und Gesetz*; Joest, *Gesetz und Freiheit*.
[88] See Roo, 'The Concept of "Works of the Law" in Jewish and Christian Literature'.

by his grace.' Justification by faith resonates with the theme of grace –
so why are believers going to be judged on the basis of their works (e.g.,
Romans 2:12; 14:10; 1 Corinthians 3:15; 2 Corinthians 5:10), which
resonates with the theme of human achievement? But this statement of
the problem fails to deal with the fact that justification is seen, not as
something in the past, but as something with future reference (Romans
2:13; 8:33; Galatians 5:4–5). It is not simply a case of being justified in
the past and judged in the future; there is a 'not yet' element to Paul's
teaching on justification, which Sanders cannot quite explain.

One possible explanation of the way in which justification and future
judgement are related involves an enhanced sensitivity towards the different contexts which the Pauline letters presuppose.[89] Paul's message
of justification is directed towards audiences with very different back-
grounds. The one doctrine finds itself applied practically for very different ends. The Corinthians appeared to be living in a state of delusion and
spiritual arrogance; Paul's objective is to break down their arrogance by
warning them of judgement. Paul does not intend the message of judgement to be his last word, but rather the word they need to hear so long
as they remain unaware of the full implications of the gospel. On the
other hand, those who exist in a state of spiritual dejection or discourage-
ment need reassurance of the unconditionality of grace. If this approach
is correct, it implies that the theme of judgement by works is not Paul's
final word to his audience; it is his penultimate word, determined by the
pastoral situation of his audience, and intended to shake up those who
exploit (and thus distort) the gospel proclamation of grace. Yet the idea
of a 'penultimate' word raises certain difficulties, not least over how one
might be reassured that it is indeed God's penultimate (and not final)
word.

We shall return to consider the 'new perspective' on Paul later in this
work, in assessing some of the challenges raised for the doctrine of justification in the later twentieth century. The debate is far from over. In this
present section, we have noted some themes of debate which emerge from
Paul's epistles, and seen at least something of the manner in which they
impacted on the western debates on the nature and means of justification.
The purpose of this survey has been, not to establish Paul's precise teaching on justification – which remains contested – but to indicate something
about the vocabulary, conceptualities and issues associated with his presentation of the doctrine. Inevitably and properly, these have played a
major, if not decisive, role in shaping Christian theological discussion
down the ages.

---

[89] See here Watson, 'Justified by Faith, Judged by Works: An Antimony?'

The remainder of this work will explore the way in which Paul's concept of justification was developed within the western theological tradition. In the case of this specific doctrine, the full exploration of its importance dates from the Middle Ages, rather than the patristic era. In this chapter, therefore, we shall consider the way in which the debates of the patristic period laid the foundations for this later consolidation, having particular regard to the significant contribution of Augustine of Hippo. To begin with, we may note some trends in the pre-Augustinian tradition.

1.3   The pre-Augustinian tradition

The patristic era is that of the exploration, and where possible the reduction, of the tension existing between the need to retain a traditional corpus of belief as the *regula fidei*,[90] and the need to expand and develop that corpus in the face of opposition from both within and without the Christian community. The earlier patristic period represents the age of the exploration of concepts, when the proclamation of the gospel within a pagan culture was accompanied by an exploitation of both Hellenistic culture and pagan philosophy as vehicles for theological advancement.[91] The use of such concepts in Christian theology was not, however, without its risks; it was not sufficient merely to baptise Plato and Plotinus, for the tension which existed between the essentially Hebraic concepts which underlie the gospel and the Hellenism of the medium employed in its early formulation and propagation remains unresolved. While it is evident that some form of adaptation may be necessary in order to give the gospel more immediate impact on its introduction to an alien culture, it is equally evident that such an adaptation may result in both compromise and distortion of the characteristic and distinctive elements of the gospel. An excellent example of the influence of a Hellenistic milieu upon Christian theology is provided by the doctrine of the impassibility of God,[92] which clearly suggests the subordination of a biblical to a philosophical view of God.

---

[90] G. G. Blum, *Tradition und Sukzession: Studien zum Normbegriff des Apostolischen von Paulus bis Irenaeus*, Berlin: Lutherisches Verlagshaus, 1963.

[91] H. Chadwick, *Early Christian Thought and the Classical Tradition: Studies in Justin, Clement, and Origen*, Oxford: Clarendon Press, 1966.

[92] J. K. Mozley, *The Impassibility of God*, Cambridge: Cambridge University Press, 1926; R. B. Edwards, 'The Pagan Doctrine of the Absolute Unchangeableness of God', *RelSt* 14 (1978) 305–13. For a criticism of this doctrine, see J. Moltmann, *Der gekreuzigte Gott: Das Kreuz Christi als Grund und Kritik christlicher Theologie*, Munich: Kaiser Verlag, 1984, especially 256–8; W. McWilliams, 'Divine Suffering in Contemporary Theology', *SJTh* 33 (1980), 33–54; K. Surin, 'The Impassibility of God and the Problem of Evil', *SJTh* 35 (1982), 97–119.

The history of early Christian doctrine is basically the history of the emergence of the Christological and Trinitarian dogmas. While the importance of soteriological considerations, both in the motivation of the development of early Christian doctrine and as a normative principle during the course of that development, is generally conceded,[93] it is equally evident that the early Christian writers did not choose to express their soteriological convictions in terms of the concept of justification. This is not to say that the fathers avoid the term 'justification'; their interest in the concept is, however, minimal, and the term generally occurs in their writings as a direct citation from, or a recognisable allusion to, the epistles of Paul, usually employed for some purpose other than a discussion of the concept of justification itself.

Furthermore, the few occasions upon which a specific discussion of justification can be found almost always involve no interpretation of the matter other than a mere paraphrase of a Pauline statement. The relationship between faith and works is explored, yet without moving significantly beyond a modest restatement of Paul's original statements,[94] in which the phrase 'works of the law' is generally interpreted as general human achievements, rather than a more specific cultic demand, peculiar to Israel's identify. Justification was simply not a theological issue in the pre-Augustinian tradition. The emerging patristic understanding of matters such as predestination, grace and free will is somewhat confused, and would remain so until controversy forced a full discussion of the issue upon the church.[95] Indeed, by the end of the fourth century, the Greek fathers had formulated a teaching on human free will based upon philosophical rather than biblical foundations. Standing in the great Platonic tradition, heavily influenced by Philo, and reacting against the fatalisms of their day, they taught that humankind was utterly free in its choice of good or evil. It is with the Latin fathers that we observe the beginnings of speculation on the nature of original sin and corruption, and the implications which this may have for people's moral faculties.[96]

Krister Stendahl put into words a thought that passed through my mind on many occasions as I wrestled with the patristic corpus for the

---

[93] Loofs, *Leitfaden zum Studien der Dogmengeschichte*, 229–32; M. F. Wiles, *The Making of Christian Doctrine: A Study in the Principles of Early Doctrinal Development*, Cambridge: Cambridge University Press, 1978, 94–113.

[94] Eno, 'Some Patristic Views on the Relationship of Faith and Works in Justification'.

[95] Beck, *Vorsehung und Vorherbestimmung*; Wörter, *Verhältnis von Gnade und Freiheit*.

[96] For an introduction to the questions involved, see S. Lyonnet, 'Le Sens de *eph'ho* en Rom v. 12 et l'exégèse des pères grecs', *Biblica* 36 (1955), 436–57; idem, 'Le Péché originel et l'exégèse de Rom v.12–14', *RSR* 44 (1956) 63–84; idem, 'Le Péché originel en Rom v.12: L'Exégèse des pères grecs et les décrets du Concile de Trente', *Biblica* 41 (1960), 325–55.

purposes of this present study. 'It has always been a puzzling fact that Paul meant so relatively little for the thinking of the church during the first 350 years of its history. To be sure, he is honoured and quoted, but – in the theological perspective of the west – it seems that Paul's great insight into justification by faith was forgotten.'[97] In part, the early patristic neglect of the Pauline writings may reflect uncertainty concerning the extent of the New Testament canon at this early stage. As the Pauline epistles came to be accorded increasing authority within the church, so their influence upon theological debate increased correspondingly. Thus the end of the period of oral tradition (c. 150) may be considered to mark a return to Paulinism in certain respects, so that writers such as Irenaeus of Lyons may be regarded as representing the gospel more accurately than Ignatius of Antioch.[98]

It must also be appreciated, however, that the early fathers do not appear to have been faced with a threat from Jewish Christian activists teaching justification by works of the law, such as is presupposed by those Pauline epistles dealing with the doctrine of justification by faith in most detail (e.g., Galatians). The only patristic work that appears to presuppose this specific threat is the tract *De his qui putant se ex operibus iustificari* of Mark the Hermit (fl. c. 431), probably dating from the early fifth century.[99] The main external threat to the early church, particularly during the second century, appears to have been pagan or semi-pagan fatalism, such as Gnosticism, which propagated the thesis that humans are responsible neither for their own sins nor for the evil of the world. It is quite possible that what some consider to be the curious and disturbing tendency of some of the early fathers to minimise original sin and emphasise the freedom of fallen humanity is a consequence of their anti-Gnostic polemic.[100] While it is true that the beginnings of a doctrine of grace may be discerned during this early period, its generally optimistic estimation of the capacities of fallen humanity has led at least some scholars to question whether it can be regarded as truly Christian in this respect.

The pre-Augustinian theological tradition is practically of one voice in asserting the freedom of the human will. Thus Justin Martyr rejects

---

[97] K. Stendahl, *Paul among Jews and Gentiles*, Philadelphia: Fortress Press, 1976, 83.

[98] Thus O. Cullmann, *The Early Church*, London: SCM Press, 1956, 96.

[99] Edition in PG 65.929–66. It is possible that this tract is part of the larger work *De lege spirituali*; see J. Quasten, *Patrology*, 3 vols., Westminster, MD: Newman Press, 1963, 3.505–6.

[100] See Wörter, *Verhältnis von Gnade und Freiheit*; T. F. Torrance, *The Doctrine of Grace in the Apostolic Fathers*, Edinburgh: Oliver & Boyd, 1948.

the idea that all human actions are foreordained on the grounds that this eliminates human accountability.[101] This argument is supplemented by an appeal to scriptural texts apparently teaching humanity's freedom of action, such as Deuteronomy 30:19: 'I have set before you life and death, the blessing and the curse; therefore choose life, that you may live.' It must be pointed out, of course, that the intellectual basis of Justin's defence of the free will does not appear to be specifically *Christian*. With the obvious exception of the use of biblical quotations, Justin's anti-fatalist arguments can be adduced from practically any of the traditional pagan refutations of astral fatalisms, going back to the second century BC.[102] Furthermore, the biblical quotations which Justin does employ can be shown to be predominantly from the Old Testament, and traditionally used in *Jewish* refutations of such fatalisms. Thus Philo of Alexandria had earlier used an anti-fatalist argument practically identical to Justin's, down to the decisive citation from Deuteronomy 30:19.[103]

While Justin's defence of the freedom of the will does not appear to have been occasioned by Gnosticism, its rise seems to have had a profound effect upon his successors. While there is still uncertainty concerning the precise nature of Gnosticism, it may be noted that a strongly fatalist or necessitarian outlook appears to be characteristic of the chief Gnostic systems.[104] Far from recognising the limitations of humanity's free will, many early fathers enthusiastically proclaimed its freedom and self-determination (*autexousia*).[105] The introduction of the *secular* concept of self-determination into the theological vocabulary of Christendom is of particular significance, particularly in view of its later application in the Macarian homilies, in which humanity's self-determination is proclaimed to be such that individuals can apply themselves either to good or to evil.[106] God cannot be said to force the free will, but merely to influence it. While God does not wish people to do evil, he cannot compel them to do good. John Chrysostom's defence of the power of the human free will was so convincing that it was taken up by many Pelagian writers: 'good and evil do not originate from human nature itself, but from the

---

[101] *I Apologia*, 43–4.

[102] Amand de Mendieta, *Fatalisme et liberté dans l'antiquité grecque*, 195–207.

[103] Amand de Mendieta, *Fatalisme et liberté dans l'antiquité grecque*, 6–7; J. Daniélou, *Philon d'Alexandrie*, Paris: Fayard, 1958, 175–81.

[104] H. Jonas, *The Gnostic Religion: The Message of the Alien God and the Beginnings of Christianity*, Boston: Beacon Press, 1958, 46–7, 270–7.

[105] Theophilus of Antioch, *Epistola ad Autolycum* ii, 27. For a discussion of the use of the term *autexousia* in early Pauline exegesis, see Schelkle, *Paulus Lehrer der Väter*, 439–40.

[106] Macarius of Egypt, *De custodia cordis* xii, PG 34.836A. See further Davids, *Das Bild vom neuen Menschen*.

will and choice alone'.[107] This localisation of the origin of sin in the mis-use of the human free will was a theological commonplace by the fourth century.

The patristic discussion of human freedom received significant development by the Cappadocians. Gregory of Nyssa distinguished two types of freedom: structural freedom, by which Adam was able to communicate with God and all of his creation; and functional freedom, by which humankind has freedom of choice. The former was lost at the Fall, but, by proper use of the latter, humans are able to regain it.[108] Nemesius of Emesa may be regarded as having developed this idea along Aristotelian lines, thus providing an important link between the latter patristic and early scholastic understandings of human freedom. Nemesius' distinction between the *voluntarium* and *involuntarium*, and his emphasis upon the role of *consilium* in decision-making, leads to his insistence that the human reason itself is the basis of humanity's freedom.

The western theological tradition was somewhat slower to develop than the eastern, and, in the course of that development, the theological vocabulary of the East became current in the West. This necessitated the translation of Greek theological terms into Latin, with inevitable shifts in their meanings as a result. It is almost certain, too, that the western theological tradition owes much of its vocabulary to Tertullian, including the Latin term which would now become the equivalent of *autexousia* – namely, *liberum arbitrium*.[109] The validity of this translation is open to question, in that *autexousia* really has to do with *exousia*, 'authority-to-act', and has at best remote associations with the concepts of 'will' and 'choice'. It may, indeed, be argued that the idea of 'will' (*voluntas*) became fully articulated only when the Latin language became the normal vehicle of Christian philosophical expression. The weakness of Pauline influence in the early church may be illustrated from the fact that non-Pauline, non-biblical terms such as *autexousia* and *liberum arbitrium* came to be introduced into the early Christian discussion of the justification of humanity before God. The 'self-determination' of the human free will is not a particularly Christian idea, being rather a philosophical idea of its early Hellenistic milieu. As we shall see, however, Augustine was able to achieve at least a degree of redirection of the concept in a more Pauline direction.

---

[107] John Chrysostom, *In epistolam ad Romanos*, Hom. xix, 6. It is significant that the Latin translations of Chrysostom's sermons were the work of the Pelagian Anianus of Celeda; see B. Altaner, 'Altlateinische Übersetzungen von Chrysostomusschriften', *Kleine patristische Schriften*, Texte und Untersuchungen 83 (1967), 416–36. Cf. PL 48.626–30.

[108] J. Gaïth, *La Conception de la liberté chez Grégoire de Nysse*, Paris: Vrin, 1953, 79–80.

[109] *De anima* 21, CSEL 20.334.27–9: 'Haec erit vis divinae gratiae, potentior utique natura, habens in nobis subiacentem sibi liberam arbitrii potestatem, quod *autexousion* dicitur.'

The earliest known Latin commentary upon the Pauline epistles is that of Ambrosiaster.[110] Most modern commentators on this important work recognise that its exposition of the doctrine of justification by faith is grounded in the contrast between Christianity and Judaism; there is no trace of a more universal interpretation of justification by faith meaning freedom from a law of works – merely freedom from the Jewish ceremonial law. The Pauline doctrine of freedom from the works of the law is given a specific historical context by Ambrosiaster, in the Jewish background to Christianity. In other respects, Ambrosiaster is more akin to Pelagius than to Augustine. The Pelagian controversy had yet to break, and much of Ambrosiaster's teaching seems strange in the light of that controversy. Like many of his contemporaries, for example, he appears to be obsessed with the idea that humans can acquire merit before God, and with the associated idea that certain labours are necessary to attain this.[111]

Similar ideas have often been detected in the writings of Tertullian, leading some commentators to suggest that his theology is merely a republication of that of Judaism, and others charging him with uniting Old Testament legalism with Roman moralism and jurisprudence.[112] His most debatable contribution to the developing western tradition on justification, his introduction of the term *liberum arbitrium* aside, is his theology of merit. For Tertullian, those who perform good works can be said to make God their debtor.[113] The understanding of the 'righteousness of God' as *reddens unicuique quod suum est* underlies this teaching. A similar tendency can be detected in his teaching that humans can 'satisfy' their obligation to God on account of their sin through penance.[114] Indeed, Tertullian has exercised a certain fascination over legal historians, who have noted with some interest his introduction into theology of legal terms such as *meritum* and *satisfactio*.[115] The concept of a divine obligation to humanity thus makes its appearance in the western theological tradition

---

[110] PL 17.45–508.

[111] A. Souter, *The Earliest Latin Commentaries on the Epistles of St Paul*, Oxford: Clarendon Press, 1927, 65, 72–3, 80.

[112] A. Nygren, *Agape and Eros*, Philadelphia: Fortress Press, 1953, 343–8.

[113] *De paenitentia* 2, CChr 1.323.44–6: 'bonum factum deum habet debitorem, sicuti et malum: quia iudex omnis remunerator est causae.'

[114] *De paenitentia* 5, CChr 1.328.32 – 329.25. It may, of course, be argued that there are grounds for suggesting the 'ingenuous use of *mereri* and *meritum*' in the pre-Augustinian tradition: see Bakhuizen van den Brink, 'Mereo(r) and meritum in Some Latin Fathers'. For an excellent study of Hilary of Poitiers' understanding of the relationship between merit and faith, see Peñamaria de Llano, *La salvación por la fe*, 191–247.

[115] A. Beck, *Römisches Recht bei Tertullian und Cyprian: Eine Studie zur frühen Kirchenrechtsgeschichte*, Halle: Niemeyer, 1930; P. Vitton, *I concetti giuridici nelle opere di Tertulliano*, Rome: Bretschneider, 1972, 50–4.

in a somewhat naive form, and once more it is due to the religious genius of Augustine that the concept was subjected to penetrating criticism.

For the first 350 years of the history of the church, its teaching on justification was inchoate and ill-defined. There had never been a serious controversy over the matter, such as those which had so stimulated the development of Christology over the period. The patristic inexactitude and occasional apparent naivety on the question merely reflects the absence of a controversy which would force more precise definition of the terms used. If the first centuries of the western theological tradition appear be characterised by a 'works-righteousness' approach to justification, it must be emphasised that this was quite innocent of the overtones which would later be associated with it. This 'works-righteousness' ceased to be innocent and ingenuous in the system of Pelagius and his followers, and came to threaten and obscure the gospel as the message of the free grace of God. It is therefore to Augustine of Hippo that we turn for the first definitive statements of the western doctrine of justification.

1.4   The fountainhead: Augustine of Hippo

No theological writer has exercised so great an influence over the development of western Christian thought as Augustine of Hippo. This influence is particularly associated with, although by no means restricted to, the theological renaissance of the twelfth century, and the Reformation of the sixteenth. Although we shall be considering Augustine's views, often at length, in discussing the medieval development of the doctrine of justification, it is clearly important to set out a general overview of his ideas at this earlier stage, before going on to present a more detailed engagment with his ideas later.

All medieval theology is 'Augustinian', to a greater or lesser extent. It is, however, remarkable that although much attention has been paid in the literature to Augustine's doctrine of *grace*, there is a virtual absence of studies dealing with his doctrine of *justification*.[116] This lacuna is all the more astonishing when the significance of Augustine's understanding of justification to his social and political thought is considered. The significance of Augustine's doctrine of justification to the present study relates to its subsequent influence upon the medieval period and beyond. Augustine's doctrine of justification is the first discussion of the matter of major significance to emerge from the twilight of the western theological

---

[116] For example, see the excellent studies of V. H. Drecoll, *Die Entstehung der Gnadenlehre Augustins*, Tübingen: Mohr Siebeck, 1999; and J. Lössl, *Intellectus Gratiae: Die erkenntnistheoretische und hermeneutische Dimension der Gnadenlehre Augustins von Hippo*, Leiden: Brill, 1997.

tradition, establishing the framework within which the future discussion of the justification of humankind before God would be conducted.

It is important to appreciate that Augustine's doctrine of justification underwent significant development. For example, prior to his elevation to the see of Hippo Regis in 395, Augustine appears to have held precisely the same opinion which he would later condemn – the Massilian attribution of the 'beginnings of faith' (*initium fidei*) to the human free will. Some thirty years after his consecration, Augustine conceded that his earlier works, particularly his *Expositio quarundam propositionum ex Epistola ad Romanos* (394), should be corrected in the light of his later insights concerning the doctrine of grace.[117] So when did Augustine change his mind on this crucial matter? Fortunately, we have his own answer to this question: it was 'in the first of two books written to Simplicianus', dating from late 396 or early 397.[118] This work is generally regarded as containing the key to Augustine's changed views on justification. In view of the fact that the Pelagian controversy would not break out until early the following century, it is important to appreciate that Augustine appears to have developed his new understanding of justification – which would henceforth bear the epithet 'Augustinian' – in a non-polemical context. It is not correct to suppose that Augustine's doctrine of justification is merely a reaction against Pelagianism, or even that it was forged in a polemical context.

Prior to 396, Augustine appears to have seen the spiritual life in Platonic terms as an ascent to perfection.[119] This understanding of the Christian life is particularly well expressed in his early conviction that humans can take the initiative in this spiritual ascent to God by believing in him and calling upon God to save them.[120] Augustine was forced to reappraise this youthful opinion in 395, when his Milanese acquaintance Simplicianus posed a series of questions relating to predestination. Why did God hate

---

[117] *De praedestinatione sanctorum* iii, 7; *Retractiones* I, xxiii, 3–4.

[118] *De praedestinatione sanctorum* iv, 8, PL 44.966a: 'Nam si curassent, invenissent istam quaestionem secundum veritatem divinarum scripturarum solutam in primo libro duorum, quos ad beatae memoriae Simplicianum scripsi episcopum Mediolanensis ecclesiae . . . in ipso exordio episcopatus mei.'

[119] P. Brown, *Augustine of Hippo*, London: Faber, 1967, 151. It is perhaps misleading for Brown to suggest that Augustine 'interpreted Paul as a Platonist' in his early period; to his dying day, Augustine never ceased to interpret Paul as a Platonist, and even died with a quotation from Plotinus on his lips. Presumably Brown intends us to understand that Augustine approached Paul with *different* Platonist presuppositions in his later period. (Thus it could be argued, for example, that his development of the doctrine of predestination reflects *Platonic* determinism as much as Pauline, in that the Neoplatonic tradition was never lacking in sympathy for determinist turns of thought, or for the attribution of human actions to transcendent forces and powers.)

[120] E.g., *De sermone Domini in monte* I, xviii, 55; *Expositio quarundam propositionum ex Epistola ad Romanos* 44.

Esau? Augustine appears to have avoided issues such as this up to this point, but was now obliged to consider the question – and as a result, he appears to have abandoned his earlier attempts to uphold the unrestricted freedom of the will.

Among the important changes in his thinking on justification as a result of his reflections on Romans 9:10–29, the following may be noted.

1. Humanity's election is now understood to be based upon God's eternal decree of predestination.[121] Augustine had earlier taught that humanity's temporal election of God is prior to God's eternal election of humanity.

2. Humanity's response of faith to God's offer of grace is now understood to be in itself a gift of God.[122] Augustine abandons his earlier teaching that the response of humans to God depends solely upon their unaided free will.

3. While conceding that the human free will is capable of many things, Augustine now insists that it is compromised by sin, and incapable of leading to justification unless it is first liberated by grace.[123]

In view of the facts that Augustine's teaching on justification appears to have altered so radically at this point, and that he is generally regarded as having worked within the same basic conceptual framework for the next thirty years,[124] it is clearly important to exclude any writings prior to his elevation to the episcopacy from our analysis of his mature doctrine of justification, which henceforth would be known as the 'classic Augustinian theology of grace'. We begin our analysis of this theology by considering one of its most difficult aspects – Augustine's teaching on the *liberum arbitrium*.

Luther's 1525 treatise *De servo arbitrio* derives its title from a phrase used in passing by Augustine in the course of his controversy with the Pelagian bishop Julian of Eclanum.[125] In selecting this phrase, Luther appears to claim the support of Augustine for his radical doctrine of the *servum arbitrium*. A consideration of Augustine's background, however, suggests that it is improbable that he held such a doctrine. He had

---

[121] *Ad Simplicianum* I, ii, 6.
[122] *Ad Simplicianum* I, ii, 12. Augustine here remarks that Paul 'ostendit etiam ipsam bonam voluntatem in nobis operante Deo fieri'; CChr 44.36.324–5.
[123] *Ad Simplicianum* I, ii, 21, CChr 44.53.740–2: 'Liberum voluntatis arbitrium plurimum valet, immo vero est quidem, sed in venundatis sub peccato, quid valet?'
[124] G. Nygren, *Das Prädestinationsproblem*, 47–8. This is not to exclude further development of significance prior to 396; thus, for example, his initial opinion that Paul was referring to unbelievers in Romans 7 later gave way to the insight that he was referring to believers.
[125] *Contra Iulianum* II, viii, 23: 'Sed vos festinatis et praesumptionem vestram festinando praecipitatis. Hic enim vultis hominem perfici, atque utinam Dei dono et non libero, vel potius servo proprie voluntatis arbitrio.'

been engaged in anti-Manichaean polemic for some time, defending the catholic teaching against its fatalist opponents. *De libero arbitrio* (388–95) was written against precisely such necessitarian teachings (e.g., that evil is natural, and not the work of the human free will). Although Augustine would later modify his earlier views on the nature of human *liberum arbitrium*, it is important to appreciate that the central thesis of the existence of such a *liberum arbitrium* was neither rejected nor radically altered.

In many respects, Pelagianism may be regarded as the antithesis of Manichaeism: whereas the latter rejected the existence of free will, the former exaggerated its role in justification. Augustine's first anti-Pelagian work, *De peccatorum meritis et remissione* (411), opened the attack against Pelagianism with the assertion that it attributed too much to the human *liberum arbitrium*, and thereby effectively denied the need for special grace. It must be stressed that Augustine does not refute the error by *denying* humanity's free will. Augustine insists that the need for grace can be defended without denying humanity's *liberum arbitrium*. His discussion of human freedom in justification proceeds upon the assumption that both grace and free will are to be affirmed, the problem requiring resolution being their precise relationship. God has given humans free will, without which they cannot be said to live well or badly,[126] and it is on the basis of their use of this *liberum arbitrium* that they will be judged. Grace, far from *abolishing* the free will, actually *establishes* it.[127] So how can this apparently inconsistent set of ideas be reconciled?

Augustine, reacting against the Pelagian exaggeration of fallen humanity's abilities, maintained that humanity possesses *liberum arbitrium*, while denying that this entailed that they also possess freedom (*libertas*).[128] The sinner has free will, but it is unable to function properly, and thus to allow them freedom. 'The free will taken captive (*liberum arbitrium captivatum*) does not avail, except for sin; for righteousness it does not avail, unless it is set free and aided by divine action.'[129] By *libertas*, Augustine means

---

[126] *De spiritu et littera* v, 7, CSEL 60.159.12–13: 'homini Deus dedit liberum arbitrium sine quo nec male nec bene vivitur'. For a more detailed analysis of Augustine's doctrine of *liberum arbitrium*, see Ball, 'Libre arbitre et liberté dans Saint Augustin'; idem, 'Les Développements de la doctrine de la liberté chez Saint Augustin'; G. R. Evans, *Augustine on Evil*, Cambridge: Cambridge University Press, 1982, 112–49.

[127] *De spiritu et littera* xxxiii, 58, CSEL 60.216.20–1: '[omnibus] adimat liberum arbitrium, quo vel bene vel male utentes iustissime iudicentur'; cf. *De spiritu et littera* xxx, 52, CSEL 60.208.16–27: 'Liberum ergo arbitrium evacuamus per gratiam? Absit; sed magis liberum arbitrium statuimus . . . quia gratia sanat voluntatem, qua iustitia libere diligatur'.

[128] *De natura et gratia* lxvi, 77.

[129] *Contra duas epistolas Pelagianorum* III, viii, 24, CSEL 60.516.24–6: 'Et liberum arbitrium captivatum non nisi ad peccatum valet, ad iustitiam vero nisi divinitus liberatum adiutumque non valet.'

the power to choose and accomplish good – a power which fallen human nature does not possess. However, this loss of *libertas* does not imply the loss of *liberum arbitrium*. The human will cannot be likened to a scale, in whose balance-pans the arguments for and against a possible course of action are carefully weighed before any action is taken (i.e., *libertas indifferentiae*), as Julian of Eclanum insisted was the case.[130] While Augustine allows that the scales in question really do exist, and are capable of operating, he argues that the balance-pans are loaded on the side of evil, yielding a judgement invariably biased towards evil. Although Adam possessed *liberum arbitrium* before the Fall, humanity's free will is now compromised by sin, so that it is now *liberum arbitrium captivatum*. The free will is not lost, nor is it non-existent; it is merely incapacitated, and may be healed by grace.[131] In justification, the *liberum arbitrium captivatum* becomes the *liberum arbitrium liberatum* by the action of this healing grace. Hence the possibility of not sinning cannot exist in fallen humankind, although Augustine is at pains to point out that this does not exclude the natural freedom of humans. God would not command us to do something unless there was free will by which we could do it. Augustine's ethics presuppose that humans' destiny is determined by merit or demerit, which together in turn presuppose – at least for Augustine – that humans possess free will. 'If there is no such thing as God's grace, how can he be the saviour of the world? And if there is no such thing as free will, how can he be its judge?'[132] Augustine's concept of *liberum arbitrium captivatum* resolves the dialectic between grace and free will without denying the reality of either.

For Augustine, the human *liberum arbitrium captivatum* is incapable of either desiring or attaining justification. How, then, does faith, the fulcrum about which justification takes place, arise in the individual? According to Augustine, the act of faith is itself a divine gift, in which God acts upon the rational soul in such a way that it comes to believe. Whether this action on the will leads to its subsequent assent to justification is a matter for humanity, rather than for God. 'The one who created you without you will not justify you without you' ('Qui fecit te sine te, non te iustificat sine te').[133] Although God is the origin of the gift which humans are able to receive and possess, the acts of receiving and possessing themselves can be said to be the humans'.

To meet what he regarded as Pelagian evasions, Augustine drew a distinction between *operative* and *co-operative* grace (or, more accurately,

---

[130] On Julian's views, see J. Lössl, *Julian von Aeclanum: Studien zu seinem Leben, seinem Werk, seiner Lehre und ihrer Überlieferung*, Leiden: Brill, 2001.
[131] See the medical image employed in *De natura et gratia* iii, 3.
[132] *Epistola* 214, 2.   [133] *Sermo* 169, 13.

between operative and co-operative modes of gratuitous divine action: Augustine does not treat them as distinct species). God *operates* to initiate humanity's justification, in that humans are given a will capable of desiring good, and subsequently *co-operate* with that good will to perform good works, to bring that justification to perfection. God operates upon the bad desires of the *liberum arbitrium captivatum* to allow it to will good, and subsequently co-operates with the *liberum arbitrium liberatum* to actualise that good will in a good action.

The justification of humanity is therefore an act of divine mercy, in that they neither desire it (because the *liberum arbitrium captivatum* is incapable of desiring good) nor deserve it (because of their sin and lack of merit). On account of the Fall, the free will of humans is weakened and incapacitated, though not destroyed. Thus humans do not wish to be justified, because their *liberum arbitrium captivatum* is incapable of desiring justification; however, once restored to its former capacities by healing grace, it recognises the goodness of what it has been given. God thus cures humanity's illness, of which the chief symptom is the absence of any desire to be cured.

This apparent contradiction has, of course, been criticised for failing to respect the free will of the humans involved.[134] In response to this, it must be pointed out that the divine justification of the sinner in the manner outlined above in no way compromises either the free will of humans, understood as *liberum arbitrium liberatum*, or their *libertas*: the only 'free will' which is compromised is the *liberum arbitrium captivatum*, itself a parody of the real thing. The compromise of the *liberum arbitrium captivatum* is necessary in order that the *liberum arbitrium liberatum* may be restored.

Once justified by divine action, the sinner does not at once become a perfect example of holiness. Humans need to pray to God continually for their growth in holiness and the spiritual life, thereby acknowledging that God is the author of both. God *operates* upon humans in the *act* of justification, and *co-operates* with them in the *process* of justification.[135] Once justified, the sinner may begin to acquire merit – but only on account of God's grace. Merit is seen to be a divine rather than a human work. Thus it is clearly wrong to suggest that Augustine excludes

---

[134] For example, the somewhat unperceptive discussion in N. P. Williams, *The Grace of God*, London: Longmans, 1930, 19–43.

[135] *De gratia et libero arbitrio* xvii, 33: 'Ut ergo velimus, sine nobis operatur; cum autem volumus, et sic volumus ut faciamus, nobiscum cooperatur.' For an earlier distinction between 'operation' and 'co-operation', see *Ad Simplicianum*, I, ii, 10, CChr. 44.35.298–301: 'ut velimus enim et suum esse voluit et nostrum: suum vocando, nostrum sequendo. Quod autem voluerimus, solus praestat, id est, posse bene agere et semper beate vivere.'

or denies merit; while merit *before* justification is indeed denied, its reality and necessity *after* justification are equally strongly affirmed. It must be noted, however, that Augustine understands merit as a gift from God to the justified sinner, and does not adopt Tertullian's somewhat legalist approach to the matter. *Hominis bona merita, Dei munera.* Eternal life is indeed the reward for merit – but merit is itself a gift from God, so that the whole process must be seen as having its origin in the divine liberality, rather than in human works. If God is under any obligation to humans on account of their merit, it is an obligation which God has imposed upon himself, rather than one which is imposed from outside, or is inherent in the nature of things.

The classic Augustinian statement on the relation between eternal life, merit and grace is the celebrated dictum of Epistle 194: 'When God crowns our merits, he crowns nothing but his own gifts.'[136] The possibility of a preparation of grace, whether meritorious or not, such as that associated with the Franciscan school in the medieval period, cannot be adduced from the mature writings of Augustine, although traces of such a doctrine may be found in his writings prior to 396.[137]

Central to Augustine's doctrine of justification is his understanding of the 'righteousness of God', *iustitia Dei*. The righteousness of God is not that righteousness by which he is himself righteous, but that by which he justifies sinners.[138] The righteousness of God, veiled in the Old Testament and revealed in the New, and supremely in Jesus Christ, is so called because, by bestowing it upon humans, God makes them righteous.[139] How is it possible for God, being just, to justify the ungodly? Augustine shows relatively little interest in this question, giving no systematic account of the work of Christ. Instead, he employs a series of images and metaphors to illustrate the purpose of Christ's mission. Of these, the most important is generally agreed to be his demonstration of the divine love for humanity (*ad demonstrandum erga nos dilectionem Dei*). Other metaphors and images which he uses to express his understanding of Christ's work include mediation, sacrifice, deliverance from the power of Satan, or an example to be imitated. It must be emphasised that it is manifestly an imposition upon Augustine's theology to develop a systematic account of the work of Christ, for the bishop is primarily concerned

---

[136] *Epistola* 194, 5, 19, CSEL 57.190: 'cum Deus coronat merita nostra, nihil aliud coronat quam munera sua'.

[137] As suggested by Dhont, *Le Problème de la préparation à la grâce*, on the basis of texts such as *De diversis quaestionibus* lxxxiii, 68, 4, CChr 44A.180.126–9: 'Praecedit ergo aliquid in peccatoribus, quo, quamvis nondum sint iustificati, digni efficiantur iustificatione: et item praecedit in aliis peccatoribus quod digni sunt obtunsione.'

[138] Studer, 'Jesucristo, nuestra justicia', 266–70.   [139] *De spiritu et littera* xi, 18.

with the question of *how* God justifies humans, rather than how God *is able* to justify them. Like Luther, he employs a wide range of images and metaphors to illustrate the nature of Christ's mission, and declines to commit himself exclusively to any one of these.

As noted above, God's prevenient grace prepares the human will for justification. Augustine understands this grace to be intimately involved with the sacrament of baptism: however, while he insists that there can be no salvation without baptism (or, more accurately, without what baptism represents), it does not follow that every baptised sinner will be justified, or finally saved. The grace of final perseverance is required if Christians are to persevere in faith until the end of their life. It is clear that this raises the question of predestination: God may give the regenerate faith, hope and love, and yet decline to give them perseverance.[140]

While Augustine occasionally appears to understand grace as an impersonal abstract force, there are many points at which he makes a clear connection between the concept of grace and the operation of the Holy Spirit. Thus regeneration is itself the work of the Holy Spirit.[141] The love of God is shed abroad in our hearts by the Holy Spirit, which is given to us in justification. The appropriation of the divine love to the person of the Holy Spirit may be regarded as one of the most profound aspects of Augustine's doctrine of the Trinity. *Amare Deum, Dei donum est.* The Holy Spirit enables humans to be inflamed with the love of God and the love of their neighbours – indeed, the Holy Spirit *is* love.[142] Faith can exist without love, on the basis of Augustine's strongly intellectualist concept of faith, but is of no value in the sight of God. God's other gifts, such as faith and hope, cannot bring us to God unless they are accompanied or preceded by love. The motif of *amor Dei* dominates Augustine's theology of justification, just as that of *sola fide* would dominate that of one of his later interpreters. Faith without love is of no value.[143]

So how does Augustine understand those passages in the Pauline corpus which speak of justification *by faith* (e.g., Romans 5:1)? This question brings us to the classic Augustinian concept of 'faith working through love', *fides quae per dilectionem operatur*, which would dominate western Christian thinking on the nature of justifying faith for the next thousand years. The process by which Augustine arrives at this understanding of

---

[140] *De corruptione et gratia* viii, 18. See G. Nygren, *Das Prädestinationsproblem*; F.-J. Thonnard, 'La Prédestination augustinienne: sa place en philosophie augustinienne', *REAug* 10 (1964), 97–123.

[141] For example, *Epistola* 98, 2. Elsewhere, Augustine criticised the Pelagians for making the grace of Christ consist solely in his example, and asserting that humans are justified by imitating him, where they are in fact justified by the Holy Spirit, who *subsequently* leads them to imitate him: *Opus imperfectum contra Julianum* II, 46.

[142] *De Trinitate* xv, xvii, 31.   [143] *De Trinitate* xv, xvii, 31; xviii, 32.

the nature of justifying faith illustrates his desire to do justice to the total biblical view on the matter, rather than a few isolated Pauline gobbets.

In *De Trinitate*, Augustine considers the difficulties arising from 1 Corinthians 13:1–3,[144] which stipulates that faith without love is useless. He therefore draws a distinction between a purely intellectual faith (such as that 'by which even the devils believe and tremble' (James 2:19)) and true justifying faith, by arguing that the latter is faith *accompanied by love*. Augustine finds this concept conveniently expressed within the Pauline corpus at Galatians 5:6: 'In Christ Jesus neither circumcision nor uncircumcision avails anything, but faith that works through love.'

Although this could be considered as being open to a Pelagian interpretation, this possibility would seem to be excluded by Augustine's insistence that both the faith and the love in question are gifts of God to humanity rather than natural human faculties – in other words, that they are *dona* rather than *data*, given over and above the natural endowment of creation. Augustine tends to understand faith primarily as an adherence to the Word of God, which inevitably introduces a strongly intellectualist element into his concept of faith, thus necessitating its supplementation with *caritas* or *dilectio* if it is to justify humanity. Faith alone is merely assent to revealed truth, itself inadequate to justify.[145] It is for this reason that it is unacceptable to summarise Augustine's doctrine of justification as *sola fide iustificamur* – if any such summary is acceptable, it is *sola caritate iustificamur*. For Augustine, it is love, rather than faith, which is the power which brings about the conversion of people. Just as *cupiditas* is the root of all evil, so *caritas* is the root of all good. The personal union of individuals with the Godhead, which forms the basis of their justification, is brought about by love, and not by faith.[146]

Augustine understands the verb *iustificare* to mean 'to make righteous', an understanding of the term which he appears to have held throughout his working life.[147] In arriving at this understanding, he appears to have interpreted *-ficare* as the unstressed form of *facere*, by analogy with *vivificare* and *mortificare*. Although this is a permissible interpretation of

---

[144] *De Trinitate* xv, xviii, 32.

[145] J. Burnaby, *Amor Dei: A Study of the Religion of St. Augustine*, London: Hodder & Stoughton, 1938, 78: 'It cannot be denied that faith, in Augustine's general usage of the term, has the predominantly intellectual connotation of the definition which he gave at the end of his life – to believe means simply to affirm in thought, *cum assensione cogitare*.'

[146] Bavaud, 'La Doctrine de la justification d'après Saint Augustin', 31–2.

[147] For example, *Expositio quarundam propositionum ex Epistola ad Romanos* 22; *Ad Simplicianum* I, ii, 3; *Sermo* 131, 9; 292, 6; *Epistola* 160, xxi, 52; *De gratia et libero arbitrio* vi, 13. Other expressions used include *efficitur iustus* (e.g., *De spiritu et littera* xxxii, 56) and *fit pius* (e.g., *Sermo* 160, 7; *In Joannis evangelium tractatus* iii, 9).

the *Latin word*, it is unacceptable as an interpretation of the *Hebrew concept* which underlies it (see 1.1). The term *iustificare* is, of course, post-classical, having been introduced through the Latin translation of the Bible, and thus restricted to Christian writers of the Latin West. Consequently, Augustine was unable to turn to classical authors in an effort to clarify its meaning, and was therefore obliged to interpret the term himself. His establishment of a relationship between *iustificare* and *iustitia* is of enormous significance, as will become clear.

Augustine's basic definition of justification may be set out in a little detail, so that its full significance can be appreciated:

What does 'justified' mean other than 'made righteous', just as 'he justifies the ungodly' means 'he makes a righteous person out of an ungodly person'? (*Quid est enim aliud, iustificati, quam iusti facti, ad illo scilicet qui iustificat impium, ut ex impio fiat iustus?*)[148]

There is no hint in Augustine of any notion of justification purely in terms of 'reputing as righteous' or 'treating as righteous', as if this state of affairs could come into being without the moral or spiritual transformation of humanity through grace. The pervasive trajectory of Augustine's thought is unambiguous: justification is a causative process, by which an ungodly person is made righteous. It is about the transformation of the *impius* to *iustus*.

Augustine has an all-embracing transformative understanding of justification, which includes both the *event* of justification (brought about by operative grace) and the *process* of justification (brought about by co-operative grace). Augustine himself does not, in fact, see any need to distinguish between these two aspects of justification; the distinction dates from the sixteenth century. However, the importance of Augustine to the controversies of that later period make it necessary to interpret him in terms of its categories at this point. The renewal of the divine image in humans, brought about by justification, may be regarded as amounting to a new creation, in which sin is rooted out and the love of God planted in the hearts of people in its place, in the form of the Holy Spirit. God's new creation is not finished once and for all in the event of justification, and requires perfecting,[149] which is brought about by co-operative grace collaborating with the *liberum arbitrium liberatum*. While *concupiscentia* may be relegated to the background as *caritas* begins its work of renewal within individuals, it continues to make its presence felt, so that renewed gifts of grace are required throughout their existence, as sin is never totally overcome in this life.[150]

---

[148] *De spiritu et littera* xxvi, 45.
[149] *De gratia et libero arbitrium* xvii, 33.   [150] *Enchiridion* I, 44.

The righteousness which God bestows upon humanity in justification is regarded by Augustine as *inherent* rather than *imputed*, to anticipate the vocabulary of the sixteenth century.[151] A concept of 'imputed righteousness', in the later Protestant sense of the term, is quite redundant within Augustine's doctrine of justification, in that humans are *made righteous* in justification. The righteousness which they thus receive, although originating from God, is nevertheless located within humans, and can be said to be *theirs*, part of their being and intrinsic to their persons. An element which underlies this understanding of the nature of justifying righteousness is the Greek concept of deification, which makes its appearance in the later Augustinian soteriology.[152] By charity, the Trinity itself comes to inhabit the soul of the justified sinner, although it is not clear whether Augustine can be said to envisage a 'state of grace' in the strict sense of the term – that is, a habit of grace, created within the human soul.[153]

It is certainly true that Augustine speaks of the real interior renewal of the sinner by the action of the Holy Spirit, which he later expressed in terms of participation in the divine substance itself. However, it seems most prudent to state that Augustine's theological vocabulary was not sufficiently developed to allow us to speak of his teaching 'created grace' in the later sense of the term. The later Augustine frequently uses phrases which are strongly reminiscent of the Cappadocians and frequently places the concepts of adoptive filiation and deification side by side in his discussion of justification. There is thus a pronounced element of participation in Augustine's later understanding of the nature of justifying righteousness, even if it is not possible to speak of a 'state of grace' in the strict sense of the term. God has given humans the power both to receive and to participate in the divine being.[154] By this participation in the life of the Trinity, the justified sinner may be said to be deified. Augustine's understanding of adoptive filiation is such that the believer not merely receives the *status* of sonhood, but *becomes* a child of God. Justification entails a real change in a person's *being*, and not merely in his or her *status*, so that

---

[151] See the important conclusions reached by J. Henninger, *S. Augustinus et doctrina de duplici iustitia*, Mödling: Sankt Gabrieler-Studien, 1935, 79: 'i. Existit aliqua iustitia, qua homo vere, intrinsecus, coram Deo iustus est; ii. Haec iustitia consistit in aliquo dono permanenti, quo homo elevatur ad aliquem statum, altiorem, ita ut sit particeps Dei, deificatus.'

[152] J. A. A. Stoop, *Die deificatio hominis in die Sermones en Epistulae van Augustins*, Leiden: Luctor et Emergo, 1952; Capánaga, 'La deificación en la soteriología agustiniana'. The theme appears to be more pronounced in Augustine's sermons than in his specifically doctrinal works.

[153] G. Philips, 'Saint Augustin a-t-il connu une "grâce créée"?' *EThL* 47 (1971), 97–116; P. G. Riga, 'Created Grace in St. Augustine', *Augustinian Studies* 3 (1972), 113–30.

[154] *De Trinitate* XIV, xii, 15; *Enarrationes in Psalmos* 49, 2; *Sermo* 192, 1.

this person *becomes* righteous and a child of God, and is not merely *treated as if he or she was* righteous and a child of God.

For Augustine, justification includes both the beginnings of humanity's righteousness before God and its subsequent perfection, the event and the process, so that what later became the Reformation concept of 'sanctification' is effectively subsumed under the aegis of justification. Although Augustine is occasionally represented, on the basis of isolated passages, as understanding justification to comprise merely the remission of sins, this cannot be sustained on the basis of a more thorough engagement with his works. It is quite clear that Augustine understands 'justification' to include the ethical and spiritual renewal of the sinner through the internal operation of the Holy Spirit. Justification, according to Augustine, is fundamentally concerned with 'being made righteous'. But what does he understand by *iustus* and *iustitia*? With this question, we come to the relation between Augustine's doctrine of justification and his ethical and political thought.

According to Augustine, the *iustitia* of an act is to be defined both in terms of the substance of the act itself (*officium*) and its inner motivation (*finis*). The correct motivation for a righteous action can come about only through operative grace and the interior action of the Holy Spirit within the believer. Righteousness, itself regarded as a gift of the Holy Spirit, consists both in the possession of a good will (effected by operative grace) and in having that potentiality actualised through co-operative grace. It will therefore be clear that Augustine understands *iustitia* participationally, rather than relationally.[155] Everyone who is incorporated into Christ can perform an action which is *iustus*. In other words, Augustine defines *iustitia* in such a manner that, by definition, only Christians may perform good actions. This is well illustrated by his famous example of the two individuals, one of whom does not hold a 'true and catholic faith in God', yet leads a morally blameless life, and another, who holds such a faith and yet leads a morally inferior existence. Which is the superior in the sight of God? For Augustine, it is the latter, on account of his faith, even though the former may be superior morally. Had the former faith, he would be the superior in the sight of God.[156] This example illustrates the difference between the inherent moral value of an act itself (*officium*), and the inner motivation which establishes the theological foundation for the righteousness of an act (*finis*). A correct inner motivation is possible only through *fides quae per dilectionem operatur*.

---

[155] *Contra Julianum* I, ix, 45.
[156] *Contra duos epistolas Pelagianorum* III, v, 14. The entire section at III, v, 14 – vii, 23 merits careful study.

It may be noted here that Augustine does *not* deny pagans the ability to perform morally good acts, as some have represented him as doing. These works are good, considered as *officium* – that is, they are good *coram hominibus*, but not *coram Deo*. The moral and meritorious realms are scrupulously distinguished by Augustine. Pagans may practise continency, temperance, even *caritas humana* – yet these are not virtues *coram Deo*.[157] The *virtutes impiorum* are righteous in terms of their *officium*, but have no value in obtaining eternal salvation. In itself, such an act may be good – but if performed outside the specific context of faith, it is sterile or even sinful. The crucial distinction between the *virtutes impiorum* and *virtutes piorum* lies in justification, by which God makes godly those who were once ungodly (*ex impio pius fit*). Thus Augustine's moral theology (i.e., his theology of *iustitia*, applied to the individual) can be seen to be closely related to his doctrine of justification. The bridge between the moral and the meritorious, between the human and the divine estimation of an act, lies in the justification of the ungodly.

Augustine's political theology (i.e., his theology of *iustitia*, applied to the community) is of considerable inherent interest, and is also closely associated with his doctrine of justification.[158] *De civitate Dei* (413–26) contains a critique of the Ciceronian understanding of the basis of social justice of decisive importance to our study. It is only within the city of God that the true divine justice, effected through justification, may be found.[159] Augustine's concept of *iustitia* within the *civitas Dei* is based on his concept of God as *iustissimus ordinator*, who orders the universe according to his will.[160] The idea of *iustitia* involved can approach that of a physical ordering of all things, and is also reflected in the right ordering of human affairs, and humankind's relationship to its environment. For Augustine, *iustitia* is practically synonymous with the right ordering of human affairs in accordance with the will of God.[161]

[157] See, for example, *De gratia et libero arbitrio* xvii, 36; *De spiritu et littera* xxvii, 48. The excellent study of J. Wang Tch'ang-Tche, *Saint Augustin et les vertus des païens*, Paris: Beauchesne, 1938, should be noted.

[158] For some interesting reflections on the rhetorical aspects of the doctrine of grace, especially in relation to the denunciation of heresy, see B. Kursawe, *Docere, delectare, movere: Die officia oratoris bei Augustinus in Rhetorik und Gnadenlehre*, Paderborn: Schoningh, 2000.

[159] On the theme of the 'two cities', see A. Lauras and H. Rondet, 'Le Thème des deux cités dans l'œuvre de saint Augustin', *Etudes Augustiniennes* 28 (1953), 99–160; Y. Congar, '"Civitas Dei" et "Ecclesia" chez S. Augustin', *REAug* 3 (1957), 1–14.

[160] *De civitate Dei* xi, 17. See also *De libero arbitrio* i, v, 2: 'iustum est, ut omnia sint ordinatissima'. The Platonic conception of justice as the right ordering of the parts of the soul is also evident in Augustine's definition of justice as *amor amato serviens et propterea recte dominans*: *De moribus ecclesiae* xv, 25.

[161] R. A. Markus, *Saeculum: History and Society in the Theology of St. Augustine*. Cambridge: Cambridge University Press, 1970, 72–104.

It may be noted that Augustine's quasi-physical understanding of justice reflects his hierarchical structuring of the order of being: *iustitia* is essentially the ordering of the world according to the order of being, itself an expression of the divine will. God created the natural order of things, and therefore this natural order of things must itself reflect *iustitia*. Thus God created humans as they ought to be – that is, he created humans *in iustitia*, the correct order of nature. By choosing to ignore this ordering, humans stepped outside this state of *iustitia*, so that their present state may be characterised as *iniustitia*. Justification is therefore essentially a 'making right', a restoration of every facet of the relationship between God and humanity, the rectitude of which constitutes *iustitia*. *Iustitia* is not conceived primarily in legal or forensic categories, but transcends them, encompassing the 'right-wising' of the God–human relationship in its many aspects: the relationship of God to humankind, of humans to their fellows, and of humans to their environment. Justification is about 'making just' – establishing the rectitude of the created order according to the divine intention. Although it is clear that justification has legal and moral ramifications, given the wide scope of Augustine's concept of *iustitia*, it is not primarily a legal or moral concept.

It is therefore clear that the interpretation of *iustitia* is dependent upon its particular context. What is *iustum* in the case of the relationship between God and humanity may not be *iustum* in the case of human relationship among their fellows, so that the analogical predication of human concepts of *iustitia* to God cannot be regarded as inherently justifiable. This point is particularly well illustrated by Augustine's critique of the Ciceronian definition of *iustitia* as *reddens unicuique quod suum est*, 'giving each what is due to them'.[162] While Augustine is prepared to use this secular definition at points, it is clear that his own concept of *iustitia* is grounded firmly in the divine will.

The importance of defining 'justice' becomes especially clear in the course of Augustine's controversy with Julian of Eclanum over the question of the justification of the ungodly. Augustine found it necessary to counter Julian's application of a secular concept of justice to the divine dispensation towards mankind.[163] Julian defined justice in terms of God rendering to each individual their due, without fraud or grace, so that God would be expected to justify those who merited his grace on the basis of their moral achievements. This approach yielded a doctrine of the justification of the *godly*, whereas Augustine held the essence of the

---

[162] For example, *De libero arbitrio* xviii, 27; *Enarrationes in Psalmos* 83, 11. For Augustine's relation to Cicero, see M. Testard, *Saint Augustin et Cicéron*, 2 vols., Paris: Etudes augustiniennes, 1958.

[163] See McGrath, 'Divine Justice and Divine Equity', for a more detailed analysis.

gospel to be the justification of the *ungodly*. In countering Julian's concept of *iustitia Dei*, Augustine appealed to the parable of the labourers in the vineyard (Matthew 20:1–16) to demonstrate that *iustitia Dei* primarily refers to God's fidelity to his promises of grace, irrespective of the merits of those to whom the promise was made.

Augustine's fundamental concept of *iustitia* is that of the submission of the individual's whole being to God. While this theme of submission to God may reflect the Neoplatonist notion of the acceptance of the established order of the universe, it is possible that Augustine's understanding of *iustitia* within the *civitas Dei* is based upon ideas similar to those to be found in the *Divinae Institutiones* of Lactantius (c. 250–317). The political theology developed by Lactantius was particularly suited to the new Christian empire, then developing under Constantine. Here *iustitia* is practically equated with *religio*: 'justice is nothing other than the pious and religious worship of the one God'.[164] This definition could be interpreted as an extension of the Ciceronian understanding of *iustitia* as 'rendering to each his due' to include the proper obligation of humans to God, whose chief part is worship. In *De civitate Dei*, Augustine revised Cicero's classic definition of the *res publica* by making *iustitia* an essential element of the *iuris consensus*: where there is no true *iustitia*, there is no true *ius*.[165] Whereas Cicero taught that *iustitia* was based on *ius*, arising from the *iuris consensus*, Augustine argued that *ius* itself must be regarded as based on *iustitia*. Thus for Augustine there can be no *res publica* without there being true *iustitia* within the community – that is, a right ordering of all its relationships in accordance with the divine purpose.[166] Where this justice does not exist, there is certainly no 'association of men united by a common sense of right and a community of interest' (as Cicero had defined the *res publica*). It is only in the *civitas Dei* that true justice exists; in the city of humans, only vestiges of this true justice may be found. It is clear that Augustine understands all human *ius*, in so far as it is just, to derive ultimately from an eternal divine law: 'there is nothing just or legitimate in temporal law save what men have derived from the eternal law'.[167] While God's law is eternal and unchanging, the positive laws which govern human relationships may vary from place to place, and yet still reflect that divine law. Although it is only in the regenerate that *vera iustitia* is possible, through their justification, there remain some *vestigia*

---

[164] Lactantius, *Divinae Institutiones* v, vii, 2, CSEL 19.419.12–14.

[165] Cicero, *De republica* 1, 39: 'Est igitur, inquit Africanus, res publica, res populi; populus autem non omnis hominim coetus quoquo modo congregatus, sed coetus multitudinis iuris consensu et utilitatis communione societatis.' See Testard, *Saint Augustin et Cicéron* 2.39–43.

[166] *De civitate Dei* XIX, 23. Cf. XIX, 21.   [167] *De libero arbitrio* I, vi, 15.

supernae iustitiae even in the unjustified, and it is such vestiges which form the basis of human ideas of justice as they find their expression in human legal and political institutions. Without such vestiges, Augustine insists, there could be no justice of any sort among humans.[168]

Augustine's discussion of *iustitia*, effected only through the justification of humanity, demonstrates how the doctrine of justification encompasses the whole of Christian existence from the first moment of faith, through the increase in righteousness before God and humans, to the final perfection of that righteousness in the eschatological city. Justification is about 'being made just' – and Augustine's understanding of *iustitia* is so broad that this could be defined as 'being made to live as God intends humans to live, in every aspect of their existence', including their relationship with God and with their fellow humans, and the relationship of their higher and lower self (on the Neoplatonic anthropological model favoured by Augustine). That *iustitia* possesses legal and moral overtones will thus be evident – but this must not be permitted to obscure its fundamentally *theological* orientation. By 'justification', Augustine comes very close to understanding the restoration of the entire universe to its original order, established at creation, an understanding not very different from the Greek doctrine of cosmic redemption. The ultimate object of humanity's justification is its 'cleaving to God', a 'cleaving' which awaits its consummation and perfection in the new Jerusalem, which is even now being established.

Augustine's contribution laid the foundation for the medieval development of the doctrine of justification. Although it would clearly be incorrect to characterise the great theological renaissance of the twelfth and thirteenth centuries as nothing other than an expansion and development of Augustine's ideas, the critical role that his theology played as both resource and norm can be overstated only with some difficulty. The standard textbook of medieval theology, still in use in the sixteenth century, was Peter Lombard's *Sentences* – a collection of patristic dicta, drawn largely from the writings of Augustine. This influential book may be regarded as developing the procedure found in Prosper of Aquitaine's *Liber sententiarum ex operibus Augustini*, which is often pointed to as an early representative of 'medieval Augustinianism' – an attempt to bring together the main features of Augustine's theology, in order that they might be identified and developed.[169] The theological renaissance of the

---

[168] F. J. Thonnard, 'Justice de Dieu et justice humaine selon Saint Augustin', *Augustinus* 12 (1967), 387–402. See further J. Rief, *Der Ordobegriff des jungen Augustinus*, Paderborn: Schoningh, 1962, 111–249.

[169] See D. M. Cappuyns, 'Le Premier Représentant de l'Augustinisme médiévale', *RThAM* 1 (1929), 309–37.

twelfth century, which may be regarded as laying the foundations for the theology of the medieval period as a whole, was largely based upon the writings of Augustine. In every major sphere of theological debate, the point of departure appears to have been the views of Augustine.[170] As David Steinmetz shrewdly observed, 'All medieval theologians, even the most Pelagian, were indebted to the great father of western theology for many of their ideas. All medieval theologians are, in some measure at least, Augustinian theologians. The question is not whether a theologian is indebted to Augustine but rather what is the degree and nature of his indebtedness.'[171]

We therefore turn to explore the great era of consolidation and development of the doctrine of justification – the Middle Ages.

[170] See M. D. Chenu, *La Théologie au XIIe siècle*, Paris: Vrin, 1957; J. de Ghellinck, *Le Mouvement théologique de XIIe siècle*, 2nd edn, Brussels: Culture et Civilization, 1969. On the twelfth-century renaissance in general, see G. Pare, A. Brunet and P. Tremblay, *La Renaissance du XIIe siècle*, Paris: Vrin, 1933.

[171] Steinmetz, *Misericordia Dei*, 33.

2   The Middle Ages: the consolidation of the doctrine

The terms 'medieval' and 'Middle Ages' are modern, signifying the period of transition between the intellectual glories of antiquity and those of the modern period. Although phrases similar to 'medieval' are encountered in the medieval period itself, their meaning is quite distinct from the modern sense of the term. Thus Julian of Toledo uses the phrase 'the middle age' or 'the middle of time' (*tempus medium*) in an Augustinian sense to refer to the period between the incarnation and the second coming of Christ.[1] Since the Renaissance, the term has been used in a somewhat disparaging sense, to mean the somewhat uninteresting period of time separating the intellectual glories of antiquity and their retrieval in the Renaissance.[2]

Historians have been vexed for some time by the question of when the 'Middle Ages' can be said to have begun, and the answers given to this question depend upon the criterion used in its definition. The practically simultaneous suppression of the Athenian Platonic academy and the establishment of Montecassino in 529 are regarded by many as marking, although not in themselves causing, the transition from late antiquity to the medieval period. For the purposes of the present study, the medieval period is regarded as having been initiated through Alaric's conquest of Rome in 410, with the resulting gradual shift in the centres of intellectual life from the Mediterranean world to the northern European world of Theodoric and Charlemagne, and later to the abbey and cathedral schools of France, and the universities of Paris and Oxford. While Augustine's world was that of the *imperium Romanum*, that of his later interpreters would be the courts and monasteries of northern Europe.[3]

---

[1] Julian of Toledo, *Antikeimenon* II, 69, PL 96.697c. Cf. Augustine, *De civitate Dei* XI, 1, where he refers to living 'in an intermediate age' (*in hoc interim saeculo*) in a similar context.
[2] For comment, see J. Trier, 'Zur Vorgeschichte des Renaissance-Begriff', *Archiv für Kulturgeschichte* 33 (1955), 45–63; J. von Stackelberg, 'Renaissance: "Wiedergeburt" oder "Wiederwunsch"? Zur Kritik an J. Triers Aufsatz über die Vorgeschichte des Renaissance-Begriffs', *BHR* 22 (1960), 406–20.
[3] See J. Marenbon, *From the Circle of Alcuin to the School of Auxerre: Logic, Theology and Philosophy in the Early Middle Ages*, Cambridge: Cambridge University Press, 1981.

Associated with this shift in the intellectual centres of Europe was a related shift in the method employed by the theologians of the medieval period. The accumulated body of tradition associated with the world of antiquity – which included both pagan philosophy and patristic theology – was assimilated and incorporated into the emerging theological literature. Prosper of Aquitaine's *Liber sententiarum ex operibus Augustini* may be regarded as an early example of this phenomenon.[4] The medieval period was characterised by its attempts to accumulate biblical and patristic material considered to be relevant to particular issues of theological interpretation, and by its attempt to develop hermeneutical methods to resolve the apparent contradictions encountered in this process.[5] These collections of patristic 'sentences' appear to have been modelled upon the codifications of the canonists, who initially grouped their collected decretals chronologically, and later according to subjects. An examination of such collections of patristic 'sentences' suggests that they were largely drawn from the works of Augustine.[6] The most famous such collection, the *Sententiarum libri quattuor* of Peter Lombard, has been styled an 'Augustinian breviary', in that roughly 80 percent of its text is taken up by a thousand citations from Augustine.[7] The high regard in which Augustine was held during the theological renaissance of the late eleventh and the twelfth centuries ensured that the framework of the medieval discussion of justification was essentially Augustinian.[8] The theology of the period may be regarded as a systematic attempt to restate and reformulate Augustine's theology to meet the needs of the new era then developing.[9] The development of the doctrine of justification during the medieval period may be considered primarily as the systematisation, clarification and conceptual elaboration of Augustine's framework of justification, where possible restating the dogmatic content of his works in the accepted categories of the day.

The period saw the concept of justification developed as the metaphor most appropriate for the articulation of the soteriological convictions and affirmations of the western church. Associated with this development

[4] D. M. Cappuyns, 'Le Premier Représentant de l'augustinisme médiévale', *RThAM* 1 (1929), 309–37.

[5] M. Colish, 'The Sentence Collection and the Education of Professional Theologians in the Twelfth Century', in N. van Deusen (ed.), *The Intellectual Climate of the Early University*, Kalamazoo: Western Michigan University, 1997, 1–26.

[6] For example, see Isidore of Seville, *Sententiae*, PL 83.537–738; Burchard of Worms, *Decretum*, PL 140.338–1058.

[7] Grabmann, *Geschichte der scholastischen Methode*, 2:385–6.

[8] H. A. Oberman, 'Tuus sum, salvum me fac: Augustinreveil zwischen Renaissance und Reformation', in C. P. Mayer and W. Eckermann (eds.), *Scientia Augustiniana: Studien über Augustinus, den Augustinismus und den Augustinerorden*, Würzburg: Augustinus Verlag, 1975, 349–94.

[9] Oberman, *Werden und Wertung der Reformation*, 82–140.

were two factors of particular importance, which we may consider briefly before turning to the development of the doctrine of justification during the period: the transference of the discussion of the salvation of humankind from the *mythological* to the *moral* or *legal* plane; and the particularly significant role of Pauline commentaries as vehicles for theological development in the earlier Middle Ages, which inevitably led to the incorporation of certain core Pauline concepts, such as justification, into the *modus loquendi theologicus* of the later medieval period.

The early patristic discussion of the redemption of humankind in Christ frequently took the form of the portrayal of a cosmic battle between God and the devil, with its *locus* in the cross of Christ. This theme would later pass into the medieval tradition in the notion of the 'Harrowing of Hell'.[10] Associated with this image of the cosmic battle fought between God and the devil over humanity are several concepts which indicate the crude realism of its mythology – for example, the ideas of the devil possessing rights over humanity (the *ius diaboli*), of God entering into a transaction with the devil, or of God deceiving the devil.[11] During the theological renaissance of the late eleventh century this structure was subjected to a devastating theological criticism, particularly by Anselm of Canterbury, largely on account of the conviction that *iustitia Dei*, the 'righteousness of God', necessarily entailed that God acted righteously in all his actions, including the redemption of humanity. This fundamental conviction led to the medieval construction of theories of redemption in which emphasis was laid upon the moral or legal propriety of both the redemption of humankind in the first place, and the means subsequently employed by God in this redemption. It is possible to argue that it is with Anselm's insights that the characteristic thinking of the western church on the means of the redemption of humankind may be said to begin.[12] The emphasis which is then laid upon the moral or legal character of God inevitably leads to increased interest in the precise nature of *iustitia Dei*, and in the question of how *iustitia Dei* and *iustitia hominis* are correlated. The recognition of the cognate relationship between *iustitia, ius* and *iustificatio* served to further enhance the importance of the concept of justification as a soteriological metaphor.

---

[10] See K. M. Ashley, 'The Guiler Beguiled: Christ and Satan as Theological Tricksters in Medieval Religious Literature', *Criticism* 24 (1982), 126–37; J. A Alford, 'Jesus the Jouster: The Christ-Knight and Medieval Theories of Atonement in Piers Plowman and the "Round Table" Sermons', *Yearbook of Langland Studies* 10 (1996), 129–43.

[11] D. M. de Clerk, 'Droits du démon et nécessité de la rédemption: les écoles d'Abelard et de Pierre Lombard', *RThAM* 14 (1947), 32–64.

[12] Thus A. B. Ritschl, *Die christliche Lehre von der Rechtfertigung und Versöhnung*, Bonn: Marcus, 1870, begins his discussion of the doctrine with reference to Anselm of Canterbury.

The importance of the influence of Pauline commentaries to the development of theology during the earlier medieval period has been well documented,[13] and it is possible to demonstrate that the development of the various theological schools of the period may be illustrated with reference to this literary genre. These commentaries are known to have been of particular importance in the early systematisation of theology during the medieval period;[14] a survey of the commentaries on Romans alone – the most important of the Pauline epistles, judged from the standpoint of the development of the doctrine of justification – suggests that practically all theologians of note during the early medieval period used such a commentary for both the positive statement and the development of their own characteristic theological positions.[15] It was therefore inevitable that these theological positions would be influenced, to a greater or lesser extent, by the Pauline material with reference to which they were developed and expounded. The discussion of questions such as the salvation of the Old Testament patriarchs, and the relation between faith and works, are but two examples of pertinent theological questions which such theologians were thus obliged to discuss with reference to the concept of justification. Thus the distinction between *iustificatio per legem* and *per fidem* was frequently used by these theologians in connection with *heilsgeschichtlich* questions such as the salvation of Abraham,[16] usually discussed with reference to Romans 4:4, while the discussion of the relation between faith and works would often involve discussion of the apparent differences on the matter between Paul and James[17] – again, with explicit reference to the concept of justification.

The early use of such Pauline commentaries as vehicles for positive theological articulation and development thus catalysed the establishment of justification as perhaps *the* most important soteriological concept, precisely because it was used by Paul in connection with those soteriological issues which attracted the attention of the theologians of the period. By the time the later *Commentaries on the Sentences* and *Summae* had replaced these commentaries, the influence of the Pauline material upon which the earlier commentaries were based was so great that it had made an indelible impression upon the emerging medieval theological vocabulary.

[13] See Landgraf, *Einführung in die Geschichte der theologischen Literatur der Frühscholastik*, 29, 39–40.
[14] C. Spicq, *Esquisse d'une histoire de l'exégèse Latine au moyen âge*, Paris: Vrin, 1944.
[15] W. Affeld, 'Verzeichnis der Römerbriefkommentare der lateinischen Kirche', *Traditio* 12 (1957), 396–406. For an exhaustive list of medieval biblical commentaries, see F. Stegmüller, *Repertorium biblicum medii aevi*, 7 vols., Madrid: Casimiro, 1950–77.
[16] For example, Robert of Melun, *Questiones de epistolis ad Romanos*, ed. Martin, 80.14 – 81.20.
[17] For example, Hervaeus of Bourg Dieu, *Commentarius in epistolas divi Pauli*, PL 181.644B – 647A.

Furthermore, the tendency of early medieval systematic works other than Pauline commentaries to use a *heilsgeschichtlich* format in presenting their material,[18] which necessitated a careful distinction between the times of the law and of the gospel, naturally led to an appeal to the Pauline concepts of *iustificatio per legem* and *per fidem* in an attempt to clarify the difference between the two periods. In other words, it is perfectly possible to view the actual systematic presentation of theology itself during the early medieval period as having further enhanced the importance attached to the metaphor of justification by medieval theologians.

The present chapter documents the development of particular aspects of the doctrine of justification during the medieval period, and illustrates how Augustine's basic insights into the framework of the doctrine of justification were preserved, while being developed to meet the needs of the new era in theology which was dawning.

2.1   The nature of justification

What is signified by the word 'justification'? As noted previously, the Latin term *iustificatio* is post-classical, and almost entirely restricted to works of Christian theology, especially those which offer translations of the Greek term *diakaiosis* – such as Pauline commentaries. (The plural *iustificationes* is occasionally encountered, when the term is used to translate *diakaiomata*.) Augustine's interpretation of *iustificare* as *iustum facere*, based on the assumption that *-ficare* was the unstressed form of *facere*, was universally accepted during the medieval period, reflecting the considerable esteem in which the opinions of the bishop were held. Although *iustificare* is occasionally interpreted as *iustum habere* ('to be held as righteous'),[19] it is clear that this is intended to refer to *iustificatio coram hominibus* rather than *coram Deo*.[20]

The characteristic medieval understanding of the nature of justification may be summarised thus: justification refers not merely to the beginning of the Christian life, but also to its continuation and ultimate perfection, in which Christians are made righteous in the sight of God and of humanity through a fundamental change in their nature, and not merely in their status. In effect, the distinction between justification (understood

---

[18] See H. Cloes, 'La Systématisation théologique pendant la première moitié du XIIe siècle', *EThL* 34 (1958), 277–329, who illustrates this point with particular reference to Hugh of St Victor's *De sacramentis*. See also V. Marcolino, *Das Alte Testament in der Heilsgeschichte: Untersuchung zum dogmatischen Verständnis des alten Testaments als heilsgeschichtliche Periode nach Alexander von Hales*, Münster: Aschendorff, 1970.

[19] For example, Atto of Vercelli, *Expositio epistolarum Pauli*, PL 134.149c; Haimo of Auxerre, *Expositio in divi Pauli epistolas*, PL 119.38IA.

[20] For example, Sedulius Scotus, *Collatio in omnes Pauli epistolas*, PL 103.41c: 'aliud est iustificari coram Deo, aliud coram hominibus'.

as an external pronouncement of God) and sanctification (understood as the subsequent process of inner renewal), characteristic of the Reformation period, is excluded from the outset. This fundamental difference concerning the *nature* of justification remains one of the best *differentiae* between the doctrines of justification associated with the medieval and the Reformation periods.[21]

An examination of the early vernacular works appears to confirm this conclusion concerning the ubiquity of the Augustinian interpretation of the significance of 'justification'. The most convenient vernacular works to study in this respect are the Old English homilies of Wulfstan (d. 1023) and Ælfric (c. 955–1020), and the Gothic Bible, the *Vulfila*. Wulfstan does not, in fact, mention the term 'justification' in his homilies, and it is with the latter works that we are chiefly concerned. The Old English church was generally able to express Christian ideas by giving new meanings to existing words in the vernacular, or by forming new compounds of words already in use.[22] Occasionally, this seems to have been impossible, with the result that 'loan words' were introduced – for example, *dēofol* (for the Latin *diabolus*) and *biscop* (for the Gallo-Roman *ebescobu* – cf. Latin *episcopus*). The theological vocabulary of Old English frequently had recourse to literal translations of Latin words – for example, *gecyrrednyss* for the Latin *conversio*. The subsequent disappearance of most of these words may be attributed to the Norman Conquest of 1066. Thus *hǣl* (salvation), *ǣrist* (resurrection) and others disappeared, while *God*, *heofon* and *hel* remained.

The Old English terms for 'justification' and its cognates appear to have suffered the former fate, *gerihtwīsung* being replaced with the Middle English *iustification*, and *gerihtwisian* with *iustifien*, both presumably derived from the Old French *justification* and *justifier*. This disappearance may be illustrated from the translation of Psalm 143:2 from a fourteenth-century vernacular source, where the Romance theological term seems out of place among its Anglo-Saxon neighbours:

> Lorde, they seruaunt dragh neuer to dome,
> For non lyuyande to the is justyfyet.[23]

Ælfric regularly translates *iustificatio* by *gerihtwīsung*,[24] and in this he follows what appears to be a traditional interpretation of the Latin text.[25] It

[21] See McGrath, 'Forerunners of the Reformation?'

[22] N. O. Halvorsen, *Doctrinal Terms in Ælfric's Homilies*, Dubuque: University of Iowa Press, 1932, 56–7.

[23] *The Pearl*, ed. Eric V. Gordon, Oxford: Clarendon Press, 1953, lines 699–700.

[24] See his translation of Romans 8:30: B. Thorpe, *The Homilies of the Anglo-Saxon Church*, 2 vols., London: Aelfric Society Publications, 1864–6, 2.367.1–3.

[25] See *The Gothic and Anglo-Saxon Gospels, with the Versions of Wycliffe and Tyndale*, ed. J. Bosworth, London: John Russell Smith, 1865, 10.29; *Libri Psalmorum versio antiqua*

is clear that the Old English term is an interpretation, rather than a mere translation, of the original Latin term. A factitive, rather than declarative, interpretation of the term is indicated by the fact that Ælfric uses the phrase *rihtwise getealde* to mean 'reckoned righteous',[26] so that the most appropriate contemporary translation of *gerihtwisung* would appear to be 'putting right', or 'rightwising'. A similar interpretation can be adduced from the Gothic version,[27] traditionally held to have been translated directly from the Greek by the Arian bishop Ulphilas (d. 383). Although the value of this source is seriously diminished by its fragmentary character, it is clear that the factitive interpretation of *dikaioun* can be demonstrated in the Gothic version of the Pauline epistles. Thus *dikaioun*, as it occurs in Galatians 2:16, is translated as *raihts wairthan*, which clearly bears the sense of 'becoming righteous'. It may be noted, however, that *dikaioun* is not translated regularly as *raihts wairthan* in the Gothic version of the gospels – for example, it is translated as the comparative *garaithoza* at Luke 18:14.

The systematic discussion of the *inner structure* of justification dates from the beginning of the twelfth century, with the conceptual exploration of the *processus iustificationis*. This discussion is an important development in the history of the doctrine of justification, as it marks an attempt to correlate the process of justification with the developing sacramental system of the church. Its beginnings may, however, be discerned at a much earlier period in the history of doctrine. Thus Augustine distinguished three aspects of the justification of the ungodly:

> In this life, justification confers these three things upon us: first, the washing of regeneration, by which our sins are forgiven; then confession of our sins, the guilt of which has been remitted; thirdly, through our prayers, in which we say 'Forgive us our sins.'[28]

Bruno the Carthusian also distinguished three aspects of the process of justification.[29] A more detailed discussion of the inner structure of justification may be found in Hervaeus of Bourg-Dieu's comments on Romans 3:20: the recognition of sin is followed by the operation of healing grace, which leads to a love for righteousness:

Latina cum paraphrasi Anglo-Saxonica, ed. B. Thorpe, Oxford: Oxford University Press, 1835, 18.8, where 'iustificati sunt' is translated 'Hi synt gerihtwisode'. See also *Homilies* 2.430.2; 472.2–3.

[26] *Homilies* 2.286.2–5.

[27] *Die gotische Bibel*, ed. W. Streitberg, 2 vols., Heidelberg: Winter, 1965. See further G. Haendler, *Wulfila und Ambrosius*, Stuttgart: Calwer Verlag, 1961.

[28] *Contra Julianum* II, viii, 23, PL 44.689B.

[29] *Expositio in Psalmos*, PL 152.1087A: 'Notandum quod haec beneficia non narrat ordine; prius enim fuit a captivitate per fidem averti, postea vero peccata operiri, et sic post iniquitatem remitti; et ad ultimum in bonis operibus et virtutibus benedici.'

For through the law comes the knowledge of sin (*cognitio peccati*); by faith comes the infusion of grace against sin; by grace somes the cleasing of the soul from the guilt of sin; through the cleansing of the soul comes freedom of the will; through the freedom of the will, the love of righteousness; and through the love of righteousness, the operation of the law.[30]

The sequential ordering of the process, with one element leading to another in a causal sequence, foreshadowed the twelfth-century discussion of the *processus iustificationis*.

Initially, the theologians of the twelfth century envisaged *the processus iustificationis* as consisting of three elements. As a study of twelfth-century works indicates, the terminology of the *processus iustificationis* is still fluid, and although the threefold structure appears fixed, its elements were still not clearly defined.[31] Peter Manducator defined the threefold sequence as follows: 'justification consists of three things, namely, the infusion of the first grace, the contrition of the heart, and the remission of sin'.[32] The *processus* is elsewhere defined as consisting of the infusion of grace, the co-operation of the free will, and its consummation.[33] Occasionally, a threefold scheme is encountered which omits any reference to the infusion of grace, such as the disavowal of sin, the intention not to sin further, and remorse for past sins.[34] Nevertheless, it is clear that a threefold process, which is initiated through the infusion of grace and terminates in the remission of sin, was widely accepted as normative. Although all three elements involved had long been recognised as closely inter-related, the increasing tendency to link the three elements together as the 'process of justification' represents an important landmark in the systematic articulation of the doctrine.

Although the threefold scheme appears to have gained considerable acceptance in the twelfth century, it was a fourfold scheme of the inner structure of justification which would finally become accepted as normative. The threefold *processus* recognised a single motion of the *liberum arbitrium*, which subsequently came to be divided into two components: a movement of the free will *towards God*, and *away from sin*. As stated by Peter of Poitiers, the scheme has the following form:

---

[30] *Expositio in epistolas Pauli*, PL 181.642D.

[31] For an excellent discussion of the *processus iustificationis* in the early medieval period, see Landgraf, *Dogmengeschichte der Frühscholastik*, 3.287–302.

[32] Cod. Paris Nat. lat. 15269 fol. 44, cited in Landgraf, *Dogmengeschichte der Frühscholastik*, 3.291 n. 11.

[33] Peter Comestor, *Sermo* 17, PL 198.1769B: 'Iustificatio etiam in tribus consistit, vel notatur; in gratia infusione, in liberi arbitrii cooperatione, tandem in consummatione; primum est incipientium, secundum proficientium, tertium pervenientium.'

[34] Cod. Vat. lat. 1174 fol. 83v; Cod. Vat. lat. 1098 fol. 151v, 157; cited in Landgraf, *Dogmengeschichte der Frühscholastik*, 3.299; cf. 298 n. 41 and 299 n. 45.

Four things take place in the justification of the ungodly: the infusion of grace, a movement arising from grace and the free will, contrition, and the remission of sin. None of these is to be regarded as taking precedence in time, although by nature the infusion of grace precedes the other three. This, however, is by nature, not in time. While any of these could be described as 'justification', no one of them can be present without the other three.[35]

The infusion of grace thus initiates a chain of events which eventually leads to justification; if any of these events may be shown to have taken place, the remaining three may also be concluded to have taken place. The fourfold *processus iustificationis* differs from the threefold scheme in including a dual, rather than a single, motion of the human free will, otherwise retaining the same overall structure. It was taken up by the first Summist, William of Auxerre, in the form *infusio gratiae, motus liberi arbitrii, contritio, peccatorum remissio*,[36] and was accepted in this form by the doctors of the early Dominican and Franciscan schools.[37] The inclusion of *contritio* in the *processus* is of no small significance, as it greatly assisted the correlation of the *processus* with the sacrament of penance in the thirteenth century.

The justification of the fourfold *processus iustificationis* within the early Dominican school is of particular interest, as it demonstrates the considerable influence of Aristotelian physics upon theological speculation within that school.[38] Albertus Magnus defined justification as a *motus* from sin to grace and rectitude.[39] Having already applied the Aristotelian theory of motion, as stated in the celebrated maxim of Aristotelian physics, *omne quod movetur ab alio movetur*, to a physical *motus* such as free

---

[35] *Sententiarum libri quinque* III, 2, PL 211.1044A–B. Peter of Poitiers was a pupil of Peter Lombard, upon whose *Sentences* his own work was modelled; see P. S. Moore, *The Works of Peter of Poitiers*, Notre Dame: University of Notre Dame Press, 1936, 1–24. He must not be confused with Peter of Poitiers of St Victor or Peter of Poitiers of Cluny; see J. W. Baldwin, *Masters, Princes and Merchants*, 2 vols., Princeton: Princeton University Press, 1970, 1.32–4; J. Kritzeck, *Peter the Venerable and Islam*, Princeton: Princeton University Press, 1964, 31–4.

[36] *Summa Aurea* lib. III tr. ii q. 1; fol. 121v.

[37] See Alexander of Hales, *In IV Sent.* dist. xvii n. 7; Albertus Magnus, *In IV Sent.* dist. xviiA a. 10; ed. Borgnet, 29.673: 'Dicitur ab omnibus, quod quattuor exiguntur ad iustificationem impii, scilicet infusio gratiae, motus liberi arbitrii in peccatum sive contritio, quod idem est, motus liberi arbitrii in Deum, et remissio peccati'; Bonaventure, *In II Sent.* dist. xxvi a. 1 dub. 3; Thomas Aquinas, *In IV Sent.* dist. xvii q. 1 a. 4; ed. Mandonnet, 4.843; idem, *Summa theologiae* IaIIae q. 113 a. 6; Odo Rigaldi, *In II Sent.* dist. xxvi membr. I q. 2 a. 3 (ed. Bouvy, 331.48 – 132.68). Matthew of Aquasparta redefines the four elements as *satisfactio, conversio, reformatio, vivificatio*: *In II Sent.* dist. xxviii a. 1 q. 1.

[38] See McGrath, 'The Influence of Aristotelian Physics upon St. Thomas Aquinas' Discussion of the "Processus Iustificationis"'. See also Flick, *L'attimo della giustificazione*, 104–54.

[39] *In IV Sent.* dist. xviiA a. 15.

fall, or to a theological problem of *motus* such as the existence of God, he applied the same principle to the analysis of the inner structure of the *motus* of justification. The explicit application of the Aristotelian theory of generation to the transition from nature to grace leads to a fourfold *processus iustificationis*, with a dual motion of the free will. This application of Aristotelian physics to the *motus* of justification is particularly associated with Thomas Aquinas. Having stated the *processus iustificationis* to be

1. the infusion of grace;
2. the movement of the free will directed towards God through faith;
3. the movement of the free will directed against sin;
4. the remission of sin.[40]

Thomas now justifies this on the basis of Aristotelian physics. By nature, the movement of the mover must come first, followed by the disposition of the matter, or the movement of that which is to be moved, followed by the final termination of the motion when the objective of the movement has been achieved. Thus the infusion of grace must precede the remission of sin, as the infusion of grace is the efficient cause of that remission. Thus the *motus* which is justification ends in the remission of sin, which may be considered as the *terminus* of the infusion of grace.[41] As every movement may be said to be defined by its *terminus*, justification may thus be said to consist of the remission of sin.[42]

Some commentators have misunderstood Thomas' occasional definition of justification solely in terms of the remission of sin, representing him as approaching a forensic concept of justification. It will be clear that this is a serious misunderstanding. Where Thomas defines justification as *remissio peccatorum*, therefore, he does not exclude other elements – such as the infusion of grace – from his definition, for the following reasons. First, justification is thus defined without reference to its content, solely in terms of its *terminus*. Such a definition is adequate, but not exhaustive, and should not be treated as if it were. Second, Thomas' understanding of the *processus iustificationis* means that the occurrence of any one of the four elements necessarily entails the occurrence of the remaining three. The definition of *iustificatio* as *remissio peccatorum* therefore expressly *includes* the remaining three elements.

Having established that the remission of sin is the final element in the *processus iustificationis*, Thomas argues that the element intervening between the initial element (i.e., *infusio gratiae*) and the final one (i.e., *remissio peccatorum*) must be the disposition of the object of justification – that is, the *motus mobilis*, the movement of that which is to be moved. As justification is *motus mentis*, this disposition must refer to the human free

---

[40] IaIIae q. 113 a. 8.   [41] IaIIae q. 113 a. 6.   [42] IaIIae q. 113 a. 6 ad 1um.

will, which precedes justification itself by nature.[43] This consideration leads to a definition of justification as 'a movement by which the human mind is moved by God from the state of sin to a state of righteousness (*quidam motus quo humana mens movetur a Deo a statu peccati in statum iustitiae*).[44] This allows a threefold *processus iustificationis* to be established: *infusio gratiae, motus liberi arbitrii, remissio peccatorum*. Tradition had by now, however, established a *dual* motion of the free will in justification: faith (directed towards God), and contrition (directed away from sin). Thomas accommodates this by applying a further axiom of Aristotelian physics – that 'in movements of the soul, the movement to the principle of understanding or to the end of the action comes first'[45] – to the *motus* of justification. Thus a movement of the *liberum arbitrium* towards God must precede its motion against sin, as the former is the cause of the latter.[46] This teaching, found in the *Summa Theologiae*, is of particular interest, as it represents an abandonment of his earlier teaching that there should be no intermediates between the influence of grace and the remission of sin.[47]

In justification, according to Thomas, humanity is translated from a state of corrupt nature to one of habitual grace; from a state of sin to a state of justice, with the remission of sin.[48] But how is this state of justice to be conceived? As noted earlier, Augustine's understanding of *iustitia* embraces practically the entire ordering of the universe, so that justification can be understood as the restoration of humans to their correct place in the hierarchy of being, including the establishment of the correct relationship between the various existential strata within humanity, on the basis of the Neoplatonist anthropological model favoured by Augustine. Thomas' discussion of the question involves a crucial distinction between the *virtue* of justice, and the *supernatural habit* of justice, infused by God. *Iustitia acquisita*, the virtue of acquired justice,[49] may be considered either as particular justice, which orders individuals' actions relating to their fellows, or as legal justice as defined by Aristotle.[50] *Iustitia infusa*, however, on the basis of which humanity is justified, comes from God himself, through grace. Failure to appreciate this distinction will lead to the quite untenable conclusion that Thomas teaches justification purely through self-endeavour or moral attainment. Justification is concerned with 'justice in the sight of God' (*iustitia quae est apud Deum*).[51]

---

[43] IaIIae q. 113 a. 8 ad 2um.   [44] IaIIae q. 113 a. 5.
[45] IaIIae q. 113 a. 8 ad 3um.   [46] IaIIae q. 113 a. 8.
[47] *De veritate* q. 28 a. 8; ed. Spiazzi 1.549: 'et ideo inter gratiae infusionem et culpae remissionem nihil cadet medium'. An identical opinion is encountered earlier: *In IV Sent.* dist. xvii q. 1 a. 4; ed. Mandonnet, 4.847.
[48] IaIIae q. 113 aa. 1, 2.   [49] IaIIae q. 63 a. 4.
[50] IaIIae q. 58 a. 5.   [51] IaIIae q. 113 a.1.

Iustitia infusa is that justice which is infused into humans by God, by which their higher faculties are submitted to God. In essence, it may be noted that Thomas' concept of infused justice is very similar to Aristotle's notion of metaphorical justice, which refers primarily to a rectitude of order within the interior disposition of humans. It is this infused justice, and this justice alone, which is the basis of the justification of humanity.

The characteristically Augustinian understanding of justification as the restoration of humanity to its proper place in the created hierarchy of being is reflected in Thomas' discussion of why justification is properly named after justice, rather than after faith or love. Although both faith and love are involved in justification, and although their supernatural habits are infused in its course, Thomas insists that the transformation which is called 'justification' is properly named after justice alone on account of the all-embracing character of the latter, which refers to the entire rectitude of order of the human soul, with all its faculties. Faith and love refer only to specific aspects of this order, whereas justice embraces the higher nature of humans in its totality.

It may be noted at this point that Thomas' understanding of justification as a *motus mentis* reflects his intellectualist understanding of human nature; if the higher nature is subordinate to God, it will be enabled to restrain the lower nature. The human intellect is restored through justifying faith, so that individuals are able to avoid *mortal* sin; although the higher nature subsequently restrains the lower, it is unable to overcome it entirely, so that they are still unable to avoid *venial* sin after justification.[52] Thus even the individual who is in a state of grace cannot be said to be free from sin. Thomas' exposition of Romans 7 is of particular interest in this respect, as he clearly understands the chapter to refer to the Christian constituted in grace. Justification is about 'being made just': the precise nature of this 'making just' is, however, carefully defined in terms of the rectitude of the human mind so that it, acting as a secondary cause, may bring all that is subordinate to it into conformity with the exemplar established for it by God. The *event* of the infusion of the habit of justice must therefore be followed by the *process* of the submission of the lower to the higher nature; in this understanding of the dual nature of justification, Thomas remains faithful to the teaching of Augustine.

Thomas' understanding of justification as a *motus mentis* allows him to apply the Aristotelian theory of motion to its presuppositions, as well as its interior structure, and is of particular interest in relation to his discussion of the need for a disposition towards justification on the part of the sinner. The early Franciscan school, however, developed a more psychological

---

[52] IaIIae q. 109 a. 8.

approach to justification, reflecting an Augustinian illuminationist epistemology which is not characteristic of the Dominican school.

The general features of the early Franciscan teaching on the nature of justification may be found in Bonaventure's *Itinerarium mentis in Deum*, which develops a hierarchical concept of justification that clearly reflects the influence of Dionysius. The three fundamental operations of grace in justification are the *purification, illumination* and *perfection* of the soul.[53] Christ performed three acts which re-established and reordered humanity's supernatural life towards God: he purged our guilt, enlightened us by his example, and perfected us by enabling us to follow in his footsteps. Christians are required to respond to these in three hierarchical acts by which they can appropriate the associated benefits.

These three aspects of the justification of the sinner correspond to the 'Three Ways' which are so characteristic of Bonaventure's spirituality,[54] distinguished by their goals rather than by their relation in time. The *stimulus conscientiae* motivates the way of purification, the *radius intelligentiae* the way of illumination, and the *igniculus sapientiae* the way of unity with God. From the moment of its first infusion, sanctifying grace takes over the substance and faculties of the soul, setting each in its respective place, and ordering the soul that it may be conformed to God.[55] The process of justification involves the destruction of the passions which threaten the development of the new life of humanity, so that humans can rediscover the image of God within themselves. Thus the soul, reconstituted by grace, can begin its ascent towards the goal of supernatural perfection. It will be clear that Bonaventure's understanding of the nature of justification differs from that of Thomas only in emphasis: both understand justification as the establishment of rectitude within the higher nature of humans, whether this be considered as *mens* or as *anima*.

Bonaventure's teaching was developed further by his Italian disciple Matthew of Aquasparta,[56] who discussed justification in terms of six stages: the hatred of sin and the love of good; regeneration; the reforming and reordering of the human nature; the generation of virtues; conversion to, and union with, God; and remission of sin.[57] His emphasis upon the regeneration of the sinner and their ultimate union with God

---

[53] *Itinerarium mentis in Deum* IV, 3.

[54] L. Bouyer, *Introduction to Spirituality*, London: Darton, Longman & Todd, 1961, 243–85.

[55] On this, see the study of Romano Guardini, *Systembildende Elemente in der Theologie Bonaventuras: Die Lehren vom Lumen Mentis, von der Gradatio Entium an der Influentia Sensus et Motus*, Leiden: Brill, 1964.

[56] For an introduction, see Z. Hayes, *The General Doctrine of Creation in the Thirteenth Century with Special Emphasis on Matthew of Aquasparta*, Munich: Schoningh, 1964.

[57] *Quaestiones disputatae de gratia* q. 2, ed. Doucet, 45–9.

points to a psychological approach to justification more characteristic of Bonaventure than Thomas.

The medieval statements concerning the nature of justification demonstrate that justification is universally understood to involve a real change in its object, so that regeneration is subsumed under justification. As John of La Rochelle pointed out, unless justification did produce a real change in humans, it would appear to serve no useful purpose:

> Persons are justified. If this places nothing within them, there has been no change on their part, nor are they any closer to their eternal good than before. If something is placed within them, I say that this is grace.[58]

This statement is of particular interest, as it involves the appeal to the reality of a change in humans arising through their justification to refute the earlier opinion, widespread in the eleventh century, that grace did not make any change to the human soul (*gratia ponit nihil in anima*).[59] While justification was universally understood to involve the regeneration of humanity, the opinion that an *ontological* change is thereby effected within humans is particularly associated with the period of High Scholasticism and the development of the concept of created grace. The earlier medieval theologians expressed the change effected in justification in terms of a particular presence of God in his creature, which did not necessarily effect an ontological change. Thus the *Summa Fratris Alexandri*, written after 1240, developed the Augustinian concept of the indwelling of God in creatures by declaring that while God is present in all creatures, only some (i.e., those who are justified) may be said to possess God.[60]

The *Summa* thus conceives a special presence of God in the justified, such that an ontological change occurs in the soul. The presence of God in the justified sinner necessarily results in *created* grace – a created grace which can be conceived as a conformity of the soul to God. This special presence of God in the souls of the justified must be distinguished from the general presence of God in the world, and from the unique union between God and humanity achieved in the hypostatic union. In this, the *Summa* makes an important advance on Peter Lombard's discussion of

---

[58] *Quaestiones disputatae de gratia* q. 7, ed. Hödl, 63.

[59] For example, *Glossa in decretum gratianis*, Cod. Bamberg Can. 13, cited in Landgraf, *Dogmengeschichte der Frühscholastik*, 1/1.210: 'Talis est gratia, quia nec vinus nec opus vel motus mentis. Et secundum hoc nichil ponit.' See Alszeghy, *Nova creatura*, for further references and discussion.

[60] *Alexandri de Hales Summa theologica* pars I inq. I tr. ii q. 3 tit. 3 membr. 2 cap. I. sol, ed. Quaracchi, 2.77: 'Dicendum quod "Deus esse per gratiam" ponit necessario gratiam creatam in creatura.'

the divine presence in all creatures; in angels and the souls of the justified through indwelling grace, and in Christ.[61]

The later medieval period saw the rise of the opinion, particularly associated with the *via moderna*, according to which the relationship between God and humans was to be understood *covenantally* rather than *ontologically*.[62] Although this opinion involves the linking of justification with the extrinsic denomination of the divine acceptation, the *de facto* necessity of a habit of grace in justification continued to be maintained. Although the ultimate reason for humanity's acceptation lies in the divine decision to accept, the fact remains that, in terms of the ordained divine manner of operation (i.e., *de potentia Dei ordinata*), the infusion of grace, the indwelling of the Holy Spirit, and the divine acceptation coincide. It is thus essential to distinguish the rejection of the metaphysical necessity of such a habit of grace from the assertion of its *de facto* necessity within the context of the covenant that governs the divine dispensation towards humankind.

The necessity of a habit of created grace in justification is thus to be considered to be radically contingent, a *necessitas consequentiae* rather than a *necessitas consequentis*; however, as theology is concerned with the articulation of the divine dispensation towards humankind as it now pertains, the justification of humans before God must be considered to involve an ontological change within them. *De potentia Dei ordinata* the habit of created grace is the middle term between sinful humans and their acceptation by God in justification; it need not have been so, but the fact remains that it is so. The essential contribution of the *via moderna* to the medieval understanding of the nature of justification is its emphasis upon the *contingent* nature of the ontological change which occurs within humans in justification. It is only by confusing the actual divine dispensation *de potentia ordinata* with a hypothetical dispensation *de potentia absoluta* that any continuity with the Reformation understandings of the nature of justification may be maintained.

Associated with the *via moderna* in particular is the weakening of the link between the elements of the traditional *processus iustificationis*. As noted above, the four elements of the process were regarded as essentially aspects of the one and the same transformation, causally linked by their very nature (*ex natura rei*). From the time of Duns Scotus onwards, this view was subjected to increasing criticism. The infusion of grace and the

---

[61] For the Christological aspects of such ideas, see Richard Cross, *The Metaphysics of the Incarnation: Thomas Aquinas to Duns Scotus*, Oxford: Oxford University Press, 2002.

[62] See Oberman, 'Wir sind pettler'; Courtenay, 'Covenant and Causality in Pierre d'Ailly'; Hamm, *Promissio, pactum, ordinatio*; McGrath, 'The Anti-Pelagian Structure of "Nominalist" Doctrines of Justification'.

remission of sin came increasingly to be seen as fundamentally distinct, coexisting and causally related only through the divine ordination (*ex pacto divino*). One may take place without the other. Scotus states four reasons why the remission of sin and the infusion of grace cannot be regarded as aspects of one and the same change (i.e., justification):

1. The remission of sin is multiple, as God forgives each committed sin individually, while the infusion of grace is single.
2. Infusion of grace can occur without remission of sin, and vice versa. Thus God infused grace into Adam in his state of innocence without remitting his sin, as he did also with the good angels.
3. There is no necessary correlation between sin and grace as opposites.
4. Sin cannot be regarded simply as the privation of grace, which would be necessary if justification were regarded as the transition from a privation to its corresponding quality.[63]

Furthermore, Scotus points out that infusion of grace is a *real* change in humans, while the remission of sin is a *mutatio rationis*, an ideal change within the divine mind and not within individuals themselves. As the concepts of the infusion of grace and the remission of sin have totally different points of reference, they cannot be allowed to be causally related as in the traditional *processus iustificationis*. Since their relationship does not derive from the nature of the elements themselves, it must derive from the divine will – i.e., it is arbitrary. Without in any way challenging the *de facto* relationship of the elements of the *processus iustificationis*, Scotus demonstrated that this relationship was itself radically contingent, the consequence of divine ordination rather than of the nature of the entities themselves. This point, which relates to the nature of the causal processes involved in justification, will be developed further in our discussion of the role of supernatural habits in justification.

The medieval concept of justification includes the renovation as well as the forgiveness of the sinner: 'in justification of souls, two things occur together, namely, the remission of guilt and the newness of life through grace'.[64] Although some theologians appear to define justification solely as the remission of sins,[65] it must be pointed out that this is a consequence of their use of Aristotelian categories in their discussion of justification: as a *motus* may be defined by its *terminus*, justification may be defined

---

[63] *Opus Oxoniense* IV dist. xvi q. 2. For important reflections on the relation between the concepts of divine acceptation associated with Scotus and the Reformation, see Pannenberg, 'Das Verhältnis zwischen der Akzeptationslehre des Duns Scotus und der reformatorischen Rechtfertigungslehre.'

[64] Thomas Aquinas, *Summa theologiae*, IIIa q. 56 a. 2 ad 4um.

[65] For example, Thomas Aquinas, *Summa theologiae*, IaIIae q. 113 a.1, 'Remissio peccatorum est iustificatio.'

as the remission of sins. Hence, the entire medieval discussion of justification proceeds upon the assumption that a *real* change in the sinner is effected thereby. This observation is as true for the *via moderna* as it is for the earlier period. It is quite untenable to suppose that the Reformation distinction between justification and regeneration can be adduced from the medieval period, when it is clear that the universal opinion is that such a distinction is excluded from the outset. Indeed, the *modernus* Gabriel Biel explicitly contrasts a forensic justification before a secular judge with justification as transformation in relation to God, the spiritual judge.[66]

In the later medieval period, the *de facto* necessity of a habit of created grace in justification is maintained, even by those theologians who otherwise stood closest to the Reformers. Even among those who use such hypothetical constructs as the 'absolute power of God' to argue that justification need not have been linked to such a created habit of grace, the consensus remained that, whatever hypothetical possibilities might be noted, the ordained order of salvation did indeed involve the transformation of humanity through grace.

Justification was about 'being made righteous'; how could such a transition take place without grace indwelling the soul of the believer? If justification involved both forgiveness and regeneration through grace (*remissio culpae et novitas vitae per gratiam*), how could one be had without the other? The excision of regeneration from the *processus iustificationis* was seen as impossible. The theologians of the *via moderna* had demonstrated that this was a theoretical possibility; yet they did not extend this theoretical critique to the revision of the existing understandings of justification. It can be argued that Luther's increasingly personalist understanding of justification, placing particular emphasis on divine acceptation, built upon the foundations laid in the fourteenth and fifteenth centuries.[67] Yet the medieval period saw no pressing reason to disentangle the notions of justification and regeneration, which they regarded as organically related.

From its beginning to its end, the medieval period saw justification as involving a real change in the sinner – an understanding which precludes any distinction between *iustificatio* and *regeneratio*. The *processus iustificationis* includes regeneration or renewal as one of its integral elements, making any such distinction intensely problematic. The notional distinction that came to emerge in the sixteenth century between *iustificatio* and *regeneratio* (or *sanctificatio*) provides one of the best ways of

---

[66] *Canonis missae expositio* 31B, ed. Oberman/Courtenay, 1.314–5.
[67] See McGrath, *Luther's Theology of the Cross.*

distinguishing between Catholic and Protestant understandings of justification, marking the Reformers' discontinuity with the earlier western theological tradition.

2.2   The righteousness of God

What is signified by the 'righteousness of God', and how is it manifested? What does it mean to affirm that God is 'righteous'? The importance of these questions was emphasised by the patristic exegesis of Romans 1:17,[68] in which Paul practically equates the revelation of the 'righteousness of God' with the gospel. An examination of the medieval exegesis of Romans 1:17 indicates that there was an early consensus among Pauline exegetes that *iustitia Dei* was to be understood as referring primarily to God's righteousness as demonstrated in the justification of the ungodly, *iustificatio impii*, in accordance with God's promises of mercy. In general, two main lines of interpretation may be distinguished in the early medieval period.

1. A subjective understanding of the construction *iustitia Dei* – that is, *iustitia Dei* is the righteousness by which God is righteous. This interpretation, which appears to stem from Ambrosiaster, emphasises the maintenance of the divine integrity in justification. God, having promised to give salvation, subsequently gives it, and as a result is deemed to be 'righteous' – faithful to what has been promised. The 'righteousness of God' is therefore demonstrated in God's faithfulness to the divine promises of salvation.[69] The gospel is thus understood to manifest the divine righteousness in that God is shown to have fulfilled the Old Testament promises, made in the prophets and elsewhere, of salvation for God's people.

2. An objective interpretation of the construction *iustitia Dei* – that is, *iustitia Dei* is the righteousness whose origin is God, given to the sinner in justification, rather than the righteousness by which God is just. This interpretation, which appears to stem from Augustine, treats the construction *iustitia Dei* as an example of *genitivus auctoris*.[70] The righteousness of God designates, not God's personal righteousness, but the

---

[68] See Holl, 'Justitia Dei in der vorlutherischen Bibelauslegung'; H. Bornkamm, 'Justitia Dei in der Scholastik und bei Luther', *ARG* 39 (1942), 1–46. See also the important analysis in E. Peretto, *La giustizia: Ricerca su gli autori cristiani del secondo secolo*, Rome: Edizioni Marianum, 1977.

[69] 'Iustitia est Dei, quia quod promisit dedit, ideo credens hoc esse se consecutum quod promiserat Deus per prophetas suos, iustum Deum probat et testis est iustitiae eius.' Ambrosiaster, *Commentarius in epistolas Pauli*, PL 17.56B. See also 17.748, 80A–B.

[70] Atto of Vercelli, *Expositio epistolarum Pauli*, PL 134.160B. See also 134.161B, 162A: 'Iustitiam Dei vocat gratiam, non qua ipse iustificatur, sed qua hominem induit.'

righteousness bestowed upon sinners in God's gracious act of acceptance or justification.

In both cases, the 'righteousness of God' is taken to refer to a gracious act of justification, rather than to an abstract divine property which stands over and against humanity. In the case of the subjective interpretation of the construction, *iustitia Dei* is understood to refer to the general framework within which the justification of humanity takes place (i.e., the promises of the Old Testament), whereas the objective interpretation of the construction refers to the immediate means by which that justification takes place (i.e., the 'righteousness' which God bestows upon sinners, in order that they may be 'made just'). It will be clear that these two interpretations of the construction *iustitia Dei* are complementary rather than mutually exclusive, and it is not uncommon to find both interpretations within the same work. *Iustitia Dei* is thus understood to be set in a soteriological context, referring to the salvation of humankind, whether as a consequence of God's faithfulness to the divine promises of mercy, or of the bestowal of divine righteousness upon the sinner.

It can, however, be shown that a third interpretation of the concept existed in the earlier medieval period, apparently corresponding to a form of popular Pelagianism. *Iustitia Dei* is here taken to refer to the divine attribute by which God rewards humans according to their just deserts. God, acting in accordance with this conception of righteousness, will reward those who act justly and punish those who act unjustly – thereby justifying the godly, and punishing the ungodly.[71] This corresponds to what might be called a 'popular catholic' understanding of justification, according to which justification is understood to be dependent upon human efforts to emulate the example which is set them in Christ. While the early exponents of this theology of justification insisted that humans cannot justify themselves,[72] it may be pointed out that the orthodoxy of this position is superficial. As justification is defined as the *divine* judgement that humankind is righteous, it follows as a matter of course that humans are not competent to pronounce this judgement themselves, in that they would thereby usurp the place of God. Justification is God's judgement upon humanity, made upon the basis of whether each has emulated the *iustitia Dei* revealed to humankind in Christ – that is, the divine standard of righteousness, which humans must imitate. It may be God's judgement – but the basis of that judgement is human achievement or status.

---

[71] 'Hieronymus', *Breviarum in Psalmos 70.2*, PL 26.1025D: 'Iustitia enim tua est, ut qui fecerit voluntatem tuam, transeat a morte in vitam, per quam et ego nunc eripi deprecor.'
[72] *Breviarum in Psalmos 30.1*, PL 26.906B: 'Quia nisi a Deo iustificemur, per nos non possumus iustificari.'

Pelagius' interpretation of the concept of the 'righteousness of God' is of particular interest in this respect. For Pelagius, this is to be taken to refer to the righteousness which God gives to humans in Christ *as their example*, so that their justification may be attributed to their own moral efforts to imitate *iustitia Dei, per exemplum Christi*, through the free and autonomous exercise of *liberum arbitrium*. A similar, although more developed, understanding of *iustitia Dei* can be found in the writings of Julian of Eclanum.[73] God deals with humanity in equity, totally impartially, considering only the merits and demerits of each in justification, 'giving each what is due to them, without deceit or favour – that is, without respect of persons' (*reddentem sua unicuique sine fraude sine gratia, id est sine personarum acceptione*).[74] In effect, Julian applies a *quid pro quo* understanding of justice to the divine dealings with humans – an understanding of *iustitia* which found its classic expression in the Ciceronian definition of the term. For Julian, God rewards humans according to their merits – otherwise, God is made guilty of a gross injustice.

Julian singles out several aspects of Augustine's theology of grace for particular criticism on the basis of this understanding of *iustitia Dei* – for example, his understanding of the nature of original sin, and the doctrine of the justification of the ungodly. If God is to reward humans *sine personarum acceptione*, God must reward them on the basis of what they *have done*, rather than on the basis of who *they are* – that is, they must be rewarded on the basis of merit. This Ciceronian understanding of *iustitia Dei* had earlier been criticised by Augustine, who pointed out that the parable of the Labourers in the Vineyard (Matthew 20:1–10) gave a more reliable insight into the divine justice than Julian's Ciceronian analogy. Every man was rewarded with his denarius, irrespective of the period he actually spent working; although the workers had no claim to the denarius in terms of the work they had performed, they *did* have a claim on account of the promise made to them by the owner of the vineyard. By analogy, humanity has no claim to grace on the basis of their works (i.e., on a *quid pro quo* basis), but does have such a claim on the basis of the obligation of God to fulfil his promise.[75]

This criticism of the predication of the Ciceronian concept of *iustitia* to God would be continued by the theologians of the early medieval period. Thus Remigius of Auxerre pointed out that human concepts of justice involved the rendering of good for good, and evil for evil; God, in marked

---

[73] On this, see McGrath, 'Divine Justice and Divine Equity'.
[74] Augustine, *Opus imperfectum contra Iulianum* III, 2, CSEL 85/1.352.6–7.
[75] Augustine, *Opus imperfectum contra Iulianum* I, 38, CSEL 85/1.28.10–35.

contrast, rendered good for evil in justifying sinful humanity.[76] If God's dealings with humans are to be rationalised on the basis of justice, human ideas of justice must give way to those of God. A somewhat different approach to the question may be found in Atto of Vercelli's gloss on Romans 1:17. Here the legal category of justice is retained, along with a Ciceronian interpretation of *iustitia* – but it is interpreted in terms of Christ's obedience to the law.[77]

This marks a development of Ambrosiaster's approach to *iustitia Dei*, in that God's faithfulness to his promise of mercy is now expressed in legal terms – that is, 'faithfulness' is interpreted in terms of 'keeping the law'. It may, however, be emphasised that while the earlier medieval period is characterised by its conviction that God's righteousness is somehow grounded in his promise of mercy, there is no real attempt to establish the precise relationship between *iustitia Dei* and *misericordia Dei*: most theologians were content merely to affirm that God, in his righteousness, was faithful to what God promises.[78]

The theological renaissance of the late eleventh and twelfth centuries saw the 'righteousness of God' being discussed in terms of two separate, although clearly related, questions:

1. What concept of *iustitia* is appropriate to characterise God's dealings with humanity?
2. How is it possible, given the limitations of human language, to speak of God being 'righteous' in the first place?

We shall consider these questions separately.

The most significant early medieval discussion of the concept of *iustitia* most appropriate to characterise God's dealings with humanity is due to Anselm of Canterbury. It must be pointed out that Anselm's soteriology has frequently been criticised as 'legalist', typical of the Latin 'impulse to carry religion into the legal sphere'.[79] This misguided and discredited criticism of Anselm, however, brings us to the very point which confronted Anselm as he began his attempt to defend the rationality of the

---

[76] PL 131.291D: 'Mea iustitia est malum pro malo reddere. Tu solus iustus, quam circa nos ostendisti, reddens bonum pro malo, qua de impio facis bonum.'

[77] Atto of Vercelli, *Expositio epistolarum Pauli*, PL 134.37A–8B.

[78] For example, Sedulius Scotus, *Collectaneum in omnes Pauli epistolas*, PL 103.18D: 'Iustitia Dei est, quia quod promisit, dedit'; Haimo of Auxerre, *Explanatio in Psalmos*, PL 116.295A; Bruno of Würzburg, *Expositio Psalmorum*, PL 140.132D, 265C. This understanding of *iustitia Dei* is reproduced in the fourteenth-century vernacular poem *The Pearl*; see A. D. Horgan, 'Justice in *The Pearl*', *Review of English Studies* 32 (1981), 173–80.

[79] Hastings Rashdall, *The Idea of Atonement in Christian Theology*, London: Macmillan, 1920, 355: 'Anselm appeals to justice . . . but his notions of justice are the barbaric ideals of an ancient Lombard king or the technicalities of a Lombard lawyer rather than the ideas which would have satisfied such a man as Anselm in ordinary human life.'

incarnation of the Son of God: what was the relationship between the 'righteousness of God' and the ideas of 'righteousness' taken from 'ordinary human life'?

God is wholly and supremely just.[80] How can he then give eternal life to one who deserves eternal death? How can he justify the sinner? This is the central question with which Anselm is concerned in *Cur Deus homo* (1098). Earlier, Anselm had wrestled with substantially the same problem in the *Proslogion* (1079).[81] Initially, Anselm locates the source of God's mercy in the divine goodness (*bonitas*), which may be contrasted with God's justice (*iustitia*). He then proceeds to argue, however, that despite the apparent contradiction, God's mercy (*misericordia*) must somehow be grounded in God's justice.

Anselm resolves this dilemma by arguing that God is just, not because God rewards humans according to their merit, but because God does what is appropriate to God, considered as the highest good (*summum bonum*).[82] Although Anselm does not identify Cicero at this point, there is no doubt that he is mounting an explicit criticism of the Ciceronian definition of *iustitia* as *reddens unicuique quod suum est* at this point. Far from endorsing prevailing secular accounts of justice, as some less perceptive critics suggested, Anselm aims to disconnect the theological discussion of redemption from preconceived human patterns of distributive or retributive justice.

A similar pattern of engagement and criticism with secular concepts of justice may be seen in *Cur Deus homo*, where Anselm notes various interpretations of the concept of *iustitia*, before selecting that which is most appropriate for his purposes. These concepts include *iustitia hominis*, which pertains under law;[83] *iustitia districta*, beyond which 'nothing more strict can be imagined' – Anselm presumably therefore understands *iustitia hominis* as *iustitia aequitatis*[84] – and supreme justice, *summa iustitia*.[85] The concept of justice which Anselm selects as most appropriate to characterise God's dealings with humankind is, as in the *Proslogion*, justice understood as action directed towards the highest good. As that highest

---

[80] On this, see McGrath, 'Rectitude'.   [81] *Proslogion* 9, ed. Schmitt, 1.106.18 – 107.3.

[82] *Proslogion* 10, ed. Schmitt, 1.109.4–5: 'Ita iustus es non quia nobis reddas debitum, sed quia facis quod decet te summe bonum.'

[83] *Cur Deus homo* I, 12.

[84] For the concept of equity as developed by the medieval canonists, see Eugen Wohlhaupter, *Aequitas Canonica: Eine Studie aus dem kanonischen Recht*, Paderborn: Schoningh, 1931; H. Lange, 'Die Wörter aequitas und iustitia auf römischen Münzen', *Zeitschrift der Savigny-Stiftung für Rechtsgeschichte*, Romanistische Abteilung, 52 (1932), 296–314; Giovanni Caron Pier, *'Aequitas' Romana, 'Misericordia' Patristica ed 'Epicheia' Aristotelica nella dottrina dell' 'Aequitas' Canonica (dalle origini al Rinascimento)*, Milan: Giuffre, 1971.

[85] *Cur Deus homo* I, 23.

good includes the redemption of fallen humankind, its salvation may be regarded as an act of divine justice. In the course of the discussion, however, it becomes clear that Anselm understands the concept of *rectitudo* to underlie that of *iustitia*, and to determine its basic meaning.

According to Anselm, justice is a 'rectitude of will served for its own sake' (*rectitudo voluntatis propter se servata*).[86] Similarly, truth must also be defined in terms of metaphysical rectitude.[87] It will thus be clear that the foundational notion for Anselm is rectitude, which is understood to have metaphysical dimensions (truth – i.e., the conforming of the mind to what it ought to be) and moral dimensions (justice – i.e., the conforming of behaviour to what it ought to be.)[88]

Anselm clearly assumes that the three concepts are closely linked, noting the intersection of their meanings.[89] The concepts of 'truth' and 'righteousness' had, of course, long been recognised to have close conceptual connections,[90] and Anselm may be regarded as establishing the conceptual foundation of both to be 'rectitude'. *Iustitia* has as its fundamental sense the moral rectitude of the created order, established by God at creation, and in itself reflecting the divine will and nature. This moral ordering of the universe extends to the relationship between humans and God, and humans and their fellows. Anselm appears to use the term *rectitudo* to describe the basic God-given ordering of the universe, and employs the term *iustitia* in a number of derivative senses, each of which may be traced back to the fundamental concept of rectitude. God's moral governing of the universe clearly involves both the divine regulation of the affairs of humans, and also the self-imposed regulation of God's dealings with human dealings. For Anselm, it is not possible to argue that the laws governing each are the same. In its fundamental sense, *iustitia* merely refers to rectitude; it remains to be seen what form this ordering may take with respect to the various aspects of creation. Thus, the justice which regulates the affairs of humans (e.g., the Ciceronian and Justinian principle of *reddens unicuique quod suum est*) cannot be considered to be identical with the justice which regulates God's dealings with humanity.

---

[86] *De veritate* 12; *De casu diaboli* 9.

[87] *De veritate* 12; ed. Spiazzi, 1.192.6–8: 'Non aliud ibi potest intelligi veritas quam rectitudo, quoniam sive veritas sive rectitudo non aliud in eius voluntate fuit quam velle quod debuit.'

[88] G. Söhngen, 'Rectitudo bei Anselm von Canterbury als Oberbegriff von Wahrheit und Gerechtigkeit', in H. Kohlenberger (ed.), *Sola Ratione*, Stuttgart: Frommann, 1970, 71–7.

[89] *De veritate* 4, ed. Spiazzi, 1.181.6–8: 'Habes igitur definitionem iustitiae, si iustitia non est aliud quam rectitudo. Et quoniam de rectitudine mente sola perceptibili loquimur, invicem sese definiunt veritas et rectitudo et iustitia.'

[90] See H. Hommel, 'Wahrheit und Gerechtigkeit: Zur Geschichte und Deutung eines Begriffspaares', *Antike und Abendland* 15 (1969), 159–86.

Humanity was created in a state of *iustitia originalis*, which was forfeited at the Fall. Anselm understands 'original justice' to refer to the initial moral rectitude of humanity within the created order. For Anselm, the basic requirement of *iustitia* is that rational creatures be subject to God,[91] which merely amounts to a statement of the place of humanity in the hierarchical moral ordering of creation. This moral ordering of creation, itself an expression of the divine will, allots a specific place to humans, with a concomitant obligation that they submit their rational nature to God. This moral ordering of the universe was violated by humans at the Fall, so that the present state of humanity is that of *iniustitia*, understood as the privation of *iustitia* rather than as a positive entity in itself. The essence of original sin is the inherited lack of moral rectitude in the will of fallen humankind.[92] The human violation of the moral order of creation means that they are no longer capable of submitting their rational nature to God – and therefore that they are incapable of redeeming themselves. If humanity is to be redeemed, a divine act of redemption is required *which must itself be consonant with the established moral order of the universe*. God, having created the moral order of the universe as an expression of his nature and will, is unable to violate it himself in the redemption of humankind.

This important point is made with particular clarity at that point in *Cur Deus homo* at which Anselm considers the question of why God cannot simply forgive sins as an act of mercy.[93] For Anselm, God's freedom in will and action is limited by God's own nature; anything that violates this nature necessarily involves contradiction. Thus what is *iustum* cannot become *iniustum* simply because God wills it, as such an alteration would involves a radical change in the divine nature itself. God's character as *summa iustitia* is expressed in the moral order of creation, and the free forgiveness of sins through mercy alone would violate this ordering. God's attributes are essential to his being, and not mere accidents which God may change at will. Anselm's fundamental theological insight is that the divine attributes must coexist within the limiting conditions which they

---

[91] *Cur Deus homo* I, 11.
[92] *De casu diaboli* 16; *De conceptu virginali et originali peccato* II, 22–3. On this, see Blomme, *La Doctrine du péché*. The earlier work of R. M. Martin, *La Controverse sur le péché originel au début du XIVe siècle*, Louvain: Spicilegium sacrum Lovaniense, 1930, is also useful. It may be noted that the influence of Anselm's concept of original sin appears to have been insignificant until Albertus Magnus defined the formal element of original sin as *privatio iustitiae*, although the same concept may be found in Odo of Cambrai, *De peccato originali*, PL 160.1071–102. In particular, the school of Laon maintained the older Augustinian understanding of original sin as concupiscence: William of St Thierry, *Disputatio adversus Abaelardum* 7, PL 180.275A; Robert Pullen, *Sententiarum libri octo* II, 27, PL 186.754B–5C.
[93] *Cur Deus homo* I, 12.

impose upon each other. The rectitude of the established moral order thus requires that God redeem humankind in such a way that God's own nature as *summa iustitia* is not contradicted.

In a very brief, but highly significant, review of the accounts traditionally given of the redemption of humankind in Christ, Anselm makes it clear that he is not satisfied with their failure to explain *why* God chose to redeem humans – at best, they were merely descriptions of *how* God redeemed them, so offering no explanation of why God should choose to redeem humans in the first place, or of the particular mode of redemption selected. Anselm therefore presents an account of the redemption of humankind, based on *iustitia*, which demonstrates

1. that the redemption of humankind is necessary *as a matter of justice*;
2. that this redemption is effected in a manner that is consonant with the divinely established moral ordering of the universe.

We shall consider these points individually.

If *iustitia Dei* is understood as a *lex talionis*, or in the Ciceronian sense of *reddens unicuique quod suum est*, it is clearly impossible, in Anselm's view, to consider God's act of redemption as an act of justice. It is for this reason that Anselm does not employ these concepts of justice in his soteriology. For Anselm, the moral ordering of the universe was violated by the sin of humans, so that the present state of affairs is that of a privation of justice – that is, *iniustitia*. As whatever is unjust is a contradiction of the divine nature, it is therefore imperative that the moral rectitude of the created order be restored. God, as *summa iustitia*, is therefore obliged, by his very nature (since to permit a state of injustice to continue indefinitely is tantamount to a contradiction of his nature) to restore the rectitude of the created order by redeeming fallen humankind – *as an act of justice*.

Anselm prefaces his discussion of the method by which God redeemed humankind by considering the rival theory of the *ius diaboli*, the 'devil's rights'. This theory may be illustrated from the tract *De redemptione humana*, attributed to Bede,[94] in which it is argued that, while the death of Christ is a free act of divine love, the choice of the means employed to effect the deliverance of humanity from the devil is necessarily dictated by the fact that the devil is *justly* entitled to punish sinners. The origins of this teaching may be traced back to Gregory the Great, who taught that the devil had acquired a legal right over sinners as a consequence of the Fall, but had no such right over anyone who was sinless. Christ therefore assumed the form of a man in order to deceive his opponent, who naturally assumed that he, like the rest of humanity, was a sinner. As

---

[94] *Aliquot quaestionum liber XV*, PL 93.471–8. On this and other aspects of the *ius diaboli*, see Rivière, *Le Dogme de la rédemption au debut du moyen âge*.

the devil thus brought about the crucifixion of the sinless Christ contrary to justice, his own legitimate power over sinners was justly abolished.[95] This theory admittedly makes an appeal to justice – but it is a concept of justice very different from that approved and employed by Anselm.

For Anselm, justice relates to the moral ordering of creation, to which the devil himself, as a rational creature, is subject. The devil clearly violated this order in his seduction of humanity, and thus cannot be regarded as having any *just* claim over humans. Himself a rational creature, the devil is obliged to submit his rational nature to God – only if he were not part of God's creation, and could therefore stand aloof from its moral ordering, could the devil claim any 'right' over humanity. By his own violation of *iustitia*, the devil had lost any claim to *ius* over humans. Anselm therefore dismisses the theory of the work of Christ which had been current for so long, and with it, an unacceptable concept of *iustitia Dei*: 'I do not see what force it has' (*non video quam vim habeat*).

Anselm's own theory may be stated as a series of propositions, if the numerous digressions are ignored. When this is one, the centrality of the concept of *iustitia* to his argument becomes apparent:

1. Humans were created in a state of original justice for eternal felicity.
2. This felicity requires the perfect and voluntary submission of the human will to God – that is, *iustitia*.
3. On account of sin, the present state of humanity is that of *iniustitia*.
4. Either this must result in the deprivation of eternal felicity, or else the situation must be rectified by an appropriate satisfaction.
5. This satisfaction must exceed the act of disobedience.
6. Humans cannot offer to God anything other than the demands of *iustitia*, and, on account of their present *iniustitia*, they cannot even do that.
7. Therefore God's purpose in creating humans has been frustrated.
8. But this is unjust, and poses a contradiction to the divine nature.
9. Therefore a means of redemption must exist if justice is to be re-established.
10. Humans cannot redeem themselves, being unable to make the necessary satisfaction for sin.
11. God could make the necessary satisfaction.
12. Since only God can, and only humans ought to, make the necessary satisfaction, it must be made by someone who is both God and human.
13. Therefore the incarnation is required as an act of justice.

---

[95] Gregory, *Moralium libri* XXXIII, xv, 31, PL 76.692D–3C.

The importance of justice at this stage in the argument is often over-looked. The 'syllogism' – Aristotle, it must be recalled, had yet to be rediscovered! – which demonstrates the 'necessity' of the incarnation may be stated thus:

A. Only humans ought to make satisfaction for sin; but they cannot.
B. Only God can make the necessary satisfaction; but God is under no obligation to do so.

It is clear that this primitive 'syllogism' could lead to two conclusions.

1. Someone who is both divine and human both cannot and ought not to make such a satisfaction.
2. Someone who is both divine and human both can and ought to make such a satisfaction.

From a purely dialectical standpoint, the work in question could equally well be entitled *Cur Deus non homo*. However, as justice demands that humanity's predicament be resolved, Anselm feels himself justified in drawing the second conclusion, and overlooking the first.

The weak point in Anselm's soteriology is generally considered to be his theory of satisfaction,[96] which we do not propose to discuss further. The essential point, however, is that Anselm considers, presumably on the basis of the established satisfaction-merit model of the penitential system of the contemporary church, that the payment of a satisfaction by the God-human would be regarded by his readers as an acceptable means of satisfying the demands of moral rectitude without violating the moral order of creation. For our purposes, this aspect of Anselm's sote-riology is subsidiary, the main element being his development of *iusti-tia Dei* as action directed towards the highest good, and thus embrac-ing the redemption of humankind. Anselm's soteriology is dominated by the understanding of justice as moral rectitude, and it marks a deci-sive turning point in the medieval discussion of the 'righteousness of God'.

The theory that the devil has rights over humanity, which God was obliged to respect, continued to influence theologians for some time after Anselm's death. Thus the school of Laon, marked by its extreme theological conservatism, taught that the devil had gained just posses-sion of humanity because humanity had freely enslaved itself to the devil as a consequence of its sin. God is therefore obliged to respect the *ius diaboli*.[97] The theological justification provided for the incarnation by

---

[96] For an excellent analysis, see F. Hammer, *Genugtuung und Heil: Absicht, Sinn und Grenzen der Erlösungslehre Anselms von Canterbury*, Vienna: Herder, 1966.
[97] Anselm of Laon, *Sententiae* 47, ed. Lottin, *Psychologie et morale*, 5.144; *Sententiae Atrebarenses*, ed. Lottin, *Psychologie et morale*, 5.414; *Sententie divinae paginae*, ed. Bliemetzrieder, 41.

the school of Laon is that it is only God who has the *ability*, and only humans who have the *obligation*, to overcome the devil; by logic similar to that employed by Anselm of Canterbury, the necessity of the incarnation is then deduced. The devil has no *ius* over the God-human, and by his abuse of his legitimate power, the devil forfeits his *ius* over humanity.[98]

More or less every aspect of Anselm's position was subjected to a penetrating theological critique by Peter Abelard. While in no way denying that the devil exercised *potestas* over humanity *de facto*, Abelard insisted that this power was not acquired or administered *de iure*. By seducing humankind, the devil acquired no rights over humans.[99] If the devil has any power over sinful humanity, he possesses it solely by divine permission, in that God has allotted him the specific and delimited function of captor of sinful humanity in the economy of salvation. Within this circumscribed realm, the devil operates only subject to divine permission, not by his own rights; outside that realm, the devil has no rights whatsoever over humankind. As the devil does not possess even this limited *potestas* by an absolute right, God is at liberty to withdraw it. A similar position is adopted by Hugh of St Victor, who argues that although humankind is justly punished by the devil, his dominion over it is held unjustly.[100] The school of Abelard, as might be expected, upheld its master's teaching that the devil had *potestas* over humankind *de facto* but not *de iure*.[101] Bernard of Clairvaux, an opponent of Abelard on so many matters, concedes that the devil's power over humans may be said to be just in that it derives from God, but unjust in that it was usurped by the devil.[102] The classic position characteristic of the later twelfth century is summarised in the teaching of Peter of Poitiers: the devil has no right to punish humans,

---

[98] Anselm of Laon, *Sententiae* 47–8, ed. Lottin, *Psychologie et morale*, 5.44–7; the School of Laon, *Sententiae* 354–5, ed. Lottin, *Psychologie et morale*, 5.269–70. Cf. Peter Lombard, *III Sent.* dist. xviii, 5.

[99] Abelard, *Expositio in epistolam ad Romanos*, PL 178.834D: 'Diabolus in hominem quem seduxit nullum ius seducendo acquisierit.' See further de Clerck, 'Droits du démon et nécessité de la rédemption'; R. E. Weingart, *The Logic of Divine Love: A Critical Analysis of the Soteriology of Peter Abelard*, Oxford: Oxford University Press, 1970, 84–8.

[100] Hugh of St Victor, *De sacramentis* I, viii, 4, PL 176.308A–B: 'Iniuste ergo diabolus tenet hominem, sed homo iuste tenetur.' On Hugh, see L. J. Taylor, *The Origin and Early Life of Hugh St. Victor: An Evaluation of the Tradition*, Notre Dame, IN: Mediaeval Institute University of Notre Dame, 1957.

[101] De Clerk, 'Droits du démon et nécessité de la rédemption', 39–45. The *Epitome theologiae Christianae* departs considerably from the 'received view' when it denies that humanity was *ever* subject to the power of the devil: *Epitome* 23, PL 178.1730D–1A: 'constat hominem sub potestate diaboli non fuisse, nec de eius servitute redemptum esse'.

[102] *Erroribus Abaelardi* v, 13–14, PL 182.10630–65B.

but on account of their sin, humans deserve to be placed under his power.[103]

The significance of this critique of the *ius diaboli* lies in the concept of *iustitia* employed to characterise God's dealings with the devil. If *iustitia* is understood to entail the respect of established *ius* – that is, the situation as it exists *de facto* – then God is obliged to respect the dominion of the devil over humankind. If *iustitia* is instead conceived primarily as conformity to the divine will, the devil has no *de iure* rights over humans, having abused the limited and conditional rights which some theologians were prepared to allow him in the context of the economy of salvation. The general rejection of the *ius diaboli* by the theologians of the twelfth century is therefore of considerable significance in the development of the articulation of the 'righteousness of God'.

A further theological development of significance is associated with Peter Abelard. Throughout his writings, there is an analogical predication to God of the definition of *iustitia* taken directly from Cicero: 'a virtue, serving the good of the community, which rewards each according to their dignity'.[104] In effect, it is this concept of *iustitia* which underlies Abelard's rejection of the *ius diaboli*: the devil, by insisting upon more than his due, stepped outside the boundaries of *iustitia*. Although Augustine had earlier subjected the theological application of the Ciceronian concept of *iustitia* to a penetrating critique, most theologians of the late twelfth century returned to the Ciceronian concept of *iustitia* to clarify the apparently related concept of *iustitia Dei*. The widespread use of the concept within the Abelardian school[105] suggests the influence of Abelard in this respect. While Godfrey of Poitiers followed Stephen Langton in distinguishing three aspects of the term *iustitia*, he appears to have introduced a significant innovation – the opinion that *iustitia reddit unicuique quod suum est* is attributed to *Augustine*.[106] William of Auxerre, the first Summist, distinguished the specifically theological use of the term from its ordinary sense,[107] noting that justice and mercy were not opposed in the former case. Simon of Hinton also reproduces the Ciceronian definition, again attributing it to Augustine.[108] The application of this concept of

---

[103] *Sententiarum libri quinque* IV, 19, PL 211.1212A. See also de Clerck, 'Droits du démon et nécessité de la rédemption', 56–7.

[104] *Expositio in epistolam ad Romanos*, PL 178.864A, 868B: *Sermo* 30, PL 178.567D; *Dialogus*, PL 178.1653A, 1654C, 1656D–7A. See Weingart, *The Logic of Divine Love*, 141–2.

[105] For example, *Epitome theologiae Christianae* 32, PL 178.1750C. See Lottin, 'Le Concept de justice', 512–13. A similar definition is due to Stephen Langton: Lottin, 'Le Concept de justice', 513–14.

[106] Lottin, *Psychologie et morale*, 5.514 n. 1.

[107] Lottin, *Psychologie et morale*, 5.514 n. 2.

[108] Lottin, *Psychologie et morale*, 5.515 nn. 1–2.

iustitia to the specific matter of justification may be illustrated from the *De virtutibus* of John of La Rochelle:

Righteousness (*iustitia*) is about rendering to each that to which they are entitled – to God, to oneself, and to one's neighbour. This is what is said in Matthew 6: 'seek first the kingdom of God and its righteousness'. This is the general righteousness by which the ungodly are justified, which has two parts: turning away from evil, and doing good.[109]

It will be clear that the justification of humanity is seen as an act of divine justice, rendering to humans their due for their efforts to avoid evil and to do good. This understanding of *iustitia Dei* is clearly closely linked to a doctrine of merit, by which the divine justification of humanity may be rationalised on the basis of justice, understood as *reddens unicuique quod suum est*. It will also be evident that this approach requires reference to the divine equity as much as to the divine justice – that is, God justifies those who merit it *sine gratia sine fraude sine personarum acceptione*.

A somewhat different approach to the matter is found in the works of Hugh of St Victor. His discussion of justification involves the distinction between *iustitia potestatis* and *iustitia aequitatis*. The former, also referred to as *iustitia secundum debitum facientis*, is such that the agent (i.e., God) is permitted to do anything within his power, provided that it is not unjust. The latter, or *iustitia secundum meritum patientis*, is that which relates to humanity as the object of the divine justification, and is such that individuals are permitted to have whatever they are entitled to, irrespective of whether they want it.[110] Applying these concepts of justice to the justification of humanity, Hugh argues that God is able to justify people justly, although it may reasonably be pointed out that Hugh's definitions of justice lead to the conclusion that whatever God wills for humanity is just, whether justification or condemnation, by virtue of the power of the divine will.[111]

A major point of transition can now be identified, arising from the introduction of the Aristotelian concept of justice to the theology of the western church in the middle of the thirteenth century. The great twelfth-century theological explorations of the theme of the 'righteousness of God' had taken place without any such reference; from this point onwards, the influence of Aristotle's *Ethics* becomes of growing and ultimately decisive importance. Thus Albertus Magnus' commentary on Book III of the *Sentences* appears to demonstrate familiarity with Book V of the *Nicomachean*

---

[109] Text as established by Lottin, *Psychologie et morale*, 5.517.13–18, from Paris Nat. lat. 14891 and 15952, and Brussels Bib. Roy. 12.042–9.
[110] *De sacramentis* I, viii, 8, PL 176.310D.
[111] *De sacramentis* I, viii, 8–9, PL 176.311A–D.

Ethics,[112] while his commentary on Book IV (1249) makes use of a translation of this work for the first time.[113] While this introduction allowed a classification of the various senses which the term *iustitia* could bear, it does not appear to have had a significant effect around this time on the medieval discussion of the 'righteousness of God'. The basic concepts employed remained much the same, despite differences in terminology. It is during the fifteenth century that some serious difficulties emerge, leading Luther to excoriate the use of Aristotelian ethics in theology on account of its implications for the doctrine of justification.

Of perhaps greater importance is the emergence of a clear distinction between the *intellectualist* and *voluntarist* approaches to the question of *iustitia Dei*, which may be illustrated from the works of Thomas Aquinas and Duns Scotus respectively. Thomas rejected the opinion that *iustitia Dei* is merely an arbitrary aspect of the divine will. To assert that *iustitia* ultimately depends upon the will of God amounts to the blasphemous assertion that God does not operate according to the order of wisdom.[114] Underlying *iustitia* is *sapientia*, discernible to the intellect, so that the ultimate standard of justice must be taken to be right reason.[115] This intellectualism is particularly evident in Thomas' discussion of the rationale of the salvation of humankind in Christ. For Thomas, the deliverance of humankind through the death of Christ is the most appropriate mode of redemption, and can be established as such on rational grounds. He mounts a critique of a voluntarist interpretation of *iustitia Dei*, according to which God's justice demanded Christ's passion as a *necessary* satisfaction for human sin. Thomas argues that human sin counts as *culpa*, and as such must be treated as coming under private, rather than public, law. If God is considered as judge (*iudex*), then he is not at liberty to remit an offence (*culpa*) without satisfaction, as the offence in question has been committed against a higher authority (e.g., the king), on whose behalf the judge is obliged to act.

However, as God is the supreme and common good of the universe (*supremum et commune bonum totius universae*), it follows that the *culpa* in question has not been committed against some authority higher than God, but against God himself. And just as it is perfectly acceptable for

---

[112] Lottin, *Psychologie et morale*, 5.521 n. 1. See also A. H. Chroust, 'The Philosophy of Law from St. Augustine to St. Thomas Aquinas', *New Scholasticism* 20 (1946), 26–71, 64–70, esp. 64 n. 141.

[113] Lottin, *Psychologie et morale*, 5.521 n. 2.

[114] *De veritate* q. 23 a. 6, ed. Spiazzi, 1.426: 'Dicero autem quod ex simplici voluntate dependeat iustitia, est dicere quod divina voluntas non procedat secundum ordinem sapientiae, quod est blasphemum.'

[115] For the arguments in full, see O. Lottin, 'L'Intellectualisme de la morale Thomiste', *Xenia Thomistica* 1(1925), 411–27.

individuals to forgive an offence against themselves without satisfaction, so God may forgive the sinner without the *necessity* of satisfaction. An interpretation of *iustitia Dei* which insists upon the absolute necessity of satisfaction – and Thomas appears to have Anselm of Canterbury in mind – is to be rejected in favour of one by which satisfaction is recognised to be most appropriate (*convenientius*) to right reason, and *universally* recognised as such by rational beings.

This point becomes clearer when the voluntarist interpretation of *iustitia Dei* is considered. Although the origins of this approach are especially associated with Duns Scotus,[116] it was more thoroughly developed in the soteriology of the *via moderna*. Gabriel Biel insists upon the priority of the divine will over any moral structures by declaring that God's will is essentially independent of what is right or wrong; if the divine will amounted to a mere endorsement of what is good or right, God's will would thereby be subject to created principles of morality. What is good, therefore, is good only if it is accepted as such by God.[117]

The divine will is thus the chief arbiter and principle of justice, establishing justice by its decisions, rather than acting on the basis of established justice. Morality and merit alike derive from the divine will, in that the goodness of an act must be defined, not in terms of the act itself, but in terms of the *divine estimation of that act*. Duns Scotus had established the general voluntarist principle, that every created offering to God is worth precisely whatever God accepts it for.[118] The consequences of this principle for the doctrine of merit will be explored later. Applying this principle to the passion of Christ and the redemption of humankind, Scotus points out that a good angel could have made satisfaction in Christ's place, had God chosen to accept its offering as having sufficient value: the merit of Christ's passion lies solely in the *acceptatio divina*.

One of the most significant developments in relation to the medieval understanding of the 'righteousness of God' took place within the *via*

---

[116] See G. Stratenwerth, *Die Naturrechtslehre des Johannes Duns Scotus*, Göttingen, Vandenhoeck & Ruprecht, 1951, where it is argued that Scotus thereby drove a conceptual wedge between the realms of natural and divine law. On Ockham, see W. Kölmel, 'Das Naturrecht bei Wilhelm Ockham', *FS* 35 (1953), 39–85; for Biel: in relation to Ockham at this point, see idem, 'Von Ockham zu Gabriel Biel: Zur Naturrechtslehre des 14. und 15. Jahrhunderts', *FS* 37 (1955), 218–59.

[117] Biel, *Canonis missae expositio* 23E, ed. Oberman/Courtenay, 1.212: 'Nihil fieri dignum est nisi de tua benignitate et misericordia volunte dignum iudicare volueris, neque enim quia bonum aut iustum est aliquid, ipsum Deus vult, sed quia Deus vult, ideo bonum est et iustum. Voluntas nanque divina non ex nostra bonitate, sed ex divina voluntate bonitas nostra pendet, nec aliquid bonum nisi quia a Deo sic acceptum.' Cf. *In I Sent.* dist. xliii q. 1 a. 4 cor., ed. Werbeck/Hoffmann, 1.746.5–7.

[118] *Opus Oxoniense* III dist. xix q. 1 n. 7: 'Dico, quod sicut omne aliud a Deo, ideo est bonum, quia a Deo volitum, et non est conversus; sic mentum illud tantum bonum erat, pro quanto acceptabatur.'

moderna, and is of particular importance in relation to the developing theology of the young Luther.[119] Gabriel Biel's doctrine of justification is based upon the concept of a *pactum* between God and humanity which defines the conditions which humans must meet if they are to be justified, as well as emphasising the divine reliability. The present order of salvation, although radically contingent, is nevertheless totally reliable and strictly immutable. Thus God, having freely and of his *liberalitas* determined to enter into such a binding contract with humanity, is now obliged to respect the terms of that covenant. God gives grace to those who 'do their best', precisely because of God's decision and promise to behave in this way.[120]

The establishment of such a reliable moral framework within which justification takes place allows Biel to resolve a difficulty which had previously impeded theologians from applying the Ciceronian definition of *iustitia* directly to God. The Ciceronian, Justinian and Aristotelian concepts of *iustitia* are based upon the notion of a contracting community, the *res publica* or *polis*, which establishes the *ius consensus*.[121] The direct application of such concepts of *iustitia* to God was rendered problematical by the absence of a theological equivalent to this contractual framework.

The postulation of a *pactum* between God and humanity eliminates this difficulty. The *pactum* effectively functions as the *iuris consensus* which is required if *iustitia Dei* is to be defined in terms of *reddens unicuique quod suum est*. Furthermore, studies of the medieval discussion of the concept of divine self-limitation (as expressed in the *pactum*) have demonstrated how the theologians of the period found the terminology of canon law – particularly *iustitia* – to be an ideal vehicle for its articulation.[122] Under the terms of the covenant (*pactum*), God is obliged to reward anyone who does *quod in se est* with grace *as a matter of justice*, in that God is to be perceived as rendering to such persons that to which they are entitled. The *pactum* determines *quod suum est*, and specifies the conditions upon which the *viator* may receive it.

Biel is thus able to correlate the divine justice and divine mercy by pointing out that the present order of salvation, to which God is now irrevocably committed as a matter of justice, is ultimately an expression of the divine mercy. *Stante lege*, God is necessarily obliged to reward the

---

[119] See McGrath, 'Mira et nova diffinitio iustitiae'; idem, *Luther's Theology of the Cross*, 95–113.

[120] *In II Sent*. dist. xxvii q. 1 a. 3 dub. 4, ed. Werbeck/Hoffmann, 2.253.7–9: 'Deus dat gratiam facienti quod in se est necessitate immutabilitatis et ex suppositione quia disposuit dare immutabiliter gratiam facienti quod in se est.'

[121] On which see B. Yack, *The Problems of a Political Animal: Community, Justice, and Conflict in Aristotelian Political Thought*, Berkeley: University of California Press, 1993.

[122] Hamm, *Promissio, pactum, ordinatia*, 462–6.

viator who does *quod in se est* with *quod suum est* – that is, justifying grace. Acting in mercy, God established an order of justice to which God is presently and irrevocably bound, not by an external necessity, but by faithfulness, consistency and integrity. What has been promised must be delivered. Failure on the part of God to honour the *pactum* would result in God being unjust, and acting unjustly, which is inconceivable.[123] Consequently, it is up to the individual, knowing the divine will, to conform to it in order to be justified.[124] It is therefore clear that Biel understands *iustitia Dei* to refer to equity within the context of the *pactum*, which defines God's manner of dealing with humanity.

It is this understanding of the 'righteousness of God' which is reproduced by Martin Luther in the earlier part of his *Dictata super Psalterium* (1513–15), as may be judged from his scholion on Psalm 9:9 (Vulgate, 10:9):

Righteousness (*iustitia*) is thus said to be rendering to each what is due to them. Yet equity is prior to righteousness, and is its prerequisite. Equity identifies merit; righteousness renders rewards. Thus the Lord judges the world 'in equity' (that is, wishing all to be saved), and judges 'in righteousness' (because God renders to each their reward).[125]

Luther here reproduces the key aspects of Biel's understanding of *iustitia Dei*: *iustitia* is understood to be based upon divine equity, which looks solely to the merits of humans in determining their reward within the framework established by the covenant. The doctors of the church rightly teach that, when people do their best (*quod in se est*), God infallibly gives grace (*hinc recte dicunt doctores, quod homini facienti quod in se est, Deus infallibiliter dat gratiam*).[126] Luther's theological breakthrough is intimately connected with his discovery of a new meaning of the 'righteousness of God', and it is important to appreciate that his earlier works are characterised by the teaching of the *via moderna* upon this matter. Luther's later view that anyone attempting to do *quod in se est* sinned mortally[127]

---

[123] *Missae canonis expositio* 59s; ed. Oberman/Courtenay, 2.446: 'Ita etiam quod stante sua promissione qua pollicitus est dare vitam eternam servantibus sua mandata, non posset sine iniusticia subtrahere eis premia repromissa.' For the possibility that *iustitia Dei* is thus understood to be purely arbitrary, see McGrath, '"The Righteousness of God" from Augustine to Luther', 72; idem, 'Some Observations concerning the Soteriology of the *Via Moderna*', *RThAM* 52 (1985), 182–93.

[124] *In II Sent.* dist. xxxvi q. unica a. 1 nota 3, ed. Werbeck/Hoffmann, 2.622.5 – 623.10.

[125] WA 55 ii.108.15 – 109.11 for the full text; for the gloss, see WA 55 i.70.9–11.

[126] WA 4.262.4–5. For Luther's concept of covenantal causality, see McGrath, *Luther's Theology of the Cross*, 85–90.

[127] See the view condemned in *Exsurge Domine*, D 1486: 'Liberum arbitrium post peccatum est res de solo titulo; et dum facit, quod in se est, peccat mortaliter.'

remains notionally within this framework, while ultimately subverting its theological plausibility.

The second question concerning the 'righteousness of God' raises the whole issue of the analogical nature of theological language. How is it possible to speak of God being 'righteous' (*iustus*)? As we noted earlier (1.2), the biblical material upon which the medieval commentators based their exegesis contained a Hebraic concept of the 'righteousness of God', which could be characterised as *iustitia salutifera*, bearing little resemblance to the concept of *iustitia distributiva* characteristic of western European thought. As such, it was difficult to argue from human to divine justice, a point which was frequently emphasised by early biblical commentators with reference to the problem of the 'transference of meaning'.[128] Peter Abelard thus urged extreme caution when employing terms borrowed from their everyday context (*translata a consuetis significationis*) in statements concerning God,[129] although he appears to have overlooked his own principle when analogically predicating human concepts of justice to God, as we noted above.

This use of human concepts of justice, applied analogically to God, was criticised by several theologians of the twelfth century, most notably by Alan of Lille. According to Alan, every term which is predicated of God is necessarily transferred from its proper meaning (*transfertur a sua propria significatione*). Recognising that God can be described as *iustus* only by an indirect transference of the term from its proper signification, Alan insists that this transference be understood to refer solely to the word (*nomen*) thus transferred, and not to its signification (*res*): when speaking of God as 'righteous', the word 'righteous' is to be understood as having been transferred from its proper context to one adapted to speaking about God, in which the signification of the original context cannot be regarded as being simultaneously transferred.[130]

In other words, the statement 'Deus est iustus' contains the term *iustus* transferred from a particular human context – but the term cannot be allowed to bear precisely the same meaning in this statement as that which it assumes in that specific human context. Even though the same term *iustus* is predicated of God in the statement 'Deus est iustus' and of Socrates in the analogical statement 'Socrates est iustus', it cannot be

---

[128] See G. R. Evans, *The Language and Logic of the Bible: The Earlier Middle Ages*, Cambridge: Cambridge University Press, 1984, 101–22.

[129] *Theologia Christiana* I, 7.

[130] *Theologicae regulae* 26, PL 210.633D. '*Deus est iustus*, hoc nomen *iustus* transfertur a sua propria significatione ad hoc ut conveniat Deo, sed res nominis non attribuitur Deo.' See G. R. Evans, *Alan of Lille: The Frontiers of Theology in the Later Twelfth Century*, Cambridge: Cambridge University Press, 1983, 29–33.

allowed to bear the same signification in each case. On account of its transference from its proper context, the word acquires a 'borrowed meaning'[131] which, although analogous to its original meaning, is not identical with it. Thus divine justice is not the same as human justice, so that the statement 'Deus est iustus' cannot be allowed to have the same point of reference as 'Socrates est iustus'. This leads to the inevitable conclusion that, since the 'borrowed meaning' of *iustus* is unknown, and almost certainly unknowable, the statement 'Deus est iustus' has no meaning. If we do not know precisely what meaning the term *iustus* assumes in the statement 'Deus est iustus', we cannot know what the statement means. Many theologians of the twelfth century thus preferred, like the Benedictine Hugh, Archbishop of Rouen, to seek refuge in the divine incomprehensibility.[132]

The question of how God may be described as *iustus* raises the related question of how his attributes may be discussed. What does it mean to speak of God's wisdom, righteousness, etc.? The rise of the Ockhamist epistemology in the late fourteenth century led to the calling into question of the existence of such attributes.[133] Henry of Ghent maintained the reality of such divine attributes. If the mental distinction between essence and attributes in God rested upon a comparison with reference to the same qualities in creatures, the existence of the divine attributes would come to be dependent upon creatures – which Henry considered impossible. Therefore the divine attributes must be considered to differ by an internal relation of reason, independent of any intellectual comparison with the same qualities among creatures. Godfrey of Fontaines, however, argued that the basis of the distinction between the divine attributes must be considered to lie in creatures rather than in God. Godfrey, like most of his contemporaries, accepted that the distinction between the divine attributes was purely mental, but insisted that the distinction must originate outside the mind. While Henry located the origin of this distinction within the divine being itself, Godfrey located it within creatures.

The distinction between the attributes must therefore rest upon a comparison within the intellect between God and the diversity which exists in his creatures, as otherwise God, being supremely simple, would be conceived only as one. The divine attributes, therefore, are contained virtually within the divine essence as the source of all perfection, and are known only by comparison with what approximates to them – that is, by

[131] G. R. Evans, 'The Borrowed Meaning: Grammar, Logic and the Problems of Theological Language in Twelfth-Century Schools', *DR* 96 (1978), 165–75.
[132] *Tractactiones in Hexamaeron* I, 12, PL 192.1252B: 'Deus enim semper est id quod est, qui determinari seu describi vel diffiniri non potest, quia incomprehensibilis est.'
[133] What follows is based on Ockham, *In I Sent.*, dist. ii q. 3, *Opera theologica* 2.50–74.

the recognition on the part of the human intellect of a similarity between God and creatures in respect of the quality involved. As such forms and qualities in creatures owe their existence and origin to the divine ideas and their perfection in God, the existence of such a similarity, albeit only to a limited and determinate extent, is to be expected.

By contrast, William of Ockham rejected both opinions. The distinction between the divine attributes on the part of the human intellect owes nothing either to any such distinction in God himself, or to any comparison with himself or anything else. According to Ockham, God's attributes, such as *iustitia*, *misericordia*, and so on, cannot be said to correspond to anything real within God, but arise purely and simply from the multiplicity of acts of human cognition involved. Thus *iustitia Dei* cannot be allowed to have any real existence within God, as it is a consequence purely of the act of cognition on the part of the human intellect. The only distinction that may be allowed among the divine attributes is that they are different concepts within the human mind; they do not denote a formal distinction within God, nor do they correspond to any distinction *in* him, or *in relation to* him. The concepts involved are neither *really* nor *formally* identical with the divine essence. The fact that such conceptual distinctions are known by the human intellect cannot be allowed to impose such a distinction upon the object of the intellect, so that any diversity which may be posited among the divine attributes cannot be allowed to correspond to a diversity within God himself, but merely to concepts which are distinguished by the intellect.

God, as supremely simple, is apprehended either totally, or not at all, and as a consequence the divine attributes are to be recognised as the product of the human intellect. Whereas God is real, the divine attributes are not (unless, of course, concepts are allowed to be real). The essence of Ockham's important criticism of the real existence of the divine attributes is that they are not founded in being. A twofold distinction must therefore be made between the divine attributes, taken absolutely for the *perfection which is God*, and taken *as concepts which can be predicated of God*.[134]

If the attributes of God are understood as in the former, there is no real distinction between them; if they are understood as in the latter, the attributal distinction is purely mental, and has no foundation in reality. Either way, it makes little sense to speak of *iustitia Dei*, and still less to speak of a tension between *iustitia* and *misericordia* in God.

Ockham's critique of the divine attributes does not appear to have had any real significance for the later medieval discussion of *iustitia Dei*, which

[134] Ockham, *In I Sent.* dist. ii q. 3, *Opera philosophica et theologica*, 2.61–2.

tended to proceed on the assumption that a real distinction could be drawn between *iustitia* and *misericordia Dei*. The problem of defining that 'righteousness', however, proved to be intractable. The medieval period can be characterised by its insistence that God's mercy, righteousness and truth were simultaneously manifested in his salvation of humankind, a point often made in connection with the Christological exegesis of the Vulgate text of Psalm 85:10 (Vulgate, 84:11): 'Mercy and truth meet together; righteousness and peace kiss each other.'

The theologians of the medieval period were convinced that God's righteousness was expressed in the redemption of humanity in Christ. The difficulties associated with this understanding of the 'righteousness of God', particularly in connection with the correlation of *iustitia Dei* and *iustitia hominis*, were never, however, entirely resolved.

2.3   The subjective appropriation of justification

The medieval theological tradition followed Augustine of Hippo in insisting that humans have a positive role to play in their own justification. Augustine's celebrated dictum 'The one who made you without you will not justify you without you' (*Qui fecit te sine te, non te iustificat sine te*)[135] virtually achieved the status of an axiom[136] in the medieval discussion of justification. The definition of the precise nature of this human role in justification was, however, the subject of considerable disagreement within the medieval theological schools. The development of the various traditional positions on the question, which forms the subject of the present section, is conveniently discussed under three headings:

1. the nature of the human free will;
2. the necessity and nature of the proper disposition for justification;
3. the origin, interpretation and application of the axiom 'God will not deny grace to those who do their best (*facienti quod in se est Deus non denegat gratiam*)'.

Before considering these three aspects of the appropriation of justification, it is necessary to make two observations.

First, it is impossible to discuss the medieval understandings of the subjective appropriation of justification without reference to the role of

---

[135] Augustine, *Sermo* 169, 13.
[136] The term 'axiom' is, of course, being used in a loose sense, rather than in the Euclidian or Boethian senses of the term; see G. R. Evans, 'Boethian and Euclidian Axiomatic Method in the Theology of the Later Twelfth Century', *Archives Internationales d'Histoire des Sciences* 103 (1980), 13–29.

the sacraments in justification, to be discussed presently. Second, the medieval discussion of the appropriation of justification is not conducted in terms of the concept of justification *by faith*. Justifying faith is universally understood to be a gift of God bestowed upon humanity as a consequence of his disposition towards justification. In effect, the possibility of justifying faith being a human work is excluded from the outset. The medieval discussion of the appropriation of justification is primarily concerned with establishing the conditions upon which justifying grace and faith are bestowed upon the individual by God. In the present section, the three aspects of the question of the subjective appropriation of justification identified above will be considered individually.

2.3.1 *The nature of the human free will*

The influence of Augustine upon the medieval discussion of justification is probably at its greatest in connection with the relation between grace and free will. Although the term *liberum arbitrium* is pre-Augustinian and unbiblical, Augustine succeeded in imposing an interpretation upon the term which allowed a profoundly biblical understanding of the human bondage to sin and the need for grace to be maintained, while simultaneously upholding the reality of human free will. This understanding of the nature of the human free will would be clarified in the course of a series of controversies immediately succeeding Augustine's death, in addition to two during his lifetime – the Pelagian and Massilian controversies.

In essence, Pelagianism must be seen as a reforming movement in the increasingly corrupt world of the later Roman empire, especially critical of the growing tendency to see in Christianity an almost magical way of obtaining salvation in the next world without undue inconvenience in the present. It was primarily against this moral laxity that Pelagius and his supporters protested,[137] apparently unaware that their chief theological opponent shared precisely the same concern. Augustine's account of the

---

[137] Recent studies have emphasised Pelagius' orthodox intentions: R. F. Evans, *Pelagius: Inquiries and Reappraisals*, London: A. & C. Black, 1968; Gisbert Greshake, *Gnade als konkrete Freiheit: Eine Untersuchung zur Gnadenlehre des Pelagius*, Mainz: Matthias-Grunewald-Verlag, 1972. The older study of G. de Plinval, *Pélage, ses écrits, sa vie et sa réforme*, Lausanne: Payot, 1943, is still helpful. On the reforming nature of Pelagianism, see the two excellent studies of Peter Brown: 'Pelagius and His Supporters: Aims and Environment', *JThS* 19 (1968) 93–114; 'The Patrons of Pelagius: The Roman Aristocracy between East and West', *JThS* 21 (1970) 56–72. Particular attention is drawn to the fact that the ascetic discipline and aims of Pelagianism are now seen as the *least* original aspects of the movement, being regarded as part of the general western reception of oriental monastic traditions through the translations of Rufinus in the late fourth century (on which see F. Winkelmann, 'Spätantike lateinische Übersetzungen christlicher griechischer Literatur', *ThLZ* 95 (1967), 229–40).

origin of the Pelagian controversy relates how Pelagius was outraged by the much cited prayer from his *Confessions*, 'Give what you command, and command what you will.'[138] To Pelagius, these words suggested that humans were merely puppets wholly determined by divine grace, thereby encouraging moral quietism of the worst order.

For Pelagius, moral responsibility presupposed freedom of the will: I ought, therefore I can. It can be argued that the fundamental doctrine of Pelagius' theological system lies in his unequivocal assertion of the autonomous and sovereign character of the human *liberum arbitrium*: in creating humans, God gave them the unique privilege of being able to accomplish the divine will by their own choice, setting before them life and death, and bidding them choose the former – but permitting the final decision to rest with the individuals themselves. Pelagius found particularly offensive the suggestion that the human *liberum arbitrium* was diseased or compromised in any way, so that it has an inherent bias towards evildoing.

While Pelagius conceded that Adam's sin had disastrous consequences for his posterity, he insisted that these arose by *imitation*, rather than by *propagation*. There is no congenital fault in humans, and no special or general influence upon them to perform evil or good. God, having created humans, is unable to exert any influence upon them, except through external, non-coercive means (i.e., *gratia ab extra*). In part, the confusion surrounding Augustine's controversy with Pelagius arises from the fact that Pelagius appears to understand by *grace* what Augustine understands by *nature*. Thus when Augustine and Pelagius agree that humanity stands in need of grace, the latter specifically means *general grace*, given in the endowment of nature (i.e., a 'given' rather than a specific 'gift'), enabling humans to perform God's will with their natural faculties.

The real locus of the Pelagian controversy lies in Augustine's doctrine of prevenient grace. Pelagius understands grace as *gratia ab extra*, an external, non-coercive grace of knowledge such as the Decalogue or the example of Christ. Humans can, if they so choose, fulfil the law of Moses without sinning. It is this concept of grace which ultimately leads to the harsh doctrine of *impeccantia*: as the law *can* be fulfilled, so it *must* be fulfilled. This 'theology of example' may be seen both in Pelagius' emphasis upon the need for *imitatio Christi* and in the assertion that it is by the *example* of Adam's sin that his posterity is injured. This is brought out clearly in Pelagius' letter to Demetrias, one of the most important sources relating to the Pelagian controversy:

---

[138] *De dona perseverentia* xx, 53. Cf. *Confessiones* x, xxix, 40 'da quod iubes et iube quod vis'.

[Instead of regarding God's commands as a privilege] we cry out at God and say, 'This is too hard! This is too difficult! We cannot do it! We are only human, and hindered by the weakness of the flesh!' What blind madness! What blatant presumption! By doing this, we accuse the God of knowledge of a twofold ignorance – ignorance of God's own creation and of God's own commands. It would be as if, forgetting the weakness of humanity – God's own creation – God had laid upon us commands which we were unable to bear. And at the same time – may God forgive us! – we ascribe to the righteous One unrighteousness, and cruelty to the Holy One; first, by complaining that God has commanded the impossible, second, by imagining that some will be condemned by God for what they could not help; so that – the blasphemy of it! – God is thought of as seeking our punishment rather than our salvation . . . No one knows the extent of our strength better than the God who gave us that strength . . . God has not willed to command anything impossible, for God is righteous, and will not condemn anyone for what they could not help, for God is holy.[139]

The Massilian controversy appears to have arisen over Augustine's doctrine of predestination. Although this is still referred to as the 'semi-Pelagian' controversy in the literature, it must be appreciated that this is a seriously misleading anachronism which has no place in such a discussion.[140] The term 'Massilian' is used by Augustine himself, and eliminates the unjustified comparison with Pelagianism implicit in the term 'semi-Pelagianism'. Augustine described the Massilians as holding doctrines which 'abundantly distinguished them from the Pelagians', which appears to amount to a rejection of Prosper of Aquitaine's description of them as the *reliquiae Pelagianorum*. He argues that their chief error lies in their teaching on predestination.[141]

Augustine's teaching on predestination met with considerable hostility in the southern regions of Gaul. Indeed, Vincent of Lérins appears to have formulated his famous 'canon' with Augustine's predestinarianism in mind. The defining characteristic of catholic doctrine is that 'it is believed everywhere, always, by everyone'.[142] As Augustine's doctrine of predestination failed to conform to this triple test of ecumenicity, antiquity, and consent, it cannot be regarded as catholic. A more positive approach to Augustine's teachings is found in the writings of John Cassian. Like Vincent, he rejected the Pelagian doctrine of the free will, apparently accepting Augustine's theology of grace in its entirety, with

---

[139] *Epistola ad Demetriadem* 16, PL 33.1110A–B. For the background, see Joanne McWilliam, 'Letters to Demetrias: A Sidebar in the Pelagian Controversy: Helenae, amicae meae', *Toronto Journal of Theology* 16 (2000), 131–9.

[140] Cf. Harnack, *History of Dogma* 5.245 n. 3. The alternative 'synergism' is similarly unacceptable: N. P. Williams, *The Grace of God*, Longman, Green & Co., 1930, 44.

[141] *De praedestinatione sanctorum* i, 2.

[142] *Commonitorium* 2, PL 50.640B: 'In ipsa item catholica ecclesia magnopere curandum est, ut id teneamus, quod ubique, quod semper, quod ad omnibus creditum est; hoc est etenim vere proprieque catholicum.'

the specific exception of his doctrines of predestination and irresistible grace.[143] In particular, it may be noted that he appears to have grasped and upheld the Augustinian concept of the dialectic between the *liberum arbitrium captivatum* and *liberum arbitrium liberatum*: 'A person is truly free only who has begun to be your prisoner, O Lord.'[144]

Cassian's emphasis upon the reality of the human free will has its context in monastic asceticism, with its characteristic stress upon the need for exertion in the spiritual life. Cassian wrote primarily for monks, who may be regarded as having been initiated into the Christian life. It may therefore be assumed that when Cassian speaks of grace, he intends *co-operative* rather than *operative* grace to be understood (to use Augustine's terms). If Cassian appears to be a 'synergist', it is because, like Augustine, he asserts the synergy of grace and free will *after* justification. Furthermore, it may be pointed out that Cassian's emphasis upon *prayer* as a means for improving the spiritual condition is a sign of the *importance* he attaches to grace, rather than of his *rejection* of its necessity, as some have supposed.

The Synod of Jerusalem (July 415) and the Synod of Diospolis (December 415) led to mild censure of Pelagianism, with the influence of Augustine much in evidence. Neither of these synods can be considered to be significant in comparison with the Council of Carthage (418),[145] whose canons would receive wide acceptance in the catholic church, and feature prominently in medieval discussions of the nature of the Pelagian error. Of these canons, the most important is the fifth, which teaches the impotence of the human free will unless aided by grace, and the further necessity of grace to enable humans to fulfil the commandments of the law.[146] The Council of Ephesus (431) condemned both Nestorianism and Pelagianism (this latter in the form associated with Caelestius), although the council does not appear to have recognised the close theological connection between the heresies so ably summarised in Charles Gore's celebrated dictum, 'The Nestorian Christ is the fitting saviour of the Pelagian man.'[147]

[143] See MacQueen, 'John Cassian on Grace and Free Will'. The two general studies of Chéné, 'Que significiaient "initium fidei"?' and 'Le Sémipélagianisme du Midi et de la Gaule', provide valuable background material.

[144] *De incarnatione* VII, i, 2.

[145] Both this council and Orange II were *local*, rather than ecumenical. For the difficulties this raises, see J. M. Todd (ed.), *Problems of Authority: An Anglo-French Symposium*, London: Darton, Longman & Todd, 1964, 63–4.

[146] *D* 227.

[147] Charles Gore, 'Our Lord's Human Example', *Church Quarterly Review* 16 (1883) 298. A similar link between Nestorius and Pelagius is identified by John Cassian (*De incarnatione* I, iii, 5). See also the somewhat scurrilous poem of Prosper of Aquitaine, *Epitaphium Nestorianae et Pelagianae haeresos*, PL 51.153.

The most specific attack upon Pelagianism to be found in a fifth-century authoritative source is that of the *Indiculus de gratia Dei* (431), usually regarded as the work of Prosper of Aquitaine. Its chapters explicitly reject the Pelagian understandings of the nature of grace and the capabilities of human free will. Individuals cannot rise from the depths of Adam's sin unless the grace of God should lift them up. Even after justification, humans require God's grace if they are to persevere. The most important statement of the document relates to the effects of grace upon free will; the *Indiculus* makes it clear that grace *liberates* rather than *abolishes* the human *liberum arbitrium*.[148]

The definitive pronouncement of the early western church on the Pelagian and Massilian controversies may be found in the Second Council of Orange (529). The council declared that to teach that the 'freedom of the soul' remained unaffected by the Fall was Pelagian.[149] Faustus of Riez's doctrine of the *initium fidei* – that is, that humans can take the initiative in their own salvation – was explicitly rejected; not only the *beginning*, but also the *increase* of faith, are alike gifts of grace.[150] While the council declared that the human *liberum arbitrium* is injured, weakened and diminished, its existence was not questioned.[151] Although the council declined to teach the doctrines of double predestination and irresistible grace, it must be pointed out that it is questionable whether these may be considered as authentically *Augustinian*, in that they are not *explicitly taught by Augustine*, even though they may appear to *follow logically* from his teaching. If the term 'Augustinian' is understood to mean 'conforming to doctrines explicitly taught by Augustine after 396', it may reasonably be suggested that Orange II endorses an Augustinian doctrine of justification.

Although it might therefore appear that the medieval period was thus bequeathed an accurate and definitive account of Augustine's teaching on justification, a number of factors conspired to generate considerable confusion over this matter. It is a curious and unexplained feature of the history of doctrine that the canons of Orange II appear to have been

---

[148] Cap. 1, *D* 239; Cap. 3, *D* 240; Cap. 9, *D* 247–8.

[149] Can. 1, *D* 371. The reference here appears to be to freedom from sin, rather than to *liberum arbitrium*.

[150] Cap. 5, *D* 375. For the terms *initium fidei* and *affectus credulitatis*, as they occur in this canon, see Chéné, 'Que significiaent "initium fidei"?'; idem, 'Le sémipélagianisme du Midi et de la Gaule'.

[151] Cap. 8, *D* 378: 'per liberum arbitrium, quod in omnibus, qui de praevaricatione primi hominis nati sunt, constat esse vitiatum . . . Is enim non omnium liberum arbitrium per peccatum primi hominis asserit infirmatum'. This is made especially clear in the 'profession of faith' appended to the canons (*D* 396).

unknown from the tenth century to the middle of the sixteenth.[152] The theologians of the medieval period thus did not have access to this definitive statement of an Augustinian doctrine of justification, and appear to have been unaware of its existence.

A further complication concerned the attribution of Pelagius' writings during the Middle Ages. Much of Pelagius' work was mistakenly ascribed to Jerome, leading some to conclude that Jerome and Augustine were thought to have radically different theologies of justification. In addition, many pseudo-Augustinian works were in circulation in the medieval period, frequently teaching a doctrine of justification which owed more to Pelagius or Faustus of Riez than to Augustine. An excellent example is provided by Pelagius' *Libellus fidei*, which, we have already noted, was attributed by some (e.g., Peter Lombard) to Jerome; elsewhere, this same Pelagian work is attributed to Augustine as *Sermo* 191. Although fourteenth-century source-critical studies achieved a certain degree of resolution of these difficulties, the fact remains that the great theological renaissance of the twelfth century would take place without access to the authentically Augustinian teaching of the sixth-century church on the relation between grace and free will.[153] This point is of particular importance in connection with the development of the teaching of Thomas Aquinas on the *initium fidei*, which will be discussed further below.

Despite these circumstances, the twelfth century witnessed considerable agreement on the issues of grace and free will. The profession of faith, composed by Leo IX in 1053, contained a clear statement of the relationship between the two: grace precedes and follows humans, yet in such a manner that it does not compromise their free will.[154] Anselm of Canterbury defined free will as the power (*potestas*) of preserving the *rectitudo voluntatis*: humanity, though fallen, still possesses this *potestas*, and can therefore be said to possess *libertas arbitrii*. However, no power is capable of actualising its potential unaided,[155] and if the *potestas* of the human free will is to be reduced to *actus* it must be actualised by God's general or special *concursus*. In effect, Anselm's definition of free will is such that a positive answer to the question of whether humans can justify themselves is excluded from the outset; as only God can convert *potestas* to *actus*, so only God can justify.

---

[152] This remarkable fact appears first to have been noticed by Bouillard, *Conversion et grâce chez S. Thomas d'Aquin*, 98–102, 114–21. See also Max Seckler, *Instinkt und Glaubenswille nach Thomas von Aquin*, Mainz: Matthias-Grunewald-Verlag, 1961, 90–133.

[153] For some of the issues, see McGrath, *The Intellectual Origins of the European Reformation*, 170–1.

[154] D 685: 'Gratiam Dei praevenire et subsequi hominem credo et profiteor, ita tamen, ut liberum arbitrium rationali creaturae non denegem.'

[155] *De libero arbitrio* 3.

This concept of the divine actualisation of *potestas* found its expression in the thirteenth-century doctrine of the *concursus simultaneus*. There was, however, considerable confusion concerning the precise means by which potency was reduced to act; according to some, the agent involved was the Holy Spirit, while others considered it to be actual or habitual grace.[156] Later, the axiom *omnis actus perfectus a forma perfecta* would be employed in the discussion of the question.[157] Underlying these developments, however, is the basic conviction, expressed by Peter Lombard in his *Sentences*, that human *liberum arbitrium* cannot do good unless it is first liberated (*liberatum*) and subsequently assisted by grace.[158] The subsequent confusion concerning the precise nature of the *concursus* unquestionably reflects a corresponding prior confusion concerning the nature of grace itself, so characteristic a feature of early scholasticism.

The medieval ignorance of the canons of Orange II is of particular importance in relation to the evaluation of the 'Pelagianism' of the teaching on human *liberum arbitrium* associated with the *via moderna*. We shall illustrate this with reference to Gabriel Biel. The relevance of Gabriel Biel's doctrine of *liberum arbitrium* to the development of Luther's doctrine of *servum arbitrium* has been emphasised by many scholars,[159] as it is now generally accepted that Luther's *Disputatio contra scholasticam theologiam* (1517) is specifically directed against Biel, rather than against 'scholastic theology' in general. Following the common teaching of the *via moderna*, Biel declines to distinguish human intellect and will, so that *liberum arbitrium*, *libertas* and *voluntas* are regarded as being essentially identical. This approach to the question leads to a strong assertion of the freedom of the will, as *libertas* is regarded as a corollary of rationality. That the will is free is evident from experience, and requires no further demonstration. For Biel, free will is the power of the soul which allows the *viator* to distinguish and choose between good and evil, by which he is distinguished from other animals.[160] The theological consequences of Biel's doctrine of *liberum arbitrium* may be stated as follows:[161]

1. The human free will may choose a morally good act *ex puris naturalibus*, without the need for grace.[162]
2. Humans are able, by the use of their free will and other natural faculties, to implement the law by their own power, but are unable to

---

[156] See Mitzka, 'Die Anfänge der Konkurslehre'. For this concept in the early Augustinian school, see Trape, *Il concorso divino del pensiero di Egidio Romano*. On the development of the concept in High Scholasticism, see Auer, *Entwicklung der Gnadenlehre*, 2.113–45.
[157] Mitzka, 'Die Anfänge der Konkurslehre', 175.
[158] *II Sent.* dist. xxv 8–9.   [159] See Grane, *Contra Gabrielem*.
[160] *In II Sent.* dist. xxv q. unica a. 1 nota 1.
[161] Ernst, *Gott und Mensch am Vorabend der Reformation*, 325–8.
[162] *In II Sent.* dist. xxviii q. unica a. 2 conc. 1.

fulfil the law in the precise manner which God intended (that is, *quoad substantiam actus*, but not *quoad intentionem praecipientis*).[163]

3. *Ex puris naturalibus* the free will is able to avoid mortal sin.[164]
4. *Ex puris naturalibus* the free will is able to love God above everything else.[165]
5. *Ex suis naturalibus* the free will is able to dispose itself towards the reception of the gift of grace.[166]

It is this final aspect of Biel's teaching on the capacities of fallen humanity's free will which has claimed most attention, and has frequently given rise to charges of Pelagianism or 'semi-Pelagianism'.[167] On careful examination in the light of the covenantal foundations of Biel's theology, however, it can be seen that these charges are quite without foundation. As Biel himself makes clear, his discussion of the role of individuals in their own justification must be set within the context of the divine *pactum*. The requirement of a minimum response on the part of humans of the divine offer of grace is totally in keeping with the earlier Franciscan school's teaching, such as that of Alexander of Hales or Bonaventure. Biel has simply placed his theology of a minimum human response to the divine initiative in justification on a firmer foundation in the theology of the *pactum*, thereby safeguarding God from the charge of capriciousness.

Biel's modern critics' surprise at the absence of contemporary criticism of his teaching as Pelagian[168] simply reflects the fact that, by the standards of the time, Biel's doctrine of justification would not have been considered Pelagian. There is a serious risk of anachronism in applying one era's understanding of 'Pelagianism' to another, which based its judgements on different criteria. The sole legitimate criteria by which the 'Pelagianism' of Biel's doctrine of justification may be judged are the canons of the Council of Carthage – the only criteria which medieval doctors then possessed, for reasons we have already noted.

---

[163] *In II Sent.* dist. xxviii q. unica a. 2 conc. 3.
[164] *In II Sent.* dist. xxviii q. unica a. 2 conc. 2.
[165] *In II Sent.* dist. xxvii q. unica a. 3 dub. 2 prop. 1.
[166] *In II Sent.* dist. xxviii q. unica a. 2 conc. 1.
[167] Thus Oberman, *The Harvest of Medieval Theology*, 176–7; H. J. McSorley, 'Was Gabriel Biel a Semi-Pelagian?', in L. Scheffczyk (ed.), *Wahrheit und Verkündigung*, 2 vols., München: Schoningh, 1967), 2.1109–20; J. E. Biechler, 'Gabriel Biel on "liberum arbitrium"', *The Thomist* 34 (1970), 114–27. For replies, see F. Clark, 'A New Appraisal of Late Medieval Nominalism', *Gregorianum* 46 (1965), 733–65; Ernst, *Gott und Mensch am Vorabend der Reformation*; McGrath, 'The Anti-Pelagian Structure of "Nominalist" Doctrines of Justification'.
[168] For example, Biechler, 'Gabriel Biel on "liberum arbitrium"', 125: 'Biel's own doctrine of justification, clearly Pelagian though it was, apparently provoked little or no pre-Lutheran opposition.' It may be pointed out that the list of forbidden books published after Trent makes no reference to Biel or other theologians of the *via moderna*; indeed, Biel was still highly regarded by the German Roman Catholic church in the late sixteenth century: Oberman, *The Harvest of Medieval Theology*, 427.

Biel's high regard for the tradition of the church is such that he accepts whatever the church defined as being *de fide*. Biel's attitude to tradition is such that, had he known of the decrees of Orange II, he would have incorporated their substance into his doctrine of justification as *determinationes ecclesiae*.[169] If Biel's theology is to be stigmatised as 'Pelagian' or 'semi-Pelagian', it must be appreciated that he suffered from a historical accident which affected the entire period up to the Council of Trent itself. If orthodoxy is to be determined with reference to *known authoritative pronouncements of the church*, orthodoxy would undergo a radical change with the rediscovery of these canons. Those who were orthodox by the standards of 1500 – among whom we may number Gabriel Biel! – may no longer have been so by 1550. Biel himself is aware of the decrees of the Council of Carthage, and makes frequent reference to Canon 5 in particular, which he states thus: 'If anyone says that we are able to fulfil the commands of God by free will without grace, it is to be condemned.'[170] Biel's careful distinction between the implementation of the law *quoad substantiam actus* and *quoad intentionem praecipientis* ensures his conformity to the teaching of this canon.

It is clear that the charge of 'Pelagianism' or 'semi-Pelagianism' brought against Biel stands or falls with the definition employed. If it is taken to mean that the *viator* can take the initiative in his own justification, the very existence of the *pactum* deflects the charge; God has taken the initiative away from humans, who are merely required to *respond* to that initiative by the proper exercise of their *liberum arbitrium*. However, neither the Pelagian nor the Massilian controversy operated with so sophisticated a concept of causality as that employed by the theologians of the *via moderna*, expressed in the *pactum* theology, so that the application of epithets such as 'Pelagian' to Biel's theology of justification must be regarded as historically unsound. In terms of the historical controversies themselves, Biel must be regarded as totally innocent of both errors.

In general, although the assertion that humanity possesses the freedom to respond to the divine initiative in justification is characteristic of the medieval period, this consensus was accompanied by widespread disagreement as to the precise nature of the freedom in question, and whether it could be regarded as given in nature or acquired through grace. This point becomes particularly clear in the medieval discussion of the axiom *facienti quod in se est Deus non denegat gratiam*, to which we shall

---

[169] For an excellent study of Biel's attitude to tradition, see Oberman, *The Harvest of Medieval Theology*, 365–408.

[170] It may be noted at this point that the conciliar collections of the medieval period generally attributed the canons of the Council of Carthage (418) to the Council of Mileve (416).

shortly return. Our attention now turns to the medieval opinions concerning the need for some kind of 'disposition' for justification.

2.3.2   The necessity and nature of the proper disposition for justification

What happens before the sinner is justified? Is justification preceded by a preparation on the part of sinners to receive the gift that God subsequently gives to them? And if this is the case, is God obliged to bestow the gift in question upon such sinners on account of their having prepared themselves to receive it? The twelfth century saw a growing conviction that a preparation was required of humans for justification. Peter of Poitiers used a domestic analogy to illustrate the role of such a preparation for justification. A person may clean out his house and decorate it in order to receive an important guest, so that all will be ready when he arrives. This preparation, however, does not necessitate the arrival of the guest, which depends only upon the guest's love for his host.[171]

The necessity of a preparation or disposition for justification was insisted upon by both the early Franciscan and the Dominican schools, although, as we shall demonstrate, for very different reasons. The pre-Bonaventuran Franciscan school demonstrates a degree of uncertainty on the question, partly due to a related uncertainty concerning the concept of created grace. Alexander of Hales may have seemed to limit the human role in justification to not resisting grace,[172] but his teaching was developed by John of La Rochelle in a significant direction. John insists upon the need for a disposition for justification in people, in that the recipients of uncreated grace – that is, of the Holy Spirit – are unable to receive it unless their souls have first been prepared for it. The need for such a disposition does not result from any deficiency on the part of God. John draws a distinction between sufficiency on the part of the agent (i.e., God) and that on the part of the recipient in justification. God is all-sufficient in justification, but the recipient of uncreated grace must first be disposed for its reception by created grace.[173]

Odo Rigaldi likewise distinguished between the gift of the uncreated grace of the Holy Spirit and the disposition of the human soul towards the reception of this gift by created grace.[174] It may be noted that Odo

[171] *Sententiarum libri quinque* III, 2, PL 211.1047A–B.
[172] *Quaestiones disputatae 'antequam esset frater'* q. 53 membr. 3, ed. Quaracchi, 2.1020.24 – 1022.7.
[173] *Quaestiones disputatae de gratia* q. 7, ed. Hödl, 64; cf. *Tractatus de gratia* q. 2 membr. 1 a. 2, ed. Hödl, 72.
[174] *In II Sent.* dist. xxvi membr. 1 q. l, ed. Bouvy, 308.89–92. See also B. Pergamo, 'Il desiderio innato del soprannaturale nelli questioni inediti di Oddone Rigaldo', *Studi Francescani* 32 (1935), 414–46; 33 (1936), 76–108.

appears unclear as to what created grace actually *is* – he seems to regard it as a hybrid species.[175] This unclarity was resolved by the *Summa Fratris Alexandri* in what appears to have been the first systematic discussion of the nature of created grace.[176] The *Summa* begins by considering the concept of uncreated grace, which transforms the human soul in justification: *gratia ponit aliquid in anima*.[177] If uncreated grace did not alter the soul in justification, there would be no difference between the justified and the unjustified sinner. Uncreated grace may therefore be considered as the *forma transformans* and created grace as the *forma transformata*.[178] This important interpretation of the nature of created grace points to its being a quality of the soul – that is, a *disposition*, rather than a *substance*. The Holy Spirit can be said to dwell in the souls of the justified as in a temple; this is impossible unless there is something within the soul which, although not itself the temple, is capable of transforming the soul into such a temple capable of receiving the Holy Spirit.[179]

This interpretation of the nature and function of created grace is closely linked with the anthropology of the early Franciscan school, according to which the human soul is not naturally capable of receiving grace. In order for the human soul to receive grace, it must first be disposed to receive it. By contrast, the early Dominican school maintained that *anima naturaliter est gratiae capax*, reflecting a quite different understanding of humanity's pristine state. The disposition of the human soul for the reception of uncreated grace is understood by the *Summa* to be a quality of the soul brought about by the action of grace, and which may be termed *created grace*. It will, however, be clear that there was still uncertainty as to whether *gratia creata* was to be considered as the *disposition towards the reception of uncreated grace* or the *result of the reception of uncreated grace*.

[175] *In II Sent.* dist. xxvi membr. 1 q. 1 ad 1um, ed. Bouvy, 308.95–105. It may be noted at this point that Thomas Aquinas never seems to use the term *gratia creata* at all, although he appears to demonstrate familiarity with the term at one point (*In II Sent.* dist. xxvi q. 1 a. 1).

[176] See E. Gössmann, *Metaphysik und Heilsgeschichte: Eine theologische Untersuchung der Summa Halensis*, Munich: Hueber, 1964; Philips, 'La Théologie de la grâce dans la "Summa Fratris Alexandri"', 100–23. This work is composite, and does not stem from Alexander of Hales; J. Auer, 'Textkritische Studien zur Gnadenlehre des Alexander von Hales', *Scholastik* 15 (1940), 63–75. For the origins of the distinction between *gratia creata* and *gratia increata*, see Auer, *Die Entwicklung der Gnadenlehre* 1.86–123.

[177] See *Summa Fratris Alexandri* pars III inq. 1 tract. 2 q. 1 cap. 1 and the following sections; *Alexandri de Hales Summa theologica* IV, 1023–60.

[178] *Summa Fratris Alexandri* pars III inq. 1 tract. 1 q. 2 cap. 1 a. 2 sol., ed. Quaracchi, 4.959. On this whole question, see Dhont, *Le Problème de la préparation à la grâce*.

[179] *Summa Fratris Alexandri* pars II inq. 2 tract. 3 sect. 2 q. 2 tit. 3 cap. 4 a. 1 ad 3um; ed. Quaracchi, 1.729. For a more detailed study of this question, see Philips, *L'Union personnelle avec le Dieu vivant*.

This basic teaching of the early Franciscan school was developed along psychological lines by Bonaventure.[180] Human nature is sufficiently frail that it is simply incapable of receiving the gift of sanctifying grace unless it is prepared beforehand.[181] This disposition towards justification is effected with the assistance of prevenient grace, *gratia gratis data*, and cannot be brought about by the unaided free will.[182] The transition from nature to grace is achieved by prevenient grace disposing the human soul to receive the supernatural gift of habitual grace.[183] Matthew of Aquasparta reports the opinion that a preparation for justification is useless and unnecessary, since grace is given to humans according to their natural aptitudes and capacities.[184] This opinion is to be rejected, he argues, as being improbable and contrary to experience; humans cannot prepare themselves for justification without *gratia gratis data*, which moves and excites the will to detest sin and desire justification. Following Bonaventure, Matthew emphasises the frailty of human nature; just as humans cannot look at the sun until they have become accustomed to its brilliance by appropriate preparation, so the free will cannot prepare itself for the light of grace unless itself moved by grace.[185] In effect, actual grace is conceived as a medium between the states of nature and supernature; it is impossible to proceed directly from one to the other, and *gratia gratis data* provides the intermediate position by which the transition may be concluded.[186]

Richard of Middleton distinguished between a *proximate* and a *remote* disposition towards justification.[187] Humans may dispose themselves towards their own justification by virtue of their own powers; this disposition, however, is remote, and not an immediate disposition towards justification, which may be effected only through actual grace exciting and illuminating the human mind.[188] It is clear that Richard understands actual grace to refer primarily to a special supernatural motion

---

[180] See Mitzka, 'Die Lehre des hl. Bonaventura von der Vorbereitung auf die heiligmachenden Gnade'.

[181] *Breviloquium* v, ii, 2.

[182] *In IV Sent.* dist. xvii pars 1 a. 2 q. 2 ad 1.2. 3um. On this point, see Mitzka, 'Die Lehre des hl. Bonaventura von der Vorbereitung auf die heiligmachenden Gnade', 64.

[183] *Quaestiones disputatae de gratia* q. 3, ed. Douchet, 69–72. The argument is based on the maxim 'naturaliter est anima gratiae capax', which is characteristic of the early Dominican school.

[184] *Quaestiones disputatae de gratia* q. 4, ed. Douchet, 94–6.

[185] *Quaestiones disputatae de gratia* q. 4, ed. Douchet, 97.

[186] *Quaestiones disputatae de gratia* q. 4, ed. Douchet, 98–9: 'Gratia enim gratis data quasi medium tenet inter naturam vel voluntatem et gratiam gratum facientem.'

[187] *In II Sent.* dist. xxix a. 1 q. 1. See further Heynck, 'Die aktuelle Gnade bei Richard von Mediavilla'.

[188] *In II Sent.* dist. xxviii a. 1 q. 2.

directly attributable to the Holy Spirit.[189] Unlike habitual grace, no disposition is required for actual grace. Thus Roger of Marston emphasised that the gift of actual grace is the first gift by which God prepares the human will for grace, and does not itself require any preparation for justification.[190]

In general, the strongly Augustinian illuminationism of the early Franciscan school led to a theology of justification in which the necessity of a disposition or preparation towards justification was maintained on the grounds of the frailty of the unaided human intellect. Just as the human intellect was incapable of attaining and comprehending divine truth unless illuminated directly by God,[191] so the human will was incapable of desiring or attaining justification unless similarly illuminated (see 2.10.2).

The early Dominican school also taught the need for a disposition for justification, but for quite different reasons. The axiom *naturaliter est anima gratiae capax* is particularly associated with the early Dominican school, and on the basis of this anthropology there would appear to be no prima facie case for the necessity of a disposition towards the reception of grace. If the human soul is naturally capable of receiving grace, there would seem to be no compelling reason to posit such a necessity. The early Franciscan school had proposed the necessity of such a disposition on the grounds that a transformation of the natural state of the human soul was required in order for it to be *capax gratiae*. It is therefore important to observe that the theologians of the school, particularly Thomas Aquinas, deduced the necessity of such a disposition *on the basis of the Aristotelian analysis of motion*.[192] Grace, being a form, exists as a disposition in the subject who receives it. Application of the Aristotelian theory of generation to this results in the deduction of a stage of preparation. Albertus Magnus did not develop this question at any length,[193] and it is with Thomas Aquinas that its full statement may be found.

In his *Commentary on the Sentences* (1254–7), Thomas considers the question *utrum homo possit se praeparare ad gratiam sine aliqua gratia*.[194] His answer involves distinguishing two understandings of grace, either as the arousal of the human will through divine providence, or as a habitual

---

[189] Hocedez, *Richard de Middleton*, 277.
[190] *Quaestiones disputatae de statu naturae lapsae* q. 2; ed. Quaracchi, 178.
[191] Martin Grabmann, *Die philosophische und theologische Erkenntnislehre des Kardinals Matthaeus ab Aquasparta*, Vienna: Mayer, 1906; E. Gilson, 'Roger Marston, un cas d'Augustinisme avicennisant', *Archives d'histoire doctrinale et littéraire du moyen âge* 8 (1952), 37–42.
[192] See McGrath, 'The Influence of Aristotelian Physics'.
[193] Doms, *Die Gnadenlehre des sel. Albertus Magnus*, 163–8.
[194] *In II Sent.* dist. xxviii q. 1 a. 4, ed. Mandonnet, 2.726–30.

gift in the soul.[195] In both cases, a preparation for grace is necessary, in that justification, being a *motus*, requires premotion on the basis of the Aristotelian theory of generation. 'Omne quod movetur ab alio movetur.' Grace, being a form, exists as a disposition in the subject who receives it. How can the human free will be prepared to receive the gift of habitual grace? Thomas points out that the preparation cannot take the form of a second habitual gift, as this would merely result in an infinite regression of habitual gifts; some gratuitous gift of God is required, moving the soul from within. While humans are converted to their ultimate end by the prime mover (God), they are converted to their proximate end (i.e., the state of justification itself) by the motion of some inferior mover.[196]

In the *Commentary on the Sentences*, Thomas had treated the premotion required for justification as being external and natural – the examples which he provides of such premotions include admonition by another person, or physical illness.[197] In the later *Quaestiones disputatae de veritate* (1256–9), however, Thomas acknowledges an internal means of premotion, *divinus instinctus secundum quod Deus in mentibus hominum operatur*,[198] although it appears that his most characteristic position remains that humans can naturally dispose themselves towards the reception of grace.

The *Summa contra Gentiles* (1258–64) is generally regarded as marking a turning point in Thomas' teaching on the nature of the preparation for justification. It appears that the pseudo-Aristotelian *Liber de bona fortuna* first came to Thomas' attention during this period,[199] as it is cited for the first time at III, 89, and frequently thereafter.[200] In this work, Thomas described the 'errors of the Pelagians' as lying in the assertion that the beginning of human justification is the work of humans, while its consummation is the work of God.[201] The crucial statement which marks Thomas' changed views on the question is the following: 'Matter does not move itself to its own perfection; therefore it must be moved by something else.' Therefore, humans cannot move themselves to receive grace, but is moved by God to receive it.[202]

The *Quodlibetum primum*, dating from the second Paris period, attributes the beginnings of human justification to an internal operation

---

[195] *In II Sent.* dist. xxviii q. 1 a. 4, ed. Mandonnet, 2.728. See further Stufler, 'Die entfernte Vorbereitung auf die Rechtfertigung nach dem hl. Thomas'.

[196] *Summa Theologiae* IaIIae q. 109 a. 6.   [197] *Summa Theologiae* IaIIae q. 109 a. 6.

[198] *De veritate* q. 24 a. 15, ed. Spiazzi, 1.467.

[199] For details of this work, which is actually an extract from the *Eudemian Ethics*, see A. Pelzer, 'Les Versions des ouvrages de morale conservés sous le nom d'Aristôte en usage au XIIIe siècle', *Revue néo-scholastique de philosophie* 23 (1921), 37–9; T. Deman, 'Le "Liber de bona fortuna" dans la théologie de S. Thomas d'Aquin', *RSPhTh* 17 (1928), 41–50.

[200] See Bouillard, *Conversion et grâce*, 114–21.

[201] *Summa contra Gentiles* III, 149, 8.   [202] *Summa contra Gentiles* III, 149. 1.

of God, by which God acts on the will internally to cause it to do good.[203] The essential difference between Thomas' early and mature opinions on the question, as determined from the *Commentary on the Sentences* and the *Summa Theologiae* respectively, is that while in both he asserted the need for premotion for the *motus mentis* of justification, the early opinion that the 'inferior mover' causing the premotion was humanity was rejected in favour of the later opinion that the 'inferior mover' was God. Human preparation for justification is thus understood to be a divine work, so that no preparation is required for the justification of humans which God does not provide.[204] The preparation for grace in humans is the work of God as the prime mover and of the free will as the passive entity which is itself moved.[205] Thomas' discussion of the justification of humanity therefore proceeds along thoroughly Aristotelian lines, presupposing that there are two unequal stages in the process: the *praemotio* (i.e., the preparation for justification as the proximate end), and the *motus* itself (i.e., the movement from the natural to the supernatural plane, with the infusion of supernatural justice). It may be noted that Thomas understands the priority of the premotion over the motion to be *by nature* and not *in time*; the two may coincide temporally, as in the case of the conversion of Paul.[206]

The later medieval period saw the need for a human disposition towards justification accepted as axiomatic. The disputed aspects of the matter related primarily to the question of whether this disposition was itself a work of grace, or a purely human act performed without the aid of grace. Thus Luther's mentor Johannes von Staupitz affirmed the necessity of a proper disposition for justification, even though he stressed the moral impotence of fallen humans and taught gratuitous election *ante praevisa menta*.[207] This brings us to the question of the *nature* of the disposition towards justification, which was practically invariably discussed in terms of the axiom *facienti quod in se est Deus denegat gratiam*. It is to this axiom that we now turn.

2.3.3 The axiom facienti quod in se est Deus non denegat gratiam

This axiom is probably best translated as 'God will not deny grace to those who do their best.'[208] The essential principle encapsulated in the axiom

---

[203] *Quodlibetum primum* q. 1 a. 7. A similar opinion may be found in the Romans *Reportatio* cap. 10 lect. 3.

[204] *Summa Theologiae* IaIIae q. 112 a. 2 ad 3um: 'nulla praeparatio exigitur quam ipse [Deus] non faciat'.

[205] IaIIae q. 112 a. 3.

[206] Iallae q. 112 a. 2 ad 2um. See J. Stufler, 'Zur Kontroverse über die *praemotio physica*', *ZKTh* 47 (1927), 533–64.

[207] See Steinmetz, *Misericordia Dei*, 93–5.

[208] Literally, 'God does not deny grace to the person who does what is in him.'

is that humans and God have their respective roles to play in justification; when humans have fulfilled theirs in penitence, God will subsequently fulfil his part. The theological principle underlying the axiom may be shown to have been current in the early patristic period – for example, it is clearly stated by Irenaeus: 'If you offer to [God] what is yours, that is faith in God and subjection, you shall receive grace, and become a perfect work of God.'[209] The medieval period saw this axiom become a dogma, part of the received tradition concerning justification. The final verbal form of the axiom can be shown to have been fixed in the twelfth century,[210] an excellent example being provided by the *Homilies* of Radulphus Ardens:

It is as if the Lord had said: 'Do what is appropriate for you, and I will do what is appropriate for me. I will make you my friend, and act for you; you, as my friends, will love me and keep my commandments.[211]

Yet does a person's action place God under an *obligation* to act in this way? Does a person's doing *quod in se est* mean that God is now coerced to bestow grace upon him or her? If so, this action could be deemed to be meritorious, at least in some sense of the term. The idea that humans could, by doing 'what lies within them' (*quod in se est*) place *God* under an obligation to reward them with grace is particularly well illustrated from the works of Stephen Langton[212] and others influenced by him in the twelfth century. The use of *debere* by an anonymous twelfth-century writer in this connection is of significance, as it specifically uses the language of *obligation* in relation to God: *si homo facit, quod suum est, Deus debet facere, quod suum est.*[213] A slightly different approach to the matter is based on James 4:8: 'Draw near to God, and he will draw near to you.' This was interpreted by some twelfth-century theologians, such as Robert Pullen, to mean that humans, by drawing near to God, placed God under an obligation to draw near to humans.[214]

The relationship between the human penitential preparation for justification and the divine justification of humanity which followed it was

---

[209] Irenaeus, *Adversus haereses* IV, xxxix, 2. Cf. Origen, *Contra Celsum* VII, 42. See J. Rivière, 'Quelques antécédents patristiques de la formule "facienti quod in se est"', *RSR* 7 (1927), 93–7.

[210] For an excellent discussion of the axiom in this period, see Landgraf, *Dogmengeschichte der Frühscholastik*, 3.249–64.

[211] *Homiliae de sanctis* 2, PL 155.1496B.

[212] For example, see his Romans commentary, cited in Landgraf, *Dogmengeschichte der Frühscholastik*, 3.251 nn. 14, 15. Cf. n. 16: 'Facite, quod vestrum est, quia Deus faciet, quod suum est.' On his concept of merit, which is closely related, see Hamm, *Promissio, pactum, ordinatio*, 109–18.

[213] Cod. Erlangen lat. 353 fol. 84; cited in Landgraf, *Dogmengeschichte der Frühscholastik*, 3.252.

[214] *Sententiarum libri octo* VI, 49, PL 186.893B. See Courtney, *Cardinal Robert Pullen*, 226–33.

the subject of considerable discussion among twelfth-century theologians. In general, the possibility of the preparation for grace being the efficient cause of justification was rejected; most theologians appear to have adopted a solution similar to that of Alan of Lille. According to Alan, the preparation of humanity for justification could be likened to opening a shutter to let sunlight into a room. The act of penitence was the *causa sine qua non* and the *occasio*, but not the *causa efficiens*, of justification:

> Penitence is indeed a necessary cause [of grace], in that unless someone is penitent, God will not forgive that person's sins. It is like the sun, which illuminates a house when a shutter (*fenestra*) is opened. The opening of that shutter is not the efficient cause of that illumination, in that the sun itself is the efficient cause of that illumination. However, it is nevertheless its occasion.[215]

In effect, the preparation of humanity for justification may be regarded as the removal of an obstacle to grace (*removens prohibens*). This analysis was placed upon a firmer basis by Hugh of St Cher, who distinguished three aspects of the remission of sin: *actus peccandi desertio, maculae sive culpae deletio, reatus solutio*. The act of sinning is an obstacle to grace, and humans, by ceasing to perform acts of sin, remove this obstacle and thus prepare the way for grace to be infused into their souls.[216] Although only God is able to forgive sin, humans are able to set in motion a series of events that culminate in forgiveness of sins by the act of ceasing to perform acts of sin, which lies within their own powers. Humans do what is asked of them, and God subsequently does the rest.

The origins of the interpretation of the axiom characteristic of the early Franciscan school can be found with John of La Rochelle. Humans cannot dispose themselves adequately for grace, so the required disposition must be effected by God. God will, however, effect this disposition, if humans do *quod in se est*. John uses Alan of Lille's analogy of the opening of a shutter to illustrate this point: the opening of the shutter permits the light of the sun to dispel darkness, just as the act of doing *quod in se est* permits the grace of God to dispel sin. Although humans do not have the power to dispel darkness, they do have the power to initiate a course of action which has this effect, by opening a shutter and thus removing the obstacle to the sun's rays; similarly, although humans do not have the ability to

---

[215] *Contra Hereticos* 1, 51, PL 210.356B. Cf. 356A: 'Nec poenitentia est causa efficiens remissionis peccati, sed tantum gratuita Dei voluntas.' See also *Theologicae regulae* 87, PL 210.666A–C.

[216] Cod. Vat. lat. 1098 Col. 155v; cited in Landgraf, *Dogmengeschichte der Frühscholastik*, 3.260.

destroy sin, they can remove the obstacles to divine grace, which then effects the required destruction of sin.[217] God continually bestows grace through his generosity, and, by doing *quod in se est*, humans remove any obstacles in the path of that grace.[218]

Odo Rigaldi similarly teaches that grace is given to those who dispose themselves to receive it by doing *quod in se est* – for example, by attrition. The subsequent gift of grace transforms this to contrition, which leads to the remission of sins.[219] While this disposition towards grace cannot be considered to be meritorious in the strict sense of the term (i.e., *de condigno*), it can be considered meritorious *de congruo*.[220] The *Summa Fratris Alexandri* considers the case of good pagans, who are ignorant of the Christian faith, and argues that if they do *quod in se est* – which is clearly understood as a purely natural act – God will somehow enlighten them, in order that they may be justified.[221] Humans prepare themselves for justification by receiving the *dignitas congruitatis* which arises from the proper use of their natural faculties of reason or free will.[222] Similarly, Bonaventure argues that, although *gratia gratis data* stirs the will, it remains within the power of the human free will to respond to or reject this excitation. Bonaventure frequently stresses that God does not justify humans without their consent,[223] giving grace in such a way that the free will is not coerced into accepting it.[224]

The interpretation of the axiom within the early Dominican school is somewhat confused, as Thomas Aquinas presents radically different interpretations of the axiom in the *Commentary on the Sentences* and the *Summa Theologiae*. In the *Commentary*, Thomas concludes his discussion of the question *utrum homo possit se praeparare ad gratiam sine aliqua gratia* with what seems to be a prima facie Pelagian interpretation of the axiom: humans can prepare themselves for justification by virtue of their own natural abilities, unaided by grace.[225] This disposition is meritorious *de congruo*;[226] Thomas emphasised that God is continuously offering his grace to humans, and anyone who does *quod in se est* necessarily receives

---

[217] *Quaestiones de gratia* q. 6, ed. Hödl, 55–6. See also *Tractatus de gratia* q. 3 membr. 2 a. 2 sol., ed. Hödl, 61.

[218] *Tractatus de gratia* q. 3 membr. 2 a. 2 sol., ed. Hödl, 60: 'Concedo igitur quod si homo faciat quod in se est, Deus necessario, id est immutabiliter dat ei gratiam.'

[219] *In II Sent.* dist. xxvi membr. 1 q. 2 a. 3, ed. Bouvy, 331.48 – 332.68.

[220] *In II Sent.* dist. xxviii membr. 1 q. 4 a. 2 ad 3um, ed. Bouvy, 86.49–52.

[221] *Summa Halensis* inq. 4 tr. 3 q. 3 tit. 1, ed. Quaracchi, 2.730–1.

[222] *Summa Halensis* inq. 4 tr. 3 q. 3 tit. 1, ed. Quaracchi, 2.731.

[223] *In IV Sent.* dist. xiv pars 1 a. 2 q. 2; dist. xvii pars 1 a. 1 q. 2.

[224] For example, *Breviloquium* v, iii, 4: 'Rursus, quoniam Deus sic reformat, quod leges naturae inditas non infirmat; ideo sic hanc gratiam tribuit libero arbitrio, ut ramen ipsum non cogar, sed eius consensus liber maneat.'

[225] *In II Sent.* dist. xxviii q. 1 a. 4.   [226] *In II Sent.* dist. xxviii q. 1 a. 4 ad 4um.

it.[227] In effect, this represents a further development of Alan of Lille's analogy of the opening of a shutter. Philip the Chancellor had earlier applied the Aristotelian categories of material and formal causality to the sun and the opening of the shutter respectively, so that the formal (i.e., the immediate) cause of justification is the human preparation for justification, understood as the removal of obstacles to grace. Thomas is thus able to formalise his causal scheme in Aristotelian terms, further enhancing the Aristotelian cast of his discussion of the doctrine of justification.

Critics of Thomas' early teaching on justification, particularly within the early Franciscan school, pointed out that he allowed a purely natural disposition towards justification, which was clearly contrary to the teaching of Augustine.[228] It is therefore important to appreciate that his mature teaching, as expressed in the *Summa Theologiae* (1266–73), is significantly different. Later commentators frequently emphasised these differences; for example, several fifteenth-century manuscripts refer to 'conclusions in which St Thomas seems to contradict himself,' or 'articles in which Thomas says one thing in the *Summa*, and something different in his writings on the *Sentences*', or – more diplomatically! – 'articles in which Thomas expresses himself better in the *Summa* than in his writings on the *Sentences*'.[229]

While Thomas continues to insist upon the necessity of a preparation for justification, and continues to discuss this in terms of people doing *quod in se est*, he now considers that this preparation lies outside purely natural human powers. Humans are not even capable of their full *natural* good, let alone the *supernatural* good required of them for justification. The preparation for justification is therefore itself to be seen as a work of grace,[230] in which God is active and humans passive. For Thomas, the axiom *facienti quod in se est* now assumes the meaning that God will not deny grace to those who do their best, in so far as they are moved by God to do this.[231] It is highly significant that Thomas does not follow the early Franciscan school in applying the axiom to the good pagan in the *Summa*, even where it would be expected at IIa–IIae q. 10 a. 1.[232] Thomas now

---

[227] *In IV Sent.* dist. xvii q. 1 aa. 3–4.
[228] Thus Roger of Marston, *Quaestiones disputatae de statu naturae lapsae* q. 1 ad 11um; ed. Quaracchi, 195.
[229] Cod. Paris Nat. lat. 14551 fol. 103r; Cod. Paris Nat. lat. 15690 fol. 228v; Klosterneuburg Cod. 322; cited in Grabmann, *Mittelalterliches Geistesleben*, 2.453–5.
[230] *Summa Theologiae* IaIIae q. 112 a. 3: 'Praeparatio ad hominis gratiam est a Deo sicut a movente, a libero autem arbitrio sicut a moto.'
[231] IaIIae q. 109 a. 6 ad 2um: 'Cum dicitur homo facere quod in se est, dicitur hoc esse in potestate hominis secundum quod est motus a Deo.'
[232] Dhont, *Le Problème de la préparation à la grâce*, 267–8. See also L. Capéran, *Le Problème du salut des infidèles*, 2 vols., Paris, Beauchesne, 1934, 2.49–57.

understands *quod in se est* to mean 'doing what one is able to do when aroused and moved by grace', thus marking a significant departure from his earlier interpretation of the concept. A similar interpretation of *quod in se est* is encountered in the writings of Peter of Tarantaise.[233]

A further development may be noted in relation to Thomas' teaching on the meritorious character of the disposition towards justification. In the *Commentary*, Thomas allows that such a disposition is meritorious *de congruo*.[234] In the later *De veritate*, however, we find an unequivocal assertion that there are no merits save *de*merits prior to justification,[235] a view which finds fuller expression in the *Summa Theologiae*. Although Thomas is prepared to allow that a justified sinner can merit *de congruo* the first grace for another person,[236] he is not prepared to allow the individual's preparation for his or her own justification to be deemed meritorious, even in this weak sense of the term.[237] Significantly, Peter of Tarantaise – who reproduces Thomas' interpretation of *quod in se est* – declines to follow him in this matter, teaching that the preparation for justification is meritorious *de congruo*.[238] It is thus clear that there was some confusion within the early Dominican school upon this matter.

An examination of the writings of later medieval theologians of the Augustinian order also reveals a significant lack of agreement concerning the interpretation of the axiom. Thomas of Strasbourg states that those who do *quod in se est* cannot be regarded as preparing themselves for justification; the role of individuals in their own justification lies in their consenting to the divine action which is taking place within them.[239] In this he is followed, as in so many other matters, by Johannes von Retz.[240] Thomas is, however, prepared to allow that this disposition towards justification is meritorious *de congruo*.[241] Retz' rejection of the possibility of a purely *natural* disposition for grace is of interest, as it proceeds upon Aristotelian presuppositions. Justification involves a transition from form to matter. Just as a natural form is converted to natural matter by a natural agent, so the conversion of a supernatural form to supernatural matter

[233] *In II Sent.* dist. xxvii q. 2 a. 4 ad 3um. Peter allows that people may dispose themselves remotely, but not proximately, to justification through their unaided powers: *In II* Sent. dist. xxviii q. 1 aa. 2, 3.

[234] *In II Sent.* dist. xxviii q. 1 a. 4, ed. Bouvy, 2.728–9.

[235] *De veritate* q. 29 a. 6, ed. Spiazzi, 1.564.   [236] *Summa Theologiae* IaIIae q. 114 a. 6.

[237] IaIIae q. 114 a. 5. Cf. IaIIae q. 112 aa. 2, 3; q. 114 aa. 3, 5.

[238] *In II Sent.* dist. xxvii q. 2 a. 2. 'Meritum impetrativum' is here to be regarded as synonymous with 'meritum de congruo'.

[239] *In II Sent.* dist. xxviii, xxix q. 1 a. 4.

[240] *Textbeilage* 119; cited in Zumkeller, 'Der Wiener Theologieprofessor Johannes von Retz'.

[241] *In II Sent.* dist. xxvi, xxvii q. 1 a. 3, conc. 2.

requires the action of a supernatural agent moving the soul – namely, divine grace.[242]

While the theologians of the Augustinian order continued the common teaching of the necessity of a disposition towards justification, older Augustinian theologians were prepared to allow that this disposition was meritorious *de congruo*, whereas theologians of the *schola Augustiniana moderna* tended to exclude this possibility. Thus Thomas Bradwardine, Gregory of Rimini, Johannes Klenkok, Angelus Dobelin, Hugolino of Orvieto and Johannes Hiltalingen of Basel rejected the opinion that the disposition for justification was meritorious *de congruo*.[243] A similar position is associated with Luther's mentor at Wittenberg, Johannes von Staupitz,[244] although his regent of studies at Erfurt, Johannes de Paltz, allowed that such a disposition was meritorious *de congruo*.[245]

The theologians of the *via moderna* adopted a much more positive attitude to the axiom *facienti quod in se est*. Underlying this attitude is the theology of the *pactum*, by which a distinction is to be made between the inherent value of a moral act and its ascribed value under the terms of the covenant between God and humanity. Just as, in today's economic system, the ascribed value of paper money has a value much greater than its inherent value on account of the covenant on the part of the issuing agency or bank to pay the bearer the equivalent sum in gold upon request, so in the Middle Ages the king appears to have been regarded as entitled to issue 'token' coinage, often made of lead, which had a negligible inherent value, but which would be redeemed at its full ascribed value at a later date.[246] In the meantime, the ascribed value of the coins was vastly greater than their inherent value, on account of the promise of the king expressed in the covenant regulating the relationship between the *valor impositus* and *valor intrinsecus*.

---

[242] *Textbeilage* 117. Here, as above, Retz is heavily dependent upon Thomas of Strasbourg – compare this with Thomas' *In II Sent.* dist. xxviii, xxix q. 1.

[243] Oberman, *Archbishop Thomas Bradwardine*, 155–9; Gregory of Rimini, *In II Sent.* dist. xxvi q. 1 aa. 1, 2; Zumkeller, 'Johannes Klenkok', 240–52; idem, 'Die Lehre des Erfurter Augustinertheologen', 32–6, 44–8, 46–8, 184–6. On the role of the *auxilium speciale Dei* in Gregory's theology of justification, see Burger, 'Das auxilium speciale Dei in der Gnadenlehre Gregors von Rimini'.

[244] Steinmetz, *Misericordia Dei*, 94–7, 114–22.

[245] Zumkeller, 'Erfurter Augustinertheologen', 54–5. For a fuller study of his theology, see M. Ferdigg, 'De vita et operibus et doctrina Ioannis de Palz', *AnAug* 30 (1967), 210–321; 31 (1968), 155–318. See also Steinmetz, *Misericordia Dei*, 94–7, 114–22.

[246] On this, see Courtenay, 'Covenant and Causality in Pierre d'Ailly'; idem, 'The King and the Leaden Coin'; Oberman, *Werden und Wertung der Reformation*, 161–200. On token coins, see W. J. Courtenay, 'Token Coinage and the Administration of Poor Relief during the Late Middle Ages', *Journal of Interdisciplinary History* 3 (1972–3), 275–95; T. J. Sargent and F. R. Velde, 'The Big Problem of Small Change', *Journal of Money, Credit and Banking*, 31 (1999), 137–61.

Such analogies from the economic system of the period lent themselves particularly well to illustrate the important distinction, characteristic of the *via moderna*, between the moral and the meritorious value of an act. Just as a major discrepancy could arise within an economic system between *bonitas intrinseca* and *valor impositus*, given a firm and binding contract on the part of the king, so a similar discrepancy could arise between the moral value of an act (i.e., its *bonitas intrinseca*) and its meritorious value (i.e., *valor impositus*), given a comparable covenant on the part of God. Although human acts have negligible inherent value in themselves by God's absolute standards, God has nevertheless entered into a *pactum* with humanity, by virtue of which such human acts have a much greater contracted value – sufficient to merit the first grace *de congruo*. Just as a king might issue a small leaden coin with negligible inherent value and a considerably greater ascribed value which permitted it to purchase goods, so human moral acts, although in themselves incapable of meriting grace, have a much greater contracted value adequate for this purpose.

The essential point emerging from this analysis of the context in which the characteristic interpretation of the axiom *facienti quod in se est* associated with the *via moderna* is set is this: the disposition of individuals cannot be said to cause their justification on account of its own nature (*ex natura rei*), but only on account of the value ascribed to it by God (*ex pacta divino*). This point is made by Ockham, again using the illustration of the king and the small lead coin.[247] A similar analogy is employed by Robert Holcot, who pointed out that a small copper coin may buy a loaf of bread, despite the much greater inherent value of the latter.[248] Failure on the part of God to honour this contractual obligation by rewarding the person who did *quod in se est* with grace would amount to a contradiction of the divine nature. While God is not bound by absolute necessity (i.e., *necessitas consequentis*) to act in this way, God has set up a situation by which there exists a conditional necessity (i.e., *necessitas consequentiae*) which God is bound to respect.

Gabriel Biel interprets the axiom *facienti quod in se est* to mean that God is under obligation to give the first grace to the person who desists from sin. However, this does not mean that humans are capable of remitting their own sin. As Biel emphasises, the link between doing *quod in se est* and the remission of sin is provided by the covenant, rather than by the nature of the entities in themselves. Alan of Lille and the early Franciscan school

---

[247] *In IV Sent.* dist. xvii q. 1c 'Sicut si rex ordinaret quod quicumque acciperet denarium plumbeum haberet certum donum, et tunc denarius plumbeus esset causa sine qua non respectu illius doni.'
[248] *Super libros Sapientiae* III, 35.

illustrated the axiom with reference to a shutter and the rays of the sun, as noted above; implicit in this analogy is an *ontological* concept of causality. The nature of the entities (i.e., the shutter and the sun's rays) is such that the removal of the obstacle permits the sunlight to enter the room. Biel and the *via moderna* operated with a concept of *covenantal* causality, by which the relationship between human action and the divine response is a consequence of the divine ordination, rather than of the nature of the entities in themselves. By the *pactum*, God has graciously ordained that such an act may be accepted as worthy of grace.[249] Biel reproduces the earlier Franciscan teaching, by which the human disposition towards justification may be regarded as removing an obstacle in the path of divine grace:

The soul, by removing an obstacle towards a good movement to God through the free will, is able to merit the first grace *de congruo*. This may be proved as follows: because God accepts the act of doing 'what lies within its powers' (*actum facientis quod in se est*) as leading to the first grace, not on account of any debt of justice, but on account of God's generosity. The soul, by removing this obstacle, ceases from acts of sin and consent to sin, and thus elicits a good movement towards God as its principle and end; and does 'what lies within its powers' (*quod in se est*). Therefore God accepts, out of his generosity (*ex sua liberalitate*), this act of removing an obstacle and a good movement towards God as the basis of the infusion of grace.[250]

Following the general teaching of the Franciscan schools, Biel holds this disposition towards justification as meritorious *de congruo*. Although humans are able to remove an obstacle to grace, Biel insists that it is God, and God alone, who remits sin – but by virtue of the *pactum*, humans are able to act in such a manner as to oblige God to respond in this way.[251]

The pastoral significance of the axiom may be illustrated with reference to the sermons of Johannes Geiler of Keisersberg, cathedral preacher at Strasbourg from 1478 to 1510. In his exposition of the Lord's Prayer, Geiler stresses that if people's prayers are to be heard, they must do *quod in se est*. Each of the seven petitions of the Lord's Prayer presupposes that humans are already doing what lies within their powers. Thus people pray to God that they might be given their daily bread, but this presupposes that they do *quod in se est* by cultivating the fields.[252] The same principle is elaborated with reference to Matthew 6:26, which refers to the birds of the air being fed by their heavenly Father. Geiler observes that this does not mean that the birds sit on their branches all day, doing nothing;

---

[249] *In II Sent.* dist. xxvii q. unica a. 3 dub. 4.
[250] *In II Sent.* dist. xxvii q. unica a. 2 conc. 4, ed. Werbeck/Hoffmann, 2.517.1–8.
[251] *In II Sent.* dist. xxvii q. unica a. 3 dub. 4.
[252] *Oratio Domini* 9B; cited in Douglass, *Justification in Late Medieval Preaching*, 144 n. 2.

they too must do *quod in se est*, going out early in the morning looking for food.[253]

It is therefore only to be expected that Geiler should apply the same principle to human justification, for which he considers preparation to be essential: 'Fools expect to have this gold without paying for it – that is, without a disposition for grace.'[254] Just as the wind does not enter into a sail until the sailsman first turns the sail directly into the wind, so the wind of the Holy Spirit enters only that soul which has been prepared to receive it. Humans must therefore dispose themselves towards the reception of grace by doing *quod in se est*.[255] The pastoral orientation of Geiler's sermons is evident from the fact that the axiom is usually expressed in the imperative form: *fac quod in te est*!

The use of the axiom remained a commonplace in the early sixteenth century, and is encountered in the earlier writings of Martin Luther.[256] Luther's continuity with the *via moderna* is particularly evident in the *Dictata super Psalterium* (1513–15), and may be illustrated from his comments on Psalm 114:1 (Vulgate, 113:1):

> The doctors rightly say that, when people do their best, God infallibly gives them grace. This cannot be understood as meaning that this preparation for grace is *de condigno* [meritorious], as they are incomparable, but it can be regarded as *de congruo* on account of this promise of God and the covenant (*pactum*) of mercy.[257]

In this, as in so many other respects, the young Luther demonstrated his close affinity with the theology of justification associated with the *via moderna.*

The discussion of the subjective appropriation of justification presented in the above section may have conveyed the impression that the theologians of the medieval period understood justification in purely individualist terms, teaching that justification is solely concerned with the individual *viator* and his or her status *coram Deo*. This is, in fact, not the case. The medieval discussion of justification proceeds upon the basis of certain explicit presuppositions concerning the community within which this justification takes place. Justification takes place within the sphere of

---

[253] *Navicula sive speculum fatuorum* 22s; cited in Douglass, *Justification in Late Medieval Preaching*, 145 n. 1.

[254] *Navicula penitentie* 28v I, cited in Douglass, *Justification in Late Medieval Preaching*, 139 n. 3.

[255] *Navicula penitentie* 18r I; cited in Douglass, *Justification in Late Medieval Preaching*, 143 n. 1.

[256] See McGrath, *Luther's Theology of the Cross*, 72–92.

[257] WA 4.262.4–7. Cf. WA 3.288.37 – 289.4. See further Grane, *Contra Gabrielem*, 296–301; R. Schwarz, *Vorgeschichte der reformatorischen Bußtheologie*, Berlin: de Gruyter, 1968, 249–59.

the church, being particularly associated with the sacraments of baptism and penance, so that it is impossible to discuss the medieval understanding of the subjective appropriation of justification without reference to the relationship between justification and the sacraments. The present section, therefore, may be regarded as having dealt with the individualist aspects of the appropriation of justification; the following section, which considers the relation between justification and the sacraments, may be considered to deal with the communal aspects of the appropriation of justification.

2.4   Justification and the sacraments

The systematic development of sacramental theology is a major feature of the medieval period, particularly between the years 1050 and 1240.[258] Associated with this development is the specific linking of justification with the *sacramenta mortuorum*, baptism and penance, and hence with the sacramental system of the church. Earlier medieval writers, such as Cassiodorus and Sedulius Scotus, had identified baptism as the justifying sacrament.[259] The ninth century, however, saw the Anglo-Irish system of private penance become widespread in Europe, with important modifications to the theology of penance following in its wake. Although earlier writers considered that penance could be undertaken only once in a lifetime, as a 'second plank after a shipwreck' (*tabula secunda post naufragiam*),[260] this opinion was gradually abandoned, rather than refuted, as much for social as for pastoral reasons. Thus the eighth-century bishop Chrodegang of Metz recommended regular confession to a superior at least once a year,[261] while Paulinus of Aquileia advocated confession and penance before each mass. Gregory the Great's classification of mortal sins became incorporated into the penitential system of the church during the ninth century, so that private penance in the presence of a priest became generally accepted.[262] Penitential books began to make

---

[258] J. de Ghellinck, 'Un Chapitre dans l'histoire de la définition des sacrements au XIIe siècle', in *Melanges Mandonnet*, Paris: Vrin, 1930, 2.79–96; N. M. Haring, 'Berengar's Definitions of *Sacramentum* and Their Influence upon Medieval Sacramentology', *Medieval Studies* 10 (1948), 109–46; D. van den Eynde, 'Les Définitions des sacrements pendant la première période de la théologie scolastique (1050–1235)', *Antonianum* 24 (1949), 183–228, 439–88; 25 (1950), 3–78.
[259] Cassiodorus, *Expositio S. Pauli epistola ad Romanos*, PL 68.417B; Sedulius Scotus, *Collatio in omnes B. Pauli epistolas*, PL 103.42D.
[260] Jerome, *Epistola* 130, 9, CSEL 56.189.4–5.
[261] *Regula canonicorum* 14, PL 89.1104A–5B.
[262] For the best study of this development, see Sarah Hamilton, *The Practice of Penance, 900–1050*, London: Royal Historical Society, 2001. See also the older study of Oscar D. Watkins, *A History of Penance*, 2 vols., New York: Franklin, 1961.

their appearance throughout Europe, similar in many respects to those which can be traced back to sixth-century Wales.

The spread of the practice in the Carolingian church appears to have been due to the formidable influence of Alcuin, who has greater claim than any to be considered the founder of the Carolingian renaissance.[263] It is therefore of considerable significance that Alcuin specifically links penance with justification.[264] Associated with this correlation between justification and penance is a maxim, representing a conflation of Ezekiel 18:21 and 33:12, which emphasised the importance of turning away from sin as a precondition for spiritual renewal, and implied a link with whatever ecclesiastical rites were linked with this process.[265] The essential feature of this development is that justification is understood to *begin* in baptism, and *to be continued* in penance.

A further development of this idea may be found in the works of Rabanus Maurus, who became the leading proponent of private confession in the Frankish church after Alcuin; justification is here linked, not merely with the act of penance, but specifically with sacerdotal confession.[266] The relationship between justification, baptism and penance was defined with particular clarity in the ninth century by Haimo of Auxerre:

> Our redemption, by which we are redeemed, and through which we are justified, is the passion of Christ, which, joined with baptism, justifies humanity through faith, and subsequently through penance. These two are joined together in such a way that it is not possible for humanity to be justified by one without the other.[267]

---

[263] For an excellent study of this development, see John Marenbon, *From the Circle of Alcuin to the School of Auxerre: Logic, Theology and Philosophy in the Early Middle Ages*, Cambridge: Cambridge University Press, 1981.

[264] *Liber de divinis officiis*, 55, PL 101.1284B: 'non dubitamus circa fidem iustificari hominem per poenitentiam et conpunctionem'. See also *De virtutibus et vitiis* 12, PL 101.622A; *De confessione peccatorum*, PL 101.652B: 'Dic tu prior iniustitias tuas, ut iustificeris.'

[265] 'In quacumque hora conversus fuerit peccator, vita vivet et non morietur.' It occurs, in various forms, throughout this period: see Alcuin, *De virtutibus et vitiis* 13, PL 101.623A; Eadmer, *Liber de S. Anselmi similitudinibus* 175, PL 159.695A; Ivo of Chartres, *Decretum* XV, 26, PL 161.862D; Bruno of Asti, *Comm. in Ioannem* II, 11, PL 165.545A; Honorius of Autun, *Speculum ecclesiae*, PL 172.881C; *Summa sententiarum* V, 7, PL 176.133A; Hugh of St Victor, *De sacramentis* II, xiv, 8, PL 176.567A; Werner of St Blasien, *Deflorationes* 2, PL 157.1184A; Zacharias Chrysopolitanus, *In unum ex quattuor* III, 99–100, PL 186.315D; Richard of St Victor, *De potestate ligandi* 19, PL 196.1171C; Ermengaudus, *Contra Waldenses* 13, PL 204.1261A; Alan of Lille, *Contra hereticos* I, I55, PL 210.358B; Peter Lombard, *IV Sent.* dist. XX 1, 5.

[266] In fact, Rabanus quotes Alcuin at some length, without acknowledgement: compare Alcuin, PL 101.6210–22B, with Rabanus, PL 101.1020–3A; and Alcuin, PL 101.622B–3A, with Rabanus, PL 101.103A–4A.

[267] *Expositio in epistolas S. Pauli*, PL 117.391C.

The possibility of constructing a totally sacramental economy of salvation was demonstrated by Bruno of Cologne in the late eleventh century. Like most of his contemporaries, Bruno defined grace in non-ontological terms, understanding it as the remission of sin, linking it specifically with baptism and penance; all sins are remitted in baptism, but sins committed subsequently may be purged through the merit of penance.[268] The emerging understanding of the *processus iustificationis* further assisted the integration of justification within the sacramental system of the church. Of particular significance in this respect is the occasional inclusion of a fifth element in the traditional fourfold *processus iustificationis* to allow the direct correlation of justification with the temporal remission of sin. Thus Hugh of St Cher suggests that the fifth and final element in the process is the human performance of an appropriate penitential act.[269]

The relationship between justification and the sacraments of baptism and penance was to preoccupy most, if not all, of the theologians of the twelfth century, with a particular concern being expressed over how this sacramental economy of salvation could take account of infant baptism. How can infants or imbeciles, who are incapable of any rational act, be justified by baptism?[270] No general solution to the problem may be said to have emerged during the period, at least in part due to the fact that there was a general failure to distinguish between habit, act and virtue. Anselm of Canterbury taught that infants are treated *quasi iusti* on account of the faith of the church.[271] In this, he was followed by Bernard of Clairvaux, who noted that, as it was impossible to please God without faith, so God has permitted children to be justified on account of the faith of others.[272] This was given some theological justification by Peter Manducator, who argued that as children are contaminated by the sins of another (i.e., Adam) in the first place, it is not unreasonable that they should subsequently be justified by the faith of others.[273] Peter Abelard was sceptical as to whether an infant was capable of an act of faith; given that this possibility appeared to be excluded, he derived some consolation from the idea that infants who die before maturity are given a

---

[268] *Expositio in omnes epistolas Pauli*, PL 153.55B–C.
[269] Hugh of St Cher, cited in Landgraf, *Dogmengeschichte der Frühscholastik*, 1/1.298 n. 41, where the fifth element is *peccati remissio quoad penam temporalem.*
[270] For an excellent discussion, see Landgraf, *Dogmengeschichte der Frühscholastik*, 3/1.279–345.
[271] *De conceptu virginali* 29, ed. Schmitt, 2.173.1–3: 'Quare si sic moriuntur: quia non sunt iniusti, non damnantur, sed et iustitia Christi qui se dedit pro illis, et iustitia fidei matris ecclesiae quae pro illis credit quasi iusti salvantur.'
[272] *Tractatus de baptismo* II, 9, PL 182.1037D.
[273] Cod. Paris Nat. lat. 15269 fol. 151v; cited in Landgraf, *Dogmengeschichte der Frühscholastik*, 3/1.289 n. 22.

perception of the glory of God at their death, so that charity may be born within them.[274] Gilbert de la Porrée is typical of the many who declined to speculate on the mysterious operation of the Holy Spirit, which none could fathom.[275]

The origins of the generally accepted solution to this difficulty date from the closing years of the twelfth century, with the introduction of the Aristotelian concept of the *habitus*. Thus Alan of Lille, one of the more speculative theologians of the twelfth century, distinguished between *virtus in actu* and *virtus in habitu*.[276] An infant may be given the habit of faith in baptism as the *virtus fidei in habitu*, which will be manifested as the *virtus fidei in actu* only when the child reaches maturity and becomes capable of rational acts. The lack of agreement which characterised the twelfth century is well illustrated from the letter of Innocent III, dated 1201, in which he declined to give any definite positive statements on the effects of baptism, merely noting two possible opinions: (1) that baptism effects the remission of sins; (2) that baptism effects the infusion of virtues as habits, to be actualised when maturity is reached.[277]

Although baptism had been recognised as a sacrament from the earliest of times, the same recognition had not always been extended to penance. Hugh of St Victor had defined a sacrament as a 'physical or material object admitted to the perception of the external senses, representing a reality beyond itself by virtue of having been instituted as a sign of it, and containing within it some invisible and spiritual grace, in virtue of having been consecrated'.[278] It is clear that this definition of a sacrament, which insists upon the presence of a physical element, leads to the exclusion of penance from the list of sacraments. Peter Lombard's definition of a sacrament[279] is therefore as interesting for what it does *not* say as for what it does, as no reference is made to the need for a 'physical or material element from without'. It is this decisive omission which allowed the Lombard to include penance among the seven sacraments – an

---

[274] *Expositio in epistolam ad Romanos* II, 3, PL 178.838B.
[275] Leipzig Universitätsbibliothek Cod. lat. 427, cited in Landgraf, *Dogmengeschichte der Frühscholastik*, 1/2.50.
[276] *Theologiae regulae* 86, PL 210.667B: 'Habentur ergo virtutes in habitu, quando homo per illas potentias quamdam habet habilitatem, et pronitatem ad utendum eis, si tempus exigerit.'
[277] D 780–1.
[278] *De sacramentis* I, ix, 2, PL 176.317D: 'Sacramentum est corporale vel materiale elementum foris sensibiliter propositum ex similitudine repraesentans, et ex institutione significans, et ex sanctificatione continens aliquam invisibilem et spiritualem gratiam.' For further comment, see A. Landgraf, 'Die frühscholastischen Definitionen der Taufe', *Gregorianum* 27 (1946), 200–19, 353–83.
[279] *IV Sent.* dist. i 1–4.

inclusion which is of major significance to the development of the doctrine of justification within the sphere of the western church.

The necessity of sacerdotal confession for the remission of sins in penance was insisted upon by many of the earlier medieval theologians. Honorius of Autun, Hervaeus of Bourg-Dieu and Bruno of Asti all use the Pentateuchal leper-cleansing ritual to illustrate the need for sacerdotal confession; the sinner's faults are cleansed only when they are confessed before a priest.[280] Just as baptism effects the remission of *original* sin, so confession effects the remission of *actual* sin.[281] This distinction leads to the obvious conclusion that regular confession is to be encouraged, in order to receive absolution. Such exhortations to confession were generally accompanied with an appeal to texts such as Isaiah 45:22, Joel 2:12 or Zechariah 1:3.[282] It must be emphasised, however, that these exhortations to confession are set within the context of the reconciliation of a lapsed believer, a justified sinner who wishes to be restored to fellowship within the church, and are not capable of a Pelagian interpretation. They refer to the restoration of justification, rather than to its inception – that is, the second rather than the first justification, to use the terms of a later period. The use of such texts indicates a growing awareness of the association of the recovery of justification with the sacrament of penance, which involves the confession of sin, penance and absolution. It may be noted, however, that there was no general agreement upon the necessity of *sacerdotal* confession: in the twelfth century, for example, the Abelardian school rejected its necessity, while the Victorine school insisted upon it.[283]

The integration of justification within the context of the sacrament of penance was greatly assisted by two developments. First, the general acceptance of Peter Lombard's *Sentences* as the basis of theological discussion during the thirteenth century led to justification being discussed with reference to the *locus* of distinction 17 of the fourth book of the *Sentences* – that is, within the specific context of the sacrament of penance.

---

[280] *Speculum ecclesiae*, PL 172.1061c; *Homilia* 13, PL 158.622b–c; *Commentarius in Lucam*, PL 165.427c–d.

[281] Honorius of Autun, *Elucidarum* II, 20, PL 172.1050c–d.

[282] 'Convertimini ad me, ait Dominus exercituum, et convertar ad vos.' See, for example, Anselm of Canterbury, *De concordia praescientiae* III, 6.

[283] Anciaux, *La Théologie du sacrement du pénance*, 164–274. For the necessity of penance in justification, see Alger of Liège, *Liber de misericordia et iustitia*, PL 180.888d; Richard of St Victor, *Sermo* 53, PL 177.1051c; Bernard of Clairvaux, *Tractatus de interiori domo*, PL 184.509b; Peter of Blois, *Liber de confessione*, PL 207.1081d; Philip of Harvengt, *In Cantica Canticorum*, PL 203.552b; Peter Lombard, *IV Sent.* dist. xiv 1. In his *Decretum*, Gratian appears to leave open the question of the necessity of confession in justification, although he notes the strong case which can be made in its favour; for example, PL 187.1532a.

Second, the conceptual elaboration of the *processus iustificationis* had led to contrition and remission of sins being identified as its third and fourth elements respectively – both of which could be correlated with the sacrament of penance. The justification of the sinner was therefore explicitly linked with the sacramental system of the church. This connection may be regarded as having been unequivocally established through the decrees of the Fourth Lateran Council (1215), which laid an obligation upon believers to confess their sins to their priest annually.[284]

The early discussion of penance involved the distinction of three elements: *contritio cordis, confessio oris, satisfactio operis*.[285] It seems that the earlier medieval discussion of the matter led to the greatest emphasis being placed upon the third element, satisfaction – an observation which is of considerable importance in connection with Anselm of Canterbury's understanding of the incarnation of the Son of God. For Anselm, the satisfaction-merit model provided by the penitential system of the church of his time provided a suitable paradigm for the divine remission of sin through the death of Christ, which his readers would have accepted as just.

By the early twelfth century, however, the focus appears to have shifted from satisfaction to contrition, with increasing emphasis being placed upon the inner motivation of the penitent, rather than on his external achievements made as satisfaction for sin. While Peter Abelard defined *poenitentia* in generally psychological terms, his respect for tradition is such, however, that he does not deny the *de facto* necessity of both confession and satisfaction, subject to qualification on account of possible mitigating circumstances.[286] This contritionism was developed by Peter Lombard, who stressed that contrition was the sole precondition for forgiveness; the function of the priest in the sacrament of penance is purely declarative, in that he merely certifies that the penitent has been justified and reconciled to the church. The priest cannot be considered to play a causative role in this matter.[287]

The precise relationship between justification and penance was the subject of considerable debate during the twelfth century. Peter of Poitiers drew attention to a possible misinterpretation of the relationship between the two: as people can lose the first grace through sin, and subsequently have it restored through penance, it might appear that the first grace can be merited by penance. Peter rejected this interpretation on the basis of its failure to recognise that humans can only *regain* the first grace in

[284] Cap. 21, *D* 812.
[285] On this, see G. J. Spykman, *Attrition and Contrition at the Council of Trent*, Kampen: Kok, 1955, 17–89.
[286] *Ethica* 18, PL 178.61A; *Ethica* 24–6, PL 178.668C–74A.   [287] *I Sent.* dist. xviii 6.

this manner; it is only the person who has already received *gratia prima* who can be justified again by penance.[288] Simon of Tournai argued that while prayers and alms qualify humans for becoming good, they cannot be said to make them good in themselves – humans become only good through the grace of God. Penance, apart from grace, does not justify. Alan of Lille similarly emphasised the unmerited character of grace in his discussion of the relation between justification and penance; the true efficient cause of justification is not penance, as might be thought, but the gracious will of God. Penance is merely the *occasio* and *conditio sine qua non* of justification.[289]

However, it will be clear that the location of any type of cause of justification within the penitent is of significance, in that it naturally leads to the discussion of the nature of the act or disposition – required of the penitent if justification is to occur. It is for this reason that the establishment of the triple order of *contritio cardis, confessio oris* and *satisfactio operis* within the sacramental system of the church is of such importance, as it allows the necessary steps for the justification of penitents to be definitely established, in order that penitents may be assured that they *have* been justified. The psychological aspects of the sacrament of penance must not be overlooked.

The classic medieval representation of the three steps leading to penitential justification may be found in Dante Alighieri's *Purgatorio*. As the poet awakes from his dream, he finds that he has been carried up to the gate of purgatory, before which lie three steps which he must first climb. The three steps represent the three penitential elements, which Dante presents in the different order of confession, contrition and satisfaction. As the poet faces the first step of polished white marble, he sees himself reflected as he really is, and so is moved to recognise, admit and confess his sin. The second step is black, cracked in the shape of a cross, symbolising the contrite heart, while the third, redder than blood spurting from a vein, symbolises Christ's atoning death, to which must be added the satisfaction of the penitent if it is to be made complete.[290]

The most important criticism of the 'contritionist' understanding of penance, associated with Peter Lombard, is due to Duns Scotus. If contrition is required as a necessary disposition for the reception of sacramental grace, the role of the *sacrament* of penance is called into question. If justification through the sacrament of penance is contingent upon an antecedent disposition of contrition, the sacrament can no longer be said to be effective *ex opere operato*, but only *ex opere operantis*.[291] The

---

[288] *Sententiarum libri quinque* III, 2, PL 201.1047C.
[289] *Contra Hereticos* I, 51, PL 210.354A–B, 356A–C.   [290] *Purgatorio* IX, 94–102.
[291] *Opus Oxoniense* IV dist. i q. 6 nn. 10–11.

alternative, according to Scotus, is 'attritionism'. Attrition is essentially repentance for sin based on fear of punishment, while contrition is a repentance for sin grounded in a love for God.[292] According to Scotus, sinners may be justified in two possible ways:

1. They may be attrite to a sufficient degree to merit grace *de congruo*.
2. They may be attrite to a minimal extent (*parum attritus*) which, although inadequate to merit justifying grace *de congruo*, is sufficient to effect justification *ex pacta divino*, as mediated through the sacrament of penance.

It will be clear that the first alternative is of major importance, as it allows the possibility of *extrasacramental justification*. If the attrition is of sufficient intensity, God informs it by grace, converting it to contrition *directly* by the extrinsic denomination of the *acceptatio divina*, and thereby effectively bypassing the sacrament of penance. In the second alternative, Scotus defines the concept of *parum attritus* as not placing an obstacle in the path of sacramental grace (*non ponere obicem*) through the avoidance of mortal sin – a teaching which has frequently been criticised for its moral laxism. This device allows the *ex opere operata* efficacy of the sacrament of penance to be maintained. Whereas Thomas Aquinas integrated contrition within the sacrament of penance, thus effectively excluding the possibility of extrasacramental justification, Scotus allows for this possibility by means of an attrition of sufficient intensity to merit *de congruo* its conversion to contrition, and thus to merit the first grace. It may be noted that the two modes of penitential justification are essentially the same, the difference lying in the fact that they are mediated through different secondary causes. Both presuppose, and are based upon, the divine acceptation.

Scotus' doctrine of the *parum attritus* appears to challenge the medieval consensus concerning the inability of the *viatores* to know with absolute certainty whether they are in a state of grace; if they can assure themselves that they are *parum attritus*, they may rely upon the *ex opere operata* efficacy of the sacrament to assure themselves that they are in a state of grace.[293] Although Scotus does indeed state that a greater degree of certitude may be achieved by this mode of justification than by the extrasacramental mode,[294] he does not retract or qualify his specific magisterial rejection of the possibility of certitude of grace made elsewhere.[295] It must therefore be assumed that Scotus did not intend to teach the absolute certitude of grace in this matter.

---

[292] *Opus Oxoniense* IV dist. xiv q. 4 n. 14.
[293] *Opus Oxoniense* IV dist. xiv q. 4 n. 14.   [294] *Opus Oxoniense* IV dist. xiv q. 4 n. 14.
[295] This point has been well brought out by V. Heynck, 'A Controversy at the Council of Trent concerning the Doctrine of Duns Scotus', *FrS* 9 (1949), 181–258.

Scotus' position was criticised by many of his contemporaries and successors, particularly by Gabriel Biel.[296] Biel insisted that justification by perfect attrition (i.e., Scotus' extrasacramental mode of justification) must always be taken as implying the intention of confession, and is therefore implicitly linked with the sacrament of penance.[297] In this, Biel appears to be reverting to a principle established by the early Franciscan school, that the intention to confess (*propositum confitendi*) is an integral element in the definition of true penance; people cannot be truly penitent if they do not wish to confess their sins to a priest. Biel does not exclude the possibility of presacramental justification, but declines to allow that this may be considered to be 'extrasacramental', a second path to justification apart from the sacrament of penance.[298]

It will be evident, however, that Biel's emphasis upon the need for contrition in penance lays him open to the same charge which Scotus earlier directed against Peter Lombard – that sacramental efficacy is thence defined *ex opere operantis* rather than *ex opere operato*. Biel himself avoids this difficulty by stating that *viatores* are able, through the use of their own natural faculties, to elicit an act of love of God for his own sake, on the basis of which the infusion of *gratia prima* takes place. It must be emphasised that this act of love of God for his own sake is to be set within the context of the sacrament of penance, even though Biel observes that it is not necessary, in principle, for justification and sacramental absolution to coincide in time; the reconciliation of humanity to the church *must* be brought about through the sacrament of penance, which is therefore necessarily implicated in justification. In effect, Biel appears to be saying that human presacramental justification must be declared *in foro ecclesiae* by sacramental absolution before it can be deemed to be justification.[299]

Like the earlier Franciscan school, Biel anchors justification to the sacrament of penance by means of the *propositum confitendi*.[300] A further criticism which Biel directs against Scotus' doctrine of the *modus meriti de congruo* (as he terms Scotus' extrasacramental mode of justification) is that it is based upon an act of attrition, whose intensity, degree and duration are unknown to anyone, and are not specified by Holy Scripture; as such, it is therefore impossible to be sure that the correct act has been performed for the correct duration.[301] Biel rejects the idea of a fixed

---

[296] Feckes, *Rechtfertigungslehre des Gabriel Biel*, 66 n. 189.
[297] *In IV Sent.* dist. xiv q. 2 a. 2 conc. 4.
[298] See Oberman, *The Harvest of Medieval Theology*, 146–60.
[299] *In IV Sent.* dist. xiv q. 2 a. 2 conc. 4. Biel uses the traditional appeal to the leper-cleansing ritual (Luke 17:14; cf. Leviticus 14) to illustrate the need for confession; see his *Sermones dominicales de tempore*, 76.
[300] *In IV Sent.* dist. xiv q. 2 a. 1 nota 2.
[301] *In IV Sent.* dist. xiv q. 2 a. 1 nota 2; cf. *Canonis Missae expositio* 26F.

duration and intensity on the part of the penitent, insisting upon the need for *amor amicitie super omnia propter Deum* in its place. It will be clear that this doctrine is essentially an extension of Biel's interpretation of *facienti quod in se est* from the *first* justification to the *second* justification. *De potentia ordinata* God is obliged to reward the individual who does *quod in se est* with grace, an obligation which exists as much in regard to the sacrament of penance as to the bestowal of the first grace. As Biel pointed out, we do penance, not so that God 'would change his judgement in response to our prayer, but so that by our prayer we might acquire the proper disposition and be made capable of obtaining what we request'.[302]

An attack of a somewhat different type was, however, developed during the fifteenth century, with potentially significant consequences for the sacramental economy of salvation. The Vulgate translated the inauguration of Christ's preaching, 'Repent (Greek, *metanoiete*) for the kingdom of God is at hand' (Mark 1:14), as follows: 'Do penance (*poenitentiam agite*), for the kingdom of God is at hand.' The double reference of the Latin *poenitentia* (i.e., it can mean 'repentance' or 'penance') served to establish a link between the sinner's inward attitude of attrition and the sacrament of penance. The rise of the new critical philology in the Quattrocento called this link into question. Thus, Lorenzo Valla challenged the Vulgate translation of New Testament texts such as the above.[303] In this, he was followed by Desiderius Erasmus, whose *Novum instrumentum omne* (1516) reproduced Valla's challenge to the Vulgate translation of *metanoiete*. Thus, in the 1516 edition, Erasmus translated the Greek imperative as *poeniteat vos* ('be penitent'), and in the 1527 edition as *resipiscite* ('change your mind'), further weakening the link between the inward attitude of repentance and the sacrament of penance. The full significance of this philological development would, however, be appreciated only in the first phase of the Reformation of the sixteenth century, and did not pose a serious challenge to the correlation of justification and the sacraments in the late medieval period.

In conclusion, it may be stated that the medieval period saw the justification of the sinner firmly linked to the sacramental life of the church, a

---

[302] *Canonis Missae expositio* 31C.

[303] Valla, *Adnotationes*, in *Monumenta politica et philosophica rariora*, Turin: Bottega d'Erasmo, 1959, 5.807 (on Matthew 3:2), 824 (on Mark 1:14), 872 (on 2 Corinthians 7:9–10). It is interesting to note that the opinion of Isidore of Seville, that there exists an etymological connection between *punire* and *poenitere* (*Etymologiae* VI, xix, 71, PL 82.258C), was generally rejected during the twelfth century. However, a close link between *poenitentia* and fear of punishment was presupposed by certain theologians, such as Anselm of Laon, possibly on the basis of this alleged etymological association: see Anciaux, *La Théologie du sacrement du pénance*, 155–7.

sound theological link having been established between justification and the sacraments.[304] This linking of justification to the sacramental system of the church has profound theological and pastoral consequences, of which the most important is the tendency to assert *iustificatio extra ecclesiam non est*.[305] Although the theologians of the medieval period were aware that God was not bound by the sacraments, the tendency to emphasise the reliability of the established order of salvation, of which the sacramental system is part, can only have served to convey the impression that the sinner who wishes to be reconciled to God must, *de facto*, seek the assistance of a priest.

The explicit statement of the sacramental economy of salvation may be regarded as complete by the thirteenth century, and as having survived the only serious theological attack to be made upon it during the medieval period. The Psalmist exhorted his people to 'enter his gates by confession'; the theology of the medieval period ensured that the only manner in which God's gates could be entered was through the sacraments of baptism and penance.[306]

This insight that the sacramental structures of the church were the sole guarantors of salvation was rapidly assimilated into church architecture. The great portals of Romanesque churches were often adorned with elaborate sculptures depicting the glory of heaven as a tactile affirmation that it was only by entering the church that this reality could be experienced. Inscriptions were often placed over the great west door of churches, declaring that it was only through entering the church that heaven could be attained. The portal was allowed to be identified with Christ for this purpose, speaking words directed to those passing by, or pausing to admire its magnificent ornamentation. An excellent example is provided by the Benedictine priory church of St.-Marcel-lès-Sauze, which was founded in 985 and extensively developed during the twelfth century. The portal to the church depicts Christ addressing these words to all who draw near:

> Vos qui transitis, qui crimina flerae venitis,
> Per me transite quoniam sum ianua vitae.[307]

> (You who are passing through, you who are coming to weep for your sins, Pass through me, since I am the gate of life.)

---

[304] Biel's linking of justification and the eucharist should be noted here: Oberman, *The Harvest of Medieval Theology*, 271–80.

[305] Cf. Augustine, *De baptismo* IV, xvii, 24: 'Salus extra ecclesiam non est.'

[306] See the use made of this text by Astesanus of Asti: H. J. Schmitz, *Die Bußbücher und die Bußdisziplin der Kirche*, Graz: Akademische Verlagsanstalt, 1958, 800.

[307] For this and other inscriptions of a similar nature, see W. M. Whitehill. *Spanish Romanesque Architecture of the Eleventh Century*, London: Oxford University Press, 1968.

Although the words are clearly to be attributed to Christ (picking up on the image of Christ as the 'gate of the sheepfold' from John 10), a tactile link has been forged with the building of the church itself. This is often reinforced visually through the physical location of the baptismal font close to the door of the church, thereby affirming that entrance to heaven is linked with the sacrament of baptism.

2.5   The concept of grace

Earlier medieval writers tended to conceive grace primarily in Augustinian terms, including elements such as the restoration of the divine image, the forgiveness of sins, regeneration and the indwelling of the Godhead.[308] In the present section, we are particularly concerned with three aspects of the development of the concept of grace which are of importance to the overall scheme of the development of the doctrine of justification. These are:

1. The development of the concept of the supernatural in the articulation of the nature and the effects of grace.
2. The distinction between *gratia gratis data* and *gratia gratum faciens*.
3. The distinction between operative and co-operative grace.

We shall consider these points individually. Before this is possible, however, a serious difficulty in terminology must be noted. The terms *gratia gratis data* and *gratis gratum faciens*, used extensively in this section, and elsewhere in this study, are conventionally translated as *actual grace* and *sanctifying grace*. These translations are, in fact, anachronisms, dating from the post-Tridentine period. *Gratia gratis data* is probably better translated as *prevenient grace*, although even this is not totally satisfactory. In view of the widespread tendency to translate *gratia gratis data* as 'actual grace', and the absence of any generally accepted alternative, however, I feel we have no alternative but to continue this practice, having drawn attention to its deficiencies.

---

[308] See Alszeghy, *Nova Creatura*; Auer, *Die Entwicklung der Gnadenlehre*; Beumer, *Gratia supponit naturam*; Doms, *Die Gnadenlehre des sel. Albertus Magnus*; Gillon, *La Grâce incréée*; Herve de l'Incarnation, 'La Grâce dans l'oeuvre de S. Leon le grand', *RThAM* 22 (1955), 193–212; Heynck, 'Die aktuelle Gnade bei Richard van Mediavilla'; R. Javelet, *Image et ressemblance au XIIe siècle de S. Anselme à Alain de Lille*, 2 vols., Paris: Letouzey et Ané, 1967; Landgraf, *Dogmengeschichte der Frühscholastik*, 1/1.51–140, 141–201; Molteni, *Roberto Holcot*; Philips, 'La Théologie de la grâce chez les préscolastiques'; idem, 'La Théologie de la grâce dans la "Summa Fratris Alexandri"'; Schupp, *Die Gnadenlehre des Petrus Lombardus*; Stoeckle, '*Gratia supponit naturam*'; Vanneste, 'Nature et grâce dans la théologie du XIIe siècle'; idem, 'Nature et grâce dans la théologie de Saint Augustin'.

The emergence of the concept of the supernatural[309] is associated with the late twelfth century. The theologians of the earlier medieval period had generally been content to assert that grace is a gift of God, which cannot be merited, and appealed to the cognate relationship of the terms *gratia*, *gratis* and *gratuita* in support of this contention. It will be clear that this discussion of the nature of grace merely postponed the inevitable question which could not be ignored: what is the relation of God's grace to God's other gifts? Grace is indeed the free gift of God – but are *all* of God's gifts to be identified as God's grace? In other words, is the characteristic feature of grace to be located purely in the fact that it is freely bestowed by God?

The eleventh- and twelfth-century discussions of this question made it clear that a careful and systematic distinction between *naturalia* and *gratuita* was required if confusion was to be avoided. The distinction which required elucidation was between *datum* (i.e., that which is already given in nature) and *donum* (i.e., the subsequent and additional gift of grace). As we have noted, confusion over precisely this point prevailed during the Pelagian controversy.

The first instance of a systematic distinction between the *datum* (i.e., nature) and *donum* (i.e., grace) may be found in the ninth century. Scotus Erigena drew a clear distinction between the natural and supernatural orders.[310] Of particular importance in this respect is Erigena's explicit reference to *gratia supernaturalis* in this context.[311] Phrases indicating that the realm of grace was increasingly conceived in supernatural terms – e.g., *supra naturam* or *ultra naturam* – are encountered with increasing frequency in the following centuries.[312] The first major step towards the definition of the concept of the supernatural may be regarded as having been taken by Simon of Tournai, who argued that the *datum* is the purely natural, while the *donum* is the purely spiritual.[313]

---

[309] Cf. Henri de Lubac, *Surnaturel: Etude historique*, Paris: Aubier, 1946.

[310] *De divisione naturae* v, 23, PL 122.904B: 'Donum gratiae neque intra terminos conditae naturae continetur neque secundum naturalem virtutem operatur, sed superessentialiter et ultra omnes creatas naturales rationes effectus suos peragit.' See further F. A. Staudenmaier, *Johannes Scotus Erigena und die Wissenschaft seiner Zeit*, Frankfurt am Main: Minerva, 1966.

[311] *Commentarius in Evangelium Johannis*, PL 122.325C; *De divisione naturae* 111.3, PL 122.631D.

[312] E.g., Hervaeus of Bourg-Dieu, *Comm. in epist. Divi Pauli*, PL 181.1446C–D; Hugh of St Victor, *De sacramentis* I, vi, 17, PL 176.237D–8A; Hugh of Amiens, *Dialogi* IV, 6, PL 192.1184A.

[313] *Quaestio* 64, ed. Warichez, 179: 'Datis autem subsistit homo, quod est et qualis est naturaliter; donis vero qualis est spiritualiter. Ex datis ergo contrahit naturalem; ex donis, spiritualem.'

This attempt to define the nature of grace in terms of the dialectic between the natural and the spiritual did not, however, really meet the problem. Neither did Peter of Poitiers' attempt to define the distinction between *naturalia* and *gratuita* in terms of their respectively human and divine origins.[314] While it is probably impossible to point to any single theologian who may be credited with making the crucial distinction between nature and supernature in defining the essence of grace, it would seem that Praepositinus of Cremona has better claim than anyone else for this innovation.

Standing at the dawn of the thirteenth century, Praepositinus argued that there must be a higher order than nature itself, and deduced its existence from considerations such as the following. Reason is the highest thing in nature, yet faith must be considered to transcend reason. Therefore faith must be regarded as transcending the natural, being itself something which is beyond nature (*supranaturam*).[315] This distinction can also be applied to the virtues. For example, in his polemic against the teaching of Hugh of St Victor, William of Auxerre distinguished a purely natural *amor amicitiae erga Deum* from a meritorious love for God.[316] On the basis of such considerations, William argued for two distinct orders of being. Even though there is a tendency here to define grace purely in terms of the meritorious, it is clear that significant progress towards the classic definition of supernature has been made. The turning point in achieving this definition appears to have been due to Philip the Chancellor, who distinguished the natural order from the 'more noble' supernatural order: to the former belong reason and natural love, to the latter faith and charity.[317] This important distinction allowed justification to be resolved into a twofold operation:

---

[314] *Sententiarum libri quinque* II, 20, PL 211.1025A: 'Naturalia dicunt illa quae habet homo a nativitate sua, unde dicuntur naturalia, ut ratio, ingenium, memoria, etc. Gratuita sunt illa quae naturalibus superaddita sunt, ut virtutes et scientiae; unde etiam dicuntur gratuita, quia a Deo homini per gratiam conferuntur.' See also the anonymous Cod. Paris Nat. lat. 686 fol. 40v, cited in Landgraf, *Dogmengeschichte der Frühscholastik*, 1.180 n. 76: 'quod dicitur natura quantum ad creationem, dicitur gratia quantum ad recreationem vel reformationem'.

[315] *Summa*, Cod. Erlangen 353 fol. 32, cited in Landgraf, *Dogmengeschichte der Frühscholastik*, 1.180: 'Fides mea est supra rationem et ratione nullum naturale bonum est homine excellentius. Ergo fides supra omnia naturalia.' Praepositinus was associated with a group of scholars upon whom the strongest influence was Peter Lombard, including Peter of Poitiers, Peter of Capua and Stephen Langton; see J. W. Baldwin, *Masters, Princes and Merchants*, 2 vols., Princeton: Princeton University Press, 1970.

[316] *Summa Aurea* lib. II tr. xiv cap 2; fol. 69.

[317] *Summa de bono*, Cod. Vat. lat. 7669 fol. 12, cited in Landgraf, *Dogmengeschichte der Frühscholastik*, 1/1.198–9 n. 84.

1. the natural: grace operates on the will, effecting its moral goodness;
2. the supernatural: grace effects the meritoriousness of human acts, raising them from the purely natural plane to that of the supernatural.

In one sense, it could be argued that this is not a new development at all, for these effects of justification had been generally accepted since the time of Augustine. Philip's achievement, however, is to distinguish the two aspects of justification in terms of two levels of being, thereby removing much of the confusion surrounding the matter. While the theologians of the earlier twelfth century tended to define grace in terms of merit, the theologians of the closing years of the century generally regarded merit as the consequence of the transference of an act from the natural (i.e., morally good) to the supernatural (i.e., meritorious) plane, in a transition effected by grace. This distinction, once made, became generally accepted; thus Thomas Aquinas stated that 'when someone is said to have the grace of God, what is meant is something supernatural (*quiddam supernaturale*) in humans which originates from God'.[318]

The earlier medieval period was characterised by confusion concerning the various manners in which grace could be understood. Peter Lombard drew a distinction between *gratia gratis dans* (i.e., the uncreated grace which is God himself) and *gratia gratis data* (i.e., the grace of justification).[319] This latter concept, however, was clearly ill-defined, and it became a task of priority to clarify what was meant by the term. Bonaventure noted the general tendency to conceive grace in the broadest of terms, and demonstrated the advantages of restricting the term to *gratis gratis data* and *gratum faciens*.[320] The distinction between *gratia gratis data* and *gratia gratum faciens* appears to have been established by the dawn of the thirteenth century, although confusion in relation to the terms employed is frequently encountered. In broad terms, *gratia gratum faciens* came to be understood as a supernatural habit within humans, while *gratia gratis data* was understood as external divine assistance, whether direct or indirect. Initially, this clarification took place by cataloguing the senses in which *gratia gratis data* could be understood.

---

[318] *Summa Theologiae* IaIIae q. 110 a. 1: 'Sic igitur per hoc quod dicitur homo gratiam Dei habere, significatur quiddam supernaturale in homine a Deo proveniens.' For the relation between grace and supernature in High Scholasticism, see Auer, *Die Entwicklung der Gnadenlehre*, 2.219–50.

[319] *II Sent.* dist. xxvii 7.

[320] *In II Sent.* dist. xxvii dub. 1, ed. Quaracchi, 2.669: 'Accipitur enim gratia uno modo largissime, et sic comprehendit dona naturalia et dona gratuita . . . Alio modo accipitur gratia minus communiter, et sic comprehendit gratiam gratis datam et gratum facientem.'

For example, Albertus Magnus distinguishes the following eight senses of the term:[321]

1. rational nature and its powers;
2. natural moral goodness;
3. Adam's supernatural gifts prior to the Fall;
4. imperfect movements towards salvation;
5. inspiration, thaumaturgy and similar gifts;
6. the assistance of the angels;
7. the indelible character received in the sacraments of baptism and confirmation;
8. the divine *concursus*.

Although Bonaventure concludes that the divine *concursus* should be excluded from this list,[322] the concept of *gratia gratis data* is still conceived in the broadest of terms, embracing virtually any means by which God interacts with humanity. It would seem that the general concept which underlies Bonaventure's catalogue of instances of *gratis gratis data* is anything which prepares or disposes humanity towards the gift of *gratia gratum faciens*. A similar degree of ambiguity is evident from the earlier writings of Thomas Aquinas. Thus Thomas uses the term *gratia gratis data* in a flexible manner, apparently regarding the concept as being beyond meaningful definition.[323] In contrast, the concept of *gratia gratum faciens* appears to have been relatively well characterised by this point.[324] Further confusion, however, existed concerning the distinction between operative and co-operative grace, an important feature of Augustine's theology of justification.[325] We shall illustrate this point with reference to the developing insights of Thomas Aquinas on this matter.

It is important to appreciate that Thomas Aquinas' understanding of both the nature and the operation of grace underwent considerable

---

[321] Doms, *Die Gnadenlehre des sel. Albertus Magnus*, 167–8.

[322] *In II Sent.* dist. xxviii a. 2 q. 1, ed. Quaracchi, 2.682.

[323] Thomas, *In II Sent.* dist. xxviii q. 1 a. 4, ed. Mandonnet, 2.728. See Stufler, 'Die entfernte Vorbereitung auf die Rechtfertigung nach dem hl. Thomas'; P. de Vooght, 'A propos de la grâce actuelle dans la théologie de Saint Thomas', *Divus Thomas* (Piacenza) 31 (1928), 386–416. Thomas elsewhere appears to regard it as a *charism* – i.e., a gift to help *others*: *Summa Theologiae* IaIIae q. 111 a. 1.

[324] For examples of such confusion, see Bonaventure, *In II Sent.* dist. xxvii a. 1 qq. 1–5; Thomas, *In II Sent.* dist. xxvi q. 1 aa. 1–6. The systematic use of the term *habitus* in this context appears to be due to the influence of Philip the Chancellor; see P. Fransen, 'Dogmengeschichtlichen Entfaltung der Gnadenlehre', in J. Feiner and M. Löhrer (eds.), *Mysterium Salutis: Grundriß heilsgeschichtlicher Dogmatik*, Einsiedeln: Beinziger, 1973, 4/2.631–722, 672–9. The first magisterial reference to grace as a *habitus* is encountered in the decisions of the Council of Vienne of 1312 (D. 483: 'et virtutes ac informans gratia infunduntur quoad habitum'), although the term is used earlier (1201) in relation to the virtues (D. 410: 'et virtutes infundi . . . quoad habitum').

[325] See Albertus Magnus, *In II Sent.* dist. xxvi aa. 6–7.

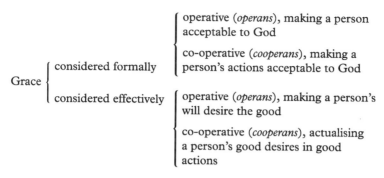

Figure 2.1

development during his lifetime. In his early discussion of grace in the *Commentary on the Sentences*, Thomas poses the following question, to answer it in the negative: whether grace is a multiple entity within the soul (*utrum gratia sit multiplex in anima*).[326] The reply given to this question illustrates his early confusion concerning the concept of actual grace. A distinction may be made between grace and the virtues: if grace is to be identified with these, it must follow that there are many graces, which is impossible. Although it might appear that the distinctions between prevenient and subsequent, operative and co-operative grace point to the multiplicity of grace, these distinctions in fact merely reflect the various effects of the one grace.

In other words, the distinction between 'prevenient grace' (*gratia praeveniens*) and other forms of grace – such as *subsequens, operans* and *cooperans* – are purely notional and not real. Grace produces in us a number of effects, and the multiplicity of the effects of grace does not necessitate the deduction of a multiplicity of graces. The effect of operative grace is to produce a good will within humans, and that of co-operative grace to actualise this good will in a good performance – which amounts to an exact restatement of the teaching of Augustine on this matter. Thus internal acts are to be attributed to operative grace, and external acts to co-operative grace. This understanding of grace may be summarised as in Figure 2.1. This simple division of grace, based simply upon the distinction between the formal and effective aspects of operative and co-operative grace, is of particular significance in that the entire analysis of the nature of grace proceeds without reference to *gratia gratis data*!

---

[326] *In II Sent.* dist. xxvi q. 1 a. 6, ed. Mandonnet, 2.682–6. For what follows, see the excellent study of Lonergan, *Grace and Reason*.

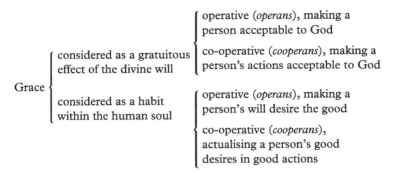

Figure 2.2

In his discussion of the matter in the later *De veritate*, a slightly different question is posed: whether in one person there is one such *gratia gratum faciens*.[327] In his answer to this question, Thomas makes an important and explicit distinction between *gratia gratis data* and *gratia gratum faciens*, the former being more a loose catalogue of various possibilities rather than a precise catalogue, and hence evidently multiple.

Gratia gratum faciens, however, is something quite different. If this type of grace is understood as referring to every aspect of the divine will, such as good thoughts or holy desires, it is clearly multiple. This simple admission of the multiplicity of *gratia gratum faciens* represents a clear and significant development in Thomas' theology of grace. In his earlier *Commentary on the Sentences*, Thomas had insisted upon the simplicity of *gratia gratum faciens*, while conceding the multiplicity of its effects. The multiplicity of the division of graces is purely notional, reflecting the effects of the one *gratia gratum faciens*. Thomas now appears to introduce a distinction between the habitual gifts of grace, and grace understood as the effects of the gratuitous will of God. This more complex division may be summarised as in Figure 2.2. Here the distinction between formal and efficient causality is retained, but is transferred from the distinction between the external and internal operation of grace (see above) to the distinction between *operation* and *co-operation*.

This has the important consequence of excluding the possibility of operative grace acting *efficiently*, which Thomas had upheld in the *Commentary on the Sentences*. It is clear, however, that the distinction between the formal and efficient causality of habitual grace leads to consequences which are merely distinct at the *notional* level, while the

---

[327] *De veritate* q. 27 a. 5, ed. Spiazzi, 1.524–8.

distinction between formal and efficient causality in the case of grace, understood as an effect of the divine will, leads to consequences which are distinct *in fact*. This clearly marks a significant departure from the Augustinian understanding of the distinction between operative and co-operative grace – indeed, it seems that Thomas is so dissatisfied with Augustine's understanding of the concepts that he practically abandons them.

Whereas Augustine taught that operative grace excites the will to desire good, and that co-operative grace subsequently actualises this good will in good deeds, Thomas now explicitly teaches that *co-operative* grace both excites the will to good desires and also externalises this in external action. This opinion would, however, soon be abandoned.

Thomas' mature discussion of the nature and divisions of grace, as presented in the *Summa Theologiae*, is of particular interest. Thomas' attempt to correlate Augustine's teaching on the relation between good will and good performance, which first appeared in the *Commentary on the Sentences*, only to be rejected in *De veritate*, makes its reappearance in the *Summa Theologiae*, although in a significantly modified form. The Augustinian distinction between operative and co-operative grace, originally introduced in a polemical context to meet the Pelagian distinction between good will and good performance, was simply inadequate to convey the metaphysical aspects of the matter which Thomas considered to be important.

Thomas introduces the distinction between *actus interior voluntatis* and *actus exterior voluntatis* to express the substance of Augustine's earlier distinction.[328] Grace is now understood either as a habit or as a motion, both of which may be either operative or co-operative. Such is the frailty of humans that, once in a state of habitual grace, they require a continual and unfailing supply of actual graces (note the deliberate use of the plural) if they are to grow in faith and charity. The new relationship of the divisions of grace arising from this may be represented diagrammatically as in Figure 2.3. Habitual grace is thus *operative*, in so far as it heals the wounded nature of humans and justifies them, rendering them acceptable to God; and *co-operative*, in so far as it is the basis of meritorious human action. Grace, understood as *motus*, operates on the human will in order that it may will good. In this matter, God is active and the free will passive. Grace, understood as *motus*, then co-operates with the will to achieve the good act itself. In this matter, the will is active, and may be said to co-operate with grace. The most important point which may

---

[328] *Summa Theologiae* IaIIae q. 111 a. 2.

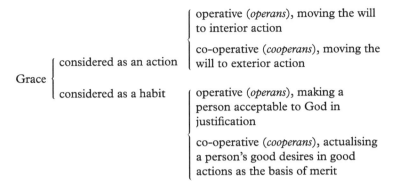

Figure 2.3

be noted concerning this new interpretation of the nature and divisions of grace is that actual grace is now assigned a definite role in human justification.

From this discussion, it will be clear that Thomas' changing views on the nature and divisions of grace are complex and difficult to follow. It is therefore important to identify any underlying factors which may explain the leading features of these changes. The decisive alteration which seems to underlie Thomas' changing views on the nature and divisions of grace appears to be his growing pessimism concerning humanity's natural faculties, which we noted earlier in relation to Thomas' teaching on the nature and necessity of human preparation for justification. In his early period, Thomas regarded a preparation for justification as necessary, yet possible without the assistance of grace. As such, the concept of *gratia gratis data* had no significant role to play in the justification of humans. In his later period, Thomas taught that the beginning of an individual's conversion must be seen as an internal operation of grace,[329] thus necessitating the implication of *gratia gratis data* prior to justification.

Further, in his early period, Thomas seems to have regarded humanity's natural capacities to be such that, once justified, no further assistance in the form of grace was required: *gratia gratum faciens* alone is treated as being *gratia operans et cooperans*.[330] Thomas cited with approval Averroes' statement to the effect that the possession of a habit allows the will to be transformed to action spontaneously.[331] Thomas, while conceding that

---

[329] *Summa Theologiae* Ia q. 62 a. 2 ad 3um; *Quodlibetum primum* I a. 7.
[330] *In II Sent.* dist. xxvi q. 1 a. 6 ad 2um, ed. Mandonnet, 2.685.
[331] Cited in *In III Sent.* dist. xxiii q. 1 a. 1, ed. Mandonnet, 3.698.

humans are far from perfect, appears to have considered this deficiency to be remedied by the possession of habitual grace.

This conclusion is confirmed by two additional considerations. First, the further interference of God in human life is to be rejected as amounting to a violation of human dignity. Second, the mere external action of God would not bring about any permanent change in humans. Divine action may make a particular action good, but it fails to achieve any fundamental alteration within the individuals themselves. Humans would remain as deficient after this external intervention as they were before it, and so a means of grace is to be rejected in favour of an internal change within humans, which is articulated in terms of the habitual gift of *gratia gratum faciens*.

Thomas' discussion of the same point in *De veritate* suggests that he is no longer content with this understanding of the nature of habitual grace. No matter how perfect the habit may be, humans are frail enough to need the continual assistance of further divine graces functioning as *gratia cooperans* – that is, acting on humans who are already in a state of habitual grace. No habit or set of habits is sufficiently efficacious to make human operations truly good,[332] as God alone is capable of perfect action. Thomas makes it clear that he now regards humans as needing actual grace before and after their conversion; the internal change wrought within them by the habit of created grace requires further supplementation by external graces. It is thus fair to suggest that Thomas' developing understanding of the divisions of grace reflects his new insights into human impotence, which we noted earlier in relation to the human disposition for justification.

The development of the concepts of *gratia gratis data* and *gratia gratum faciens* in the later medieval period still remains to be clarified at present, as it is not clear how the precise relationship between the habit of created grace and the extrinsic denomination of the divine acceptation was understood in the fourteenth and fifteenth centuries.[333] We shall return to this question in connection with the related topic of the formal principle of justification. We conclude the present section by summarising the classic Thomist understanding of the nature and divisions of grace, as stated in the *Summa Theologiae*. Grace may be defined according to whether it is *actual* or *habitual*, and according to whether it *operates upon humans, or*

---

[332] *De veritate* q. 27 a. 5 ad 3um, ed. Spiazzi, 1.52–7. Thomas emphasises that this arises 'non quidem propter defectum gratiae, sed propter infirmitatem naturae'. Cf. q. 24 a. 7.
[333] For an introduction to the problem, see Janz, 'A Reinterpretation of Gabriel Biel on Nature and Grace'.

co-operates with them. Actual grace, *gratia gratis data*, may be conceived as a series of transient effluxes of divine power or influence, given over and above the realm of nature, which impinge upon human will in order to incline it or assist it to particular actions. The earlier distinction between *prevenient* and *subsequent* grace must therefore be understood to apply only to *actual* grace. Quite distinct from this is habitual or sanctifying grace, *gratia gratum faciens*, which takes the form of a permanent habit of the soul, infused into humans by God, and which may be considered to amount to a participation by humanity in the divine being. Although permanent in the individual who has been justified, the habit may be lost by mortal sin, and must be regained in penance. The combination of these categories leads to four main categories of grace:

1. *Actual operative grace*, which inclines the human will to desire good, and operates without the need for a response from humans.
2. *Actual co-operative grace*, which assists the renewed will to actualise its good intentions in the form of external actions, and requires the co-operation of the will.
3. *Habitual operative grace*, which is the formal principle of justification within the Thomist understanding of the process.
4. *Habitual co-operative grace*, which is the formal principle of merit within the Thomist system, and requires humanity's co-operation.

It is to the question of merit that we now turn.

2.6   The concept of merit

The medieval discussion of merit may be regarded as based upon Augustine's celebrated maxim. When God crowns the merits of humanity, he merely crowns his own gifts to humans,[334] rather than some attribute of humanity which it is obliged to acknowledge, respect and reward. The early Latin fathers, prior to the Pelagian controversy, do not appear to have considered merit to involve any real claim on the part of humans to divine reward on the basis of their efforts.[335] Merit appears to have been understood simply as a divine gift to the justified sinner, relating to the bestowal of eternal life rather than of the first grace, and based upon divine grace rather than upon divine justice or an obligation

---

[334] Augustine, *De gratia et libero arbitrio* vi, 15: 'si ergo Dei dona sunt bona merita tua, non Deus coronat merita tua tanquam merita tua, sed tanquam dona sua'. See also *Epistola* 194.19.

[335] Bakhuizen van den Brink, 'Mereo(r) and meritum in some Latin Fathers'; Peñamaria de Llano, *La salvación por la fe*, 191–211. See also the earlier study of K. H. Wirth, *Der 'Verdienst'-Begriff in der christlichen Kirche* I: *Der 'Verdienst'-Begriff bei Tertullian*, Leipzig: Dorffling & Franke, 1892; II: *Der 'Verdienst'-Begriff bei Cyprian*, Leipzig: Dorffling & Franke, 1901.

arising from the nature of merit in itself.[336] Despite the semantic associations of the Latin term *meritum*, the early use of the term appears to
have been quite innocent of the overtones of 'works-righteousness' which
would later be associated with it.

The theological renaissance of the eleventh and twelfth centuries saw
several developments of decisive importance in connection with the concept of merit. Of these, the most significant is the shift in the context
in which merit was discussed. For Augustine, the purpose of humanity's temporal existence was 'to win the merit by which we may live in
eternity'.[337] The context in which Augustine's doctrine of merit is set is
clearly that of the final gaining of eternal life, rather than of the initial
justification of humans. When God 'crowns merits', God does so, not by
justifying humans, but by bestowing upon them *eternal life*. For Augustine,
merit both presupposes and expresses grace. The eleventh and twelfth
centuries, however, saw the question of merit discussed within a quite
different context – the gratuity of *gratia prima*. Is humanity capable of
meriting its initial justification? The fact that this question was universally answered in the negative at this stage is at least in part a consequence
of the Augustinian background to the early medieval discussion of merit,
in that merit is seen to be, by definition, a consequence of grace.[338]

The Augustinian interpretation of merit as *gratis pro gratia* can be illustrated from many works of the eleventh and twelfth centuries,[339] but is
particularly associated with Gilbert de la Porrée (sometimes referred to
as 'Gilbert of Poitiers') and his school,[340] among whom we may number

---

[336] Augustine, *Sermo* 111, iv, 4, PL 38.641A: 'Non debendo enim sed promittendo debitorem se Deus fecit.' For an excellent discussion of this aspect of Augustine's theology,
see Hamm, *Promissio, pactum, ordinatio*, 11–18.

[337] Augustine, *Epistola* 130, 14.

[338] For example, Hervaeus of Bourg-Dieu, *Commentarius in epistolae Pauli*, PL 181.1052B–
D; Anselm of Canterbury, *De casu diaboli* 17; *De veritate* 12; Peter Abailard, *Expositio
in Epistolam ad Romanos*, PL 178.903A, 919B, 920A–B; Bernard of Clairvaux, *De gratia et libero arbitrio* vi, 16, PL 182.1010C; Honorius of Autun, *Elucidarum* 11, 3, PL
172.1135D; Robert Pullen, *Sententiarum libri octo* v, 9, PL 186.837B–C; Peter of Poitiers,
Sententiarum libri quinque III, 2, PL 211.1045A–D; Alan of Lille, *Theologicae regulae* 86,
PL 210.665C–6A; Hugh of St Victor, *De sacramentis* I, vi, 17, PL 176.247G–D; Richard
of St Victor, *In Apocalypsim Joannis* VII, 8, PL 196.883G–D; Peter Lombard, *II Sent.*
dist. xxvii, 7.

[339] The remark of 'Magister Martinus' (Martin of Fougères) is typical of many: 'Cum Deus
coronat nostra merita, quid aliud coronat quam sua munera'; Cod. Paris Nat. lat. 14556
fol. 314, cited in Landgraf, *Dogmengeschichte der Frühscholastik*, 1.185. 'Master Martin'
was one of a group of theologians, including Alan of Lille and Simon of Tournai, who
owed a particular debt to Gilbert de la Porrée; see J. W. Baldwin, *Masters, Princes and
Merchants*, 2 vols., Princeton: Princeton University Press, 1970, 1.44.

[340] See Landgraf, 'Untersuchungen zu den Eigenlehren Gilberts de la Porrée'; idem, 'Mitteilungen zur Schule Gilberts de la Porree'; idem, 'Neue Funde zur Porretanerschule';
idem, 'Der Porretanismus der Homilien des Radulphus Ardens'.

Cardinal Laborans, Odo of Ourscamp, Alan of Lille and Radulphus Ardens. The axiom *Christus solus meruit* is of particular importance in this connection, as it summarises the opinion, characteristic of the *Porretani*, that only Christ may be said to merit anything in the strict sense of the term.[341]

The systematisation of theological discourse during the twelfth century, however, led to a growing realisation that the strict sense of merit as *meritum debitum* was quite inadequate to deal with the spectrum of meanings of the term if the utter gratuity of justification and the necessity of a human disposition or preparation for justification were to be simultaneously upheld. It can be shown that a distinction came to be drawn between the concepts of *merit* and *congruity*: while humanity cannot be said to merit justification by any human actions, the preparation for justification of humans could be said to make their subsequent justification 'congruous' or 'appropriate'. Thus a manuscript source of the late twelfth century makes a clear distinction between the two concepts: 'digno, dico, non dignitate meriti, sed dignitate congrui'.[342] The sense which is clearly intended here is that of a congruity which cannot be considered meritorious in the strict sense of the term.

This concept of merit appears to have found its most important application in connection with the question of whether, and in what sense, Mary can be said to have merited the honour of bearing the saviour of the world.[343] The most widely accepted answer was that Mary could not be thought of as having merited this distinction in the strict sense of the term, although it was appropriate or 'congruous' that she should have been favoured in this manner. The concept of *meritum congruitas* or *meritum interpretativum* thus passed into general circulation, being understood as a form of merit in the weakest sense of the term.

This distinction between merit in the strict sense of the term and in its weaker sense of 'propriety' passed into the theological vocabulary of the thirteenth century as the concepts of *meritum de condigno* and *meritum de congruo*. Although these precise terms can be shown to have been used occasionally in the late twelfth century,[344] they do not always bear

---

[341] Alan of Lille, *Theologicae regulae* 82, PL 210.663C: 'Solus Christus proprie nobis meruit vitam aeternam'; cf. Hamm, *Promissio, pactum, ordinatio*, 32–4. Cardinal Laborans' critique of the theological application of *civil* concepts of merit should also be noted here: Hamm, *Promissio, pactum, ordinatio*, 47–66.

[342] Cod. British Museum Harley 957 fol. 179v; cited in Landgraf, *Dogmengeschichte der Frühscholastik*, 1/1.271.

[343] For example, Cod. British Museum Royal 9 E XII fol. 95v; Cod. Vat. lat. 4297 fol. 24, cited in Landgraf, *Dogmengeschichte der Frühscholastik*, 1/1.272 nn. 17, 18.

[344] For example, as used in Geoffrey of Poitiers's *Summa*: Brugge Bibliothèque de la Ville Cod. lat. 220 fol. 114v, cited in Landgraf, *Dogmengeschichte der Frühscholastik*, 1/1.276 n. 35: 'Et ita patet, quod non meretur de congruo. Et certum est, quod nec de condigno.'

precisely the same meaning as they would in later periods. Furthermore, the concept of congruous merit, which was initially used chiefly in connection with the question of the propriety of Mary's bearing the Saviour of the world, came to be used increasingly in a quite distinct context – that of the meritorious character of the human disposition towards justification. Thus whenever a theologian of the twelfth century concedes merit prior to justification, the 'merit' in question is not to be understood as merit in the strict sense of the term, but rather as *meritum de congruo*.[345]

The concept of congruous merit has been the subject of considerable criticism on the part of Protestant historians of doctrine. For Adolf von Harnack, the concept represented the total disintegration of the Augustinian doctrine of grace.[346] It is, of course, possible to sustain this rather extravagant thesis with reference to certain more maverick theologians of the period, who are not representative of the theological trends of the era. Thus Durandus of St Pourçain appears to have regarded *meritum de congruo* as *meritum ante gratiam*; the sole difference between *meritum de congruo* and *meritum de condigno* is that the former exists prior to grace, and the latter subsequent to it.[347] However, an analysis of the origins of the concept, and of the intentions which underlie it, conspires to invalidate such criticism. In particular, three points may be noted.

First, the pastoral intention of the concept cannot be overlooked.[348] Although humanity has no claim to justification on the basis of divine justice, humans may look towards the divine generosity and kindness for some recognition of their attempts to amend their lives in accordance with the demands of the gospel. It may be pointed out that the concept of a disposition towards justification which is meritorious *de congruo* is particularly associated with the Franciscan order and the school of theology which came to be associated with it. The pastoral emphasis upon God's kindness towards sinful humanity finds its appropriate expression in the concept of congruous merit.

Secondly, the human activity, which counts as the disposition towards justification, must be regarded as being already set within the context of grace.[349] Even in the later *via moderna*, the axiom *facienti quod in se est Deus non denegat gratiam* is always understood as an expression and a consequence of divine grace. Those theologians who taught that humans could prepare themselves for justification in a manner which was meritorious

---

[345] Landgraf, *Dogmengeschichte der Frühscholastik*, 3.238–302.
[346] Harnack, *History of Dogma*, 6.275–317.   [347] *In II Sent.* dist. xxvii q. 2.
[348] Auer, *Die Entwicklung der Gnadenlehre*, 2.85: 'Es war das religiöse und vielleicht seelsorgliche Bedürfnis, aus der Güte Gottes die Möglichkeit einer wirksamen Vorbereitung auf die Gnade zu erweisen.'
[349] Auer, *Die Entwicklung der Gnadenlehre*, 2.86.

de congruo invariably insisted that this be understood as a consequence of divine grace. Human justification must be seen as a divine *gift*, rather than as a divine *reward*.

In the third place, most theologians of the period explicitly taught that humans require the assistance of actual grace before they are capable of disposing themselves *proximately* towards justification, although they might concede that humans are capable of disposing themselves *remotely* towards justification through the proper exercise of their unaided natural faculties. Those theologians who held that a proximate disposition towards justification was meritorious *de congruo* thus presupposed the implication of *gratia gratis data* (and not merely the *concursus generalis*) in effecting this necessary disposition.

The concept of condign merit was employed to express the notion of a self-imposed obligation upon the part of God to reward human efforts. The notion of obligation, which is essential to the concept of merit *de condigno*, may be detected in the early twelfth century. Peter the Chanter explicitly implicated the notion of obligation in his definition of merit: 'mereri est de indebito debitum facere'.[350] In this, he was followed by Alan of Lille, who listed four elements essential to true merit, especially the concept of being placed under an obligation.[351]

This notion of being placed under obligation (*de indebito debitum facere*) is taken up by theologians of the early thirteenth century, such as Stephen Langton[352] and Godfrey of Poitiers,[353] and is stated with particular clarity by William of Auvergne.[354] Merit is now defined as an act performed by humans that places God under an obligation to them. It must be pointed out, however, that this obligation on the part of God is usually understood to arise as a consequence of the gracious decision by which God chooses to be placed under an obligation to humans in this manner.[355] A similar

---

[350] *De tropis loquendi*, Cod. Vat. lat. 1283 fol. 38r, cited in Landgraf, *Dogmengeschichte der Frühscholastik*, 3.270 n. 5. On this work, see Gillian R. Evans, 'Peter the Chanter's *De Tropis Loquendi*: The Problem of the Text', *New Scholasticism* 55 (1981), 95–103.

[351] *Theologicae regulae* 82, PL 210.663B–C. 'Ad hoc enim, ut aliquis proprie dicatur aliquid mereri, quattuor concurrunt: ut opus quod agit eius proprie sit; ut apud alium mereatur; ut apud talem qui potestatem habet remunerandi; ut de indebito fiat debitum.'

[352] Cod. Salzburg St Peter a. x 19 fol. 25, cited in Landgraf, 'Untersuchungen zu den Eigenlehre Gilberts de la Porrée', 201–2 and n. 7.

[353] *Summa*, Cod. Paris Nat. lat. 15747 fol. 42v, cited in Landgraf, *Dogmengeschichte der Frühscholastik*, 3.276 n. 37.

[354] *De meritis*, in *Opera omnia* 1.310 aF: 'Meritum ergo proprie et rectissima diffinitione obsequium est retributionis obligatorium, hoc est quod recipientem sive illum, cui impenditur, retributionis efficit debitum.'

[355] This point is emphasised by Hamm, who distinguishes two distinct senses in which the concept of self-limitation was understood: an *absolute* sense (Hamm, *Promissio, pactum, ordinatio*, 41–103) and a *restricted* sense (104–249). This useful distinction permits much of the earlier confusion on this matter to be resolved.

definition of merit may be shown to have characterised the writers of the early Franciscan school, such as Odo Rigaldi[356] and Bonaventure,[357] as well as the first Summist, William of Auxerre.[358]

The introduction of Aristotelian physics had a pronounced and profound effect upon the early Dominican school. We have already noted the considerable influence of Aristotelian physics upon Thomas Aquinas' teaching upon both the nature of justification and the necessity of a disposition for justification. It can be shown that Aristotelian considerations also exercised a considerable influence upon the early Dominican school's teaching on merit. Roland of Cremona's definition of merit locates its essence in its being a *motus* intermediate between humanity's initial state and the final state of eternal life.[359] In this, we can see the beginnings of the tendency, which would become particularly clear in the writings of Thomas Aquinas, to conceive merit *ontologically*, rather than in terms of a personal obligation of God to the individual Christian. Whereas the earlier medieval theologians had understood merit to refer essentially to the obligation of God towards humanity, the theologians of the early Dominican school tended to understand merit in terms of ontological participation in the divine nature itself. This may be contrasted with the teaching of the early Franciscan school, which retained the older personal understanding of merit.[360]

A significant feature of the medieval understanding of condign merit is that merit and its reward are understood to be proportionally related. Thus Roland of Cremona states that merit *de condigno* is not called merit *de digno* precisely because the initial *cum* indicates the association between the merit and its reward.[361] This idea is picked up by others around this time, and inevitably leads to the notion, first clearly encountered in the writings of William of Auxerre, that the relation between merit and reward can be established as a matter *of justice*.[362] This idea is developed by Thomas Aquinas, who stresses that the divine reward of human merit is to be regarded as an 'act of justice' on God's part. Thomas, however,

---

[356] *In II Sent.* dist. xxviii q. 4 a. 1 arg. 1, ed. Bouvy, 82.10.
[357] *In III Sent.* dist. xviii a. 1 q. 2 resp.
[358] *Summa Aurea* lib. III tr. 2 q. 6 arg. 1; fol. 136d: 'Mereri ex condigno est facere de indebito debitum vel de debito magis debitum.'
[359] *Summa* 35, 2, ed. Cortesi, 117: 'Mereri est motum ex virtute gratuita et libero arbitrio elicere in via militiae; et aliquem mereri sibi est motum virtu tis pro se elicere.'
[360] Cf. Thomas Aquinas, *In II Sent.* dist. xxvi q. 1 a. 3.
[361] Roland of Cremona, *Summa* 347, 66, ed. Cortesi, 1050: 'ipsum autem cum adiungitur ibi ad notandum associationem meriti cum praemio'. Auer's distinction between *Würdigkeit* (i.e., 'worth') and *Verdienst* (i.e., 'merit') is valuable here: Auer, *Die Entwicklung der Gnadenlehre*, 2.150.
[362] *Summa Aurea* lib. III tr. 16 q. 2 arg. 7; fol. 221c.

emphasises that the term 'justice' is used in this context in a sense significantly different from its normal use.[363]

Although merit *de condigno* is often referred to as 'true' merit, to distinguish it from merit *de congruo*, it must be appreciated that Thomas understands neither type of merit to represent a just claim on the part of humans before God. Justice, in the strict sense of the term, can exist only among equals. Just as Aristotle excluded animals and gods from his concept of justice on the grounds that there existed too great a dissimilarity between them and humans to allow their inclusion in the contracting political community, so Thomas argues that there is too great a dissimilarity between humans and God to allow anyone to speak of humanity having a 'just' claim before God. 'It is obvious that there is the greatest inequality between God and humans, for they are infinitely different, and all of humanity's good comes from God.'[364] Thus one cannot speak of *iustitia secundum absolutam aequalitatem* in this context, but only of *iustitia secundum proportionem quandam*. Although one can speak of justice and merit in terms of the relationship between God and humanity, it must be appreciated that merit in this context must be understood as merit on the basis of *iustitia secundum praesuppositionem divinae ordinationis*, rather than on the basis of *iustitia secundum absolutam aequalitatem*.

The merit in question is thus merit *secundum quid* – a merit before God which, though in some sense analogous to human merit, is nevertheless sharply to be distinguished from it. Merit before God is based upon a divine ordination according to which God will reward a particular work with a specified reward. God cannot be thought of as being in debt to humanity, in any sense of the notion; God's faithfulness, understood as self-obligation rather than obligation to humanity, is reflected in the divine ordination that God will reward such acts in this manner.[365] Merit arises from grace, in that God can be said to bestow quality upon his creatures in an act of grace. Merit is therefore not based upon strict justice, but upon *iustitia secundum quid*, 'a sort of justice', which is based upon God's decision to reward creatures. In effect, Thomas develops Augustine's principle, that merit is based upon the divine promise, to the effect that *all* merit before God is 'improper' merit, in the sense that it is not based upon strict justice between equals.

---

[363] *Summa Theologiae* IaIIae q. 114 a. 1: 'Unde sicut reddere iustum pretium pro re accepta ab aliquo, est actus iustitiae; ita etiam recompensare mercedem operis vel laboris, est actus iustitiae.' See also *In II Sent.* dist. xxvii q. 1 a. 3; *In III Sent.* dist. xviii a. 2.

[364] *Summa Theologiae* IaIIae q. 114 a. 1.

[365] *Summa Theologiae* IaIIae q. 114 a. 1 ad 3um. This important section is frequently overlooked by Thomas' critics.

It is possible to distinguish between an *intellectualist* and a *voluntarist* approach to the relation between the moral and the meritorious. The former, which is particularly associated with the theologians of the twelfth century and the early Dominican and Franciscan schools, recognises a direct correlation between the moral and the meritorious value of an act, the transition between the two being effected by grace or charity. This relationship is frequently indicated by the use of terms such as *comparabilis*, *associatio*, *aequiparari* or *proportionalis*. While there was general agreement that the merit of an act *coram Deo* was a consequence of God's graciousness and liberality in accepting it as such, rather than of its inherent value, there was division between the early Dominican and Franciscan schools on whether this merit was to be conceived *ontologically* or *personally*. Although the intellectualism of the early Franciscan school stands in contrast to the voluntarism of the later Franciscan school, an essential continuity between the schools is demonstrated in their mutual tendency to conceive merit in *non-ontological categories*.

The voluntarist position is particularly associated with the later Franciscan school and the *via moderna*. Its fundamental and characteristic feature is the recognition of a discontinuity between the moral and the meritorious realms, the latter being understood to rest entirely upon the divine will itself. For Scotus, every created offering is worth exactly what God accepts it for, and nothing more.[366] The meritorious value of an act need therefore have no relation to its moral value, as it rests upon God's estimation alone. This position is developed with particular clarity in the works of William of Ockham, and we shall illustrate it with reference to these.

For Ockham, the decision as to what may be deemed to be meritorious or demeritorious lies entirely within the scope of the divine will, and no reference whatsoever need be made to the moral act in question. There is a fundamental discontinuity between the moral value of an act (i.e., the act, considered in itself) and the meritorious value of the act (i.e., the value which God chooses to impose upon the act). Moral virtue imposes no obligation upon God, and where such obligation may be conceded, it exists as the purely contingent outcome of a prior uncoerced divine decision. This aspect of Ockham's teaching has been the subject

---

[366] *Opus Oxoniense* III dist. xix q. 1, 7: 'Dico, quod sicut omne aliud a Deo, ideo est bonum, quia a Deo volitum, et non est converso: sic meritum illud tantum bonum erat, pro quanto acceptabatur.' This view should be contrasted with that of Peter Aureoli, *In I Sent.* dist. xvii q. 1 a. 2: 'ex quo patet quod ex divino amore debetur actibus nostris ut habeant meriti rationem *intrinsice et ex natura rei*' (my italics: note the assertion of *ex natura rei* causality).

of considerable criticism, as it appears to suggest that the relation between the moral and the meritorious domains is purely arbitrary.[367] Although Ockham insists that an act can be meritorious only if it is performed in a state of grace, it appears that he regards this as merely a *conditio sine qua non* for merit, secondary in importance to the divine acceptation.[368] For Ockham, an act can be meritorious *de potentia ordinata* only if it is performed in a state of grace – but the meritorious *value* of that act is determined solely through the divine will. God is not bound by the moral value of an act, but is free to impose upon that act whatever meritorious value he may deem appropriate. The relationship between the moral and meritorious values of an act is thus to be regarded as purely contingent, a consequence of the divine will, and not merely a necessary consequence of the nature of the act itself which God is obliged to respect. Ockham's concept of *covenantal causality* necessitates his rejection of an *ex natura rei* causal relationship between the moral and meritorious realms. Ockham uses the dialectic between the two powers of God to demonstrate that *de potentia absoluta* an act which is now deemed meritorious might have been demeritorious, even though precisely the same act is involved in each case.[369]

Ockham's discussion of the nature of congruous merit appears to underlie the criticisms of Thomas Bradwardine and Gregory of Rimini directed against the 'modern Pelagians'. According to Ockham, God rewards virtuous acts performed outside a state of grace with congruous merit.[370] However, Ockham insists that this 'merit' carries with it no claim to eternal life; such a claim can be held to arise only on account of merit *de condigno*.[371] All that Ockham intends to convey by the notion of congruous merit is that humans are capable of acting in such a way that God may bestow upon humanity a habit of grace – which, as we noted earlier, is the general understanding of the concept at the time. The *function* of the concept within the context of Ockham's soteriology is that it forms the necessary (understood as *necessitas consequentiae*, rather than *necessitas consequentis*) bridge between the state of nature and of grace, and between the moral and theological virtues.

It is often asserted that Ockham's optimism concerning human abilities leads him into Pelagianism or 'semi-Pelagianism'; it may, however, be pointed out that Ockham's optimism concerning humanity relates solely to its *moral* capacities, and that the radical discontinuity which Ockham recognises between the moral and meritorious values of an act means

---

[367] See especially Iserloh, *Gnade und Eucharistie*, 64–7.
[368] Iserloh, *Gnade und Eucharistie*, 111.   [369] *In III Sent.* q. 12.   [370] *In IV Sent.* q. 9.
[371] *In IV Sent.* q. 9: 'Et dico quod respectu gratie nullus actus est meritorius de condigno nisi ille qui est respectu eterne beatitudinis.'

that the moral abilities of humans are largely irrelevant, as the ultimate grounds of merit lie outside of humanity, in the extrinsic denomination of the divine acceptation. As we have pointed out, the meritorious value of an act lies in the divine estimation of that act rather than in its inherent moral value. Ockham's theology of merit allows him to take a favourable view of human moral capacities, while at the same time totally destroying the theological foundation upon which human acts might be considered capable of meriting grace or eternal life.

One of the most brilliant and original aspects of Ockham's theology of merit is that he permits the moral acts of humans to have a considerable inherent moral value, while simultaneously establishing that the moral value of an act is irrelevant in determining its meritorious value, by locating the *ratio meriti* in the extrinsic denomination of the *acceptatio divina*. Ockham's teaching on this matter has been subject to a considerable degree of misrepresentation and misunderstanding by both contemporary and modern critics.[372] Of Ockham's contemporary critics, his fellow Englishman Thomas Bradwardine may be singled out for particular comment. Bradwardine totally rejected the concept of congruous merit prior to grace,[373] insisting that merit was the consequence of grace; unless the tree is itself good, it cannot bear good fruit.

A similar position is associated with Gregory of Rimini.[374] In response to the opinion which was more associated with Ockham's followers than with Ockham himself, that humans can merit justification *de congruo* by an act of contrition,[375] Gregory denies that contrition is a possibility apart from grace. A rather different, and somewhat startling, approach to the question is associated with John Wycliffe, the later English follower of Bradwardine. Wycliffe totally rejected the concept of *condign* merit, even after the bestowal of grace, on the grounds that the concept implied that God rewarded human acts *de pura iustitia*, as if they were entirely

---

[372] Leff's early study of Bradwardine seriously misrepresents Ockham: G. Leff, *Bradwardine and the Pelagians: A Study of 'De Causa Dei' and its Opponents*, Cambridge: Cambridge University Press, 1957, 188–210. His later *William of Ockham* acknowledges and corrects these misunderstandings; see especially *William of Ockham*, 470 n. 85.

[373] *De causa Dei* I, 39. Cf. Oberman, *Archbishop Thomas Bradwardine*, 155–9; Leff, *Bradwardine and the Pelagians*, 75–7. Leff is incorrect when he states that Bradwardine denied congruous merit *totally*.

[374] See Manuel Santos-Noya, *Die Sünden- und Gnadenlehre des Gregor von Rimini*, Frankfurt am Main: Peter Lang, 1990. For the key texts, see *In II Sent.* dist. xxvi, xxvii, xxviii q. 1 a. 1. For an analysis of Gregory's *Commentary on the Sentences*, see P. Bermon, 'La *Lectura* sur les deux premiers livres des Sentences de Grégoire de Rimini O.E.S.A. (1300–1358)', in G. R. Evans (ed.), *Medieval Commentaries on Peter Lombard's Sentences*, 2 vols., Leiden: Brill, 2001, 1.267–85.

[375] For example, Robert Holcot, *In IV Sent.* q. 1 a. 8: 'Nam peccator meretur de congruo iustificationem per motum contritionis.'

performed by the humans themselves without the assistance of divine grace. Wycliffe defines congruous merit as merit which arises through God's rewarding those human acts which result from the influence of divine grace – and hence altogether excludes the concept of condign merit from consideration.[376]

Unlike Bradwardine, who conceded both congruous and condign merit after justification, Wycliffe conceded *only* congruous merit, and that *only after* justification. A similar position is associated with Huss, who pointed out that *pura iustitia* implied an equality between God and humanity which simply did not exist, except in the form of *equalitas proportionis*.[377] It is therefore impossible for humans to merit eternal life *de condigno*, even when in a state of grace.[378]

It is instructive to recall that Thomas Aquinas made a similar observation concerning the concept of *iustitia* implied by the concept of condign merit, but did not feel that the *secundum quid* character of the resulting merit was sufficient reason to reject the concept. The criticisms of Wycliffe and Huss appear to be directed against a misunderstanding or misrepresentation of the nature of condign merit which does not correspond to the teaching of any of the theological schools of the period, in that the existence of a proportional relationship between an act and its reward was not held to imply an equality between humankind and God.

The later *via moderna* may be regarded as continuing the teaching of Ockham on the nature of merit. Gabriel Biel emphasised that the concept of congruous merit is based upon the divine liberality rather than on the divine justice. The disposition of humanity towards justification is regarded as meritorious *non ex debito iusticie sed ex sola acceptantis liberalitate*.[379] As we have already noted, the teaching of the *via moderna* concerning congruous merit was criticised in certain quarters as exhibiting Pelagian tendencies. It is therefore of particular interest to note the defence of the doctrine provided by the distinguished early sixteenth-century Tübingen exegete Wendelin Steinbach. Steinbach points out that the early church was confused concerning the concept of merit, but that

---

[376] *De sciencia Dei*, cited in J. A. Robson, *Wyclif and the Oxford Schools*, Cambridge: Cambridge University Press, 1961, 209 n. 1. It is, of course, possible that Wycliffe means that congruous merit results from God's prevenient grace prior to justification.

[377] *In II Sent.* dist. xxvii q. 5, ed. Flajshans, 2.307–9: 'Qui ergo dicunt, quod non potest homo mereri vitam aeternam de condigno, attendunt equalitatem quantitatis; qui autem dicunt, quod homo potest mereri de condigno attendunt equalitatem proporcionis.'

[378] *In II Sent.* dist. xxvii q. 5, ed. Flajshans, 308: 'non potest pura creatura de condigno mereri vitam eternam'.

[379] *In II Sent.* dist. xxvii q. 1 a.1 nota 3.

the concept was now sufficiently well understood to avoid a Pelagian misunderstanding of the concept of congruous merit.[380]

The continuity between the late medieval and Reformation periods may also be demonstrated from John Calvin's teaching concerning the merits of Christ. The later Franciscan school, the *via moderna* and the *schola Augustiniana moderna* regarded the *ratio meriti* as lying in the divine good pleasure; nothing was meritorious unless God chose to accept it as such. This teaching was extended to include the work of Christ; the *merita Christi* were regarded as being grounded in the *acceptatio divina*. There are excellent reasons for suggesting that Calvin himself encountered such a teaching during his formative Paris years.[381] It is therefore of some considerable interest that Calvin reproduces the essential features of this late medieval understanding of the *ratio meriti Christi*. This point can fully be appreciated only by considering the *Institutio* of 1559 (XI.xvii.1–5), a section which is based upon an exchange of letters between Calvin and Laelius Socinus. In 1555, Calvin responded to questions raised by Socinus concerning the merit of Christ and the assurance of faith,[382] and appears to have incorporated these replies into the 1559 *Institutio* without significant modification. In the course of this correspondence, Calvin's strongly voluntarist understanding of the *ratio meriti Christi* becomes apparent. Although the evident similarity between Calvin and Scotus on this question has been noted in the past,[383] it has not been fully appreciated that Scotus merely marks a point of transition in the medieval discussion of the question of the *ratio meriti*, so that the main theological schools of the fourteenth and fifteenth centuries adopted a similarly voluntarist understanding of the criterion of merit. In other words, there has been a tendency in the past to assume that this similarity between Scotus and Calvin reflects the specific influence of Scotus upon Calvin, whereas it actually reflects a much more general influence of currents of thought prevalent within later medieval theology.[384] Calvin insists that 'apart from God's good pleasure, Christ could not have merited

---

[380] Steinbach, *Opera exegetica* 1.136.4–6: 'Tamen hodie non est absonum dicere, quod peccator mereatur bonis operibus de genere vel impetret de congruo a Deo iustificari et graciam sibi infundi.'

[381] On this, see A. E. McGrath, 'John Calvin and Late Medieval Thought'.

[382] The replies are incorporated into the 1559 edition of the *Institutio* at the following points: II.xvii.1–5; III.ii.11–12. See the marginal notes in *Ioannis Calvini Opera Selecta*, ed. Barth and Niesel, 3.509; 4.20–2.

[383] For example, see A. Gordon, 'The Sozzini and their School', *ThRev* 16 (1879), 293–322.

[384] For the importance of this point, see McGrath, *The Intellectual Origins of the European Reformation*, 29–33, 67–103.

anything'.[385] Christ's work is meritorious *pro nobis* because God has ordained that it will be so, and accepted it as such. The fact that Calvin's discussion of the *ratio meriti Christi* is continuous with that of the *via moderna* suggests that Calvin encountered such an opinion at Paris, perhaps through the influence of John Major. Whatever the historical explanation of this continuity with later medieval thought may be, however, it serves to indicate that there is a closer relationship between late medieval theology and that of the Reformation than many have realised.

2.7   The dialectic between the two powers of God

From the discussion of merit presented above, it will be clear that the concept of God's being under an obligation to justify humans if they do *quod in se est* is a commonplace in the later medieval discussion of justification. But in what sense may God be said to be under an *obligation* to humans? Is not this a compromise of the divine freedom and omnipotence? It is this question which forms the context of the dialectic between the two powers of God, which is one of the most important and most frequently misrepresented aspects of the late medieval discussion of justification.

The problem identified above is recognised by Augustine, who presented the outlines of a solution which would be taken up and developed by the theologians of the medieval period, particularly by those of the *via moderna*. For Augustine, the divine *obligation* to humanity arises purely from the divine *promises* made to humans: 'non debendo enim, sed promittendo debitorem se deus fecit, id est non mutuo accipiendo'.[386] If God is under any obligation to humans, it is as a consequence of God's free, non-coerced decision to enter into such an obligation by means of the promises made to humanity. We have already noted the significance of the divine promises to humanity in relation to Augustine's understanding of *iustitia Dei*.

It is clear that Augustine understands the concept of divine obligation to humanity as an expression of the divine sovereignty, as it demonstrates God's ability to extend that authority to limit God's own course of action.[387] This point was taken up and developed during the theological renaissance of the twelfth century, but assumed a new significance in the thirteenth century as a consequence of Averroist determinism.

---

[385] *Institutio* II.xvii.1, ed. Barth and Niesel, 3.509: 'nam Christus nonnisi ex Dei beneplacito quidquam mereri potuit'.

[386] *Sermo* 110, iv, 4, PL 38.641A.

[387] See Hamm, *Promissio, pactum, ordinatio*, 15: 'Der promissio-Begriff hat somit im Zusammenhang der Vorstellung von Gott als Schuldner die spezifische Funktion, Gottes Selbstverpflichtung als Ausdruck seiner Souveränität zu interpretieren.'

Thus Thomas Aquinas points out that, while God is omnipotent, there are many things which God *could* do which but nevertheless wills *not* to do. From an initial set of possibilities, limited only by the condition that the outcome must not involve contradiction, God willed to actualise only a specific subset. In that God could have willed a different subset of possibilities, and was not coerced in this selection, the subset selected for actualisation cannot be regarded as resulting from absolute necessity. However, in that God has chosen to act in this particular manner, the subset of unwilled possibilities must be considered as being set aside as only hypothetically possible.[388]

These two sets of possibilities represent the two spheres of the power of God. God's *absolute* power refers to the initial set of possibilities which are open to divine actualisation, which is limited only by the condition that their actualisation does not involve contradiction. Of these initial possibilities, only a small number are selected for actualisation. Their actualisation results in the present order as we know it, which is defined as the realm of God's *ordained* power. This realm represents the subset of possibilities which God chose to actualise – and, having chosen to act in this way, God abides by these decisions. Thus there is no absolute necessity for God to choose any particular course of action within the context of the ordained order; however, having chosen to establish the present order, God is under a self-imposed, personal obligation to respect it. Such considerations underlie the important distinction between *necessitas consequentis* (a necessity which arises through the inherent nature of things) and *necessitas consequentiae* (a necessity which arises through the establishment of a contingent order of existence). This important distinction between an *absolute* necessity and *self-imposed conditional* necessity is of vital importance to a correct understanding of the medieval discussion of justification.

The thirteenth century saw the rise of Averroist determinism at Paris, posing a serious threat to the concept of the divine freedom. Among the propositions which were condemned at Paris in 1277 were several which denied or seriously questioned the omnipotence and freedom of God.[389] According to Siger of Brabant, God *necessarily* produces everything which God creates.[390] The essential problem which these opinions raise may be stated in terms of two propositions:

---

[388] *Summa Theologiae* Ia q. 25 a. 5 ad 1um.

[389] For a useful discussion, see Etienne Gilson, *History of Christian Philosophy in the Middle Ages*, London: Sheed & Ward, 1978, 406–8.

[390] For the thesis in question, see P. Mandonnet, *Siger de Brabant et l'Averroisme Latin au XIIIe siècle*, 2 vols., Louvain: Institut supérieur de philosophie de l'Université, 1908–11, 2.195.

God is free, and not bound by any external factors in acting.

God acts *reliably* in dealing with humanity.

The Averroist controversy made it a matter of urgency to develop a conceptual framework within which both these propositions could be maintained simultaneously. In its original form, the dialectic between the two powers of God was conceived as a solution to this dilemma, and is particularly associated with Henry of Ghent and Duns Scotus.

For Scotus, the divine freedom may be upheld in connection with his primordial decision as to which of the possibilities open to initial actualisation would subsequently be actualised. God's freedom in this respect is demonstrated by the non-coerced character of this decision, in that God was free from external constraints (save that contradiction must not result) in any decisions concerning the nature of the present established order. Scotus is thus able to reject the idea that God acts of absolute necessity – that is, *necessitas consequentis*. Once having determined the nature and character of the established order, however, God is under a contingent, conditional and self-imposed obligation to respect the order thus established – which may therefore be regarded as totally reliable. The present obligation to humanity on the part of God is a consequence, as well as an expression, of the divine freedom. God's absolute power (*de potentia absoluta*) affirms the divine freedom to act; God's ordained power (*de potentia ordinata*) affirms the present reliability of divine actions. The two propositions noted above may therefore be maintained simultaneously without contradiction.

The development of this dialectic between the absolute and ordained power of God is particularly associated with William of Ockham.[391] Like Scotus, Ockham uses the tension between what is *de facto* and what might have been *de possibili* to safeguard the divine freedom in the face of Greco-Arabian determinism. Although Ockham frequently refers to the first article of the Creed, 'Credo in deum patrem *omnipotentem*',[392] it is clear that he understands this omnipotence to have been qualified and circumscribed by the uncoerced divine decision to create. Ockham does not teach that God is currently able to do one thing *de potentia absoluta*, and the reverse *de potentia ordinata*; as he frequently emphasises, there exists only one power in God at present, and that is the ordained power, itself

---

[391] See M. A. Pernoud, 'Innovation in William of Ockham's References to the *Potentia Dei*', *Antonianum* 65 (1970), 65–97; Bannach, *Die Lehre van der doppelten Macht Gottes bei Wilhelm van Ockham.*

[392] *Quodlibetum primum* VI q. 6, *Opera theologica* 9.604.13–16: 'Credo in Deum patrem omnipotentem. Quem sic intelligo quod quodlibet est divine potentiae attribuendum quod non includit manifestam contradictionem.'

an expression of the contingent and uncoerced divine decision to create the established order.[393]

Where Ockham appears to go further than Scotus is in the *use* he makes of the dialectic between the powers of God. For Ockham, the dialectic between the powers of God was a critical tool for theological analysis; we shall illustrate this point shortly by exploring his critique of the necessity of created habits in justification. Thus while Peter Aureole insisted upon the absolute necessity of a created habit in justification, on account of the nature of things, Ockham pointed out that God was free to choose an alternative mode of justification. Without rejecting their *de facto* implication in justification, Ockham demonstrated that created habits were not involved as a matter of *absolute* necessity.

Ockham's use of the dialectic between the two powers of God as a critical theological tool was misunderstood at an early stage. In 1326 a commission of six theologians censured fifty-one articles taken from Ockham's writings, including a number of relevance to the doctrine of justification. Some six centuries later, this report was rediscovered,[394] allowing us to establish the precise nature of the condemned propositions, as well as the reasons for their condemnation. The four propositions which concern us are the following:

1. *De potentia Dei absoluta* individuals may make good use of their will by their purely natural powers, which God may accept as meritorious.[395] The *magistri* pronounced this to be Pelagian 'or worse', as it overthrew the habit of charity altogether.[396]
2. *De potentia absoluta* God may accept individuals *ex puris naturalibus* as worthy of eternal life without their possessing habitual grace, or damn them without their having sinned.[397]

---

[393] *Quodlibetum primum* VI q. 1, *Opera theologica* 9.585.14 – 586.24: 'Circa primum dico quod quaedam potest Deus facere de potentia ordinata et aliqua de potentia absoluta. Haec distincto non est sic intelligenda quod in Deo sint realiter duae potentiae quarum una sit ordinata et alia absoluta, quia unica est potentia in Deo ad extra, quae omni modo est ipse Deus. Nec sic est intelligenda quod aliqua potest Deus ordinate facere et aliqua potest absolute et non ordinate, quia Deus nihil potest facere inordinate. Sed est intelligenda quod "posse aliquid" quandoque accipitur secundum leges ordinatas et institutas a Deo; et illa dicitur Deus posse facere de potentia ordinata.'

[394] See A. Pelzer, 'Les 51 articles de Guillaume d'Occam censurés en Avignon en 1326', *Revue d'histoire ecclésiastique* 18 (1922), 240–70. A second, briefer version of the list of articles is now known: J. Koch, 'Neue Aktenstücke zu dem gegen Wilhelm von Ockham in Avignon geführten Prozess', *RThAM* 8 (1936), 168–97. The list of 56 articles drawn up by John Lutterell, along with his appended comments, has been edited by Fritz Hoffmann, *Die Schriften des Oxforder Kanzlers Johannes Lutterell*, Leipzig: St Benno, 1959, 3–102.

[395] Pelzer, 'Les 51 articles de Guillaume d'Occam censurés en Avignon en 1326', 250–1.

[396] Pelzer, 'Les 51 articles de Guillaume d'Occam censurés en Avignon en 1326', 251: 'Dicimus quod iste longus processus in predicto articulo contentus est erroneus et sapit heresim Pelagianam vel peius.'

[397] Pelzer, 'Les 51 articles de Guillaume d'Occam censurés en Avignon en 1326', 253.

3. *De potentia absoluta* God may accept humans *ex puris naturalibus* as worthy of eternal life without their possessing a habit of charity. Taking these two propositions together, the *magistri* pronounced that they were Pelagian, in that they taught that humans could be accepted to eternal life by their natural abilities.

4. *De potentia absoluta* God may remit sin without the infusion of grace.[398] This proposition follows from the others, and the *magistri* duly repeat their charge of Pelagianism.

The text of the condemned propositions makes it explicit that they are intended to be understood as discarded hypothetical possibilities, pertaining *de potentia absoluta* but not *de potentia ordinata*. Ockham's critics at Avignon, however, insisted that the addition of the phrase *de potentia Dei absoluta* made no difference to the sense of the propositions.[399] This seems to amount to a culpable misunderstanding of Ockham's intentions; Ockham merely exploits the tension between what *might have been* and what *actually is* the case to demonstrate the contingency and reliability of the established order. As we have noted, Ockham insists that there is only one power in God. If both the absolute and ordained powers of God were understood to be in force now, the charge of Pelagianism against Ockham could be regarded as justified. The fact remains, however, that this is not what Ockham meant.

That Ockham is not guilty of Pelagianism in these propositions may be confirmed by considering the position of Gregory of Rimini, one of the most ferociously anti-Pelagian theologians of the medieval period, on the same questions. Like Ockham, Gregory emphasises that, while God is not bound by any absolute necessity to accept individuals to eternal life if they possess a habit of charity, God has ordained that *de potentia ordinata* the possession of such a habit will result in the glorification of the *viator*. Gregory thus draws three conclusions:[400]

1. *De potentia absoluta* God may accept a person as *gratus* without a habit of created grace.

2. *De potentia absoluta* God is not obliged to accept as *gratus* the *viator* who is in possession of such a habit.

3. *De potentia absoluta* God may accept an act as meritorious even if it is performed outside a state of grace.

It is clear that these ideas broadly correspond to Ockham's views, as condemned at Avignon, and that they represent hypothetical possibilities

---

[398] Pelzer, 'Les 51 articles de Guillaume d'Occam censurés en Avignon en 1326', 253.

[399] Pelzer, 'Les 51 articles de Guillaume d'Occam censurés en Avignon en 1326', 252: 'Nec potest excusari per illam addicionem, quam ponit: de potentia Dei absoluta, quia argumentum suum eque procedit absque illa condicione sicut cum illa. Propositio autem, quam assumit, est heretica et conclusio heretica.'

[400] Gregory of Rimini, *In I Sent.* dist. xvii q. 1 a. 2.

de potentia Dei absoluta which do not pertain *de facto.* Furthermore, a careful examination of the writings of the *modernus* Pierre d'Ailly suggests that the critique of the necessity of grace in justification, conducted via hypothetical speculation *de potentia absoluta*, is specifically aimed at *created habits of grace*, and not at the uncreated grace of the Holy Spirit.[401]

In effect, the proposed necessity of a created infused habit of grace in justification may be regarded as the consequence of the intrusion of Aristotelianism within the sphere of the doctrine of justification, and the application of 'Ockham's Razor' – in this case, supported by a critique based upon the dialectic between the two powers of God – leads to the rejection of the absolute necessity of such a habit. The fact that the Tridentine decree on justification declines to affirm the necessity of a created habit of grace or charity in justification may be regarded as demonstrating that the hypothetical critique of the concept had made its point well.

The soteriological point which theologians of the *via moderna* used the dialectic between the two powers to emphasise is that the present established order of salvation, although radically contingent, is totally reliable. The established order of salvation, to which Scripture and tradition bear witness, is an expression of the divine will, and circumstances under which God would act contrary to this established and revealed will can never arise. To the objection that, because the present order depends upon the divine will, the possibility that God might revoke this order through a further act of will cannot be ignored, the theologians of the *via moderna* responded by appealing to the unity of intellect and will within God; God's actions are always totally consistent and reliable.

The use of the dialectic between the two powers of God within the *via moderna* has often been illustrated with reference to the writings of Gabriel Biel, and it is necessary to challenge a serious and influential misrepresentation of Biel's teaching on the *potentia Dei absoluta.* Carl Feckes argues that Biel used the absolute power of God as a convenient vehicle for conveying his own true theology, while retaining traditional teaching in connection with the ordained power of God. In other words, Biel states *de potentia absoluta* what he would have otherwise stated *de potentia ordinata*, were it not for fear of recrimination by the ecclesiastical authorities.[402] This criticism of Biel is impossible to sustain, particularly when

---

[401] See Courtenay, 'Covenant and Causality in Pierre d'Ailly', 107–9.

[402] Feckes, *Die Rechifertigungslehre des Gabriel Biel*, 12: 'Darum retten sich die Nominalisten gern auf das Gebiet der potentia absoluta hinüber, wenn die Konsequenzen ihrer Prinzipien mit der Kirchenlehre in Konflikt zu geraten drohen.' On the basis of this presupposition, Feckes argues (22) that Biel developed two essentially independent doctrines of justification, one according to God's absolute power (which represents Biel's own teaching), and one according to God's ordained power (which represents the teaching of the church).

it is appreciated that the use to which Biel puts the tool of the dialectic between the two powers of God is that of not merely *defending* the established order of salvation against divine capriciousness, but also of providing a firm theological foundation (in the concept of the *pactum*) upon which the established order of salvation may be more securely grounded.

This misrepresentation of Biel's thought has also had considerable influence in connection with the related question of the influence of later medieval theology upon the young Martin Luther: if what Biel *really* meant is to be determined from his statements concerning the *absolute* power of God, then Luther's early opinions should be compared with Biel's opinions *de potentia Dei absoluta*. This inevitably leads to the simplistic and quite unjustifiable conclusion that Luther merely states *de potentia ordinata* what Biel stated *de potentia absoluta* – which is as much a caricature of Luther's thought as it is of Biel's.[403]

Feckes' interpretation of Biel appeared in 1925; the first significant criticism of his approach appeared in 1934, with the publication of Paul Vignaux's highly influential study on fourteenth-century theology, which included a careful study of Ockham's 'voluntarism'.[404] The established order of salvation is not arbitrary but rational, and its rationality can be demonstrated on the basis of probable, though not necessary, arguments. According to Vignaux, the hypothetical order *de potentia absoluta* represents the order of divine logic, in that the possibilities open to divine actualisation are non-contradictory; the actual order *de potentia ordinata* is the order of divine mercy, in that God has voluntarily made himself a debtor to those who possess divine grace in order that they may be justified. Vignaux developed this point further in a highly acclaimed study of the young Luther, in which he emphasised that it was a total misrepresentation of Biel's thought to argue that the absolute power pertained to the order of reason and law, while the ordained order pertained solely to the arbitrary *de facto* situation.[405] The established order, Vignaux stressed, demonstrates simultaneously the divine justice and the divine mercy.

On the basis of reading Biel within this conceptual framework, subsequent studies have emphasised the innocence of Biel's use of the dialectic

---

[403] On the question of Luther's relationship to the theology of the *via moderna*, see McGrath, *Luther's Theology of the Cross*, 72–147.

[404] Vignaux, *Justification et prédestination*, 127–40. Particular attention should be paid to the comments made concerning Seeberg and Feckes: 132 n. 1.

[405] Vignaux, *Luther, Commentateur des Sentences*, 78: 'La *potentia absoluta* ne représente pas la raison et le droit, ni la *potentia ordinata*, une pure donnée de fait: toute interprétation de ce genre trahirait la pensée de Gabriel Biel . . . [L'ordre établi] est un ordre fait de libéralité à la fois et de la justice.'

between the two powers of God,[406] although criticism has frequently been directed against the amount of theological energy wasted on hypothetical speculation *de potentia Dei absoluta*.[407] Similar criticism was directed against the device in the fifteenth century, as may be seen from Erasmus' comments concerning the theological questions which were perplexing the Paris *théologastres* in the final decade of the century.[408] Two such questions may be noted:

Can God undo the past, such as making a harlot into a virgin?

Could God have become a beetle or a cucumber, instead of a human?

In fact, both these questions raised serious theological issues, similar to the question of the necessity of created habits in justification, which could not be resolved without the appeal to the dialectic of the two powers of God.[409]

The understanding of divine self-limitation associated with the *via moderna* is particularly linked to a 'covenant' (*pactum*) between God and humanity. It must be emphasised that this *pactum* should not be confused with the early form of the social-contract theory which is so characteristic a feature of the political thought of Marsilius of Padua. The *pactum* is ordained and instituted unilaterally by God, as an act of kindness and generosity towards humanity. Strictly speaking, it is necessary to recognise two covenants: one pertaining to the natural order, relating to all humanity, by which God is committed to upholding the created universe and the laws which govern it; the other pertaining to the theological order, relating to the church, by which God is committed to the salvation of sinful humanity.

It is with this latter covenant that we are chiefly concerned. At the heart of this concept of the covenant lies a major break with the rationalistic limitations of the Aristotelian concept of God, and a return to a more biblical concept of God who, though omnipotent, has entered into a covenant with the descendants of Abraham. The existence of this covenant affirms God's commitment both to the salvation of humankind and to the means

---

[406] For example, R. Weijenborg, 'La Charité dans la première théologie de Luther', *Revue d'histoire ecclésiastique* 45 (1950), 615–69, 617.

[407] Iserloh, *Gnade und Eucharistie*, 137–46. It may be noted that Heiko Oberman's early emphasis upon the priority of the *potentia absoluta* (e.g., see H. A. Oberman, 'Some Notes on the Theology of Nominalism with Attention to its Relation to the Renaissance', *HThR* 53 (1960), 47–76) is later replaced by a much more balanced approach in his *Harvest of Medieval Theology*, 30–47.

[408] Erasmus, *Opera omnia*, 6.927B–C.

[409] See W. J. Courtenay, 'John of Mirecourt and Gregory of Rimini on whether God can Undo the Past', *RThAM* 39 (1972) 244–56; 40 (1973), 147–74; A. E. McGrath, '*Homo assumptus*? A Study in the Christology of the *Via Moderna*, with Particular Reference to William of Ockham', *EThL* 61 (1985), 283–97.

ordained towards this end, particularly the sacramental system of the church. It is this *pactum* which forms the fulcrum about which the doctrines of justification associated with the *via moderna* turn.[410]

The most important use to which the dialectic between the two powers of God was put in the medieval period was the demonstration of the radical contingency of the role of created habits in justification, associated with which is the development of the concept of 'covenantal causality'. This topic will be further explored later. Our attention is now claimed by the question of the relationship between predestination and justification.

2.8   The relation between predestination and justification

The first systematic discussion of the relation between predestination and justification is encountered in the works of Augustine of Hippo. Although earlier writers appear to have realised that Paul's discussion of the rejection of Israel, contained in Romans 9—11, raised the question of predestination,[411] their chief concern appears to have been the defence of what they understood to be an authentically Christian understanding of free will in the face of astral fatalisms, such as Gnosticism. The confusion between the concepts of predestination and fatalism or determinism unquestionably served to lessen patristic interest in the idea of *divine* predestination, with the inevitable result that the early patristic period is pervaded by a theological optimism quite out of character with the Pauline corpus of the New Testament. It is with Augustine that attention is first directed to the idea that God exercises more control over the entire process of salvation than might at first seem to be the case.

As noted earlier, Augustine appears to have first confronted the problem of predestination in the course of his correspondence with Simplicianus of Milan.[412] Around 395, Simplicianus found himself perturbed by several issues arising from his reading of Romans 9—11. Why did God hate Esau? And was the idea that God hardened Pharaoh's heart compatible with the Christian understanding of the nature of God and of human freedom? Frustrated by Ambrose of Milan's failure to discuss the problem properly, Simplicianus turned to Augustine for guidance. By doing so, he appears to have been the occasion for the emergence of the characteristic theological position generally known as 'Augustinianism',

---

[410] On this, see Oberman, 'Wir sind pettler'; Courtenay, 'The King and the Leaden Coin'; McGrath, 'The Anti-Pelagian Structure of "Nominalist" Doctrines of Justification'.

[411] For example, Schelkle, *Paulus Lehrer der Väter*, 336–53, 436–40.

[412] *Das Prädestinationsproblem in der Theologie Augustins*, 41–8.

which would have so incalculable an effect upon subsequent western theological speculation concerning the relation between predestination and justification.

The essence of Augustine's position upon this question may be summarised in the statement that the *temporal* election, or justification, of humanity is the consequence of God's *eternal* election, or predestination.[413] Thus Augustine interprets the hardening of Pharaoh's heart as a consequence of divine predestination, understood as a positive action on God's part. However, Augustine totally excludes the possibility of an arbitrary *fiat* on the part of God in this respect by emphasising that predestination is based upon and is ultimately an expression of divine justice. Augustine demonstrates that the hardening of Pharaoh's heart is based upon justice in three ways:[414]

1. The hardening of Pharaoh's heart must be seen as a consequence of his previous sins.
2. The hardening of Pharaoh's heart is not totally a work of God; Pharaoh must be regarded as having contributed to the hardening of his heart by his own free will. Even in his discussion of predestination, Augustine insists upon the reality of the human free will.
3. God's judgement, whether open to public scrutiny or not, is always a matter of justice.

Even in the famous letter to Sixtus, written at the close of the Pelagian controversy, Augustine insists upon the total justice of divine predestination. God determines the destinies of humans on the basis of justice. Augustine frequently emphasises the role of the divine wisdom in predestination, intending by this to draw attention to the distinction between predestination and fatalism.[415] The total sovereignty of God in election is maintained: the justification of humans is preceded by the stirring of their will by God; and God, in his wisdom, has determined to prepare the wills of only a few.[416] For Augustine's critic Julian of Eclanum, any such teaching called into question the divine justice; Julian, however, employed a secularised concept of *iustitia Dei* which Augustine was not prepared to sanction.[417]

---

[413] *Ad Simplicianum* I, ii, 6, CChr 44.30.165 – 31.198.

[414] For example, see *De gratia et libero arbitrio* xx, 41; xxi, 42–3; xxiii, 45.

[415] Augustine makes it clear that wisdom is to be understood as the antithesis of fate: *Epistola* 194, ii, 5. It is interesting to note Ælfric's rejection of the fatalist associations of the Old English term *wyrd* in precisely the same context: *The Homilies of the Anglo-Saxon Church*, ed. B. Thorpe, 2 vols., London, 1864–6, 1.114.13.

[416] For example, *Epistola* 194, ii, 3–4. Cf. A. Sage, 'Praeparatur voluntas a Deo', *REAug* 10 (1964), 1–20.

[417] See McGrath, 'Divine Justice and Divine Equity in the Controversy between Augustine and Julian of Eclanum'.

Augustine declined to draw from his doctrine of predestination the conclusion that God predestined some to eternal life and others to damnation, or the related conclusion that Christ died only for the elect. These conclusions, however, would be drawn – and opposed! – with considerable frequency thereafter. The first theologian who can legitimately be styled 'predestinarian' is the fifth-century Gallic priest Lucidus, whose views were condemned at the Council of Arles (473). Of particular importance are his assertions that Christ did not die for all humans, that the divine grace is irresistible, and that those who are lost, are lost through God's will.[418] This condemnation was endorsed by Orange II (529), which specifically anathematised anyone who believed that some are predestined to evil by God.[419] Although some have argued that the council's condemnation was directed against Augustine, the fact remains that Augustine did not explicitly teach a doctrine of *double* predestination.

The most significant predestination controversy of the medieval period erupted in the ninth century, centring on the Benedictine monk Godescalc of Orbais (often incorrectly referred to as 'Gottschalk'). Until recently, our knowledge of this controversy stemmed chiefly from the accounts of Godescalc's supporters and opponents. The original text of Godescalc's principal writings was rediscovered in the first half of the twentieth century, with the result that we are now in a position to assess the significance of the great predestinarian controversy of the ninth century with some accuracy.[420]

Godescalc's doctrine of double predestination, *praedestinatio gemina*, is a logical consequence of a fundamentally Augustinian understanding of the relation between nature and grace. Where Godescalc appears to have differed from Augustine is in the rigour with which he deduced the necessity of double predestination from the prevenience of grace in justification. All rational creatures, whether human or angelic, continually need divine grace if they are to be acceptable to God. This necessity of grace extends also to the proper functioning of the human free will, which is unable to will or to do good apart from grace. With total fidelity to

---

[418] *D* 332–3. Both the date and the status of this council are open to question: it may date from 475, and it appears to represent the private judgement of a group of individuals, rather than that of the church. '[Lucidus] dicit quod Christus Dominus et Salvator noster mortem non pro omnium salute suscepit; qui dicit quod praescientia Dei hominem violenter impellat ad mortem, vel quod Dei pereant voluntate qui pereunt.'

[419] *D* 397. See also the confirmation of the pronouncements of Orange II on this matter by Boniface II in 531: *D* 398–400.

[420] G. Morin, 'Gottschalk retrouvé', *Revue Bénédictine* 43 (1931) 302–12. The contents of MS Berne 83 were published by Lambot, *Œuvres théologiques et grammaticales de Godescalc d'Orbais*.

Augustine, Godescalc asserted that the free will of humans is truly free only when it has been liberated by grace.[421]

It seems that the fundamental principle upon which Godescalc based his doctrine of double predestination is that of the divine immutability.[422] If there is in God no new judgement or decision, then all must be predestined. The possibility of any such new judgements or decisions is excluded on the grounds that 'if God does something which he has not done through predestination, he will have to undergo change' – which is unthinkable, given Godescalc's doctrine of the immutability of God. If God damns anyone, God must have determined to do so from all eternity, in that God is otherwise subject to change. Therefore, Godescalc concluded, both the salvation of the elect and the reprobation of the damned are predestined from all eternity. It is possible that this radical departure from the teaching of Augustine on this matter may have been occasioned by the teaching of Isidore of Seville, who explicitly taught that 'there is a double predestination, of the elect to rest and of the damned to death. Both are caused by divine judgement.'[423] Godescalc frequently refers to the great Spanish bishop with approval in relation to his teaching on predestination.[424]

If some are predestined to evil, it follows that Christ cannot have died for all people, but only for those predestined to life. This conclusion is unhesitatingly accepted by Godescalc.[425] The text frequently cited against him in relation to this point was 1 Timothy 2:4, which refers to God's desiring 'all people to be saved'. Godescalc rejected the suggestion that this reference implied that God desired all people in general to be saved, interpreting it instead as an affirmation that whoever is saved, is saved by divine predestination.[426]

The most sophisticated critique of Godescalc's doctrine of predestination was that of the Irish head of the cathedral school in Paris, John Scotus Erigena. In his *De divina praedestinatione*, written in about 850, Scotus criticised Godescalc for his misinterpretation and improper use of theological language. Terms such as 'predestination' and 'foreknowledge' are predicated of God metaphorically (*translative de deo predicari*),

---

[421] *De praedestinatione* 13, ed. Lambot, 234; *Responsa de diversis* 6, ed. Lambot, 148.

[422] *Confessio brevior*, ed. Lambot, 52: 'Credo et confiteor deum omnipotentem et incommutabilem praescisse et praedestinasse angelos sanctos et homines electos ad vitam gratis aeternam.'

[423] Isidore of Seville, *Sent.* ii, vi, 1, PL 65.656A.

[424] For example, Godescalc, *Confessio brevior*, ed. Lambot, 54: 'Unde dicit et sanctus Isidorus: Gemina est praedestinatio sive electorum ad requiem, sive reproborum ad mortem'; *Responsa de diversis* 7, ed. Lambot, 154–5.

[425] *Opuscula theologica* 20, ed. Lambot, 279–82.

[426] *De praedestinatione* 14, ed. Lambot, 238. The same conclusion was expressed more forcefully by Servatus Lupus, *Quaestiones*, PL 119.646A–B.

so that the precise meaning of the term 'predestine' cannot be assumed to be the same in the following statements:

1. God has predestined the elect to salvation.
2. God has predestined the wicked to damnation.

Although this would not satisfy Prudentius of Troyes,[427] it served to draw attention to some of the difficulties attending the debate.

The most implacable opponent of the views of Godescalc was Hincmar of Reims, who accused *isti moderni praedestinatiani* of teaching that 'the necessity of salvation has been imposed upon those who are saved, and the necessity of damnation upon those who perish'.[428] This was unacceptable to him, as it appeared to deny the reality of human free will, which Hincmar asserted to be real, even if weakened by the Fall (*per se sufficiens sibi ad malum, languidum autem atque invalidum ad omne bonum*).[429] Hincmar also asserted that Godescalc's statements amounted to a contradiction of the teaching of Augustine, and appealed to the pseudo-Augustinian treatise *Hypognosticon* in support of his refutation of the Benedictine. Citing this work as 'Augustine's book on predestination', Hincmar insisted that predestination and foreknowledge must be distinguished.[430] As Florus of Lyons – a moderate supporter of Godescalc – pointed out, this restricted predestination to the elect, while allowing the divine foreknowledge to apply to both the elect and damned.[431] Florus himself had no difficulty in rejecting the Augustinian provenance of the treatise in question.[432]

In 849, Hincmar convened a synod at Quiercy, which condemned the opinions of Godescalc, and deprived him of his orders. The synod was reconvened by Hincmar in 853, and issued a renewed censure of predestinarianism, based on four fundamental statements.[433]

1. Predestination is to be distinguished from foreknowledge. God can be said to predestine to eternal life, but cannot be said to predestine to punishment. A distinction is thus made between the predestination *of* punishment, and predestination *to* punishment. In effect, this amounts to a restatement of the teaching of the pseudo-Augustinian *Hypognosticon*, noted above. For Hincmar, 'God had predestined what divine equity was going to render, not what human iniquity was going to commit'[434] – that

---

[427] See G. R. Evans, 'The Grammar of Predestination in the Ninth Century', *JThS* 33 (1982), 134–45; idem, *The Language and Logic of the Bible: The Earlier Middle Ages*. Cambridge: Cambridge University Press, 1984, 111–13.

[428] *De praedestinatione* 26, PL 125.270B.   [429] *De praedestinatione* 23, PL 125.209C.

[430] *Hypognosticon* VI, ii, 2, PL 45.1657D. Hincmar cites this work in *Epistola* 37b, *MGH.Ep* 8.17–18.

[431] *Liber de tribus epistolis* 34, PL 121.1043C.

[432] *Liber de tribus epistolis* 35, PL 121.1044–7. The *Liber de tribus epistolis* is of considerable importance in connection with our knowledge of the Synod of Quiercy.

[433] D 621–4.   [434] Hincmar, *Epistola* 37b, *MGH.Ep* 8.19.

is, God has predestined that evil will be rewarded with punishment, but *not* the evil that will be thus punished.

2. The human *libertas arbitrii*, which was lost in Adam, has been restored in Christ. This section appears to confuse *liberum arbitrium* and *libertas arbitrii* – that is, natural and acquired freedom. A similar weakness may be noted in the first section, which asserts that God created humans 'righteous, without sin, and endowed with *liberum arbitrium*'.[435] As Florus of Lyons pointed out, this statement of free will failed to implicate divine grace in human freedom.[436] Florus found a similar weakness in the present section, in that it appeared to make grace a mere consequence of divine foreknowledge.[437] This failure to clarify the relation of nature and grace is one of the most striking features of the opening two statements of this synod.

3. God wills to save all humans, rather than just the elect.

4. Jesus Christ died for *all* humans, and not just for a limited section of humanity. Once more, this amounts to a restatement of Hincmar's position that Christ had suffered and died for all humans, even if they refused to accept his gift of redemption.[438] For Hincmar, God was evidently guilty of injustice if Christ was permitted to die for the elect alone.[439] This teaching was criticised by Florus of Lyons on the grounds that it implied that the blood of Christ was shed in vain (*esse inane et vacuum*) if it was shed for those who did not believe in it.[440] Florus himself argued that Christ's blood was not shed for all men, but for his church, that is, 'all believers in Christ who have been or now are or ever will be'.

Florus drew up seven 'rules of faith' in which he made a careful distinction between the concepts of predestination and foreknowledge, for which he claimed the authority of both Scripture and the fathers:[441]

1. The predestination and foreknowledge of God are, like God, eternal and unchangeable.
2. There is nothing in all creation which is not foreknown or predestined by God.
3. Anything which may be said to have been predestined may also be said to have been foreknown, just as whatever may be said to have been predestined may also be said to have been foreknown. Nothing

---

[435] *D* 621: 'Deus omnipotens hominem sine peccato rectum cum libero arbitrio condidit.'
[436] Florus of Lyons, *De tenenda scriptura veritate* 3, PL 121.1087C–D.
[437] *De tenenda scriptura veritate* 4, PL 121.1091B–92B.
[438] Hincmar, *De praedestinatione* 32, PL 125.309B: 'Sanguis Christi redemptio est totius mundi.'
[439] *De praedestinatione* 34, PL 125.350A.
[440] Florus of Lyons, *Liber de tribus epistolis* 16, PL 121.1015C.
[441] *Liber de tribus epistolis* 1–6, PL 121.989–98.

exists which can be said to have been predestined but not foreknown, and vice versa.

4. The good works of both humans and angels may be said to be fore-known and predestined by God, while their evil works may be said to be foreknown, but not predestined, by God. The tension between this statement and the previous two is not discussed at any length.

5. God's foreknowledge and predestination cannot be said to impose necessity upon anyone. This point had been made against Hinc-mar by supporters of Godescalc, such as Ratramnus[442] and Servatus Lupus.[443]

6. These concepts of foreknowledge and predestination are implied by Holy Scripture, even at those points at which they are not explicitly stated.

7. None of those who are elect may ever perish, just as none of those who are damned can ever be saved.

The pronouncements of the Synod of Quiercy were overturned by the Council of Valence (855).[444] Whereas Quiercy had insisted that there is *una Dei praedestinatio tantummodo*, Valence asserted a double predestina-tion, *praedestinatio electorum ad vitam et praedestinatio impiorum ad mortem*. It must be emphasised that the council understood this latter predesti-nation to be essentially different from the predestination of the elect.[445] The canons of Valence were reaffirmed four years later at a local synod held in Langues. In that same year, it is reported that Nicholas I issued a declaration endorsing the doctrine of double predestination, and the associated teaching that Christ died only for the elect.[446] It is impossible to confirm this report, as no such papal declaration is known to exist. Hincmar, writing in 866, declared his belief that the alleged declaration was a fraud.[447]

The ninth-century debate on predestination was not carried over into the tenth century, which is generally regarded as a period of stagnation or decline, or into the theological renaissance of the late eleventh and the twelfth centuries. While the subject was not debated with the intensity of the ninth century at this time, two general schools of thought concerning the motivation of divine predestination may be discerned.

1. The *majority* opinion recognised that there was no basis whatso-ever in humanity for either predestination to glory or reprobation, the

---

[442] Ratramnus, *De praedestinatione* 2, PL 121.54D, 69B–C.
[443] Servatus, *Epistulae* 3, 4, *MGH.Ep* 6.110–12.   [444] *D* 625–33.
[445] Can. 3, *D* 628: 'In electione tamen salvandorum misericordiam Dei praecedere meritum bonum; in damnatione autem periturorum meritum malum praecedere iustum Dei iudicium.'
[446] The report may be found in the *Annals of Saint-Berlin* 859, as cited in *MGH.SRG* 31.53.
[447] Hincmar, *Epistola* 187, *MGH.Ep* 8.196.

difference resting solely in the divine will itself. This opinion was supported by Peter Lombard in his *Sentences*,[448] and in this he was followed by the majority of the theologians of High Scholasticism, and particularly by the theologians of the early Dominican school. Thus Thomas Aquinas taught that the divine decision in humanity's election was necessarily free and uncoerced, made without reference to foreseen human merit or demerit.[449]

2. The *minority* opinion held that there was some ground in humanity itself for both predestination and reprobation. This opinion is particularly associated with the early Franciscan school, such as Alexander of Hales and Bonaventure. Predestination is understood as an act of intellect, rather than of will; the divine will must be informed by the intellect before the decision to elect or reject, and the information supplied by the intellect relates to the foreseen use of the grace granted to the individual in question.[450]

Duns Scotus departed from the early Franciscan school's teaching on predestination by insisting that predestination was an act of the divine *will* rather than of the divine *intellect*. Predestination is understood as an act of will by which God, in electing rational creatures, ordains them to grace and glory, or the act of intellection which *accompanies* (and not, as in the case of the earlier Franciscan school, *precedes*) this election.[451] Scotus understands predestination as *praedestinatio ad vitam*, to be distinguished from reprobation. One of the most important aspects of Scotus' doctrine of predestination is the means by which he deduces the gratuity of predestination.

Scotus appears to be the first theologian to use the principle that the end is willed before the means to that end (*omnis ordinate volens prius vult finem quam ea quae sunt ad finem*) to demonstrate the utter gratuity of

---

[448] *I Sent.* dist. xl, xli.

[449] *De veritate* q. 6 a. 1, ed. Spiazzi, 1.114: 'Praeexigitur etiam et electio, per quam ille qui in finem infallibiliter dirigitur ab aliis separatur qui non hoc modo in finem diriguntur. Haec autem separatio non est propter diversitatem aliquam inventam in his qui separantur quae possit ad amorem incitare: quia antequam nati essent aut aliquid boni aut mali fecissent, dictum est: Iacob dilexi, Esau odio habui.' However, predestination includes *propositum*, *praeparatio* and *praescientia exitus* (*In I Sent.* dist. xl q. 1 a. 2, ed. Mandonnet, 1.945), whereas reprobation is merely *praescientia culpae et praeparatio poenae* (*In I Sent.* dist. xl q. 1 a. l, ed. Mandonnet, 1.954). Cf. *De veritate* q. 6 a. 3; *Summa Theologiae* Ia q. 23 aa. 3, 5.

[450] Pannenberg, *Die Prädestinationslehre des Duns Skotus*, 30–3, 77–9. For a reliable summary of the two main medieval traditions on the *ratio praedestinationis*, see Johannes Eck, *Chrysopassus praedestinationis* I, 2.

[451] *Opus Oxoniense* I dist. xl q. unica n. 2. For an excellent analysis of Scotus' doctrine of predestination, see Pannenberg, *Die Prädestinationslehre des Duns Skotus*, 54–68, 90–119, 125–39.

predestination.[452] Before Scotus, the gratuity of predestination had been deduced from the gratuity of grace. For Scotus, however, the volition of the end itself must precede the volition of the means to that end – that is, God wills the final glorification of humanity before willing the means by which this end may be achieved. As grace is merely the means to the end of predestination, it is improper to deduce the gratuity of predestination from that of grace, in that grace is logically posterior to predestination. Therefore the election of a soul to glory must precede the foreknowledge of merits, and hence be grounded entirely within the divine will. The logical priority of predestination over the means by which it is attained inevitably means that predestination is totally gratuitous, in that it represents an act of divine will, uninformed by the intellect's analysis of any *ratio praedestinationis in creatura*. The *processus praedestinationis* is therefore such that eternal life precedes merit in terms of its logical analysis, but is consequent to it in terms of its execution in time.[453]

This analysis runs into difficulty in the case of reprobation. Following the teaching of the early Franciscan school, Scotus refuses to concede that God actively wills reprobation. Scotus argues that the foreknowledge of sin must precede reprobation.[454] As all good is to be attributed principally to God, and all evil to people, Scotus argues that different causal processes operate in predestination and in reprobation.[455] As predestination is an act of the divine will, rather than of the divine intellect, Scotus rejects the opinion that foreknowledge is a cause of predestination; the decision of God to predestine a soul to glory does not depend upon information about the soul in question being made available to the divine will by the divine intellect. It is clear that predestination is thus understood to be an active decision on the part of God, rather than the essentially passive endorsement of a prior human decision. This stands in contrast to Scotus' teaching on reprobation, which is understood to be a passive act of divine permission in regard to human sin.

The distinction may be illustrated by considering the cases of Peter and Judas. The former was predestined by God independently of foreknowledge of his merit; God prepared for Peter the means of grace by which he might be glorified. In the case of Judas, however, God merely recognises his sin and punishes him for it. This points to an important

---

[452] H. Lennerz, 'De historia applicationis principii "omnis ordinate volens prius vult finem quam ea quae sunt ad finem"'. As Lennerz notes (245), there is no hint in the text (*Opus Oxoniense* I dist. xli q. unica n. 11) to suggest that Scotus accepted this on the basis of an earlier authority.

[453] Pannenberg, *Die Prädestinationslehre des Duns Skotus*, 90–3.

[454] Pannenberg, *Die Prädestinationslehre des Duns Skotus*, 95–100. The discussion of the question in the later Paris *Reportata* is significantly different (103–11).

[455] *Opus Oxoniense* I dist. xli q. unica n. 12.

difference between Aquinas and Scotus: for the former, God predestines first to grace and subsequently to glory; for the latter, God predestines first to glory and then to grace. It also illustrates a significant difference between the intellectualism and the voluntarism of the early and later Franciscan schools respectively. The intellectualist approach to predestination involves the intellect informing the will concerning the foreseen use an individual will make of a gift of grace, thus permitting the will to make an informed decision. The *ratio praedestinationis* and *ratio reprobationis* are both located in the creature. The voluntarist approach, however, necessarily locates the *ratio praedestinationis* in the divine will, and Scotus' fidelity to the teaching of the earlier Franciscan school on the *ratio reprobationis* appears to involve him in a serious contradiction, in that his voluntarist presuppositions dictate that it should also be located in the divine will.

Scotus' doctrine of predestination has important consequences for his soteriology in general. As is well known, Scotus regards the fall of humans and the incarnation of the Son of God as being essentially independent of each other. The incarnation did not occur as a consequence of human sin; only after the divine foreknowledge of the fall of humanity was Christ's incarnation ordained as a remedy for the sin of humans. Scotus supports this teaching by arguing that a physician necessarily wills the health of his patient before he specified the remedy which will cure them.[456] In other words, the elect are predestined to grace and glory *before* (both *logically* and *chronologically*) Christ's passion was ordained as a means to that end.

This doctrine of predestination was developed in a significant direction by William of Ockham, who also remained faithful to the Franciscan teaching that reprobation is based upon a quality within humanity, rather than upon an act of divine will. For Ockham, *praedestinare*, in its active mood, refers to the future bestowal of eternal life upon individuals, just as *reprobare* refers to the infliction of punishment upon them. It is clear that both verbs have a specifically future reference, so that any proposition which contains the verbs must necessarily refer to the future.[457] Thus the proposition *Petrus est praedestinatus* is not necessarily true, as the verb here appears with reference to the past. The statement can refer only to a future instant during which God will bestow eternal life upon

---

[456] *Opus Oxoniense* III dist. xix q. unica n. 6.
[457] *Tractatus de praedestinatione* q. 1 N, ed. Boehner, 13: 'Quarta suppositio: Quod omnes propositiones in ista materia, quantumcumque sint vocaliter de praesenti vel de praeterito, sunt tamen aequivalenter de futuro, quia earum veritas dependet ex veritate propositionum formaliter de futuro.' Cf. Boehner's analysis of this text: ed. Boehner, 49.

Peter – and only at that instant can the proposition be said to be true. Of course, its truth at that instant guarantees its truth in the past, so that the proposition is then recognised always to have been true. However, the fundamentally eschatological orientation of Ockham's concept of predestination prevents any positive statement concerning the truth of the proposition from being made until that point has been reached. For Ockham, predestination signifies three entities: God, humanity, and eternal life. Ockham rejects any understanding of predestination as a real relation additional to God's own necessary being, or as a *relatio realis* added to humans by virtue of their being predestined. Predestination is defined solely in terms of the final gift of eternal life, given by God to humans.

Ockham's discussion of the *cause* of predestination is generally regarded as being extremely difficult to follow. First, it may be noted that Ockham's understanding of predestination is such that, strictly speaking, it is impossible to speak of its having a cause in the first place. Ockham is prepared to discuss predestination only in terms of the priority of propositions. Ockham provides the following causal sequence of propositions, apparently in the form of an enthymene, to illustrate this point:[458]

1. This person will finally persevere.
2. Therefore this person will be predestined.

The non-syllogistic character of the argument may, of course, be rectified by supplying the assumed major premise: 'A person who finally perseveres will be predestined.' While this constitutes the only permissible statement on the relationship between predestination and human merit which is possible, given Ockham's definitions of the terms, it must be pointed out that there are several passages in which he refers to the relationship between predestination and merit in more traditional terms. On the basis of a careful examination of such passages, it appears that Ockham allows both a general *praedestinatio cum praevisis meritis* and a special and distinct *praedestinatio ex gratia speciali*, both possible *de potentia ordinata*. Some will be saved on account of their merits, as without acting freely they would not merit their salvation. As predestination is equivalent to being given eternal life, these individuals may be said to have merited their predestination, *provided that* the explicitly future reference of this statement is acknowledged. Only when eternal life is finally bestowed upon individuals can they be said to be predestined, and only then can the causality of the matter be properly discussed. In the case of other individuals (St Paul being isolated as a specific example), predestination

---

[458] *Tractatus de praedestinatione* q. 4 B, ed. Boehner, 36.

is regarded as arising for no other reason than that God desires their salvation without merit.

The obscurity surrounding Ockham's pronouncements upon predestination has led to the drawing of a number of questionable conclusions in connection with them. Oberman concludes that Ockham taught predestination *post praevisa merita*,[459] which, in addition to being a questionable interpretation of Ockham's teaching in the first place, compounds the confusion still further by introducing the terminology of Protestant orthodoxy where it is clearly totally out of place and seriously misleading. As we have argued elsewhere,[460] Ockham's doctrine of predestination is best approached through the writings of Gabriel Biel, which may be treated as a commentary upon Ockham. Biel himself pronounced his *Collectorium* to be an attempt to summarise the leading themes of Ockham's works. In fact, Biel's discussion of predestination represents a considerable expansion, rather than an abbreviation, of Ockham's statements on the matter.[461] We therefore propose to analyse Biel's doctrine of predestination as an influential late-medieval interpretation of Ockham's teaching on the matter.

Heiko A. Oberman's analysis of Biel's doctrine of predestination is confused by his use of the categories of predestination *post praevisa merita* and *ante praevisa merita*. Biel, naturally, uses neither phrase,[462] nor does he employ the conceptual framework within which Protestant orthodoxy discussed the doctrine of justification. Biel, it must be emphasised, is entitled to be interpreted by the standards, and within the context, of his own conceptual framework, rather than having an alien framework imposed upon him. Following Ockham, Biel understands the term predestination to have a specifically future reference. If individuals receive eternal life, they may be said to be predestined *at that moment* – but not before. If God chooses to accept *viatores* to eternal life at the end, they may be said to be predestined from that moment, and from that moment only. Of course, their predestination at that moment demonstrates their predestination at earlier points – but it is impossible to verify the statement

---

[459] Oberman, *The Harvest of Medieval Theology*, 211. Oberman here finds himself in conflict with Seeberg and Vignaux, both of whom correctly find a concept of predestination in the strict sense in Ockham's thought (206–11).

[460] McGrath, 'The Anti-Pelagian Structure of "Nominalist" Doctrines of Justification', 108–10.

[461] On Biel's relation to Ockham, see M. L. Picascia, *Un occamista quattrocentesco, Gabriel Biel*, Florence: La Nuova Italia, 1971, 37–41. Cf. *In I Sent.* dist. xli q. unica a. 2 conc. 3.

[462] As pointed out by F. Clark, 'A New Appraisal of Late Medieval Nominalism', *Gregorianum* 46 (1965), 733–65. Oberman appears to be dependent upon Feckes at this point: see Feckes, *Die Rechtfertigungslehre des Gabriel Biel*, 88 n. 268.

until the actual bestowal of eternal life takes place. The statement 'A is predestined' cannot be verified until A actually has eternal life bestowed upon him by God.[463]

Oberman asserts that Biel cannot have a meaningful doctrine of predestination, on the grounds that his Pelagian doctrine of justification makes predestination not merely superfluous, but actually destructive.[464] Oberman's criticism of Biel may be rejected, however, for two reasons. First, it is dependent upon Oberman's prior conviction that Biel teaches a Pelagian doctrine of justification, which we have already seen to be highly questionable. Second, Oberman misunderstands Biel to refer predestination to *justification*, whereas it is clear that Biel refers it to the final bestowal of eternal life. This misunderstanding appears to have arisen through Oberman's approaching Biel through the later Protestant understanding of the nature of predestination, evident in his unjustifiable use of terms such as *praedestinatio ante praevisa menta*. The justification of sinners does not demonstrate their predestination, which is demonstrated only by their final glorification. The justification of humans does not necessarily imply their future glorification.

A consideration of Biel's discussion of the grounds of merit (*ratio meriti*) makes Oberman's thesis even more improbable. Eternal life cannot be merited *de congruo*, but only *de condigno* by the *viator* in possession of a habit of grace.[465] The ultimate grounds of merit, however, lie in the divine will, which leads to a hiatus between the moral and the meritorious realms. The *ratio meriti* lies outside of humanity, in the extrinsic denomination of the divine acceptation. Applying these observations to Biel's doctrine of predestination, we find that we are forced to draw a conclusion very different from that of Oberman. Like Ockham, Biel recognises two modes of predestination, which may be termed *praedestinatio cum praevisis meritis* and *praedestinatio ex gratia speciali*. The former term is to be preferred to Oberman's anachronistic and misleading *praedestinatio post praevisa merita*. It will be evident that if an individual, such as St Paul, is predestined *ex gratia speciali*, the *ratio praedestinationis* will lie outside humans.

Some commentators, however, appear to assume that the general mode of predestination *cum praevisis meritis* locates the *ratio praedestinationis* within humans, so that humans may be said to occasion their own predestination. It will be evident that this is not the case. Even in this mode of predestination, the *ratio praedestinationis* lies outside of humanity, precisely because the *ratio meriti* lies outside of humans in the extrinsic

---

[463] *In II Sent.* dist. xxvii q. unica a. 3 dub. 4, ed. Werbeck/Hoffmann, 2.523.11–16.
[464] Oberman, *The Harvest of Medieval Theology*, 196.
[465] *In II Sent.* dist. xxvii q. unica a. 1 nota 1.

denomination of the *acceptatio divina*. If the grounds of human predestination by this mode is merit, it must be conceded immediately that the grounds of this merit lie outside of humanity, in the extrinsic denomination of the *acceptatio divina*.

This observation leads to the following important conclusion: predestination *cum praevisis meritis* is itself predestination *ex gratia speciali* mediated through the secondary cause of merit. The two types of predestination are essentially the same, except that one proceeds directly, and the other indirectly through secondary causes. The situation may be represented as follows:

1. Predestination *ex gratia speciali*:
   acceptatio divina → *ratio praedestinationis*.
2. Predestination *cum praevisis meritis*:
   acceptatio divina → *ratio meriti* → *ratio praedestinationis*.

In both cases, the ultimate grounds of predestination lie outside of humanity, in the extrinsic denomination of the divine acceptation. Viewed from the standpoint of the divine acceptation, the two modes are essentially the same; the only difference between them is that one proceeds directly, the other indirectly. In both cases, however, the *ratio praedestinationis* is one and the same, the *acceptatio divina*, external to humans and outside their control.

A very different understanding of the nature of divine predestination, however, emerged during the fourteenth century, and is particularly associated with the academic Augustinian revival at Oxford, and especially at Paris, usually known as the *schola Augustiniana moderna*.[466] In many respects, the *schola Augustiniana moderna* may be regarded as developing a doctrine of predestination similar to that of Godescalc of Orbais. Although it can be argued that Augustine himself did not explicitly teach a doctrine of double predestination,[467] there were those who argued that it represented the logical outcome of his doctrine of grace, and hence claimed the support of the African bishop for their teaching. The origins of this sterner understanding of predestination are usually considered to

---

[466] See McGrath, *Intellectual Origins of the European Reformation*, 82–8. Among older works, see Oberman, *Werden und Wertung*, 81–90; M. Schulze, "'Via Gregorii' in Forschung und Quellen', in H. A. Oberman, ed., *Gregor von Rimini: Werk und Wirkung bis zur Reformation*, Berlin: de Gruyter, 1981, 1–126, 25–64.

[467] As Walter von Loewenich points out, doctrines such as double predestination or irresistible grace are 'tatsächlich bedenkliche Elemente in Augustins Gnadenlehre'; *Von Augustin zu Luther*, 111. Oberman labours under the mistaken apprehension that Augustine's most characteristic teaching on predestination is *praedestinatio gemina*, which goes some considerable way towards explaining his simplistic designation of Bradwardine's theology as 'Augustinian'; Oberman, *Archbishop Thomas Bradwardine*, 145 n. 1.

lie in the anti-Pelagian polemic of the English secular priest, Thomas Bradwardine.

Bradwardine's chief work, *De causa Dei contra Pelagianum*, is a somewhat tedious, rambling work aimed at certain unnamed *Pelagiani moderni*, presumably the Oxford circle based upon Merton College in the fourteenth century, noted for their Ockhamism.[468] According to Bradwardine's own account of the history of his religious opinions, he himself was attracted to Pelagianism in his early days as a philosophy student at Oxford. However, this youthful espousal of some form of Pelagianism – and Bradwardine never favours us with an explicit definition of the term – was to evaporate when confronted with Romans 9:16, which was to become the leading theme of his mature theology. While Bradwardine's theological sources in *De causa Dei* are primarily scriptural, it is clear that his interpretation of these sources is based upon Augustine, whom he values above all others as their interpreter.[469]

Although Bradwardine follows Augustine faithfully in defending the existence of a weakened free will against those, such as *vani astrologi*, who maintained a psychological determinism, he departs significantly from Augustine's teaching in relation to the Fall. For Bradwardine, the human need for grace is a consequence of human creatureliness, rather than of the Fall; even when in Paradise, humanity was impotent to do good. This departure from Augustine is also evident in connection with his teaching on predestination. Although Bradwardine follows Augustine in discussing predestination within the context of the question of final perseverance, his explicit teaching on *double* predestination at once distinguishes him from the authentic teaching of Augustine. Bradwardine's doctrine of predestination is essentially supralapsarian, although it may be noted that he is careful to locate the origin of evil in secondary causes, so that God may be said to predestine *to* evil, but not to *predestine* evil. We may observe in this respect that Bradwardine's discussion of contingency appears to contain several novel elements: contingency is understood not merely to include the non-necessary, but also to express the principle that events may occur at random or by chance, apart from God's providential direction. In rejecting this understanding of contingency, Bradwardine appears to teach that all things happen of necessity, in that God may be said to cause and direct them. On the basis of such presuppositions, it may be conceded that Bradwardine's doctrine of double predestination expresses a metaphysical, rather than a theological, principle.

In the nineteenth century, Bradwardine was widely regarded as having prepared the way for the Reformation through the questions which he

---

[468] For details of this important group based on Merton, see Courtenay, *Adam Wodeham*.

[469] *De causa Dei* I, 35. More generally, see J.-F. Genest, *Prédétermination et liberté créée à Oxford au XIVe siècle: Buckingham contre Bradwardine*, Paris: Vrin, 1992.

raised, and through the influence which he mediated through Wycliffe and Huss.[470] This view cannot be maintained in its original form. While Bradwardine emphasised the role of the divine will in predestination, Wycliffe saw predestination as a form of divine truth, known to God by means of the ideas themselves before their actualisation. Thus Wycliffe's doctrine of predestination is not based upon a free decision of the divine will; his understanding of necessity is such that the reprobate are damned by foreknowledge, rather than by an unconditional act of divine will.[471] Wycliffe's determinism at this point may reflect the influence of Bradwardine. It is also quite possible that Wycliffe's determinism is a necessary consequence of his doctrine of real universals and possibilities.[472] The attribution of Wycliffe's form of determinism to the influence of Bradwardine is rendered questionable by two considerations. First, Bradwardine's understanding of *necessitas antecedens* presupposes the real existence of human free will – a freedom which Wycliffe explicitly rejects. Second, Bradwardine explicitly condemns as *heretical* the thesis that everything which occurs, takes place by absolute necessity – yet it is precisely this thesis which, some argue, Wycliffe derived from Bradwardine. A more realistic estimation of Bradwardine's significance is that he established an academic form of Augustinianism, based primarily upon his anti-Pelagian writings, which eventually became characteristic of the *schola Augustiniana moderna*. Two factors, however, combined to reduce Bradwardine's influence over this school. First, Bradwardine was not a member of a religious order, which would propagate his teaching. By contrast, Gregory of Rimini's teaching was extensively propagated within the Augustinian order. Second, the Hundred Years War resulted in Oxford becoming isolated as a centre of theological study, with Paris gaining the ascendancy. The *schola Augustiniana moderna* thus came to be based on Paris, even though it is possible to argue that its origins lay at Oxford.

---

[470] For example, Harnack, *History of Dogma* 6.169–70. Harnack is unduly and unwisely dependent here upon the earlier study of Gotthard Lechler, *Johann van Wiclif und die Vorgeschichte der Reformation*, Leipzig: Friedrich Fleischer, 1873.

[471] See Laun, 'Die Prädestination bei Wiclif und Bradwardin'. Note especially *De domino divino* I, 14: 'In primis suppono cum doctore secundo, quod omnia quae eveniunt sit necessarium evenire', which apparently refers to *De causa Dei* III, 1: 'omnia quae eveniunt de necessitate eveniunt'. This thesis, however, is condemned by Bradwardine as heretical: *De causa Dei* III, 12. For the important distinction between *antecedent* and *absolute* necessity, as used by Bradwardine, see Oberman, *Archbishop Thomas Bradwardine*, 70–5. Wycliffe's thesis, that everything happens by absolute necessity, was condemned by the Council of Constance on 4 May 1415, and again in papal bulls of 22 February 1418: D 1177.

[472] On which see S. E. Lahey, *Philosophy and Politics in the Thought of John Wycliffe*, Cambridge: Cambridge University Press, 2003, 90. For the understanding of necessity in later medieval thought, see B. R. de la Torre, *Thomas Buckingham and the Contingencies of Futures*, Notre Dame, IN: University of Notre Dame Press, 1987, 41–103.

A doctrine of double predestination, similar in respects to that of Bradwardine, is associated with Gregory of Rimini.[473] Predestination is defined as the divine decision to grant eternal life, and reprobation as the decision not to grant it – and *both* are understood to be acts of divine will. Predestination and reprobation are not based upon foreknowledge of the use made of free will, nor of whether an obstacle will be placed in the path of grace:

It is clear to me from the statements of Scripture and of the saints that the following conclusions must be accepted as true, and taught and preached as such. First, that no-one is predestined on account of the good use of the free will, which God foreknows and considers to his advantage. Second, that no-one is predestined because it is foreknown that he will not finally place any obstacle in the path of habitual or actual grace. Thirdly, that whoever God predestines, is predestined in a manner which is gracious and merciful. Fourthly, that no-one is condemned on account of the evil use of the free will, which is foreknown by God. Fifthly, that no-one is condemned because it is foreseen that he will finally place an obstacle in the path of grace.[474]

The exclusive location of both predestination and reprobation in the divine will runs counter to the general opinion of the period, which tended to locate the cause of reprobation at least partly in humanity itself. Gregory's views were widely propagated within the Augustinian order by theologians such as Hugolino of Orvieto, Dionysius of Montina, Johannes Hiltalingen of Basel, Johannes Klenkok and Angelus Dobelinus.[475]

The renewed interest in, and increasing understanding of, Augustine in the fourteenth and fifteenth centuries are reflected in the increasingly critical approach adopted to the dictum widely attributed to Augustine: *Si non es praedestinatus, fac ut praedestineris*, 'If you are not predestined, endeavour to be predestined!' Johannes Eck, later to be Luther's opponent at the Leipzig Disputation of 1519, described this dictum as a 'teaching of Augustine which is better known than the history of Troy'.[476] In adopting

---

[473] For the best study, see M. Santos-Noya, *Die Sünden- und Gnadenlehre des Gregor von Rimini*, Frankfurt am Main: Peter Lang, 1990. For the older literature, which is still useful, see especially M. Schuler, *Prädestination, Sünde und Freiheit bei Gregor von Rimini*, Stuttgart: Kohlhammer, 1934, 39–69; Vignaux, *Justification et prédestination*, 141–75.

[474] *In I Sent.* dist. xl, xli q. 1 a. 2, ed. Trapp, 3.326.17–26.

[475] On which see Zumkeller, 'Hugolin von Orvieto'; idem, *Dionysius de Montina*, 77–8; idem, 'Der Augustinertheologe Johannes Hiltalingen von Basel', 81–98; idem, 'Johannes Klenkok', 259–66; idem, 'Der Augustiner Angelus Dobelinus', 77–91.

[476] Eck, *Chrysopassus praedestinationis* I, 66: 'Ex data distinctione clare potest haberi verus sensus propositionis divini Augustini, quae est notior alias historia Troiana: "Si non es praedestinatus, fac ut praedestineris" . . . Recipit ergo veritatem, quando intelligitur de praedestinatione secundum quid et secundum praesentem iusticiam, et est sensus*:* Si *non es praedestinatus*, scilicet per praesentam gratiam, *fac* poenitendo et displicentiam de peccatis habendo *ut praedestineris* gratiam acquirendo, a qua diceris praedestinatus secundum praesentem iusticiam.'

this approach to the *ratio praedestinationis*, Eck appears to have believed that he was remaining faithful to the teaching of the early Franciscan school. For Eck, the dictum represented a significant development of the axiom *facienti quod in se est Deus non denegat gratiam*. *Viatores*, by doing *quod in se est*, could ensure that they received the grace necessary to be 'predestined'. Predestination may therefore be regarded as the divine counterpart to people doing *quod in se est*, so that *viatores* may reassure themselves concerning their predestination by performing good works. It is, of course, significant that Eck refers predestination to justification, rather than to the final future bestowal of eternal life.

The non-Augustinian character of this dictum was increasingly recognised during the closing years of the medieval period. For example, Johannes Altenstaig's celebrated theological dictionary of 1517 attributes the maxim to an unnamed doctor: 'if you are not predestined, then get yourself predestined'.[477] In the same year, Johannes von Staupitz published his famous series of lectures on predestination, *Libellus de exsecutione aeternae praedestinationis*, in which he supported his argument to the effect that the temporal election of humanity is posterior to the eternal divine election with a denial of the Augustinian provenance of the maxim.

Finally, it is appropriate to inquire into the *function* of doctrines of predestination within the context of medieval theologies of justification. This function is best demonstrated by considering the profile of Duns Scotus' doctrine of justification. Scotus' doctrine of justification resembles an Iron Age settlement, containing a highly vulnerable central area surrounded by defensive ditches. The two defensive ditches in Scotus' doctrine of justification are his doctrines of absolute predestination and divine acceptation, which emphasise the priority of the divine will in justification. The central area, however, is highly vulnerable to the charge of Pelagianism, in that Scotus insists upon the *activity* of the human will in justification. Any study of Scotus' doctrine of justification which does not take account of the theological context in which it has been placed (i.e., the doctrines of the *acceptatio divina* and absolute predestination) will inevitably conclude that Scotus is guilty of Pelagianism or some kindred heresy. The charges of Pelagianism or 'semi-Pelagianism' brought against Scotus by an earlier generation of scholars are now seen to be somewhat wide of the mark,[478] although it is relatively easy to understand how

---

[477] Johannes Altenstaig, *Vocabularius theologiae* (Hagenau, 1517), art. 'Praedestinatio'.
[478] As first demonstrated by Parthenius Minges, *Die Gnadenlehre des Johannes Duns Scotus auf ihren angeblichen Pelagianismus und Semipelagianismus geprüft*, Münster: Aschendorff, 1906. See further W. Dettloff, 'Die antipelagianische Grundstruktur der scotischen Rechtfertigungslehre'.

these arose. It will, of course, be evident that a weakening of these outer defences without a concomitant strengthening of the inner structure of the doctrine of justification will make such a doctrine increasingly vulnerable to a Pelagian interpretation. It is the opinion of several scholars of the later medieval period that precisely such a weakening may be detected in the soteriology of the *via moderna*,[479] although some reservations are still to be expressed concerning such conclusions. In effect, the theologians of the *via moderna* appear to have recognised the close interconnection between the doctrines of predestination and divine acceptation, with the result that the two outer ditches have become merged into one, although the basic profile of their doctrines of justification remains similar to that of Scotus.

2.9   The critique of the role of supernatural habits in justification

We have already noted how justification is invariably understood to involve a real change in the sinner, and not merely an external pronouncement on the part of God. This change was generally regarded as involving the infusion of a supernatural habit of grace into the souls of humans. It will be clear, however, that there remains an unresolved question concerning the relationship between these aspects of justification. Are these habits infused into humans in order that the humans may be regarded as acceptable by God? Or are humans regarded as acceptable by God, as a result of which the supernatural habits are infused? Although these two may be regarded as being essentially simultaneous, there still remains the question of their *logical* relationship. Is the infusion of supernatural habits theologically prior or posterior to the divine acceptation? It is this question which lay at the heart of the fourteenth-century debate on the role of supernatural habits in justification, which forms the subject of the present section.

The starting point for this discussion is generally agreed to be Peter Lombard's identification of the *caritas* infused into the soul in justification with the Holy Spirit.[480] For Thomas Aquinas, this opinion is impossible to sustain, as the union of the uncreated Holy Spirit with the created human soul appeared to him to be inconsistent with the ontological distinction which it was necessary to maintain between them.[481] Thomas therefore located the solution to the problem in a created gift which is itself

---

[479] For example, Oberman, *The Harvest of Medieval Theology*, 196.
[480] *I Sent.* dist. xvii, 6.   [481] Thomas Aquinas, *In I Sent.* dist. xvii q. 1 a. 1.

produced within the soul by God, and yet is essentially indistinguishable from him – the supernatural habit.[482] The general teaching of the early Dominican and Franciscan schools is that the immediate or formal cause of justification, and hence of divine acceptation, is the infused habit of grace. This opinion is also characteristic of the *schola Aegidiana*, the early school within the Augustinian order, as may be illustrated from the position of Thomas of Strasbourg on this matter: 'nobody can be formally pleasing to God unless informed by created grace from God'.[483] The possibility of a purely extrinsic acceptation is rejected on the grounds that a real change must occur in humans if they are to be acceptable to God, and that such a change is effected solely by a created habit of grace. Grace is *aliquid creatum in anima*, which alone renders humans acceptable to God. The general consensus of the thirteenth century was thus that *gratiae infusio* was prior to *acceptatio divino*.

The fourteenth century saw this consensus shattered through the systematic application of the dialectic between the two powers of God and the concept of covenantal causality. The origins of this critique of the role of supernatural habits in justification is generally regarded as owing its origins to Duns Scotus, whose teaching on the matter we shall consider in detail.[484] The terms *acceptatio* or *acceptio* are used by Scotus primarily to refer to the divine acceptation which not merely wills a thing to be, but also accepts it according to the greater good.[485] Scotus' interpretation of the Lombard at this point is based upon two explicitly acknowledged presuppositions: the reality of the justification of sinners (*iustificatio impii*), and the real possibility of human merit. It is significant that Scotus regards these as *articuli fidei*, and derives them from the Apostles' Creed. The theological problem that requires resolution is the following: how *can* God justify sinners and permit human merit? The explicit linking of these two questions is of considerable significance, as essentially the same solution emerges to both: the *ratio iustificationis* and *ratio meriti* are identical, in that they must both be located in the extrinsic denomination of the *acceptatio divino*.

---

[482] See Iserloh, *Gnade und Eucharistie*, 81: 'Besonders Thomas hatte noch betont, daß das Prinzip des übernatürlichen Handelns dem Menschen innerlich zu eigen sein muß, damit die Handlung freiwillig und verdienstlich ist. Deshalb könne sie nicht vom Heiligen Geist unmittelbar hervorgebracht sein, sondern müße einer dem Menschen inhärierenden Form entspringen.' Cf. T. Bonhoeffer, *Die Gotteslehre des Thomas von Aquin*, Tübingen: Mohr, 1961, 87–97.

[483] *In II Sent.* dist. xvii q.1 a. l.

[484] We here follow Dettloff, *Die Lehre von der acceptatio divina bei Johannes Duns Skotus.*

[485] *Reportata Parisiensis* I dist. xvii q. 2 n. 4. For the biblical provenance of the term, see Dettloff, *Die Lehre von der acceptatio divina bei Johannes Duns Skotus*, 3 nn. 6–21.

Scotus' insistence upon the unity and the simplicity of the divine will leads him to the conclusion that the divine will cannot be altered from within. If God wills to accept something, or if he wills not to accept something else, the reason for the distinction must be regarded as lying outside the divine will itself, if a serious internal contradiction is not to result. That God should choose to save *this* person and to reject *that* person must reflect a fundamental difference between the two people in question, as the divine will is unable, according to Scotus, to move itself to accept one and not the other without external causes. Whether a person is accepted or not must depend upon the individual themselves. (The obvious difficulties which this assertion raises in relation to his teaching on predestination are not discussed.) Therefore, Scotus argues, there must be a habit within humans, by which they can be accepted at a given moment in time, whereas previously they were not regarded as acceptable. This difference, Scotus argues, is the habit of charity.[486] This is the first of four arguments which Scotus brings forward in support of his contention that a habit of charity is required *de potentia ordinata* for justification. His second argument is based upon the immutability of the divine will, and has already been touched upon above. As the divine will is immutable, the diversity apparent in the fact that God accepts some, and not others, must arise on account of a similar diversity within the individuals in question. There must therefore be something inherent within the individual which leads to this diversity of judgement – and Scotus identifies this as the presence, or absence, of the created habit of charity. His third argument is based upon privation. Humans are not born in a state of justice, so they are unable to increase in justice unless it is by means of a supernatural habit. If this were not the case, a human could be both a friend and an enemy of God, both loved and not loved. Therefore there must exist a supernatural habit which can account for this transition from being an enemy of God to being a friend of God – and this is the habit of charity.[487] Finally, Scotus argues that those who deny the necessity of such a habit *de potentia Dei ordinata* must be considered as asserting that an individual is as acceptable to God *before* penitence as *afterwards* – which is heretical.[488] Scotus thus insists that a habit of charity is required for justification *de potentia Dei ordinata*.

Having established this conclusion, Scotus begins to employ the dialectic between the two powers of God to qualify his conclusions. By God's absolute power, God was not under any compulsion whatsoever to accept

---

[486] *Reportata Parisiensis* I dist. xvii q. 1 n. 3.
[487] *Reportata Parisiensis* I dist. xvii q. 1 n. 4.
[488] *Reportata Parisiensis* I dist. xvii q. 1 n. 4.

a soul to eternal life on account of its possession of a created habit of charity, or to employ such intermediates in justification in the first place. God need not do anything by second causes which could be done directly without them. God has ordained, however, that such a habit of charity is required for acceptation and justification. But this necessity arises, not through the nature of divine acceptation itself (*ex natura rei*), but merely on account of the laws which God has established through the divine ordained will (*ex pacto divino*). By God's absolute power, a quite different set of laws might have existed in connection with divine acceptation. While the laws relating to divine acceptation through created habits may be considered to be utterly reliable, they must also be considered to be equally contingent.

This leads to Scotus' important discussion of whether this created habit of charity can be said to be the formal cause of justification, in which the maxim *nihil creatum formaliter est a Deo acceptandum* plays an important role. Scotus begins his discussion by citing Augustine in support of the general consensus of the period to the effect that those who are accepted by God are distinguished from those who are not by their possession of a created habit of charity.[489] This does not, however, mean that the created habit of charity may be regarded as the formal cause of divine acceptation, considered from the standpoint of the one who elicits the act of acceptation (i.e., God), as this must be regarded as lying within the divine will itself.[490] A distinction must be made between the primary cause of divine acceptation (i.e., a *necessary* cause, arising out of the nature of the entities in question) and the secondary cause of divine acceptation (i.e., a *contingent* cause, which has its *esse* solely in the divine apprehension). On the basis of this distinction, Scotus argues that the created habit of charity must be regarded as a secondary cause of divine acceptation. God ordained from all eternity that the created habit of charity should be the *ratio acceptandi*, so that its importance in this connection is contingent, rather than necessary, deriving solely from the divine ordination, and not from any universally valid law. In effect, this amounts to an unequivocal statement of the concept of *covenantal causality*, noted earlier. The inner connection between acceptation and the habit of charity lies in neither the nature of acceptation nor the habit of charity, but solely in the divine ordination that there should be a causal relationship between them, which has now been actualised *de potentia Dei ordinata*.

A further aspect of Scotus' teaching on acceptation which should be noted is his distinction between divine acceptation of a person and divine

---

[489] *Reportata Parisiensis* I dist. xvii q. 2 n. 2: 'sed per solam caritatem distinguitur acceptus Deo a non accepto'.
[490] *Reportata Parisiensis* I dist. xvii q. 2 n. 5.

acceptation of his acts. The *acceptatio personae* takes priority over the *acceptatio actus*.[491] As it is the acceptation of the person which gives rise to the acceptation of their acts, it will be clear that the *ratio meriti* lies outside humanity in the divine acceptation itself. Furthermore, a distinction must be drawn between acceptation to eternal life and to grace. The former relates to the *end* of justification, the latter to its *means*. In keeping with the general Scotist principle that the end is willed before the means to this end, it follows that acceptation to grace is posterior to acceptation to eternal life. Acceptation to grace is merely *acceptatio secundum quid*, as it presupposes *acceptatio simpliciter* – that is, acceptation to eternal life. As we noted earlier (see 2.8), the general profile of Scotus' doctrine of justification is thus such that the fundamental gratuity of justification and predestination are maintained, despite the apparent threat posed to this gratuity by Scotus' insistence upon the activity of the human will.

Scotus' teaching on the secondary and derivative role of the created habit in justification was criticised by Peter Aureole,[492] who is generally regarded as being the most important theologian in the period between Scotus and Ockham. He appears to have been dissatisfied with the Aristotelianism of his period, in that both his psychology and his noetic are fundamentally Augustinian in character. Peter is heavily dependent upon Durandus of St Pourçain, mediated through the quodlibetal questions of Thomas of Wilton.[493] While Peter's epistemology is characterised by his rejection of any realist understanding of universal concepts, it is inaccurate to characterise his epistemology as 'nominalist' in the usual sense of the term; his understanding of the role of *conceptio* in cognition suggests that his particular form of 'nominalism' should be styled *conceptualism*. Peter's theology of justification is of particular interest on account of his explicit and penetrating criticism of Scotus on two matters: the type of denomination required for divine acceptation, and the role of the divine will in predestination.

In marked contrast to Scotus, Peter maintains that, for a soul to be *accepta Deo*, a habit of charity is necessary. In his rejection of Scotus' maxim *nihil creatum formaliter est a Deo acceptandum*, Peter argues that the necessity of the intrinsic denomination of the habit of charity for divine acceptation is itself the consequence of a primordial divine ordination. His teaching on the matter may be summarised in the three propositions which he advances in support of this contention:[494]

---

[491] Dettloff, *Die Lehre von der acceptatio divina bei Johannes Duns Skotus*, 159–60.
[492] See Vignaux, *Justification et prédestination*, 43–95.
[493] As pointed out by A. Maier, 'Literarhistorische Notizen über Petrus Aureoli, Durandus und den "Cancellarius"', *Gregorianum* 29 (1948), 213–51.
[494] For an excellent analysis, see Dettloff, *Die Entwicklung der Akzeptations- und Verdienstlehre*, 29–36.

1. divine acceptation is the natural and necessary result of the presence of a created form in the soul;[495]
2. this form is not itself the consequence of divine acceptation, but itself renders the soul acceptable to God by the application of the divine love;[496]
3. this form, by which the soul is accepted, is some habitual love of God, which is directly infused into the soul by God, and does not arise from natural human powers.[497]

Peter then identifies this *aliqua forma creata* as the habit of charity, directly infused by God himself into the soul of the *viator*. Thus the extrinsic denomination of the divine acceptation is itself based upon the intrinsic denomination of the infused habit of charity.

Peter's criticism of Scotus' doctrine of absolute predestination is based on related considerations. Scotus had taught that God first predestined a soul to glory, and then to grace *quasi posterius*. For Peter, this failed to do justice to the universal saving will of God. The divine will must extend to the salvation of all humans, not merely to those who are predestined. Peter eliminates this apparent arbitrariness on the part of God by insisting that the formal cause of divine acceptation must be considered to be the intrinsic denomination of the habit of charity. By doing this, he effectively reduces predestination to an act of divine power, based upon foreknowledge.[498]

It will be clear that the fundamental disagreement between Peter and Scotus relates to the question of the causality of the supernatural habit of charity. For Scotus, the causality of the habit in connection with divine acceptation is *covenantal*, reflecting the divine ordination that such a causality should exist. For Peter, the causality is *ex natura rei*, itself a consequence of the nature of the created habit of charity and the act of divine acceptation. The nature of the entities implicated in the act dictates that such a causal connection is necessary, independent of any divine ordination concerning it. Once the habit of charity has been infused into the soul of the *viator*, God is obliged, by the very nature of things, to accept that *viator*.

Peter's association of the priority of habit over act was rejected by William of Ockham. The first thesis which Ockham critiques is that a created form in the soul is by its very nature (*ex natura rei*) pleasing to

---

[495] *In I Sent.* dist. xvii q. 1 a. 2; 408 bD: 'Quod est aliqua forma creata a Deo quae ex natura rei et de necessitate cadit sub Dei complacentia et cuius existentiam in anima ipsa gratificetur et sit Deo accepta et dilecta aut cara.'
[496] *In I Sent.* dist. xvii q. 1 a. 2; 410 aD: 'Quod huiusmodi forma qua ex natura ei redditur anima Deo grata non profluit ex divina acceptatione in anima.'
[497] *In I Sent.* dist. xvii q. 1 a. 2; 410 bG: 'Quod forma qua anima sit accepta est quaedam habitualis dilectio, quae ab ipso infunditur nec ex pulis naturalibus generatur.'
[498] *In I Sent.* dist. xl a. 1.

God, so that it results in divine acceptation and the bestowal of grace. Ockham immediately demonstrates the *contingency* of this thesis: *de potentia absoluta*, God may bypass created habits, preparing and accepting the soul to eternal life in the absence of any such habit. God's granting eternal life and the beatific vision to an individual is in no way a consequence of or dependent upon the possession of such a created habit.[499] To those who object that it is only by virtue of the possession of such a habit that a *viator* becomes worthy of eternal life, Ockham replies that all that is actually necessary is that God disposes the *viator* towards eternal life.

Ockham's second argument against Peter is that both being loved and being hated by God are effects of the divine will. To be hated by God, however, does not necessarily result in *aliqua forma creata detestabilis* formally inhering within the soul of the *viator* who is hated by God. It is therefore inconsistent to assert that such a created form is required within the soul of a *viator* if he is to be *loved* by God, while not simultaneously asserting that such a form is required if he is to be *hated* by God. The inconsistency involved is further emphasised by Ockham in connection with the action of the sacrament of baptism. If Peter's thesis is valid, according to Ockham, it must follow that a sinner who is newly converted and baptised would be loved and hated *at the same time*, as the habits of mortal sin and charity would coexist.

Ockham's critique of Peter continues with a strong statement of the priority of acts over habits. The meritorious nature of an act is not located in the fact that the *viator* is in possession of a created habit of charity. Merit has its origin in the uncoerced volition of the moral agent. The criterion of merit or demerit is what God chooses to accept or reject, lying outside the moral agent, and not reflecting any quality (such as a created habit) inherent in the *viator*. God can do directly what he would normally do by a supernatural habit. Although God is *now* obliged to justify humans by means of created supernatural habits, this does not reflect the nature of things, but simply the divine ordination. After considering the opinion of Thomas Aquinas on the *ratio meriti*, Ockham concludes by insisting that, if a created habit is indeed implicated in divine acceptation, this arises purely *ex pacto divino*, not *ex natura rei*.[500] While not questioning the *de facto* necessity of such habits in justification, Ockham demonstrated their

---

[499] *In I Sent.* dist. xvii q. 1. On this, see Vignaux, *Justification et prédestination*, 99–118.

[500] *In I Sent.* dist. xvii q. 2, *Opera theologica* 3.471.15 – 472.5: 'Ideo dico aliter ad quaestionem, quod non includit contradictionem aliquem actum esse meritorium sine omni tali habitu supernaturali formaliter informante. Quia nullus actus ex puris naturalibus, nec ex quacumque causa creata, potest esse meritorius, sed ex gratia Dei voluntari, et libere acceptante. Et ideo sicut Deus libere acceptat bonum motum voluntatis tamquam meritorium quando elicitur ab habente caritatem, ita de potentia sua absoluta posset acceptare eundem motum voluntatis etiam si non infunderet caritatem.'

radical contingency, and thus undermined the conceptual foundations upon which the *habitus* theology had been established in the thirteenth century.

Ockham's basic position was defended by Gabriel Biel, who maintained the *de facto* necessity of habits in justification, while rejecting their absolute necessity.[501] That habits are implicated in the divine acceptation is a matter of theological contingency, in that nothing that is created may be held to necessarily elicit a specific divine action.[502] Biel, however, defends the traditional teaching on the role of created habits in justification with considerable skill. Particular attention should be paid to his argument that actual grace is inadequate to cope with the ravages of human sin: as God cannot accept indifferent or sinful acts, the *viator* would be required to avoid these totally at all times – which is clearly an impossibility. Biel stresses the reality of venial sin, and points out that the concept of *habitual* grace allows for a certain degree of indifference of sinfulness to coexist with acceptability.[503] It must be conceded, however, that the precise significance of the concept of created grace within the context of the soteriology of the *via moderna* is open to question, in that the theological foundations of the concept, laid in the earlier medieval period when the concept of ontological (i.e., *ex natura rei*) causality had been regarded as self-evident, appear to have been quite demolished through the application of the dialectic between the two powers of God and the concept of covenantal (i.e., *ex pacto divino*) causality. The arguments for the necessity of created grace originally rested upon the apparent necessity of created habits in effecting a person's transformation from *homo peccator* to *homo iustus* and his or her acceptance by God. The new emphasis upon the priority of acts over habits called this presupposition into question.

The theologians of the *schola Aegidiana* (i.e., the early school of theology within the Augustinian order, based upon the teaching of Giles of Rome) taught that divine acceptation was contingent upon a created habit of grace. We have already noted this point in relation to Thomas of Strasbourg. This teaching is maintained by several later theologians of the Augustinian order, such as Johannes von Retz.[504] The *schola Augustiniana moderna*, however, followed Scotus and the *via moderna*

---

[501] On this, see Vignaux, *Luther Commentateur des Sentences*, 45–86; Oberman, *The Harvest of Medieval Theology*, 160–84.

[502] *In I Sent.* dist. xvii q. 3 a. 3 dub. 2, ed. Werbeck/Hoffmann, 1.433.5: 'nihil creatum potest esse ratio actus divini'.

[503] *In II Sent.* dist. xxvii q. unica a.1 nota 1.

[504] Zumkeller, 'Der Wiener Theologieprofessor Johannes von Retz', Textbeilage 48: '[nullus] potest esse formaliter carus vel gratus nisi informatus gratia a Deo creata'. Cf. Thomas of Strasbourg, *In II Sent.* dist. xxvi, xxvii q. 1 a. 1.

in teaching the priority of the act of divine acceptation over the possession of created habits. This development is associated with the theologian
usually regarded as having established the theological foundations of the
schola Augustiniana moderna, Gregory of Rimini, who distinguished two
modes by which a soul is accepted by God:[505]

1. an *intrinsic* mode, by a habit of grace informing the soul;
2. an *extrinsic* mode, by which the divine will accepts the soul directly to
   eternal life.

Grace may therefore be understood either as an intrinsic created gift, or as
the extrinsic divine acceptation. The former, however, must be regarded
as contingent, in that God must be at liberty to do directly what he would
otherwise do indirectly, through created intermediates. Thus God normally accepts the *viator* on the basis of created grace informing the soul;
however, as God is the prime cause of the secondary cause of acceptation (i.e., the habit of created grace), God must be regarded as at liberty
to bypass the intrinsic mode of acceptation altogether. Distinguishing
between created and uncreated grace, Gregory argues that the uncreated
gift itself (i.e., the Holy Spirit) is sufficient for acceptation without the
necessity of any created form or habit. Gregory is thus able to maintain
the possibility of a purely extrinsic justification by simple acceptation;
a habit bestowed upon the *viator* bestows no benefits which cannot be
attributed to the Holy Spirit himself.[506]

This logico-critical approach to the role of created habits in justification
was developed by Hugolino of Orvieto, who is distinguished in other
respects as being one of the most conservative anti-Pelagian theologians
of the Augustinian order.[507] Like Gregory, Hugolino was concerned to
preserve the divine freedom in the justification of humanity, particularly in
relation to created habits. The primacy of acts over habits is maintained
uncompromisingly: no created grace, whether actual or habitual, can
render a person *gratus*, *carus*, or *acceptus ad vitam aeternam* before God as
its formal effect. In common with Gregory, Hugolino regards the formal
cause of justification as being the extrinsic denomination of the divine
acceptation.[508] If the possession of a habit of charity were the formal cause
of justification, Hugolino argues, it would follow that a creature (i.e.,

---

[505] *In I Sent.* dist. xvii q. 1 a. 2. On this, see Vignaux, *Justification et prédestination*,
142–53.

[506] *In I Sent.* dist. xvii q. 1 a. 2: 'alioquin . . . caritas creata natura sua aliquam dignitatem in
respectu ad vitam aeternam tribueret animae quam nullo modo posset sibi per seipsum
tribuere Spiritus sanctus'.

[507] Zumkeller refers to him as 'der Vertreter eines ausgesprochenen Augustinianismus';
Zumkeller, 'Hugolin von Orvieto', 110.

[508] Zumkeller, 'Hugolin von Orvieto', 120–1.

the created habit) would effect what was appropriate to the uncreated grace of the Holy Spirit, which is unthinkable. Hugolino thus assigns a minimal role to created habits in justification, tending to see justification as a direct personal act of God himself. Hugolino's extensive use of the dialectic between the two powers of God has raised the question of the influences of the *via moderna* upon his theology, although it is difficult to demonstrate its positive influence upon it. Hugolino's views on divine acceptation appear to be derived from Scotus, probably via Gregory of Rimini, rather than from Ockham.

A similar critique of the role of created habits in justification can be shown to characterise the writings of later theologians of the Augustinian order. Hugolino's teaching was developed by his junior in the order, Dionysius of Montina, who lectured on the *Sentences* at Paris in the academic year 1371–2.[509] A similar critique was developed by Alphonsus of Toledo. Johannes Klenkok insisted that God could undoubtedly remit sin without the necessity for any created qualities within the soul.[510] A similar conclusion is drawn by Johannes Hiltalingen of Basel.[511] The position of Angelus Dobelinus is less certain, although he is clearly unhappy about the underlying rationale for the necessity of created habits in justification. Dobelinus himself clearly attached considerably greater importance to the uncreated gift of the Holy Spirit than to created habits.[512] In this, he may be regarded as having been followed by Johannes von Staupitz, who emphasised the priority of *gratia increata* over *gratia creata*; the movement of the soul towards God in justification is effected by none other than the Holy Spirit himself. Indeed, there are grounds for suspecting that Staupitz may have abandoned the concept of a created habit of grace altogether.[513]

This late medieval critique of the role of created habits in justification, with an increased emphasis upon the role of uncreated grace in the person of the Holy Spirit, constitutes the background against which Luther's early critique of the role of habits in justification should be seen.[514] Luther argues that the habit required in justification is none other than the Holy Spirit: 'habitus adhuc est spiritus sanctus'.[515] There is every reason to suppose that Luther's critique of the role of created habits in justification, and his emphasis upon justification as a personal encounter of the

---

[509] Zumkeller, *Dionysius de Montina*, 76–81.
[510] Zumkeller, 'Johannes Klenkok', 255–6.
[511] Zumkeller, 'Der Augustinertheologe Johannes Hiltalingen von Basel', 136 n. 246.
[512] Zumkeller, 'Der Augustiner Angelus Dobelinus', 118–19.
[513] Steinmetz, *Misericordia Dei*, 106–7.
[514] See McGrath, *Luther's Theology of the Cross*, 81–5.
[515] WA 9.44.1–4; cf. WA 9.43.2–8.

individual with God, reflect a general disquiet concerning the theological foundations of created grace, and a decisive shift away from created grace towards the uncreated grace of the Holy Spirit in the late medieval period.

The question of the nature of the formal, or immediate, cause of justification is of particular significance to the historian of medieval theology, in that it offers a means by which otherwise very similar theological schools of thought may be differentiated. Thus it allows the *schola Aegidiana* to be distinguished from the *schola Augustiniana moderna*, as well as from the early and later Franciscan schools. It emerged as an important issue in its own right at the Council of Trent, whose discussion of the question can be understood only in the light of these medieval debates.

2.10   The medieval schools of thought on justification

In the course of the late eleventh and early twelfth centuries there was a remarkable advance and consolidation within the church and society as a whole, in literature, science, philosophy and theology.[516] In part, this renaissance must be regarded as a direct consequence of increasing political stability in western Europe, a fact which is recognised by several writers of the period, such as Andrew of St Victor, who shrewdly observed that it was difficult to pursue wisdom in the midst of wars and civil unrest.[517] The rise of canonical theology had been greatly stimulated by the emergence of the church as a unifying social force during the Dark Ages, and its development was to reach its zenith during the twelfth century, under Gratian of Bologna and Ivo of Chartres.[518] The Berengarian and Investiture controversies further stimulated the need for systematic codification in theology. This need for theological development and codification was met by the monastic and cathedral schools, which quickly became the intellectual centres of a rapidly developing society. It is a simple matter to demonstrate that each of these schools developed its own particular and characteristic stance on theological and spiritual matters, and it is the purpose of the present section to document the different interpretations of the doctrine of justification which emerged from such schools in the medieval period.

---

[516] R. L. Benson, *Renaissance and Renewal in the Twelfth Century*, Oxford: Clarendon Press, 1982; R. N. Swanson, *The Twelfth-Century Renaissance*, Manchester: Manchester University Press, 1999.

[517] MS 45, Pembroke College, Cambridge; cited in B. Smalley, *The Study of the Bible in the Middle Ages*, Notre Dame, IN: University of Notre Dame Press, 1970, 116 n. l.

[518] E. A. Friedberg, *Die Canones-Sammlungen zwischen Gratian und Bernhard von Pavia*, Graz: Akademische Verlagsanstalt, 1958.

The ninth century saw the development of St Gall, Reichenau, Tours, Mainz, Corbie, Laon and Reims as theological centres.[519] The rise of the great cathedral schools in the eleventh century appears to be largely due to the instructions issued in 1079 to his bishops by the reforming pope Gregory VII, to the effect that all bishops should 'cause the discipline of letters to be taught in their churches'.[520] By the year 1197, which witnessed the death of Peter the Chanter,[521] Paris had become established as the theological centre of Europe.[522] During the course of the twelfth century, the Parisian schools of the Ile de la Cité and the abbeys of the Left Bank would far surpass in importance those of Léon, Chartres, Bec, Reims and Orléans, which had dominated the eleventh century.[523] The rise of the Left Bank schools was largely a consequence of the migration of masters from the Ile de la Cité to evade the jurisdiction of the chancellor. The masters' practice of placing themselves under the jurisdiction of the independent congregation of St Geneviève would receive formal papal authorisation only in 1227, but was widespread in the late twelfth century. The second half of the twelfth century was dominated by the schools based upon masters such as Peter Abailard, Gilbert of Poitiers, Peter Lombard and Hugh of St Victor. These schools were, however, of relatively little significance in connection with the development of the doctrine of justification.

A development which, though not theological in itself, was to have an incalculable effect upon the course of the medieval understanding of justification, was the establishment of the Dominican and Franciscan schools at Paris in the early thirteenth century. The Friars Preachers arrived at Paris in 1218 and the Friars Minor the following year. Until the arrival of the friars at Paris, teaching at the University of Paris had been solely the responsibility of the secular clergy. Neither the Dominicans nor the Franciscans can be regarded as having come to Paris with the object

---

[519] See J. J. Contreni, *The Cathedral School of Laon from 850 to 930*, Munich: Arbeo 1978; J. Marenbon, *From the Circle of Alcuin to the School of Auxerre*, Cambridge: Cambridge University Press, 1981.

[520] 'Ut omnes episcopi artes litterarum in suis ecclesiis docere faciant': cited in P. Delhaye, 'L'Organisation des écoles au XII siècle', *Traditio* 5 (1947), 240.

[521] J. W. Baldwin, *Masters, Princes and Merchants: The Social Views of Peter the Chanter and his Circle*, 2 vols., Princeton: Princeton University Press, 1970.

[522] This is demonstrated, rather than contradicted, by the infamous condemnations of 1277: see J. Aertsen et al. (eds.), *Nach der Verurteilung von 1277: Philosophie und Theologie an der Universität von Paris im letzten Viertel des 13. Jahrhunderts*, Berlin: de Gruyter, 2001.

[523] On the role of Parisian masters at this time, see W. J. Courtenay, *Teaching Careers at the University of Paris in the Thirteenth and Fourteenth Centuries*, Notre Dame, IN: University of Notre Dame, 1988. There is also some useful material in M. M. McLaughlin, *Intellectual Freedom and Its Limitations in the University of Paris in the Thirteenth and Fourteenth Centuries: The Academic Profession*, New York: Arno Press, 1977.

of founding theological schools, which makes subsequent events all the more significant. By the year 1229, both orders were established at their Parisian houses, at which they carried out teaching in addition to their other work. Theology was taught at the university by secular masters, who held eight chairs of theology according to the decree of Innocent III of 14 November 1207.[524] By 1229, this number had risen to twelve, of which three were reserved for canons of Notre Dame.[525]

In 1229 a dispute arose which led to the 'Great Dispersion' of masters and students between March 1229 and April 1231. Although the masters left Paris for other centres of study, the friars continued their work. As they were not subject to the normal university discipline, they were not obliged to join the general exodus. Among those who left Paris for Cologne was a certain Boniface, who left vacant his chair of theology. His place appears to have been taken by Roland of Cremona, a Dominican student of the secular master John of St Giles. Roland was granted his licence in theology by William of Auvergne, bishop of Paris, over the head of his chancellor.

The second Dominican chair was established the following year, when John of St Giles himself entered the Dominican order on 22 September 1230. This second chair of theology would thereafter be known as the 'external' chair, reserved for Dominican masters from outside Paris. The Franciscan chair was established in 1236 or 1237, when an English secular master, Alexander of Hales, caused a sensation by joining the Friars Minor. By 1237, therefore, three of the twelve chairs in theology at the University of Paris were reserved for members of the Dominican or Franciscan orders. The establishment of these chairs may be regarded as marking the first phase of the conflict between the friars and the secular masters which was so characteristic a feature of the university during the thirteenth and fourteenth centuries; the secular masters appear to have been convinced that the friars deliberately remained in Paris during the Dispersion to take advantage of their absence.[526]

The significance of the University of Paris to our study may also be illustrated from the later medieval period, in that both the *via moderna*

---

[524] *Chartularium Universitatis Parisiensis*, ed. H. Denifle and E. Chatelain, 4 vols., Paris: Delalain, 1889–97, 1.65 n. 5.

[525] *Chartularium Universitatis Parisiensis*, 1.85 n. 27. The number of chairs over the period was as follows: 1200–18, 8; 1218–19, 10; 1219–21, 11; 1221 onwards, 12. For details, see P. Glorieux, *Répertoire des Maîtres en théologie de Paris au XIII siècle*, 2 vols., Paris: Vrin, 1933–4.

[526] H. Rashdall, *The Universities of Europe in the Middle Ages*, 3 vols., London: Oxford University Press, 1935, 1.370–6; P. R. McKeon, 'The Status of the University of Paris as *Parens Scientiarum*: An Episode in the Development of its Autonomy', *Speculum* 39 (1964), 651–75; M.-M. Dufeil, *Guillaume de Saint-Amour et la polémique universitaire parisienne 1250–1259*, Paris: Picard, 1972, 146–282.

and the *schola Augustiniana moderna* were well represented in its faculties in the fourteenth and fifteenth centuries. The faculty of arts at Paris initially attempted to stem the influence of the *via moderna*; on 29 December 1340, a statute condemning the *errores Ockanicorum* took effect.[527] Henceforth any candidate wishing to supplicate for the degree of Master of Arts at Paris would have to swear that, in addition to being under the age of twenty-one and having studied arts for six years, he would observe the statutes of the faculty of arts *contra scientiam Ockamicam*, and abstain from teaching such doctrines to their pupils. Paris would remain a stronghold of the *via moderna* until the sixteenth century. During the fourteenth century, the *schola Augustiniana moderna* appears to have become established at the university through the activity of Gregory of Rimini and his followers, such as Hugolino of Orvieto.[528] The historical significance of both these movements, however, is largely due to their influence upon the development of the Reformation in general, and the theology of Martin Luther in particular, with the result that they are usually discussed in relation to the late medieval universities of Germany, rather than Paris itself.

In the following sections, we shall characterise and compare the five main schools of thought on justification during the medieval period. In view of the importance of the *via moderna* and *schola Augustiniana moderna* to the development of the theology of the Reformation, we propose to consider these in more detail than the other three.

2.10.1 The early Dominican school

On 24 June 1316, a decree of the provincial chapter of the Dominican order in Provence was promulgated, stating that the works of Albertus Magnus, Thomas Aquinas and Peter of Tarantaise were to be regarded as normative in doctrinal matters. Of these three doctors, however, it is quite clear that Thomas himself was regarded as pre-eminent; in 1313, the general chapter of the order ruled that no friar of the order was to be permitted to undertake theological studies at Paris without three years' study of the works of Thomas, and that no *lector* was to be permitted to mention opinions contrary to his teaching, unless such opinions were refuted immediately.

---

[527] For the text, see R. Paqué, *Das Pariser Nominalistenstatut: Zur Entstehung des Realitätsbegriffs der neuzeitlichen Naturwissenschaft*, Berlin: de Gruyter, 1970, 8–12.

[528] For a list of the doctors of this school, see A. Zumkeller, 'Die Augustinerschule des Mittelalters: Vertreter und philosophisch-theologische Lehre', *AnAug* 27 (1964), 167–262, especially 174–6. The close association of the school with Paris will be evident.

It will be clear that these rulings were made without apparent reference to the diversity of opinion which may be found within Thomas' writings, some of which we have noted during the course of the present study. Thus his doctrine of justification as stated in the *Commentary on the Sentences* (1252–6) is quite distinct from that stated in the *prima secundae* of the *Summa Theologiae* (1270). There appears to have been some confusion within the early Dominican school as to which of these works should be used in ascertaining the authentic position of the Angelic Doctor. It may be pointed out that the distinctive contribution of Johannes Capreolus to the development of the later Thomist school was his insistence that the *Summa* represents the final determination and retraction of Thomas' earlier statements.[529]

Along with other Parisian masters of the period, Roland of Cremona is known to have developed an interest in Aristotle, and this interest is reproduced by his successors within the early Dominican school. Of particular importance in this respect is his ontological interpretation of merit (see 2.6), and his definition of justification as a *motus* from sin to rectitude. The Aristotelian foundations of Thomas Aquinas' teaching on the *processus iustificationis* (see 2.1) and the necessity of a disposition towards justification (see 2.3) are particularly significant examples of the theological influence of Aristotle over the emerging theology of the early Dominican school. The positive estimation of Aristotle is one of the most prominent features of the early Dominican school, and is particularly evident when contrasted with the strong Augustinianism of the early Franciscan school.

One of the most important aspects of the early Dominican school's teaching on justification relates to the question of 'original justice', *iustitia originalis*. The thirteenth century witnessed considerable discussion of the question of whether the first human was created in a state of grace or a purely natural state. The general consensus in the earlier part of the period was that Adam was created in the integrity of nature, but not in a state of grace. If Adam received the gift of sanctifying grace, he did so voluntarily.[530] In his earlier works, Thomas Aquinas appears to register a hesitant disagreement with the opinion of Albertus Magnus on this question. It seems clear that Thomas favoured the opinion that Adam received grace at the instant of his creation, as judged from his discussion of the

[529] See M. Grabmann, 'Johannes Capreolus O.P., der "Princeps Thomistarum" und seine Stellung in der Geschichte der Thomistenschule', in L. Ott, ed., *Mittelalterliches Geistesleben*, Munich: Hueber, 1955, 3.370–410.
[530] This is the position of Peter Lombard, Alexander of Hales, Albertus Magnus and Bonaventure; see R. Garrigou-Lagrange, *La Synthèse Thomiste*, Paris: Desclée de Brouwer, 1947, 305–11.

matter in the *Commentary on the Sentences*.[531] This opinion is unequivocally stated in the later disputed questions *De malo*,[532] which affirms that
iustitia originalis, which Adam received at the moment of his creation,
included sanctifying grace (*gratia gratum faciens*).[533]

Much the same view is advocated in the *Summa Theologiae*, in an important discussion of the Old Testament locus which usually constituted the
point of departure for speculation on this matter: *Deus fecit hominem rectum* (Ecclesiastes 7:30). What can this mean except that God created
humanity, and then bestowed original justice upon it? The basis of this
original justice must be considered to be the supernatural submission of
the will to God, which can be effected only through sanctifying grace.[534]
This original justice pertains to the essence of the soul, and is inherent
within humans. Thomas is careful to point out this does not amount to
an equation of nature and grace. For Thomas, the *status naturae inte-
grae* is merely an abstraction; not even Adam could ever be said to have
existed in this state, for at the instant of his creation he was endowed with
the *donum supernaturale* of *gratia gratum faciens*. Although nature must
be regarded as being good, it is nevertheless incomplete, and requires
ordering towards its principal good (i.e., the enjoyment of God) through
the aid of supernatural grace. It therefore follows that original sin may
be formally defined as the privation of original righteousness. Although
Thomas follows Albertus Magnus in adopting Anselm of Canterbury's
definition of original sin as *privatio iustitiae originalis*, it is necessary to
observe that he uses the term *iustitia* in a significantly different sense
from Anselm.

The prime effect of the first sin, according to Thomas, is thus the
instantaneous fall of Adam from the *supernatural* plane to which he had
been elevated at the moment of his creation through *gratia gratum faciens*
to the purely *natural* plane. The human nature which is transmitted to
us from Adam is thus nature deprived of the supernatural gifts once
bestowed upon Adam, but capable of receiving such gifts subsequently –
a principle expressed succinctly in the theological maxim *anima naturaliter
capax gratiae*.

The general characteristics of the early Dominican school at Paris, as
exemplified by Thomas Aquinas, may be summarised as follows.
1. The possibility of humanity's meriting justification *de congruo* is
   rejected on the basis of the general principle that all merit presupposes grace. It must be pointed out that this opinion is characteristic

---

[531] *In II Sent.* dist. xx q. 1 a. 3 appears to avoid any firm statement on the matter. A more
definite statement may be found later: *In II Sent.* dist. xxix q. 1 a. 2.
[532] *De malo* q. 4 a. 2 ad 17um.   [533] *Summa Theologiae* Ia q. 95 a. l.
[534] *Summa Theologiae* Ia q. 100 a. 1 ad 2um.

of the *Summa Theologiae* but *not* of the earlier *Commentary on the Sentences*, in which a congruously meritorious disposition for justification is upheld. There appears to have been some confusion within the early Dominican school upon this matter.

2. The possibility of humans' knowing with absolute certitude whether they are in a state of grace is rejected.[535] God is totally beyond human comprehension, and although believers may know in a conjectural manner whether they have grace – for instance, by observing whether they take delight in God – they cannot know *beyond doubt* whether they are in a state of grace. It may be noted that this represents the general medieval opinion on this question, rather than the peculiar teaching of the early Dominican school.

3. Original righteousness is understood to include the gift of sanctifying grace, so that the formal element of original sin may be defined as *privatio iustitiae originalis*.

4. The formal cause of justification is defined as being the habit of created grace.

5. The principle of merit is understood to be the habit of created grace.

6. The necessity of a human disposition towards justification is maintained, on the basis of the Aristotelian presupposition that motion implies premotion.

7. A strongly maculist position is adopted in relation to the conception of Mary.[536] Mary, in common with the remainder of humanity, is understood to be affected by sin as a *macula animae* (Stephen Langton).

2.10.2   The early Franciscan school

The early Franciscan school of theology owed its origins to its first great Parisian master, Alexander of Hales. The work which is generally known as the *Summa Fratris Alexandri*, long thought to be an authentic work of Alexander's, is now regarded as being composite.[537] Alexander's authentic lectures on the *Sentences*, generally considered to date from the period 1222–9, were discovered in the form of students' notes in 1946.[538] On

[535] *Summa Theologiae* IaIIae q. 112 a. 5. Thomas elsewhere teaches that the grace of final perseverance is a further gift of God to the elect, which cannot be merited: IaIIae q. 114 a. 9.

[536] See, for example, *Summa Theologiae* IIIa q. 27 a. 2 ad 3um. This question is discussed further below in 2.10.3.

[537] See the classic work of J. Auer, 'Textkritische Studien zur Gnadenlehre des Alexander von Hales', *Scholastik* 15 (1940), 63–75.

[538] Published as *Glossa in Quatuor Libros Sententiarum Petri Lombardi*. For an excellent introduction, see *Glossa* 4, 18*–44*. Alexander is of particular significance in that it was through him that Peter Lombard's *Sentences* was divided into its present divisions, and became the standard text in the schools; see I. Brady, 'The Distinctions of the Lombard's Book of Sentences and Alexander of Hales', *FrS* 25 (1965), 90–116.

the basis of these, and a series of disputed questions which antedate his joining the Franciscan order, it is possible to argue that the main features of the early Franciscan school's teaching on justification are essentially identical with the early teaching of Alexander of Hales. In other words, Alexander does not appear to have modified his theology significantly upon joining the Friars Minor, and subsequent Franciscan masters perpetuated his teachings as the authentic teaching of their order. This may be illustrated with reference to his teaching on original justice.

Alexander notes that there are two opinions concerning Adam's pristine state: the first is that he was created in a purely natural state; the second that he was created in a state of *gratia gratum faciens*.[539] The opinion adopted is once more based on Ecclesiastes 7:30, *Deus fecit hominem rectum*. Alexander draws a distinction between natural and gratuitous justice, and argues that the verse in question clearly refers to a state of natural justice.[540] In this, he was followed by Odo Rigaldi, who taught that Adam was created in a state of purely natural justice and innocence, relying upon actual grace (*gratia gratis data*) rather than *gratia gratum faciens*.[541] Bonaventure similarly states that humans were not endowed with *gratia gratum faciens* at their creation,[542] while recognising their endowment with *gratia gratis data*.

The characteristic features of the early Franciscan school's teaching on justification are the following.

1. The possibility of humanity's meriting justification *de congruo* is upheld.
2. The possibility of absolute certitude of grace is rejected.
3. Original righteousness is understood to include the gift of actual grace; the opinion that the gift included *gratia gratum faciens* is rejected.
4. The formal cause of justification is understood to be a created habit of grace.
5. The formal principle of merit is understood to be a created habit of grace.
6. The necessity of a human disposition towards justification is maintained upon Augustinian psychological grounds, rather than upon the basis of an Aristotelian analysis of the nature of *motus*.
7. A maculist position is adopted in relation to the conception of Mary.

The early Franciscan school can be shown to have found itself in difficulty towards the end of the thirteenth century in relation to its understanding

---

[539] *In II Sent.* dist. xxiv n.1, 2.206.9–11.
[540] *In II Sent.* dist. xxiv n.1, 2.207.14–19.   [541] *In II Sent.* dist. xxix q.1, 90.57–88.
[542] *In II Sent.* dist. xxxiv pars 2 a. 3 q. 2 ad 3um. For a useful summary of the differences between Bonaventure and Thomas, see Bruch, 'Die Urgerechtigkeit als Rechtheit des Willens nach der Lehre des hl. Bonaventuras', especially 193–4. See further Kaup, 'Zum Begriff der justitia originalis in der älteren Franziskanerschule'.

of the relationship between nature and grace. The Augustinianism of the early school is not restricted to its soteriology and psychology, but extends also to its epistemology. The early Franciscan school adopted the Augustinian doctrine of divine illumination,[543] which is actually an elaboration of a metaphor which Augustine himself used in an attempt to explain how God makes himself understood to humanity. God is to the human mind what the sun is to the physical world. Just as a physical object cannot be seen without the light of the sun, so the mind is unable to perceive spiritual truths without divine illumination. Just as the sun is the source of the light by which humans are able to see physical objects, so God is the sourse of the spiritual light by which humans are able to apprehend divine truth.

It will be evident that this concept has considerable affinity with the Platonic notion of the Good as the sun of the intelligible world. The fundamental difficulty which faced the early Franciscan proponents of divine illumination was that it was far from clear as to whether this illuminating influence of God was to be considered as a *natural* or a *supernatural* light: was it *naturalia* or *gratuita*? Scotus' radical criticism of Henry of Ghent's illuminationism[544] led to the characteristically abstractionist epistemology of the later Franciscan school, and considerable unease concerning illuminationism may be detected in the final years of the early Franciscan school. Thus Peter Olivi stated that he supported the doctrine of divine illumination merely because it happened to be the traditional teaching of his order, while even Matthew of Aquasparta was unable to decide whether divine illumination counted as a 'somewhat general influence' or a 'special influence' of God. The essential problem underlying this question is that of the relationship between nature and grace, and it is precisely this difficulty which emerged from the early Franciscan discussion of the nature and necessity of a human disposition for justification. The essential difficulty facing the early Franciscan theologians was that the transition from nature to grace was prima facie impossible. The transition between opposites was held to be impossible without an intervening stage. But how is this *tertium quid* to be understood?

---

[543] See M. Grabmann, 'Zur Erkenntnislehre des älteren Franziskanerschule', *FS* 4 (1917), 105–18; E. Gilson, 'Sur quelques difficultés de l'illumination augustinienne', *Revue néoscolastique de philosophie* 36 (1934), 321–31; idem, 'Roger Marston, un cas d'Augustinisme avicennisant', *Archives d'histoire doctrinale et littéraire du moyen âge* 8 (1952), 37–42; P. A. Faustino Prezioza, 'L'attività del soggetto pensante della gnoseologia di Matteo d'Acquasparte e di Ruggerio Marston', *Antonianum* 25 (1950), 259–326.

[544] *Opus Oxoniense* I dist. iii q. 4 aa. 1–3. For an outstanding study of Scotus' critique of Henry of Ghent's illuminationism, see P. C. Vier, *Evidence and Its Function according to John Duns Scotus*, New York: Franciscan Institute, 1951. The early Dominican school, it may be noted, was also critical of Augustine's illuminationism; see the classic study of E. Gilson, 'Pourquoi S. Thomas a critiqué S. Augustin', *Archives d'histoire doctrinale et littéraire du moyen âge* 1 (1926–7), 5–127.

The concept of *gratia gratis data* did not appear to resolve the difficulty, as the ontological chasm between nature and grace remained. It must be emphasised that this difficulty arises through the early Franciscan understanding of *iustitia originalis*; for the early Dominican school, humans were *naturally* capable of grace, having been created with this facility; for the Franciscans, however, the possession of *gratia gratum faciens* was not included in the original endowment of nature. The problem of the ontological transition implicit in justification had not been resolved by the time Richard of Middleton's *Commentary on the Sentences* appeared at some point shortly after 1294. The period of the early Franciscan school may be regarded as closing at this point, in that a new approach to the problem was being developed which would avoid this difficulty. The solution to the problem, however, involved the abandonment of much of the earlier Franciscan presuppositions concerning the nature of grace and its role in justification, and the period of the later Franciscan school may thus be regarded as beginning at this point.

2.10.3   The later Franciscan school

The early Franciscan school looked to Bonaventure for its inspiration and guidance; the later Franciscan school substituted for him the colossal figure of Duns Scotus. Although there are undoubtedly Augustinian elements in Scotus' theology, it is quite clear that there has been a decisive shift away from Augustinianism towards Aristotelianism. Furthermore, Scotus' discussion of justification is quite distinct from that of Bonaventure at points of major importance, among which may be noted his teaching on the relationship between the elements of the *processus iustificationis*, on the possibility of extrasacramental justification, on the cause of predestination and on the formal principle of merit and justification.

This latter point is of particular significance in relation to the difficulties we noted in the previous section, which arose in connection with the early Franciscan school's teaching on the relationship between nature and grace. For Scotus, the volition of the end necessarily precedes the volition of the means to that end, so that the precise means by which justification occurs is of secondary importance to the fact that God has ordained that it *will* occur. The increasing emphasis upon the priority of the extrinsic denomination of the divine acceptation over the possession of a habit of grace inevitably led to a marked reduction in interest in the question of how such a habit came about in the soul.

Furthermore, Scotus' concept of covenantal causality eliminated the ontological difficulty felt by the theologians of the early Franciscan school over the possibility of the transition from nature to grace; for Scotus, God had ordained that this transition could be effected through a congruously

meritorious disposition towards justification, so that there was no difficulty in abolishing the hiatus between the states of nature and grace.
Scotus' approach to the question which posed such difficulties for his predecessors in the Franciscan order may therefore be said to have resolved
the problem in two ways. First, the question was discussed in a significantly different context: for Scotus, the divine acceptation was prior to the
possession of a habit of grace, whereas the theologians of the early Franciscan school regarded divine acceptation as posterior to, and contingent
upon, the possession of a habit of grace. Second, the *ex natura rei* concept
of causality, which posed such difficulties for the theologians of the early
Franciscan school, was replaced with an *ex pacto divino* concept, which
eliminated the difficulty at once. These alterations, however, resulted in
significant changes in Franciscan teaching on justification, which will be
noted below.

Scotus' theology of justification, which may be regarded as characteristic of the later Franciscan school, has already been discussed at some
length in terms of its individual aspects. There remains, however, one
aspect of his teaching which was the subject of considerable confusion
in the medieval period itself, and which requires further discussion. This
is the question of the possibility of the certitude of grace. The Council of Trent witnessed a significant debate among the assembled prelates
over Scotus' teaching on this matter, reflecting the considerable difficulty
in interpreting Scotus' pronouncements concerning it.[545] This difficulty
chiefly arises from the fact that Scotus never treats the matter *ex professo*,
although he comments upon it briefly in his discussion of the possibility of extrasacramental justification (see 2.5). In general, however, it is
clear that Scotus rejects the possibility of such certitude. Individuals who
are conscious of having elicited an act of love for God are not able to
conclude that they are in possession of an infused habit of charity as a
result. They cannot deduce this either from the substance or the intensity of the act itself, or from the pleasure or ease with which they elicit
the act. If such a conclusion were possible, believers could know for certain that they were in a state of charity.[546] It is, however, impossible for
believers to know whether they are worthy of love or hate. The impossibility of such certitude is particularly emphasised by Scotus in connection
with the reception of the sacraments.[547] It seems safe to conclude that
Scotus adopts the general position of the twelfth and thirteenth centuries

---

[545] See Heynck, 'A Controversy at the Council of Trent concerning the Doctrine of Duns
Scotus'.
[546] *Opus Oxoniense* IV dist. xvii q. 3 n. 21.
[547] *Reportata Parisiensis* IV dist. ix q. unica n. 2.

by declining to allow anything other than *conjectural* certainty of grace, and rigorously excluding the possibility of *absolute* certitude.

A development of major importance within the later Franciscan schools concerns the doctrine of the immaculate conception.[548] The importance of this doctrine is subsidiary to the development of the doctrine of justification, in that it relates to the extent of Christ's redeeming work. Nevertheless, it came to represent one of the most reliable means of distinguishing the later Franciscan school from its forebears. Prior to Scotus, there appears to have been a general consensus that Mary shared the common human sinful condition. The theologians of the early Dominican school, such as Albertus Magnus and Thomas Aquinas, argued that the exemption of Mary from sin would limit the perfection of the work of Christ, who must be considered to have died for *all* humankind without exception. It is a reflection of Scotus' subtlety that he is able to turn this argument *against* the doctrine into an argument *for* it.

If Christ is the most perfect redeemer, Scotus argued, it must be conceded that he is able to redeem at least one person in the most perfect manner possible. As it is more perfect to preserve someone from sin than to liberate them from it, it follows that the most perfect mode of redemption is preservation from sin. Turning his attention to the pressing question of who that single person might be, Scotus argues that it is appropriate that the person concerned should be the mother of the redeemer himself.[549] Scotus supports this argument with an appeal to the general principle, widely accepted within contemporary theological circles, that the highest possible honour consistent with Scripture and tradition should be ascribed to Mary.[550]

Scotus' influence within the Franciscan order was such that the doctrine of the immaculate conception had become the general teaching of the order by the middle of the fourteenth century,[551] and rapidly became accepted within the *via moderna* and *schola Augustiniana moderna*. The

---

[548] See I. Brady, 'The Development of the Doctrine of the Immaculate Conception in the Fourteenth Century after Aureoli', *FrS* 15 (1955), 175–202; K. Balic, 'Die Corredemptrixfrage innerhalb der franziskanischen Theologie', *FS* 39 (1957), 218–87. See further P. de Alcántara, 'La redención de Maria y los méritos de Cristo', *Estudios franciscanos* 55 (1954), 229–53; M. Mückshoff, 'Die mariologische Prädestination im Denken der franziskanischen Theologie', *FS* 39 (1957), 288–502.
[549] *Opus Oxoniense* III dist. iii q. 1 n. 4.   [550] *Opus Oxoniense* III dist. iii. q. 1 n. 10.
[551] The best study is G. Ameri, *Doctrina Theologorum de Immaculata B. V. Mariae Conceptione Tempore Concilii Basileensis*, Rome: Academia Mariana Internationalis, 1954. For a survey of opinions, see F. de Guimarens, 'La Doctrine des théologiens sur l'Immaculée Conception de 1250 à 1350', *Etudes Franciscaines* 3 (1952), 181–203; 4 (1953), 23–51, 167–87; A. di Lella, 'The Immaculate Conception in the Writings of Peter Aureoli', *FrS* 15 (1955),146–58; E. M. Buytaen, 'The Immaculate Conception in the Writings of Ockham', *FrS* 10 (1950), 149–63.

doctrine is particularly useful in distinguishing the later Franciscan and Dominican schools of theology, although Dominican theologians associated with the *via moderna* – such as Robert Holcot – appear to have experienced some difficulty in accommodating the tension between the teaching of their orders and their schools.[552]

The leading features of the later Franciscan school's teaching on justification may be summarised as follows:

1. The possibility of humans' meriting justification *de congruo* is upheld.
2. The possibility of absolute certitude of grace is rejected.
3. Original righteousness is understood to refer to the gift of actual, rather than habitual, grace.
4. The formal cause of justification is understood to be the extrinsic denomination of the divine acceptation. The intrinsic denomination of the created habit of charity is relegated to the status of a *secondary* formal cause of justification.
5. The formal principle of merit is understood to be the extrinsic denomination of the divine acceptation. Every act of humans is worth precisely what God chooses to accept it for.
6. The necessity of a preparation for justification is upheld. The psychological justification for this preparation, associated with the earlier Franciscan school, now appears to have been abandoned.
7. Mary must be regarded as exempt from the common human condition of original sin, and thus as standing outside the scope of Christ's normal mode of redemption. This does not, however, mean that Scotus denies that Christ redeemed Mary, as some have suggested; rather, a different mode of redemption is envisaged in this specific case.

2.10.4 *The* via moderna

The term *via moderna* is now widely used to refer to the theological school based upon the teachings of William of Ockham, including such theologians as Pierre d'Ailly, Robert Holcot, Gabriel Biel and Wendelin Steinbach, and has more or less completely displaced the potentially misleading term 'Nominalism', frequently employed in the past to designate this school of thought.[553]

The *via moderna* shows signs of having developed a considerable degree of local heterogeneity in the late medieval period, so that making generalisations concerning its theological distinctives is somewhat

---

[552] *Super libros Sapientiae* lect. 160c.
[553] For details of this important historiographical transition, see McGrath, *The Intellectual Origins of the European Reformation*, 67–88.

hazardous. However much the historian may desire to simplify complex situations and depict 'nominalism' as an essentially well-defined and relatively homogeneous movement throughout western Europe, the evidence suggests that the *via moderna* actually developed local characteristics associated with the intellectual centres at which it was based. Although William of Ockham may be credited with the initiation of the movement, its specific local forms at the Universities of Oxford, Paris, Heidelberg and Tübingen were shaped by personalities with differing concerns and emphases. At Paris, the movement was specifically associated with Jean Buridan and Nicolas Oresme; at Heidelberg, with Marsilius of Inghen; at Tübingen, with Gabriel Biel and Wendelin Steinbach.[554]

Although the theologians of the *via moderna* generally adopted a nominalist epistemology, in common with their contemporaries, their characteristic soteriological opinions were quite independent of this nominalism. The characteristic features of the doctrines of justification associated with the theologians of the *via moderna* are similar to those of the later Franciscan school. Despite the nominalism of the former and the realism of the latter, their doctrines of justification are substantially identical. Where differences exist between the two schools, they are primarily concerned with the *conceptual framework* within which the justification of the *viator* was discussed, rather than with the *substance* of their teaching on justification. Indeed, the *via moderna* may be regarded as having exploited the dialectic between the two powers of God and the concept of the *pactum* to place the teaching of the later Franciscan schools upon a firmer conceptual foundation. Furthermore, the differences which exist between the later Franciscan school and the *via moderna* in relation to the conceptual framework within which justification was discussed do not appear to have any *direct* bearing upon the epistemological differences between the schools.

The context within which the question of the possibility of the justification of the *viator* is set by the theologians of the *via moderna* is that of the *pactum* between God and humanity. God has ordained that he will enter into a covenantal relationship with humanity, by virtue of which God chooses to accept human acts as being worthy of salvation, even though

---

[554] On which see such studies as L. M. de Rijk, *Jean Buridan (c. 1292–c. 1360): Eerbiedig ondermijner van het aristotelisch substantie-denken*, Amsterdam: Koninklijke Nederlandse Akademie van Wetenschappen, 1994; P. Souffrin and A. Segonds, *Nicolas Oresme: Tradition et innovation chez un intellectuel du XIVe siècle*, Paris: Editions Les Belles Lettres, 1988; M. J. F. M. Hoenen and P. J. J. M. Bakker, *Philosophie und Theologie des ausgehenden Mittelalters: Marsilius von Inghen und das Denken seiner Zeit*, Leiden: Brill, 2000. The question of Jean Gerson's relationship to the *via moderna* has been the subject of much discussion; see Jan Pinborg, *Logik und Semantik im Mittelalter: Ein Überblick*, Stuttgart: Frommann-Holzboog, 1972, 77–126.

their intrinsic value is negligible. This distinction between the *intrinsic* and *imposed* value of moral acts is of decisive importance, as it permits the axiom *facienti quod in se est Deus non denegat gratiam* to be interpreted in a sense which allows individuals to play a positive role in their own justification, without elevating that role to Pelagian proportions.

In this way, the theologians of the *via moderna* were able to maintain the teaching of both the early and later Franciscan schools concerning the meritorious disposition of humans towards justification, while establishing a conceptual framework within which this teaching could be safeguarded from the charge of Pelagianism. Linked with this was the related concept of *covenantal causality*, by which the theologians of the *via moderna* were able to avoid the ontological difficulties experienced by the early Franciscan school concerning the transition from nature to grace.

One aspect of the soteriology of the *via moderna* which is of particular interest is the Christological lacuna within their understanding of the economy of salvation.[555] It is quite possible to discuss the justification of the *viator* within the terms set by the theologians of the *via moderna* without reference to the incarnation and death of Christ. This point is best seen by considering the following question: what, according to the theologians of the *via moderna*, is the difference between the justification of humans in the period of the Old Testament and in the period of the New? Biel's understanding of the covenant between God and humans is such that God rewards the person who does *quod in se est* with grace, irrespective of whether this pertains under the old or new covenant.

The Old Testament character of the ethics of the *via moderna* has frequently been noted;[556] it does not appear to have been fully appreciated, however, that this arises from the simple fact that, according to the *via moderna*, the Old Testament scheme of justification is essentially the same as that of the New. Both the Old and the New Testaments hold out the promise of rewards to those who do good. While the new covenant abrogates the ceremonial aspects of the old, the moral law of the Old Testament remains valid. Christ is therefore more appropriately described as *Legislator* than as *Salvator*, in that he has fulfilled and perfected the law of Moses in order that he may be imitated by Christians.[557] The justice

---

[555] See McGrath, *'Homo Assumptus?'*; idem, 'Some Observations concerning the Soteriology of the *Via Moderna*', *RThAM* 52 (1986), 182–93.

[556] For example, Oberman, *The Harvest of Medieval Theology*, 108–11; McGrath, *Luther's Theology of the Cross*, 110–11.

[557] Biel, *In III Sent.* dist. xl q. unica a. 3 dub. 3; ed. Werbeck/Hoffmann, 3.704.18–19. It is this understanding of Christ's function which appears to underlie Luther's early theological difficulties; see WA 38.148.12; 40/1.298.9; 40/1.326.1; 41.653.41; 45.482.16; 47.590.1.

which is required of humans in order that they may be justified is the same in the old and new dispensations.[558]

The characteristic features of the doctrines of justification associated with the *via moderna* may be summarised as follows. It must be emphasised that the following features pertain *de potentia Dei ordinata*.

1. The necessity of humanity's meriting justification *de congruo* is maintained, this being regarded as effecting the transition between the moral and the meritorious planes within the terms of the *pactum*.

2. The possibility of humans' knowing with absolute certitude whether they are in possession of grace is rejected, although various degrees of conjectural certainty are conceded. In view of the total reliability of the *pactum*, however, the uncertainty is understood to arise through the inability of humans to know whether they have done *quod in se est*.[559]

3. Original righteousness is understood to include the gift of actual, but not sanctifying grace. The state of pure nature is thus understood to include the *influentia Dei generalis* alone.

4. The formal cause of justification is defined as the extrinsic denomination of the divine acceptation. It is not clear what role created habits play within the soteriology of the *via moderna*.

5. The formal principle of merit is defined as the extrinsic denomination of the divine acceptation.

6. The necessity of a human disposition towards justification is maintained, on the grounds that it constitutes the contracted link between the realms of nature and grace within the terms of the *pactum* – that is, within the context of *ex pacto divino* causality, it functions as the cause of the infusion of grace. The difficulties associated with the early Franciscan school – which arise from an *ex natura rei* understanding of causality – are thus avoided.

7. A strongly immaculist approach is generally adopted to the question of the conception of Mary.

2.10.5 The medieval Augustinian tradition

Just as the questionable presuppositions and methods of earlier generations of Reformation historians led to a distorted understanding of the nature and influence of the *via moderna*, a similarly misleading impression of the 'medieval Augustinian tradition' has also arisen for similar reasons.

---

[558] For example, see *Sermones Dominicales de tempore* 32D.

[559] Biel, *In II Sent.* dist. xxvii q. unica a. 3 dub. 5; ed. Werbeck/Hoffmann, 2.525.11–14: 'Homo non potest evidenter scire se facere quod in se est, quia hoc facere includit in se proponere oboedire Deo propter Deum tamquam ultimum et principalem finem, quod exigit dilectionem Dei super omnia, quam ex naturalis suis homo potest elicere.'

The tendency on the part of an earlier generation of historians to approach the late medieval period with the concerns and presuppositions of the Reformation itself (particularly in relation to Martin Luther) resulted in the identification of 'Nominalism' and 'Augustinianism' as two theological movements within the later medieval period which were totally and irreconcilably opposed. In particular, the conflict between the 'Nominalism' of Gabriel Biel and the 'Augustinianism' of Johannes von Staupitz was assumed to be a general feature of the period between the death of Duns Scotus and Luther's revolt against the theology of Gabriel Biel in 1517. A study of the interaction between 'Nominalists' and 'Augustinians' in the fourteenth and fifteenth centuries, however, indicates that this dichotomy is more easily suggested than demonstrated. The highly questionable methods of earlier Reformation historiographers thus resulted in deducing an estimation of pre-Reformation catholicism which reflects solely or largely the interests, concerns and presuppositions of modern Luther scholars.[560]

Recently, this trend has been reversed, with increasing attention being paid to the theology of the later medieval period as a subject of importance in its own right, independent of its relation to the Reformation, with a considerable number of important studies being published on medieval Augustinian theologians. As a result, we are now in a position to evaluate the nature and influence of the 'medieval Augustinian tradition'. In the present section, we propose to consider whether any 'medieval Augustinian tradition' can be identified with a coherent teaching on justification.

As noted in the previous section, there is a growing tendency to reject the idea of 'Nominalism' as a homogeneous school of thought during the later medieval period. It is not generally appreciated, however, that this has important consequences for the definition of 'Augustinianism' during the same period, in that the latter was usually *defined in relation to 'Nominalism'*. Once the idea of a homogeneous school of 'Nominalism' is rejected, the point of reference for the definition of 'Augustinianism' is removed. The vast amount of research undertaken on theologians of the Augustinian order during recent decades has made it clear that a dichotomy between 'Augustinianism' and 'Nominalism' is quite untenable. A phenomenally wide spectrum of theological opinions existed at the time, so that the use of the terms 'Nominalist' and 'Augustinian' *as correlatives* is now obviously inappropriate.

---

[560] For detailed discussion, see McGrath, *Intellectual Origins of the European Reformation*, 82–8.

This confusion is particularly well illustrated by the attempt of A. V. Müller to demonstrate that Luther stood within a school of theologians which represented a theology more Augustinian than that of Thomas Aquinas or Bonaventure.[561] In particular, Müller argued that Luther's concept of *iustitia duplex* could be traced back to a theological school which included Simon Fidati of Cascia (d. 1348), Hugolino of Orvieto (d. 1373), Agostino Favaroni (d. 1443) and Jacobus Perez of Valencia (d. 1490). A similar thesis was defended, although for rather different reasons, by Eduard Stakemeier, who argued that the doctrine of double justification associated with Girolamo Seripando during the Tridentine proceedings on justification represented an Augustinian theological tradition which could be properly understood only when set within the context of the theological tradition of the Augustinian order – to which both Seripando and Luther belonged.[562] It is, however, quite impossible to sustain the thesis that both Luther and Seripando represent possible variations on a basically Augustinian theology of justification, in Stakemeier's sense of the term.[563] There are, in fact, serious difficulties attending *any* attempt to characterise the theology of any later medieval thinker as 'Augustinian' (in the sense of corresponding to the thought of Augustine himself), as we shall make clear in what follows.

The criterion usually employed in establishing the 'Augustinianism' of a theologian is whether he taught that anything in humans themselves could be said to cause their subsequent justification. The rejection of any such *ratio iustificationis ex parte creaturae* is usually taken as evidence of a theologian's 'Augustinianism'. This criterion, however, is open to question, as such a rejection may arise for thoroughly non-Augustinian reasons.

This may be illustrated with reference to Thomas Bradwardine, who rejects the thesis that anything in humanity is the cause of its justification. God is the efficient, formal and final cause of everything which occurs concerning his creatures, so that the creature has no role to play in the causal sequence whatsoever.[564] The reasons for Bradwardine's rejection of any *ratio iustificationis ex parte creaturae* are thus Aristotelian in nature, rather than Augustinian, and clearly raise questions relating to the role of the Fall in this theology. The human need for grace is a consequence of their creatureliness, rather than of their sinfulness as a result of the

---

[561] A. V. Müller, *Luthers theologische Quellen: Seine Verteidigung gegen Denifle und Grisar*, Giessen: Topelmann, 1912.
[562] E. Stakemeier, *Der Kampf um Augustin*.
[563] McGrath, *The Intellectual Origins of the European Reformation*, 82–4, 103–11.
[564] *De causa Dei*, 174.

Fall. There is thus no fundamental difference between the pristine and fallen states of humanity in this respect, as, in both, humans are creatures. It is difficult to see how such a theologian can be deemed to be 'Augustinian', in view of the critical role of the Fall and human sin in Augustine's theology. It is almost certain that Gregory of Rimini, the great fourteenth-century theologian of the Augustinian order, singles out Bradwardine for special criticism for his un-Augustinian views on the Fall.[565]

A more sustained critique of Bradwardine upon this point may be illustrated from the writings of other members of the Augustinian order at the time, such as Johannes Klenkok, who studied at Bradwardine's university, Oxford, in the decades following the appearance of *De causa Dei*. Klenkok's critique of Bradwardine is very similar to that of his fellow Augustinian Hugolino of Orvieto; both Augustinian theologians regarded Bradwardine as perpetrating a metaphysical determinism which owed nothing to Augustine.[566] Similar criticisms were made by the later Augustinians Johannes Hiltalingen of Basel and Angelus Dobelinus, the first professor of theology at the university of Erfurt.[567]

A more significant approach to the 'medieval Augustinian tradition' is to study theological currents prevalent within the Augustinian order during the later medieval period. When this is done, it is possible to distinguish two main schools of thought within the order during the period: the *schola Aegidiana* and the *schola Augustiniana moderna*. We shall consider these two schools individually.

The school of thought which developed during the fourteenth century, based upon the writings of Giles of Rome, was known as the *schola Aegidiana*, suggesting that Giles was regarded as a theological authority by those who followed in his footsteps within the order. Although the theory that members of the Augustinian order were obliged to swear fidelity to the teachings of Giles of Rome at the time of their profession has not stood up to critical examination, it is nevertheless clear that a school of thought developed within the order which remained faithful to his teaching. This fidelity is particularly clear in relation to his teaching on original righteousness.[568] Thus Dionysius de Burgo regarded Giles of Rome and Thomas Aquinas as being theological authorities of equal importance, although his occasional preference for *doctor noster Aegidius*

---

[565] Gregory refers critically to (an unnamed) *unus modernus doctor* in this context: *In II Sent.* dist. xxxix q. 1 a. 1. The name 'Bradwardine' is inserted in the margins to two manuscripts (Paris Nat. lat. 15891 and Mazarin 914).

[566] Zumkeller, 'Johannes Klenkok', 266–90; idem, 'Hugolin von Orvieto', 175–82.

[567] Zumkeller, 'Der Augustinertheologe Johannes Hiltalingen von Basel', 115–18; idem, 'Der Augustiner Angelus Dobelinus', 97–103.

[568] G. Diaz, *De peccati originalis essentia in Schola Augustiniana Praetridentina*, Real Monasterio de El Escorial: Biblioteca La Ciudad de Dios, 1961.

is noticeable.[569] Thomas of Strasbourg refers to Giles as *doctor noster*, and cites him with sufficient frequency to suggest that he regards him as a theological authority of some considerable weight.[570] Johannes von Retz, the second member of the Augustinian order to become professor of theology at Vienna, cited both Giles of Rome and especially his follower Thomas of Strasbourg extensively.[571] Johannes Hiltalingen of Basel considered that the theologians of the Augustinian order could be regarded as constituting a distinct theological school, although he neglected to mention which particular features were characteristic of this putative 'school'.

The characteristic features of the *schola Aegidiana* are due to Giles of Rome himself, the strongly Augustinian character of his theology being slightly modulated with Thomism at points.[572] The strongly Augustinian cast of the *schola Aegidiana* may be particularly well seen in the emphasis placed upon the priority of *caritas* and *gratia* in justification.[573]

The *schola Aegidiana* gradually gave way to the *schola Augustiniana moderna* during the fourteenth century. It is generally accepted that the period of medieval Augustinian theology can be divided into two periods, the first encompassing the period between Giles of Rome and Thomas of Strasbourg, and the second the period between Gregory of Rimini and the early sixteenth century. The theologians of the Augustinian order appear to have been significantly influenced by theological currents from outside their order, as may be seen from their changing understandings of the nature of the conception of Mary. The earlier theologians of the *schola Aegidiana*, such as Giles of Rome, Albert of Padua, Augustinus Triumphus of Ancona and Gregory of Rimini, were strongly maculist in their Mariological persuasions.[574]

However, from the late fourteenth century onwards, the theologians of the Augustinian order came to adopt the immaculist position. Thus, beginning with Johannes Hiltalingen of Basel, Henry of Freimar and Thomas of Strasbourg, and continuing into the fifteenth and early sixteenth centuries with Jacobus Perez of Valencia, Johannes de Paltz and Johannes von Staupitz, the theologians of the Augustinian order

---

[569] Trapp, 'Augustinian Theology of the Fourteenth Century', especially 156–7.

[570] For example, *In I Sent.* dist. xvii q. 2.

[571] For example, see Zumkeller's edition of Retz, 'Der Wiener Theologie professor Johannes von Retz', 540–82, Textbeilage 126, citing Thomas of Strasbourg, *In II Sent.* dist. xxviii, xxix q. 1 a. 3.

[572] J. Beumer, 'Augustinismus und Thomismus in der theologischen Prinzipienlehre des Aegidius Romanus', *Scholastik* 32 (1957), 542–60.

[573] A. Zumkeller, 'Die Augustinerschule des Mittelalters: Vertreter und philosophisch-theologische Lehre (Übersicht nach dem heutigen Stand der Forschung)', *AnAug* 27 (1964), 167–262, especially 193–5.

[574] Oberman, *The Harvest of Medieval Theology*, 286–92.

moved away from the teaching of the *schola Aegidiana* in this respect. Although similar divergences from other characteristic teachings of the *schola Aegidiana*, such as their understanding of *iustitia originalis*, may also be detected, the most fundamental difference relates to the method employed in theological speculation.

In the late fourteenth century, a polarisation between the methods and presuppositions of the *via antiqua* and *via moderna* took place within the Augustinian order itself.[575] While the *antiqui* were primarily concerned with accurately establishing the opinions of writers such as Augustine on the basis of historico-critical studies, the *moderni* employed the logico-critical device of the dialectic between the two powers of God to 'correct' such opinions.[576] One such 'correction' was the critique of the role of created habits in justification. Although the theologians of the *schola Aegidiana* held that the formal cause of justification was the created habit of grace, the theologians of the *schola Augustiniana moderna* adopted the characteristic position of the later Franciscan school and the *via moderna –* that the *ratio iustificationis* was the extrinsic denomination of the divine acceptation.[577]

By the late fifteenth century, a theology of justification had developed within certain sections of the Augustinian order which can only be regarded as a hybrid species, retaining much of the authentic theological emphases of Augustine (e.g., the emphasis upon human depravity, and the priority of *caritas* in justification), while employing methods (such as the dialectic between the two powers of God) which owed more to the *via moderna*. (This does not, of course, imply that the *schola Augustiniana moderna* derived these methods from the *via moderna*; it seems that both schools ultimately derived them from Duns Scotus, the former via Gregory of Rimini and the latter via William of Ockham.)

It will therefore be clear that it is impossible to speak of a single homogeneous 'medieval Augustinian tradition' during the Middle Ages in relation to the doctrine of justification. If anything, it is necessary to draw a distinction between two such traditions, as follows:

1. The school of thought often referred to as the *schola Aegidiana*, which is based upon the teaching of Giles of Rome, which understood the created habit of grace to be the grounds of justification.

2. The later school of thought, usually referred to as the *schola Augustiniana moderna*, mediated through Gregory of Rimini and Hugolino of

---

[575] Trapp, 'Augustinian Theology of the Fourteenth Century'.
[576] Trapp makes the important point that no theologian of the Augustinian order uses the dialectic between the two powers of God in the unorthodox manner associated with *moderni* such as John of Mirecourt and Nicholas of Autrecourt; Trapp, 'Augustinian Theology of the Fourteenth Century', 265.
[577] For documentation of this transition, see McGrath, '"Augustinianism"?'.

Orvieto, which had serious reservations concerning the role of created habits in justification, and which placed increasing emphasis upon the uncreated grace of the Holy Spirit and the extrinsic denomination of the divine acceptation. It is within this latter tradition that Martin Luther's early critique of the role of created habits in justification should be located and interpreted.[578]

This naturally leads us to consider the Reformation debates over justification, in which the medieval debate over how justification came about was extended to consider something even more fundamental – what the term 'justification' itself actually denoted.

[578] See McGrath, *Luther's Theology of the Cross*, 81–5.

3 Protestantism: the Reformation debates on justification

The leading principle of the Reformation is generally considered to be its doctrine of justification. While there is unquestionably much truth in this statement, it requires careful modification to do justice to the historical evidence. It is certainly true that the *articulus iustificationis* is the leading feature of the theology of Martin Luther.[1] It was never, however, accepted within the more radical wing of the Reformation, which stressed the importance of obedience and discipleship, adopting doctrines of grace which stressed human responsibility and accountability towards God, rather than God's transformation of the individual.[2]

Nevertheless, the considerable personal influence of Luther over the majority of the evangelical factions within Germany and elsewhere inevitably led to his personal high estimation of the doctrine of justification being adopted elsewhere,[3] and becoming a determinative and distinctive mark of the mainline Reformation. Thus by the beginning of the seventeenth century the *articulus iustificationis* appears to have been generally regarded as the *articulus stantis et cadentis ecclesiae*, the 'article by which the church stands or falls'.[4]

As will become clear in the present study, however, the origins of the Reformed church seem to owe little, if anything, to Luther's insights into justification. The relation between Luther's own theological insights and the dawn of the Reformation itself is now seen to be a historical question of the utmost complexity, and it must be emphasised that it is no longer possible to assert with any degree of historical or theological precision

---

[1] See E. Wolf, 'Die Rechtfertigungslehre als Mitte und Grenze reformatorischer Theologie', *EvTh* 9 (1949–50), 298–308; Schwarz, 'Luthers Rechtfertigungslehre als Eckstein der christlichen Theologie und Kirche'.

[2] See Beachy, *The Concept of Grace in the Radical Reformation*.

[3] There is, of course, a genuine difficulty in establishing the precise causal relationship between the origins of Luther's own theology and that of the Reformation as a whole; see H. A. Oberman, 'Headwaters of the Reformation'; McGrath, *Luther's Theology of the Cross*, 24 n. 45, 52–3, 142.

[4] Schwarz, 'Luthers Rechtfertigungslehre als Eckstein der christlichen Theologie und Kirche'.

that the Reformation, considered as a movement, began as a fundamental consequence of Luther's new insights into human justification *coram Deo*, although it is unquestionably true that Luther's own personal theological preoccupations centred upon this matter.

The present chapter is concerned with the documentation and critical analysis of the understandings of justification associated with the Reformation in Germany and Switzerland – in other words, with the origins and subsequent development of the Lutheran and Reformed churches. In view of the crucial importance of the development of Martin Luther's theological insights to any account of the origins of the Reformation, we begin by considering his break with the theology of the medieval period associated with his 'discovery of the righteousness of God', and the leading features of his doctrine of justification.

The Reformation is often portrayed as a rediscovery of the Bible, particularly of the Pauline corpus. Although there is undoubtedly truth in this description, it is considerably more accurate to portray it as a rediscovery of Augustine's doctrine of grace, with a subsequent critique of his doctrine of the church. In an age which witnessed a general revival of Augustinian studies, this new interest in Augustine must be regarded as an aspect of the Renaissance in general, rather than as a feature peculiar to the Reformers. What was unquestionably new, however, is the use to which the Reformers put Augustine. The most accurate description of the doctrines of justification associated with the Reformed and Lutheran churches from 1530 onwards is that they represent a radically new interpretation of the Pauline concept of 'imputed righteousness' set within an Augustinian soteriological framework.

It is clearly of importance to account for this new understanding of the nature of justifying righteousness, with its associated conceptual distinction between justification and sanctification. Attempts on the part of an earlier generation of Protestant apologists to defend this innovation as a recovery of the authentic teaching of Augustine, and of their Catholic opponents to demonstrate that it constituted a vestige of a discredited and ossified Ockhamism, can no longer be taken seriously. It is the task of the historian to account for this new development, which marks a significant break with the tradition up to this point.

It must be made clear that it is quite inadequate to attempt to characterise the doctrines of justification associated with the Reformation by referring merely to their anti-Pelagian structure. Such doctrines of justification can be adduced from practically every period in the history of doctrine, particularly in the later medieval period (such as within the *schola Augustiniana moderna*). The notional distinction, necessitated by a forensic understanding of justification, between the external act of God in pronouncing sentence, and the internal process of regeneration, along with the associated insistence upon the alien and external nature of justifying righteousness, must be considered to be the most reliable *historical* characterisation of Protestant doctrines of justification. As the Osiandrist controversy made clear, an anti-Pelagian doctrine of justification could still be rejected as unrepresentative of the Reformation *if justifying righteousness was conceived intrinsically.*[5]

Indeed, precisely this controversy may be considered to have exercised a decisive influence in establishing the concept of forensic justification as characteristic of the Reformation. As the history of the Reformation itself demonstrates, the criterion employed at the time to determine whether a given doctrine of justification was Protestant or not was whether justifying righteousness was conceived extrinsically. This criterion served to distinguish the doctrines of justification associated with the magisterial Reformation from those of Catholicism on the one hand and from the radical Reformation on the other.

In view of the significance of the concept of the imputation of righteousness both as an idea itself and as a criterion of the Protestant character of a doctrine of justification, much of the present chapter is concerned with documenting its development within the churches of the Reformation. The importance of the concept is also reflected in other parts of the present volume, particularly in the attention paid to the late sixteenth- and early seventeenth-century disputes over the formal cause of justification.

The present chapter begins by considering whether there can be said to be 'precursors' or 'forerunners' of the distinctive Reformation views on justification during the later Middle Ages.

3.1   Forerunners of the Reformation doctrines of justification?

It is clearly of great interest to establish the relationship between the doctrines of justification associated with the emerging churches of the Reformation of the sixteenth century and those associated with earlier periods in the history of doctrine. The historical importance of this question will be self-evident, in that the character, distinctiveness and final significance of any movement in intellectual history is invariably better appreciated when its relationship to comparable movements which preceded it are positively identified. It is for this reason that considerable attention is currently being directed towards establishing the precise relationship between the thought of the late medieval period and that of

---

[5] On which see Hauke, *Gott-Haben, um Gottes Willen.*

the Reformation. It must be appreciated, however, that scholarly interest in the *historical* aspects of the question concerning the continuity of the late medieval and Reformation periods has tended to obscure the theological aspect of the question, which was thought to be more significant at the time of the Reformation itself.

The fundamental theological question which is thus raised is the following: can the teachings of the churches of the Reformation be regarded as truly catholic? In view of the centrality of the doctrine of justification to both the *initium theologiae Lutheri* and the *initium Reformationis*, this question becomes acutely pressing concerning the doctrine of justification itself. If it can be shown that the central teaching of the Lutheran Reformation, the fulcrum about which the early Reformation turned, the *articulus stantis et cadentis ecclesiae*, constituted a theological novelty, unknown within the previous fifteen centuries of catholic thought, the Reformers' claim to catholicity would be seriously prejudiced, if not totally discredited.

The question of the historical continuity between the teaching of the churches of the Reformation and that of earlier periods in relation to justification thus became acutely pressing. For the Roman Catholic opponents of the Reformation, such teachings represented theological innovations. For Bossuet, the Reformers had significantly altered the common teaching of the catholic church upon this central doctrine and, by doing so, had forfeited their claims to orthodoxy and catholicity:

The church's doctrine is always the same . . . the Gospel is never different from what it was before. Hence, if at any time someone says that the faith includes something which yesterday was not said to be of the faith, it is always *heterodoxy*, which is any doctrine different from *orthodoxy*. There is no difficulty about recognising false doctrine: there is no argument about it: it is recognised at once, whenever it appears, merely because it is new.[6]

This was such a serious charge that the theologians of the Reformation were obliged to meet it, which they did in two manners.[7]

1. The claim was rejected out of hand, it being asserted that the Reformation represented a long-overdue return to the truly catholic teaching of the church, which had become distorted and disfigured through the questionable theological methods of later medieval theology. Particular

---

[6] Bossuet, *Première Instruction pastorale* xxvii; cited in O. Chadwick, *From Bossuet to Newman: The Idea of Doctrinal Development*, Cambridge: Cambridge University Press, 1957, 17.

[7] On which see the detailed study of I. Backus, *Historical Method and Confessional Identity in the Era of the Reformation (1378–1615)*, Leiden: Brill, 2003.

emphasis was laid upon the alleged concurrence of the Reformation teachings on justification with those of Augustine.[8]

2. The claim was conceded, to varying extents, but was qualified in an important respect. The doctrines of justification associated with the Reformation represent innovations only if orthodoxy is determined by the decrees of the corrupt late medieval church. A dichotomy was posited between the corrupt official teaching of the church, and the faithful catholic teaching of individual 'proto-Reformers', which would eventually triumph at the time of the Reformation.[9] It is this thesis which is usually stated in terms of the existence of 'forerunners of the Reformation'.[10] In the present section, we are particularly concerned with the historical task of establishing areas of continuity and discontinuity between the late medieval period and that of the Reformation. In view of the theological importance of the question, however, we shall examine both of the positions identified above.

From the analysis of the late medieval schools of thought on justification presented in the present study, it will be clear that there existed considerable diversity of opinion on this issue during the later medieval period. This diversity represents a particular instance of the general pluralism of late medieval religious thought, which, it is usually argued, originates from the fourteenth century.[11] The Tridentine decree on justification may be regarded as an attempt to define the limits of this pluralism, if not to impose a unity upon it. But are the characteristic features of the Reformation doctrines of justification foreshadowed in the doctrinal pluralism of the late medieval period? Before attempting to answer this question, the characteristic features of such teachings must first be identified.

The first era of the Reformation witnessed a broad consensus emerging upon both the *nature* of justification and the *context* in which it was set. The following three features are characteristic of Protestant understandings of the *nature* of justification over the period 1530–1730:

1. Justification is defined as the forensic *declaration* that believers are righteous, rather than the process by which they are *made* righteous, involving a change in their *status* rather than in their *nature*.

---

[8] Thus Philip Melanchthon, CR (Melanchthon), 2.884: 'So man nun fragt, warum sondert ich euch denn von der vorigen Kirchen? Antwort: wir sondern uns nicht von der vorigen rechten Kirchen. Ich halte es eben das, welches Ambrosius und Augustinus gelehret haben.'

[9] Thus Flacius Illyricus, initially in his *Catalogus testium veritatis* (1556), and subsequently in his celebrated *Magdeburg Centuries* (1559–74).

[10] On which see McGrath, *The Intellectual Origins of the European Reformation*, 29–33.

[11] H. A. Oberman, 'Fourteenth Century Religious Thought: A Premature Profile', *Speculum* 53 (1978), 80–93.

2. A deliberate and systematic distinction is made between *justification* (the external act by which God declares the sinner to be righteous) and *sanctification* or *regeneration* (the internal process of renewal within humans). Although the two are treated as inseparable, a notional distinction is thus drawn where none was conceded before.

3. Justifying righteousness, or the formal cause of justification, is defined as the alien righteousness of Christ, external to humans and imputed to them, rather than a righteousness which is inherent to them, located within them, or which in any sense may be said to belong to them. God's judgement in justification is therefore *synthetic* rather than *analytic*, in that there is no righteousness within humans which can be considered to be the basis of the divine verdict of justification; the righteousness upon which such a judgement is necessarily based is external to humans.[12]

In suggesting that these three features should be considered as being characteristic of Protestant understandings of justification, I am aware that neither Martin Luther nor Huldrych Zwingli can be said to have understood justification in precisely this manner. The consolidation of these features as characteristic of Protestantism appears to have been achieved in the late 1530s through the considerable influence of Philip Melanchthon. It is nevertheless clear that Luther's doctrine of the *iustitia Christia aliena* laid the conceptual foundation for such a doctrine of forensic justification.[13]

In effect, Luther must be regarded as a transitional figure, standing at the junction of two rival understandings of the nature of justification. As we demonstrated earlier, the medieval theological tradition was unanimous in its understanding of justification as both an act and a process, by which both the status of humans *coram Deo* and their essential nature underwent alteration. Although Luther regarded justification as an essentially unitary process, he nevertheless introduced a decisive break with the western theological tradition as a whole by insisting that, through their justification, humans are *intrinsically* sinful yet *extrinsically* righteous. It is at this point that it is possible to distinguish the otherwise similar teachings of Luther and Johannes von Staupitz on justification.[14]

It must be emphasised that it is totally unacceptable to characterise the doctrines of justification associated with the Reformation solely with reference to their anti-Pelagian character or to their associated doctrines of predestination. Although an earlier generation of scholars argued that

---

[12] For an exploration of the general issue, see Härle, 'Analytische und synthetische Urteile in der Rechtfertigungslehre'.
[13] See McGrath, *Luther's Theology of the Cross*, 133–6.
[14] As pointed out by Oberman, *Werden und Wertung*, 110–12.

the Reformation resulted from the sudden rediscovery of the radical anti-Pelagianism of Augustine's soteriology, it is clear that this judgement cannot be sustained. The emergence of the *schola Augustiniana moderna* in the fourteenth century was essentially an academic movement based upon the anti-Pelagian writings of Augustine,[15] and the possibility that both Calvin and Luther, as well as other Reformers such as Peter Martyr Vermigli, demonstrate continuity with this late medieval Augustinian school calls this judgement into question.[16] In its radical anti-Pelagianism, the Reformation, in its first phase, demonstrated a remarkable degree of continuity with well-established currents in late medieval thought. This is not, of course, to say that the Reformation was *typical* of the late medieval period, but merely to observe that the Reformation demonstrates strong affinities with one of the many theological currents which constituted the flux of late medieval theology.

Equally, the Reformers unhesitatingly rejected the necessity of created habits of grace in justification, a tendency which is evident from Luther's *Randbemerkungen* of 1509–10 onwards.[17] By doing so, they reflected the general tendency of the period, particularly within the *via moderna* and *schola Augustiniana moderna*, to locate the *ratio iustificationis* primarily in the extrinsic denomination of the divine acceptation (see 2.9). It may also be argued that the covenantal (rather than ontological) and voluntarist (rather than intellectualist) foundations of late medieval theology passed into the theology of the first phase of the Reformation. It will therefore be clear that many of the fundamental presuppositions of the soteriology of the late medieval period passed into the early theology of the Reformation. Within the flux of late medieval theology, currents may easily be identified which demonstrate various degrees of continuity with the emerging theologies of justification associated with the first phase of the Reformation.

These areas of continuity, nevertheless, relate primarily, if not exclusively, to the *mode* of justification rather than to its *nature*. Despite the disagreement within the various theological schools concerning the manner in which justification came about, there was a fundamental consensus on what the term 'justification' itself signified. Throughout the entire medieval period, justification continued to be understood as the process by which humans are made righteous, subsuming the concepts of 'sanctification' and 'regeneration'. *Iustificare* was understood to signify *iustum*

---

[15] Oberman, *Werden und Wertung*, 82–140, especially 83–92.
[16] McGrath, *Luther's Theology of the Cross*, 36–40, 63–71; idem, 'John Calvin and Late Medieval Thought'.
[17] Vignaux, *Luther Commentateur des Sentences*, 5–44; McGrath, *Luther's Theology of the Cross*, 81–5.

facere throughout the period. Albrecht Ritschl is thus correct when he states:

We shall . . . search in vain to find in any theologian of the Middle Ages the Reformation idea of justification – the deliberate distinction between justification and regeneration . . . Their deliberate treatment of the idea of justification proceeds rather on the principle that a real change in the sinner is thought of as involved in it – in other words, the Reformation distinction between the two ideas is at the outset rejected.[18]

The significance of the Protestant distinction between *iustificatio* and *regeneratio* is that a fundamental intellectual discontinuity has been introduced into the western theological tradition through the recognition of a difference, where none had previously been acknowledged to exist. There is no doubt that a small number of medieval writers, such as Duns Scotus, explored the conceptual possibilities of separating these notions; yet despite such notional analysis, justification was not conceptually detached from the process of regeneration.[19] Despite the astonishing theological diversity of the late medieval period, a consensus relating to the *nature* of justification was maintained throughout.

The Protestant understanding of the *nature* of justification thus represents a theological *novum*, whereas its understanding of its *mode* does not. It is therefore of considerable importance to appreciate that the *criterion employed in the sixteenth century* to determine whether a particular doctrine of justification was Protestant or otherwise was *whether justification was understood forensically*. The fury surrounding the Osiandrist controversy only served to harden the early Protestant conviction that any doctrine of justification by inherent righteousness was intrinsically anti-Protestant.[20] The history of the Reformation itself, especially as it concerns Osiander and Latomus, demonstrates that the criterion employed *at the time* to determine whether a given doctrine was Protestant or otherwise primarily concerned the manner in which justifying righteousness was understood. It would therefore appear to be historically unsound to use any other criterion in this respect.

Once this point is conceded, we may return to a consideration of the two main lines of defence of the catholicity of Protestant doctrines of justification encountered during the first phase of the Reformation. The first

---

[18] A. B. Ritschl, *A Critical History of the Christian Doctrine of Justification and Reconciliation*, Edinburgh: Edmonston & Douglas, 1872, 90–1.
[19] Pannenberg, 'Das Verhältnis zwischen der Akzeptationslehre des Duns Skotus und der reformatorischen Rechtfertigungslehre.'
[20] See here W. Niesel, 'Calvin wider Osianders Rechtfertigungslehre', *ZKG* 46 (1928), 410–30; W. Koehler, *Dogmengeschichte als Geschichte des christlichen Selbstbewußtseins*, Zurich: Niehan, 1951, 354.

such approach, which is particularly associated with Philip Melanchthon, is to argue that the Reformation understandings of justification represent a legitimate interpretation of the theology of Augustine, so that the Lutheran Reformation may be regarded as recovering the authentic teaching of the African bishop from the distortions of the medieval period.[21] However, it will be clear that the medieval period was astonishingly faithful to the teaching of Augustine on the question of the nature of justification, where the Reformers departed from it. Melanchthon himself appears to have been unaware of this point, as Latomus pointed out with some force.[22]

If the catholicity of Protestant understandings of the nature of justification is to be defended, it is therefore necessary to investigate the possible existence of 'forerunners of the Reformation doctrines of justification' – that is, writers from the later medieval period itself who, in conscious opposition to what they deemed to be the corrupt teaching of the contemporary church, foreshadowed the teaching of the Reformers on the point at issue. Although this approach yields valuable results in the area of sacramental theology and ecclesiology, particularly in connection with the opinions of Wycliffe and Huss, it fails in relation to the specific question of the nature of justification and justifying righteousness. It is, of course, possible to argue that later medieval teaching on *predestination* establishes the case for 'forerunners of the Reformation doctrines of justification'.[23] However, as we shall indicate below, this appears to rest upon a fallacy.

In an important study, Oberman argued that Dettloff was unable to distinguish the 'nominalistic' and 'scotistic' traditions on justification (i.e., the teachings of the *via moderna* and the late Franciscan school),

because he concentrated on the doctrine of justification, which in the late medieval sources is always associated and connected with a discussion of predestination. These differences do not appear in an analysis of the *content* of statements on justification, but rather in the different *context* of justification, namely, in the diverging ways of understanding the doctrine of predestination.[24]

This point is unquestionably valid: precisely because there was a fundamental continuity within the medieval tradition concerning the *content* of

---

[21] See McGrath, 'Forerunners of the Reformation?', 228–36.

[22] Latomus, *Duae Epistolae*, Antwerp, 1544, 38.

[23] It is interesting to note that Oberman's case for 'forerunners' of the Reformation doctrines of justification is nowhere stated explicitly, but appears to rest upon certain writings pertaining to predestination: Oberman, *Forerunners of the Reformation*, 121–41.

[24] H. A. Oberman, '"Iustitia Christi" and "Iustitia Dei". Cf. idem, *The Harvest of Medieval Theology*, 185–7, especially 185: 'It is a reliable rule of interpretation for the historian of Christian thought that the position taken with respect to the doctrine of predestination is a most revealing indicator of the understanding of the doctrine of justification'.

justification, differences between theologians had to be sought elsewhere, in their discussion of its *context*. It may, however, be noted that analysis of the doctrine of predestination does not exhaust an analysis of a writer's views on the context of justification, which must also be taken to include his statements concerning the possibility or otherwise of extrasacramental justification.

Nevertheless, this cannot be regarded as an adequate scholarly foundation for dealing with the relationship between the doctrines of justification of the late medieval period and the Reformation – precisely because there exist such significant differences between their understandings of the *nature* of justification that an inquiry into its *mode* is no longer necessary. The appeal to writers' statements concerning *predestination* in an attempt to elucidate their doctrines of *justification* is legitimate *only when their statements are otherwise indistinguishable*. In the case of the later Franciscan school and the *via moderna*, such statements are near-identical, so the appeal is proper. Nevertheless, in the case of late medieval theology and the theology of the first phase of the Reformation, statements concerning justification are immediately distinguishable without the necessity of appealing to their statements concerning predestination.

In this case, there is a remarkable degree of continuity between the statements of certain strands of late medieval thought (e.g., the *schola Augustiniana moderna*) and that of the Reformation, despite the fact that their statements pertaining to the *content*, as opposed to the *context*, of justification (to use Oberman's terms) are grossly different. It will therefore be clear that the application of this method to study the continuity between the thought of the later medieval period and the first phase of the Reformation is seriously misleading, as well as being unjustifiable.

The essential distinguishing feature of the Reformation doctrines of justification is that a deliberate and systematic distinction is made between *justification* and *regeneration*. Although it must be emphasised that this distinction is purely notional, in that it is impossible to separate the two within the context of the *ordo salutis*, the essential point is that a notional distinction is made where none had been acknowledged before in the history of Christian doctrine. A fundamental discontinuity was introduced into the western theological tradition where none had ever existed, or ever been contemplated, before. The Reformation understanding of the *nature* of justification – as opposed to its *mode* – must therefore be regarded as a genuine theological *novum*.

Like all periods in the history of doctrine, the Reformation demonstrates both continuity and discontinuity with the period which immediately preceded it. Chief among these discontinuities is the new understanding of the nature of justification, whereas there are clearly extensive areas of continuity with the late medieval theological movement as a whole, or well-defined sections of the movement, in relation to other aspects of the doctrine, as noted above. That there are no 'forerunners of the Reformation doctrines of justification' has little theological significance today, given current thinking on the nature of the development of doctrine, which renders Bossuet's static model, on which he based his critique of Protestantism, obsolete. Nevertheless, the historical aspects of the question continue to have relevance. For what reasons did the Reformers abandon the catholic consensus on the nature of justification? We shall discuss this matter in what follows.

3.2   Luther's discovery of the 'righteousness of God'

In an earlier section, I pointed out that during the period 1508–14 the young Luther appears to have adopted an understanding of the 'righteousness of God' essentially identical to that of the *via moderna*. The continuities between the young Luther and late medieval theology over the period 1509–14 include several matters of significance to his understanding of justification. Thus the young Luther rejected the implication of supernatural habits in justification, following both the *via moderna* and the *schola Augustiniana moderna* in doing so. Of particular importance is the observation that in this period he developed an understanding of human involvement in justification which is clearly based upon the *pactum* theology of the *via moderna* and upon the interpretation of the axiom *facienti quod in se est Deus non denegat gratiam* characteristic of this school of thought.[25] Over the period 1514–19, however, Luther's understanding of justification underwent a radical alteration. The nature and date of this alteration have remained a matter of controversy within contemporary Luther scholarship, justifying extensive discussion of the question in the present section.

One of the most important sources for our understanding of this radical alteration in Luther's doctrine of justification is the 1545 autobiographical fragment in which Luther records his intense personal difficulties over the concept of the 'righteousness of God'.

I had certainly been overcome with a great desire to understand St Paul in his letter to the Romans, but what had hindered me thus far was not any 'coldness of the blood' so much as that one phrase in the first chapter: 'the righteousness of God (*iustitia Dei*) is revealed in it.' For I had hated that phrase 'the righteousness

---

[25] WA 3.289.1–5; 4.261.32–9; 262.2–7. Cf. O. Bayer, *Promissio: Geschichte der reformatorischen Wende in Luthers Theologie*, Göttingen: Vandenhoeck & Ruprecht, 1971, 119–23, 128–43, 313–17; McGrath, *Luther's Theology of the Cross*, 85–92.

of God', which, according to the use and custom of all the doctors, I had been taught to understand philosophically, in the sense of the formal or active (as they termed it) righteousness by which God is righteous, and punishes unrighteous sinners.[26]

The modern preoccupation of scholars with this autobiographical fragment dates from 1904, when the distinguished Catholic historian Heinrich Denifle argued that Luther's discussion of the term *iustitia Dei* indicated a near-total theological ignorance and incompetence.[27] In a remarkable appendix to his intensely hostile study of the development of Lutheranism, Denifle produced a detailed analysis of the exposition of Romans 1:16–17 by some sixty doctors of the western church, indicating that not one of them, from Ambrosiaster onwards, understood *iustitia Dei* in the sense Luther notes in the above citation.[28] However, the conclusion which Denifle drew from this demonstration – that Luther was either ignorant of the Catholic tradition, or else deliberately perverted it – was clearly unjustified.

It is quite obvious that Luther intended to make no global reference to the tradition of the western church upon the matter, but was referring specifically to the doctors who taught him – an unequivocal reference to the *moderni* at Erfurt, under whom he received his initial theological education. There is every indication that Luther is referring to the specific concept of *iustitia Dei* associated with the *via moderna*: God is righteous in the sense that God rewards the person who does *quod in se est* with grace, and punishes the person who does not. In view of Gabriel Biel's unambiguous assertion that individuals cannot know for certain whether they have, in fact, done *quod in se est*,[29] there is clearly every reason to state that Luther's early concept of *iustitia Dei* was that of the righteousness of an utterly scrupulous and impartial judge, who rewarded or punished humans on the basis of an ultimately unknown quality.

The autobiographical fragment clearly indicates that Luther's difficulties over the concept of the 'righteousness of God' were resolved *by*

---

[26] WA 54.185.12 – 186.21. For the debate over this passage in the literature, see Gerhard Pfeiffer, 'Das Ringen des jungen Luthers um die Gerechtigkeit Gottes', *Luther-Jahrbuch* 26 (1959), 25–55; Regin Prenter, *Der barmherzige Richter: Iustitia Dei passiva in Luthers Dictata super Psalterium 1513–1515*, Copenhagen: Aarhus, 1961; Albrecht Peters, 'Luthers Turmerlebnis', *ZSTh* 3 (1961), 203–36; Bornkamm, 'Zur Frage der Iustitia Dei beim jungen Luther'; Oberman, '"Iustitia Christi" and "Iustitia Dei"'; McGrath, *Luther's Theology of the Cross*.

[27] Heinrich Denifle, *Luther und Luthertum in der ersten Entwickelung, quellenmäßig dargestellt*, 2 vols., Mainz, Kirchheim, 1904, especially 392–5, 404–15.

[28] Denifle, *Die abendländischen Schriftausleger bis Luther über Iustitia Dei (Röm. 1.17) und Iustificatio*, Mainz: Kircheim, 1905.

[29] Biel, *In II Sent.* dist. xxvii q. unica a. 3 dub. 5; ed. Werbeck/Hoffmann, 2.525.11 – 526.17: 'Homo non potest evidenter scire se facere quod in se est.'

(although not necessarily *in*) the year 1519.[30] An analysis of Luther's lectures on the Psalter (1513–15), on Romans (1515–16) and on Galatians (1516–17) indicates that Luther's understanding of 'the righteousness of God' in particular, and his theology of justification in general, appear to have undergone a significant alteration over the period 1514–15, with the crucial step apparently dating from 1515.

Luther's early understanding of justification (1513–14) may be summarised as follows: humans must recognise their spiritual weakness and inadequacy, and turn in humility from their attempts at self-justification to ask God for his grace. God treats this humility of faith (*humilitas fidei*) as the precondition necessary for justification under the terms of the *pactum* (that is, as the *quod in se est* demanded of humans), and then fulfils God's obligations under the *pactum* by bestowing grace upon them.[31] It is clear that Luther understands humans to be capable of making a response towards God without the assistance of special grace, and that this response of *iustitia fidei* is the necessary precondition (*quod in se est*) *for* the bestowal of justifying grace.[32]

Although some Luther scholars have argued that Luther's understanding of the term *iustitia Dei* appears to have undergone a significant alteration during the course of his exposition of Psalms 70 and 71, it is clear that Luther has merely clarified the terminology within his *existing* theological framework, so that the precise relationship of the various *iustitiae* (specifically, the *iustitia* which humans must possess if they are to be justified (that is, *iustitia fidei*) and the *iustitia* by which God is obliged to reward this righteousness with grace (that is, *iustitia Dei*)) implicated in the process of justification is clarified. Luther still expounds with some brilliance the *pactum* theology of the *via moderna*.

A decisive break with this theology of justification is evident in the Romans lectures of 1515–16. Three major alterations may be noted, leading to this break. First, Luther insists that humans are *passive* in their own justification.[33] Although not denying that humans have *any* role in their justification, Luther clearly states that they are not capable of initiating, or collaborating with, the process leading to justification. Whereas, in the *Dictata super Psalterium*, humans were understood to be *active* in the process of their justification (in that they were able to turn to God in humility

---

[30] For a detailed analysis of the nature, date and theological significance of this 'discovery', see McGrath, *Luther's Theology of the Cross*, 95–147, 153–61. This is an essential supplement to the briefer discussion presented in the present work.

[31] WA 3.124.12–14; 3.588.8; 4.91.4–5; 111.33–7; 262.2–7. Cf. Bayer, *Promissio*, 128; Bizer, *Fides ex auditu*, 19–21; McGrath, *Luther's Theology of the Cross*, 89–92.

[32] For the argument, see McGrath, *Luther's Theology of the Cross*, 113–19.

[33] WA 56.379.1–15.

and faith, and cry out for grace), Luther now unequivocally states that it is God who converts humans. Second, he insists that human will is held captive by grace, and is incapable of attaining righteousness unaided by divine grace.[34] One should speak of *servum potius quam liberum arbitrium*, as Augustine reminded Julian of Eclanum. Third, and perhaps most significant of all, Luther states that the idea that humans can do *quod in se est* is nothing more and nothing less than Pelagian, even though he once held this position himself.[35] Despite the fact that his theology of justification up to this point was based upon the explicitly stated presupposition that humans were capable of doing *quod in se est*, he now concedes the Pelagianism of the opinion that salvation is dependent upon a decision of the human will.[36] Even though he will continue to identify *fides* and *humilitas* for some time to come, it is clear that a genuine and radical alteration in his theology of justification has taken place. Although he may not have arrived at any dramatically new understanding of the *nature* of faith, he has certainly arrived at a radically new understanding of *how faith comes about in the first place*.

The recognition that God bestows the precondition of justification upon humanity inevitably involves the abandonment of the soteriological framework underlying the *pactum* theology of the *via moderna*. Luther's early interpretation of *iustitia Dei* was based upon the presupposition that God, who acts according to equity (*equitas*) rewarded the person who had done *quod in se est* with justifying grace, *sine acceptione personarum*. The divine judgement is based solely upon the divine recognition of an individual's possessing or achieving a quality that God is under an obligation to reward.

Yet if it is God who bestows this quality upon humanity – rather than humanity that achieves or acquires it – then the framework of *equitas* and *iustitia* essential to the *pactum* theology of the *via moderna* and the young Luther can no longer be sustained, in that God suddenly becomes open to the charge of *inequitas*, *iniustitia* and *acceptio personarum*. The essential feature of Luther's theological breakthrough is thus the destruction of the framework upon which his early soteriology was based, and *thence* the necessity of reinterpretation of the concept of *iustitia Dei*. It is therefore clear that an important change in Luther's understanding of justification took place at some time in the year 1515.

---

[34] WA 56.385.15–22. Note the explicit usage of the term *servum arbitrium*.
[35] WA 56.382.26–7; 502.32 – 503.5.
[36] Luther's marginal comments on Biel are of importance here; unfortunately, their date remains uncertain: H. Volz, 'Luthers Randbemerkungen zu zwei Schriften Gabriel Biels: Kritische Anmerkungen zu Hermann Degerings Publikation', *ZKG* 81 (1970), 207–19.

How, then, does this relate to the experience described in the autobiographical fragment of 1545? The first point which should be noted
is that the fragment does not state that Luther's discovery *took place* in
1519, or that it was essentially the recognition that *iustitia Dei* was none
other than *iustitia qua nos Deus induit, dum nos iustificat*, as some more
superficial discussions appear to suggest; if this were the case, we should
be forced to conclude that Luther merely came to a conclusion identical to that already reached by Karlstadt in 1517, in a work known to
have been read by Luther. Rather, the fragment states that his theological insights were *complete* by 1519, and also that these insights involved
the rethinking of the specific concepts, not merely of *iustitia Dei*, but
also of *sapientia Dei*, *fortitudo Dei* and *gloria Dei*. Second, it is clear that
the concept of *iustitia Dei* as *iustitia activa* which Luther describes in the
fragment is that associated with the soteriology of the *via moderna*.[37] As
we suggest elsewhere, however, Luther's discovery of the 'wonderful new
definition of righteousness' is essentially programmatic,[38] and capable
of being applied to other divine attributes, such as those referred to in
the autobiographical fragment, leading ultimately to the *theologia crucis*,
the 'theology of the cross', in which there is currently such considerable
interest in systematic-theological circles.

Although Luther indeed recognises that *iustitia Dei* is not to be understood as the righteousness by which God is himself just, but the righteousness by which he justifies the ungodly, this does not exhaust his
understanding of the concept, nor is it sufficient to characterise it adequately. Indeed, Luther's unique interpretation of the 'righteousness of
God' could not be distinguished from Augustine's interpretation of the
same concept if it were. The following characteristics of Luther's concept of *iustitia Dei* may be established on the basis of an analysis of the
later sections of the *Dictata super Psalterium* (1513–15), and the Romans
lectures (1515–16). *Iustitia Dei* is, according to Luther:
1. a righteousness which is a gift from God, rather than a righteousness
   which belongs to God;
2. a righteousness which is revealed in the cross of Christ;
3. a righteousness which contradicts human preconceptions.
While the first of these three elements unquestionably corresponds to
an important aspect of Augustine's concept of *iustitia Dei*, the remaining two serve to distinguish Luther and Augustine on this point. For
Luther, the 'righteousness of God' is revealed exclusively in the cross,
contradicting human preconceptions and expectations of the form that

---

[37] McGrath, *Luther's Theology of the Cross*, 100–13.
[38] McGrath, 'Mira et nova diffinitio iustitiae'.

revelation should take. This insight is essentially methodological, as the autobiographical fragment indicates, and is capable of being extended to the remaining divine attributes – such as the 'glory of God', the 'wisdom of God', and the 'strength of God'. All are revealed in the cross, and all are revealed *sub contrariis*, contradicting human expectations. It is this understanding of the nature of the revelation of the divine attributes which underlies Luther's *theologia crucis*, and which distinguishes the 'theologian of glory' from the 'theologian of the cross'.

Initially, Luther could not understand how the concept of a 'righteous God' was gospel, in that it appeared to offer nothing other than condemnation for sinful humanity. On the basis of the Ciceronian concept of *iustitia* as *reddens unicuique quod suum est*, underlying the concept of *iustitia Dei* associated with the *via moderna*, the individual who failed to do *quod in se est* was condemned. The fundamental presupposition at the heart of this soteriology is that humans are indeed capable of *quod in se est* – in other words, that humans are capable of meeting the fundamental precondition of justification through their own unaided faculties. The essential insight encapsulated in Luther's breakthrough of 1515 is that God himself meets a precondition which humans cannot fulfil – in other words, that God himself bestows upon humankind the gift of *fides Christi*. It is this insight which underlies Luther's remarks of 1517, paralleling the statements of the 1545 fragment:

A wonderful, new definition of righteousness! This is usually described thus: 'righteousness is a virtue which renders to each their due (*virtus reddens unicuique, quod suum est*).' This truly says: 'Righteousness is faith in Jesus Christ.'[39]

Having considered the origins of Luther's new theology of justification, we must now turn to deal with its mature statements.

3.3   Luther's mature theology of justification

Perhaps the most distinctive feature of Luther's mature doctrine of justification is the emphasis he places on its theological centrality. It was Luther above all who saw the *articulus iustificationis* as *the* word of the gospel, to which all else was subordinate. The doctrine of justification which he propounded was to cause him to reject the papacy and the church of

---

[39] Scholion to Galatians 2:16, WA 57.69.14–16; cf. WA 2.503.34–6. Note also the 1516 statement: 'Iustitia autem ista non est ea, de qua Aristoteles 5. Ethicorum vel iurisperiti agunt, sed fides seu gratia Christ iustificans' (WA 31 1.456.36). (I have taken the liberty of correcting the clearly incorrect '3. Ethicorum'.) It is Luther's critique of the concept of *iustitia* underlying the soteriology of the *via moderna* which lies at the heart of his later critique of Aristotle; see McGrath, *Luther's Theology of the Cross*, 136–41.

his day, not on the basis of any *direct* ecclesiological argument, but upon the basis of his conviction that the church of his day was committed to doctrines of justification which were nothing less than Pelagian.[40] The priority of his soteriology over his ecclesiology is particularly evident in his remarkable statement of 1535, to the effect that he will concede the Pope his authority if the latter concedes the free justification of sinners in Christ.[41]

The cornerstone of both Luther's theological breakthrough and his subsequent controversy with the church of his day appears to have been his insight that humans cannot initiate the process of justification, and his conviction that the church of his day had, by affirming the direct opposite, fallen into the Pelagian error. It is, of course, obvious that this was not the case: he appears to have been familiar with the academic theology of the *via moderna* at first hand, and does not seem to have known any of the rival soteriologies – such as that of the *schola Augustiniana moderna* (despite his being a member of the Augustinian order). In view of the fact that the soteriology of certain Reformed theologians (such as Peter Martyr Vermigli and John Calvin) may reflect precisely this soteriology, it is necessary to treat Luther's inadequate and ill-informed generalisations concerning the theology (especially the *pastoral* theology) of the late medieval church with considerable caution.

Following his decisive break with the soteriology of the *via moderna* in 1515, the general lines of the development of Luther's theology are clear. The important concept of *iustitia Christi aliena*, the 'commerce of exchange' between Christ and the sinner, and the *totus homo* theology all make their appearance in the Romans lectures of 1515–16; the *theologia crucis* emerges over the period 1516–19; the place of good works in justification is clarified in the 1520 *Sermo von den guten Werken*; and the crucial distinction between forgiving grace and the gift of the Holy Spirit is made clear in what is perhaps the most impressive of Luther's early works, *Rationis Latomianae confutatio* (1521). We shall consider these points individually.

It is important to appreciate that Luther's theology of justification cannot be characterised solely with reference to the strongly anti-Pelagian cast which that theology increasingly assumed from 1515 onwards. One of its most distinctive features is its explicit criticism of Augustine, evident from the same period. This point emerges from Karl Holl's interpretation of Luther's understanding of justification as a progressive *reale Gerechtmachung*.[42] For Holl, the solution to 'the riddle of Luther's

---

[40] WA 56.502.32 – 503.5 is particularly significant here.   [41] WA 40/I.357.18–22.
[42] Holl, 'Die Rechtfertigungslehre in Luthers Vorlesung über den Römerbrief mit besonderer Rücksicht auf die Frage der Heilsgewißheit', in *Gesammelte Aufsätze* 1.111–54.

doctrine of justification' lay not in a doctrine of double justification, nor in a juxtaposition of *Rechtfertigung* and *Gerechtmachung*, but in a proleptic understanding of the basis of the analytic divine judgement implicit in the process of justification. Holl illustrated this concept with reference to the analogy of a sculptor and his vision of the final product which motivates and guides him as he begins work on a block of crude marble; similarly, God's present justification of sinners is based upon his anticipation of their final sanctification, in that the present justification of humans takes place on the basis of their foreseen future righteousness.

This influential interpretation of Luther was, according to some critics, actually a confusion of Luther's views with those of early Lutheran orthodoxy, requiring modification on the basis of the 1521 treatise *Rationis Latomianae confutatio*, to which we shall shortly return. Nevertheless, Holl's exposition of the dialectic between the sinner's state *in re* and *in spe* does indeed correspond closely to the sanative concept of justification, frequently employed by Luther in the 1515–16 Romans lectures. This clearly raises the question of precisely what *was* distinctive about Luther's early teaching on justification.

This question has been raised recently by the 'Finnish school', whose interpretation of Luther places particular emphasis upon the believer's *actual participation in the divine life* through union with Christ.[43] Christ is present within the believer in faith, and is through this presence identical with the righteousness of faith. Such ideas are found in the 1520 writing *The Freedom of a Christian*:

Faith does not merely mean that the soul realises that the divine word is full of all grace, free and holy; it also unites the soul with Christ (*voreynigt auch die seele mit Christo*), as a bride is united with her bridegroom. From such a marriage, as St Paul says (Ephesians 5:32–32), it follows that Christ and the soul become one body, so that they hold all things in common, whether for better or worse. This means that what Christ possesses belongs to the believing soul; and what the soul possesses, belongs to Christ. Thus Christ possesses all good things and holiness; these now belong to the soul. The soul possesses lots of vices and sin; these now belong to Christ.[44]

This approach, while recognising forensic elements within Luther's theology of justification, stresses its transforming aspects, especially the idea of a real, physical union with Christ. On this reading of Luther, there is a

[43] On which see C. E. Braaten and R. W. Jenson, *Union with Christ: The New Finnish Interpretation of Luther*, Grand Rapids: Eerdmans, 1998.
[44] WA 7.25.26 – 26.9.

much greater degree of affinity between his theology of justification and the eastern notion of divinisation.[45]

The key to Luther's distinctive early understanding of the process of justification, particularly his difference with Augustine, lies in his anthropology.[46] Departing radically from Augustine's Neoplatonist anthropology, Luther insists that the Pauline antithesis between *caro* and *spiritus* must be understood theologically, rather than anthropologically. On an anthropological approach to the antithesis, *caro* is the 'fleshly', sensual or worldly side of humanity, while *spiritus* represents the higher human nature, orientated towards striving towards God. For Luther, it is the whole person (*totus homo*) who serves the law of God and the law of sin at one and the same time, and who thus exists under a double servitude.[47] The one and the same person is spiritual and carnal, righteous and a sinner, good and evil.

Since the saints are always conscious of their sin, and seek righteousness from God in accordance with his mercy, they are always reckoned as righteous by God (*semper quoque iusti a Deo reputantur*). Thus in their own eyes, and as a matter of fact, they are unrighteous. But God reckons them as righteous on account of their confession of their sin. In fact, they are sinners; however, they are righteous by the reckoning of a merciful God (*re vera peccatores, sed reputatione miserentis Dei iusti*). Without knowing it, they are righteous; knowing it, they are unrighteous. They are sinners in fact, but righteous in hope (*peccatores in re, iusti autem in spe*).[48]

It is on the basis of this anthropology that Luther bases his famous assertion that the believer is *simul iustus et peccator*.

How, then, may the believer be distinguished from the unbeliever on the basis of this anthropology? The answer lies in the frame of reference from which the *totus homo* is viewed – *coram Deo* or *coram hominibus*. For Luther, the believer is righteous *coram Deo*, whereas the unbeliever is righteous *coram hominibus*. The believer is thus *iustus apud Deum et in reputatione eius*, but not *iustus coram hominibus*. The justified sinner is, and will remain, *semper peccator, semper penitens, semper iustus*. This point is important, on account of the evident divergence from Augustine. For Augustine, the righteousness bestowed upon humans by God in their justification was recognisable as such by humans – in other words, the justified sinner was *iustus coram Deo et coram hominibus*. It will therefore be clear that Luther was obliged to develop a radically different understanding of the

---

[45] On which see J. Heubach, *Luther und Theosis*, Erlangen: Martin-Luther-Verlag, 1990; R. Flogaus, *Theosis bei Palamas und Luther: Ein Beitrag zum ökumenischen Gespräch*, Göttingen: Vandenhoeck & Ruprecht, 1997.

[46] H.-M. Barth, 'Martin Luther disputiert über den Menschen: Ein Beitrag zu Luthers Anthropologie', *KuD* 27 (1981), 154–66.

[47] WA 56.347.2–11.   [48] WA 56.343.16–19.

nature of justifying righteousness if he was to avoid contradicting the basic presuppositions implicit in his *totus homo* anthropology. This new understanding is to be found in the concept of *iustitia Christi aliena*, which is perhaps the most characteristic feature of his early understanding of justification.

For Luther, the gospel destroys all human righteousness, in that humans are forced to recognise that they are totally devoid of soteriological resources, and thus turn to receive these resources *ab extra*. Humans are justified by laying hold of a righteousness which is not, and can never be, their own – the *iustitia Christi aliena*, which God mercifully 'reckons' to humans. 'The Christ who is grasped by faith and lives in the heart is the true Christian righteousness, on account of which God counts us righteous and grants us eternal life.'[49] The essence of justifying faith is that it is *fides apprehensiva* – a faith which seizes Christ, and holds him fast, in order that his righteousness may be ours, and our sin his. Thus Luther interprets *semper iustificandus* as 'ever to be justified anew', while Augustine treats it as meaning 'ever to be made more and more righteous'. Luther does not make the distinction between justification and sanctification associated with later Protestantism, treating justification as a process of becoming: *fieri est iustificatio*.[50]

Justification is thus a 'sort of beginning of God's creation', *initium aliquod creaturae eius*, by which Christians wait in hope for the consummation of their righteousness.[51] This sanative aspect of his early teaching on justification corresponds closely to the teaching of Augustine on the matter. Justification is regarded as a healing process which permits God to overlook the remaining sin on account of its pending eradication. This is especially clear from the famous analogy of the sick person under the care of a competent physician: like a sick person under the care of a doctor, who is ill *in re* yet healthy *in spe*, the Christian awaits in hope the final resolution of the dialectic between righteousness and sin.

It is like the case of a man who is ill, who trusts the doctor who promises him a certain recovery and in the meantime obeys the doctor's instructions, abstaining from what has been forbidden to him, in the hope of the promised recovery (*in spe promissae sanitatis*), so that he does not do anything to hinder this promised recovery . . . Now this man who is ill, is he healthy? The fact is that he is a man who is both ill and healthy at the same time (*immo aegrotus simul et sanus*). As a matter of fact, he is ill; but he is healthy on account of the certain promise of the doctor, whom he trusts and who reckons him as healthy already, because he is sure that he will cure him. Indeed, he has already begun to cure him, and no longer regards him as having a terminal illness. In the same way, our Samaritan, Christ, has brought this ill man to the inn to be cared for, and has begun to cure

---

[49] WA 40/I.229.28; cf. 229.4.   [50] WA 56.442.3.   [51] WA 40/II.24.2–3.

him, having promised him the most certain cure leading to eternal life . . . Now is this man perfectly righteous? No. But he is at one and the same time a sinner and a righteous person (*simul iustus et peccator*). He is a sinner in fact, but a righteous person by the sure reckoning and promise of God that he will continue to deliver him from sin until he has completely cured him. And so he is totally healthy in hope, but is a sinner in fact (*sanus perfecte est in spe, in re autem peccator*). He has the beginning of righteousness, and so always continues more and more to seek it, while realising that he is always unrighteous.[52]

There is thus clearly a proleptic element in this understanding of justification, as Holl suggests. However, Luther's equation of *iustitia* and *fides Christi* – foreshadowed in the concept of *iustitia fidei* in the *Dictata super Psalterium* – is potentially misleading at this point. The distinction between Luther and Augustine on this aspect of justification is best seen from Luther's discussion of the relation between grace and faith.

Luther's concept of faith represents a significant departure from Augustine's rather intellectualist counterpart. The strongly existentialist dimension of faith is brought out with particular clarity in the 1517 Hebrews lectures. Whereas a purely human faith acknowledges that God exists,[53] or is prepared to concede that 'Christ appears before the face of God for others', a true justifying faith recognises, in a practical manner, that 'Christ appears before the face of God for us' (*Christus apparuit vultui Dei pro nobis*).[54] Only this latter faith can resist the assaults of temptation and despair – ideas that Luther expresses in his classic notion of *Anfechtung*. Whereas a *fides informis* is like a candle, all too easily extinguished by the winds of *Anfechtung*, true justifying faith is like the sun itself – unaffected by even the most tempestuous of winds.[55] For Luther, the grace of God is always something external to humanity, and an absolute, rather than a partial, quality. Humans are either totally under grace or totally under wrath.

In contrast to this, faith (and its antithesis, sin) are seen as internal and partial, in that the person under grace may be partially faithful and partially sinful. Faith is thus seen as the means by which individuals under grace may develop and grow in their spiritual life. Luther thus abandons the traditional understanding of the role of grace in justification by interpreting it as the absolute favour of God towards an individual, rather than a quality, or a series of qualities, at work within the human

[52] WA 56.272.3–21.
[53] WA 57.232.26. Cf. Schwarz, *Fides, spes und caritas beim jungen Luther*, 50, where Luther is shown to have employed the traditional understanding of *fides* in 1509–10.
[54] WA 57.215.16–20.
[55] WA 57.233.16–19. See further H. Beintker, *Die Überwindung der Anfechtung bei Luther: Eine Studie zu seiner Theologie nach den Operationes in Psalmos 1519–21*, Berlin: Evangelische Verlagsanstalt, 1954.

soul. Grace is no longer understood as a new nature within humans. This latter role is now allocated to *fides Christi*.

It is important to appreciate that Luther insists that the distinguishing mark of faith is the real and redeeming presence of Christ. Faith is *fides apprehensiva*, a faith which 'grasps' Christ and makes him present. By arguing that grace and faith are given in Christ, Luther is able to assert at one and the same time that the righteousness of believers is, and will remain, extrinsic to them,[56] while Christ is none the less really present within believers, effecting their renovation and regeneration. Furthermore, by insisting that faith is given to humans *in* justification, Luther avoids any suggestion that humans are justified *on account of* their faith; justification is *propter Christum*, and not *propter fidem*.

The reinterpretation of grace as an absolute external quality, and of faith as a partial internal one, permits Luther to maintain what is otherwise clearly a contradiction within his theology of justification – his simultaneous insistence upon the external nature of the righteousness of Christ and upon the real presence of Christ in the believer. Although Luther does not develop a theology of *iustitia imputata* at this point, it is clear that his anthropological presuppositions dictate that justifying righteousness be conceived extrinsically, thus laying the foundations for the Melanchthonian doctrine of the imputation of the righteousness of Christ to the believer. The origins of the concept of 'imputed righteousness', so characteristic of Protestant theologies of justification after the year 1530, may therefore legitimately be considered to lie with Luther.

One of the most significant aspects of Luther's break with the soteriology of the *via moderna* lies in his doctrine of the *servum arbitrium*.[57] The 1517 *Disputatio contra scholasticam theologiam* asserted that the unjustified sinner can only will and perform evil.[58] The Heidelberg disputation of the following year included the assertion that the 'free will after sin exists in name only, and when it does *quod in se est*, it sins mortally'.[59]

It is difficult, at this stage, to draw any clear distinction between Augustine and Luther on the powers of the *liberum arbitrium post peccatum*, partially because it is not clear precisely what Luther understands by the term

---

[56] WA 56.279.22: 'Ideo recte dixi, quod extrinsecum nobis est omne bonum nostrum, quod est Christus.'

[57] On which see H. J. McSorley, *Luther – Right or Wrong?*, 217–73, 297–366.

[58] WA 1.224 Thesis 4. On Luther's attack on the *via moderna*, personified by Gabriel Biel, see Grane, *Contra Gabrielem*, 369–85.

[59] WA 1.354 Thesis 13. Cf. *D* 1481: 'In omni opere bono iustus peccat'; *D* 1486: 'Liberum arbitrium post peccatum est res de solo titulo; et dum facit, quod in se est, peccat mortaliter.' See further H. Roos, 'Die Quellen der Bulle "Exsurge Domine"', in J. Auer and H. Yolk (eds.), *Theologie in Geschichte und Gegenwart: Festschrift für Michael Schmaus*, 3 vols., Munich: Zink, 1957, 3.909–26.

liberum arbitrium (e.g., if it is assumed that he is referring to Augustine's *liberum arbitrium captivatum*, the proposition is clearly Augustinian). It is therefore important to observe that the condemnation of Luther's teaching in the papal bull *Exsurge Domine* of 15 June 1520 is curiously phrased, and should probably be interpreted to mean that the condemned forty-one propositions are *variously* heretical or scandalous or false or offensive to pious ears or misleading to simple minds, rather than that each and every proposition is to be condemned on all five grounds.[60] The thirty-sixth proposition, which appears to affirm an essentially Augustinian doctrine, may therefore be regarded as having been condemned for stating an orthodox Catholic dogma in an offensive or potentially misleading manner.

In his subsequent pronouncements upon free will, however, Luther appears to move increasingly away from Augustine. Both in his defence of the thirty-sixth proposition and in the anti-Erasmian *De servo arbitrio* of 1525, Luther appears to adopt a form of necessitarianism, either as the main substance of his defence of the *servum arbitrium*, or at least as an important supporting argument. His assertions that Wycliffe was correct to maintain that all things happen by absolute necessity,[61] and that God is the author of all evil human deeds,[62] have proved serious obstacles to those who wish to suggest that Luther was merely restating an Augustinian or scriptural position.

In particular, three significant points of difference between Augustine and Luther should be noted:
1. For Luther, it is God who is the author of sin. For Augustine, it is humans who are the author of sin.
2. The slavery of human will is understood by Luther to be a consequence of humans' creatureliness, rather than of their sin (the affinities with Thomas Bradwardine here are evident).[63]
3. Luther explicitly teaches a doctrine of double predestination, whereas Augustine was reluctant to acknowledge such a doctrine, no matter how logically appropriate it might appear.

Some scholars have argued that Luther's doctrine of justification and of the *servum arbitrium* are related as the two sides of a coin,[64] so that a statement of the one amounts to a statement of the other. It must, however,

[60] See *D* 1491, and compare with the *in globo* condemnation of *D* 910–16 and 1235. See McSorley, *Luther: Right or Wrong?*, 251–3.
[61] WA 7.146.6–12; 18.615.12–17.   [62] WA 7.144.34 – 145.4; 18.709.28–36.
[63] WA 18.615.13–16 seems to leave no room whatsoever for contingency on the part of any created being, including humans, whether they are sinners or not.
[64] For example, G. L. Plitt, 'Luthers Streit mit Erasmus über den freien Willen in den Jahren 1525–25', *Studien der evangelisch-protestantischen Geistlichen des Grossherzogthums Baden* 2 (1876), 205–14.

be pointed out that Luther's doctrine of justification is not exhausted or adequately characterised by a statement of the doctrine of the *servum arbitrium*. Essential to his understanding of justification is the concept of *iustitia Christi aliena*, which is not necessarily implied by the doctrine of the unfree will. If human free will is enslaved, it is certainly true that humans cannot justify themselves – but this does not place God under any obligation to justify them by means of an extrinsic righteousness, provided the source of justifying righteousness is conceded to be none other than God himself. That the will of humans is enslaved is one matter; that God should choose to justify them in one specific manner as a result is quite another.

As we shall show, the history of Lutheran theology indicates that a wedge was driven between the concepts of an alien justifying righteousness and an enslaved will at a comparatively early stage, the former being consistently maintained as *de fide*, the latter being abandoned or reduced to the mere assertion that humans cannot justify themselves – a far cry from its original meaning. This implicit criticism of Luther by Lutheranism may be taken as demonstrating that there is no fundamental theological connection between the two concepts. They are two essentially independent statements about justification, related only by the personality of Luther. With his death, that relation ceased to exist within Lutheranism.

A point upon which Luther has been consistently misunderstood concerns the relationship between faith and works in justification. Luther's theological breakthrough was intimately linked with the realisation that humanity was justified not upon the basis of any human work, but through the work of God within humans.[65] Luther's intense hostility towards anyone who wished *per legem iustificari* led him to develop an understanding of the relationship between law and gospel which allocated the former a specific, but strictly circumscribed, role in the Christian life.[66]

Luther does not, as he is frequently represented, reject the necessity of good works in justification: 'works are necessary for salvation, but do not cause salvation, in that faith alone gives life'.[67] He frequently appeals to the biblical image of the good tree which bears good fruit, that fruit demonstrating rather than causing its good nature.[68] In his later period,

[65] See B. Lohse, *Ratio und Fides: Eine Untersuchung über die Ratio in der Theologie Luthers*, Göttingen: Vandenhoeck & Ruprecht, 1958, 82–6; B. A. Gerrish, *Grace and Reason: A Study in the Theology of Martin Luther*, London: Oxford University Press, 1962, 84–99; McGrath, *Luther's Theology of the Cross*, 136–41.
[66] Modalsi, *Das Gericht nach den Werken*; Peters, *Glaube und Werk*.
[67] WA 39/I.96.6–8.   [68] WA 39/I.254.27–30.

particularly in those writings dating from 1534–5, Luther distinguished two dimensions to justification: justification in the sight of God, and in the sight of the world.[69] It is clear that he is not developing a doctrine of what would later be known as 'double justification' at this point, but merely identifying one element of the *usus legis in loco iustificationis*. The good works of the justified demonstrate the believer's justification *by God*, and cannot be considered to cause it.[70]

Before documenting the manner in which Luther's doctrine of justification was appropriated or modified within the early Reformation, it is important that we should attempt to establish the points of contact with the earlier medieval tradition. Luther represents a figure of theological transition, standing between two eras, and it is clearly of some interest to characterise the modifications which took place in relation to two clear sources of influence upon Luther: Augustine and the *via moderna*. Although sympathetic to the former and critical of the latter, he stands in continuity with both.

It is possible to outline the relation between Luther and Augustine on justification as follows:

1. Luther and Augustine both interpret *iustitia Dei* as the righteousness by which God justifies sinners, rather than as the abstract divine attribute which stands over and against humankind, judging on the basis of merit. In this respect, Luther is closer to Augustine than to the *via moderna*, although the nature of Luther's understanding of *iustitia Dei* is more complex than is usually appreciated.[71]

2. Augustine understands *iustitia Dei* to be contiguous with *iustitia hominum*, in that it underlies human concepts of *iustitia*. For Luther, *iustitia Dei* is revealed only in the cross of Christ, and, if anything, contradicts human conceptions of *iustitia*. Whereas Luther's doctrine of justification is based upon the concept of *servum arbitrium*, Augustine's is based upon that of *liberum arbitrium captivatum*, which becomes *liberum arbitrium liberatum* through the action of *gratia sanans*.

3. Luther does not appear to envisage a liberation of the *servum arbitrium* after justification, in that the servitude of human will is seen as a consequence of the creatureliness of humans, rather than their sinfulness. The differences between Luther and Augustine on predestination, noted above, also reflect this point. Although the phrase *servum arbitrium* derives from Augustine, it is not typical of his thought.

---

[69] WA 39/I.208.9–10: 'Duplex in scripturis traditur iustificatio, altera fidei coram Deo, altera operum coram mundo.'
[70] WA 39/I.96.9–14.
[71] For a more detailed discussion, see McGrath, *Luther's Theology of the Cross*, 95–147, especially 113–19.

4. Luther and Augustine concur in understanding justification as an all-embracing process, subsuming the beginning, development and subsequent perfection of the Christian life. This is one of the clearest *differentiae* between Luther and later Protestantism, and places Luther closer to the position of the Council of Trent than is generally realised.

5. Whereas Augustine understands the believer to become righteous in justification, participating in the divine life and being, Luther is reluctant to admit that humanity becomes righteous in justification. If anything, humans become more and more aware of their sinfulness, and of their need for the alien righteousness of Christ. Intrinsically humans are, and will remain, sinners, despite being extrinsically righteous. Luther explicitly criticises Augustine on this point. Although Luther makes frequent reference to the righteousness of believers, his equation of *iustitia* and *fides Christi* makes it clear that he is not referring to the morality of believers, but to the real and redeeming presence of Christ. The strongly Christological orientation of Luther's concept of the righteousness of believers sets him apart from Augustine on this point.

6. Luther and Augustine work with quite different anthropological presuppositions, with important consequences for their understandings of faith and sin.

7. Luther expresses the divine soteriological priority by speaking primarily in terms of 'justification by faith', thus using the Pauline imagery of Romans 5:1 and related passages. Augustine expresses this same notion by speaking of 'salvation by grace', thus picking up the Pauline imagery of Ephesians 2:8. This divergence in vocabulary is of considerable importance, and has not been satisfactorily explained to date.

It will therefore be clear that Luther's relation to Augustine is ambivalent. While one can point to elements in his thought which are clearly Augustinian, there are points – particularly his doctrine of *iustitia Christia aliena* – where he diverges significantly from Augustine.

Luther's relation to the *via moderna* is rather more complex, and remains the subject of investigation. There can be no doubt that Luther's early theology, up to the year 1514, as well as some elements which persist until 1515, is essentially that of the *via moderna*. This is particularly evident in the case of his understanding of the covenantal foundations of justification, his interpretation of the axiom *facienti quod in se est Deus non denegat gratiam*, his understanding of the notion of *iustitia Dei*, and his critique of the implication of created habits in justification. It is also clear that Luther's 1517 dispute against 'scholastic theology' is actually directed specifically against Gabriel Biel. The question which remains to be answered, however, is whether Luther appropriated any elements of the theology of the *via moderna* in his *later* theology of justification.

At one stage, it was considered that Luther's doctrine of the imputation of righteousness and the non-imputation of sin represented one such element. Thus de Lagarde suggested that the background to Luther's doctrine was to be found in the dialectic between the two powers of God.[72] *De potentia sua absoluta*, God may accept a person without the grace of justification. Thus Luther may be regarded as stating *de potentia ordinata* what Biel stated *de potentia absoluta* concerning divine acceptation. It may, however, be pointed out that where Biel and Ockham understand the locus of the doctrine of the *acceptatio divina* to be the divine will, Luther actually locates it Christologically. A similar argument was advanced by Feckes, based upon the presupposition that Biel actually states *de potentia absoluta* what he would like to have stated *de potentia ordinata*, but could not on account of possible criticism from the ecclesiastical authorities.[73] As Feckes' attempt to relate Biel and Luther is based upon this discredited understanding of Biel, it cannot be sustained. Furthermore, as Vignaux has pointed out, this possibility appears to be excluded by Luther himself, particularly by theses 56 and 57 of the *Disputatio contra scholasticam theologiam*.[74] Neither Biel nor Ockham, of course, develops a doctrine of the imputation of righteousness, which enormously weakens the case for any putative positive influence from the *via moderna* in this respect. We must look elsewhere for the origins of Luther's understanding of the *reputatio* of the *iustitia Christi aliena* to believers.

The influence of the *schola Augustiniana moderna* upon Luther is much more difficult to assess. It is clear that there are excellent reasons for believing that Luther did not encounter this school, even in the person of Johannes von Staupitz, during his theological education.[75] Furthermore, Luther does not appear to have encountered Gregory of Rimini's writings until 1519.[76] It is therefore impossible to maintain that his distinctive views on justification derive from this school. Thus Luther and Staupitz, although having a common Augustinian soteriological framework, differ totally on the question of the nature of justifying righteousness: for Staupitz, justifying righteousness is *iustitia in nobis*, whereas for Luther it is *iustitia extra nos*.[77]

Whatever the origins of Luther's distinctive ideas on justification, it is clear that they exercised an immediate influence upon the development

---

[72] F. de Lagarde, *Naissance de l'esprit laïque au déclin du Moyen Age*, 6 vols., Paris: Presses Universitaires de France, 1948, 6.86–8.

[73] C. Feckes, *Die Rechtfertigungslehre des Gabriel Biels*, 12.

[74] Vignaux, 'Sur Luther et Ockham'.

[75] See McGrath, *Luther's Theology of the Cross*, 27–40, 63–71.

[76] As established by Leif Grane, 'Gregor von Rimini und Luthers Leipziger Disputation'. The crucial text is *Resolutiones Lutherianae super propositionibus suis Lipsiae disputatis*: WA 2.394.31 – 395.6.

[77] See Oberman, *Werden und Wertung der Reformation*, 110–12.

of the Lutheran Reformation at Wittenberg. Nevertheless, Luther's ideas were not accepted without modifications, some subtle. This gradual process of critical appropriation and nuanced redirection in the years leading up to the Formula of Concord is itself of considerable scholarly interest. In the following section, we shall consider the origins and subsequent development of this process of modification of Luther within Lutheranism.

3.4   Justification in early Lutheranism, 1516–1580

The year 1516 witnessed considerable discussion within the theological faculty at the University of Wittenberg concerning the nature of Augustine's teaching on justification. In a disputation of 25 September 1516, Luther had suggested that Karlstadt should check the teachings of the *scholasticos doctores* against the writings of Augustine to discover the extent to which they diverged from him.[78] Setting off for Leipzig on 13 January 1517, Karlstadt managed to equip himself with a copy of the works of Augustine, and hence realised the radical discrepancy between his own position and that of Augustine. As a result, Karlstadt was moved to arrange a public disputation on 26 April 1517, in which, to Luther's delight, he defended 151 Augustinian theses.[79] His particular attraction to Augustine's strongly anti-Pelagian *De spiritu et litera* led to his lecturing, and subsequently publishing a commentary, upon this important work. The result of Karlstadt's conversion to the *vera theologia* in 1517 was that the Wittenberg theological faculty was committed to a programme of theological reform by the year 1518, based extensively upon the anti-Pelagian writings of Augustine.

It is at this point that differences between Luther and Karlstadt become clearly discernible. In his works dating from this early period, Karlstadt appears as a remarkably faithful interpreter of Augustine, where Luther often appears as his critic. Thus Karlstadt follows Augustine in developing an antithesis between law and *grace* rather than *gospel*, and emphasises the priority of *grace* rather than *faith*.[80] Most significantly of all, the Augustinian understanding of the *nature* of justification is faithfully reproduced. Of particular importance is his unequivocal assertion that

---

[78] McGrath, *Luther's Theology of the Cross*, 44–6. For Karlstadt's own account, see Karlstadt, *De spiritu et litera*, ed. Kähler, 4.13–28.

[79] For the text of these theses, see *De spiritu et litera*, 11*–37*. He also published 405 theses partly directed against Eck: *Vollständige Reformations-Acta und Documenta*, ed. V. E. Löscher, 3 vols., Leipzig, 1720–3, 2.79–104.

[80] For example, *De spiritu et litera*, 28*, Theses 103–5. Karlstadt actually uses the term 'gospel' infrequently over the period 1516–21, and it is somewhat misleading for Kriechbaum to devote an important section of her work to the antithesis of 'law and gospel'; Kriechbaum, *Grundzüge der Theologie Karlstadts*, 39–76.

justifying righteousness is inherent to humans, and that it *makes* them righteous.[81] It is clear that Karlstadt follows Staupitz in this understanding of the nature of justifying righteousness, and either knows nothing of Luther's concept of justifying righteousness as *iustitia Christi aliena* or chooses to ignore it altogether. Indeed, the Christological emphasis evident in Luther's theology of justification by this stage is quite absent from Karlstadt's theology of justification,[82] which continues to be primarily a theology of the *grace of God*. It will also be clear that this passage calls into question the suggestion that Luther discovered an essentially *Augustinian* concept of *iustitia Dei* in late 1518 or early 1519; precisely this concept of *iustitia Dei* is faithfully reproduced in Karlstadt's lectures and published commentary on Augustine. Similarly, Karlstadt follows Augustine in defining justification in terms of the non-imputation of sin, rather than the imputation of righteousness. In his writings for the period 1519–21, Karlstadt faithfully reproduces the Augustinian concept of justification as the non-imputation of sin and the impartation of righteousness, and does not adopt Luther's extrinsic conception of justifying righteousness.[83] As we indicated earlier, Luther's extrinsic conception of justifying righteousness is partly a consequence of his *totus homo* anthropology, which differs significantly from Augustine's Neoplatonist understanding of humans. Karlstadt adopts an essentially Augustinian anthropology, in which justification is conceived as a renewal of human nature through a gradual eradication of sin. Although this is clearly similar to Luther's assertion that the justified believer is *simul iustus et peccator*, it is evident that the two theologians interpret the phrase differently. For Luther, what is being stated is that the believer is *extrinsically righteous* and *intrinsically sinful*; for Karlstadt, what is being affirmed in this manner is precisely what Augustine intended when he stated that the justified sinner is *partly* righteous and *partly* sinful (*ex quadam parte iustus, ex quadam parte peccator*).[84]

---

[81] *De spiritu et litera*, 69.27–31: 'Non est sensus, quod illa iusticia dei sit per legem testificata, qua deus in se iustus est, sed illa, qua iustificat impium, qua induit hominem, qua instaurat imaginem dei in homine; de hac iusticia, qua deus suos electos iustos et pios efficit, tractamus.' Cf. 55.32 – 56.2.

[82] *De spiritu et litera*, 43*. Cf. Kriechbaum, *Grundzüge der Theologie Karlstadts*, 42–5.

[83] In his study of Karlstadt, Sider appears to misunderstand the term 'forensic justification', apparently regarding it as synonymous with 'the merciful pardoning of sins': Sider, *Andreas Bodenstein von Karlstadt*, 67–8, 122–5, 258–9. Although Sider frequently refers to the concept of 'imputed righteousness', the texts which he adduces do not support his interpretation of the concept. Furthermore, he recognises that Karlstadt continues to emphasise the interior regeneration implicit in justification; for example, see 126–9, 258. Karlstadt's doctrine of justification is no more forensic than that of Augustine, which he reproduces remarkably faithfully.

[84] Augustine, *Ennarationes in Psalmos* 140.15. See further Nygren, 'Simul iustus et peccator bei Augustin und Luther'.

There are therefore excellent reasons for suggesting that Karlstadt's doctrine of justification over the period 1517–21 is essentially Augustinian, lacking the novel elements which distinguish Luther's teaching of the time from that of the African bishop. A similar conclusion must be drawn concerning the theology of Johann Bugenhagen over the period 1521–5.[85] In his 1525 lectures on Romans, Bugenhagen identifies the three elements of justification as *remissio peccatorum, donatio spiritus* and *non-imputatio peccati.*[86] Even when commenting on Romans 4:5–6, where Erasmus had corrected the Vulgate translation *reputatio iustitiae* to *imputatio iustitiae*, Bugenhagen still interprets the text as referring to the *non-imputation of sin* rather than the *imputation of an alien righteousness.*[87] Where Bugenhagen speaks of *imputatio* in a specifically *Christological* context, he is referring to the fact that the sin of believers is not imputed to them on account of Christ: *iusti non imputante deo propter Christum peccatum.* More generally, however, his concept of the non-imputation of sin is discussed in a pneumatological context; the renewing work of the Holy Spirit within humans permits God not to impute their sin.

Although Bugenhagen thus develops a doctrine of justification which is essentially Augustinian, omitting any reference to the imputation of the alien righteousness of Christ, it is clear that he has moved away from Augustine on certain points of significance.[88] In particular, he follows Luther in arguing that grace is to be conceived extrinsically, as *favor Dei.*[89] At this point, Bugenhagen is clearly dependent upon Melanchthon's 1521 *Loci.*[90] In view of Melanchthon's importance in establishing a forensic concept of justification as normative within Protestantism, it is appropriate to consider his contribution at this point.

Although an Erasmian on his arrival at Wittenberg in 1518, Melanchthon appears to have adopted Luther's *totus homo* anthropology at an early stage,[91] regarding sin as permeating even the higher faculties of humans. While his baccalaureate theses of September 1519 appear to develop a theology of justification which parallels that of Luther rather

---

[85] R. Kötter, 'Zur Entwicklung der Rechtfertigungslehre Johannes Bugenhagens 1521–1525', *ZKG* 105 (1994), 18–34.

[86] Holfelder, *Ausbildung von Bugenhagens Rechtfertigungslehre*, 24–42. For the concept of the non-imputation of sin in his commentary on the Psalter, see Holfelder, *Tentatio et consolatio*, 173–98.

[87] As pointed out, with documentation, by Holfelder, *Solus Christus*, 23 n. 25.

[88] For a good account of the issues, see R. Kötter, *Johannes Bugenhagens Rechtfertigungslehre und der römische Katholizismus: Studien zum Sendbrief an die Hamburger, 1525*, Göttingen: Vandenhoeck & Ruprecht, 1994.

[89] Bugenhagen, *Annotationes im epistolas Pauli* (1525), cited in Holfelder, *Solus Christus*, 24.

[90] Cf. Melanchthon, *Locus de gratia* (1521), StA 2.85.16 – 88.4.

[91] H. Bornkamm, 'Humanismus und Reform im Menschenbild Melanchthons', in *Das Jahrhundert der Reformation*, Göttingen: Vandenhoeck & Ruprecht, 1961, 69–87.

than that of Karlstadt,[92] it is clear from his writings of the period 1519–20 that he still tends to conceive justification ethically at points, as 'mortification of the flesh and our affections'.[93]

In his earlier works, Melanchthon portrays justification in predominantly factitive, rather than declarative, terms. Thus a conspicuous feature of these works is his emphasis upon the role of the *person* of Christ in justification; for example, the 1523 *Annotationes in Evangelium Iohannis* develops the idea that justification involves a personal union between Christ and the believer.[94] This contrasts significantly with his later emphasis upon the more abstract concept of the *work* of Christ associated with his doctrine of forensic justification, which becomes particularly evident from his writings dating from after 1530.

Nevertheless, by 1521 Melanchthon appears to have grasped much of Luther's distinctive understanding of justification, and incorporated it into the first edition of the *Loci communes* of that year.[95] This is particularly clear in the *Locus de gratia*, in which grace is unequivocally defined extrinsically as *favor Dei*: 'for grace, if it is to be very precisely defined, is nothing other than the benevolence of God towards us'.[96]

In his writings subsequent to 1530, Melanchthon increasingly emphasises the notion of *iustitia aliena* – an alien righteousness, which is imputed to the believer. Justification is then interpreted as *Gerechtsprechung*, being 'pronounced righteous' or 'accepted as righteous'. A sharp distinction thus comes to be drawn between justification, as the external act in which God pronounces or declares the believer to be righteous, and regeneration, as the internal process of renewal in which the believer is regenerated through the work of the Holy Spirit.

Whereas Luther consistently employed images and categories of personal relationship to describe the union of the believer and Christ (such as the *commercium admirabile* of a human marriage paralleling that between the soul and Christ), Melanchthon increasingly borrowed images and categories from the sphere of Roman law. Thus Melanchthon illustrates

[92] *StA* 1.24 Thesis 9: 'Ergo Christi beneficium est iustitia'; Thesis 10, 'Omnis iustitia nostra est gratuita dei imputatio.'
[93] *Annotationes in Evangelium Matthaei, StA* 4.173.5–6. But see Bizer, *Theologie der Verheißung*, 123–8.
[94] For example, see CR (Melanchthon) 14.1068, 1080. Cf. Bornkamm, 'Humanismus und Reform in Menschenbild Melanchthons'.
[95] For Lutheran polemical accounts of justification dating from this period, see Hohenberger, *Lutherische Rechtfertigungslehre in den reformatorischen Flugschriften der Jahre 1521–2.*
[96] *StA* 2.86.23–5; cf. 2.86.26–8, 106.20–2. See W. Maurer, *Der junge Melanchthon zwischen Humanismus und Reformation 2. Der Theologe*, Göttingen: Vandenhoeck & Ruprecht, 1969, 361–8.

the concept of forensic justification with reference to a classical analogy: just as the people of Rome declared Scipio to be a free person, so God declares the sinner to be righteous before God.[97] Significantly, Erasmus had used the forensic concept of *acceptilatio* (the purely verbal remission of a debt without payment) in the *Novum instrumentum omne* of 1516 as an illustration of the meaning of the verb *imputare*.[98]

The growing emphasis upon the concept of forensic justification in early Lutheranism raises the question of the origins of the concept. It is clear that the extrinsic conception of justifying righteousness which is fundamental to the notion of forensic justification is due to Luther himself. Although Luther incorporates traces of legal terminology into his discussion of justification,[99] it seems that the origins of the concept actually lie in Erasmus' 1516 translation of the New Testament. Erasmus' *Novum instrumentum omne* of 1516 provided not merely a new Latin translation of the Greek text of the New Testament, but also extensive notes justifying departure from the Vulgate text, which often appeal to classical antecedents. Of particular interest are his alterations to Romans 4:3. Where the Vulgate read 'Credidit Abraham Deo et reputatum est illi ad iustitiam', Erasmus altered the translation to 'Credidit aut Abraham Deo et imputatum est ei ad iustitiam.' The potentially forensic implications of this new translation of the Greek verb *logizomai* were pointed out by Erasmus himself; the basic concept underlying 'imputation' was termed 'acceptilation' by the jurisconsults.[100]

The concept of forensic justification is particularly well illustrated by the analogical concept of *acceptilatio* – indeed, this latter concept was frequently employed by the theologians of later Protestant orthodoxy in their discussion of the nature of forensic justification. As we noted above, 'acceptilation' is a Roman legal term, referring to the purely verbal

---

[97] The analogy first appears in the 1533 edition of the *Loci*; CR (Melanchthon) 21.421. For the 1555 edition, see *StA* 2.359.10–18. For the differences between Luther and Melanchthon at this point, see R. Stupperich, 'Die Rechtfertigungslehre bei Luther und Melanchthon 1530–1536', in *Luther und Melanchthon: Referate und Berichte des Zweitens Internationalen Kongresses für Lutherforschung*, Göttingen: Vandenhoeck & Ruprecht, 1961, 73–88; L. Haikola, 'Melanchthons und Luthers Lehre von der Rechtfertigung', in *Luther und Melanchthon*, 89–103; Greschat, *Melanchthon neben Luther*.

[98] For an exploration of the extent and significance of the differences between Luther and Melanchthon, see R. Flogaus, 'Luther versus Melanchthon? Zur Frage der Einheit der Wittenberger Reformation in der Rechtfertigungslehre', *ARG* 91 (2000), 6–46.

[99] W. Elert, 'Deutschrechtliche Züge in Luthers Rechtfertigungslehre', *ZSTh* 12 (1935), 22–35.

[100] Erasmus, *Novum Instrumentum omne*, 429: 'Accepto fert: logizetai, id est, imputat sive acceptum fert. Est autem acceptum fere, debere, sive pro accepto habere, quod non acceperis, *quae apud jure consultos vacatur acceptilatio.*'

remission of a debt, as if the debt has been paid – whereas, in fact, it has not. In view of the fact that Melanchthon knew and used Erasmus' New Testament text – the best of its age – he could hardly have failed to notice the forensic implications of the concept of 'imputation' as the purely verbal remission of sin, *without* – as with Augustine, Karlstadt and Bugenhagen – the prior or concomitant renewal of the sinner. It would therefore have been a remarkable coincidence, to say the least, that Erasmus should choose to illustrate the meaning of the term 'imputation' with a classical analogy which would later become normative within Protestant orthodoxy in the definition of the concept of forensic justification – although the concepts of *acceptatio* and *acceptilatio* were frequently confused! – if his original use of the analogy had not been taken up and developed by Melanchthon. A forensic doctrine of justification, in the proper sense of the term, would result from linking Erasmus' interpretation of the concept of imputation with Luther's concept of an extrinsic justifying righteousness – and it seems that Melanchthon took precisely this step.

The Augsburg Confession (1530) contains a brief statement on justification in its fourth article. This does not actually refer to the imputation of the alien righteousness of Christ at all, but instead merely restates the Pauline idea (Romans 4:5) of 'faith being reckoned as righteousness'.[101] The use of the formula *propter Christum per fidem* is significant, in that it defines the correct understanding of the formula 'justification *sola fide*'. The sole ground for human justification lies, not in humans themselves or in anything which they can do, but in Christ and his work alone. Humanity is not justified on account of faith (which would represent a doctrine of justification *propter fidem*), nor must faith be seen as a human work or achievement; strictly speaking, faith is a reception by humans of the gracious deed of God in Christ.

In the *Apologia* (1530) for the Confession, Melanchthon develops the concept of imputation – hinted at, but not explicitly stated, in the above article – in a significant direction. Just as a person might pay the debt of a friend, even though it is not his own, so the believer may be reckoned as righteous on account of the alien merit of Christ.[102] Making Luther's critique of Augustine's concept of justifying righteousness explicit, Melanchthon states that justification is to be understood forensically, as the declaration that the believer is righteous on account

---

[101] *BSLK* 56.1–10.
[102] 26 *Apologia* art. 21 para. 19, *BSLK* 320.40–6: 'Ut si quis amicus pro amico solvis aes alienum, debitor alieno merito tamquam proprio liberatur. Ita Christi menta nobis donantur, ut iusti reputemur fiducia meritorum Christi, cum in eum credimus, tamquam propria merita haberemus.'

of the alien righteousness of Christ.[103] Thus justification does not signify 'making righteous', but 'pronouncing righteous'.[104] There is no righteousness within humans, or inherent to them, which can be regarded as the basis of their justification; humans are justified on the basis of an external and alien righteousness, which is 'reputed' or 'imputed' to them. It will be clear that these statements of the imputation of righteousness go far beyond the traditional Augustinian statements concerning justification as the non-imputation of sin, and contradict such statements which define justification as 'making righteous'. It might, therefore, appear reasonable to conclude that the teaching of the Lutheran church with respect to justification had been defined and distinguished from that of Augustine at this point. In fact, this is not actually the case. Alongside statements which explicitly define the forensic character of justification, and which clearly *exclude* a factitive interpretation of justification, we find occasional statements which seem to define justification in more factitive terms. Significantly, such statements tend to be found near the beginning of the *Apologia* for the fourth article, whereas those denying the factitive character of justification tend to be found towards its end.[105]

The subsequent history of the evangelical faction within Germany, particularly in the aftermath of Luther's death (1546), the defeat of the Smalkadic League (1547) and the imposition of the Augsburg Interim (1548) is characterised by bitter controversy over more or less every aspect of the doctrine of justification. These controversies related to three main areas of the doctrine: the objective grounds of justification (the Osiandrist and Stancarist controversies); the necessity of good works after justification (the antinomian and Majorist controversies); and the subjective appropriation of justification (the synergist and monergist controversies). In view of their importance, we shall consider each of these areas individually.

3.4.1   The objective grounds of justification: the Osiandrist and Stancarist controversies

Among Melanchthon's contemporary critics was Andreas Osiander, leader of the evangelical faction in Nuremburg from 1522 to 1547. For Osiander, the Melanchthonian concept of justification as merely 'declaring righteous' was totally unacceptable: saving righteousness was none

---

[103] *Apologia* art. 4 para. 305, *BSLK* 219.43–5.
[104] *Apologia* art. 4 para. 252, *BSLK* 209.32–4.
[105] For example, *Apologia* art. 4 para. 72, *BSLK* 174.37–40. For a careful analysis and attempt to resolve this puzzling ambiguity, see Pfnür, *Einig in der Rechtfertigungslehre?*, 155–81, especially 157–68, 178–81.

other than the essential indwelling righteousness of Christ, arising from his divinity rather than from his humanity.[106] Justification must therefore be understood to consist of the infusion of the essential righteousness of Christ. We see here an unequivocal reassertion of a fundamentally Augustinian understanding of the *nature* of justification, especially in relation to the real interior transformation of an individual through the indwelling of God.[107] Although some of his critics, such as Martin Chemnitz, argued that this made justification dependent upon sanctification, it is clear that this is not actually the case. Osiander merely reacted against what he regarded as the unacceptably extrinsic conception of justification in the *Apologia* by emphasising those scriptural passages which speak of Christ dwelling within the believer.

Furthermore, Osiander claimed, not without reason, the support of Luther in his views on the significance of the indwelling of Christ; the increasing emphasis within the German evangelical faction upon the work of Christ imputed to humanity inevitably led to a reduction in interest in the role of the person of Christ within humans, and thus to a certain indifference to Luther's high estimation of this aspect of the justification of humanity. Indeed, the new 'Finnish school' of Luther interpretation may be regarded as an indirect vindication of Osiander's reading of Luther. However, Osiander's views merely served to harden German Protestant opinion against the concept of justification by inherent righteousness, and it was left to Calvin to demonstrate how Osiander's legitimate protest against the externalisation of Christ might be appropriated while maintaining a *forensic* doctrine of justification.[108]

Francesco Stancari maintained a totally antithetical position, and cited Melanchthon in his support (to the latter's horror). Whereas Osiander maintained that Christ's *divinity* was the ground of the justification of humanity, Stancari argued that the implication of Christ's divinity in this justification was quite unthinkable, involving logical contradiction (such as the fact that Christ's divine nature had to function both as mediator and as offended party). The objective basis of the justification of humanity was therefore Christ's *human* nature alone. On account of Christ's obedient suffering upon the cross in his human nature, his *acquired* (not *essential!*) righteousness was imputed to humans as the basis of their justification.[109] These controversies thus identified the need

---

[106] See Hauke, *Gott-Haben, um Gottes willen.*
[107] As demonstrated by P. Wilson-Kastner, 'Andreas Osiander's Theology of Grace in the Perspective of the Influence of Augustine of Hippo', *SCJ* 10 (1979), 72–91.
[108] Niesel, 'Calvin wider Osianders Rechtfertigungslehre'.
[109] Perhaps the best account of the views and influence of Stancari may be found in C. A. Selig, *Vollständige Historie des Augsburger Confession*, 3 vols. Halle, 1730, 2.714–947.

for clarification of the Augsburg Confession's unclear statements on the nature of justifying righteousness and the person of the Redeemer.

3.4.2   The role of works in justification: the antinomian and Majorist controversies

Perhaps through his emphasis on the priority of faith in justification, Luther had often seemed to imply that good works were of no significance in the Christian life (see 3.3). His fundamental position on this matter, particularly as clarified in his later writings, is that works are a condition, but not a cause, of salvation.[110] Luther is prepared to concede that if no works follow faith, it is certain that the faith in question is dead, and not a living faith in Christ. The 1520 sermon on good works states that 'faith in Christ is the first, highest and most sublime good work', adding that 'works are not pleasing on their own account, but on account of faith'.[111]

Melanchthon, however, always entertained a much more positive understanding of the role of the law in the Christian life. Melanchthon defined justification in terms of a new capacity to fulfil the law, and Christian freedom as a new freedom to fulfil the law spontaneously.[112] The 1527 *Articuli de quibus egerunt per visitatores* reproduced these views, and placed the preaching of the law at the heart of Christian instruction, insisting that without the law, both repentance and faith were impossible. These views were criticised by Johann Agricola, who argued that repentance was to be seen as a consequence of the gospel, not of the law.[113]

The Majorist controversy arose over Georg Major's support for the failure of the Leipzig Interim to stress the exclusive role of faith in justification. Although it is clear from his 1552 tract *Auf des ehrwürdigen Herrn Nikolaus van Amsdorfs Schrift Antwort* that Major was totally committed to the principle of justification *sola fide*, he nevertheless stated his conviction that, within this context, Luther taught that good works were necessary for salvation. Flacius immediately pointed out that this excluded both infants and the dying from being saved. Nikolaus von Amsdorf replied to Major initially with the assertion that the law had no role in justification whatsoever, and subsequently with the suggestion that good works might

---

[110] WA 1.96.6–8: 'Opera sunt necessaria ad salutem, sed non causant salutem, quia fides sola dat vitam.' Cf. WA 30/II.663.3–5; 39/I.254.27–30. For an excellent study, see Modalsi, *Gericht nach den Werken*, 83–9.

[111] WA 6.204.25–6; 206–36.   [112] *StA* 2.148.22–4; 149.19–21; 4.153–4.

[113] On which see T. J. Wengert, *Law and Gospel: Philip Melanchthon's Debate with John Agricola of Eisleben over Poenitentia*, Grand Rapids: Baker, 1997.

actually be detrimental to salvation.[114] The related dispute *de tertio usus legis* arose over similar views expressed by Luther's pupils Andreas Poach and Anton Otho.[115] By 1560, it was clear to all that the sixth article of the Augsburg Confession required clarification if serious internal disunity on this point were to be brought to an end.

3.4.3 The subjective appropriation of justification: the synergist and monergist controversies

Luther's insistence upon the utter passivity of humans in justification, especially evident in his defence of the thirty-sixth proposition and *De servo arbitrio*, remained characteristic of his teaching on justification throughout his life. It is therefore important to note Melanchthon's growing unease concerning this aspect of Luther's theology. The 1535 edition of the *Loci* suggested, and the 1543 edition made explicit, that Melanchthon no longer agreed with Luther on this point: justification was now to be attributed to three contributing factors – the Word of God, the Holy Spirit, and the faculty of the human will. For Melanchthon, humans possess the *facultas applicandi se ad gratiam* prior to justification. As a result, people are not drawn to God unless they wish to be drawn.[116] Similarly, Melanchthon's early commitment to the doctrine of predestination *ante praevisa merita* in the 1521 edition of the *Loci* is replaced by that of predestination *post praevisa merita* in the edition of 1535. It is possibly this change of heart which underlies the omission of any article dealing specifically with the contentious question of predestination in the Augsburg Confession.

Melanchthon's views were defended by Strigel on the one hand, and subjected to heavy criticism by Amsdorf and Flacius on the other.[117] The occasion of the synergist controversy was the publication of Johann Pfeffinger's *Propositiones de libero arbitrio* (1555), which asserted that the reason that some responded to the gospel and others did not was to

---

[114] Amsdorf, *Das die propositio (Gute werck sind sur Seligkeit schedlich) eine rechte ware christliche propositio sey* (Magdeburg, 1559). In his preface to Luther's sermons on John 18–20, published in 1557, Amsdorf represented Luther as teaching that good works were unnecessary and harmful: WA 28.765–7. See further Kolb, *Nikolaus von Amsdorf*, 123–80, especially 158–62.

[115] W. Joest, *Gesetz und Freiheit: Das Problem des tertius usus legis bei Luther und neutestamentliche Parainese*, Göttingen: Vandenhoeck & Ruprecht, 1961.

[116] T. J. Wengert, *Human Freedom, Christian Righteousness: Philip Melanchthon's Exegetical Dispute with Erasmus of Rotterdam*, New York: Oxford University Press, 1998.

[117] Both Amsdorf and Flacius were strident defenders of the 'Gnesio-Lutheran' principle of absolute predestination, which they held to be compromised by Pfeffinger: Kolb, *Nikolaus van Amsdorf*, 188–201. See further O. K. Olson, *Matthias Flacius and the Survival of Luther's Reform*, Wiesbaden: Harrassowitz, 2002.

be found within humans themselves, rather than in an extrinsic prior divine decision. Thus the ultimate difference between David and Saul, or between Peter and Judas, must lie in their respective free wills. Although Pfeffinger was careful to insist that God retains the initiative (and, indeed, the upper hand) in justification, he nevertheless stated that it is the human free will which decides whether or not the Holy Spirit enters into an individual's life.

This concept of *liberum arbitrium in spiritualibus* was violently opposed by the monergists Amsdorf and Flacius, with the result that the matter came to a head at the Weimar Colloquy (1560). In this dispute, Strigel suggested that the human free will was injured and weakened through original sin, although not completely destroyed. He illustrated this Augustinian position by comparing the effect of sin upon the free will with that of garlic juice upon a magnet: once the obstruction has been removed, the power of the magnet is restored.

This analogy is of interest in its own right, and deserves further comment.[118] It is based on an observation in the writings of the Greek scholar Plutarch (46–119), who notes that 'a lodestone will not attract iron if it is rubbed with garlic'.[119] The illustration appears several decades later in the writings of the astronomer Claudius Ptolemy.[120] We find it elaborated still further in a tenth-century collection of writings entitled *Geoponica*, which includes a short work headed 'On Physical Sympathies and Antipathies': 'The magnetic stone, known as the "lodestone", attracts iron, but loses this power when it is rubbed with garlic. However, this is recovered once more when the blood of a goat is poured on to it.'[121] This assertion is regularly repeated throughout the early modern period. Even as late as 1636, Bernardo Cesi was insisting that he and his readers 'know by everyday experience that the power of a magnet is weakened by garlic (*retundi vires magnetis allio, experimentis discimus quotidianis*).[122] Yet the experimental basis of this analogy had been disproved conclusively by Giambattista della Porta, who demonstrated that it was without empirical warrant.[123] Its theological application in the intra-Lutheran debates of the late sixteenth century is an interesting anomaly.

Flacius replied by accusing Strigel of externalising sin and proceeded to develop Luther's analogy of the passivity of humanity in justification

---

[118] See D. Lehoux, 'Tropes, Facts and Empiricism', *Perspectives on Science* 11 (2003), 326–45.
[119] Plutarch, *Quaestiones conviviales* 641 c5.
[120] Ptolemy, *Tetrabiblos* I.iii.13.   [121] *Geoponica* xv.i.28.2.
[122] B. Cesi, *Mineralogia sive naturalis philosophiae thesauri*, Leiden, 1636, 40.
[123] B. della Porta, *Magiae naturalis libri xx*, Naples, 1589.

in a manner which seemed Manichaean to those observing the debate.[124] Nevertheless, it was once more clear that clarification of the role of humans in their own justification was required if further internal dissent was to be avoided.

Clarification of these three areas would be provided by the Formula of Concord, drawn up in March 1577, which gave the doctrine of justification a critical role in relation to Lutheran self-definition.[125] Before considering the manner in which the Formula settled these disputes, it is necessary to return to the question of the nature of justification and justifying righteousness, in order to note that substantial internal agreement had been reached within Lutheranism and the Reformed church on this matter in the intervening period.

This is best illustrated from Martin Chemnitz' *Examen Concilii Tridentini* (1563–73), an authoritative work which clearly established the difference between the Lutheran church and Augustine on these points. Chemnitz notes that there are two approaches to the term 'justification': the Latin approach, which interprets justification as *iustum facere*, and the Hebrew approach, which interprets it as *absolutio a peccato seu remissio peccatorum et imputatio iustitiae Christi*.[126] The former corresponds to that of Augustine and subsequently the Roman Catholic approach, and the latter to the Lutheran. The Latin approach involves the interpretation of justification as the infusion of righteousness,[127] whereas Chemnitz argues, on the basis of an analysis of secular Greek sources, that the verb must be interpreted in a forensic sense. As a result, Augustine is guilty of misrepresenting Paul, particularly in relation to the matter of the imputation of righteousness.[128]

This position was endorsed by the third article of the Formula of Concord.[129] Justification is here defined in explicitly forensic terms, and it is made clear that it is not faith which is reckoned as justifying righteousness, but the righteousness of Christ imputed to us.

The term 'justification' in this discussion means 'to pronounce righteous, to absolve from sin and the eternal consequences of sin, on account of the righteousness of Christ, which is imputed by God through faith'.[130]

---

[124] For useful background, see I. Dingel, 'Flacius als Schüler Luthers and Melanchthons', in G. Graf (ed.), *Vestigia Pietatis: Studien zur Geschichte der Frömmigkeit in Thüringen und Sachsen*, Leipzig: Evangelische Verlagsanstalt, 2000, 77–93.

[125] T. Kaufman, 'Die "kriteriologische Funktion" der Rechtfertigungslehre in den lutherischen Bekenntnisschriften', *ZThK* 10 (1998), 47–64.

[126] Chemnitz, *Examen* 129.a 7–16.   [127] Chemnitz, *Examen* 130.b 15–18.

[128] Chemnitz, *Loci theologici*, Pars II, 626, 642; *Examen* 130.b 24–48; 131.a 39–41; 131.b 18–23; 132.b 1–3.

[129] *BSLK* 913–36.

[130] *Solida declaratio* III.17, *BSLK* 919.24–9: 'Vocabulum igitur *iustificationis* in hoc negotio significat iustum pronuntiare, a peccatis et aeternis peccatorum suppliciis absolvere, propter iustitiam Christi, quae a Deo fidei imputatur.'

The individual teachings of both Osiander and Stancari are rejected, in favour of justification by the mediatorial righteousness of Christ, grounded in both his divinity and his humanity.[131]

The Majorist controversy was resolved through the fourth article of the Formula, which asserted that good works were obligatory, in that they are commanded, as well as being an appropriate expression of faith and gratitude to God; they are not, however, mandatory or necessary *for salvation*. Works are and remain the effects of justifying faith, and must not be confused with the cause of that faith.[132]

The synergist and monergist controversies were ended with the explicit condemnation of the synergist position. Strigel's analogy of the magnet and garlic juice is explicitly rejected.[133] The text (John 6:44) which Melanchthon had interpreted (though with the aid of Chrysostom) to mean that God drew to himself only those who wished to be drawn, is now interpreted in an anti-Melanchthonian sense, meaning that the free will is totally impotent and dependent upon grace. Whereas, since 1535, Melanchthon had recognised three concurrent causes of justification (the Word, the Holy Spirit, and the human will), thus permitting humans a say in their own justification, the Formula recognised only one such cause – the Holy Spirit.[134]

It might therefore be thought that the Formula endorses the monergist position. In fact, it does not, as may be seen from its statements on predestination. The doctrine of double predestination – so important a feature of Luther's *De servo arbitrio* – is explicitly rejected in favour of a doctrine of predestination based upon the *benevolentia Dei universalis*. A careful distinction is made between *praedestinatio* and *praescientia*: the former extends only to the children of God, whereas the latter extends to all creatures as such.[135] The *causa perditionis* is defined as being humanity, rather than God[136] – a conclusion, incidentally, which stands in contrast to Luther's 1525 assertion that the only centre of freedom which cannot be said to be necessitated by another is God himself. Furthermore, Luther's doctrine of the *servum arbitrium* is radically undermined by the assertion that the free will may, under the influence of grace, assent to faith.[137] Although the Formula specifically rejects any suggestion of

---

[131] *Solida Declaratio* III.4; III.12; III.56, *BSLK* 914.19 – 916.3; 918.10–12; 933.36 – 934.11.

[132] *Epitome* IV.16, *BSLK* 789.15–20.

[133] *Epitome* I.15, *BSLK* 773.28: 'cum magnes allii succo illinitur'.

[134] *Epitome* II.6, *BSLK* 778.4–14. See the classic study of E. F. Fischer, *Melanchthons Lehre von der Bekehrung: Eine Studie zur Entwicklung der Anschauung Melanchthons über Monergismus und Synergismus*, Tübingen: Mohr, 1905.

[135] *Solida Declaratio* XI.4; XI.5, *BSLK* 1065.2–6, 23–7.

[136] *Solida Declaratio* XI.81, *BSLK* 1086.26–41: 'enim Deus non est causa peccati'. Cf. XI.41 (1076.4–16), where the possibility that the reprobate's contempt for the Word of God as a consequence of divine predestination is also rejected.

[137] *Epitome* II.18, *BSLK* 780.30 – 781.3. Cf. II.83, 906.5–24.

co-operation between human will and the Holy Spirit, it is clear that this is directed against Melanchthon's opinion that humans can co-operate with God *apart from grace*. The Formula envisages the human *liberum arbitrium* as being liberated by grace, whereas Luther regarded it as being permanently enslaved through human creatureliness.

It will therefore be clear that the Formula of Concord not only marked the ending of an important series of controversies in the Lutheran church immediately after Luther's death; it also marked the victory and consolidation of the critique of Luther from within Lutheranism itself. Luther's concept of justification, his concept of the presence of Christ within the believer, his doctrine of double predestination, his doctrine of *servum arbitrium* – all were rejected or radically modified by those who followed him. It would be improper to inquire into whether this critique and modification were warranted; it is, however, right and proper to note that they took place, as it is only on the basis of this recognition that the full significance of the contribution of Lutheran orthodoxy to the development of our doctrine may be appreciated.

Before turning to consider the course of the doctrine in Lutheran and Reformed orthodoxy, however, we must examine how the doctrine unfolded within the wing of the Reformation associated with Zwingli and Calvin.

3.5   Early Reformed theology, 1519–1560

Although Luther's influence on the historical and theological shaping of the Reformation was immense, it is important to appreciate that reforming currents developed in other parts of Europe around the same time, often on the basis of quite different perceptions of the nature and mode of reform. Eastern Switzerland is a case in point. The reforming movement in this region in the 1510s and early 1520s was closely linked with humanist sodalities active in the region, particularly at the Universities of Basel and Vienna. The reforming agenda in this region was not linked with any perception that the medieval church had misconstrued its soteriology; rather, the driving force for reform focussed on the life and morals of the church and of individual Christians.

From its outset, the Swiss Reformation was characterised by a vision for the future of the church that envisaged reform primarily as a reformation of life and morals.[138] Doctrinal reform was not regarded as necessary or important; the central issues concerned the revitalisation of the vision of the church, and a realignment of its structures and morality with those

---

[138] See the important study of E. Ziegler, 'Zur Reformation als Reformation des Lebens und der Sitten', *Rorschacher Neujahrsblatt* (1984), 53–71.

envisaged by the New Testament – a vision of reform that can clearly be seen in Zwingli's early sermons at Zurich during the year 1519.

There are strong and significant – if often overlooked – affinities between the early reforming theology of Zwingli and that of more radical thinkers. Zwingli's characteristic suspicion of the doctrine of original sin was echoed by radical theologians such as Peter Riedemann.[139] Redemption was about inner transformation, ensuing in a life of discipleship. Luther's emphasis on justification appeared to erode this demand for obedience, making acceptance unconditional. Zwingli echoed similar concerns, although the necessities of theological diplomacy may have caused him to underplay them.

The influence of humanism over early Reformed theology was significant,[140] and has important implications for understanding the lack of interest in issues of soteriology typical of the movement in its early stages. Although Erasmus' interest in the doctrine of justification appears to have been minimal, his general approach to the issues is basically moralist in tone.[141] For Erasmus, the importance of the New Testament relates to the teaching of Jesus as the *lex Christi*, so that the New Testament is to be regarded as the primary instrument in a religiously educative and formative process. Erasmus thus emphasises the importance of the moral sense of Scripture, by which he is able to demonstrate the continuity of the *lex evangelica* from the Old Testament to the New.[142]

This brings us to one of the most decisive differences between the early Reformed tradition and Luther. For Bucer and Zwingli, the Jewish law is to be seen as a good thing now fulfilled, rather than (as in much Lutheran thought of the 1520s and beyond) a bad thing which is now abolished. The influence of Erasmus over both Zwingli and Bucer at this point appears to have been considerable,[143] and may go some way towards explaining the strongly moralist doctrines of justification associated with

---

[139] See J. Friedmann, 'Peter Riedemann on Original Sin and the Way of Redemption', *Mennonite Quarterly Review* 26 (1952), 210–15.

[140] See B. Moeller, 'Die deutschen Humanisten und die Anfänge der Reformation', *ZKG* 70 (1959), 46–61; idem, 'Die Ursprünge der reformierten Kirche', *ThLZ* 100 (1975), 642–53.

[141] See E.-W. Kohls, *Die Theologie des Erasmus*, 2 vols., Basel: Reinhard, 1966, 1.43–58.

[142] For a useful discussion of Erasmus' moralist exegesis of Scripture, see H. G. Reventlow, *The Authority of the Bible and the Rise of the Modern World*, London: SCM Press, 1984, 39–48.

[143] For example, see J. F. G. Goeters, in M. Greschat and J. F. G. Goeters (eds.), 'Zwinglis Werdegang als Erasmianer', in *Reformation und Humanismus: Robert Stupperich zum 65. Geburtstag*, Witten: Luther-Verlag, 1969, 225–71; F. Krüger, *Bucer und Erasmus: Eine Untersuchung zum Einfluß des Erasmus auf die Theologie Martin Bucers*, Wiesbaden: Steiner, 1970; R. Stauffer, 'Einfluß und Kritik des Humanismus in Zwinglis "Commentarius de vera et falsa religione"', *Zwingliana* 16 (1983), 97–110; Christine Christ, 'Das Schriftverständnis von Zwingli und Erasmus im Jahre 1522', *Zwingliana* 16 (1983), 111–25.

these two key theologians of the early Reformed church.[144] Nevertheless, both theologians clearly regard their positive attitude towards the law as grounded in the Old and New Testaments themselves, rather than in the moralist presuppositions of the various forms of humanism which impacted on their theological development at this point.[145]

In his early humanist period, Zwingli's understanding of justification appears to have been primarily ethical. His contemporaries within the Swiss humanist movement regarded him as a fine exponent of the *philosophia Christi*, with its distinctive emphasis upon moral integrity.[146] For Zwingli, the 'righteousness of faith', based upon obedience to God, must be contrasted with 'self-righteousness', based upon self-confidence. The similarities between Erasmus and Zwingli on the *lex evangelica* can be seen particularly clearly in their subordination of justification to regeneration. Zwingli rarely uses the term 'justification' or 'justified', tending to use the term *rechtglöbig* ('right-believing') instead. Thus he indicates that *der rechtglöbige Mensch* submits himself to the law willingly, in contrast to the unbeliever.

Zwingli's emphasis upon the moral character of the 'new person' (*wiedergeborene und neue Menschen*) thus leads him to understand justification to be based upon an *analytic*, rather than a *synthetic*, divine judgement. Once more, the similies with the radical wing of the Reformation at this point must be noted.[147] Radical reformers preferred to speak of *Gerechtmachung* or *Fromm-machung* to stress that the believer is required to imitate Christ rather than merely to trust in God's promises.[148]

Whereas, for Luther, the question of how one might find a gracious God led to his intense personal preoccupation with the doctrine of justification, Zwingli's concerns appear to have been primarily with the reform and revitalisation of the church – in other words, with the humanist vision of *Christianismus renascens*. Far from regarding the doctrine of justification as the centre of the gospel, and the foundation of a coherent programme of theological reform, Zwingli appears to have adopted a form of moralism, demonstrating clear and significant affinities with Erasmus' *philosophia*

---

[144] On the impact of Roman law on sixteenth-century humanism, of no small importance at this point, see M. L. Monheit, 'Guillaume Budé, Andrea Alciato, Pierre de l'Estoile: Renaissance Interpreters of Roman Law', *JHI* 68 (1997), 21–40.

[145] For the Jewish roots of Bucer's approach, see G. M. Hobbs, 'Martin Bucer on Psalm 22: A Study in the Application of Rabbinical Exegesis by a Christian Hebraist', in O. Fatio and P. Fraenkel (eds.), *Histoire de l'exégèse au XVIᵉ siècle*, Geneva: Droz, 1978, 144–63.

[146] For example, see CR 7.328.17–20. See Rich, *Anfänge*, 56–70.

[147] Beachy, *The Concept of Grace in the Radical Reformation*.

[148] For this theme in the works of Kaspar Schwenckfeld, see A. Séguenny, *Homme charnel, homme spirituel: étude sur la christologie de Caspar Schwenckfeld (1489–1561)*, Wiesbaden: Steiner Verlag, 1975.

Christi.[149] Zwingli's programme of reform initially corresponds to that of the circle of Swiss humanists to which he belonged; his divergence from that programme is probably to be dated from around the year 1520, after his arrival at Zurich and the inauguration of his reforming ministry.[150]

A similarly moralist approach to justification may be found in the writings of Johannes Oecolampadius, whose strong emphasis upon the importance of regeneration in the Christian life inevitably led to the subordination of humans' justification to their regeneration. As Oecolampadius remarks in the course of his comments on Hebrews 10:24, Christians must continually examine themselves to see if the faith which they profess is manifested in good works. Henri Strohl has noted that Oecolampadius' chief concern appears to have been the ethical dimension of faith.[151] Similarly, Christ's death upon the cross exemplifies the divine love for humanity, which is intended to move humans to moral excellence. Here, as with Zwingli, we find the moral protests of the early Swiss Reformers passing into their theology: the person who has true faith is the person of moral integrity. Similarly, Heinrich Bullinger insisted that justification meant, not the imputation of righteousness, but the actualisation of righteousness.[152] As with later Pietism, the justification of humans is confirmed by their moral actions.

The most significant exposition of the doctrine of justification within the early Reformed church is due to Martin Bucer, and it is here that we find the still-inchoate moralism of Zwingli being developed into a demonstrably Erasmian approach. Even from his earliest period, Bucer was strongly inclined towards Erasmianism.[153] Although Bucer was clearly influenced by Luther, following their meeting at Heidelberg in 1518, it is significant that Bucer tended to interpret much of Luther's teaching in Erasmian terms, and to pass over many of his more distinctive reforming ideas altogether.[154] Bucer's preoccupations are clearly moralist, as may be

---

[149] McGrath, 'Humanist Elements in the Early Reformed Doctrine of Justification'.

[150] For the question of the date of Zwingli's inception as a theological reformer, see Neuser, *Die reformatorische Wende bei Zwingli*, 38–74.

[151] H. Strohl, *La Pensée de la Réforme*, Neuchâtel: Delachaux & Niestle, 1951, 107. Cf. E. Staehelin, *Das theologische Lebenswerk Johannes Oecolampadius*, Leipzig: Heinsius, 1939; E. G. Rupp, *Patterns of Reformation*, London: Epworth, 1969, 3–48.

[152] Bullinger, *Sermonum decades quinque* 157b. Note too the emphasis upon the consonance of Paul and James, also evident in *De gratia dei iustificante* 65–7.

[153] This is clearly seen from his early preoccupation with the works of Erasmus: M. Greschat, 'Martin Bucers Bücherverzeichnis', *Archiv für Kulturgeschichte* 57 (1975), 162–85.

[154] This is well brought out by K. Koch, *Studium Pietatis: Martin Bucer als Ethiker*, Neukirchen: Neukirchener Verlag, 1962, 10–15, on the basis of his correspondence with Beatus Rhenanus.

seen from his reduction of 'doctrine' to 'ethics' on the basis of his philological exegesis of the concept of *torah*: for Bucer, the whole of Scripture
is to be seen as law.[155] This moralist approach to Scripture is reflected in
his doctrine of justification, which represents a significant modification
of that of Luther.

Bucer develops a doctrine of *double* justification: after a 'primary justification', in which the sins of humans are forgiven and righteousness
imputed to them, there follows a 'secondary justification', in which
humanity is *made* righteous; the *iustificatio impii*, expounded by Bucer
on the basis of St Paul, is followed by the *iustificatio pii*, expounded on
the basis of St James.[156] While Bucer is concerned to maintain a forensic
concept of primary justification, he stresses the need for this to be manifested as good works in the secondary justification. Although the primary justification of humans takes place on the basis of faith alone (*sola
fide*), their secondary justification takes place on the basis of their works.
While Bucer maintains the forensic nature of the primary justification,
he stresses the need for this to be manifested in good works. Although
this secondary justification appears to be equivalent, in respects, to the
later concept of sanctification, it is still conceived in primarily moralist
terms.

The question which necessarily follows from this analysis is this: did
Bucer actually teach a doctrine of double justification in the strict sense –
in other words, that the formal cause of justification is both imputed
and inherent righteousness? Bucer's involvement in the drawing up of
the 'Regensburg Book' (*Liber Ratisboniensis*), with its important article
on justification, is certainly highly suggestive in this respect.[157] The most
adequate answer to this question appears to be that Bucer did not for-
mulate his doctrine of justification in such a way that it might serve an
eirenic purpose, as Gropper and Pighius appear to have intended, but
rather wished to forge a secure theological link between the totally gratuitous justification of sinners and the moral obligations which this subsequently placed upon them. The righteousness and good works which
are effected by the Holy Spirit are to be seen as the visible evidence of
humanity's unmerited acceptance in the sight of God. Just as a good tree

---

[155] *Enarrationes in sacra quattuor evangelia* (1530), 48 B–C; 49 C. Cf. Koch, *Studium Pietatis*, 67.
[156] *Metaphrasis et enarratio in epist. D. Pauli ad Romanos*, 231 A–B; 232 D–E. Elsewhere in the same work, he notes a threefold scheme, which includes the final glorification of the sinner as its third element: 119 A–B. See J. Müller, *Martin Bucers Hermeneutik*, Gütersloh: Mohn, 1965, 122 n. 184.
[157] Stuperich, 'Der Ursprung des Regensburger Buches von 1541 und seine Rechtferti-gungslehre'.

produces good fruit, so the justified sinner must produce good works.[158] It is on account of his anxieties over the potentially negative ethical implications of the doctrine of justification *sola fide* that Bucer has been styled 'the Pietist among the Reformers'.[159] Bucer clearly considers the role of piety in the Christian life to be of sufficient importance to require explicit incorporation into a doctrine of justification. Faith must produce 'die ganze Frommheit und Seligkeit', and Bucer ensures this by setting out the following *ordo salutis*:[160]

praedestinatio → *electio* → *vocatio* → *iustificatio* → *glorificatio*

in which *iustificatio* is understood to have two elements: an initial justification by faith, and a subsequent justification by works.

The important point to be emphasised is that Bucer locates the theological sphere of human moral action under justification, whereas others (such as Melanchthon) located it under regeneration or sanctification, which was understood to be a quite distinct element in the *ordo salutis*. Bucer does not, as one of his recent interpreters suggests, include sanctification in the *ordo salutis*;[161] what was later termed *sanctificatio* by Calvin is termed 'secondary justification' or *iustificatio pii* by Bucer.

It is widely agreed that the most significant contribution to the development of the early Reformed doctrine of justification was due to John Calvin.[162] Although the 1536 edition of the *Christianae religionis institutio* contains a few scant lines on justification, that of 1539 and subsequent

[158] *Metaphrasis et enarratio in epist. D. Pauli ad Romanos*, 11–14. Cf. W. P. Stephens, *The Holy Spirit in the Theology of Martin Bucer*, Cambridge: Cambridge University Press, 1970, 48–100, especially 55–61.

[159] A. Lang, *Der Evangelienkommentar Martin Butzers und die Grundzüge seiner Theologie*, Leipzig: Dieterich, 1900, 8, 137, 377–8. Unfortunately, Lang's assertion that Bucer was devoid of humanist influence has not stood up to critical evaluation. However, Bucer's ideological flexibility may go some way towards explaining difficulties in interpretation at such points: see M. Greschat, 'Der Ansatz der Theologie Martin Bucers', *ThLZ* 103 (1978), 81–96.

[160] For example, *Metaphrasis et enarratio in epist. D. Pauli ad Romanos*, 405 c. It is not clear whether this should be understood as a logical or a chronological sequence: Stephens, *Martin Bucer*, 30, suggests it is logical, although the more careful analysis of Müller, *Martin Bucers Hermeneutik*, 24 n. 38, suggests it is chronological.

[161] Stephens, *Martin Bucer*, 99, states that 'there is an unbreakable link holding together predestination, vocation, justification, *sanctification* and glorification' (our italics); the reference given makes no mention of sanctification (99 n. 2). Similarly, Stephens' entire section on 'sanctification' (71–98) represents the imposition of an alien structure upon Bucer's thought, and cannot be supported on the basis of the texts cited.

[162] Although the main features of Calvin's theology of justification may be found in his exegetical works (for example, see H. P. Santmire, 'Justification in Calvin's 1540 Romans Commentary', *ChH* 33 (1963), 294–313), we propose to develop our analysis upon the basis of the 1559 edition of the *Institutes*. It is only in this later work that the distinction between Calvin and Osiander on the nature of the believer's relation

editions describe the doctrine of justification as the 'main hinge upon which religion turns', and the 'sum of all piety'. The terse statements of that first edition concerning justification are, however, significant, in that justification is clearly defined in forensic terms. To be 'justified' does not mean that we become righteous, but that we are reckoned to be righteous on account of Christ.[163]

This brief affirmation of forensic justification is developed further in subsequent editions of the *Institutes*. Humanity is not made righteous in justification, but is accepted as righteous, not on account of its own righteousness, but on account of the righteousness of Christ located outside of humans. Calvin's brief discussion of the nature of imputation parallels that of Erasmus' *Novum instrumentum omne* (1516), noted above. For Calvin, persons may be said to be justified when they are accepted by God as if they were righteous:

We therefore interpret 'justification' simply as the acceptance by which God receives us in grace and treats us as righteous, consisting of the remission of sins and the imputation of the righteousness of Christ.[164]

Calvin himself has no hesitation in acknowledging the strongly forensic character of this concept of justification, particularly in his polemic against Osiander.[165] It will also be clear that the emphasis placed by Calvin upon the *acceptatio divina* parallels that of the *via moderna* and the *schola Augustiniana moderna*, suggesting an affinity with the voluntarism and extrinsicism of these late medieval movements.[166]

Calvin insists that, as there is no basis in humans for their divine acceptation, their righteousness in justification is always *extra seipsum*; our righteousness is always *non in nobis sed in Christo*.[167] Although Calvin may be regarded as following the lead of Melanchthon in this matter,[168] he

to Christ is fully clarified. Furthermore, the propagation of Reformed theology in the later sixteenth century was largely due to the 1559 *Institutes*, either in translation or in a condensed edition, rather than to his biblical commentaries.

[163] *Christianae religionis institutio*, Basel, 1536, III, *OS* 1.73. The 1539 edition contains a chapter (*VI. De iustificatione fidei et meritis operum*) which represents a massive expansion of the brief comments of the first edition.
[164] *Institutes* (1559) III.xi.2, *OS* 4.183.7–10.
[165] *Institutes* III.xi.11, *OS* 4.193.2–5; 193.17 – 194.21. On Calvin's critique of Osiander, see Zimmermann, 'Calvins Auseinandersetzung mit Osianders Rechtfertigungslehre', *KuD*.
[166] See McGrath, 'John Calvin and Late Medieval Thought', for an analysis. Calvin's doctrine of the *meritum Christi* – of importance in this respect – was discussed earlier in this volume in relation to the late medieval doctrine of merit.
[167] *Institutes* III.xi.23, *OS* 4.206.29–32. Thus Calvin criticises Augustine's own intrinsic concept of justifying righteousness, as well as its Osiandrian variant: *Institutes* III.xi.15, *OS* 4.199.25 – 200.6.
[168] For Calvin's attitude to the Augsburg Confession, see Willem Nijenhuis, 'Calvin en de Augsburgse Confessie', *Nederlands Theologisch Tijdschrift* 15 (1960–1), 416–33.

nevertheless preserves an important aspect of Luther's understanding of justification which Melanchthon appeared to have abandoned – the personal union of Christ and the believer in justification, which has been retrieved so successfully by the modern Finnish interpreters of Luther. Thus Calvin speaks of the believer's being 'grafted into Christ', so that the concept of *incorporation* becomes central to Calvin's understanding of justification. The *iustitia Christi*, on the basis of which humanity is justified, is treated as if it were that of humanity within the context of the intimate personal relationship of Christ and the believer.[169] Calvin's polemic against Osiander concerns the fundamental nature, rather than the existence, of the union of Christ and the believer. Where Osiander understands the union to be physical, Calvin considers it to be purely spiritual.[170]

The two consequences of the believer's incorporation into Christ are *iustificatio* and *sanctificatio*, which are distinct and inseparable.[171] Thus where Bucer speaks of *iustificatio pii* or 'secondary justification', Calvin speaks of *sanctificatio*; where Bucer links the first and second justifications on the basis of the regenerating activity of the Holy Spirit, Calvin relates them on the basis of the believer's *insitio in Christum*. Justification and sanctification are aspects of the believer's new life in Christ, and just as one receives the whole Christ, and not part of him, through faith, so any separation of these two soteriological elements – which Calvin refers to as *les deux principales grâces* – is inconceivable.[172] It is instructive to compare Bucer and Calvin on the *ordo salutis*:

Bucer: *electio* → *iustificatio impii* → *iustificatio pii* → *glorificatio*

Calvin: *electio* → *unio mystica* → $\begin{cases} iustificatio \\ sanctificatio \end{cases}$ → *glorificatio*

The strength of Calvin's understanding of justification is that justification is now conceived *Christologically*, thus permitting the essentially

---

[169] *Institutes* III.xi.10, *OS* 4.191.31 – 192.4.

[170] See Niesel, 'Calvin wider Osianders Rechtfertigungslehre'. Calvin's attitude to the concept of 'union with Christ' of Bernard of Clairvaux is of interest here; see D. E. Tamburello, *Union with Christ: John Calvin and the Mysticism of St. Bernard*, Louisville: Westminster John Knox Press, 1994. Also of relevance here is Calvin's attitude to the Regensburg article of justification (1541): see W. H. Neuser, 'Calvins Urteil über den Rechtfertigungsartikel des Regensburger Buches', in Greschat and Goeters (eds.), *Reformation und Humanismus*, 176–94.

[171] *Institutes* III.xi.1, 6. For further discussion and references, see Boisset, 'Justification et sanctification chez Calvin'; Stadtland, *Rechtfertigung und Heiligung*; McGrath, 'Humanist Elements in the Early Reformed Doctrine of Justification', 14–16.

[172] For the phrase, see CR (Calvin) 50.437–8.

moral conception of justification associated with Zwingli and Bucer to be discarded. Where Zwingli and Bucer tended to make justification dependent upon believers' regeneration through the renewing work of the Holy Spirit, which enabled them to keep the law and imitate the (external) example of Christ, Calvin understands both justification and sanctification to be the chief *beneficia Christi*, bestowed simultaneously and inseparably upon believers as a consequence of their *insitio in Christum*. Sanctification is not the effect of justification; both justification and sanctification are effects of union with Christ. Notice also how sanctification is now conceived Christologically, in terms of 'becoming what we are' – that is to say, actualising our new status in Christ in our lives through the process of being conformed to Christ.

Calvin thus implicates Christ *intrinsically*, where Zwingli and Bucer implicated him *extrinsically*, in the *ordo salutis*. This new approach to justification may be regarded as a recovery – probably intentional – of Luther's realist conception of justification as the personal encounter of the believer with God in Christ, while simultaneously retaining the extrinsicism of the Melanchthonian concept of justification. Like Luther, Calvin stresses that faith is implicated in justification only to the extent that it grasps and appropriates Christ.[173] Indeed, faith may be said to play its part in justification by insisting that it does *not* justify, attributing all to Christ.[174] In other words, the possibility that the slogan 'justification *sola fide*' will be understood as 'justification *propter fidem*' is excluded from the outset: justification can only be *propter Christum*. Faith is merely the vessel which receives Christ – and the vessel cannot be compared in value with the treasure which it contains. Faith may thus be said to be the instrumental cause of justification.[175] It will, however, be clear that Calvin is actually concerned, not so much with justification, as with incorporation into Christ (which has, as one of its necessary consequences, justification). It is this point that goes some considerable way towards explaining the lack of importance which Calvin appears to attach to justification in the 1559 *Institutes*.

It is a well-known fact that, in the 1559 edition of this work, Calvin defers his discussion of justification until Book III, and it is then found only after a detailed exposition of sanctification. This has proved a serious embarrassment to those who project Luther's concern with the *articulus iustificationis* on to Calvin, asserting that justification is the 'focal centre' of the *Institutio*. In fact, Calvin's concern is with the manner in which the individual is incorporated into Christ, and the personal and corporate

[173] *Institutes* III.xi.7.   [174] *Institutes* IV.xvii.42; III.xvii.11; III.xviii.10.
[175] *Institutes* III.xi.7.

consequences of this *insitio in Christum* – of which justification is but one. Calvin thus expresses systematically what Luther grasped intuitively – that the question of justification was essentially an aspect of the greater question of the relation of humanity to God in Christ, which need not be discussed exclusively in terms of the category of justification.[176] In effect, all the watchwords of the Reformation relating to this theme – *sola fide*, *sola gratia*, and even *sola scriptura* – may be reduced to their common denominator: justification is *through Christ alone*.

Calvin may be regarded as establishing the framework within which subsequent discussion of justification within the Reformed school would proceed, as well as exemplifying a trend which becomes increasingly evident in the Protestantism of the following century – the increasing diminution of the perceived significance of the *locus iustificationis*. Calvin did not, however, initiate this trend; as we have argued in the present section, the early Reformed church never attached the same importance to the *articulus iustificationis* as did the early evangelical faction within Germany (apparently on account of the personal influence of Luther). Zwingli's early concern with *Christianismus renascens* and Bucer's Erasmian concept of *lex Christi* had little bearing on the doctrine of justification, and, if anything, appear to have exercised a negative influence upon its evaluation. The supposition that the Reformation was homogeneously concerned with the *articulus iustificationis*, even in its initial phase, cannot be sustained on the basis of the evidence available, in that this evidence indicates that the high estimation of and concern for this article were restricted to the initial phase of the German Reformation.

With the death of Calvin, a new phase in the development of Reformed theology took place, which resulted in the emphasis shifting still further away from justification. The rise of Reformed scholasticism led to the recognition of predestination as the central dogma of the Reformed church,[177] even though this emphasis is absent from Calvin's 1559 *Institutio*. Whereas the Lutheran church was initially faced with a series of controversies relating to justification, those now facing the Reformed church would primarily concern predestination. In the following section, we shall consider the development of the doctrine of justification within

---

[176] That this is also the case with early Scottish Reformed theology (for example, that of John Knox or the *Scots Confession* of 1560) has been brought out by T. F. Torrance, 'Justification: Its Radical Nature and Place in Reformed Doctrine and Life', *SJTh* 13 (1960), 225–46, especially 225–7.

[177] See Alexander Schweizer, *Die protestantischen Centraldogmen in ihrer Entwicklung innerhalb der reformierten Kirche*, 2 vols., Zurich: Orell & Fuessli, 1854–6. Schweizer, however, argues that Calvin treats the doctrine of predestination as central – a conclusion which modern Calvin scholarship has not endorsed.

Lutheran and Reformed orthodoxy, and establish their points of convergence and divergence.

3.6   The English Reformation: from Tyndale to Hooker

The Reformation in England drew its inspiration primarily from its continental counterpart, although the Lollard movement had done much to encourage the development of anticlerical and anti-sacramental attitudes upon which the English Reformers would base their appeal to the doctrine of justification *sola fide*.[178] The strongly political cast of the English Reformation tended to result in attaching a secondary and derivative importance to theological issues, which goes some way towards accounting for the theological mediocrity of the movement. Furthermore, the English Reformers appear to have busied themselves chiefly with eucharistic controversies – unnecessarily drawing attention to their differences in doing so – rather than with the doctrine of justification. It is, however, clear that the doctrines of justification circulating in English reforming circles in the 1520s and early 1530s were quite distinct from those of the mainstream continental Reformation, thus raising the question of the sources of these doctrines. Although the Cambridge 'White Horse circle' met to discuss the works of Luther in the 1520s, it is clear that relatively few of the Reformer's distinctive ideas became generally accepted in England.

There are excellent reasons for supposing that essentially Augustinian doctrines of justification were in circulation in England independently of the influence of Luther, and that the doctrines of justification which developed as an indirect consequence of such influence appear to have omitted the idea of the *reputatio iustitiae Christi alienae* – a central feature of Luther's conception of justification – altogether. Thomas Bilney, for example, a leading figure of the 'White Horse circle', developed a concept of justification framed solely in terms of the non-imputation of sin, omitting any reference to the concept of the 'imputation of righteousness'.[179] Similarly, William Tyndale, although making extensive use of Luther in his early polemical works, still tends to interpret justification as 'making righteous'. Tyndale's emphasis upon the renewing and transforming work of the Holy Spirit within humans is quite distinct from Luther's emphasis upon faith, and clearly parallels Augustine's transformational concept of

---

[178] J. F. Davis, 'Lollardy and the Reformation in England', *ARG* 73 (1982), 217–37.
[179] Rupp, *The Making of the English Protestant Tradition*, 161; Knox, *The Doctrine of Faith in the Reign of Henry VIII*, 106–9.

justification.[180] John Frith reproduces a sanative concept of justification, clearly Augustinian in its structure. Frith's most characteristic definition of justification is that it consists of the non-imputation of sin, omitting any references to the imputation of righteousness.[181]

The first clear and unambiguous statement of the concept of the imputation of righteousness to be found in the writings of an English Reformer may be found in the 1534 edition of Robert Barnes' *Supplication unto King Henry VIII*. The vague statements of the 1531 edition on this matter[182] are expanded to yield an unequivocal statement of the concept of imputed righteousness.[183] Barnes, however, was exceptional in his understanding of, and affinity with, Lutheranism; the early English Reformation as a whole appears to have been characterised by theologies of justification which demonstrate many points of contact with their continental counterparts, except in their understanding of the *nature* of justification. In 1531, George Joye defined justification thus:

> To be justified, or to be made righteous before God by this faith, is nothing else but to be absolved from sin of God, to be forgiven, or to have no sin imputed of him by God.[184]

The assertion that justification is the forgiveness or non-imputation of sin *without* the simultaneous assertion that righteousness is imputed to the believer, or *with* the assertion that justification is to be understood as *making* righteous, appears to be characteristic of the English Reformation until the late 1530s.

[180] For example, see the *Prologue to Romans*, *Works*, 493–4, which emphasises that faith 'altereth a man, and changeth him into a new spiritual nature'. See further *Mammon*, *Works*, 53–5. In his later works, such as his *Exposition of Matthew V VI VII*, he appears to reproduce the basic features of the concept of the *imputatio iustitiae*.

[181] See Knox, *The Doctrine of Faith*, 43–51, 44. There is one isolated passage in which Frith refers to Christ's righteousness being 'reputed unto us for our own': *Workes*, 49. The parallelism between Adam's sin and Christ's righteousness is evidently constructed on the basis of Augustinian presuppositions, rather than on those of later Lutheranism. His statement that, although believers are righteous in Christ, they continue to be sinners in fact, seems to be based upon a proleptic understanding of justification associated with Augustine, and reproduced by Luther in his 1515–16 *Romans* lectures: 'Bulwark against Rastell', *Workes*, 72.

[182] For example, *Supplication* (1531), fol. liiir: 'the faith of Christ Jesus which is imputed unto them for justice'. For an incomplete list of the differences between the two editions, see W. D. J. Cargill Thompson, 'The Sixteenth Century Editions of *A Supplication unto King Henry VIII* by Robert Barnes D. D.', *Transactions of the Cambridge Bibliographical Society* 3 (1960), 133–42.

[183] For example, *Supplication* (1534), *Workes*, 242A: 'Wherefore we say with S. Paul, that faith only justifies *imputative*; that is, all the merits and goodness, grace and favour, and all that is in Christ, to our salvation, is imputed and reckoned unto us.'

[184] George Joye, *Answer to Ashwell* (London, 1531), B3.

The years between Henry VIII's break with Rome and his death saw the publication of a series of formularies of faith, which attempted to define the theological position of the new national church: the Ten Articles (July 1536); the Bishops' Book (August 1537); the Six Articles (statute enacted June 1539); and the King's Book (published May 1543). While these formularies of faith give insights perhaps more into the political than into the theological concerns of the period, their statements on justification are particularly interesting to the extent that they refer to the *nature* of that concept.

The Ten Articles of July 1536 deal with justification and the three sacraments, among other matters. Although the influence of Lutheranism upon these articles, mediated through the Wittenberg Articles of the same year, is well established, this influence appears to have been minimal in relation to their statements on justification. Justification is defined in an Augustinian manner, as follows:

> Justification signifieth remission of our sins, and our acceptation or reconciliation into the grace and favour of God, that is to say, our perfect renovation in Christ.[185]

Although grace is clearly conceived extrinsically as the *favor Dei*, justification continues to be defined non-forensically, in strongly transformational terms. This definition of justification is, in fact, based upon part – but only part – of Philip Melanchthon's definition, as set out in 1535 *Loci communes*:

> Justification signifies the remission of sin and the reconciliation of acceptance of a person to eternal life. Now according to its Hebrew sense, 'to justify' is a forensic term; it is as if one were to say that the people of Rome justified Scipio when accused by the court, that is, absolved him, and pronounced him to be righteous.[186]

It is clearly significant that the entire second sentence, which contains an unequivocal assertion of the *forensic* character of justification, has

---

[185] Hardwick, *A History of the Articles of Religion*, 250; Lloyd, *Formularies of Faith*, xxvi. For the political factors shaping the development of such formularies of faith around this time, see D. MacCulloch, *Thomas Cranmer: A Life*, New Haven: Yale University Press, 1996, 161–6.

[186] CR (Melanchthon) 21.421. See R. W. Dixon, *History of the Church of England*, 3rd edn., 6 vols., London: Oxford University Press, 1895–1902, 1.415; P. Hughes, *The Reformation in England*, 3 vols., London: Burnes & Oates, 1963, 2.29 n. 2. It may also be noted that the scriptural citations (Romans 8:12 – note that Lloyd wrongly attributes it to the tenth chapter – and Matthew 19:17) in Article Five are taken from Melanchthon's 1535 *Locus de bonis operibus*, which follows immediately after the *Locus de gratia et de iustificatione*. Tyndale's definition of justification parallels Melanchthon's closely, but omits any reference to its forensic dimension: *Prologue to Romans, Works*, 508: 'By justifying, understand no other thing than to be reconciled to God, and to be restored unto his favour, and to have thy sins forgiven thee.'

been omitted, and a final phrase ('perfect renovation in Christ') substituted which completely eliminates any possibility of a distinction between *iustificatio* and *regeneratio*. This article was subsequently incorporated verbatim into the Bishops' Book of the following year.[187] Elsewhere, the Bishops' Book emphasised the *communication* – and not the *imputation* – of the righteousness of Christ to the believer:

> He hath planted and grafted me into his own body, and made me a member of the same, and he hath communicated and made me participant of his justice, his power, his life, his felicity, and all of his goods.[188]

Although this Book contains extracts from William Marshall's 1535 *Primer*, which is widely believed to be based upon Luther's 1523 *Betbüchlein*, remarkably few distinctively Lutheran ideas appear to have been incorporated into the work.

The King's Book of 1543 contained an entirely new article on justification, abandoning the previous definition, based partly on Melanchthon, in favour of a definition which could be taken directly from the works of Augustine himself:

> Justification . . . signifieth the making of us rightous afore God, where before we were unrighteous.[189]

The phrase 'afore God' here appears to reflect the Augustinian and medieval *apud Deum*, rather than the Lutheran *coram Deo*. Elsewhere in the book, the teachings of baptism as the first justification, and of 'restoration to justification' through penance, may be found – clearly indicative of a concept of justification continuous with the medieval Catholic tradition.

A work of particular importance in establishing the position of the early English national church on the nature of justification is the *Homily of Salvation*, usually regarded as the work of Thomas Cranmer himself.[190] In many respects, the *Homily* is Melanchthonian – note, for example, the obvious similarity between the explanations of Cranmer and Melanchthon concerning the correct interpretation of the phrase *sola fide*, and the striking verbal correspondence between Melanchthon and Cranmer on the role of the law.[191] However, Melanchthon's influence

---

[187] Lloyd, *Formularies of Faith*, 209–10.   [188] Lloyd, *Formularies of Faith*, 35.
[189] Lloyd, *Formularies of Faith*, 364. For the full text of the article, see 363–9.
[190] For the text of the *Homily*, see *The Two Books of Homilies appointed to be read in Churches*, Oxford, 1859, 24–35. For the best study, see C. Stacey, 'Justification by Faith in the Two Books of Homilies (1547 and 1571)', *Anglican Theological Review* 83 (2001), 255–79.
[191] Cranmer: 'no man can fulfil the law, and therefore by the law all men are condemned' *(Homily* 32.3–5); Melanchthon: 'nemo legem satisfaciet; lex accusat omnes', CR (Melanchthon) 21.426.

does not appear to extend to Cranmer's discussion of the nature of jus- tification. Cranmer interprets justification to mean 'making righteous', which clearly reflects the strongly factitive Augustinian concept of justi- fication evident in the collection of patristic texts assembled by Cranmer in support of the position he develops in the *Homily*. Although Cranmer rejects Augustine's doctrine of justification on the basis of *fides quae per dilectionem operatur*, excluding charity from his account of the justification of humanity, it is highly significant that he does not extend this criticism to Augustine's understanding of the *nature* of justification.

This raises an important point. The English Reformers seem to have understood that their continental colleagues developed a doctrine of jus- tification *by fayth onely*, and that its leading feature was the total exclusion of human works from justification. Several of them also apparently under- stood this faith to be 'reputed' as righteousness, possibly drawing on the use of this term in the *Apologia* for the Augsburg Confession. They do not, however, appear to have realised precisely what was meant by the very different concept of the imputation of righteousness, or its potential theological significance. In general, the English Reformers seem to have worked with a doctrine of justification in which humanity was understood to be *made* righteous *by fayth onely*, with good works being the natural consequence of justifying faith. This is clearly a possible interpretation of the Lutheran teaching, as stated in the important confessional documents of 1530; it is, however, not the most reliable such interpretation.

The year 1547 marked the beginning of the reign of Edward VII, and the dawning of new possibilities for the English Reformers to consoli- date the Protestantism of the national church. Cranmer wrote to various continental Reformers, inviting them to England to supervise the reli- gious developments which he envisaged – including the clarification of significant points of doctrine. Of these, one of the most important was the following question: does justification make individuals really righ- teous, or does it merely make them acceptable to God *as though* they were really righteous? By 1549, Bucer and Fagius felt able to write to their colleagues in Strasbourg to the effect that 'the doctrine of justifica- tion is purely and soundly taught' in England. It is not clear what moved them to this judgement; even as late as 1571, the teaching of the English church on this matter was unclear.

The 1552 article *De hominis iustificatione* affirms that 'justification *ex sola fide Iesu Christi*, in the sense in which it is explained in the *Homelia de iustificatione*', is the most important and healthy doctrine of Christians.[192]

---

[192] *BSRK* 509.24–8 (left-hand column).

The fact that this article refers interested readers to the *Homily of Justification* (almost certainly Cranmer's *Homily of Salvation*) for further details, when this homily simultaneously develops an Augustinian concept of justification and a Melanchthonian doctrine of justification *per solam fidem*, further indicates that, at least in this respect, the English Reformation had yet to assimilate the teaching of its continental counterpart.

It is, of course, possible that the English Reformers were misled through the occasional references in the *Apologia* of the Augsburg Confession which do indeed refer to justification as 'making righteous', and which use the term 'repute', rather than 'impute'.[193] Although the *Homily* clearly states the doctrine of justification *per solam fidem* in an orthodox Melanchthonian sense (apparently with extracts from the *Loci* being worked into the text), it is significant that the crucial concept of imputed righteousness is still not explicitly stated.

The 1563 Articles, however, contain an important addition. The reader is referred to the *Homily* merely for details of *the manner in which faith justifies*; justification itself is defined in terms of 'being reputed as righteous before God' (*iusti coram Deo reputamur*).[194] This is clearly a much more precise statement of the Melanchthonian doctrine of justification *per solam fidem*; indeed, this entire sentence could be constructed from Melanchthon's statements in the 1530 *Apologia*.

Despite this clear alignment with the Lutheran Reformation, rather than with the Swiss Reformations of Zurich or Geneva, the Elizabethan period witnessed a general decline in the fortunes of Lutheranism in England.[195] The returning Marian exiles, many of whom were promptly elevated to the episcopacy in the aftermath of the deprivations of 1559, had generally spent their time of exile in cities (such as Zurich, Strasbourg and Geneva) strongly influenced by the Reformed, rather than Lutheran, theology. Although Elizabeth herself had read Melanchthon's *Loci* as a girl (the 1538 edition was dedicated to her father), and in 1559 expressed the wish that the 'Augustanean Confession' be maintained in the realm, it is clear that the Reformed theology made considerable headway in England during the final decades of the sixteenth century. The tension between episcopalians and presbyterians (both of whom were obliged to

---

[193] For example, *BSLK* 174.34–44; 175.37–9. For the significance of these passages in relation to the doctrine of the *Apology* as a whole, see Pfnür, *Einig in der Rechtfertigungslehre?*, 155–81.

[194] *BSRK* 509.20–4 (right-hand column).

[195] For a careful study of the decline in Luther's influence, see Basil Hall, 'The Early Rise and Gradual Decline of Lutheranism in England (1520–1600)', in D. Baker (ed.), *Reform and Reformation: England and the Continent c. 1500–c. 1750*, Oxford: Blackwell, 1979, 103–31.

consider themselves members of the same church as a result of the Act of Uniformity) led to the appearance of a number of important apologetic works justifying the existence and teachings of the episcopal national church.

The most important of these for our purposes are Richard Hooker's sermons on the book of Habakkuk, preached in 1586, although not published until 1612.[196] In these sermons, Hooker addresses himself to issues such as the 'grand question which hangeth yet in controversy between us and the Church of Rome, about the matter of justifying righteousness'.[197] In his response, it is clear that Hooker attempts to construct a mediating doctrine of justification between Catholicism and Protestantism which avoids the discredited eirenicon of double justification.

Hooker considers that the chief error of his Catholic opponents is their teaching that a habit of grace is infused into humans at their first justification to produce an inherent and real righteousness within, which may subsequently be increased, by merit acquired through good works, in the second justification.[198] For Hooker, God bestows upon humans justifying and sanctifying righteousness in their justification at one and the same time; the distinction between the two lies in the fact that the former is external to humans, and imputed to them, while the latter is worked within them by the Holy Spirit.

Hooker thus distinguishes habitual and actual sanctifying righteousness, the former being the righteousness with which the soul is endowed through the indwelling of the Holy Spirit, and the latter the righteousness which results from the action of that Spirit. At the instant of their justification, humans are simultaneously accepted as righteous in Christ and given the Holy Spirit, which is the formal cause of their subsequent actual sanctifying righteousness. Hooker interprets the phrase 'justification by faith alone' as follows:

We teach that faith alone justifieth: whereas we by this speech never meant to exclude either hope and charity from being always joined as inseparable mates with faith in the man that is justified; or works from being added as necessary duties, required at the hands of every justified man: but to shew that faith is the only hand that putteth on Christ unto justification; and Christ the only garment, which being so put on, covereth the shame of our defiled natures, hideth the imperfections of our works, preserveth us blameless in the sight of God, before whom otherwise the very weakness of our faith were cause sufficient to make us culpable.[199]

---

[196] *Works*, 3.469–81; 483–547. For an analysis of these sermons, see Gibbs, 'Richard Hooker's *Via Media* Doctrine of Justification'.
[197] *Works*, 3.486.   [198] *Works*, 3.487–9.   [199] *Works*, 3.530.

As Hooker concedes, however, faith is itself a work of the Holy Spirit within humans,[200] so that faith is both the prerequisite and consequence of justification.[201]

It will thus be evident that Hooker's understanding of the nature of justification is similar to that of Calvin. Humankind is justified *per fidem propter Christum*. Justification is to be conceived Christologically, in terms of the appropriation of the personal presence of Christ within believers through the Holy Spirit, on account of which they are declared righteous and the process of sanctification is initiated. A clear distinction is thus drawn between justification through imputed righteousness, and sanctification through inherent righteousness. The importance of this distinction will become apparent in the section that follows.

3.7   Protestant orthodoxy

The remarkable ease with which a new form of scholasticism established itself within the churches of the Reformation is one of the more significant aspects of the intellectual history of that period.[202] The need to systematise both Reformed and Lutheran dogmatics was partly a consequence of the perceived need to defend such theologies and to distinguish them, not merely from that of the Council of Trent, but also from one another. The rise of Confessionalism led to a new emphasis upon doctrinal orthodoxy as conformity to the confessional documents of Protestantism, and to the use of increasingly subtle and refined concepts in order to defend their theological coherence.[203] This is particularly evident in the case of the doctrine of justification, in which the differences between the two chief Protestant confessions were well established by the year 1620.

Reformed theology was quicker to develop a new scholasticism than its Lutheran counterpart. The general drift of Reformed theology into a form of Aristotelian scholasticism is generally thought to have begun

---

[200] *Works*, 3.515. Note the reference to the passivity of humans in their justification, 'working no more than dead and senseless matter, wood, or stone or iron'; *Works*, 3.531.
[201] For a discussion of this paradox, see *Works*, 3.508.
[202] See the excellent collection of studies assembled in C. R. Trueman and R. S. Clark, *Protestant Scholasticism: Essays in Reassessment*, Carlisle: Paternoster, 1999.
[203] For the impact of Confessionalism on church, society and universities, see Thomas Kaufmann, *Universität und lutherische Konfessionalisierung: Die Rostocker Theologieprofessoren und ihr Beitrag zur theologischen Bildung und kirchlichen Gestaltung im Herzogtum Mecklenburg zwischen 1550 und 1675*, Gütersloh: Vandenhoeck & Ruprecht, 1997; Heiko E. Janssen, *Gräfin Anna von Ostfriesland: Eine hochadelige Frau der späten Reformationszeit (1540/42–1575): Ein Beitrag zu den Anfängen der reformierten Konfessionalisierung im Reich*, Münster: Aschendorff, 1998.

with Beza,[204] and represents a significant shift from Calvin's position on a number of matters of importance. The tendency to base theology upon the basis of deductive reasoning from given principles to yield a rationally coherent system had three significant consequences for the development of the doctrine of justification in Reformed theology:

1. The Christological emphasis evident in Calvin's soteriology is replaced by a theocentric emphasis, as the basis of theological speculation shifts from an inductive method based upon the Christ-event to a deductive method based upon the divine decrees of election.
2. A doctrine of limited atonement is unequivocally stated. Although it may be argued that this doctrine is merely the logical conclusion of Calvin's soteriology, the fact remains that Calvin chose not to draw that conclusion.[205]
3. Predestination is considered as an aspect of the doctrine of *God*, rather than as an aspect of the doctrine of *salvation*.

This process of modification of Calvin under Bezan inspiration culminated in the Five Articles of the Synod of Dort (1619). The English-speaking world has paid a curious tribute to the bulb-growers of the Netherlands in the TULIP mnemonic for these five soteriological points, summed up in the doctrines of: (T) total depravity; (U) unconditional election; (L) limited atonement; (I) irresistible grace; (P) perseverance of the elect.[206] Against this, the Remonstrants argued that Christ was the saviour of the world, not merely of the elect, having died for each and every person, and obtained for them remission of sins.

One of the most significant features of the doctrines of justification associated with Reformed orthodoxy, distinguishing them from both that of Calvin on the one hand and those of Lutheranism on the other, is that of the covenant between God and humans. This development can be traced to the Zurich reforming theology of the 1520s, but was restated in terms of a *double* covenant by Gomarus, Polanus and Wollebius.[207] It is this later form of the concept which would become normative within later Reformed orthodoxy and Puritanism.[208] So significant a role did the federal foundations of justification assume within the Reformed theological

---

[204] The best study here is J. Mallinson, *Faith, Reason, and Revelation in Theodore Beza, 1519–1605*. Oxford: Oxford University Press, 2003.
[205] For the reasons, see the second of the *Treze Sermons*: CR (Calvin) 58.31–44.
[206] *BSRK* 843.15 – 861.8. On the final point, see J. Moltmann, *Prädestination und Perseveranz: Geschichte und Bedeutung der reformierten Lehre 'de perseverantia sanctorum'*, Neukirchen: Neukirchener Verlag, 1961, especially 110–62.
[207] Schrenk, *Gottesreich und Bund im älteren Protestantismus*, 63.
[208] For Calvin's role in this development, see P. A. Lillback, *The Binding of God: Calvin's Role in the Development of Covenant Theology*, Grand Rapids: Baker, 2001.

tradition that the covenant concept was frequently defined as the 'marrow (*medula*) of divinity'.

The essential features of the concept may be found outlined in the works of Ursinus, who distinguished between the *foedus naturae*, known naturally to humans and offering salvation upon condition of absolute obedience to God, and the *foedus gratiae*, known to humans by revelation and offering salvation upon condition that they believe in Jesus Christ. Polanus, by redefining Ursinus' *foedus naturae* as the *foedus operum*, established the general outlines of the theology which would become normative within the early Reformed school. The concept of the covenant between God and humans eventually came to replace Calvin's Christological solution to the problem of the relationship between the totally gratuitous justification of the sinner and the demands of obedience subsequently laid upon them, without resorting to the moralist solution associated with Zwingli and Bucer. The *foedus gratiae* was grounded Christologically, with Christ as *testator*, thus retaining the emphasis, if not the substance, of Calvin's position.

The general outlines of the pre-Cocceian theology of the double covenant may be studied from Wollebius' *Christianae theologiae compendium* (1626). A fundamental distinction is drawn between God's dealings with humans in their innocent and in their lapsed states. In the former, God entered of his own free and sovereign decision into a covenant of works with humans, which promised them eternal life upon condition that they were obedient to God.[209] The fall of humankind led to the establishment of a new covenant with humanity, as an expression of the divine graciousness. The *foedus gratiae* must be distinguished from the universal covenant made by God with all creatures, and the *foedus operum* made with Adam; it is the covenant established between God and his elect, by which God promises himself as their father in Christ, provided that they live in filial obedience to him. Although the *foedus gratiae* is offered to all people, the explicit particularism of the later Reformed soteriology permits only the elect to enjoy its benefits.

It is important to appreciate that the *foedus gratiae* is understood to have operated throughout the period of both the Old and the New Testaments. The Old Testament may be considered as the covenant of grace, as it was administered until the time of Christ, and may be divided into three periods. Between Adam and Abraham, the covenant was expressed simply in terms of the promises of God made to all people, unsupported in any external manner, and marked by the ritual of sacrifice. Between

---

[209] For a careful analysis, see H. Faulenbach, *Die Struktur der Theologie des Amandus Polanus von Polansdorf*, Zurich: EVZ-Verlag, 1967.

Abraham and Moses, the covenant was expressed in terms of the promises of God to the children of Abraham, supplemented by demands of obedience and the ritual of circumcision. Between Moses and Christ, the covenant assumed a more testamentary character, being marked by the ritual of Passover and other types of the death of Christ, who may be regarded as the testator of the *foedus gratiae*, and hence of both the Old and New Testaments. In effect, both the Old and New Testaments may be regarded as the same in substance, in that both contain the promise of grace linked with the demand of obedience; their difference lies primarily in the manner in which the covenant is administered. The dialectic between law and gospel, so characteristic of contemporary Lutheranism, is thus conspicuously absent.

The covenant theology of Reformed orthodoxy received a significant development through Cocceius, who emphasised the potential theological significance of the term *testamentum*, which tended to be used interchangeably with *foedus*.[210] Cocceius located the difference between the *foedus operum* and the *foedus gratiae* by affirming that the latter alone may be allowed the character of a divine testament (in the sense of a 'will'), ratified beforehand by God to Christ, by which God appointed a heavenly inheritance for his children, to be acquired through the intervening death of Jesus Christ. The contracting parties to this testament are God as Redeemer, humanity as sinners, and Christ as the federal mediator between them. The testament is actually contracted in eternity between God and Christ, in which God exacted from Christ the condition of perfect obedience to the law in return for the elect as his own inheritance. This development served to distinguish the covenant of works from that of grace, emphasising the novel character of the latter, in that it alone has the status of a testament. Furthermore, the existence of the intratrinitarian pact between Father and Son was held to justify the doctrine of limited atonement, thus further increasing its influence within later Reformed orthodoxy.

The doctrine of a threefold covenant between God and humanity is particularly associated with the Salmurian Academy. In April 1608, John Cameron published *De triplici Dei cum homine foedere theses*, in which he developed an analysis of salvation history based upon three distinct covenants between God and humanity: the *foedus naturae*, *foedus gratiae subserviens* and *foedus gratiae*. The *foedus gratiae subserviens* was regarded by Cameron as a preparation for the *foedus gratiae*, and appears to have represented an attempt to incorporate the Lutheran distinction between

---

[210] For the best study, see W. J. van Asselt, *The Federal Theology of Johannes Cocceius (1603–1669)*, Leiden: Brill, 2001.

law and gospel within the context of a federal scheme. Cameron seems to have regarded the harmonisation of law and gospel implicit in the orthodox Reformed twofold covenant scheme as compromising the doctrine of justification *sola fide*. The importance of this threefold scheme derives from its adoption by Moses Amyraut as the basis of his distinctive theology.[211]

Amyraut's 'hypothetical universalism' and his doctrine of the triple covenant between God and humanity is unquestionably a direct consequence of his emphasis upon the priority of justification over other Christian doctrines.[212] The Pauline dialectic between law and gospel, underlying Cameron's covenant scheme, causes Amyraut to revise the traditional *foedus operum* or *foedus legale* by interpreting the term *lex* in a radically restricted sense. In his disputation *De tribus foederibus divinis*, Amyraut developed a theory of progressive revelation, culminating in the period of the covenant of grace. The first covenant (the 'natural covenant') pertained to humanity in the earthly paradise; the second covenant (the 'legal' covenant) to the people of Israel; and the third (the 'covenant of grace') to the church under the gospel.[213]

It is possible to confuse the Cocceian and Salmurian interpretations of the federal foundations of justification if it is not realised that the Salmurian academicians recognised the three covenants as being *actualised in time*. The Cocceian covenant theology may be restated in the form of three covenants, of which one is made in eternity: the eternal intratrinitarian covenant between Father and Son precedes the temporal covenants of works and of grace. The Salmurian academicians recognised no such eternal intratrinitarian covenant, regarding all three covenants as pertaining to human history. The *foedus naturale* was made directly – without a mediator – between God and Adam, promising a continued blessed existence in Eden upon condition of perfect obedience to the law of nature. The *foedus legale* was made through Moses between God and Israel, and promised a blessed existence in the promised land of Canaan upon condition of perfect obedience to the law of nature *as clarified by the written law and ceremonies*. The *foedus gratiae* was made through Christ between God and all humankind, promising salvation and eternal life upon condition of faith. It is at this point that Amyraut's 'hypothetical universalism' becomes evident: Amyraut states that *Christ intended to die for all men*, although he concedes that the will of God which desires

---

[211] See Moltmann, 'Prädestination und Heilsgeschichte bei Moyse Amyraut'; Laplanche, *Orthodoxie et prédication*; Armstrong, *Calvinism and the Amyraut Heresy*.
[212] Armstrong, *Calvinism* and *the Amyraut Heresy*, 222–40.
[213] Thesis 2; in *Syntagma thesium theologicarum*, 2 vols., Saumur, 1641, 1.212.

universal salvation also specifies that the condition of faith must be met before this is possible.[214]

Seventeenth-century Lutheran orthodoxy was primarily concerned with the elucidation and defence of the doctrine of justification to be found in the Formula of Concord. Although the concept of forensic justification was maintained with the utmost rigour, attention shifted to the question of the subjective appropriation of justification. Like Reformed orthodoxy, Lutheranism came to adopt scholastic terminology and categories in discussions of justification, although the increasing emphasis upon the practical aspect of justification led to its being discussed as a matter of practical theology (*gratia applicatrix*). Although the extrinsic and forensic aspect of justification was thus maintained formally, it is clear that interest in this aspect of the concept was now overshadowed – particularly as the threat posed by Pietism loomed large – by the practical and experiential dimensions of conversion.[215]

The distinctive positions of Lutheran and Reformed orthodoxy on justification are most easily expounded and compared when considered under three headings: the nature of justification; the objective grounds of justification; the subjective appropriation of justification. We shall consider each of these points individually.

3.7.1   The nature of justification

Both confessions understand justification to be the forensic declaratory act of God (*actus Dei forensis in foro coeli*), subsequent to vocation and prior to sanctification.[216] Justification consists of two elements: the

---

[214] *Défense de la doctrine de Calvin sur le sujet de l'élection*, Saumur, 1644, 544. The whole of this chapter (512–68) should be studied. Note also 312–13, where Amyraut makes it clear that he regards the doctrine of election as functioning as an *ex post facto* explanation of why some believe and others do not, rather than as a speculative principle of deductive theology. For the manner in which Amyraut reconciles the universality of the offer of salvation and the particularity of faith, see *Brief traitté de la prédestination*, Saumur, 1634, 89–90; Laplanche, *Orthodoxie et prédication*, 87–108.

[215] See W. Dantine, *Die Gerechtmachung der Gottlosen: Eine dogmatische Untersuchung*, Munich: Kaiser, 1959, 15–29.

[216] On the Lutheran side, see Hafenreffer, *Loci theologici*, 664; Koenig, *Theologia positiva acroamatica*, §562; 208; Brochmand, *Universae theologiae systema*, 1.471. On the Reformed, see Heidegger, *Medulla theologiae christianae* XXII, 4; 169; XXI, 6; 169; XXII, 2.6; 183; Wollebius, *Christianae theologiae compendium* I.XXX.2.; 234; Bucanus, *Institutiones theologicae* XXXI, 6; 332; Alsted, *Theologia scholastica didactica* IV.XXVI.1; 709; Musculus, *Loci communes*, 2.62–3. Note the explicit criticism of Augustine evident in certain of these citations (e.g., Musculus). For an analysis of the Aristotelian foundations of Johann Gerhard's understanding of the causality of justification, see R. Schröder, *Johann Gerhards lutherische Christologie und die aristotelische Metaphysik*, Tübingen: Mohr, 1983, 69–96. For a description of Quenstedt's doctrine of justification, which illustrates Lutheran orthodoxy at its best, see R. D. Preuss, 'The Justification of a Sinner before God as taught in Later Lutheran Orthodoxy', *SJTh* 13 (1960), 262–77.

remission of sins (or the non-imputation of sin, which is treated as identical with the remission of sins), and the imputation of the obedience of Christ. The Augustinian concept of justification as both event and process, still evident in Luther, is rejected by later Lutheranism. Thus the divine judgement implicit in justification is understood to be *synthetic*, rather than *analytic*. The Reformed school is able to justify its emphasis upon the *iudicium Dei secundum veritatem* through the application of the principle of the *unio mystica* between Christ and the believer, as well as the federal relationship between them, so that the alien righteousness of the former may be imputed to the latter.[217] The absence of a corresponding principle or federal basis within Lutheranism leads to a weakness at this point, with justification tending to be treated as a legal fiction.

The forensic dimension of justification is emphasised by the use of the term *acceptilation*. This concept, taken from Roman private law, refers to the dissolution of an obligation (such as a debt) by a verbal decree on the part of the one to whom the debt was due, without any form of payment having taken place or necessarily being envisaged as taking place in the future. Justification is thus conceived analogically, as the remission of sins and imputation of righteousness by a purely verbal decree *in foro divino*, without any change in the sinner having taken place with reference to which this verdict could be supported. The term *acceptilation*, so frequently used in this context, appears to be misunderstood by several Reformed theologians, such as Alsted, who confuses it with the Scotist concept of *acceptation*.

An important distinction is made by the Reformed theologians between active and passive justification. The distinction refers to the act of God by which the sinner is justified (active justification), and the subjective feeling of grace subsequently evoked in the conscience of the justified sinner. God *acts* to justify, and humanity is *passive* in receiving this justification. The importance of the distinction lies in the fact that God's act of justification, in which the sinner is declared righteous, is perfect, accomplished once and for all, whereas the realisation by humans of this state of justification is imperfect, in so far as it is based upon the *feeling* of grace evoked in their conscience. While the two coexist simultaneously in the formal act of justification, the extent of the consciousness of justification may vary from one individual to another. The absence of a corresponding distinction within Lutheranism led to considerable confusion concerning the precise causal relationship

---

[217] See Bucanus, *Institutiones theologicae* XXXI, 27; 341: 'Iustitia Christi aliena est, quatenus extra nos est . . . sed aliena non est, quatenus nobis destinata est . . . Est etiam nostra illa iustitia, quatenus illud ipsum eius subjectum, nempe Christus, noster est adeoque spiritualiter per fidem factus est unus nobiscum.' Cf. Polanus, *Syntagma* IV, 27; 781.

of faith and justification, whereas the Reformed theologians were able to state that faith was posterior to objective, and prior to subjective, justification.

3.7.2   The objective grounds of justification

Both confessions agree that the objective grounds of justification are to be located in the satisfaction offered by Christ by virtue of his fulfilment of the law and his passion. A distinction was drawn between the *obedientia activa Christi* (his obedience to and fulfilment of the law in his life) and the *obedientia Christi passiva* (his obedience in his suffering and death upon the cross). Both Lutheran and Reformed thinking on this question was stimulated by the controversies surrounding the views of Piscator and Socinus. In his *Theses theologicae*, Piscator developed the views of the Lutheran Parsimonius, who had hindered the Stancarist cause somewhat by arguing that, if the obedience of humanity to the law was still necessary, it followed that the *obedientia activa* had no substitutionary value. Piscator observed that, as believers are clearly still under an obligation to fulfil the law, Christ's active obedience cannot be directly imputed to them.[218] *Remissio peccatorum* and *imputatio iustitia* were thus both understood to be based upon the *iustitia Christi passiva*.

Piscator was refuted in a variety of manners. The Lutheran Johann Gerhard argued that, as justification included both *remissio peccatorum* and *imputatio iustitiae*, the former could be held to be based upon the *obedientia passiva* and the latter upon the *obedientia activa*. However, Gerhard conceded that this suggestion was valid only *secundum rationem*, and did not reflect a theological relationship between the concepts;[219] as Baier pointed out, this would imply – *secundum rationem* – the priority of *imputatio iustitia* over *remissio peccatorum*. The Reformed reply to Piscator was somewhat different, and requires careful analysis. According to the Lutheran understanding of the *communicatio idiomatum*, the incarnation of the Word may be said to result in the participation of the humanity of Christ in *all* the divine attributes, including that of superiority to the law (the so-called *exlex*). Thus Christ, as a human being, is under no positive obligation to fulfil the law, and his subsequent fulfilment of the law must therefore be seen as a vicarious act on his part. If this act is to have any

---

[218] It is not strictly correct to suggest that Piscator denied that Christ's active obedience was totally devoid of satisfactory value. Piscator asserted that the active obedience of Christ affected the satisfactory value of his death, in that without Christ's sinless and obedient life, his passion could not have had any satisfactory value. Thus the *obedientia activa* may be said to possess *indirect* satisfactory value.

[219] *Loci theologici*, ed. Cotta, 7.260–1.

value, that value must relate to others, rather than to Christ himself. Thus the *obedientia activa* is of purely vicarious satisfactory value.

While insisting that the *obedientia activa* is vicarious (in other words, of value to those for whom Christ became incarnate), the Reformed theologians operated with a significantly different understanding of the *communicatio idiomatum*; the Lutheran understanding of the principle is rejected as practically dissipating the humanity of Christ. The Reformed Christology attempted to preserve the distinction between the human and divine natures at this point, and replaced the Lutheran understanding of the *communicatio idiomatum* with the quite distinct principle of the *unctio spiritus sancti*. The incarnation itself must be seen as an act of exinanition, involving the setting aside of certain divine attributes – including the so-called *exlex* – as a result of which the humanity of Christ retains its primary characteristics, with the exception of humanity's innate sinfulness. Thus Christ, as a human being, is under obligation to the law,[220] so that the *obedientia activa* is not necessarily vicarious.

The vicarious character of the *obedientia activa* arises through the rigorously Christological understanding of justification associated with Reformed orthodoxy, expressed in the doctrine of Christ as *caput et sponsor electorum*, by which the elect may be said to participate in all the benefits of Christ as if they had obtained them through their own efforts. The *obedientia activa*, in that it is of benefit to Christ, is also of benefit to the elect. It is this concept of Christ as *caput et sponsor electorum* – ultimately representing a central element of Luther's soteriology which Lutheranism failed to appropriate – which underlies the Reformed insistence that the verdict of justification is *iudicium Dei secundum veritatem*, and has misled many into concluding that later Reformed orthodoxy is based upon an *analytical* understanding of the divine judgement in justification. It could thus be argued that the Reformed understanding of the *obedientia activa* involves a concept of derivative or transferred vicariousness.

The two confessions concur in their understanding of the priestly office of Christ, by which he made satisfaction for the sins of humankind, and in their mutual opposition to Socinianism. Socinus had denied that God required any form of satisfaction in order to remit sin; God is to be conceived as a private creditor, able to remit debts of any kind without the necessity of the imposition of any penalty.[221] Although Socinus retains

---

[220] It should be noted here that federal theologians, such as Burmann, discussed the *obedientia activa* in terms of Christ's *natural* submission to the law as on account of his *being* a man, and his *federal* submission to the law by virtue of his *becoming* human on behalf of the elect.

[221] The best study of Socinianism remains Fock, *Der Socianismus nach seiner Stellung*. A useful analysis in English is to be found in R. S. Franks, *The Work of Christ*, London: Nelson, 1962, 362–77.

the traditional threefold office of Christ as prophet, priest and king, he restricts the office of priest to that of intercession (whereas it had traditionally included satisfaction), shifting the emphasis to the prophetic office, by which Christ revealed the will of God to humankind. A general statement of the common Protestant understanding of the satisfaction of Christ takes the following form. Humans, having fallen into sin, are liable to death, because God, the righteous judge, is under obligation to punish sin. As humans cannot provide the necessary satisfaction for sin, this satisfaction is provided by the incarnate God, whose sinlessness absolves him from the common human lot of suffering and death. Christ was obedient to the law in his suffering and death on the cross, and this obedience was adequate as a satisfaction for the sins of humanity. The strongly Anselmian basis of this scheme will be evident, although Anselm did not envisage the merit of Christ functioning as a basis for the imputation of righteousness.[222] Both confessions assert the theanthropic nature of the mediation of Christ[223] – in other words, that Christ is mediator as the God-human, and not as either God or human separately.

The confessions diverge dramatically over the question of the extent of the redeeming work of Christ. Lutheranism asserted that Christ's merit, won by his obedience, was sufficient for all people, although efficacious only in the case of those who, after their regeneration, respond to the Word and are thus justified. The *errores Calvinianorum* are located by Gerhard in their concept of predestination, which underlies their teaching on justification.[224] In effect, Lutheran orthodoxy interpreted the concept of election as God's affirmation of that which he foreknows will occur within the sphere of his ordained will – in other words, election takes place on the basis of *fides praevisa*. Through the regeneration of humans, their *liberum arbitrium* is restored, enabling them to respond freely to the Word of the gospel – whether they accept it or not is up to the individual. This affirmation that *vocatio* is *resistibilis et universalis* is characteristic of later Lutheran orthodoxy, and raises significant questions to which we shall

---

[222] There appears to have been considerable confusion within Lutheranism upon the relation of Christ's merits and satisfaction. Gerhard appears to treat the concepts as identical, although a distinction between them emerges later; see Koenig, *Theologia positiva acroamatica*, §§219–20; §§150–1. See also Ritschl, *Justification and Reconciliation*, 261.

[223] On the Lutheran side, see Koenig, *Theologia positiva acroamatica*, §217; 150; §232; 153; Brochmand, *Universae theologiae systema*, 1.709–11; Gerhard, *Loci theologici*, in *Opera* 7.70. On the Reformed, see Heidegger, *Medulla theologiae christianae* xix, 15; 53; Wollebius, *Christianae theologiae compendium*, lxvii.4; 117; Polanus, *Syntagma*, vi, 27; 266–82.

[224] *Loci theologici*, locus xvii, *De iustificatione per fidem, prooemium*, ed. Cotta, 7.1: 'Calviniani errant in articulo praedestinationis; ergo et in articulo iustificationis, quia iustificatio est praedestinationis executio.'

return in our discussion of the subjective appropriation of justification (3.7.3).

The Reformed divines, while conceding the universal sufficiency of the work of Christ, emphasised the particularity of its efficacy. This opinion represents a development of the views of Calvin, who did not teach limited atonement, but affirmed that the gospel was offered by God for all humankind. Hence, in his critical discussion of the Tridentine decree on justification, Calvin raised no objection to the explicit statement that Christ died for all.[225] Beza, however, explicitly stated that Christ died only for the elect, and not for all people.[226] As later orthodoxy would put it, Christ died *sufficienter* for all, but *efficienter* only for the elect. A distinction must be drawn between God's general love, exercised towards all of humanity, and his saving love, by which he wills to redeem them. There is thus a clear distinction between the Lutheran concept of the general divine intention to save all, actualised in the case of those who believe, and the Reformed doctrine of an efficacious individual election.

3.7.3   *The subjective appropriation of justification*

One of the most significant developments in seventeenth-century Lutheran dogmatics was the affirmation that faith was itself a cause of justification. Although it was emphasised that faith was a *causa impulsiva minus principalis iustificationis*, it was clearly stated that faith was logically prior to justification in the *ordo salutis*. This affirmation was interpreted to mean that justification was dependent upon a change in humans, and resulted in the placing of justification towards the end of an *ordo salutis* which included elements such as *illuminatio, regeneratio* and *conversio*. Although justification is still defined *forensically*, it is understood to be predicated upon a prior alteration within humans – namely, that they believe. Where Luther had understood justification to concern the *unbelieving sinner*, orthodoxy revised this view, referring justification to the *believing sinner*. Thus Calov and Quenstedt defend the following *ordo salutis*:

vocatio → *illuminatio* → *regeneratio* → *conversio* → *iustificatio*

The final Lutheran doctrine of justification, as stated by Hollaz, has the following form: humans, in their natural state, are spiritually dead. By the means of grace, especially through the agency of the Word, humans receive new powers, the illumination of their understanding, and the

---

[225] T. W. Casteel, 'Calvin and Trent: Calvin's Reaction to the Council of Trent in the Context of His Conciliar Thought', *HThR* 63 (1970), 91–117.
[226] Beza, *Tractationes theologicae*, 1.344, 363, 418.

excitement of good desires. This brings about the restoration of the *liberum arbitrium*, so that the *arbitrium liberatum* is now enabled, should individuals so wish, to believe. Humans thus possess the *facultas applicandi se ad gratiam* before their justification, and their justification is contingent upon precisely such *applicatio gratiae*. If individuals choose to do so, they may, although they need not, use these powers consequent to their regeneration to repent and believe, and as a result to be justified.[227] It will be clear that there are thus considerable affinities between later orthodoxy and Pietism on the relationship between faith and justification.

In part, the later Lutheran insistence on the priority of regeneration and conversion over justification represents a reaction against the Reformed doctrine of irresistible grace, a leading feature of Reformed spirituality in the post-Dort period. In order to avoid such a teaching, it is necessary to develop a theology of justification which simultaneously asserts the inability of humans to justify themselves *sine gratia* and their ability to reject the possibility of justification once this arises. The affirmation of the priority of regeneration over justification thus permits the later Lutheran divines to maintain the necessity of grace in justification (in that it is necessary for the regeneration of humans), while restricting its efficacy (in that human regeneration is understood to involve the repristination of their volitional faculties, by which they are able to determine whether or not to respond to their call). It will, however, be clear that the result is a theology which places regeneration prior to faith, and faith prior to justification.

The Reformed understanding of the matter is much simpler and more coherent. The justification of humanity is the temporal execution of the decree of election, brought about through grace. The fact that this proceeds through a complex causal sequence does not alter the truth that the entire sequence of events is to be directly attributed to God. Faith is to be seen as a divine gift effected within humans, functioning as the instrument by which the Holy Spirit may establish the *unio mystica* between Christ and the believer, whose threefold outcome is justification, sanctification and glorification. The role of humans at each and every stage of the *ordo salutis* is purely passive, in that the elect are called and accepted *efficaciter*. This observation goes some considerable way towards explaining the low status accorded to justification within Reformed dogmatics; justification is merely an aspect of the temporal execution of the eternal decree of election. God exercises his providential rule over creation

---

[227] Interestingly, Koenig does not even include *iustificatio* in his *ordo salutis: Theologia positiva acroamatica*, §426; 184 (although it is possible that he intends to subsume it under *regeneratio* – cf. §447; 188). See further B. Hägglund, 'Rechtfertigung – Wiedergeburt – Erneuerung in der nachreformatorischen Theologie', *KuD* 5 (1959), 318–37.

through the efficacious justification of the elect. It is interesting to observe that, although the objective grounds of justification fall under the aegis of the priestly office of Christ in Reformed dogmatics, the subjective appropriation of justification is dealt with under the aegis of the kingly office.

It will be clear that the Lutheran and Reformed understandings of the *nature* of justification are similar; the chief differences between them emerge in relation to the question of the objective grounds and subjective appropriation of justification. The Reformed doctrines of absolute and unconditional predestination and limited atonement, linked with the federal understanding of the basis of justification, distinguish the doctrines of justification associated with that school from those of Lutheranism. Significantly, the Reformed school is considerably closer to Luther (especially the 1525 Luther) than Lutheranism is. Given that both confessions adopted a strongly forensic concept of justification, which set them apart from Luther on this point, the strongly predestinarian cast of Reformed theology approximates to that of Luther to a far greater extent than Lutheran orthodoxy does. Similarly, the strongly Christological conception of justification to be found in Luther's writings is carried over into Reformed theology, particularly in the image of Christ as *caput et sponsor electorum*, where it is so evidently lacking in Lutheran orthodoxy. In terms of both its substance and its emphasis, the teaching of later Lutheran orthodoxy bears little relation to that of Luther.

3.8   Anglicanism: the Caroline Divines

Just as the seventeenth century witnessed the consolidation of the two main theological streams of the Continental Reformation in the shape of Lutheran and Reformed orthodoxy, so the theological developments initiated by the English Reformation may be regarded as having been consolidated in the century that followed. The 'golden age of Anglican divinity' took place in a century which witnessed considerable change in England, including the turmoil and the uncertainty occasioned by the Civil War and Interregnum, and the theological and ecclesiological changes introduced by the Westminster Assembly.

Despite the political revolution of 1688, and the no less significant, and practically simultaneous, revolution in the world of ideas accompanying the publication of Newton's *Principia mathematica* and Locke's *Essay concerning Human Understanding*, the Church of England appeared to remain relatively unaltered, retaining both her episcopal system of church government and the reigning monarch as her head. Nevertheless, significant changes had taken place within Anglican theology; for example, the origins of Deism may be detected in the writings of certain post-Reformation divines.

In the present section, we propose to illustrate an important discontinuity in Anglican thinking on justification over the period 1600–1700, and assess its significance.[228] The seventeenth-century churchmen collectively known as the Caroline Divines may, in general, be regarded as exponents of an Arminianism which immediately distinguishes them from their Puritan opponents, whom we shall consider presently. In May 1595, William Barrett, a fellow of Caius College, Cambridge, preached a sermon which touched off the predestinarian controversy which ultimately led to the nine Lambeth Articles of 1595. These strongly predestinarian articles never had any force, other than as the private judgement of those who drafted them. The seventeenth century saw their failing to achieve any authority within the Church of England, particularly when the Puritan representative John Reynolds was unable to persuade the Hampton Court Conference of 1604 to append them to the Thirty-Nine Articles of Religion. This left Article XVII – easily harmonised with an Arminian doctrine of election – as the sole authoritative pronouncement of the Church of England on the matter.

Although there can be little doubt that the Reformed doctrine of election continued to be widely held, particularly within Puritan circles, increasing opposition to the doctrine, largely from academic sources, was evident in the early seventeenth century. Thus Richard Hooker at Oxford, and Launcelot Andrewes at Cambridge, developed an 'Arminianism before Arminius', which received considerable impetus through the influence of William Laud, subsequently translated to Canterbury. Like Vincent of Lérins, Andrewes declined to support the latest continental speculation on predestination precisely because he felt it to be an evident innovation.

The Arminianism of the leading divines of the period – and the intense hostility towards them from Puritans – is perhaps best illustrated from the controversy surrounding the publication of Henry Hammond's *Practical Catechism* in 1644.[229] This work may be regarded as a classic statement of the soteriological convictions of the Laudian party, asserting unequivocally that Christ died for all people.[230] This view was variously described

---

[228] See C. F. Allison, *The Rise of Moralism: The Proclamation of the Gospel from Hooker to Baxter*, London: SPCK, 1962. On the distinctive themes of the 'Caroline Divines', see G. Thomann, *Studies in English Church History: Essays in the Piety and Liturgical Thought of the Caroline Divines and the Nonjurors*, Nurnberg: Thomann, 1992.

[229] J. W. Packer, *The Transformation of Anglicanism 1643–1660*, Manchester: Manchester University Press, 1969, 26–8.

[230] *A Practical Catechism*, 2nd edn, London, 1646, 9.

by his opponents: Cheynell accused him of subscribing to the doctrine of universal salvation; others charged him with Arminianism. The response of Clement Barksdale to this latter charge is particularly significant:

> You are mistaken when you think the Doctrine of Universall Redemption Arminianisme. It was the Doctrine of the Church of England before Arminius was borne. We learne it out of the old Church-Catechisme. I believe in Iesus Christ, Who hath redeemed mee and all mankind. And the Church hath learned it out of the plaine Scripture, where Christ is the Lamb of God that taketh away the sinnes of the world.[231]

In this, Barksdale must be regarded as substantially correct. The Bezan doctrine of limited atonement was somewhat late in arriving in England, by which time the older Melanchthonian view had become incorporated into the confessional material of the English national church – such as the catechism of 1549. This evidently poses a nice problem in relation to terminology: should one style men such as Peter Baro (d. 1599) as an 'Arminian *avant la lettre*', or accept that their teaching was typical of the period before the Arminian controversy brought the matter to a head and a new theological term into existence? Most Anglican divines in the late sixteenth and early seventeenth centuries appear to have based their soteriology on the dialectic between universal redemption and universal salvation, declining to accept the Bezan solution of their Puritan opponents. More significantly, the early Caroline Divines appear to have been unanimous in their rejection of the doctrine of justification by inherent righteousness.

In 1701, two letters of Thomas Barlow (1607–71), sometime Bishop of Lincoln, were published. Addressed to a priest in his diocese, the letters condemn the tendency to harmonise Paul and James to yield a doctrine of justification by faith *and* works, particularly on account of its associated denial of the imputation of the righteousness of Christ in justification. As we shall indicate later in the present section, this doctrine is characteristic of the post-Reformation Caroline Divines. The real significance of the letters, however, lies in their historical insight. Barlow states that Anglican divines

> who have writ of our justification *coram Deo* before the late unhappy rebellion, such as Bishop Jewel, Hooker, Reynolds, Whittaker, Field, Downhant, John White, etc., do constantly prove and vindicate the imputation of our blessed Saviour's Righteousness against the contrary doctrine of Racovia and Rome, Papists and Socinians. So that in truth it is only you, and some Neotericks who (since the year 1640) deny such imputation.[232]

---

[231] Packer, *The Transformation of Anglicanism*, 53–6, 56. Cf. *BSRK* 523.3.
[232] *Two Letters Written by the Rt Rev. Thomas Barlow*, 139.

In this respect, Barlow must be judged correct. In the case of every divine that he mentions, the doctrine of justification by imputed righteousness is defended, reflecting the general theological consensus upon this point in the Caroline church up to 1640. Had he so desired, Barlow could have added Ussher, Hall, Jackson, Davenant, Cosin and Andrewes to his list.[233] Thus George Downham defined justification as 'a most gracious and righteous action of God whereby he, imputing the righteousness of Christ to a believing sinner, absolveth him from his sinnes and accepteth him as righteous in Christ'.[234]

In common with his contemporaries, Downham distinguished between the *imputation* of the righteousness of Christ, as the formal cause of the justification of humans, and the *infusion* of righteousness in their subsequent sanctification. The Tridentine doctrine of justification by inherent righteousness (or, more strictly, the doctrine that the formal cause of justification was inherent righteousness) was criticised on six counts,[235] closely paralleling similar criticisms made of the Tridentine teaching – particularly as presented in the writings of Bellarmine – by Lutheran and Reformed apologists. Indeed, in the period 1590–1640, the Caroline Divines may be regarded as developing an understanding of justification which parallels that of Lutheran orthodoxy, and as criticising both Rome (on the formal cause of justification) and Geneva (on the nature of predestination) on grounds similar to those by then well established within Lutheranism.

Isolated traces of an emerging discontinuity may be detected in the final years of the troubled reign of Charles I. Henry Hammond reverted to the more Augustinian definition of justification associated with the earlier period of the English Reformation, including the non-imputation of sin, but *not* the imputation of righteousness, among its elements. In his *Practical Catechism*, Hammond defines justification as

God's accepting our persons, and not imputing our sins, His covering or pardoning our iniquities, His being so reconciled unto us sinners, that He determines not to punish us eternally.[236]

A similar understanding of justification may be found in the works of William Forbes, particularly his posthumously published *Considerationes*. In this work, Forbes reverts to the Augustinian understanding of justification as 'an entity, one by aggregation, and compounded of two, which by

---

[233] Ussher, *Whole Works*, 13.250–1, 264; Hall, *Works*, 9.322; Jackson, *Works*, 5.118; Davenant, *A Treatise on Justification*, 164–5; Cosin, *Works*, 2.49; Andrewes, *Works*, 5.104–26, especially 116–17.
[234] *A Treatise of Justification*, 2.   [235] See Allison, *The Rise of Moralism*, 181–2.
[236] Hammond, *A Practical Catechism*, 78. Note also his criticism of the priority of justification over sanctification (78–83).

necessary conjunction and co-ordination are one only' – in other words, justification subsumes both the forgiveness of sins and the regeneration of humans through inherent righteousness.[237] The 'whole sanctification or renewal of humanity ought to be comprehended in the expression "forgiveness of sins"'.[238]

The idea of justification *sola fide* is also criticised by the same authors. Hammond agrees that regeneration must be regarded as a precondition of justification,[239] while Forbes, conceding that faith justifies 'in a singular manner', denies that it is faith *and faith alone* which justifies. Works cannot be excluded from justification, precisely because faith is itself a work.[240] This understanding of the implication of both faith and works in justification is, of course, a necessary consequence of the reversion to the Augustinian concept of justification, which subsumes the new life of the believer under the aegis of justification rather than of sanctification.

The leading features of the doctrines of justification characteristic of the leading Anglican divines in the period of the Restoration may thus be shown to have been anticipated in the earlier part of the century. These leading features are as follows.

1. Justification is treated as both an event and a process, subsuming regeneration or sanctification.
2. The formal cause of justification is held to be *either* imputed righteousness, *or* inherent and imputed righteousness – but *not inherent righteousness alone*.
3. The teachings of Paul and James are harmonised in such a manner that both faith and works are held to be involved in the justification of humanity, frequently on the basis of the explicitly stated presupposition that faith is itself a work.

The most significant expositions of this understanding of justification are Jeremy Taylor's Dublin sermons of 1662[241] and George Bull's *Harmonia Apostolica* (1669–70) – the 'apostles' in question being, of course, Paul and James.[242]

Of particular interest is Bull's apparent awareness that his views on justification are at variance with those of an earlier generation of Anglican divines; he acknowledges significant points of disagreement with Hooker on the question of justifying righteousness.[243] Nevertheless, whatever its relationship with the earlier Caroline divinity may have been, it is clear

---

[237] Forbes, *Considerationes*, 1.174, 204.   [238] *Considerationes*, 1.216.
[239] See Allison, *The Rise of Moralism*, 98–106.   [240] Forbes, *Considerationes*, 1.54.
[241] *Works*, 8.247–302, especially 284–90 (on the relation between Paul and James). See H. R. McAdoo, *The Structure of Caroline Moral Theology*, London: Longmans, Green & Co., 1949; Allison, *The Rise of Moralism*, 64–95.
[242] See Allison, *The Rise of Moralism*, 118–37.   [243] *Harmonia Apostolica*, 279–80.

that the 'theology of holy living' came to exercise a profound influence over later Caroline theology in general, and particularly its moral theology. This is not to say that there were no critics of this new theology of justification among the later Caroline Divines; Barlow, Barrow and Beveridge, for example, argued that Paul was referring to justification *coram Deo* and James to justification *coram hominibus*, thus challenging the *harmonia apostolica* of the 'holy living' school. Similarly, many of the earlier Caroline Divines – such as Bramhall and Sanderson – survived until the period of the post-Restoration Caroline church, maintaining the older view of the nature of the formal causes of justification.[244]

In his *Learned Discourse of Justification*, delivered towards the end of the sixteenth century, Richard Hooker spoke of 'that grand question, which hangeth yet in controversy between us and the Church of Rome, about the matter of justifying righteousness'. The following century saw disagreement concerning precisely this 'grand question' arise within the Church of England itself. Whereas the Anglican tradition had been virtually unanimous upon this and related questions until about 1640 (the earlier Caroline divines following Hooker himself in insisting that justifying righteousness was imputed to humanity; that faith was not a work of humans; and that justification and sanctification were to be distinguished), the later period of Caroline divinity came to be dominated by the theology of 'holy living', with a quite distinct – indeed, one might go so far as to say totally different – understanding of justification (justifying righteousness is inherent to humans; faith is a work of humans; justification subsumes sanctification). Although the intervention of the Puritan Commonwealth between these two periods of Caroline divinity suggests that the new directions within the Anglican theology of justification may have arisen as a conscious reaction against that of the Westminster divines, the origins of these new directions may be found in the earlier Caroline period. Even in the later period, however, significant support for the older view persisted.

These observations are clearly of significance in relation to John Henry Newman's polemical attempt to construct a *via media* doctrine of justification on the basis of the teachings of the later Caroline Divines, such as Bull and Taylor. Newman's own doctrine of justification, as expounded in the 1837 *Lectures on Justification*, is essentially coterminous with that of the later Caroline Divines just mentioned. However, Newman appears to appreciate that his own teaching on justification is at variance with some of the pre-Commonwealth divines. Thus Newman appeals to 'the

---

[244] Bramhall, *Works*, 1.56; Sanderson, *Sermons*, 1.543.

three who have sometimes been considered the special lights of our later church, Hooker, Taylor and Barrow';[245] while he feels able to claim the support of the latter two for his own teaching, he is obliged to report that Hooker 'decides the contrary way, declaring not only for one special view of justification . . . but that the opposite opinion is a virtual denial of gospel truth'.[246] This 'opposite opinion' bears a remarkable resemblance to the position carefully established by Newman himself. Furthermore, it is questionable, to say the least, whether Barrow may be cited as an antecedent of Newman's position, on account of his strong affinities with the earlier Caroline theology of justification; Newman merely cites Barrow to demonstrate the latter's awareness of the confusion and uncertainty concerning the terminology of justification, and his cautionary comments arising as a consequence;[247] this does not, however, inhibit Barrow from unequivocally affirming the earlier Anglican teaching of justification by imputed rather than inherent righteousness, and by faith rather than by works.

Newman's claim to present an 'Anglican' theology of justification appears to involve the unwarranted restriction of 'Anglican' sources to the 'holy living' divines, with the total exclusion of several earlier generations of Anglican divines – men such as Andrewes, Beveridge, Davenant, Downham, Hooker, Jewel, Reynolds, Ussher and Whittaker. The case for the 'Anglican' provenance of Newman's *via media* doctrine of justification thus rests upon the teachings of a small, and unrepresentative, group of theologians operating over a period of a mere thirty or so years, which immediately followed the greatest discontinuity within English history – the period of the Commonwealth.

It is therefore quite unacceptable to suggest that certain divines of the Restoration period in any way represent a classic statement of the essence of 'Anglican' thinking on justification; to do so manifests an arbitrary historical positivism. Anglicanism cannot be defined with reference to the teachings of such a small group of theologians, operating over so short a period of time, contradicting a previously well-established tradition, and subject to considerable contemporary criticism. If any such group *could* be singled out in this manner, it is the group of *earlier* Anglican theologians, operating in the period immediately following the Elizabethan Settlement – for whom Hooker is generally regarded as spokesman.

---

[245] Newman, *Lectures on the Doctrine of Justification*, 400.
[246] Newman, *Lectures on the Doctrine of Justification*, 402.
[247] Newman, *Lectures on the Doctrine of Justification*, 400–1. See Barrow, *Theological Works*, 162–79.

We shall return to consider Newman's views in a little more detail later (3.11). Our attention is now claimed by what is probably the most significant contribution of the English Reformation to Christian theology and church life: Puritanism.

3.9   Puritanism: from the Old World to the New

The term 'Puritan' is notoriously difficult to define, this difficulty unquestionably reflecting the fact that it was a term of stigmatisation used uncritically in a wide variety of social contexts over a long period of time. As early as 1565, Catholic exiles from Elizabethan England were complaining of the 'hot puritans of the new clergy', and it is possible that Shakespeare's Malvolio (1600) exemplifies the stereotyped puritan of the new 'character' literature, particularly in the aftermath of the Marprelate Tracts.

For the purposes of the present study, the term 'Puritanism' may be regarded as the English manifestation, especially during the period 1564–1640, of Reformed theology which laid particular emphasis upon both the experimental basis of faith and the divine sovereignty in election.[248] In this period, Puritans may be regarded as those members of the English national church who, although critical of its theology, church polity and liturgy, chose to remain within it; terms such as 'Brownist', 'Separatist' or 'Barrowist' were used to refer to those who, though criticising the same church for substantially the same reasons, did so from without its bounds. Although some historians have suggested that Puritanism is the 'earlier and English form of that mutation from the Protestantism of the Reformation which on the Continent is called Pietism',[249] it must be emphasised that the Arminianism which is so characteristic a feature of Pietism is rejected by Puritan theologians in favour of the *decretum absolutum*. Indeed, the term is recorded as being used in 1622 to refer specifically to anti-Arminian elements.

More recently, the particular form of predestinarianism associated with Puritanism has been characterised as 'experimental predestinarianism',[250] thus capturing the twin elements of the characteristic Puritan understanding of justification. It is perfectly legitimate to suggest that perhaps the most important feature of Puritan spirituality – the quest

---

[248] See J. van der Berg, 'Het puriteinse ethos en zijn bronnen', *Vox Theologica* 33 (1963), 161–71; 34 (1964), 1–8.

[249] B. Hall, 'Puritanism: The Problems of Definition', in G. J. Cuming (ed.), *Studies in Church History* II, Leiden: Brill, 1965, 283–96.

[250] R. T. Kendall, *Calvin and English Calvinism to 1649*, Oxford: Oxford University Press, 1979, 8–9.

for assurance – results from the tension inherent between the emphasis simultaneously placed upon an emotional searching for communion with God (unquestionably paralleling later Pietism in this respect) and upon the divine sovereignty in election.

The tension between Anglicanism and Puritanism led to the great exodus of pilgrim fathers from the old England to the new. The early American Puritans were refugees from an intolerant England. An old theology thus came to be planted in the New World, where it developed unhindered. The legacy of Puritanism is to be sought chiefly in American, where its influence upon the piety and culture of a new nation, with no indigenous theology or culture to oppose it, was incalculable. Just as no student of European history can neglect the Reformation, so no student of American history can neglect the Puritans, who shaped a nation in the image of their God.

One of the most important features of Puritan theologies of justification is the federal foundation upon which they are based. The concept of a covenant initially associated with the Reformed theologian Heinrich Bullinger and subsequently with the Heidelberg theologians Zacharias Ursinus, Kaspar Olevianus and Girolamo Zanchius appears to underlie that which became distinctive of Puritanism. The introduction of the covenant concept into the English church appears to have been largely due to the influence of Heinrich Bullinger, whose *Decades* were published in English translation in 1577, and subsequently commended by Archbishop Whitgift. In the same year, John Knewstub delivered a series of lectures in London, in which he expounded the soteriological benefits of the 'league' between God and humans.[251]

The first clear statement of the decisive concept of the *double* covenant may be found in Dudley Fenner's highly influential *Theologia sacra* (1585), but passed into general circulation through William Perkins' *Armilla aurea* (1590). Although Perkins' theology is essentially Bezan, his piety is overwhelmingly Puritan, demonstrating the intense concern with casuistry and personal election so characteristic of Cambridge Puritanism at the time. The *Armilla*, based largely upon Beza's *Summa totius theologiae*, did much to promote the Bezan doctrines of election and limited atonement in the period before the Synod of Dort, and its perhaps most famous feature – the 'chart of salvation', resembling an early map of the London Underground – permitted those who found theologising difficult to follow the course of their election along well-established Bezan paths with the minimum of effort. Perkins declared that the outward means of election is the covenant, which is God's

---

[251] Knewstub, *Lectures upon the Twentieth Chapter of Exodus*, 5–6.

contract with men concerning the obtaining life eternall upon a certain condition. This covenant consisteth of two parts: God's promise to man, man's promise to God. God's promise to man is that whereby he bindeth himself to man to be his God, if he perform the condition. Man's promise to God is that whereby he voweth his allegiance unto his Lord and to perform the condition betweene them.[252]

Following the Heidelberg theologians, he distinguishes between a covenant of works and a covenant of grace, this latter being 'that, whereby God, freely promising Christ and his benefits, exacteth againe of man that he would by faith receive Christ and repent of his sinnes'.[253]

In general, the English Puritans may be regarded as following Reformed orthodoxy in their teaching on justification, particularly in relation to the doctrines of election and the imputation of the righteousness of Christ. The strongly anti-Arminian character of English Puritanism is best illustrated from the writings of John Owen, evident in his first work, *A Display of Arminianism*.[254] In this work, Owen reduced the Arminian teaching to two points: first, the precise object of Christ's death; second, the efficacy and end of his death. The controversy was thus defined in terms of the identity of those on whose behalf Christ died, and what he merited or otherwise obtained on their behalf.

Both these points were developed at greater length in *Salus electorum, sanguis Jesu* (1647). Although Owen displays the usual Puritan veneration for Scripture, it is significant that this work is essentially a logical analysis of the Arminian doctrine of universal redemption. Owen argues that the Arminian proposition 'Christ died for all people' contains within itself the further proposition 'Christ died for nobody', in that no people are actually and effectively saved by his death. For Owen, it is beyond dispute that all people are not saved; therefore, if Christ died to save all people, he has failed in his mission – which is unthinkable.[255] For Owen, the Arminians subscribe to a doctrine of conditional redemption, so that God may be said to have given Christ to obtain peace, reconciliation and forgiveness of sins for all people, 'provided that they do believe'. Thus the Arminians treat the 'blood of Christ'

as a medicine in a box, laid up for all that shall come to have any of it, and so applied now to one, then to the other, without any respect or difference, as though it should be intended no more for one than for another; so that although he hath obtained all the good that he hath purchased for us, yet it is left indifferent and uncertain whether it shall ever be ours or no.[256]

---

[252] *Workes*, 1.32.   [253] *Workes*, 1.71.   [254] *Works*, 5.41–204.   [255] *Works*, 5.284–90.
[256] *Works*, 5.320–1. Owen thus styles the Arminian Christ 'but a half-mediator' (323), in that he procures the end, but not the means thereto. Similarly, he ridicules the Arminian condition of salvation (i.e., faith) as an impossibility: it is 'as if man should promise a blind man a thousand pounds upon condition that he will see' (323).

For Owen, 'salvation indeed is bestowed conditionally, but faith, which is the condition, is absolutely procured'.[257]

Although Owen himself taught that the formal cause of justification was the imputation of the righteousness of Christ, the controversy surrounding Baxter's *Aphorisms of Justification* (1649) served to demonstrate the remarkable variety of opinions within Puritanism on this question. For Baxter himself, the formal cause of justification was the faith of the believing individual, imputed or reputed as righteousness on account of the righteousness of Christ.[258] Underlying this doctrine is a federal scheme characteristic of Puritanism, in which a distinction is drawn between the old and new covenants. According to Baxter, Christ has fulfilled the old covenant, and has therefore made it possible for humans to be justified on the basis of the somewhat more lenient terms of the new. The righteousness of Christ in fulfilling the old covenant is thus the meritorious cause of justification, in that it is on account of this fulfilment that the faith of the believer may be the formal cause of justification under the new covenant.

A similar teaching may be found in John Goodwin's *Imputatio fidei* and George Walker's *Defence*, although these two writers differed on the grounds on which human faith could be treated as righteousness; for Walker, the faith of humans is reckoned as righteousness only because it apprehends Christ as its object,[259] whereas Goodwin argued that the remission of sin implied that the sinner was 'compleately and perfectly righteous',[260] and thus did not require the imputation of the righteousness of Christ. In many respects, the disagreements over the formal cause of justification within seventeenth-century Puritanism parallel those within contemporary Anglicanism. Nevertheless, it is clear that the most favoured view was unquestionably that adopted by John Owen and others – that the formal cause of justification was none other than the imputed righteousness of Christ,[261] thus aligning the English movement with continental Reformed orthodoxy.

In the year 1633, the *Griffin* set sail from Holland for the New World, carrying with her two refugees from Laudian England: Thomas Hooker and John Cotton. Both were to prove of considerable significance in the establishment of Puritanism in New England. It was not, however, merely English Puritanism, but also the tensions within English Puritanism, which sailed with the *Griffin* to America, there to flare up once more

---

[257] *Works*, 5.324.   [258] Baxter, *A Treatise of Justifying Righteousness*, 29, 88, 129–30.
[259] *Defence of the True Sense*, 15.   [260] *Imputatio fidei*, 3–4. Cf. 212.
[261] For example, John Eedes, *The Orthodox Doctrine concerning Justification* (London, 1642), 56–62; William Eyre, *Vindiciae iustificationis gratuitae* (London, 1654), 7; Thomas Gataker, *An Antidote against Error* (London, 1670), 37–8; Owen, *Works*, 11.214–15, 258–60.

with renewed vigour. Of particular significance was the issue of 'prepa-rationism', to which we now turn.

We have already noted the importance of assurance as both a theo-logical and a practical aspect of Puritan spirituality, and the tendency to treat the experimental aspects of the Christian life (such as faith or regeneration) as grounds of assurance. During his period as a preacher in the Surrey parish of Esher, Hooker was called to counsel one Mrs Joan Drake, who was convinced that she was beyond salvation. Although we have no record of Hooker's advice to her – which succeeded where that of others had failed – it is probable that it is incorporated into the 1629 sermon *Poor Doubting Christian drawne unto Christ*.[262] In this sermon, Hooker rejected the experimental basis of assurance:

A man's faith may be somewhat strong, when his feeling is nothing at all. David was justified and sanctified, and yet wanted this joy; and so Job rested upon God, when he had but little feeling . . . Therefore away with your feeling, and go to the promise.[263]

Having rejected experience as the foundation and criterion of assur-ance, Hooker substituted the process of preparation in its place. It is within the natural powers of humans to be sufficiently contrite to permit God to justify them: 'when the heart is fitted and prepared, the Lord Jesus comes immediately into it'.[264] The absence of Christian experi-ence is therefore of secondary importance in relation to the matter of assurance; developing an argument which parallels the federal theol-ogy of the *via moderna*, Hooker argues that, once humans have satisfied the minimum precondition for justification, they may rely upon God's faithfulness to his promises of mercy to ensure their subsequent justi-fication and assurance of the same. The human preparation for justifi-cation (the 'fitting of the sinner for his being in Christ'), in which the heart is 'fitted and prepared for Christ', thus constitutes the grounds of assurance.

A similar understanding of the relation of the preparation of humans for grace and their assurance of the same may be found in the early writings of John Cotton. In an early discussion of Revelation 3:20, he argued that conversion consists of an act of God, knocking at the door of the human heart, followed by an act of humanity, opening the door in order that God

---

[262] T. Hooker, *Writings in England and Holland*, 152–86; Kendall, *Calvin and English Calvin-ism*, 125–38.

[263] *Writings in England and Holland*, 160–2.

[264] *The Soules Humiliation*, 170. Cf. *The Unbeleevers Preparing for Christ*, 1, 104; *The Soules Preparation for Christ*, 165. Note also the important statement to the effect that not every *saving* work is a *sanctifying* work: *Writings in England and Holland*, 145.

may enter.[265] Once humans have performed this necessary act, they may rest assured that God will do the rest – which he, and only he, may do. In an intriguing exposition of Isaiah 4:3–4, he declares: 'if we smooth the way for him, then he will come into our hearts'.[266]

Before his departure from England, however, Cotton's theology appears to have undergone a significant alteration. Prior to this point, Cotton and Hooker had assumed that humans were naturally capable of preparing themselves for justification (once more, it is necessary to point out the similarity with the soteriology of the *via moderna* on this point). But what if human depravity was such that they could not prepare themselves? In a development which parallels that of Luther over the period 1513–16, Cotton appears to have arrived at the insight that there is no saving preparation for grace prior to union with Christ; Christ is offered in a promise of free grace without any previous gracious qualification stipulated. In other words, humans cannot turn to God of their own volition; they require God to take hold of them. Christ is given to the sinner upon the basis of an absolute, rather than a conditional, promise. As a result, Cotton makes faith itself the basis of the assurance of humans, rather than preparation or sanctification. Cotton's rejection of sanctification as the basis of assurance was founded upon his conviction that this was to revert to the covenant of works from the covenant of grace.

Unfortunately for Cotton, his views appear to have been misunderstood by some of his more intimate circle, most notably by Mrs Anne Hutchinson. Prior to her demise at the hands of the Indians in late 1643, Mrs Hutchinson suggested that every minister in Massachusetts Bay – with the exception of Cotton – was preaching nothing more and nothing less than a covenant of works. The resulting controversy did not seriously damage his reputation. More significant, however, was his evasion of the crucial question which Hooker had addressed so directly; although Cotton implies that believers know that they have faith, he has nothing to say concerning how that faith may be obtained in the first place.

The controversy over 'the heart prepared' is of importance in a number of respects, particularly as it indicates the manner in which Puritan thinking on justification and assurance were related. Although Hooker and Cotton adopt very different theologies of justification (the former asserting the activity, the latter the passivity, of humans prior to their justification), they share a common desire to establish the grounds of assurance within the context of that theology. It is therefore vital to note

---

[265] Cotton, *Gods Mercie Mixed with his Iustice*, 10–12. See also N. Pettit, *The Heart Prepared: Grace and Conversion in Puritan Spiritual Life*, New Haven: Yale University Press, 1966, 129–79; Kendall, *Calvin and English Calvinism*, 110–17, 167–83.
[266] *Christ the Fountaine of Life*, 40–1.

that the grounds of assurance are the consequence of a prior understanding of the mode in which humans are justified.

The later seventeenth and early eighteenth centuries saw New England Puritanism in decline. The emphasis upon human impotence in the face of the divine omnipotence, a cornerstone of mainstream Puritan thought, tended to induce religious paralysis rather than renewal. As a consequence, subsequent generations of New Englanders were largely unconverted, obliging the churches to introduce the 'Half-Way Covenant', by which baptised persons of moral character would be treated as church members, save in certain respects. The emphasis on the 'means of grace' – apparently peculiar to New England – permitted pastors to admit the unregenerate to church services on the basis of the principle that the public reading of the Bible, the preaching of the Word (and, in the Stoddardean system, the attending of the Lord's Supper) were means by which divine grace could be bestowed upon humanity.

This situation was radically altered through the 'Great Awakening', particularly associated with Jonathan Edwards.[267] In 1734, Edwards preached a series of sermons on the theme of 'justification by faith'. Although these sermons contained nothing which could be described as radical innovations, the earnestness with which they were preached appears to have proved decisive in achieving their astonishing and celebrated effects. The intense emphasis placed by Edwards and others upon the need for spiritual rebirth was such that it became the criterion of church membership, thus ensuring the demise of the Half-Way Covenant.

The Great Awakening was based upon a covenant theology similar to that which had long been accepted in New England. God is understood to have entered into an agreement with humans, by which he promised to pardon those who have faith in him, upon condition that humans promise to work towards their sanctification. Edwards' discussion of the covenant of grace parallels that of Reformed orthodoxy; God has made a covenant of redemption with Christ from all eternity, by which humanity would be redeemed, and the covenant of grace is the temporal manifestation of this eternal covenant.[268] Just as the imputation of the sin of Adam to his posterity is the consequence of his being the federal representative of all humankind in the covenant of works, so the imputation of the

[267] For an excellent analysis of Edwards' reaction to Stoddardeanism, see John F. Jamieson, 'Jonathan Edwards' Change of Position on Stoddardeanism', *HThR* 74 (1981), 79–99.

[268] *Works*, 2.950b. For Samuel Willard's views on the covenant, see E. B. Lowrie, *The Shape of the Puritan Mind: The Thought of Samuel Willard*, New Haven: Yale University Press, 1974, 160–85. For the importance of the covenant concept to Puritan theology in the period, see the classic study of P. Miller, 'The Marrow of Puritan Divinity', in *Errand into the Wilderness*, Cambridge, MA: Harvard University Press, 1956, 48–98.

righteousness of Christ to the elect is the consequence of his being their federal representative in the covenant of redemption, actualised in the covenant of grace.

Edwards' somewhat traditional presentation of the federal basis of justification was developed and modified by his followers. Joseph Bellamy modified the Bezan foundations of the 'New England Theology' by following Grotius in insisting that Christ's sufferings were a penal example stipulated by God as the moral governor of the universe, rather than a satisfaction rendered to God as the offended party. Samuel Hopkins explicitly rejected the 'Old Calvinist' emphasis upon the 'means of grace' – the principle upon which the Half-Way Covenant was based – although his chief contribution to the development of the movement was his understanding of the positive role of sin within the economy of salvation.[269]

Of particular significance was the rise of federal Arminianism within New England Puritanism. Recognising that the federal condition required of humans for justification was faith (which the 'Old Calvinists' regarded as a divine gift to humanity), the Arminians regarded faith as a condition, equivalent to obedience, capable of being met by all people. In many respects, the Arminian party within the Puritan movement may be regarded as the direct equivalent of European Pietism, the one significant difference between Puritanism and Pietism (the doctrine of election) having been abandoned. Indeed, there are excellent grounds for suggesting a direct link between the two movements through the correspondence between Cotton Mather and the Halle Pietists.[270] The Arminians thus followed the 'Old Calvinists' in relation to the principle of the 'means of grace': grace was understood to be available to all humanity, particularly through 'means' such as reading the Bible, attending public worship and hearing the proclamation of the Word. As Jonathan Mayhew stated this principle: 'Tho' God is omnipotent, yet he seldom or never works wholly without means.' The Arminians thus sided with the 'Old Calvinists' over the question of unregenerate church membership, proclaiming the universality of grace:

The Gospel takes no Notice of different Kinds or Sorts of grace – Sorts of Grace specifically different, – one of which may be call'd *special* and the other not so; – one of which, from the peculiar and distinguishing Nature of it, shall prove converting and saving, and the other not.[271]

---

[269] Hopkins, *The Wisdom of God in the Permission of Sin* (Boston, 1759).

[270] K. Francke, 'The Beginning of Cotton Mather's Correspondence with August Hermann Franke', *Philological Quarterly* 5 (1926), 193–5.

[271] John Tucker, *Observations on the Doctrines and Uncharitableness of the Rev Mr Jonathan Parsons of Newbury* (Boston, 1757), 5.

The emphasis upon the necessity of both faith and works in justification was usually supported with reference to the need to harmonise the opinions of Paul and James, with both faith and works being understood 'as the *gracious Terms* and *Conditions*, appointed by the Redeemer, without which we shall not be *pardon'd* and *accepted*'.[272]

Although the effects of the Great Awakening in New England were to extend far beyond the purely religious sphere, the revival in preaching and intense interest in personal conversion and religious experience thus resulted in the exposing of a number of differences on the question of justification within New England Puritanism, in many respects paralleling similar developments within continental Protestant theology.

3.10   The Pietist critique of Protestant orthodoxy

The period of Lutheran orthodoxy was marked by considerable opposition from the increasingly influential Pietist movement, particularly associated with the university of Halle.[273] At its best, the Pietist movement may be regarded as a reaction on the part of a living faith against the empty formulas of a dead orthodoxy. The term 'Pietism' is particularly applied to the movement within Lutheranism associated with Philipp Jakob Spener, characterised by its insistence upon the active nature of faith and its critique of the orthodox doctrine of forensic justification. Such criticism was foreshadowed in many quarters, including sections of the Radical Reformation.[274] The English Quaker Robert Barclay taught that justification is identical with regeneration, whose formal cause is 'the revelation of God in the soul, changing, altering and renewing the mind'.[275] On account of being made a partaker of the divine nature, humanity is *made* righteous.[276] A similar, although more extended, critique of the orthodox doctrine of justification is to be found in the writings of Jakob Böhme.[277]

---

[272] Samuel Webster, *Justification by the Free Grace of God* (Boston, 1765), 27. It will be obvious that this opened the Arminians to the charge that they were preaching justification by works – a charge which they vigorously denied: Lemuel Briant, *Some Friendly Remarks upon a Sermon Lately Preached at Braintree* (Boston, 1750), 10; Charles Chauncy, *Twelve Sermons* (Boston, 1765). 12; Jonathan Mayhew, *Striving to Enter In at the Strait Gate* (Boston, 1761), 19–20.

[273] See N. Hinske and C. Ritterhoff (eds.), *Halle, Aufklärung und Pietismus*, Heidelberg: Schneider, 1989.

[274] See A. J. Beachy, *The Concept of Grace in the Radical Reformation*, especially 28–9, who demonstrates the transformational concept of justification widely employed within the movement, generally articulated in terms of the concept of 'deification'.

[275] Robert Barclay, *An Apologie for the True Christian Divinity*, 13th edn, Manchester, 1869, 136.

[276] *Apologie*, 131.

[277] E. Hirsch, *Geschichte der neuen evangelischen Theologie*, 5 vols., Gütersloh: Mohn, 1949–51, 2.245–9.

As Ritschl has observed,[278] Pietism maintained the doctrine of *reconciliation* in a thoroughly orthodox form (in other words, humanity was understood to be alienated from God through original sin), while subjecting the doctrine of *justification* to extensive modification on the basis of the pastoral concern for personal holiness and devotion.[279] The concept of participation in the divine nature, usually expounded on the basis of 2 Peter 1:4, appears to have become characteristic of Pietist understandings of the nature of justification at an early stage.

Five important modifications were made by the Pietists to the orthodox doctrine of justification, each corresponding to a distinctive aspect of the movement's agenda.

1. Faith is understood to be active, rather than passive, in justification. The Pietist assertion of the activity of faith in justification was particularly criticised by the Lutheran Valentin Löscher, who appealed to Luther's insistence upon the passivity of justifying faith.[280] Löscher's criticisms were rejected by Anton and Lange, who argued that faith must be active if it is to lay hold of Christ. Francke himself argued that the activity of faith in justification was not inconsistent with God's being the author of justification.

2. The intense emphasis placed by Pietism upon the necessity for personal piety led to the articulation of the doctrine of Christian perfection, a concept without any counterpart within – indeed, which was excluded by – orthodoxy.

3. The concept of vicarious satisfaction is rejected as detrimental to personal piety. This criticism of the orthodox understanding of the objective foundations of justification can be instanced from the writings of Spener, although it is particularly associated with John Wesley. To Wesley, the assertion that Christ had fulfilled the law on the behalf of humanity appeared to imply that humans were no longer under any obligation to fulfil it. It is this consideration which underlies Wesley's discussion of the law *sub loco sanctificationis*.

4. The concept of imputed righteousness, which is an essential feature of the orthodox understanding of justification, is generally rejected as being destructive of piety.[281] Thus, in his *Theses credendorum*, Breithaupt argued for the necessary implication of inherent righteousness

---

[278] Ritschl, *Justification and Reconciliation*, 515.
[279] J. Baur, *Salus Christiana: Die Rechtfertigungslehre in der Geschichte des christlichen Heilsverständnisses*, Gütersloh: Mohn, 1969, 87–110; E. Peschke, 'Speners Wiederburtslehre und ihr Verhältnis zu Franckes Lehre von der Bekehrung', in W. Zeller (ed.), *Traditio – Krisis – Renovatio aus theologischer Sicht*, Marburg: Elwert, 1976, 206–24.
[280] On this controversy, see H.-M. Rotermund, *Orthodoxie und Pietismus: Valentin Ernst Löschers 'Timotheus Verinus' in der Auseinandersetzung mit der Schule August Hermann Franckes*, Berlin: Evangelische Verlagsanstalt, 1960, 48–51.
[281] See Baur, *Salus Christiana*, 91–5.

in justification.[282] In his sermon *A Blow at the Root, or Christ Stabbed in the House of his Friends*, Wesley described the teaching 'that Christ had done as well as suffered all; that his righteousness being imputed to us, we need none of our own' as 'a blow at the root of all holiness, all true religion . . . for wherever this doctrine is cordially received, it leaves no place for holiness'.[283] This criticism was expanded in the Standard Sermon *Justification by Faith*:

> Least of all does justification imply that God is deceived in those whom he justifies; that he thinks them to be what, in fact, they are not; that he accounts them to be otherwise than they are. It does by no means imply that God judges concerning us contrary to the real nature of things; that he esteems us better than we really are, or believes us righteous when we are unrighteous . . . [or] . . . judges that I am righteous, because another is so.[284]

5. The Pietist emphasis upon the need for personal holiness appeared to be threatened by the orthodox doctrine that humans might repent at any time of their choosing, which frequently led to 'deathbed conversions' on the part of notorious sinners who had evidently chosen to postpone their conversion until the last possible moment.

Although the early Pietists such as Spener or Francke were more concerned with the promotion of personal piety than with the restructuring of Christian doctrine, it is an inescapable fact that the Pietist emphasis upon regeneration led to a re-evaluation of the received teachings of Lutheran orthodoxy in terms of their promotion of piety. The emphasis upon the necessity of regeneration led to the assertion of the priority of regeneration over justification – a tendency already evident within Lutheran orthodoxy itself, which was thus ill prepared to meet this development.

The Pietist emphasis upon the priority and necessity of piety, virtue and obedience on the part of believers is also significant for another reason, in that it provides a direct link with the moralism of the Enlightenment. If an 'active faith' is to be accepted as the arbiter and criterion of justification, in the quasi-Arminian sense often found in the writings of the Pietists, it may be concluded that the practice of piety by individuals is an adequate demonstration of their faith. In other words, the ethical renewal of individuals both causes and demonstrates their justification. This important

---

[282] Rotermund, *Orthodoxie und Pietismus*, 56–7. Löscher saw in this development a revival of the Osiandrist position.

[283] Wesley, *Works*, 10.366. On the importance of this issue, see K. J. Collins, 'John Wesley's Doctrine of the New Birth', *Wesleyan Theological Journal* 32 (1997), 53–68.

[284] Wesley, *Standard Sermons*, 1.120. Baur notes the general Pietist hostility towards the *als-ob-Theologie* of Lutheran orthodoxy: *Salus Christiana*, 94. On the specific question of Wesley's attitude towards the notion, see W. W. Whidden, 'Wesley on Imputation: A Truly Reckoned Reality or Antinomian Polemical Wreckage?', *Asbury Theological Journal* 52 (1997), 63–70.

observation goes some considerable way towards explaining the rise of legalism within the Pietist theological faculty at Halle towards the end of the eighteenth century, and also points to a fundamental affinity with the moralism of the theologians of the Enlightenment.

3.11   The Anglo-Catholic critique of the Reformation

Finally, we turn to consider a development which is chronologically located in the early nineteenth century, but theologically represents a reversion to the agenda of the seventeenth century – namely, the criticisms of Luther's doctrine of justification associated with the rise of the Oxford Movement, and particularly with John Henry Newman.

As noted earlier, the Restoration of Charles II in 1660 appears to have been the occasion for the introduction of a new Anglican theology of justification, which asserted the positive role of inherent righteousness in justification, with faith being understood as a human work. If these later Anglican divines believed in justification *sola fide*, it was in the sense that faith justifies *in its own particular manner*. These features of the later Caroline understanding of justification were emphasised by the 'High Churchmen' of the later eighteenth century in their polemic against the possibility that their Evangelical counterparts might cause the faithful to become complacent or negligent of good works through their preaching of the doctrine of justification *sola fide*.

The nineteenth century saw the theological differences between High Churchmen and Evangelicals on this matter fairly well established, and not the subject of major controversy. Indeed, both parties to the debate emphasised the need for personal holiness as a result of justification, showing a remarkable uniformity in their respective teachings on piety. It is a fact which is often overlooked, that many Evangelicals – such as C. R. Sumner – followed the early stages of the Oxford Movement with great sympathy.

This relative calm was shattered through the publication (1834–7) of the *Remains* of Alexander Knox, a lay theologian of some considerable talent. The *Remains* included his 1810 essay 'On Justification',[285] in which Knox argued that the Church of England, far from teaching a doctrine of *forensic* justification in her Homilies and Articles, was actually committed to a doctrine of *moral* justification. 'In the judgement of the Church of England justification by faith contains in it the vitalisation which vera et viva fides (true and lively faith) produces in the subject; as well as the

---

[285]   Originally a letter to D. Parker, dated 16 April 1810, entitled 'On Justification': *Remains*, 1.281–317.

reputation of righteousness, which follows coram Deo (before God).'[286] Noting Cranmer's frequent references to patristic writers in the *Homily of Salvation*, and the failure of the church historian Joseph Milner to demonstrate that such writers taught a forensic doctrine of justification, Knox suggested that the patristic consensus favoured a doctrine of moral justification.[287]

In 1837, Newman – the editor of Knox's *Remains* – delivered a series of lectures in the Adam de Brome chapel of the University Church of St Mary the Virgin, Oxford, on the theme of justification. The lectures are of significance in a number of respects. In them, Newman defined what he took to be a *via media* understanding of justification, which allowed an authentically *Anglican* concept of justification to be defended in the face of the distortions of both Protestantism and Roman Catholicism.[288] Newman thus declared his intention to 'build up a system of theology out of the Anglican divines', and indicated that the lectures were a 'tentative inquiry' towards that end.[289] They belong to a cluster of writings, including *The Arians of the Fourth Century* (1833) and *Lectures on the Prophetical Office of the Church* (1837), in which historical analysis serves as a means of clarifying the distinctive position of the Church of England.

Newman envisaged his *Lectures on Justification* as one of a series of works which was intended to illustrate 'what has often been considered to be the charateristic position of the Anglican church, as lying in a supposed *Via Media*, admitting much and excluding much both of Roman and of Protestant teaching'.[290] In view of the importance of Newman's historical analysis for the future development of Anglicanism, his views on the doctrine of justification are of considerable interest.

Newman's theology of justification rests primarily upon a historical analysis of the doctrines of justification associated with Luther (and to a much lesser extent, with Melanchthon), with Roman Catholic theologians such as Bellarmine and Vásquez, and with the Caroline Divines. It is therefore of the utmost importance to appreciate that in every case, and supremely in the case of Luther himself, Newman's historico-theological analysis appears to be seriously and irredeemably inaccurate. In other

---

[286] *Remains*, 1.308. Note the deliberate avoidance of the term 'imputation'. Cf. 1.298–9.
[287] G. S. Faber's *Primitive Doctrine of Justification Investigated*, London: Seeley & Burnside, 1837, attempted to disprove Knox on this point, while at the same time suggesting that Knox was Tridentine, rather than Anglican, in his personal view on justification.
[288] For a useful introduction, see Sheridan, *Newman on Justification*.
[289] Newman, *Apologia pro vita sua*, London: Everyman, 1964, 86. Note the statement that the 'essay on Justification' was 'aimed at the Lutheran dictum that justification by faith only was the cardinal doctrine of Christianity'.
[290] Newman, *Lectures on the Doctrine of Justification*, ix. These comments were added to the third edition.

words, Newman's construction of a *via media* doctrine of justification seems to rest upon a fallacious interpretation of both the extremes to which he was opposed, as well as of the Caroline divinity of the seventeenth century, which he regarded as a prototype of his own position. We shall develop these criticisms at the appropriate point in the present section.

The essential feature of Newman's understanding of the nature of justification is his insistence upon the real presence of the Trinity within the soul of the justified believer, conceived in broadly realist terms which undoubtedly reflect his interest in and positive evaluation of the Greek fathers, such as Athanasius.[291] It is this understanding of the nature of justification which underlies the most difficult stanza of his most famous hymn:

> And that a higher gift than grace,
>   Should flesh and blood refine;
> God's presence and his very self,
>   And essence all-divine.[292]

It is God himself, the 'essence all-divine', who dwells within and thus 'refines' sinful humans, in the process of justification. '*This* is to be justified, to receive the Divine Presence within us, and be made a Temple of the Holy Ghost.'[293] Justification thus refers to a present reality, the 'indwelling in us of God the Father and the Word Incarnate through the Holy Ghost'.[294] Although this divine presence is to be understood in Trinitarian terms, Newman makes it clear that it is most appropriately conceived as the presence of Christ himself. 'If to justify be to impart a certain inward token of our personal redemption, and if the presence of God within us is such a token, our justification must consist in God's coming to us and dwelling in us.'[295]

This real presence of the Trinity within the soul of the believer has certain associated and necessary consequences, which Newman identifies as being *counted righteous* and being *made righteous*. Both justification and sanctification are bestowed simultaneously with the gift of the divine presence within the souls of the justified. In other words, Newman understands the primary and fundamental sense of the term 'justification' to be the indwelling of the Trinity within the soul of believers, which has

[291] C. S. Dessain, 'Cardinal Newman and the Eastern Tradition', *DR* 94 (1976), 83–98.
[292] 'Praise to the Holiest in the height', *English Hymnal* no. 471; *Hymns Ancient and Modern Revised* no. 185. The hymn first appeared in 1865, as part of the *Dream of Gerontius*.
[293] *Lectures on the Doctrine of Justification*, 144. Cf. 150–1.
[294] *Lectures on the Doctrine of Justification*, 144.
[295] *Lectures on the Doctrine of Justification*, 149.

as its necessary consequence those aspects of their conversion which are traditionally (although Newman feels *inappropriately*) termed 'justification' (that is, being counted as righteous) and 'sanctification' (that is, being made righteous).[296] This is made clear in what is probably the most important passage in the *Lectures*:

We now may see what the connection really is between justification and renewal. They are both included in that one great gift of God, the indwelling of Christ in the Christian soul. That dwelling is *ipso facto* our sanctification and justification, as its necessary results. It is the divine presence which justifies us, not faith, as say the Protestant schools, not renewal, as say the Roman. The word of justification is the substantive and living Word of God, entering the soul, illuminating and cleansing it, as fire brightens and purifies material substances. He who justifies also sanctifies, because it is He. The first blessing runs into the second as its necessary limit; and the second being rejected, carries away with it the first. And the one cannot be separated from the other except in idea, unless the sun's rays can be separated from the sun, or the power of purifying from fire or water.[297]

Justification is therefore *notionally distinct* from sanctification, although inseparable from it, in that they are both aspects of one and the same thing – the indwelling of the Holy Trinity within the soul of the believer. This distinction between justification and renewal allows Newman to maintain a proleptic relation between them: 'Justification is at first what renewal could but be at last; and therefore is by no means a mere result or consequence of renewal, but a real, though not a separate act of God's mercy.'[298] The distinction between justification and sanctification is thus 'purely mental',[299] relating to the single act of divine mercy, and does not necessitate the division of that act itself.

In his tenth lecture, Newman turns his attention to the vexed question of the precise role of faith in justification. Newman rejects a purely fiduciary interpretation of faith as excluding other Christian virtues, such as love or obedience. While Newman would not go so far as to state 'that there is no such thing as a trusting in Christ's mercy for salvation, and a comfort resulting from it',[300] he insists that this is inadequate to characterise true Christian faith. The evil and good alike can

---

[296] Newman here distances himself from Knox, who suggested that justification concerned being *made righteous*, and sanctification being *made holy*: Knox, *Remains*, 1.307–9.

[297] *Lectures on the Doctrine of Justification*, 154.

[298] *Lectures on the Doctrine of Justification*, 74. This also permits the earlier statement (63) to be understood correctly: 'justification and sanctification [are] in fact substantially one and the same thing; . . . in order of ideas, viewed relatively to each other, justification followed upon sanctification'.

[299] *Lectures on the Doctrine of Justification*, 112.

[300] *Lectures on the Doctrine of Justification*, 263.

trust in God's mercy, whereas the good and the evil are distinguished on account of the former's charity, love and obedience. The Protestant understanding of faith, as Newman perceives it, is thus not so much wrong, as incomplete.[301] Following later Caroline divines such as Bull and Taylor, Newman argues that faith and works must both be said to justify, although in different manners.[302] Thus the fact that all acknowledge that it is Christ who justifies does not prevent the simultaneous assertion that faith justifies, nor does the fact that faith justifies exclude works from justifying:

> It seems then, that whereas faith on our part fitly corresponds, or is the correlative, as it is called, to grace on God's part, sacraments are but the manifestation of grace, and good works are but the manifestation of faith; so that, whether we say we are justified by faith, or by works or by sacraments, all these but mean this one doctrine, that we are justified by grace, which is given through sacraments, impetrated by faith, manifested in works.[303]

Newman's use of the later Caroline divines to determine what constitutes an authentically Anglican doctrine of justification is deeply problematic. The theology of justification of the post-Restoration divines, such as Bull and Taylor, by no means represents a unanimous or even the *majority* opinion within contemporary Anglicanism. Yet Newman appears to suggest that the theology of justification is characteristic of Anglicanism, and may be taken to define the *via media* between Protestant and Roman Catholic. Put crudely, but none the less accurately, Newman appears to believe that Protestants taught that humanity was justified on account of faith (which, as we have seen, is an Arminian rather than an orthodox view) and that Roman Catholics taught that humans were justified on account of their works or renewal – and therefore that the *via media* consisted in the affirmation that humans are justified on account of both faith and works. This view corresponds with that of the 'holy living' school within later Caroline divinity, which appears to establish the 'Anglican' character of this mediating doctrine. However, as we have seen, the discontinuity within Anglicanism over the period 1550–1700 on precisely this point is sufficient to negate any attempt to characterise such a position as 'Anglican'.

Newman's superficial engagement with Roman Catholic theologies of justification cannot be allowed to pass without comment. Newman nowhere attempts a detailed analysis of the teaching of Bellarmine and Vásquez, forcing us to base our tentative conclusions upon the few passing

---

[301] *Lectures on the Doctrine of Justification*, 262.
[302] *Lectures on the Doctrine of Justification*, 275–6.
[303] *Lectures on the Doctrine of Justification*, 303.

statements made in the *Lectures* concerning Roman Catholicism in general. Newman clearly believes the Roman Catholic teaching to be that humans are justified on account of their renewal.[304] Like many contemporary Evangelicals, Newman appears to have assumed that the notion of factitive justification implies that the analytic divine verdict of justification is based upon the inherent righteousness of the individual, *achieved through moral renewal* – whereas the reference is, of course, to the *infusion* of *divine* righteousness which is the *cause* of subsequent moral renewal, and is not identical with that renewal itself. The evidence contained within the body of the *Lectures* suggests (though it is not conclusive) that Newman simply did not understand the Tridentine doctrine of justification.

Both in the *Lectures* and in the earlier *Arians of the Fourth Century*, Newman uses historical theology as little more than a thinly veiled foil for his own theological and ecclesiological agenda, which is firmly wedded to the realities of the Church of England in the 1830s. In each case, Newman's enemy is not so much the stated subject of his inquiry – whether Arians or Luther – but Protestantism in general, and evangelicalism in particular. Equally, in each case the scholarship is flawed, even to the point of involving what I must regrettably describe as deliberate misrepresentation. Rowan Williams, in his excellent study of Arius, points out the severe limitations of Newman's historical scholarship:

> One must charitably say that Newman is not at his best here: a brilliant argument, linking all sorts of diverse phenomena, is built up on a foundation of complacent bigotry and historical fantasy. However, setting aside for the moment the distasteful rhetoric of his exposition, it should be possible to see something of what his polemical agenda really is. *The Arians of the Fourth Century* is, in large part, a tract in defence of what the early Oxford Movement thought of as spiritual religion and spiritual authority.[305]

In both his *Arians of the Fourth Century* and his *Lectures on Justification*, Newman's critique of Protestantism is subtle and largely indirect, tending to proceed by 'eccentric, superficial and prejudiced'[306] historical analysis of the past, on the basis of an assumed linkage between disliked individuals of the past (Arius and Luther) and the evangelicalism of the 1830s.

Newman's summary of Luther's failings, which concludes this course of lectures, runs as follows:

---

[304] *Lectures on the Doctrine of Justification*, 154.
[305] Rowan Williams, *Arius: Heresy and Tradition*, London: Darton, Longman & Todd, 1987, 4–5.
[306] Williams, *Arius*, 6.

Luther found in the Church great moral corruptions countenanced by the highest authorities; he felt them; but instead of meeting them with divine weapons, he used one of his own. He adopted a doctrine original, specious, fascinating, persuasive, powerful against Rome, and wonderfully adapted, as if prophetically, to the genius of the times which were to follow. He found Christians in bondage to their works and observances; he released them by his doctrine of faith; and he left them in bondage to their feelings. He weaned them from seeking assurance of salvation in standing ordinances, at the cost of teaching them that a personal consciousness of it was promised to every one who believed. For outward signs he substituted inward; for reverence towards the church contemplation of self.[307]

We have here a series of puzzling assertions concerning Luther, of which I shall note a few, and indicate the responses which any Oxford undergraduate studying Luther's works for the Final Honour School of Theology would be able to make.

1. 'He found Christians in bondage to their works and observances . . . he left them in bondage to their feelings.' This is untenable. Luther's *theologia crucis* is aimed precisely at any form of reliance upon feelings. Luther has no doubt that theology must relate to experience, but the nature of that relationship is construed in terms of the primacy of theology over experience.[308]

2. 'He weaned them from seeking assurance of salvation in standing ordinances, at the cost of teaching them that a personal consciousness of it was promised to every one who believed.' Once more, Luther's 'theology of the cross' flatly contradicts this point. For Luther, the grounds of Christian certainty most emphatically do *not* lie in any 'personal consciousness of salvation', but only in the objective promises of God.[309] For Luther, security comes from looking outside of oneself to the gracious promises of God delivered and secured in Christ, and made visible and tangible in the sacraments. Luther argues that the essence of sin is that humanity is *incurvatus in se*, 'bent in on itself', in that it seeks both the grounds of salvation and reassurance in itself, rather than in Christ.

3. 'For outward signs he substituted inward.' I assume that this is to be interpreted as meaning that Luther puts personal consciousness of salvation above the sacraments. Precisely the opposite is true. Luther consistently declares that the sacraments are objective signs and reassurances of the promises of God, which are to be trusted and relied upon irrespective of the personal feelings and emotions of the believer.

4. '. . . for reverence towards the church contemplation of self'. Newman here seems to have bought into the Enlightenment view that Luther

[307] *Lectures on the Doctrine of Justification*, 339–40.
[308] See the exhaustive analysis in McGrath, *Luther's Theology of the Cross*.
[309] See Randall C. Zachman, *The Assurance of Faith: Conscience in the Theology of Martin Luther and John Calvin*, Minneapolis: Fortress Press, 1993.

is a rugged and lonely individualist, who spurned the church in order to contemplate himself. The popular view of Luther's doctrine of justification is that it obviates the need for church, sacraments and ministry. Luther's view on this matter was, of course, rather different.

At this point, we must make several comments which may help us view Newman's inept treatment of Luther in a more kindly manner than might otherwise be the case.

1. The full scholarly edition of Luther's works was begun in 1883, in celebration of the 400th anniversary of Luther's birth. Neither Newman nor his contemporaries could have hoped to have access to the full range of Luther's writings in their original language. In one sense, the modern study of Luther dates from after the First World War, when it became possible to engage with the primary sources in a level of detail which had hitherto been impossible.

2. A number of the English translations of Luther which would have been familiar to Newman were notoriously inaccurate. For example, the most widely used translation of Luther's 1535 *Commentary on Galatians* (a work, it hardly needs to be added, which is of fundamental importance to the doctrine of justification) had its origins in 1575, and was reworked and reprinted until it achieved its final rescension in 1807 under 'the Rev. Erasmus Middleton, BD, Rector of Turvey, Bedfordshire'. The Middleton translation offers what I can only describe as a somewhat free and imaginative rendering of Luther, adding ideas which the translators clearly feel that Luther ought to have included and omitting those which they felt were unhelpful. To convey an idea of its general tone, we may look at its translation of four words. At one point, Luther refers to *missis, vigiliis, & c.* The natural English translation of this phrase would be 'masses, vigils, and so on'. Middleton, however, offers a more imaginative translation: 'masses, vigils, trentals, and such trash'.

3. It is entirely possible that Newman is viewing Luther through the lens of the evangelicalism that he knew within the Church of England during the 1830s. In other words, Newman is to be understood as critiquing the then prevailing Evangelical image of Luther, rather than the views of Luther himself. Initially, this option is quite attractive. There is no doubt that the evangelicalism of the period was inclined to place considerable emphasis upon personal experience, and to take a generally low view of the sacraments and the church. It is a simple matter of fact that such Evangelicals tended to adopt an iconic rather than a historically and theologically informed view of Luther. It would therefore be entirely proper to read the *Lectures on Justification* as a critique of contemporary evangelicalism – were it not for the fact that Newman explicitly identifies Luther himself, rather than any portrayal of Luther, as the object of his criticisms.

A further difficulty in understanding Newman's intentions should be noted at this point. As we have seen, it is clear that Luther himself is Newman's primary target in the *Lectures on Justification*. Yet it is generally conceded that evangelicalism within the Church of England at this time tended to draw upon Calvinist, rather than Lutheran, inspiration. The influence of Luther may have been considerable within the English church of the mid-sixteenth century; thereafter, it declined substantially.[310] The assumption that evangelicalism drew directly upon Luther for its views on justification is simply not historically warranted. Although many Evangelicals of the period make positive reference to Luther, this often rests on little more than a perception that Luther set in motion a much-needed reform of the church. Where matters of theological substance are concerned, the evangelicalism that Newman knew tended to look to Reformed sources, more often indirectly than directly.

Yet Newman makes it clear that his primary concern is to engage with Luther and the 'Lutheran' teachings on justification, on the basis of the assumption that Evangelicals within the Church of England grounded their views upon his. At this point, I must confess that it is not entirely obvious to me (and possibly was not to Newman either) whether he intends us to understand 'Lutheran' to mean 'the tradition proceeding from, and partly based upon, Luther', or 'the views of Luther himself'. This point is important, in that Newman tends to interpret Luther from the perspective of later Lutheranism. This is particularly apparent in relation to his treatment of the relationship between faith and Christ, which we may profitably explore.

Newman argues that Luther's fundamental belief is that the righteousness of Christ is imputed to believers through faith. This would suggest that Luther sees justification in abstract terms, expressed as the impersonal imputation of qualities or benefits of Christ to the believer rather than personal tranformation through the indwelling of Christ. While it is entirely proper to suggest that some such criticism may be directed against Luther's later followers, such as Philip Melanchthon, Luther cannot fairly be critiqued at this juncture. In setting out this criticism, Newman draws heavily (yet somewhat selectively) upon the 1535 Galatians commentary. Yet that same commentary contains substantial sections dealing with the manner in which faith achieves a personal and living relationship between the believer and Christ. 'The Christ who is grasped by faith and lives in the heart is the true Christian righteousness, on account of which God counts us righteous, and grants us eternal life.'[311] It is quite clear that Luther understands faith, not purely as 'fiduciary assent' or 'trust',[312]

---

[310] See Hall, 'The Early Rise and Gradual Decline of Lutheranism in England (1500–1600)'.

[311] WA 4/I.229.28–9.   [312] *Lectures on the Doctrine of Justification*, 256.

but as the means by which a real, personal and living relationship is established between Christ and the believer. Luther's strongly personalist understanding of the relation of Christ and the believer is particularly clearly set out in the 1520 work *The Freedom of a Christian*:

> Faith does not merely mean that the soul realises that the divine word is full of all grace, free and holy; it also unites the soul with Christ, as a bride is united with her bridegroom. From such a marriage, as St Paul says (Ephesians 5:32), it follows that Christ and the soul become one body, so that they hold all things in common, whether for better or worse. This means that what Christ possesses belongs to the believing soul; and what the soul possesses, belongs to Christ. Thus Christ possesses all good things and holiness; these now belong to the soul. The soul possesses lots of vices and sin; these now belong to Christ.[313]

I have set out this passage in full, as it clearly raises some difficulties for Newman's interpretation of Luther. Note in particular the unequivocal assertion that faith is more than cognitive assent or trust: 'Faith does not merely mean that the soul realises that the divine word is full of all grace, free and holy; it also unites the soul with Christ, as a bride is united with her bridegroom.'

Newman's presentation of Luther is also puzzling for another reason – namely, the extent to which Newman cites passages from Luther with ellipses indicating the omission of sections. For example, in the final lecture, he cites from Luther's Galatians commentary to make a point.[314] At two places in this citation, Newman indicates, through the use of ellipses (. . .), that material has been omitted. On consulting the original text to establish what has been omitted, one is left with the disconcerting discovery that the omitted material forces one to the conclusion that Luther has been less than fairly treated by Newman – assuming, of course, that Newman encountered the full version of Luther's text, and modified it for his own purposes.

The most serious case of such misrepresentation demands particular attention. Newman's view on justification is that faith and works both justify, although in different manners.

> It seems, then, that whereas faith on our part fitly corresponds, or is the correlative, as it is called, to grace on God's part, sacraments are but the manifestation of grace, and good works are but the manifestation of faith; so that, whether we say we are justified by faith, or by works or sacraments, all these but mean this one doctrine, that we are justified by grace, which is given through sacraments, impetrated by faith, manifested in works.[315]

---

[313] WA 7.25.26 – 26.9.
[314] *Lectures on the Doctrine of Justification*, 331–3. Compare this with the full text: WA 40/1.282.
[315] *Lectures on the Doctrine of Justification*, 303.

This view is to be contrasted with Luther's view, which is that faith (understood as trust) alone justifies.

In a remarkable section, Newman then asserts that Luther corroborates this (that is, Newman's view), 'not willingly . . . but in consequence of the stress of texts urged against him'. This frankly rather patronising statement is followed by a citation from Luther's 1535 Galatians commentary, as follows. In view of the seriousness of the charge which I am about to lay against Newman, I will cite the passage in full:

'It is usual with us', he says, 'to view faith, sometimes apart from its work, sometimes with it. For as an artist speaks variously of his materials, and a gardener of a tree, as in bearing or not, so also the Holy Ghost speaks variously in Scripture concerning faith; at one time of what may be called abstract faith, faith as such: at another of concrete faith, faith in composition, or embodied. Faith, as such, or abstract, is meant, when Scripture speaks of justification, as such, or of the justified. (Vid. Rom. and Gal.). But when it speaks of rewards and works, then it speaks of faith in composition, concrete or embodied. For instance: "Faith which worketh by love"; "This do, and thou shalt live"; "If thou wilt enter into life, keep the commandments"; "Whoso doeth these things, shall live in them"; "Cease to do evil, learn to do well". In these and similar texts, which occur without number, in which mention is made of doing, believing doings are always meant; as, when it says, "This do, and thou shalt live", it means, "First see that thou art believing, that thy reason is right and thy will good, that thou hast faith in Christ; that being secured, work".' Then he proceeds: – 'How is it wonderful, that to that embodied faith, that is, faith working as was Abel's, in other words to believing works, are annexed merits and rewards? Why should not Scripture speak thus variously of faith, considering it so speaks even of Christ, God and man; sometimes of his entire person, sometimes of one or other of his two natures, the divine or human? When it speaks of one or other of these, it speaks of Christ in the abstract; when of the divine made one with the human in one person, of Christ as if in composition and incarnate. There is a well-known rule in the Schools concerning the "communicatio idiomatum", when the attributes of his divinity are ascribed to his humanity, as is frequent in Scripture; for instance, in Luke ii the angel calls the infant born of the Virgin Mary "the Saviour" of men, and "the Lord" both of angels and men, and in the preceding chapter, "the Son of God". Hence I may say with literal truth, That infant who is lying in a manger and in the Virgin's bosom, created heaven and earth, and is the Lord of angels. . . . As it is truly said, Jesus the Son of Mary created all things, so is justification ascribed to faith incarnate or to believing deeds.'[316]

This passage, as cited, clearly indicates that Luther concedes that justification is to be ascribed to 'believing deeds', an excellent summary of Newman's own position, as well as that of certain earlier Anglican divines, including George Bull. On the basis of the biblical passages

---

[316] *Lectures on the Doctrine of Justification*, 300–1.

noted, Newman declares that Luther is obliged – against his will, it would seem – to accept this inevitable conclusion. Luther's doctrine of justification by faith alone is thus to be set aside as irreconcilable with Scripture on the one hand, and with Luther's own words on the other. The strategic location of the citation within Lecture 12 – it is the final and clinching argument – indicates that Newman is aware of its importance. Like a conjurer producing an unexpected rabbit from a hat, Newman surprises his readers with the news that even Luther had to concede the case on this one.

But notice a curious feature of this passage. It has been cited extensively without any omissions. Yet suddenly, towards the end, we encounter an ellipsis, in the form of three periods. All of us who indulge in scholarship use this device, generally to save weary readers from having to wrestle with textual material which is not totally germane to the issue under discussion. Perhaps Newman has omitted part of a sentence, or maybe even a sentence or two, which is not relevant to the interpretation of the final dramatic sentence. Such, I imagine, would be the conclusion of many of his readers, although some would be puzzled as to the need for verbal economy at this stage, given the generous nature of the citation up to this point.

But to anyone familiar with Luther, the line of argumentation is suspicious. It is simply not what Luther consistently maintains throughout his extensive body of writings; nor would it be the kind of statement he would have made in such a significant work as the 1535 Galatians commentary. It is with sadness that I have to point out that the omitted portion is not a sentence but a section – and a section which so qualifies the meaning of the final sentence as to exclude Newman's interpretation of it. In what follows, we shall pick up Newman's citation at the penultimate sentence, and insert the omitted material, before proceeding to the final sentence. For the sake of clarity, the material which Newman included has been printed in italics:

Hence I may say with literal truth, That infant who is lying in a manger and in the Virgin's bosom, created heaven and earth, and is the Lord of angels. I am indeed speaking about a man here. But 'man' in this proposition is obviously a new term, and, as the sophists say, stands for the divinity; that is, this God who became man created all things. Here creation is attributed to the divinity alone, since the humanity does not create. Nevertheless, it is correct to say that 'the man created', because the divinity, which alone creates, is incarnate with the humanity, and therefore the humanity participates in the attributes of both predicates. [A list of biblical passages relating to this point follows.] Therefore the meaning of the passage 'do this and you will live' is 'you will live on account of this faithful doing; this doing will give you life solely on account of faith. *Thus justification* belongs to faith alone, just as creation belongs to the divinity. *As it is truly said, Jesus the Son of Mary created all things, so is justification ascribed to faith incarnate or to believing deeds'.*

Throughout this analysis, we find Luther insisting that 'faith alone justifies and does everything'; works are implicated only in a derivative manner. The significance of the passage which is omitted is that it unequivocally qualifies the final sentence so that its only meaning can be that of 'faith alone justifies'.

This observation forces us to confront a most difficult and vexing question: did Newman himself deliberately and knowingly omit the critical section of the passage, or did he encounter the passage in this mutilated form? My suspicion is that the latter option is much more probable, although I cannot prove this. None of us is infallible, and Newman may simply have copied the passage in this distorted version from another source. Evidence supportive of this suggestion can be found in the generally inaccurate citations which he provides from Luther, which suggest borrowing from secondary sources rather than an engagement with the original.

3.12   Conclusion

In this chapter we have surveyed the complex development of the Protestant understandings of justification. As this analysis will have made clear, the Reformation gave rise to a new appreciation of the importance of the concept of justification in enunciating the Christian doctrine of salvation. Yet that new understanding of the nature and modalities of justification would be challenged, as an increasingly confident and theologically articulate church began to counter its Protestant critics. In what follows, we shall consider the background to the Council of Trent's magisterial pronouncements on justification, before offering a detailed analysis of this most important document.

4   Catholicism: the Council of Trent on justification

The Catholic church was ill prepared to meet the challenge posed by the rise of the evangelical faction within Germany and elsewhere in the 1520s and 1530s. Luther's doctrine of justification attracted considerable attention in the 1520s, not all of it unsympathetic. According to Schmidt, three reasons may be suggested to explain the remarkable importance which came to be attached within contemporary Catholicism to the doctrine of justification *sola fide*.[1] First, it required an internalisation of the religious life, thus sharply contrasting with the prevailing external forms of Christian existence. Second, it restored an emphasis upon the priority of the divine role in justification, against the prevailing tendency to concentrate upon the human role. Third, it amounted to an implicit declaration of war upon the Roman curia. Relatively few works dealing with the doctrine of justification were published within Catholicism in the period 1520–45, with notable exceptions such as Tommaso de Vio Cajetan's *De fide et operibus* (1532).[2] A survey of such works suggests that the Lutheran doctrine of justification was simply not understood by the early opponents of the Reformation,[3] although the rise of polemical theology in the 1530s served to clarify points of importance. Early anti-Lutheran polemic tended to fasten upon points which Luther regarded as trivial – such as Luther's views on the papacy, indulgences or the sacraments – while failing to deal with such crucial questions as the concept of *servum arbitrium* or the nature of justifying righteousness. Indeed, Luther singled out Erasmus alone as identifying the real theological issues involved in his protest.[4]

[1] H. Schmidt, *Brückenschlag zwischen den Konfessionen*, Paderborn: Schoningh, 1951, 162.
[2] Pfnür, *Einig in der Rechtfertigungslehre?*, 369–78.
[3] The full implications of the forensic dimension of the Melanchthonian concept of justification occasionally appear to have been recognised – for instance, in the case of Johannes Dietenberger, *Phimostomus Scripturariorum* (1530), and Johannes Mensing, *Antapologie* (1535); see Pfnür, *Einig in der Rechtfertigungslehre?*, 280 n. 66, 359–60.
[4] See WA 18.786.26–8. Luther's polemical intentions at this point cannot, however, be overlooked.

The task facing the theologians assembled at Trent was thus not merely the clarification of Catholic teaching on justification, but also the definition of Catholic dogma in relation to the perceived errors of Protestantism. In fact, however, views on justification remarkably similar to those associated with the northern European Reformers penetrated deep into the hierarchy of the Italian church in the period 1520–45, and are widely thought to have been espoused by several of those present during the Tridentine debate on justification. What those views were, and whence they originated, are the subject of the following section.

4.1   Developments within Catholicism, 1490–1545

The late fifteenth and early sixteenth centuries saw the emergence of numerous groups agitating for reform within the church, frequently adopting theologies of justification which foreshadowed the Augustinianism of the Wittenberg Reformation. In the present section, we are particularly concerned with developments in Italy, and the origins and significance of the doctrines of justification associated with Gropper and Contarini, which exercised some influence over evangelical–Catholic attempts at reconciliation in the period 1536–41 and emerged as an issue at the Council of Trent.

The rise of Augustinianism in the late fifteenth and early sixteenth centuries is perhaps best illustrated from developments within Spain. The rise of the *alumbrados* is one of the more remarkable features of the period, and the records of the Spanish Inquisition indicate that radically theocentric views on justification were in circulation within the movement by 1511.[5] Although there are clear divergences between *alumbramiento* and early Lutheran ideas, the polemical context was such that recognition of affinities between certain *alumbrados* and Luther was sufficent to lead to the suppression of the movement in the 1520s.

The most significant figure of the Spanish religious renaissance for our purposes is Juan de Valdés, whose *Diálogo de doctrina cristiana* (1529) developed a theocentric doctrine of justification which came to serve as a model for Italian Evangelism in the 1530s. The central problem posed by the doctrine of justification is identified by Valdés in *Las ciento diez divinas consideraciones* as follows:

---

[5] The relevant portions of the confessions of Pedro Ruiz de Alcaraz and Isabella de la Cruz should be noted; see M. Serrano y Sanz, 'Pedro Ruiz de Alcaraz, illuminado alcarreno del siglo XVI', *Revista de archivos, bibliotecas y museos* 8 (1903), 1–16, 126–39; A. Selke de Sánchez, 'Alguno datos nuevos sobre los primeros alumbrados: El edicto de 1525 y su relación con el proceso de Alcaraz', *Bulletin Hispanique* 54 (1952), 125–52.

It is useful to humanity that God is omnipotent, generous, wise, strong, merciful and pious; but it does not seem useful that God is *righteous*, in that if God is righteous and humanity is unrighteous, we have no hope of salvation through the judgement of God.[6]

Valdés then proceeds to develop a concept of *la justicia de Dios* based upon the principle 'once in jeopardy' which is somewhat different from that of Augustine and the Wittenberg Reformers: God, having punished Christ, and hence humanity, for the sins of humankind, may be relied upon not to punish twice for the same offence.[7] It is therefore necessary for believers to recognise that they are righteous in Christ (although they are sinners in themselves), in that the penalty for sin has been laid upon Christ, not upon them.[8] This marks a significant departure from the Erasmian anthropology, although it must be noted that Valdés' statement of the principle *simul iustus et peccator* parallels neither that of Augustine nor that of Luther exactly. Valdés' arrival in Italy in 1531 led to his subsequently exercising considerable influence over Italian reforming circles, to which we now turn.

The late fifteenth and early sixteenth centuries witnessed a revival of interest in the theology of Augustine, accompanying extensive publication of editions of his works.[9] In Italy, this Augustinian renaissance was accompanied by a new interest on the part of Italian humanists in the Pauline corpus of the New Testament.[10] It is against this background that the conversion experience of Gasparo Contarini must be seen. Contarini was a member of a group of Paduan-educated humanists, including Paolo Giustiniani, who debated the means by which salvation might be attained. The contemporary confusion within the Catholic church concerning the doctrine of justification was reflected within this group: after much soul-searching, some eventually chose to enter a local hermitage as the only possible means of expiating their sins, while others – including Contarini – preferred to remain in the world, believing that some means must exist for the salvation of those who elected to exist in this manner.

The correspondence between Contarini and Giustiniani, dating from 1510–11, indicates their shared concern for problems remarkably similar

---

[6] *Las ciento diez divinas consideraciones*, ed. Idígoras, 85.

[7] *Las ciento diez divinas consideraciones*, 85–6.

[8] *Las ciento diez divinas consideraciones*, 291.

[9] See P. O. Kristeller, 'Augustine and the Early Renaissance', in *Studies in Renaissance Thought and Letters*, Rome: Storia e letteratura, 1956, 355–72, for details of such works.

[10] For a careful study, see R. Cessi, 'Paolinismo preluterano', *Rendiconti dell' Academia nazionale dei Lincei*, Classe di scienze morali, storiche e filologe Ser. VIII, 12 (1957), 3–30. Note also that Valdés was regarded as an avid student of Augustine; see J. N. Bakhuizen van den Brink, *Juan de Valdés réformateur en Espagne et en Italie*, Geneva: Droz, 1969, 16.

to those which so preoccupied Luther at the same time.[11] For Contarini, the sacrifice of Christ upon the cross was more than adequate as a satisfaction for human sin, in which humans must learn to trust utterly.[12] It is utterly impossible for humans to be justified on the basis of their works; humans are justified through faith in Christ, as a result of which the righteousness of Christ is made ours.[13] Contarini's theological breakthrough may be dated in the first half of 1511, thus placing it before that of Luther and even before the alleged 'discovery' by Pietro Speziali of the doctrine of justification by faith in 1512.

The Contarini–Giustiniani correspondence is of importance in that it illustrates the doctrinal confusion of the immediate pre-Tridentine period in relation to the doctrine of justification. Giustiniani was convinced that it was necessary to withdraw from the world and to lead a life of the utmost austerity in order to be saved, whereas Contarini came to believe that it was possible to lead a normal life in the world, trusting in the merits of Christ for salvation. But which of these positions represented, or approximated most closely to, the teaching of the Catholic church? The simple fact is that this question could not be answered with any degree of confidence. This doctrinal confusion concerning precisely the issue over which the Reformation was widely held to have begun inevitably meant that the Catholic church was in no position to attempt a coherent systematic refutation of the teaching of the evangelical faction in its crucial initial phase.

It must be appreciated that there are important differences between Luther and Contarini. Although both emphasise the role of faith and the 'alien' righteousness of Christ, the exclusivity of Luther's solafideism and extrinsicism is not to be found with Contarini. Contarini's primary concern, both in his early letters and in his more mature writings of the 1520s and 1530s, appears to have been the elimination of human self-confidence, which he regarded as an impediment to justification; he does not exclude the possibility of human co-operation with God, nor does he consider the proper emphasis upon faith to entail the elimination of *caritas* from justification.

---

[11] C. Furey, 'The communication of friendship: Gasparo Contarini's letters to hermits at Camaldoli', *Church History* 72 (2003), 71–101. For details of the correspondence, discovered in 1957, see Hubert Jedin, 'Contarini und Camaldoli', *Archivio italiano per la storia della pietà* 2 (1959), 51–117. For the comparison with Luther, see Jedin, 'Ein Turmerlebnis des jungen Contarini', in *Kirche des Glaubens – Kirche de Geschichte*, 2 vols., Freiburg: Herder, 1966, 1.167–80.

[12] The episode of Easter Eve 1511, which he recounts to Giustiniani in a letter of 24 April of that year (Jedin, 'Contarini und Camaldoli', 64), should be studied in full.

[13] Jedin, 'Contarini und Camaldoli', 117. This letter, dated 7 February 1523, is the last surviving letter in the collection discovered by Jedin.

In some respects, Contarini's later views on justification – particularly those dating from 1541 – parallel those of the Cologne theologian Johannes Gropper, whose *Enchiridion* was published in 1538. This work has often been regarded as developing a doctrine of double justification, based on the concept of *duplex iustitia*.[14] In fact, this view appears to rest upon a serious misunderstanding of Gropper's views, possibly arising from Bellarmine's later polemical attempt to discredit those present at Regensburg for political reasons.[15]

In his influential study on the background to Regensburg, Stupperich appears to follow Bellarmine's analysis of the relation of Bucer, Pighius and Gropper,[16] and concluded that Gropper explicitly taught a doctrine of double justification. This conclusion requires modification. The concept of a 'double righteousness' – but *not* of a double formal cause of justification – is to be found in the earlier medieval discussion of justification, where a clear distinction is drawn (particularly within the early Dominican, and subsequently the Thomist, school) between *iustitia infusa* and *iustitia acquisita*. Justification takes place upon the basis of *iustitia infusa*, with the subsequent establishment of *iustitia acquisita*.

This is not a doctrine of double justification, in the proper sense of the term. Gropper draws a careful distinction between the righteousness which functions as the formal cause of justification (*iustitia infusa* or *iustitia inhaerens*) and the righteousness which subsequently develops within the believer through his co-operation with grace; in other words, although justification involves *duplex iustitia*, these *iustitiae* are understood to be implicated in totally different manners within the overall scheme of

---

[14] For example, see S. Ehses, 'Johannes Groppers Rechtfertigungslehre auf dem Konzil von Trient', *Römische Quartalschrift* 20 (1906), 175–88, 184; Hanns Rückert, *Die theologische Entwicklung Gasparo Contarinis*, Bonn: Marcus & Weber, 1926, 97 n. 1. The suggestion that Kaspar Schatzgeyer developed a doctrine of *duplex iustitia* rests upon a misunderstanding of the significance of the Scotist analysis of the elements of justification; see Valens Heynck, 'Bemerkungen zu dem Buche von O. Müller, *Die Rechtfertigungslehre nominalistischer Reformationsgegner*', FS 28 (1941), 129–51, especially 145–50. There is no convincing evidence that Contarini's views on justification derive from Gropper's *Enchiridion*, see Rückert, *Die theologische Entwicklung Gasparo Contarinis*, 102–4, where it is shown that there are excellent reasons for supposing that Contarini reflects theological currents prevalent in Italy in the 1530s. The discovery of the Contarini–Giustiniani correspondence some thirty years after Rückert's investigation has enormously strengthened his conclusions.

[15] Bellarmine, *Disputationum de controversiis Christianae fidei*, Ingolstadt, 1601, 1028, cf. 1096–7. Bellarmine may base his views upon the vote of Seripando at Trent, in which Contarini, Cajetan, Pighius, Julius Pflug and Gropper are identified with the doctrine of 'double justification': CT 5.487.33–4.

[16] Robert Stupperich, *Der Humanismus und die Wiedervereinigung der Konfession*, Leipzig: Hensius, 1936, 11–36. Cf. Walter Lipgens, *Kardinal Johannes Gropper (1503–1559) und die Anfänge der katholischen Reform in Deutschland*, Münster: Aschendorff, 1951, 100–8, 192–203.

justification. A doctrine of 'double justification', in the strict sense of the term (as it is encountered during the Tridentine proceedings on justification), is essentially a doctrine of a *double formal cause of justification*; in other words, justification takes place on account of *duplex iustitia*.

Stupperich has tended to confuse *iustitia inhaerens* with *iustitia acquisita* in his exposition of the relationship of Gropper's concepts of *iustitia imputata* and *iustitia inhaerens*, with a concomitant misunderstanding both of Gropper's doctrine of justification and its relationship to Melanchthon and to Catholicism.[17] The assertion of the inseparability of forgiveness and renewal is most emphatically *not* equivalent to a doctrine of 'double justification', and this confusion over the definition of terms has enormously impeded the proper evaluation of the significance of Gropper. In the *Enchiridion*, it is clear that Gropper merely develops an earlier medieval insight in such a manner as to correct the perceived shortcomings of the Melanchthonian doctrine of justification, while at the same time indicating the common ground between the Lutheran and Catholic doctrines.

The chapter of the *Enchiridion* entitled *De iustificatione hominis* opens by defining justification in terms of two components: the remission of sin, and the internal renewal of the mind.[18] Gropper criticises Melanchthon's concept of forensic justification, which he illustrates with specific reference to the latter's analogy of the people of Rome declaring Scipio to be free.[19] For Gropper, justification is inextricably linked with the internal renewal of the individual: 'nobody is justified, unless through the renewal of the will'.[20] Where Gropper so evidently differs from the traditional Catholic account of justification is in his use of the concept of imputed righteousness. It appears, however, that Gropper interprets this concept in a non-Melanchthonian sense, tending to regard it as equivalent to divine acceptation.[21] Justification is not regarded as identical with the forensic pronouncement that the individual is righteous, and Gropper's divergence from Melanchthon at this point is unequivocal. It appears that Gropper regards the divine acceptation of believers through their renewal (expressed in terms of *remissio peccatorum et renovatio interior*

---

[17] As pointed out by Braunisch, *Die Theologie der Rechtfertigung im 'Enchiridion' (1538) des Johannes Gropper*, especially 419–38.

[18] *Enchiridion Christianae institutione*, Cologne, 1538, fol. 163r. Cf. fol. 163v: 'Nam quis iustificatum dixerit eum, cui tantum sunt remissa peccata, non autem voluntas etiam commutata, nempe ex mala facta bona? Quemadmodum nemo servum nequam, ob id tantum, quod ei indulgens dominus noxam clementer remiserit iustificatum dixerit, nisi is bonam quoque voluntatem (qua posthac servus non inutilis sed frugi esse contendat) ceperit?'

[19] *Enchiridion*, fol. 163r (margin).   [20] *Enchiridion*, fol. 163v (margin).

[21] For example, *Enchiridion*, fol. 129v, treats *imputatio iustitiae* and *acceptatio* as synonymous.

voluntatis) as equivalent to the imputation of righteousness, and thus merely restates the standard later medieval concept of *acceptatio divina* in language which he feels to be more acceptable to his Lutheran opponents. Far from developing a doctrine of 'double justification', Gropper merely states the inseparability of *remissio peccatorum* and *renovatio* in a thoroughly Augustinian sense.

Those who hold that Gropper develops a doctrine of 'double justification' in the proper sense of the term are obliged to assert that the *Enchiridion* explicitly teaches a *double formal cause of justification*.[22] This is simply not found to be the case. Gropper clearly propounds a single formal cause of justification, which he defines in terms of *misericordia et gratia Dei nos innovans*.[23] Gropper rigorously excludes the possibility, necessarily associated with a doctrine of 'double justification', that believers are justified on account of (*propter*) their renewal.[24] It is evident that Gropper is merely restating the traditional medieval teaching that justification *includes*, but does not *take place on account of*, the interior renewal of the believer. Although Gropper's discussion of habitual grace is difficult to follow, it is evident that *gratia Dei nos innovans* – which he defines to be the single formal cause of justification – is functionally identical with the Thomist concept of *iustitia infusa seu inhaerens*, thus establishing the continuity between Gropper and the medieval tradition upon this point. Although Gropper clearly identifies important areas of continuity between the Catholic and Protestant understandings of justification, he cannot be regarded as a pre-Tridentine exponent of 'double justification' in the proper sense of that term.

Views similar to those expressed in Gropper's *Enchiridion* may be found in Contarini's *Epistola de iustificatione*, written from Regensburg on 25 May 1541. For Contarini, justification involves both becoming righteous (*iustum fieri*) and being counted as righteous (*iustum haberi*).[25] Contarini thus develops a theology which, like that of Gropper, has tended to be interpreted as a pre-Tridentine statement of the doctrine of 'double justification', explicitly recognising two types of righteousness implicated in the process of justification:

---

[22] For example, W. van Gulik, *Johannes Gropper (1503–1559): Ein Beitrag zur Kirchengeschichte Deutschlands*, Freiburg: Herder, 1906, 54 n. 5.

[23] *Enchiridion*, fol. 167v. For an excellent critical analysis, see Braunisch, *Die Theologie der Rechtfertigung im 'Enchiridion' (1538) des Johannes Gropper*, 360–72, 381–98, especially 394–6.

[24] *Enchiridion*, fol. 167v (margin).

[25] Contarini, *Epistola de iustificatione*, in Corpus Catholicorum VII, ed. F. I. Hünermann, Münster, 1923, 24.1–2. Those at Rome who read the letter were sceptical about its catholicity; see *Epistolae Reginaldi Poli Cardinalis* 5 vols., Brescia, 1744–57, 3.ccxxxi–x.

We therefore attain a double righteousness (*duplex iustitia*), one dwelling within us, by which we begin to be righteous, are made 'partakers in the divine nature', and have love shed abroad in our hearts; and another which is not inherent, but is given to us with Christ – that is, the righteousness of Christ and all his merit.[26]

Which of these is prior to the other is, according to Contarini, a useless scholastic disputation; the important point is that the inherent righteousness of humanity, which is initially inchoate and imperfect, is supplemented by *iustitia Christi* as a preliminary anticipation of the state which subsequently arises through the agency of *iustitia inhaerens*.[27] The evident similarity between the views of Gropper and Contarini on justification goes some considerable way towards explaining the 'agreement' reached on justification at the Diet of Regensburg (often referred to in its Latinised form 'Ratisbon') in 1541.

Gropper's *Enchiridion* appears to have formed the basis of Article 5 of the *Liber Ratisboniensis*, which formed the basis of the discussion between Protestants and Catholics at Regensburg.[28] Although agreement on the matter of justification was reached between those present at the Diet, it is clear that these individuals were simply not regarded as representative by their respective institutions; whatever personal agreement might be found to exist on the matter of justification between men such as Bucer, Contarini and Gropper, this was more than outweighed by the institutional differences between Lutheranism and Catholicism. Furthermore, the agreement appears to have been reached by a process of *zusammenleimen* – 'tacking together' (to use Luther's term) – which merely placed opposing views side by side, without reconciling, or even addressing, the underlying questions.

The fifth article, on justification, seems to represent a juxtaposition of the Catholic and Protestant positions, without any significant

---

[26] *Epistola de iustificatione*, 28.12–18.

[27] *Epistola de iustificatione*, 29.19–38; see further Rückert, *Die theologische Entwicklung Gasparo Contarinis*, 93. Rückert's suggestion (86 n. 2) that Contarini affirms that *iustitia inhaerens* and *iustitia imputata* function as the double formal cause of justification cannot be sustained on the basis of the text cited in its support: the adverb *formaliter* is transferred from its proper clause to one subsequent, from which it does not appear to have been elided.

[28] Text of the article in CR (Melanchthon) 4.198–201. The parallels between the two documents have been brought out by Stupperich, 'Der Ursprung des Regensburger Buches von 1541 und seine Rechtfertigungslehre'. For an excellent analysis, see Lane, 'Cardinal Contarini and Article 5 of the Regensburg Colloquy (1541).' It may be noted that three of the five major theological figures present were amenable to this doctrine of *duplex iustitia* – Bucer, Contarini and Gropper. Eck was critical of the document, and Melanchthon more favourably disposed towards it. For Luther's attitude to Regensburg on justification, see von Loewenich, *Duplex Iustitia*, 48–55; for Calvin's, see Neuser, 'Calvins Urteil über den Rechtfertigungsartikel des Regensburger Buches'.

attempt to resolve the serious theological issues at stake.[29] The failure of Regensburg was of considerable political consequence, as it eventually led to the general discrediting of the Italian reforming movement known as 'Evangelism', to which we may now turn.

The term 'Evangelism' has become widely used to refer to an indigenous reforming movement within the Italian church, which possessed some of the theological and spiritual characteristics of northern European Protestantism, yet declined to follow its ecclesiological implications through to their potentially schismatic implications.[30] It is not an entirely satisfactory designation, in that the movement is clearly a form of what would now be described as 'evangelicalism'.[31] Evangelism was an undogmatic and transitory movement, originating within Italy itself (and the importance of Contarini's experience of 1511 should not be overlooked), rather than from Protestant currents north of the Alps.[32] The strongly Augustinian and individualist theologies of justification associated with the movement in its early phase paralleled those emerging elsewhere within Catholic Europe at the time. There can, however, be no doubt that the movement rapidly came under Protestant influence through the dissemination of printed works of the Reformers.[33]

One of the most intriguing questions concerning this movement relates to the anonymous work *Trattato utilissimo del beneficio di Giesu Cristo crocifisso*, the second edition of which (1543) achieved a significant circulation throughout Europe.[34] Its first four chapters expound the doctrine of justification by faith with some vigour, and it is significant that the mediating position associated with Contarini and the Regensburg delegates appears

---

[29] See P. Matheson, *Cardinal Contarini at Regensburg*, Oxford: Clarendon Press, 1972, 181: 'The dialogue between Protestantism and Catholicism at the Diet of Regensburg in 1541 did not fail. It never took place.'

[30] S. M. Taylor, 'Hoping for Religious Reform in Italy: Background and Description of Italian Evangelism', *Fides et Historia* 28 (1996), 8–24; E. G. Gleason, 'On the Nature of Sixteenth-Century Italian Evangelism: Scholarship, 1953–1978', *SCJ* 9 (1978), 3–25.

[31] See, for example, its emphasis on biblical spirituality, noted by writers such as B. Collett, *Italian Benedictine Scholars and the Reformation: The Congregation of Santa Giustina of Padua*, Oxford: Clarendon Press, 1985.

[32] *Contra* P. McNair, *Peter Martyr in Italy: An Anatomy of Apostasy*, Oxford: Clarendon Press, 1967, 1–50, especially 8.

[33] See Carlo de Frede, 'La stampa nel Cinquecento e la diffusione della Riforma in Italia', *Atti della Accademia Pontiniana* (Napoli) 13 (1963–64), 87–91; idem, 'Per la storia della stampa nel Cinquecento in rapporto con la diffusione della Riforma in Italia', in *Gutenberger Jahrbuch* 1964 (Mainz, 1964), 175–84; E. L. Gleason, 'Sixteenth Century Italian Interpretations of Luther' *Archiv für Reformationsgeschichte* 60 (1969), 160–73. The Viterbo Circle appears to have been of particular importance in this respect in the 1530s and early 1540s: see Dermot Fenlon, *Heresy and Obedience in Tridentine Italy: Cardinal Pole and the Counter Reformation*, Cambridge: Cambridge University Press, 1972, 69–99, for an excellent introduction.

[34] See *Il Beneficio di Cristo*, ed. Caponetto, 469–96, for details of the work.

to have been abandoned in favour of an account of the mode of justification which parallels that associated with Juan de Valdés. Its doctrine of justification *sola fide* affirms that it is through faith that Christ and his righteousness become the believer's, and on the basis of the union of the believer with Christ that God treats the former as righteous.[35]

The strongly personalist understanding of justification associated with both Luther and Calvin appears throughout the work. Through faith, the believer is united with Christ, clothed with his righteousness, and thence accepted as righteous and worthy of eternal life by God. Although there are unquestionably further recognisable allusions to the writings of northern European Reformers in the work, it is clear that the dominant influence is the form of Augustinian individualism associated with Valdés – evident, for example, in the complete omission of any reference to the implication of the church as an institution in the process of justification. Furthermore, the concept of *imputatio iustitiae* is not to be found in the work in its distinctively Protestant form.

Most significant, however, is the outright rejection of the mediating theology of justification by faith *and* works associated with the members of the Viterbo circle.[36] This point is important, as it indicates the development of a more radical faction within the Italian reforming movement in the period immediately before its suppression, critical of the mediating Regensburg theology. Although the work develops a doctrine of justification *sola fide*, it is clear that the formula is understood in a sufficiently flexible manner to accommodate those such as Reginald Pole, who retained the verbal formula, while interpreting the concept of faith in an Augustinian sense, as *fides quae per dilectionem operatur*. For Pole, the faith by which humans alone were justified was a faith active through love, in contrast to the fiduciary notion of faith associated with Luther.[37] This mediating approach appears to have exercised some restraint within the Viterbo circle, restraining its more radical members (such as Flaminio, Priuli and Vitoria) from action which could have proved prejudicial to the future conciliar pronouncement (which, Pole appears to have assumed, would broadly parallel his own mediating formula).[38]

The period of Italian Evangelism came to a close in 1542. Rather like the 'Prague Spring' of 1968, the period 1520–42 represented a brief interval in which ideas could be freely debated before an external authority intervened to prohibit such discussion. In 1542, Paul III, alarmed by religious unrest in Lucca, Modena and Venice, published the bull

[35] *Il Beneficio di Cristo*, 38.281–9.   [36] *Il Beneficio di Cristo*, 46.514–47.515.
[37] R. Pole, *De concilio*, Rome: Manutius, 1562, 24f–v.
[38] See Fenlon, *Heresy and Obedience*, 203–4.

Licet ab initio, re-establishing the Roman Inquisition. While the influence of the northern European Reformers upon Evangelism in its later phase is undeniable, there are excellent reasons for suggesting that a form of doctrine of justification *sola fide* initially originated – independent of reforming movements in northern Europe – and subsequently achieved widespread circulation in the highest ecclesiastical circles in Italy. The failure of Regensburg to mediate between Catholicism and Protestantism forced the issue of definition of Catholic dogma upon the church, with the inevitable possibility that the temporary estrangement of the evangelical faction might become permanent schism. The convening of the Council of Trent was intended to provide the definition of Catholic doctrine so urgently required. Before dealing with this crucial period in the development of the doctrine of justification, it is necessary to consider the theologies of justification associated with the main schools of thought represented at the Council, and particularly the question of whether there existed an 'Augustinian' school, often held in older works of scholarship to be represented by Girolamo Seripando.

4.2   The theological schools at Trent during the debate on justification

The Council of Trent was faced with a group of formidable problems as it assembled to debate the question of justification in June 1546. The medieval period had witnessed the emergence of a number of quite distinct schools of thought on justification, clearly incompatible at points, all of which could lay claim to represent the teaching of the Catholic church. The Council of Trent was concerned, not with settling long-standing debates between the various Catholic schools of theology, but with attempting a definition of the Catholic consensus on justification in the face of the Protestant challenge. The suggestion of the Bishop of Vaison, that the theologians present at Trent to debate the matter of justification should initially meet as separate orders under their respective generals,[39] was rejected, presumably because this procedure would merely heighten the differences between the schools of thought present at Trent. In this section, we are concerned with the identification of the main schools present at Trent, as this has an important bearing upon the relation of the final decree to late medieval Catholic theology in general.

In an important study in 1936, Eduard Stakemeier argued for the existence of three theological schools at Trent during the proceedings on

[39] CT 5.259.3–6.

justification: the Thomist, Scotist and Augustinian schools.[40] This division of the theological schools present at Trent has exercised considerable influence over subsequent discussion, and does not appear to have been subjected to anything even approaching the critical examination that such an ambitious hypothesis would seem to require. It is, in fact, quite difficult to establish the precise allegiance of many of the speakers during the proceedings on account of the similarities between the schools in relation to the points under discussion.

It is beyond question that a significant Thomist school was represented at Trent. The revival of the Thomist school had taken place in the fifteenth century under Capreolus,[41] who had established the fundamental principle that Thomas Aquinas' views should be determined on the basis of the *Summa Theologiae*, rather than on that of the earlier *Commentary on the Sentences*. As we noted in chapter 2, Thomas' views on justification altered significantly in the intervening period, with the result that Capreolus' maxim led to a more Augustinian understanding of justification being defined as 'Thomist' than would have been regarded as legitimate previously. It is this presupposition which underlies Cajetan's use of Thomas. In addition, Capreolus appears to have drawn upon the ferociously anti-Pelagian writings of Gregory of Rimini to emphasise the Augustinian elements of Thomas' doctrine of justification,[42] with the result that a theology of justification based jointly upon Augustine and Thomas Aquinas came to be current within Catholic circles. The authority with which Thomas was invested may be judged from the fact that he was cited more than any theologian – other than Augustine – during the course of the Tridentine debate on justification, despite the fact that only seven of the fifty-five theologians involved in the debates were card-carrying Dominicans.[43]

---

[40] E. Stakemeier, 'Die theologische Schulen'. The older study of H. Lennerz, 'Das Konzil von Trient und die theologischen Schulmeinungen', *Scholastick* 4 (1929), 38–53, should also be noted. A major deficiency of Stakemeier's study is the implication that the proceedings on justification were of interest only to academic theologians, whereas it is clear that many bishops regarded the matter as of practical and spiritual importance; see Giuseppe Alberigo, *I vescovi italiani al Concilio di Trento (1545–7)*, Florence: Sansoni, 1959, 337–94.

[41] M. Grabmann, 'Johannes Capreolus O. P., der "princeps Thomistarum", und seine Stellung in der Geschichte des Thomistenschule', in L. Ott (ed.), *Mittelalterliches Geistesleben: Abhandlungen zur Geschichte der Scholastik und Mystik* III, Munich: Hueber, 1956, 370–410.

[42] This was first pointed out by Friedrich Stegmüller, 'Gratia sanans: Zur Schicksal des Augustinismus in der Salmantizienerschule', in M. Grabmann and J. Mausbach (eds.), *Aurelius Augustinus: Festschrift der Görres-Gesellschaft zum 1500. Tod des heiligen Augustinus*, Cologne: Bachem, 1930, 395–409.

[43] See the *Index nominum et rerum* of CT 5.1053–72. On the Thomist school at Trent, see E. Stakemeier, 'Die theologischen Schulen', 199–207, 322–31.

Table 4.1 *Analysis of theologians involved in the Tridentine proceedings*

Religious order	Present at opening session	Present at sixth session
Franciscans	34	29
Dominicans	9	7
Jesuits	2	2
Carmelites	15	4
Servites	19	1
Augustinians	14	4
Secular priests	11	8

The Salamantine school in Imperial Spain, which developed under Francisco de Vitoria, represented an approach similar to that of Thomas.[44] It is therefore significant that Charles V chose the Thomist Domingo de Soto, who held the chair of theology at Salamanca in the period 1532–45, as the Imperial theologian at Trent. The most significant position associated with the Thomist faction present at Trent is the total and unequivocal rejection of a meritorious disposition towards justification.[45]

The Franciscan theologians were particularly prominent in the Tridentine proceedings on justification. Table 4.1 indicates the preponderance of the Franciscan contingent.[46] As noted earlier, the Franciscans were not unanimous in recognising a single authoritative doctor of their order, and it is clear that several doctors were treated as authoritative during the course of the Tridentine proceedings, representing the early Franciscan school (such as Alexander of Hales and Bonaventure), the later Franciscan school (Duns Scotus), and even the *via moderna* (such as Gabriel Biel). The obvious reluctance on the part of certain Franciscans to concede the precedence of Scotus over Bonaventure[47] serves to emphasise the importance of this point. The most important Franciscan theologian present at Trent during the proceedings on justification was the Spanish Observant Andrés de Vega, whose *Opusculum de iustificatione*

[44] See Stegmüller, 'Zur Gnadenlehre des spanischen Konzilstheologen Domingo de Soto'; Becker, *Die Rechtfertigungslehre nach Domingo de Soto.*

[45] See Becker, *Die Rechtfertigungslehre nach Domingo de Soto*, 141–53. On this question, with particular reference to Francisco de Vitoria, see Xiberta, 'La causa meritoria de la justificación'.

[46] Those present at the opening session were ascertained from the list published in CT 5.1041–4. The list published at CT 5.819–20 is misleading, as it notes only those present at the closing session on 13 January 1547; the numbers given for the sixth session are based upon an analysis of those actually taking part in the debate.

[47] See the comments of Bonaventura Pius de Costacciaro, dated 28 December 1546: CT 5.741.28–32.

was conveniently published in time for it to be in the hands of those involved in the debate.

In this work, Vega defends the notion of the necessity of a human disposition towards justification which is meritorious *de congruo*. The extreme opinions on this question, according to Vega, are the Pelagian concept of justification *ex meritis*, and the Thomist denial of all merit prior to justification.[48] Vega argues for what he considers to be the *via media*: the denial of merit *de condigno* and recognition of merit *de congruo* prior to grace – a doctrine which he associates with Duns Scotus and Gabriel Biel, among other recent theologians.[49]

It is clear that Vega is drawing upon the common teaching of the Franciscan order, and it is worth recalling that the whole medieval Franciscan tradition taught that the disposition for justification was meritorious *de congruo*.[50] Stakemeier appears to designate the common Franciscan teaching on this question 'Scotist' on the basis of certain presuppositions which more recent scholarship has explicitly called into question – for example, Hünermann's restriction of possible theological alternatives within Catholicism to either Thomism or Scotism.[51] More seriously, Stakemeier appears to be indirectly dependent upon Carl Stange's essays of 1900 and 1902, in which he argued that the theology of the medieval period was essentially a theology of orders:[52] the monastic vow was taken as implying obedience to the official doctor of the order, which, according to Stange, implied recognition of the authority of Thomas Aquinas in the case of the Dominicans, and of that of Duns Scotus in the case of Franciscans. As both Thomas and Scotus represented the *via antiqua*, Stakemeier was able to suggest that the influence of the *via moderna* at Trent was minimal.[53]

However, although Stakemeier notes Hermelink's response to Stange of 1906, he seems to overlook its totally destructive significance, in that it

[48] *Opusculum de iustificatione*, fols. 146–8. See further Sagués, 'Un libro pretridentino de Andrés de Vega sobre la justificación'. Perhaps with Capreolus in mind, Vega links Thomas Aquinas and Gregory of Rimini together as exponents of the 'no merit whatsoever prior to justification' school.

[49] *Opusculum de iustificatione*, fol. 148: 'theologi recentiores, Gabriel, Maiores, Almanyus et similes; et ante illos, ne adeo nova existemetur, videtur iam tempore doctoris subtilis fuisse haec opinio communis in scholis'.

[50] Heynck, 'Der Anteil des Konzilstheologen Andreas de Vega O.F.M. an dem ersten amtlichen Entwurf des Trienter Rechtfertigungsdekretes', 57.

[51] Hünermann, *Wesen und Notwendigkeit der aktuellen Gnade nach dem Konzil von Trient*, 5 n. 1; cf. E. Stakemeier, 'Die theologischen Schulen', 341.

[52] Carl Stange, 'Über Luthers Beziehungen zur Theologie seines Ordens', *Neue kirchliche Zeitschrift* 11 (1900), 574–85; idem, 'Luther über Gregor von Rimini', *Neue kirchliche Zeitschrift* 13 (1902), 721–7.

[53] E. Stakemeier, 'Die theologischen Schulen', 342–3.

was demonstrated that medieval theology was better designated a theology of *universities* rather than of *orders*.[54] Thomas Aquinas may well have been regarded as authoritative at the Dominican house in Cologne, where the *via antiqua* was dominant in the local university, but at Erfurt, where the *via moderna* was in the ascendancy in the university faculty of arts, it was to Ockham that the Dominicans looked for guidance. Although Ockham is hardly referred to at Trent by Franciscan theologians – the Avignon condemnation (1326) of his theology as 'Pelagian or worse' doubtless hardly commending him as a reliable theological source – they made frequent reference to two doctors of the Franciscan order, Bonaventure and Scotus,[55] as well as occasional reference to two others (Alexander of Hales and Gabriel Biel). Since Bonaventure and Scotus represent very different understandings of the doctrine of justification (particularly in relation to the role of supernatural habits in justification), it is clear that the Franciscan contingent found itself in difficulty on occasion. In view of this broad theological foundation upon which the Franciscan contingent based their opinions, it is both unduly restrictive and quite inappropriate to designate this contingent as 'the *Scotist* school'.[56]

The third school which Stakemeier identified at Trent was the 'Augustinian school'.[57] His views on this school, developed in a later study,[58] may be summarised as follows. The General of the Augustinian order, Girolamo Seripando, defended a doctrine of *duplex iustitia* during the Tridentine proceedings on justification, which represented a theology of justification characteristic of the theologians of the Augustinian order during the later medieval period. The 'Augustinian school' at Trent could therefore be regarded as adopting a position on justification, exemplified by Seripando, representing a theological tradition within the Augustinian order since the time of Simon Fidati of Cassia and Hugolino of Orvieto. Stakemeier's thesis has exercised considerable influence upon accounts of the Tridentine debate on justification, and it is therefore necessary to call its foundations into question.

---

[54]   H. Hermelink, *Die theologische Fakultät in Tübingen vor der Reformation*, Tübingen: Mohr, 1906. Stakemeier merely notes this study: E. Stakemeier, 'Die theologischen Schulen', 342 n. 3.

[55]   As noted by Stakemeier himself: for example, 'Die theologischen Schulen', 344–5.

[56]   The controversy at Trent over Scotus' views on the certitude of grace raises further questions over the 'Scotism' of the Franciscan contingent; see Heynck, 'A Controversy at the Council of Trent'. Heynck correctly notes (257) the much greater faithfulness of the Conventuals than of the Observants to the earlier Franciscan tradition.

[57]   For a detailed account of the latest scholarly understanding of late medieval Augustinianism, and its strongly negative implications for Stakemeier's position, see McGrath, *The Intellectual Origins of the European Reformation*, 82–8.

[58]   E. Stakemeier, *Der Kampf um Augustin*.

A careful study of Stakemeier's references to the Augustinian theologians whom he adduces as earlier representatives of this theological tradition indicates that he was familiar with their writings only at second hand, his immediate source being the highly controversial study of A. V. Müller on Luther's theological sources.[59] In this study, Müller had argued that Luther was the heir of precisely such a theological tradition within the Augustinian order – a view which Stakemeier emphatically rejects in the case of Luther, only to attach it to the Augustian contingent at Trent.[60] His evidence for this suggestion is quite unconvincing. Not only was this conclusion premature;[61] it has not stood up to subsequent critical examination. The theologians of the Augustinian order involved in the Tridentine debates on justification appear to have followed the person, rather than the theology, of their general in their voting, making it impossible to suggest that there was a coherent 'school' of thought, characteristic of the Augustinian order as a whole, represented during the Tridentine proceedings on justification.

Thus, in the debate of 8 October 1546, Seripando cites the Augustinian Giles of Viterbo as an earlier proponent of the doctrine of 'double justice', also suggesting that Jacobus Perez of Valencia is to be associated with the doctrine. However, it is significant that nowhere does he justify this assertion; the only theologian whom he cites verbatim is Gropper, and Contarini is cited inaccurately. Seripando appears merely to present a version of Gropper's theology, which is not of Augustinian provenance.[62] It is not merely impossible to defend the view that the doctrine of *duplex iustitia* was of Augustinian provenance; it is impossible to provide convincing evidence for an 'Augustinian *school*' at Trent.

There is thus no reason for continuing the discredited practice of reporting the presence of an 'Augustinian school' during the Tridentine proceedings on justification. This is not to deny that the Augustinian contingent at Trent espoused certain specific theological attitudes; it is to call into question the implication that these attitudes were representative of the Augustinian order as a whole, or that they corresponded to a tradition or school of thought peculiar to that order.

---

[59] A. V. Müller, *Luthers theologische Quellen: Seine Verteidigung gegen Denifle und Grisar*, Giessen: Topelmann, 1912; cf. W. Werbeck, *Jacobus Perez von Valencia: Untersuchungen zu seinem Psalmenkommentar*, 212 n. 6.

[60] E. Stakemeier, *Der Kampf um Augustin*, 21–2.

[61] As Jedin pointed out in his review of Stakemeier's book, the sources required for such a conclusion were simply not available in 1937: H. Jedin, in *Theologische Revue* 37 (1938), 425–30. See further our discussion of Gropper, 312–14.

[62] The study of Anselm Forster, *Gesetz und Evangelium bei Girolamo Seripando*, Paderborn: Verlag Bonifacius-Druckerei, 1963, demonstrates the generally conventional character of much of Seripando's theology of justification.

The Tridentine proceedings on justification suggest that the neo-Thomist school, the early Franciscan school and the later Franciscan school were all represented at Trent, along with a variety of other positions which defy rigid classification. While Trent appears to have taken some care to avoid censuring, or judging between, the traditional teachings associated with the major orders (a policy particularly evident during the proceedings on original sin), these teachings appear to have exercised considerably less influence upon the proceedings on justification than might be expected.

One possible explanation of this observation is that the whole matrix of traditional disputed questions concerning justification was recognised as occasionally having little bearing on the crucial new questions thrown up by the rise of the evangelical faction within Germany. The new questions thus raised demanded new answers, with the result that the appeal to the traditional positions of the theological schools associated with the orders had to give way to speculation concerning the most appropriate responses to these questions. A further consideration, however, is the rise of an increasingly independent intellectual environment, particularly in Italy, which enabled theologians to break free from the thought patterns of the medieval theological schools.[63]

In the following section, we shall consider the Tridentine debates on certain crucial aspects of the doctrine of justification, with a view to casting further light upon the proper interpretation of the final decree on justification itself.

4.3   The Tridentine debates on justification

The Council of Trent was the final outcome of a prolonged attempt by the papacy to convene a reforming council. The continuation of the war in Europe between the Emperor and the King of France had led to the postponement of the projected council at Mantua (1537) and the abortive convocation at Trent (1542–3). Only when the Habsburg–Valois conflict was settled by the Peace of Crépy in 1544 was there any real possibility of convening an ecumenical council. Two months after the conclusion of peace, when it became clear that there was a real possibility of a permanent cessation of hostilities, Paul III issued the bull *Laetare Ierusalem*, announcing his intention to convene a general council for the removal of religious discord, the reform of the church, and the liberation

---

[63] See Alberigo, *I vescovi italiani*, 388–9. Alberigo is primarily concerned with the intellectual climate in Italy, from which most of those involved in the Tridentine proceedings on justification were drawn. His conclusions, however, would appear to have a wider validity.

of the faithful from the Turk. Although it had been hoped that the council might open in March, the unsettled relations between the Emperor and the Pope delayed this until 13 December 1545. These difficulties arose partly from the Emperor's wish that the council should discuss the reform of the church, whereas the Pope desired doctrinal clarification. A judicious compromise led to both these questions being considered in parallel.

The initial doctrinal debates concerned the relation of Scripture and tradition, and original sin.[64] It was, however, recognised that the doctrine of justification was of peculiar importance. A number of crucial questions required clarification in the light of the Protestant challenge.[65] First, is justification merely *remissio peccatorum*, or does it necessarily include intrinsic sanctification through the action of grace within humans? Second, what is the precise relation between faith and good works? This question required a careful response to the Protestant doctrine of justification *sola fide*. Third, what is the precise nature of the active role of the human will in justification, given the general Protestant tendency to assert the passivity of the will? Fourth, what is the relationship between justification and the *sacramenta mortuorum* of baptism and penance? Fifth, can believers know with any degree of certitude whether they are, in fact, justified? Finally, is it necessary for humans to dispose themselves towards justification, and if so, is this disposition to be considered meritorious in any sense?

The council initially set itself the task of dealing with six questions. On 22 June 1546, a commission of theologians laid down the following questions for discussion:[66]

1. What is justification, nominally and actually (*quoad nomen et quoad rem*), and what is to be understood when it is said that 'humanity is justified' (*iustificari hominem*)?
2. What are the causes of justification? What part is played by God? And what is required of humans?
3. What is to be understood when it is said that 'humanity is justified by faith' (*iustificari hominem per fidem*)?

---

[64] The importance and inseparability of the doctrines of original sin and justification had been stressed in the legates' report of 15 April 1546 (CT 10.548–60). However, the two doctrines were eventually discussed in isolation.

[65] For a slightly different list, see Jedin, *Geschichte des Konzils von Trient*, 2.142–4. It should be borne in mind that the council was committed to the simultaneous discussion of the questions of residence and of translation.

[66] CT 5.261.26–35. For background information to such congregations, see H. Lennerz, 'De congregationibus theologorum in Concilio Tridentino', *Gregorianum* 26 (1945), 7–21. For similar information in relation to votes, see idem, 'Voten auf dem Konzil von Trient', *Gregorianum* 15 (1934), 577–88.

4. What role do human works and the sacraments play in justification, whether before, during or after it?
5. What precedes, accompanies and follows justification?
6. By what proofs is the Catholic doctrine supported?

Although this approach would eventually prove to be inadequate, in that it omitted important questions such as the certitude of grace, it served as a useful point of departure for the initial discussion leading up to the first draft of the decree on justification.

In the six congregations held in the period 22–28 June 1546, some thirty-four theologians addressed themselves to the questions set for discussion. Although it is far from clear upon what basis the speakers were called, it is apparent that their initial concern was with the question of the *nature* of justification. Most of the speakers addressed themselves to this point, with a variety of concepts of justification being employed.[67] Despite this remarkable variety of definitions, it is clear that there existed a consensus concerning the factitive and transformational character of justification.[68] Two possible exceptions to this consensus may be noted: the Dominican Marcus Laureus and the Franciscan Observant Andrés de Vega.

Marcus Laureus defined justification as *remissio peccatorum per gratiam*,[69] significantly omitting any reference to the concomitant spiritual regeneration or moral transformation of the believer. This might be taken as indicating that Laureus approached the Protestant position at this point. In fact, this conclusion cannot be drawn without further corroborating evidence, which we do not possess. As noted in an earlier discussion, Thomas Aquinas had demonstrated, on Aristotelian grounds, that a process could be defined in terms of its *terminus*, with the result that the *processus iustificationis* could be defined simply as *remissio peccatorum*, the final element in this process. Thomas' occasional statements to the effect that *iustificatio* may be defined as *remissio peccatorum* have occasionally been misinterpreted as implying that he did not include *infusio iustitiae* as an element of justification, which is evidently incorrect. Laureus must therefore, in the absence of any evidence to the contrary, be regarded as restating the position of the chief doctor of his order in the congregation of 23 June 1546.

---

[67] To give a few illustrations: the Conventual Sigismondo Fedrio da Diruta defined the term *iustificatio* as *motus quidam spiritualis de impietate ad pietatem*, and *iustificari* as *ex nocente fieri innocens*. Richard of Le Mans defined *iustificatio* as *adhaesio Dei*, and *iustificari* as *redire in gratiam Dei*. Gregory of Padua defined *iustificatio* in Augustinian terms, as *de impio pium facere vel iniusto iustum*, and *iustificari* as *fieri Deo gratus*.

[68] See, for example, CT 5.263.9–10, 22–3, 27–9, 31–2; 264.1–5; 264.43 – 265.2; 265.12–14; 272.40–1; 273.11–12, 45–6; 274.35–6, 275–6.

[69] CT 5.264.31–2.

Andrés de Vega defined justification in a noticeably extrinsicist manner, in terms of three elements: absolution from sin, possession of divine
grace, and acceptance to eternal life.[70] Vega's conception of justification
clearly parallels that of the later Franciscan school, and is reflected in the
statements of other Franciscan theologians in these congregations.[71] The
weakening of the ontological link between *remissio peccatorum* and *infusio
gratiae*, characteristic of both this school and the *via moderna*, places them
closest to the extrinsicism of the Reformers at this point. Nevertheless,
it is important to appreciate the heterogeneity of the Franciscan contingent at Trent over this point; other Franciscans defined justification in
strongly intrinsicist and transformational terms, such as *regeneratio hominis interioris*,[72] or *mutatio quaedam spiritualis in peccatorem a Deo facta per
infusionem iustitiae habitualis*,[73] paralleling those of the earlier Franciscan
school. Although this understanding of justification does not exclude the
infusion of grace and the transformation of humanity, the priority of the
extrinsic denomination of the divine acceptation over such intrinsic qualities was rigorously upheld. This observation is of importance in relation
to the question whether there existed a *Scotist* school at Trent; as noted
earlier, the evidence strongly suggests that the theological tension already
present within the Franciscan order (particularly between the early and
later Franciscan schools) is evident during the Tridentine debates on
justification.

The general agreement over the nature of justification was summarised
by Marcus Laureus as follows:

For all theologians agree on the matter, even if they diverge verbally. They affirm
that, as a theological term, 'justification' means *iustifactio*, 'a making righteous',
and that 'to justify' means 'to become righteous before God (*iustum fieri coram
Deo*).' Justification is therefore the remission of sin by God through grace.[74]

The discussion of the question of the nature of justification was greatly
facilitated by the distinction of three stages (*status*) of justification, which
permitted three different senses of the term *iustificatio* to be distinguished,
thus avoiding some of the confusion evident in the initial discussions. The
first *status* has to do with the justification of sinners, in which they are
transformed from a state of unbelief and sin to one of faith and grace; the
second concerns the increase in righteousness of justified believers, and

---

[70] CT 5.275.9–11: 'Hominem iustificari est absolutum esse a peccatis et gratiam Dei
habere. Et acceptum ad vitam aeternam.'
[71] For example, Antonio Delfini, CT 5.274.21–30. See further Santoro, 'La giustificazione
in Giovanni Antonio Delfini'.
[72] CT 5.278.20–1.   [73] CT 5.278.1–2.   [74] CT 5.279.27–31.

their perseverance in the Christian life; the third concerns the justification of lapsed believers.[75]

This general consensus on the nature of justification is reflected in the first draft of the decree on justification, dating from 24 July 1546. Although it was once thought that this draft version was the work of Andrés de Vega, this judgement is now generally regarded as unreliable.[76] The first draft consists of a brief introduction, three chapters, and a series of eighteen canons.[77] No formal definition of justification is given, although it is possible to deduce such a definition from the material appended to the first two canons. The first three canons make clear the distinction between the Catholic and Protestant understanding of the nature of justification in the following manner.

First, the opinion that a sinner may be justified solely as a matter of reputation or imputation, while remaining a sinner in fact, is rejected.

Therefore, if anyone says that a sinner (*impium*) who is justified by God through Jesus Christ, is or remains unrighteous, but is somehow reputed to be righteous, rather than becoming righteous, so that this justification is only the imputation of righteousness, let him be condemned.[78]

Justification is thus defined in terms of a person becoming, and not merely being reputed as, righteous (*sic vere non modo reputatur, sed efficitur iustus*). Although this manifestly excludes the concept of a 'legal fiction' in justification, it is somewhat unclear whether it affects mainstream Protestant teaching on the question, in view of the purely notional distinction this envisaged between justification and regeneration. For Melanchthon, the notional separation of justification and sanctification did not entail their division, as if one could be justified without subsequently being sanctified. It is, however, evident that there was a consensus throughout the Tridentine debates that the Protestants did, in fact, restrict the meaning of the term *iustificatio* to *iustum reputatio*. This is particularly apparent from the

[75] See the list of errors noted at CT 5.281–2. The subsequent discussion follows this division, with interest focussing particularly on the *primus status*: for example, see CT 5.287–96, 298–310.
[76] See the careful study of Heynck, 'Der Anteil des Konzilstheologen Andreas de Vega an dem ersten amtlichen Entwurf des Trienter Rechtfertigungsdekretes'.
[77] CT 5.384–91. The numeration of the canons is confusing, and errors of reference are frequent in the secondary literature. The Görres edition numbers the chapters and canons consecutively, without distinguishing them, so that the paragraph numbered '4' is actually Canon 1, and that numbered '18' is Canon 15, etc. It is clear from the *notationes theologorum* (CT 5.392.1 – 394.6) that the first three chapters were actually treated *as canons*. Thus a reference to 'Canon 18' (CT 5.393.36) refers to the section numbered '18' (CT 5.390.22–40), even though, strictly speaking, this is actually the *fifteenth* canon.
[78] Canon 1, CT 5.386.12–14.

comments of the Spanish Jesuit Alfonso Salmeron, who clearly failed to understand the significance of Melanchthon's distinction between *iustificatio* and *regeneratio*.[79] The fact that Melanchthon understood by 'justification' *and* 'regeneration' what Catholics understood by 'justification' alone does not appear to have been appreciated. As the Catholics understood *iustificatio* to refer to Christian existence in its totality, the Protestant exclusion of *regeneratio* from *iustificatio* appeared to amount to the exclusion of any transformational dimension from Christian existence altogether.

The Protestant concept of justification *per solam fidem* presents a similar difficulty, as the Tridentine theologians generally seem to have understood it to exclude works from Christian existence (whereas the Protestants, operating with a quite distinct concept of justification, understood it merely to refer to the exclusion of works from the *initiation* of the Christian life). We shall return to this point below; it is, however, essential to appreciate that the full significance of the new understanding of the nature of justification associated with Melanchthon was not wholly grasped by his Catholic opponents, with important consequences for the interpretation of the relevance of the Tridentine pronouncements for Protestant theologies of justification.

Second, the opinion that justification consists solely in the remission of sins, and not in the *donatio iustitiae*, is condemned.[80] Third, the opinion that the righteousness bestowed upon believers in their justification is the righteousness of Christ won on the cross is condemned.[81] This point is of particular interest, and appears to be directed against the Lutheran doctrine of *imputatio iustitiae alienae Christi*. The righteousness on the basis of which humanity is justified is defined as *habitus divinae gratiae*, which is bestowed *by God through Christ* – in other words, God effects what Christ merited. This statement clarifies the relationship between *iustitia Christi* and *iustitia Dei*, indicating that the former is to be understood as the meritorious cause of justification, and the latter as the formal cause.[82]

The general consensus concerning the necessity of works subsequent to the first justification, evident in the earlier discussions, led to the condemnation of solafideism. With the recognition, however, that the phrase *iustificari hominem per fidem* had a legitimate place in the Catholic exposition of the first justification, the condemnation of solafideism was phrased in a slightly unusual manner, which made the Catholic objection to the perceived meaning of the concept unambiguous:

[79] CT 5.266.3–28.   [80] Canon 2, CT 5.386.18–20.
[81] Canon 3, CT 5.386.25–7.   [82] CT 5.386.28–33.

330 The Council of Trent on justification

If anyone says that faith alone, without works, justifies the ungodly – that is, brings about their justification – in the sense in which the heretics of this age profess, as if nothing is required on the part of humanity except that they should believe, let him be condemned.[83]

Throughout the Tridentine debates on justification, there was a general consensus that Protestants employed the terms *fides* and *credere* in a highly unorthodox sense. Alfonso Salmeron critiqued Melanchthon's interpretation of the term *fides* as *fiducia divinae misericordiae*, thus excluding the Catholic notion of *fides quae per dilectionem operatur*.[84] It is clear that the initial Catholic hostility to the Lutheran doctrine of justification *per solam fidem* at Trent was based upon a quite specific understanding of the concepts both of *fides* and of *iustificatio*.

Although the July debate on this draft proved inconclusive,[85] the debate of 17 August made clear that there was still some considerable way to go before any agreement was possible.[86] The document which was to form the basis of a revised draft was presented to the legates by Seripando on 11 August 1546.[87] This document remedied a major deficiency of the first draft – its omission of a formal definition of the term *iustificatio hominis*. Justification is now defined unequivocally in transformative terms:

When we speak of the 'justification of humanity', we mean nothing other than their translation, through a new spiritual birth, from that state in which they are born according to the flesh, as sons of the first Adam, under the wrath and hostility of God, to the state of adoption as children of God through the second Adam, Jesus Christ.[88]

Dissatisfied with this first draft, Seripando presented a second version on 29 August.[89] The new version of the decree took a form radically different from that of its predecessors. In its customary form, such a decree consisted of a long series of canons, with a short introduction or introductory chapters. The new draft consisted of fifteen chapters, and a mere eight canons. The significance of the document, however, lies not only in its new form, but also in its views on the formal cause of justification.

---

[83] Canon 9, CT 5.387.40–2.   [84] CT 5.268.43–4.

[85] CT 5.392–4. Perhaps the only positive achievement was the recognition of significant difficulties concerning the existing draft of Canon 11, dealing with the certitude of grace (396.36–41).

[86] CT 5.408–14. The postponement of the debate occurred primarily on account of political considerations, rather than because of concerns about the quality of the document under consideration.

[87] Seripando's draft is to be found in CT 5.821–8.   [88] Cap. 4, CT 5.823.6–9.

[89] CT 5.828–30. The first four chapters correspond to those of the draft of 11 August. The date given in the Görres edition (19 August) is incorrect, and should be amended to 29 August.

In his first draft, Seripando explicitly rejected the Lutheran doctrine that the only basis upon which justification may take place is *imputatio iustitiae Christi*.[90] However, Seripando revised his views on the matter in his second draft. The fourth canon repeats the substance of the second canon of the draft of 11 August, in that it censures the opinion that we are justified 'only by the imputation of the righteousness of Christ to the exclusion of the righteousness diffused in our hearts'.[91] Although the obvious interpretation of this statement is that humanity is justified on the basis of an infused or intrinsic righteousness, it seems clear that Seripando intended this merely as the rejection of the opinion that humanity is justified *solely* on the basis of the imputation of the righteousness of Christ.[92]

The September draft of the decree omits any explicit reference to *duplex iustitia*, and develops the teaching of Canon 3 of the July draft in such a manner as to exclude the opinion that the Christian possesses one *iustitia* deriving from God and another deriving from Christ.[93] Nevertheless, Canon 7 of the September draft still follows the wording of Seripando's original version closely, and condemns only the opinion that the imputed righteousness of Christ *alone* is the basis of the justification of humanity, if this is understood to exclude an inherent righteousness through the action of the Holy Spirit.[94] The opinion that humans are justified on the basis of *duplex iustitia* – that is, *iustitia imputata* and *iustitia inhaerens* – is thus not explicitly condemned, and might even be considered to be condoned.

This should not be understood to imply a Tridentine consensus on this issue, as if the theologians present at Trent were prepared to allow that sinners were justified on the basis of both an intrinsic and an imputed righteousness, following the lead given some years earlier at the Diet of Regensburg. In fact it is quite clear, from the records of the proceedings in the period 27 September – 8 October 1546, that many of the delegates found themselves unable to make sense of the phrasing of the seventh chapter.[95] There were growing calls for clarification of the ambiguities of

[90] Canon 3, CT 5.824.33–5. This canon also condemns the doctrine of justification *sola fide*.

[91] CT 5.832.27–8; cf. 824.33–4.

[92] To appreciate this point, compare the official draft of this text with Seripando's two drafts: CT 5.386.13–14; 824.33–4; 832.27–8. The substitution of *solius* for *sola* enables Seripando to open the way to a doctrine of justification on the basis of *iustitia duplex* – both *iustitia imputata* and *iustitia inhaerens*.

[93] Cap. 7, CT 5.423.34–6. See further Pas, 'La Doctrine de la double justice au Concile de Trente'.

[94] Canon 7, CT 5.427.1–7.

[95] For example, see Pas, 'La Doctrine de la double justice au Concile de Trent', 20–3.

the September draft, and the elimination of the confusion that they were creating. The case for replacing the ambiguous *non sunt duae iustitiae* with the more explicit *una est iustitia* was pressed with some force,[96] forcing Seripando and his supporters – including the Augustinians Aurelius of Rocca Contrata, Marianus Feltrinus and Stephen of Sestino, the Servite Lorenzo Mazocchi, and the Spanish secular priest Antonio Solis[97] – to make their views on the matter explicit, and to defend their provenance. Yet a close reading of their votes on this question raises serious doubts as to whether their doctrine of 'double justification' can be regarded as Augustinian – or, indeed, whether establishing that it could be defended, either from Augustine or from leading writers of the Augustinian order, was seen as a matter of importance.

In his defence of the doctrine, Aurelius of Rocca Contrata merely recapitulates previous statements of his general, Seripando, without developing his arguments in any manner.[98] Stephen of Sestino emphasised the imperfection and inadequacy of human works in a manner which parallels Gropper's argument in the *Enchiridion* to such an extent that dependence upon this source is a probability.[99] The vote of the third Augustinian, Feltrinus, exists only in the outline of Massarelli,[100] and appears to parallel the views of Sestino. It is thus significant, in view of the hypothesis that an authentically Augustinian theology of justification is implicit in these statements, to note the clear priority given to the arguments of Gropper over Augustinian theologians such as Jacobus Perez of Valencia.

The remaining supporters of the doctrine appear to have based their views upon considerations so disparate that generalisations are impossible. The vote of Solis survives only in a form which is too brief to permit analysis;[101] that of Sarra, although longer, is difficult to categorise.[102] Mazocchi's vote is something of an enigma;[103] although Mazocchi appears to have given his fellow delegates the impression that

---

[96] For example, CT 5.492.10–11; 496.2: 'Tenet quod una sit iustitia tantum, qua iustificamur, videlicet nobis inhaerens.' The objections recorded at CT 5.505.26–7 should also be noted. To the twenty-two votes recorded in the Görres edition of the *Acta* should be added those of Salmeron and Hervet: see J. Olazarán, 'En el IV centenario de un voto tridentino del jesuito Alfonso Salmeron sobre la doble justicia', *EE* 20 (1946), 211–40; idem, 'Voto tridentino de Gentian Hervet sobre la certeza de la gracia y la doble justicia', *Archivio Teológico Granadino* 9 (1946), 127–59.

[97] It is possible that another Spanish secular priest, Pedro Sarra, should be considered a supporter of the doctrine.

[98] See Aurelius' vote of 19 October 1546: CT 5.561.47 – 564.12. For the similarities, compare CT 5.563.4–13 with 12.665.2–12; 5.563.35–6 with 12.667.46 – 668.9; 5.563.37–42 with 12.635.37–42 and 5.374.10–15.

[99] For example, compare CT 5.609.22–7 with Gropper, *Enchiridion*, fol. 132v; 5.611.17–24, with *Enchiridion*, fol. 168r–v.

[100] CT 5.599.4–10.   [101] CT 5.576.31–5.

[102] CT 5.547.8 – 549.43.   [103] CT 5.581.17 – 590.19.

he supported Seripando, his vote actually gives little, if any, indication of endorsing the doctrine of *duplex iustitia*.

The majority opinion was, however, unequivocal. Although demonstrating a near-total ignorance of the historical origins of the doctrine of *duplex iustitia*,[104] there was a general conviction that the concept of *iustitia imputata* was a theological novelty, unknown to Catholic theology throughout its existence.[105] Furthermore, the concept of imputed righteousness was widely regarded as something approaching an irrelevance, on account of the renovation of humans in justification; if God made people righteous in justification, what was the point of imputed righteousness? It seemed to be completely redundant theologically.[106] Although Seripando actually employed the term *imputare* rarely (and never in his votes at Trent),[107] it seems that the demand on the part of many of his colleagues for an explicit condemnation of conceptions of justification grounded on imputed righteousness is to be seen as an indirect attack upon his position.[108] There also appears to have been a general consensus that Seripando's appeal to *iustitia Christi* undermined the foundation of human merit.

On 31 October 1546, the September draft of the decree was rewritten in the light of the preceding debate, in which the overwhelming hostility to the concept of *duplex iustitia* (or *duae iustitiae*) had been made clear. The demand for an explicit condemnation of justification on the basis of *iustitia imputata* was met by an unequivocal assertion that humanity was justified on the basis of an internal righteousness:

> The justification of the ungodly consists at one and the same time in the removal of sins, sanctification, and the infusion of gifts. . . . [Its formal cause is] the one righteousness of God, by which we are renewed by the spirit of our minds, and not by reputation, but we are named, and really are, righteous.[109]

Although this new statement undermined any idea of justification by both inherent and imputed righteousnesses, Seripando's position could still be accommodated if it were conceded that there was more than one formal

---

[104] There is no specific reference to Gropper or his *Enchiridion*, or to the Diet of Regensburg, throughout the entire debate. However, the personal association of Reginald Pole with similar views was known to many delegates: see Fenlon, *Heresy and Obedience*, 161–95.

[105] For example, see CT 5.564.38–9; 569.8; 579.5–6; 602.37–42; 617.27–9.

[106] CT 5.541.45–6: 'Non quod tunc nova fiat imputatio, ut quidam falso imaginantur, quia, ut patet sufficienter ex praemissis, ista imputatio nulla ratione requiritur.' For a full study of the main lines of criticism directed against Seripando's position, see Pas, 'La doctrine de la double justice', 31–43.

[107] For example, see CT 5.489.31–2; 12.671.16–32.

[108] For example, CT 5.643.31–2; 644.34; 644.31–2; 647.12–15; 649.10–11.

[109] CT 5.512.12–20.

cause of justification. It is this ambiguous understanding of the formal cause of justification which became incorporated into the draft of the decree presented on 5 November 1546.[110] This led some to press for changes which would exclude the doctrine of *duplex iustitia*, as defended by Seripando.[111]

A revised version of the eighth chapter of the decree was drawn up for discussion on 11 December 1546, and avoided any ambiguity concerning the formal cause of justification. There was only one formal cause of justification – and this was the righteousness of God, by which God makes us righteous in his sight.[112] This unequivocal statement to the effect that the *single* formal cause of justification was the righteousness of God, in the sense defined, was approved in general congregation the same day,[113] and eventually incorporated into the final version of the decree on justification.[114] It is only at this point that the rejection of Seripando's concept of *duplex iustitia* may be considered to be complete and unambiguous.

The question of the formal cause of justification was one of a number of highly contentious issues to be debated at Trent; another was the assurance of salvation, a highly significant issue for the Reformers, and particularly for Luther.[115] The medieval consensus on this matter was that such assurance was an impossibility, thus placing clear blue theological water between Trent and Lutheranism. This manifest difference of opinion, along with its polemical potential, made it impossible for the theologians assembled at Trent to ignore the matter, despite its absence from the initial agenda for their discussions.[116]

Initially, little interest was shown in the question of assurance. The records of the congregations of 22–28 June 1546 demonstrate that only

---

[110] CT 5.636.30 – 637.11. Note especially 35–6: 'formalis iustitia una Dei'.

[111] For example, in the congregation of 23 November, Claude Le Jay proposed that the phrase 'causa formalis iustitia una Dei' should be replaced with 'causa formalis una iustitia Dei'. CT 5.658.24–6.

[112] CT 5.700.25–8: 'Demum unica formalis causa est iustitia illa Dei, non qua ipse iustus est, sed qua nos coram ipso iustos facit, qua videlicet ab eo donati renovamur spiritu mentis nostrae et non modo reputamur, sed vere iusti nominamur et sumus.'

[113] CT 5.701.14 – 704.14.

[114] Cap. 7, *D* 1528–9. There is a slight alteration in the wording, which does not affect the fundamental sense of the statement in question.

[115] For example, see H. J. Iwand, *Nachgelassene Werke*, v: *Luthers Theologie*, Munich: Kaiser Verlag, 1974, 64–104, especially 90–104.

[116] For the general problem at Trent, see Guerard des Lauriers, 'Saint Augustin et la question de la certitude de la grâce au Concile de Trente'; Heynck, 'Zur Kontroverse über die Gnadengewissheit auf dem Konzil von Trient'; Huthmacher, 'La Certitude de la grâce au Concile de Trente'; Schierse, 'Das Trienterkonzil und die Frage nach der christliche Gewissheit'; A. Stakemeier, *Das Konzil van Trient über die Heilsgewissheit*.

two speakers deemed the matter worthy of consideration. The very different approaches adopted by Andrés de Vega[117] and Antonius Frexius[118] were indicative of the divisions which would subsequently be exposed on this question, and it is significant that these apparently extreme contributions were not included in the *summarium* of Marcus Laureus.[119] Although the Lutheran doctrine of assurance is included among the list of proscribed errors concerning the second *status iustificationis* tabled for discussion on 30 June, little attention was paid to it.[120]

The emergence of the question of assurance as a serious issue dates from the July 1546 draft of the decree, which included as its fifteenth canon an explicit condemnation of the Lutheran doctrine of assurance as an assertion contrary to proper Christian humility.[121] It was clear, however, that this canon provoked considerable disquiet. There was obviously serious disagreement on the matter among the theologians, as well as a general desire to discuss the matter further.[122] As a result, Costacciaro invited the Conventual Antonio Delfini to prepare an expert opinion on the question whether Christians might have certainty over whether they were in a state of grace, and to clarify the position of Duns Scotus on this contentious matter.[123] In this document, Delfini interprets Scotus from the not entirely appropriate perspective of Gabriel Biel,[124] indicating that Scotus cannot be regarded as an exponent of the Lutheran doctrine of assurance. Costacciaro himself clearly considered that Scotus upheld the possibility of the certitude of grace on account of the *ex opere operato* character of the sacrament of penance.[125] Zannetino, however, disagreed, and cited John Fisher as an accurate and reliable interpreter of Scotus on this

---

[117] CT 5.275.14–16, which rejects this possibility, apart from special divine revelation.

[118] CT 5.277.42–3, which upholds the possibility of certitude.

[119] CT 5.279.6 – 281.15.

[120] For the briefing material, see CT 5.282.24–5: '9. Quod iustificatus tenetur credere, se esse in gratia et sibi non imputari peccata, et se esse praedestinatum.' For the somewhat tentative response to this, see CT 5.324.34–42. Seripando noted the point (CT 12.634.31 – 635.11), but did not permit his views to be included in the general discussion.

[121] CT 5.390.22–40, especially 37–40. On the numeration of the canons, see n. 74 above.

[122] See, for example, CT 5.393.36–41.

[123] CT 5.410 n. 1. The reference to Scotus is significant; as Heynck has shown, there was considerable confusion among the delegates (particularly the Franciscans) concerning Scotus' views on the certitude of grace; Heynck, 'A Controversy at the Council of Trent', passim. On Delfini, see Friedrich Lauchert, *Die italienischen literarischen Gegner Luthers*, Freiburg: Herder, 1912, 487–536; Santoro, 'La giustificazione in Giovanni Antonio Delfini'.

[124] For the document, see CT 12.651.22 – 658.14. For the appeal to Biel's interpretation of Scotus, see CT 12.657.53 – 658.11.

[125] CT 5.404.41–3. He appears to have been supported in this assertion by the General of the Carmelites (CT 5.404.50) and Martellus of Fiessole (CT 5.406.16–18).

point.[126] By 17 August, it was apparent that there was a serious division of opinion on the matter within the council, with the Dominicans implacably opposed to any suggestion that *certitudo gratiae* was possible, and others affirming precisely such a possibility, with due divergence over the degree of certainty that was possible.[127] In view of this difficulty, a general congregation of 28 August 1546 determined to proceed directly merely to the condemnation of the Lutheran position, while leaving unresolved the question of the Catholic position on the matter.[128] This principle was observed in the drawing up of the September draft of the decree.

The September draft refers to the question of the certitude of grace at two points. The seventh chapter rejects the opinion, which it attributes to 'heretics and schismatics', that it is possible to know with confidence and certainty that one's sins have been forgiven.[129] While rejecting the Lutheran position, no clarification on the Catholic teaching is provided. Canon 8 explicitly rejects any suggestion that believers may know with certainty that they are among the predestined, or that they will persevere to the end, apart from special divine revelation.[130] Once more, it proved easier to reject Protestant views than to provide an authoritative statement of the Catholic alternative, because of the diversity of views represented at Trent on the question.

The compromise of 28 August was soon recognised as unsatisfactory, and the debate on the question was resumed on 12 October 1546.[131] Discussion of this matter over the period 15–26 October 1546 further emphasised the divisions within the council at this point; of the thirty-seven theologians who expressed their opinions, twenty were in favour of the possibility of certitude of grace, fifteen against, and two undecided.[132]

---

[126] CT 10.586.22 – 587.20.
[127] Thus the Generals of both the Conventuals and the Observants spoke in favour of the latter: CT 5.410.1–2, 5–6. The English bishop Richard Pate, himself suspected by many of Lutheranism, also spoke in support of this latter position on 28 August 1546: CT 5.419.18–19. His views were expressed even more forcefully on 13 November: CT 5.648.4–5: 'Homo iustificatus secundum praesentem iustitiam potest esse certus certitudine fidei, se esse in gratia Dei.'
[128] CT 5.418.1–9; 419.44.   [129] Cap. 7, CT 5.424.12–13.
[130] Canon 8, CT 5.427.8–11. Note the term *praedestinatio* is here used in the positive sense of 'predestination to life'.
[131] Note especially the comments of del Monte, CT 5.497.3–4; cf. 497.12–15. For further comments on the chapter and canon, see CT 5.505.46–51; 508.40–2.
[132] For the names of the theologians in each group, see Massarelli's lists at CT 5.632.31 – 633.10. We have taken the liberty of transferring the secular priest Andrés de Navarra from the list of supporters of *certitudo fidei, se esse in gratia* to that of its opponents. His vote (CT 5.559.14 – 561.46) clearly opposes the concept; we are unable to account for Massarelli's error at this point.

Without exception, the Dominican theologians were opposed to the possibility of *certitudo fidei, se esse in gratia* – despite the recent arrival at the Council of the Dominican bishop Ambrogio Catharino, an outspoken supporter of the possibility.[133] The Franciscan contingent, by contrast, was deeply divided, the seven Conventuals supporting the possibility, and the Observants more or less equally divided.

The third draft of the decree was submitted for consideration on 5 November 1546, with a revised statement on the question incorporated into the decree in the form of its ninth chapter.[134] Its substance parallels that of the equivalent statement in the second draft, with an intensification of its opening affirmation:[135]

September draft: *not all* have such confidence and certainty
November draft: *no-one* has such confidence and certainty

Although this went some way towards meeting the demands of some delegates that the condemnation of *certitudo fidei, se esse in gratia* be strengthened and made more explicit, the new chapter still failed to win general approval. By 17 December, the issue, although forcefully contested on both sides, was still unresolved. In view of the serious delays this difficulty was occasioning, del Monte proposed that the council should merely condemn the Lutheran position, and leave further discussion of the Catholic position until a future date.[136] Despite opposition from some who did not wish to see the results of months of discussion come to nothing, the procedure was approved.

On 9 January 1547, four days before the final decree was published, a small group of senior officials met to attempt to establish a last-minute consensus on the ninth chapter on the certainty of grace.[137] After three hours' debate, a compromise formula was finally agreed: 'no one can know with a certainty of faith, which cannot be subject to error, that he has obtained the grace of God' (*nemo possit esse certus certitudine fidei, cui non potest subesse falsum, se esse in gratia Dei*).[138] The formula was

---

[133] His vote of 22 November 1546 is of particular importance: CT 5.655.34 – 657.18. See further Olazarán, 'La controversia Soto-Caterino-Vega sobre la certeza de la gracia'; Beltrán de Heredia, 'Controversia de certitudine gratiae entre Domingo de Soto y Ambrosio Catarino'; Hernández, 'La certeza del estado de gracia según Andrés de Vega'.

[134] Cap. 9, CT 5.637.12–21. The contents of Canon 8 of the September draft are to be found in Canons 12 and 13, CT 5.649.39–42. A new canon on the subject follows: Canon 14, CT 5.649.43–4.

[135] September draft, cap. 7, CT 5.424.13; November draft, cap. 9, CT 5.637.14–15.

[136] CT 5.727.1–11.   [137] CT 5.772.10 – 773.5.

[138] CT 5.773.4–5. The relief was evident.

immediately incorporated into the fifth draft of the decree, submitted for consideration on the same day,[139] and finally approved.

With the resolution of the questions of the cause of justification and the certitude of grace, the Council of Trent was able to proceed with its extensive pronouncements concerning the Catholic teaching on justification, contained in the chapters of the final decree, as well as with its specific condemnation in the canons of the errors of Protestantism. Although, strictly speaking, the decree could not be considered binding upon Catholics until the papal ratification of the council after its closure in 1563, the decisions were widely regarded as immediately valid – despite Reginald Pole's refusal to sign the document. By 1547, therefore, the teaching of the Catholic church on justification may be regarded as fixed, in the sense that the approved formulas (which permitted a certain degree of latitude of interpretation at crucial points) had been established. In the following section, we shall outline the main features of the decree itself, before considering the interpretation of the decree in the immediate post-Tridentine period.

4.4   The Tridentine decree on justification

The Tridentine decree on justification marks a significant development in conciliar history. Up to that point, conciliar decisions had tended to be framed largely in terms of explicit condemnation, in the form of canons, of specific opinions, without substantial exposition of the Catholic teaching on the matter in question. Perhaps on account of the peculiar importance with which, it was recognised, the doctrine of justification was invested, the Tridentine decree on justification devotes sixteen initial chapters to a point-by-point exposition of the Catholic teaching before proceeding to condemn thirty-three specific opinions deemed to be unacceptable to the Catholic church. As will become clear from the following section, there was considerable disagreement in the immediate post-Tridentine period concerning the precise interpretation of the decree. In the present section, we propose to indicate the broad range of opinions on justification which the Council of Trent recognised as authentically Catholic. In establishing these, the following principles have been employed.

1. In that the council was primarily concerned with distinguishing Catholic teaching from that of the Reformers, and not to settle disputed matters within the Catholic schools of theology, it follows that the previously professed theological positions of these schools may continue to be held, unless they are explicitly excluded.

---

[139] CT 5.777.1–10.

2. The final decree is to be interpreted in the light of the debates which led to its formulation, in order to establish what the Tridentine fathers intended particular terms and phrases to mean.[140] Although the attempt to interpret any historical document is notoriously difficult, we possess sufficient documentary evidence to clarify the intended meaning of at least certain otherwise obscure statements.

With these points in mind, we may turn to the analysis of the decree and its canons.

The final arrangement of the decree reflects the three 'stages of justification' which emerged during the earlier debates. The first nine chapters discuss the 'first justification', in which humanity's initial transition from a state of sin to righteousness is described. This is followed by four chapters dealing with the 'second justification' – how humans, once justified, may increase in righteousness. The final three chapters deal with the *status tertius*, indicating how persons may forfeit their justification and subsequently regain it through penance, and clarifying the manner in which this differs from the first stage of justification.

The decree opens with an analysis of the fallen condition of humanity, inevitably incorporating certain matters touched upon in the fifth session *de peccato originali*. On account of original sin, which is a condition affecting the entire human race, humans are incapable of redeeming themselves. Free will is not destroyed, but is weakened and debilitated by the Fall.[141] The council thus reaffirmed the position of Augustine and Orange II on this crucial point, and implicitly rejected Luther's statement that 'free will after sin exists in name only'. The particularism implicit in Luther's teaching on election is excluded by the unequivocal assertion that Christ died for all people, granting grace through the merits of his passion in order that humans might be born again, and hence justified. Justification is defined in transformational terms, including reference to necessary alterations in human status and nature:

The justification of the ungodly is a translation from that state in which humanity is born a child of the first Adam, to the state of grace and of the adoption of the sons of God through the second Adam, Jesus Christ, our Saviour (*translatio ab eo statu, in quo homo nascitur filius primi Adae, in statum gratiae et 'adoptionis filiorum' Dei, per secundum Adam Iesum Christum Salvatorem nostrum*).[142]

The fifth and sixth chapters deal with the necessity and the mode of preparation towards justification. Humans are called through prevenient

---

[140] A failure to deal with the decree in its proper historical perspective is one of the most significant (and irritating) shortcomings of Hans Küng's analysis of the Tridentine decree; Küng, *Rechtfertigung*.
[141] Cap. 1, *D* 1521.   [142] Cap. 4, *D* 1524.

grace, without reference to their merits, to dispose themselves towards justification. As a consequence of humans' assenting to and co-operating with this call, God touches their hearts through the illumination of his Holy Spirit.[143] The traditional medieval terminology usually employed in the discussion of the necessity for a disposition towards justification is studiously avoided, exemplifying the general tendency to avoid scholastic language wherever possible. Indeed, the decree on justification is notable for its marked preference to appeal directly to Scripture, passing over the vocabulary of the medieval period altogether.

The preparation for justification is then defined in terms of humans' believing the truth of divine revelation and the divine promises (particularly the promise that God will justify the ungodly through his grace), and thence being moved to detest their sins and repent of them. This culminates in the sacrament of baptism, in which individuals declare their intention to lead a new life and observe the divine commandments.[144] Once more, the nature of the disposition towards justification is discussed in terms drawn directly from Scripture, rather than from the medieval theological schools.

The seventh chapter presents a careful analysis of the causes of justification.[145] It reaffirms the transformational character of justification (*non est sola peccatorum remissio, sed et sanctificatio et renovatio interioris hominis*), setting out the causes of justification as follows:

final cause	the glory of God and eternal life
efficient cause	the mercy of God
meritorious cause	the passion of Christ
instrumental cause	the sacrament of baptism
formal cause	the righteousness of God

Although this might appear to be a reversion to the somewhat mechanical theological vocabulary of scholasticism, the decree is merely clarifying the various contributing factors to the justification of humanity in the most convenient manner possible. The most significant statement concerns the formal cause of justification. The assertion that the *single* formal cause of justification (*unica formalis causa*) is 'the righteousness of God, not

---

[143] Cap. 5, *D* 1525.
[144] Cap. 6, *D* 1526. The charge of 'neo-semi-Pelagianism' brought against the decree at this point is really quite unsustainable: Loofs, *Leitfaden zum Studium der Dogmengeschichte*, 668–9. A similar criticism must be levelled at the study of A. T. Jörgenssen, 'Was verstand man in der Reformationszeit unter Pelagianismus?', *ThStK* 83 (1910), 63–82, in which any theology of justification which recognises the necessity of a preparation for justification is improperly (both historically and dogmatically) treated as 'semi-Pelagian'.
[145] Cap. 7, *D* 1528–31.

by which he himself is righteous, but by which he makes us righteous (*iustitia Dei, non qua ipse iustus est, sed qua nos iustos facit*)',[146] represents a deliberate and conscious attempt to exclude the possibility that there exists more than one formal cause – the opinion particularly associated with Seripando during the proceedings on justification. The statement implicitly excludes the possibility that *iustitia imputata* is a contributing cause to human justification.

Perhaps more significantly, the entire medieval debate over whether the formal cause of justification was an intrinsic created habit of grace or the extrinsic denomination of the divine acceptation was circumvented by a reversion to the Augustinian concept of *iustitia Dei*. This does not resolve the medieval debate on this matter one way or the other, and represents an attempt to establish the common basis of both medieval understandings of the matter without using the terminology of the period. The linking of the 'first justification' with the sacrament of baptism continues the common medieval tradition of excluding the possibility of extrasacramental justification, and parallels the subsequent linking of the recovery of justification with the sacrament of penance.

The eighth chapter deals with the concepts of 'to be justified by faith' (*iustificari per fidem*) and 'to be justified freely' (*gratis iustificari*).[147] Both these terms are to be interpreted according to the Catholic tradition; faith is to be seen as the beginning of human salvation, the foundation and root of all justification, without which it is impossible to please God. This gift is given freely (*gratis*) in the sense that none of the things which precede justification (including faith, as well as works) can be said to merit justification:

> We are therefore said to be justified *by faith*, because faith is the beginning of human salvation, the foundation and the root of all justification, without which it is impossible to please God, and to enter into the fellowship of his children; but we are therefore said to be justified *freely*, because none of those things which precede justification – whether faith or works – themselves merit the grace of justification.

Although this statement clearly excludes the possibility that humans may merit justification *de condigno*, it does not – and was not intended to – exclude the possibility that they may merit it *de congruo*. In other words, although the traditional teaching of the Franciscan order (that humanity's disposition towards justification is meritorious *de congruo*) is not explicitly permitted, there was a manifest intention that it should not be excluded either.

---

[146] The reference is to Augustine, *De Trinitate*, XLV.xii.15.   [147] Cap. 8, D 1532.

The ninth chapter deals with the question of the certitude of faith.[148] This question having been the subject of intense debate at Trent, the chapter is worded with some care. *Fiducia* on the part of the believer concerning the mercy of God, the merit of Christ and the efficacy of the sacraments is certainly appropriate; what is inappropriate is the 'mad confidence of the heretics' concerning the individual's justification.

Just as no pious person ought to doubt the mercy of God, the merit of Christ, or the virtue and efficacy of the sacraments, nevertheless everyone, on consideration of themselves and their own weakness and indisposition, should have fear and apprehension concerning their own grace, in that no one can know with a certainty of faith, which cannot be subject to error, that they have obtained the grace of God.[149]

The tenth chapter opens the section of the decree dealing with the second justification, in which humanity increases in righteousness. This second justification is seen as a positive duty placed upon humans by virtue of the first justification. There are clear connections between the Tridentine concept of the second justification and the Reformed concept of sanctification. Whereas in the first justification, grace operates upon humans, in the second, humans co-operate with grace. It is thus both possible and necessary to keep the law of God.[150] The opinion that such good works as are involved in the second justification are sinful is rejected. The Augustinian doctrine of final perseverance is reaffirmed: in this mortal life, no one may know whether he is among the number of the predestined, except through special revelation.[151] Although the sacrament of baptism is linked with the first justification, and that of penance with the restoration of justification, it is significant that there is no specific mention of any of the remaining sacraments in connection with the second justification.

The final three chapters deal with those who have fallen from the grace of justification through mortal sin. Those who are moved by grace may regain the grace of justification through the sacrament of penance, on account of the merit of Christ.[152] It is important to appreciate that it is only grace, and not faith, which is lost by mortal sin; the lapsed individual remains a believer. The final chapter deals with the question of merit, and goes some considerable way towards meeting Protestant criticism of the concept.[153] While insisting upon the biblical principle that good works

[148] Cap. 9, *D* 1533–4.
[149] Cap. 9, *D* 1534. For some of the issues that this statement raises, see Jorissen, 'Einig in der Rechtfertigungslehre'.
[150] Cap. 11, *D* 1536–9.   [151] Cap. 12, *D* 1540. Cf. Cap. 13; D. 1541.
[152] Cap. 14, *D* 1542–3.   [153] Cap. 16, *D* 1545–9.

are rewarded by God, Trent emphasises that merit is a divine gift to humanity, excluding human boasting. Merit remains, however, the result of the free efforts of humans.

Although the grace of Christ precedes and accompanies human efforts, those efforts are real nevertheless. Believers, by their co-operation with grace, are entitled to receive merit and to increase in justification. The individual who perseveres until the end may be said to receive eternal life as a reward, the crowning gift promised by God to those who persevere. The question of the ultimate foundation of merit (*ratio meriti*), a subject of some controversy in the medieval schools, is answered in non-scholastic terms (such as the union of the believer with Christ) that permit the traditional views to be retained.

The thirty-three canons appended to the decree condemn specific heretical opinions, by no means restricted to Protestantism. The specific condemnation of Pelagianism in the opening canons was especially significant, as it represents a much needed magisterial clarification in this area. However, it appears that it is certain caricatures of Protestantism which are actually condemned, rather than Protestantism itself. There seems to have been considerable confusion as a consequence of the different understandings of the *nature* of justification associated with Protestants and Catholics. Canon 11 may be singled out as being of particular importance in this respect:

If anyone says that people are justified, either by the sole imputation of the justice of Christ, or by the sole remission of sins, to the exclusion of the grace and the charity poured forth in their hearts by the Holy Spirit and inherent in them; or even that the grace, whereby we are justified, is only the favour of God: let him be condemned.[154]

It is clear that this condemnation is aimed against a purely extrinsic conception of justification (in the Catholic sense of the term) – in other words, the view that the Christian life may begin and continue without any transformation or inner renewal of the sinner. In fact, the canon does not censure any magisterial Protestant account of *iustificatio hominis*, in that the initial (extrinsic) justification of humans is either understood (as with Melanchthon) to be inextricably linked with their subsequent (intrinsic) sanctification, so that the concepts are notionally distinct, but nothing more; or else both the extrinsic justification and intrinsic sanctification of humanity are understood (as with Calvin) to be contiguous dimensions of the union of the believer with Christ. Underlying this canon appears to be the view that Protestants denied that transformation and renewal

---

[154] Can. 11, *D* 1561.

were of the *esse* of Christian existence, an error primarily due to terminological confusion, but compounded by Luther's frequently intemperate (and occasionally obscure) statements on the matter.

The degree of latitude of interpretation incorporated into the Tridentine decree on justification at points of importance makes it impossible to speak of 'the Tridentine doctrine of justification', as if there were *one such doctrine*. In fact, Trent legitimated a range of theologies as Catholic, and any one of them may reasonably lay claim to be a 'Tridentine doctrine of justification'. Trent may be regarded as endorsing the medieval catholic heritage on justification, while eliminating much of its technical vocabulary, substituting biblical or Augustinian phrases in its place. Trent thus marks a point of transition in our study, in that it denotes the deliberate and systematic rejection of much of the *terminology* of the medieval schools, while retaining the *theology* which it expressed. It is possible to argue that Trent indicates the end of the medieval discussion of justification, in the sense that it established a new framework within which subsequent discussion of the matter was increasingly obliged to proceed.

It will, however, be clear that the degree of latitude of interpretation implicitly endorsed by Trent did more than permit the traditional teaching of the medieval schools to be considered Catholic; it also caused uncertainty concerning the precise interpretation of the decree. The result of this uncertainty may be seen in the immediate post-Tridentine period, in which it transpired that the debate on justification within Catholicism was renewed, rather than settled. It is to this period that we now turn.

4.5   The post-Tridentine debates on justification

The Tridentine decree on justification remains the most significant statement on the matter ever to have been made by a Christian church. The question of its correct interpretation is therefore of considerable importance. In his still influential account of the Tridentine debate on justification, Hans Rückert argued that the final decree, particularly in relation to its statements concerning the meritorious nature of the disposition towards justification, ultimately represented a victory for Thomism.[155] This judgement was not universally accepted in the immediate aftermath of Trent, nor is it accepted today. In the present section, I propose to

---

[155] Rückert, *Die Rechtfertigungslehre auf dem Tridentinischen Konzil*, 185. Cf. Gonzáles Rivas, 'Los teólogos salmantinos y el decreto de la justificación.'

consider the interpretation of the Tridentine statement on the meritorious nature of the disposition towards justification to illustrate the difficulties associated with interpreting the decree, before proceeding to a brief discussion of some issues raised by Baianism, Molinism and Jansenism.

The eighth chapter of the Tridentine decree on justification makes the following statement:[156]

> We are therefore said to be justified *freely*, because none of those things which precede justification – whether faith or works – themselves merit the grace of justification (*nihil eorum, quae iustificationem praecedunt, sive fides, sive opera, ipsam iustificationis gratiam promeretur*).

As noted earlier, there was a substantial body of opinion within the Franciscan order which held that humanity could merit justification *de congruo*. Is this opinion excluded by this statement?

An emphatically negative answer to this question was given in the present century by Heiko A. Oberman, who drew attention to the use of the somewhat unusual verb *promereri* in the place of the more usual *mereri* in the above statement.[157] Oberman suggests that a contrast between *mereri* and *promereri* had become well established within Catholicism by the time of the Council of Trent, the latter meaning 'merit in the full sense of the term'. He thus argued that, during the Tridentine proceedings on justification, the verb *mereri* was associated with *meritum de congruo*, and *promereri* with the weaker sense of merit associated with the concept of *meritum de condigno*. The statement cited above should therefore be interpreted as follows: none of the acts which precede justification, whether faith or works, merit the grace of justification *de condigno*. On this reading of the text, the possibility of a disposition towards justification which is meritorious *de congruo* is thus not excluded by the decree.

This highly problematic distinction between *promereri* and *mereri* has been rejected by subsequent commentators. Rückert drew attention to the fact that the Council of Trent was anxious to break away from the vocabulary of medieval theology, including such terms as *meritum de congruo* and *meritum de condigno*.[158] Phrases such as *mereri ex debitum* or *proprie et vere mereri* were used extensively in lieu of *mereri de condigno*. Oberman suggests that *promereri* was understood by the Tridentine

---

[156] Cap. 8, *D* 1532.

[157] Oberman, 'Das tridentinische Rechtfertigungsdekret'. The verb *promereri* also occurs at one additional point in the decree itself (cap. 16, *D* 1546: 'consequendam vere promeruisse censeantur'), and in canon 2 (*D* 1552: 'facilius homo iustus vivere ac vitam aeternam promereri possit'). The qualification of *promereri* with *vere* in chapter 16 ought itself to be sufficient to raise doubts concerning Oberman's thesis.

[158] Rückert, 'Promereri'.

fathers to mean nothing more and nothing less than *proprie et vere mereri*, and that their use of this term in place of the more usual *mereri* was intended to emphasise this hardening in meaning. This suggestion rests upon inadequate documentary evidence. There are no grounds for supporting the belief that such a distinction was current in the later medieval period, or that it was recognised or employed by those present at Trent. Indeed, the supplementation of *promereri* with *vere* at points during the Tridentine proceedings suggests that the verbs *mereri* and *promereri* were regarded as synonymous.[159] Elsewhere, ample evidence is to be had that the terms were not distinguished in the manner Oberman suggests.[160] Oberman himself concedes the critically important point that Domingo de Soto does not distinguish the two terms.[161] Furthermore, his suggestion that this distinction is made by Andrés de Vega has now been shown to be untenable.[162]

In what follows, we shall consider several interpretations of the Tridentine decree on justification dating from the period, including two from the pens of influential theologians present during the Tridentine debates. In his 1547 *de natura et gratia*, the Dominican theologian Domingo de Soto argued that Trent denied that the disposition of humans towards justification was meritorious *de congruo*. Conceding the necessity of some kind of disposition towards justification,[163] Soto argues that humans cannot dispose themselves towards grace without the *auxilium speciale Dei*.[164] Although a purely natural disposition towards justification is conceivable, Soto insists that this is merely *dispositio impropria seu remota*.[165] Merit, in any sense of the term, prior to justification is rigorously excluded, even in its weaker form of merit *de congruo*.[166] Soto thus understands Trent to have explicitly rejected the doctrine of a congruously meritorious disposition towards justification. In this, he was followed by the English Catholic émigré Thomas Stapleton, who rejected the concept of congruous merit as long since discredited.[167] The Tridentine

---

[159] See the proceedings of 2 January 1547, CT 5.753.17–20; and those of 9 January 1547, CT 5.777.16–19.

[160] CT 5.737.15–16, 20–1.

[161] Oberman, 'Das tridentinische Rechtfertigungsdekret', 278–9.

[162] See Heynck, 'Die Bedeutung von "mereri" und "promereri" bei dem Konzilstheologen Andreas de Vega O.F.M.'.

[163] *De natura et gratia*, ii.1, fol. 96r.   [164] *De natura et gratia*, ii.3, fol. 102r.

[165] *De natura et gratia*, ii.3, fol. 101r–v.

[166] *De natura et gratia*, ii.4, fol. 109r–111v. Soto's views on congruous merit prior to justification were defended by Suárez (although the latter was reluctant to concede any form of disposition, however remote, towards justification); *De gratia*, vii.vii.9; *Opera* 9.339–42.

[167] *De universa iustificationis doctrina*, viii.16, *Opera omnia* 2.265B. See further Seybold, *Glaube und Rechtfertigung bei Thomas Stapleton*.

decree is unequivocal on this matter, according to Stapleton; merit can exist only in the case of the regenerate.[168]

A very different interpretation of the Tridentine decree is associated with the Franciscan Andrés de Vega. Although Vega emphatically denied that people could merit prevenient grace,[169] it is clear that he understands this to refer to merit *de condigno*.[170] He thus expounds the eighth chapter of the Tridentine decree as follows:

> And this the fathers affirmed when they stated that neither faith 'nor any good works preceding justification merit (*promereri*) this grace of justification'. No sinner is justified as a matter of debt, or as a matter of rigorous justice, or on account of the condignity of his works; but all who are justified are justified freely by God in his grace and mercy, without any merit or condignity of their works.[171]

It is clear that Vega understands Trent to have excluded the opinion that humans can make a claim on God *ex debito* or *ex rigore iustitiae* – but not that they may rely upon the divine benevolence and generosity. 'It is therefore obvious that the words of our council assert nothing contrary to merit *ex congruo*.'[172] Vega understands the terms *meritum* and *mereri* to refer solely to merit in its strictest sense but does not extend their use to *congruous* merit. In other words, the Tridentine rejection of merit prior to justification is merely a rejection of the Pelagian doctrine of justification *ex meritis* – that is, justification on the basis of condign merit. The Franciscan doctrine of a congruously meritorious disposition towards justification is thus unaffected by the Tridentine statements, whether these employ the verb *promereri* or *mereri* – Vega understands *both* to mean 'merit in the strict and proper sense of the term'.

In fact, there are excellent reasons for suggesting that the Tridentine fathers intended this latitude of interpretation. The council was concerned to exclude the possibility that humans could merit – in the strict sense of the word – their own justification. This teaching was, in their view, clearly Pelagian, and hence unacceptable. Yet the Council of Trent was not concerned with resolving the long-standing debate within the Catholic schools of theology on whether the immediate disposition towards justification could be deemed meritorious in a weaker sense of the term. The presence of so large a contingent of Franciscan theologians at Trent, and particularly the prominent position which

---

[168] See the references collected by Seybold, *Glaube und Rechtfertigung bei Thomas Stapleton*, 89 n. 189.
[169] *De iustificatione doctrina universa*, vi.10, fol. 86.
[170] *De iustificatione doctrina universa*, vii.8, fol. 137.
[171] *De iustificatione doctrina universa*, viii.10, fol. 192.
[172] *De iustificatione doctrina universa*, viii.10, fol. 194.

they assumed during the proceedings on justification, made it improbable that the traditional teaching of their own order would be censured. In effect, both the Thomist and the Franciscan (whether inclined to accept Bonaventure or Scotus as mentor) could claim that Trent condoned their characteristic views on this matter.

The success enjoyed by early Protestant catechisms, such as Luther's *Kleiner Catechismus* of 1529, made a Catholic catechetical response imperative. Two such unofficial responses appeared soon after the Tridentine decree on justification. Peter Canisius produced his *Catechismus Major* in 1555,[173] while his work in Germany was paralleled by that of Edmund Augerius in France. Work on an official catechetical response to the Reformers began in 1547, but does not appear to have been taken seriously until 1563 – the year which saw both the closure of the Council of Trent and the publication of the influential Reformed *Heidelberg Catechism*.

The definitive catechism of the Catholic church, the *Catechismus Romanus*, appeared in October 1566, with a subtitle (*Catechismus ex decreta Tridentini*) clearly implying that it provided an exposition of the Tridentine decrees. In fact, however, the work is an exposition of the creed, the sacraments, the decalogue and the Lord's Prayer, rather than of the Council of Trent. It is, however, possible to determine the work's teaching on justification by correlating its various elements as they are found at sundry points in its course.[174] Grace always precedes, accompanies and follows the works of humans, and merit is impossible apart from grace.[175] The catechism makes no distinction between condign and congruous merit, however, and its statements on merit are thus open to precisely the same latitude of interpretation as the Tridentine decree itself; once more, this appears to be deliberate.

The Council of Trent did not produce a definitive and exhaustive account of the Catholic doctrine of justification, and must be regarded as a response to past errors rather than as an anticipation of those of the future. In particular, the council was content to affirm the reality of the human free will and the universal necessity of grace, without specifying the precise manner in which these notions might be reconciled. As with the council's teaching on congruous merit, it seems that a certain degree of latitude of interpretation was envisaged by the Tridentine fathers in regard to their statements on these matters. A general feature

---

[173] *Summa doctrina Christianae* (Vienna, 1555); a shorter version appeared the following year.

[174] See G. Bellinger, *Der Catechismus Romanus und die Reformation*, Paderborn: Bonifacius-Druckerei, 1958, 95–8. Bellinger's suggestion (97–8) that the catechism teaches the necessity of a disposition for justification, based on faith and penitence, does not appear to be borne out by the evidence he assembles.

[175] *Catechismus Romanus*, II.v.68, Leipzig: Tauchnitz, 1852, 247.

of the post-Tridentine period was its patristic positivism, particularly the renewed interest in the writings of Augustine of Hippo. That the reality of the human *liberum arbitrium* and the necessity of divine grace had been reconciled by Augustine was generally accepted – but the African bishop had many post-Tridentine interpreters, eventually forcing the church to determine which represented the closest approximation to his thought.

The first major post-Tridentine controversy to arise concerning the doctrine of justification was Baianism, characterised by its rejection of *supernaturale quoad essentiam*, and the cognate distinction between 'natural' and 'supernatural'.[176] The main features of Baius' theology may be deduced from his basic assertion that humans were created *rectus* by God, and that this defines their natural state.[177] Abandoning the concept of *natura pura* (whose characteristics, particularly concerning the grace with which it had been endowed, had been the subject of a long-standing debate between the Dominican and Franciscan schools), Baius lays down three principles upon the basis of which the characteristics and qualities of the natural state of humanity may be established.[178] First, the quality involved must not compromise the exigencies of human nature. Second, any quality which is necessarily implicated in the specific elements of human nature must be considered as 'natural' to humanity. Third, a quality must be considered 'natural' to humans when their nature requires it as its necessary complement, so that without it their nature suffers privative evil. Thus Adam's innocence was not a supernatural gift, but the essential complement of his human nature. These principles may be illustrated with reference to Baius' assertion that Adam was given the Holy Spirit at his creation.

As it is part of the nature of human beings that they should be alive, Baius argues that they are necessarily endowed with whatever is necessary to life – and includes the Holy Spirit among such endowments on basic theological presuppositions. The absence of the Holy Spirit would have resulted in a privation, and hence in evil. Furthermore, those powers and faculties which lead to the completion of nature must, according to Baius, be considered as part of nature itself. The subjection of the lower nature of humans to their higher spiritual nature, and of the *totus homo* to God, is immediately dependent upon the inhabitation of the Holy Spirit in humans *ex natura rei*. As it is unthinkable that God would deny to Adam

---

[176] On this, see Abercrombie, *The Origins of Jansenism*, 87–93, 137–42. On the more specifically theological issues, see Alfaro, 'Sobrenatural y pecado original en Bayo'; Kaiser, *Natur und Gnade im Urstand*; H. de Lubac, *Augustinisme et théologie moderne*, Paris: Aubier, 1965, 15–48.

[177] *De prima hominis iustitia*, 1, *Opera*, 49.

[178] *De prima hominis iustitia*, 9, *Opera*, 62–3. Cf. Kaiser, *Natur und Gnade im Urstand*, 69–157.

anything essential to the completion of his being, it may be concluded that he was endowed with the Holy Spirit at creation.

This approach to the 'natural' state of humans has a number of important consequences. Adam's perseverance would have resulted in his receiving beatitude as a reward; there is no need to involve divine grace in this matter, because people have certain rights over God *ex natura rei*. Thus 'natural' humanity receives eternal life as a reward, not as a gift. 'Natural' humanity has certain rights before God; the divine assistance which humans require must be considered to arise from an obligation on God's part, rather than from his generosity, in that this assistance must be regarded as an integral aspect of their 'natural' state. It is instructive to compare Augustine and Baius on this point. Both agree that humans are created in such a manner as to require divine assistance, and reject the possibility that they may attain their destiny unaided, by virtue of their own powers and abilities. Augustine, however, affirms that this divine assistance is bestowed gratuitously, in order that they may obtain their *supernatural* destiny (although Augustine does not use this precise term), where Baius insists that God is under an obligation to bestow such assistance, in order that humans may attain their *natural* state. The comparison with Pelagius is also instructive. Where Pelagius asserted the total autonomy of human nature, Baius simultaneously asserted its *impotence apart from grace* and the *divine obligation to bestow grace as and when required*. Where Pelagius affirms human independence of God, Baius affirms humans' total dependence upon God, and thus their entitlement – in the manner of litigants rather than of beggars – to demand their due assistance from God.

Baius' definition of Adam's original state carries with it the implication that Adam possessed nothing other than that which was essential to his nature, so that the deprivation of any quality of this state could only result in its vitiation. As a consequence of the Fall, humanity now exists in an 'unnatural' state, in that its innocence is destroyed through the privation of essential natural qualities, to be replaced with 'viciousness'. Original sin is defined in terms of a *habitus concupiscentiae*, which prevents humans from breaking free from sin unaided. Indeed, Baius' radical dichotomy between *concupiscentia* and *caritas* leads to his asserting that all works prior to justification are sinful – far exceeding the more cautious statements of Augustine on this point, and tending to approach the more radical views of the Reformers.

The problem of justification, as stated by Baius, thus comes to concern the means by which the transition from a state of concupiscence to a state of charity may be effected. However, it must be emphasised that justification is conceived in purely natural terms; it is essentially a restoration of the state of innocence and natural faculties by which humans are enabled to lead a moral existence. It is this principle which underlies the proposition, subsequently condemned by Pius V, that the *ratio meriti* is not the Holy Spirit, but obedience to the law.[179]

It is clear that Baius' theology of justification is radically different from that of Augustine, despite his attempt to recover the latter's views from the adumbrations of the medieval period. This departure from Augustine appears to arise from the rejection of the concept of *supernaturale quoad essentiam*, from which most of Baius' views ultimately derive. Although Augustine does not employ the *term* 'supernatural', this cannot be taken as an indication that the *concept* is not implicitly present in his theology of justification. The medieval development of Augustine's theology of grace may be regarded as making this concept explicit within, rather than imposing it as an alien concept upon, this theology. By rejecting the concept of the supernatural altogether, Baius inevitably reduced Augustine's theology to pure naturalism.

Further controversy developed between the Dominican and Jesuit orders in Spain, such as the acrimonious Valladolid confrontation of 1582 between Prudentius Montemayor and Domingo Báñez. This controversy entered a new phase with the publication of Luis de Molina's *Concordia* in 1588.[180] This work takes the form of a commentary upon certain sections of Thomas Aquinas' *Summa Theologiae*, and reconciles human freedom and grace by denying the efficacy of *gratia ab intrinseco*, and substituting the efficacy of grace in the divine foreknowledge *de scientia media* of human co-operation with the gift of grace.

Rejecting Thomas Aquinas' teaching on the causal relation of grace and free will,[181] Molina develops a theory of the relation between primary and secondary causes which has important consequences for his discussion of the concord between grace and the human free will in justification. God foreknows all that comes to pass, freely and contingently, through secondary causes.[182] This foreknowledge compromises neither the contingency of the present order of things nor the autonomy of the human free will. Molina defines the knowledge of the behaviour of every

<hr/>

[179] Proposition 13, *Opera*, 51; cf. *D* 1913: 'Opera bona, a filiis adoptionis facta, non accipiunt rationem meriti ex eo, quod fiunt per spiritum adoptionis inhabitantem corda filiorum Dei, sed tantum ex eo, quod sunt conformia legi, quodque per ea praestatur oboedientia legi.'

[180] The best study remains G. Schneemann, *Die Entstehung und Entwickelung der thomistisch-molinistischen Kontroverse*, 2 vols., Freiburg: Herder, 1879–80. More recently, see F. Stegmüller, *Geschichte des Molinismus*, Münster: Aschendorff, 1935.

[181] As stated in *Summa Theologiae*, Ia q. 105 a. 5; Molina, *Concordia liberi arbitrii cum gratiae donis*, Lisbon, 1588, disp. 26; 167–71.

[182] *Concordia*, disp. 47; 298.

autonomous secondary cause in all circumstances as *scientia media*.[183] This *scientia media* relates to the hypothetical and the contingent – which includes the decisions of an individual free will under a given set of circumstances.

God thus knows infallibly how each individual will respond to the grace that is offered to him or her, without compromising the autonomy of that individual. Molina uses this concept of the *scientia media* to reconcile the two propositions:

God decreed from all eternity that Paul should go to Macedonia.
Paul went to Macedonia of his own free will.

God knew infallibly, by his *scientia media*, that if Paul went to Troas, and thence received a call to go to Macedonia, he would obey this call. Therefore, Molina argues, God created the world with such circumstances that Paul would find himself in Troas at an opportune moment, and thence proceed to Macedonia – thus maintaining both the divine sovereignty and human freedom. The efficacy of grace is thus maintained, but is understood to arise on account of something extrinsic to grace (the consent of the human will) rather than the intrinsic nature of grace itself.[184]

This view was sharply attacked by Spanish Thomists, particularly Báñez, who upheld the notion of intrinsically efficacious grace. In contrast to sufficient grace, which confers upon humans a capacity to act, efficacious grace moves human will to action. Báñez and his supporters were particularly critical of Molina's assertion that God foreknew something because it would happen contingently through free will, and his rejection of the opinion that something happened on account of the divine foreknowledge.[185] The doctrine of *scientia media* was thus rejected in favour of the Báñezian *praemotio physica*. It is interesting to note that the term 'semi-Pelagian' was introduced during the course of this dispute by the

---

[183] *Concordia*, disp. 50; 329–30. Molina distinguishes this *scientia media* from *scientia visionis* (by which God knows realities) and *scientia simplicis intelligentiae* (by which God contemplates the realm of the unreal). The objects apprehended by the *scientia media* thus fall between the categories of the real and unreal – that is, *futurabilia*, which exist only if certain preconditions are realised.

[184] Molinism is paralleled at this point by Congruism, particularly associated with Roberto Bellarmine and Francisco de Suárez: see F. Stegmüller, *Zur Gnadenlehre des jungen Suárez*, Freiburg: Verlagsbuchhandlung, 1933. This teaching should be distinguished from that of Gabriel Vásquez; see J. A. de Aldama, 'Un parecer inédito del P. Gabriel Vásquez sobre la doctrina agustiniana de la gracia eficaz', *EE* 23 (1949), 515–20.

[185] Báñez, *Apologia*, i.xxiii.1; in V. Beltrán de Heredia, *Domingo Báñez y las controversias sobre la gracia: Textos y documentos* Madrid: Consejo Superior de Investigaciones Científicas, Instituto Francisco Suárez, 1968, 210–11.

followers of Báñez to describe the teachings of their Molinist opponents. The controversy between Jesuits and Dominicans at Valladolid in 1594 eventually became so heated that the papal nuncio at Madrid was obliged to impose silence upon the disputing parties, and referred the matter to Rome for resolution. A commission was appointed in November 1597 to consider the matter.

The celebrated *Congregatio de auxiliis* began at Rome in 1598, and continued, without great enthusiam, over two pontificates until 1607.[186] Although the commission was initially in favour of censuring Molinism, pressure from representatives of both the King of Spain and the Society of Jesus led to a widening of the commission's membership and terms of reference, and the eventual declaration on 5 September 1607 that the Báñezian teaching was not Calvinist, nor the Molinist Pelagian. The Jesuit and Dominican orders were permitted to defend their own teachings on the matter, but were forbidden to criticise each other, pending a final settlement of the question.[187] No definitive settlement was ever proposed, and there the matter has rested.

The inconvenience of this soteriological stalemate was, however, overshadowed by the rise of Jansenism and the political threat which this posed to the papal influence in France.[188] Jansen's *Augustinus*, published posthumously in 1640, shows strong affinities with Baianism, particularly in its rejection of the concept of 'pure nature', and the corresponding distinction between 'nature' and 'supernature'. Jansen defines the grace conferred upon Adam at his creation as *adiutorium sine quo non*, which he distinguishes from *adiutorium quo*.[189] The former, bestowed upon Adam at his creation, is the divine grace without which he could do nothing. Just as human eyes require illumination if they are to function correctly, so human *liberum arbitrium* requires *adiutorium sine quo non* before it too can function correctly. This *adiutorium* is thus an essential part of the original nature of humans.[190]

The Fall robbed humans of *adiutorium sine quo non*, with a resulting radical vitiation of their nature. However, on account of the profound effects

---

[186] The classic account of the congregation remains J. H. Serry, *Historia congregationum de auxiliis divinae gratiae*, Antwerp, 1709.

[187] D 1997.

[188] For the history of the controversy, see L. Ceyssens, *Sources relatives aux débuts du jansénisme et de l'antijansénisme 1640–1643*, Louvain: Bibliothèque de l'Université, 1957; Abercrombie, *The Origins of Jansenism. Augustinus* is divided into three parts, and reference will be made to the part by name rather than by number. The edition used in the present study is that published at Paris in 1641. For a convenient synopsis of the work in English, see Abercrombie, *The Origins of Jansenism*, 126–53.

[189] *De gratia primi hominis*, 10–12; 51A–59A.

[190] Despite terminological differences, Jansen's *adiutorium sine quo non* appears to correspond broadly to the general medieval concept of *concursus generalis*.

of the Fall on their faculties, which are now reduced from the natural to the subnatural level, humans now require more than light to restore their vision; they require a cure for their blindness.

Jansen thus rejects the Molinist concept of *gratia sufficiens* as an absurdity; on account of the radically vitiated nature of humanity arising from the Fall, such grace would be sufficient only if it actually and effectually cured the will of humans, thereby restoring their health and permitting them to do good. Such grace was adequate in the case of Adam's natural state – but in the case of fallen humanity, healing grace (*gratia sanans*) was required in the form of *adiutorium quo*.[191] Jansen then proceeds to demonstrate that *gratia sanans* is necessary, efficacious and non-universal.[192]

The second and third points are of particular importance. Jansen argues that Augustine never uses the term 'grace' unless he intends it to mean 'efficacious grace': if grace is given, the performance of the work for which it was given necessarily follows; if no such grace is given, no corresponding work results. Jansen's rejection of the universality of grace leads to his criticism of certain accounts of the effects of Christ's death, particularly those which suggested that Christ died for all. According to Jansen, Augustine never concedes that Christ died for all humankind without exception, but only for those who benefited by his death.[193] When Christ is said in certain scriptural passages to have died for all, this should be understood to mean that he died for all *types* of people (such as kings and subjects, nobles and peasants; or people of all nations or languages).[194] Augustine does not speak of Christ as being a redemption for all people, unless this is interpreted as meaning all *the faithful*. In all the writings of Augustine, Jansen stated that he found no reference to Christ dying for the sins of those unbelievers who remain in unbelief.[195] Although Christ's work is sufficient for all, it is efficacious only for some. Jansen thus rejects the opinion that God must confer his grace upon the individual who does *quod in se est*, claiming the support of Augustine for this conclusion.[196]

It was clear, in the light of the rise of Jansenism, that the Tridentine decree on justification required supplementation. On 31 May 1653, Innocent X condemned five Jansenist propositions in the bull *Cum*

---

[191] *De gratia Christi salvatoris*, ii.5; 36bE.   [192] *De gratia Christi salvatoris*, ii–iii.
[193] *De gratia Christi salvatoris*, iii.20; 161bc-D; 161bE–162aA.
[194] *De gratia Christi salvatoris*, iii.20; 162aE.
[195] *De gratia Christi salvatoris*, iii.20; 162bD.
[196] This interpretation of Augustine goes back to Baius, and had been challenged by Suárez: Suárez, *De gratia*, I.xxi.l; *Opera*, 1.468–9.

occasione.[197] This was followed by more extensive condemnation of Jansenist positions (as stated by Pasquier Quesnel) in the 1713 papal constitution *Unigenitus filius Dei.*[198] The strongly political overtones to the condemnation of Jansenism, particularly evident in the association of the movement with Gallicanism,[199] lend weight to the suggestion that *Unigenitus* should be seen as a political, rather than a theological, document.

The post-Tridentine debates on justification ended with the magisterial toleration of the various forms of Thomism and Molinism, and the rejection of Jansenism and Baianism. Although individual Catholic theologians have subsequently written extensively on the question of justification, the broad outlines of the Catholic teaching on the matter may be regarded as having been finally fixed by 1713.

Two points may be noted in closing this chapter. First, it may be emphasised that, despite the considerable degree of convergence evident at points between Jansenism and Protestantism, the entire post-Tridentine Catholic tradition (including those otherwise considered heterodox, such as Baianists and Jansenists) continued to regard justification as a process in which humanity was made righteous, involving the actualisation rather than the imputation of righteousness. The Protestant conception of justification was not adopted even by those who came closest to Protestant understandings of the mode in which justification came about. The continuity within the western tradition concerning the nature of justification was upheld by its post-Tridentine representatives on all sides of the debates.

Second, the very term 'justification' itself appears to have been gradually marginalised, if not completely eliminated, from the homiletical and catechetical literature of Catholicism. Although the term is employed extensively in Catholic polemical works of the sixteenth century, and may still be encountered in sermons of the seventeenth,[200] it seems that

---

[197] *D* 2001–7. For the background, see L. Ceyssens, *La Première Bulle contre Jansénius: sources relatives à son histoire* (1644–53), 2 vols., Rome: Institut historique belge de Rome, 1961–2.

[198] *D* 2400–502. See further J. D. Thomas, *La Querelle de l'Unigenitus*, Paris: Presses universitaires de France, 1950; J. A. G. Tans, *Pasquier Quesnel et les Pays-Bas: correspondance, publiée avec introduction et annotations*, Groningen: Wolters, 1960.

[199] V. Martin, *Les Origines du Gallicanisme*, 2 vols., Paris: Bloud & Gay, 1939; M. Vaussard, *Jansénisme et Gallicanisme aux origines religieuses du Risorgimento*, Paris: Letouzey & Ané, 1959.

[200] A study of sermons preached in seventeenth-century Spain on the theme of justification indicates the considerable difficulties encountered in explaining the council's pronouncements on the matter to the laity; see H. D. Smith, *Preaching in the Spanish Golden Age: A Study in Some Preachers of the Reign of Philip III*, Oxford: Oxford University Press, 1978, especially 140–5.

the associations of the term led to an increased reluctance to employ it from the late seventeenth century onwards – despite the extensive use of the concept by the Council of Trent. The dating of this elimination suggests that it may have been a reaction to internal developments within Catholicism, rather than to external threats – in other words, that it arose in response to Jansenism, rather than in reaction to Protestantism.

The culmination of this trend can be seen in the *Catechism of the Catholic Church* (1992), one of the most significant magisterial publications of the church. In 1985, an extraordinary Synod of Bishops gathered in Rome to celebrate the twentieth anniversary of the Second Vatican Council, and find ways to develop its work. There was considerable pressure for the production of a new vernacular catechism reflecting the needs of the church in the late twentieth century. The synod noted that

There were many who expressed the wish that a catechism or a compendium of all Catholic doctrine regarding both faith and morals be prepared so that it could serve as a kind of point of reference for catechisms or compendia prepared in different regions. The presentation of doctrine should be biblical and liturgical. It is to embody a sound doctrine applied to the present life of Christians.

The *Catechism of the Catholic Church* was the direct result of this wish. The work was published in 1992, and soon established itself as a major teaching resource. The process by which the catechism was produced was lengthy, reflecting the many issues which its compilers had to face. John Paul II appointed an *ad hoc* commission to undertake the work on 15 November 1986. It was not until 14 February, 1992 that it concluded its work. The resulting catechism was accepted by the Pope on 25 June of the same year.

The two features of modern Catholic discussion of justification we have just described are absolutely characteristic of this work. On the relatively few occasions where any reference is made to justification, it is defined in factitive, transformational terms.[201] Justification is 'not only the remission of sins, but also the sanctification and renewal of the interior man'; it is the 'acceptance of God's righteousness through faith in Jesus Christ', so that 'faith, hope, and charity are poured into our hearts'. Although the catechism continues to speak of grace in traditional terms – for example, its definition of sanctifying grace as 'an habitual gift, a stable and supernatural disposition that perfects the soul itself to enable it to live with God'[202] – more personalist ways of conceiving grace, such as those typical of early Lutheranism, are also acknowledged and affirmed. 'Grace is *favour*, the free and undeserved help that God gives us to respond

[201] *Catechism of the Catholic Church*, articles 1987–1995.
[202] *Catechism of the Catholic Church*, article 2000.

to his call to become children of God, adoptive sons, partakers of the divine nature and of eternal life.'[203]

Yet perhaps the most striking thing about the catechism's discussion of justification is the remarkable lack of attention that is paid to the concept, the term, and the history of the debate within Christianity over the matter, especially during the sixteenth century. The question of how individuals are reconciled to God is framed primarily in terms other than justification.

4.6   Conclusion

The material presented in this chapter has concerned the Catholic church's response to the theological agenda of the Reformation in formulating its distinctive doctrines of justification. The debates of that era continue to be a significant issue in contemporary Christianity, as the agenda of ecumenical dialogues reminds us. Yet although Lutheranism, Calvinism, the Council of Trent and Pietism entertained significantly different understandings of how justification came about, certain shared assumptions remained deeply embedded within their debates – such as that humanity was alienated from God, and required reconciliation to God to achieve its true potential. Although movements such as Socinianism called such assumptions into question, these criticisms were generally seen as peripheral. All that, however, would change.

In the following chapter, we shall explore how the rise of the Enlightenment called into question many of the most fundamental aspects of the Christian doctrine of justification, forcing a radical new agenda upon the churches. No longer was justification a matter for dispute between Christian groups; it was a matter of debate between Christianity and a secular culture which was increasingly of the view that humanity did not require reconciliation to anything or anyone, for any reason.

---

[203] *Catechism of the Catholic Church*, article 1996.

5   The modern period

Practically every period in human history since the Italian Renaissance may lay claim to having initiated the 'modern' period in some way, and to some extent. For instance, it is often argued that Renaissance Italy laid the foundations of modern political theory,[1] marking the transition from the medieval to the 'modern' understanding of this particular matter. The question thus arises: when may the transition to the 'modern' understanding of the theology of justification be deemed to have taken place?

To answer this question, we need to identify the defining themes of the modern era, an enterprise which is not without its difficulties. Nevertheless, there can be little doubt that one of the most distinctive themes of the modern era is its shift from a fundamentally theocentric to an anthropocentric frame of reference, defined by a new emphasis upon human autonomy, in relation to both revelation and salvation.[2] As Jeffrey Stout notes, 'modern thought was born in a crisis of authority, took shape in flight from authority, and aspired from the start to autonomy from all traditional influence whatsoever'.[3] This desire for intellectual and political emancipation was often linked with the mythical figure of Prometheus, who came to be seen as a symbol of liberation in European literature.[4] Prometheus was now unbound, and humanity poised to enter a new era of autonomy and progress – independent of God.

[1] See especially Q. Skinner, *The Foundations of Modern Political Thought*, Cambridge: Cambridge University Press, 1978; J. F. Rundell, *Origins of Modernity: The Origins of Modern Social Theory from Kant to Hegel to Marx*, Madison: University of Wisconsin Press, 1987; S. A. McKnight, *Sacralizing the Secular: The Renaissance Origins of Modernity*, Baton Rouge: Louisiana State University Press, 1989.
[2] For the importance of this theme in modern theology, particularly in relation to Barth, see T. Gundlach, *Selbstbegrenzung Gottes und die Autonomie des Menschen*, Frankfurt: Peter Lang, 1992.
[3] J. Stout, *The Flight from Authority: Religion, Morality and the Quest for Autonomy*, Notre Dame: University of Notre Dame Press, 1981, 2–3.
[4] On the literary significance of Prometheus, see R. Trousson, *Le Thème de Prométhée dans la littérature européenne*, Geneva: Droz, 1976; L. M. Lewis, *The Promethean Politics of Milton, Blake and Shelley*, London: University of Missouri Press, 1992.

This radical shift can be seen as having two important implications. First, the doctrine of justification – traditionally regarded as addressing the question of how humanity may establish a transcendent dimension to existence through relating to the divine – is to a greater or lesser extent subverted by the Enlightenment's emphasis upon self-actualisation as the goal of human existence. This has led, both directly and indirectly, to a growing perception that the traditional Christian soteriological agenda is implausible for modernity. Perhaps the most visible sign of this was anxiety within Lutheran circles in the second half of the twentieth century as to whether Luther's celebrated quest for a gracious God was relevant to modern culture.[5]

Secondly, classic formulations of the doctrine of justification took the sinfulness of humanity as a 'given'. The Enlightenment emphasis upon the autonomy of humanity called this into question, often suggesting that notions such as 'original sin' were irrational, ecclesiastically contrived, and designed to enslave humanity to certain patterns of belief and behaviour.[6] With the advent of modernity, such arbitrary and oppressive ideas could be swept to one side as outmoded superstition, and replaced by more enlightened approaches to human nature. Far from running a soteriological deficit, humanity was in full possession of whatever rational resources were necessary for self-fulfilment and self-legitimation.

It is certainly true that some have argued that the modern discussion of the question originates from the Protestant Reformation.[7] Nevertheless, it will be clear from the analysis thus far that the Protestant Reformers discussed the question of the justification of humans *coram Deo* within the same general theological framework as their medieval counterparts, and also that there existed a substantial number of uncontroverted presuppositions relating to the doctrine – such as the presupposition of the necessity of the reconciliation of humanity to God, traditionally expressed in the dogma of original sin. The growing recognition of the medieval character of the Reformation in general must be extended to include its theologies of justification. The theocentricity underlying Luther's so-called 'Copernican Revolution' was not an innovation,[8] but was a well-established feature of certain schools of thought in the late medieval period, and cannot be considered to represent a permanent universal alteration in

---

[5] A good example is E. Leppin, 'Luthers Frage nach dem gnädigen Gott – heute', *ZThK* 61 (1964), 89–102.

[6] C. A. Holbrook, 'Original Sin and the Enlightenment', in R. E. Cushman (ed.), *Heritage of Christian Thought*, New York: Harper & Row, 1965, 142–65. For the critique of the doctrine of original sin associated with the French Enlightenment, see Ernst Cassirer, *The Philosophy of the Enlightenment*, Boston: Beacon Press, 1960, 137–60.

[7] Gerhard Ebeling, 'Luther und der Anbruch der Neuzeit', *ZThK* 69 (1972), 185–213.

[8] *Contra* Althaus, 'Gottes Gottheit als Sinn der Rechtfertigungslehre Luthers'.

theological outlook which parallels that attending the recognition of the heliocentricity of the solar system. The rise of anthropocentric theologies of justification within both the Lutheran and Reformed traditions in the late seventeenth century, apparently to attain a dominant position in the eighteenth and nineteenth centuries, effectively calls into question the suggestion that Luther's theocentricity can be deemed quintessentially 'modern'.

If there is a 'modern' period in the development of the doctrine of justification, that period must be regarded as having been initiated by the Enlightenment in England, France and Germany in the eighteenth century. It was this movement which called into question the presuppositions (such as the dogma of original sin) upon which theologies of justification, whether Protestant or Catholic, had until then been based, and which dictated the means by which such presuppositions might be defended. We therefore begin our discussion of the 'modern period' with an analysis of the significance of the Enlightenment for the development of the doctrine.

5.1   The Enlightenment critique of orthodox doctrines of justification

The origins of the Enlightenment critique of orthodox doctrines of justification may be located in the new emphasis upon the autonomy of humans as moral agents so characteristic of the movement. The new optimism concerning the capacity of the natural human faculties to understand and master the world led to suspicion of those moral and religious systems which called into question the autonomy of humans. The particular hostility demonstrated by the theologians and philosophers of the Enlightenment towards the orthodox dogma of original sin was ultimately a rejection of the implied heteronomous conditioning and moral inadequacy of the individual. In that an orthodox theology of justification – whether Lutheran, Reformed or Catholic – presupposed the essential natural alienation of individuals from God (in other words, that individuals enter the world already alienated from God, rather than that they become alienated from God through their subsequent actions), it will be evident that a serious challenge was posed to such theologies by the rise of the moral optimism and rationalism of the Enlightenment. In the present section, we are particularly concerned with the critique of orthodox Protestant theologies of justification associated initially with English Deism, and subsequently with the German *Aufklärung*.

The founder of English Deism is usually, although incorrectly, considered to be Edward Herbert, Lord Cherbury.[9] Herbert's influential treatise *De veritate religionis* (1624) set out the idea of a religious aspect to human nature, informed by a rational awareness of the divine presence and nature. John Toland's *Christianity not Mysterious* rejects the view that human reason is corrupted through original sin to such an extent that it is unable to recognise the truths of the gospel.[10] Similarly, John Locke (upon whom Toland is clearly dependent) earlier rejected the idea of original sin as unworthy of God.[11] The person who is totally obedient to God is the person who attains eternal life. Locke, however, concedes the weakness of human nature, and permits any deficiencies in human obedience to the law of God to be supplemented:

> The rule therefore, of right, is the same that ever it was; the obligation to observe it is also the same: the difference between the law of works, and the law of faith, is only this: that the law of works makes no allowance for failing on any occasion . . . But by the law of faith, faith is allowed to supply the defect of full obedience: and so the believers are admitted to life and immortality, as if they were righteous.[12]

Although he defines the *theological* element of faith to be belief that 'Jesus is the Messiah',[13] it must be emphasised that Locke insists upon the necessity of a *moral* element in faith. The theological element of faith is itself inadequate to justify, and must be supplemented with the moral element.[14] 'These two, faith and repentance, i.e., believing Jesus to be the Messiah, and a good life, are the indispensable conditions of the new covenant, to be performed by all those who would obtain eternal life.'[15] It is clear that Locke reduces the dogmatic content of Christianity to a single statement, in order to permit the believer to lead a moral life untroubled by intricate matters of doctrine. Thus the work of Christ may be defined in terms of the 'great encouragement he brought to a virtuous and pious life'.[16]

---

[9] D. Pailin, 'Should Herbert of Cherbury Be Regarded as a "Deist"?', *JThS* 51 (2000), 113–49.

[10] Toland, *Christianity not Mysterious*, ed. Gawlick, 58–63. See further F. Heinemann, 'John Toland and the Age of Reason', *Archiv für Philosophie* 4 (1950), 35–66.

[11] Locke, *The Reasonableness of Christianity*, *Works* 7.6.

[12] *The Reasonableness of Christianity*, *Works* 7.14, cf. 112.

[13] *The Reasonableness of Christianity*, *Works* 7.101, 110. Cf. L. Stephen, *History of English Thought in the Eighteenth Century*, 3rd edn, 2 vols., London: Smith Elder & Co., 1902, 1.95–6.

[14] *The Reasonableness of Christianity*, *Works* 7.101–3.

[15] *The Reasonableness of Christianity*, *Works* 7.105.

[16] *The Reasonableness of Christianity*, *Works* 7.148.

The moralist understanding of the divine nature so characteristic of Latitudinarianism and the later Deism may be regarded as being substantiated by the theological method which Locke developed in his *Essay concerning Human Understanding* (1690).[17] The basic theological method employed by him in the *Essay* leads to the establishment of the moral character of God by the projection of human ideas of good, justice, and so forth, *ad infinitum* – and thus inevitably leads to the endorsement, rather than the critique, of human concepts of morality.[18] In an age increasingly dominated by rationalism, it was inevitable that God should be deemed to act according to precisely such concepts, and should be modelled upon the institution which was increasingly being recognised as the ultimate arbiter of justice – the state.

According to Thomas Hobbes, the state imposes certain restrictions upon humans in order that they may benefit as a consequence. The ultimate reality to be reckoned with is the claim of the individual to self-preservation and happiness. As all people have a natural claim to all things, the only restraining factor that can be brought into operation to prevent universal war is the rational acceptance of certain self-imposed restrictions. The subjective right of the individual is therefore transposed into an objective right by a *translatio iuris*, by which each individual transfers to the state a portion of his individual rights.[19]

In effect, the state may be regarded as representing the general will of the individuals which compose it, offering them protection and promising to each his due. 'For Justice, that is to say, Performance of Covenant, and giving to each their due, is a Dictate of the Law of Nature.'[20] The state is thus conceived as *persona civilis*, whose function is to promote the happiness and well-being of humans. The application of such insights leads to an empirically derived concept of God modelled on the state as the philanthropic preserver of humankind, and the rejection of theological notions (such as that of eternal punishment) which cannot be justified on the basis of this criterion of preservation.

---

[17] On which see P. A. Schouls, *The Imposition of Method: A Study of Descartes and Locke*, Oxford: Oxford University Press, 1980, 149–85.

[18] See the analysis of G. A. J. Rogers, 'Locke, Law and the Laws of Nature', in R. Brand (ed.), *John Locke: Symposium Wolfenbüttel*, Berlin: de Gruyter, 1981, 146–62.

[19] See G. Schedler, 'Hobbes on the Basis of Political Obligation', *Journal of the History of Philosophy* 15 (1977), 165–70. On the concept of 'contract' in Hobbes's theory of cession, see M. T. Delgano, 'Analysing Hobbes' Contract', *Proceedings of the Aristotelian Society* 76 (1975–6), 209–26.

[20] Hobbes, *Leviathan*, London, 1651, II.xxvi.4; 138. For the concept of 'covenant' employed, see Delgano, 'Analysing Hobbes' Contract'; for the concept of the 'Law of Nature', see P. E. Moreau, 'Loi divine et loi naturelle selon Hobbes', *Revue internationale de philosophie* 33 (1979), 443–51.

Precisely such a eudaemonistic concept of God is to be found in the Deist writings, such as Tindal's *Christianity as Old as the Creation*. God's commands are given purely in order to benefit humankind:

Nothing can be a Part of the Divine Law, but what tends to promote the common Interest, and mutual Happiness of his rational Creatures . . . As God can require nothing of us, but what makes for our Happiness; so he . . . can forbid us those Things only, which tend to our Hurt.[21]

The later phase of Deism involved not merely the rejection of the concept of original sin and an emphasis upon the moral character of Christianity, but a sustained attack upon central dogmas of the Christian faith which were held to be at variance with reason. Significantly, most of these dogmas related to the Christological dimension of the doctrine of justification. In *The True Gospel of Jesus Christ* (1738), Thomas Chubb asserted the identity of the *lex Christi* with the eternal law of reason. Chubb thus summarised the 'Gospel of Jesus Christ, or the Christian revelation', in three propositions:[22]

1. People must ground their lives and actions on the eternal and unchangeable rule of action that is grounded in the reason of things.
2. God requires repentance and reformation of individuals who depart from this rule of life if they are to be forgiven.
3. God will judge humans on the basis of whether they have lived in accordance with this rule.

Christ has a place in this soteriological scheme only in so far as he established the laws with reference to which humanity must live – laws that may be established equally well on the basis of unaided reason. 'Christ preached his own life, if I may so speak, and lived his own doctrine.'[23] Thus Chubb argues that the essential moral simplicity of Christianity has been compromised by certain unjustifiable theological beliefs – such as the doctrine of imputed righteousness, and the vicarious significance of the death of Christ. The only manner in which Christ could effect the salvation of humans was by summoning them to repentance and conversion.[24] Thus Paul's statement that the 'blood of Christ takes away sin' is to be understood in the sense that the moral example of the death of Christ moves sinners to repentance, and hence entails their forgiveness on this account.[25] Christ saves humans 'by his working a personal change in them', in that this alteration leads to their becoming worthy of divine

[21] *Christianity as Old as the Creation*, ed. Gawlick, 14–15.
[22] *Posthumous Works* 2.18, 104–5, 140–1.   [23] *Posthumous Works* 2.55.
[24] *Posthumous Works* 2.32, cf. 43–9, 112–20. For his critique of the doctrine of original sin, see 2.164.
[25] *Posthumous Works* 2.150.

forgiveness and salvation. The basis upon which God favours one rather than another lies in the individual themselves.

The strongly naturalist and rationalist cast of Chubb's analysis parallels the general outlook of later Deism. Thus Thomas Morgan argued that Christianity represented the 'best rendering' of the law of nature,[26] and that Christ was a moral legislator superior to Moses, Zarathustra, Confucius or Mahomet. For Morgan, it is axiomatic that God acts and legislates only in such a manner as is 'necessary to the Well being and Happiness of Mankind throughout the whole period of their existence'.[27] The essential feature of the Deist soteriology was the rejection of the concept of the *mediatorship* of Christ in favour of the 'republication' by Christ of the laws of nature. Although the notion of the mediation of Christ between God and humanity was defended with some vigour, particularly in Joseph Butler's influential *Analogy of Religion* (1736), the Deist critique of this and related ideas was received with some sympathy, initially in England, and subsequently in France and Germany. The traditional structure of the Christian doctrine of justification was discarded, occasionally on the basis of criticisms paralleling those made earlier by Socinus, in favour of a purely moral conception of the matter. Humans are justified *propter fidem*, in the Arminian sense – in other words, they are justified on the basis of their unaided act of repentance, inspired by the moral example and teaching of Christ, and motivated by the knowledge of the good which this repentance will bring them. The strongly eudaemonistic cast of Deist ethics lent weight to the assertion that morality was the foundation and criterion of religion, thus inverting the traditional understanding of the relation of the two.

The indirect influence of Pietism on rationalist critiques of orthodox doctrines of justification should be noted carefully. Many of the representatives of the German Enlightenment (*Aufklärer*) were of Pietist origins, and appear to have been familiar with the standard Pietist critique of the '*als-ob*' theologies of justification of Protestant (especially Lutheran) orthodoxy – namely, that they were ultimately fictitious rather than actual, and did not encourage moral regeneration. For the Pietist, the object of justification was potentially or actually morally regenerate individuals, whose moral regeneration both caused and demonstrated their justification. This emphasis upon the moral dimension of justification, and the rejection of the view that justification entailed a synthetic, rather than an analytic, judgement, is also characteristic of the early *Aufklärung*.[28] Thus

---

[26] Morgan, *The Moral Philosopher* 1.439, cf. 412.   [27] *The Moral Philosopher* 3.150.

[28] On the soteriologies of the *Aufklärung* see F. C. Baur, *Die christliche Lehre von der Versöhnung in ihrer geschichtlichen Entwicklung*, Tübingen: Osiander, 1838, 478–530; Baur, *Salus Christiana*, 111–79.

Johann Franz Budde makes no reference to the concept of *iustificatio impii* where it might be expected, and insists that it is the regenerate alone who may be justified: 'it is certain that there is some change in the person who is justified'.[29]

For Protestant orthodoxy, justification entailed a synthetic judgement – namely, a judgement that brought about the right relationship that the verdict of justification presupposed. For Pietism, justification rested on an analytic judgement, which acknowledged that the requisite change (*motus*) had already taken place.[30] Budde argues that the object of the divine justification must therefore possess an inherent quality, or undergo a transformation (*mutatio*) bringing about such a quality, which legitimates this divine pronouncement: 'this change, which occurs through regeneration, is presupposed in justification, so that no one is justified without being renewed'.[31]

Although justification is understood as a forensic divine declaration, this is taken to be based on a presently existing moral quality within humans. In his *Elementa theologiae dogmaticae* (1758), Lorenz von Mosheim explicitly stated the transformational concept of justification underlying his moralist soteriology: 'justification is an act of God, by which God changes an unrighteous person so that he becomes righteous'.[32] The divine judgement implicit in the process of justification is necessarily *iudicium secundum veritatem*, and thus depends on the pre-existing presence in the object of justification of those qualities which such a judgement presupposes.

In many respects, the early German Enlightenment (*Aufklärung*) paralleled later Pietism in its theology of justification, retaining the concept of justification as *actus forensis Dei*, while substituting an analytical concept of the divine judgement in place of orthodoxy's synthetic equivalent. Yet a major divergence was already in the process of emerging, focussing on the role of Christ in justification. One of the most significant theological achievements of the Enlightenment was the systematic dismantling of the entire soteriological framework established by Anselm of Canterbury in the eleventh century, which played such a decisive role in

---

[29] *Institutiones theologiae dogmaticae* IV.iv.4; 956. Cf. IV.iv.12; 978: 'neminem nisi regenitum iustificari'.

[30] For the theological distinction, see Härle, 'Analytische und synthetische Urteile in der Rechtfertigungslehre'.

[31] *Institutiones theologiae dogmaticae* IV.iv.4; 956. As Stolzenburg emphasises, both Budde and Pfaff presuppose that humans are naturally capable of receiving grace without the necessity of *satisfactio Christi* (in the orthodox sense): A. F. Stolzenburg, *Die Theologie des J. Fr. Buddeus und des Chr. M. Pfaff: Ein Beitrag zur Geschichte der Aufklärung in Deutschland*, Aalen: Scientia, 1979, 211.

[32] *Elementa theologiae dogmaticae* 819.

shaping traditional understandings of the work of Christ. This dismembering of the traditional framework of the doctrine of atonement took place across a broad front, involving a critique of such notions as original sin, the vicarious satisfaction of Christ, and the retributive justice of God.

Earlier, we noted the theological significance of emerging theories of the nature and function of the state (such as that of Hobbes). Such theories represented the state as the means towards the end of the welfare of the individual, and this understanding of the *persona civilis* had been extended to include God as the moral governor of the universe, working towards the end of its welfare. Hobbes had extended this teleological understanding of the state to include a rationale for the state punishment of individuals; given that the state exists as a means towards the end of the welfare of individuals, the function of punishment is essentially to deter individuals from committing acts which are detrimental to their own welfare, or to reform them should such deterrence fail.[33] The *Aufklärung* is particularly significant, in that this understanding of the basis of punishment came to be applied to God, with important consequences for the Christian doctrine of justification. The explicit transfer of Hobbes' understanding of the basis of punishment from the theory of the state to the theology of justification is particularly associated with Johann Konrad Dippel, and we propose to consider it in some detail.[34]

Dippel transferred to God the function of the state – that is, the well-being of the individual, along with the understanding of the rationale of punishment within this context. On this basis, Dippel argued that God could not conceivably wish to destroy sinners, since this is at variance with his understanding of the divine purpose, but merely to eradicate their sin and reform them. For Dippel, the consequences of sin relate solely to humans, in that their well-being is affected by its existence. In marked contrast to Anselm of Canterbury and Protestant orthodoxy, Dippel argued that sin has no effect upon God whatsoever, except indirectly, in that his love for humankind is grieved by the disadvantages which sin is perceived to bring to them.

There is therefore no need for God to punish sin, in that sin brings its own natural punishment with it, on account of its dysteleological character. If God does threaten humans with punishment – as Dippel reluctantly concedes to be the case – it is solely with the object of deterring them

---

[33] Hobbes, *Leviathan* ii.xxvii; 161–7.
[34] See S. Goldschmidt, *Johann Konrad Dippel (1673–1734): Seine radikalpietistische Theologie und ihre Entstehung*, Göttingen: Vandenhoeck & Ruprecht, 2001.

from sin. God's threats against humanity do not arise from sin being committed *against* God, but on account of the potential frustration of the divine purposes in creating humankind in the first place. God, in his love for humans, works actively towards their well-being – and is therefore obliged, as is the state, to discourage inherently self-destructive actions, which pose a threat to their well-being. Thus Dippel prefers not to speak of 'retributive' or 'vindictive justice', and is reluctant to speak of the divine 'wrath', lest this be misunderstood as divine wrath against *sinners*, rather than against *sin*.

The consequences of this understanding of the nature of God for Dippel's understanding of the doctrine of reconciliation are considerable. First, Dippel departs from the orthodox understanding of the scheme of reconciliation, in that he declines to allow a divine wrath directed against sinners, which the death of Christ can be said to appease or satisfy. Second, as sin is accompanied by its own natural punishments, it is clear that there is no sense in which Dippel may speak of Christ's having removed the human punishment for sin. Dippel understands Christ's passion and death as a model for human conquest of sin, which has no soteriological significance until it is successfully imitated. Christ's death cannot be said to remit the divine punishment of the sins of humanity, in that sin has its own natural punishment, which God cannot remove, save by abrogating the natural order.[35]

Although Dippel's criticisms of the orthodox doctrine of reconciliation made relatively little impact at the time of their publication, similar criticisms made later were to have considerable effect. An excellent example of the latter is to be found in Johann Gottlieb Töllner's celebrated criticism of the satisfactory value of the active obedience of Christ.[36] In his monograph *Der thätige Gehorsam Christi untersucht* (1768), Töllner rejected the thesis of the independent satisfactory value of the active obedience of Christ with a rigour never before encountered. Earlier, Piscator had argued that Christ's active obedience (that is, his obedience to the law) was essentially a presupposition of his passive obedience (that is, his suffering and death upon the cross). Töllner's thesis is far more radical,

---

[35] It is of interest to note that the most penetrating contemporary criticism of Dippel's views was that of Wolffian I. G. Kanz. Unlike Dippel, who regarded the divine government of humankind as the means towards the well-being of humans, Kanz retained the Leibnizian concept of the *civitas Dei* as an end in itself. The establishment of moral order among humankind is thus an end in itself, rather than a means to an eudaemonistic end. Kanz is thus able to follow Leibniz in retaining the concept of the retributive justice of God, in addition to the purely natural punishment for sin which Dippel allowed.

[36] See M. Pfizenmaier, *Mit Vernunft glauben: fides ratione formata. Die Umformung der Rechtfertigungslehre in der Theologie der deutschen Aufklärung dargestellt am Werk Johann Gottlieb Töllners (1724–1774)*, Stuttgart: Calwer Verlag, 1986.

and is based upon the analysis of the concepts of the person and office of Christ, and the nature of vicarious satisfaction itself.

Töllner argues that Christ, as a man, was under the common human obligation to obey the law.[37] As such, he was able to fulfil the law only for himself, and not for others. This thesis thus calls into question the Lutheran doctrine of *exlex*, according to which Christ was under no such obligation whatsoever. The possibility that the *obedientia Christi activa* possessed any independent vicarious satisfactory value can thus be maintained only if it can be shown that one of two conditions has been satisfied. Either Christ must be the authorised federal representative of humankind, so that the actions which he performs on behalf of humankind may be duly accredited to them; or else Christ's obedience must be accepted by God as if it were performed on behalf of those whom he represents.

Although Töllner gives no indication that he is familiar with the Reformed teaching on this question, it will be clear that the specified conditions correspond to the Reformed understanding of Christ as *caput et sponsor electorum* (see 3.7.2), by which the union between Christ and the believer, in justification, permits a *commercium admirabile* between them, as a result of which Christ's righteousness and merit become the believer's, and the latter's sin and guilt Christ's. Töllner, however, rejects the first condition as unprovable, and accordingly feels able to deny the notion that Christ's active obedience could be of benefit to humans.

On the basis of this conclusion, Töllner argues that the concept of vicarious satisfaction for sin may be rejected.[38] Töllner then argues, in the manner noted above, that it is the renewal (*Heiligung*) of the individual which leads to the bestowal of grace (*Begnadigung*), rather than the satisfaction of Christ. The obedience of Christ is an essentially moral quality, which inspires a corresponding moral quality within humans – upon the basis of which they are forgiven and justified. Thus Töllner explicitly appeals to the Socinian critique of the satisfaction doctrine of orthodoxy. Those who are justified are morally regenerate individuals, whose justification depends, not upon the allegedly 'objective' value of the death of Christ, but upon the subjective moral influence which it exerts upon them.[39]

---

[37] *Der thätige Gehorsam*, 419–21. For a useful analysis, see Baur, *Salus Christiana*, 132–44.

[38] *Der thätige Gehorsam*, 42: 'nun ist es augenscheinlich, wie ohne den ganzen thätigen Gehorsam Christi die vertretende Genugthuung desselben unmöglich gewesen wäre'. Cf. 631–2, especially 632: 'Ich stelle mich vor, daß Gott zur Begnadigung an sich niemals eine Genugthuung gefordert oder veranstaltet haben würde: und daß wir daher gar nicht auf dem rechten Wege sind, wenn wir sie als eine zur Begnadigung der Menschen nöthig befundne Veranstaltung betrachten.'

[39] *Der thätige Gehorsam*, 685.

Töllner thus draws the conclusion that all explanations of the significance of the death of Christ (*alle Erklärungsarten vom versöhnenden Tode
Christi*) actually reduce to one essential point: that Christ's death is the
ground of our assurance of God's graciousness towards us, and con-
firms the reliability of previous divine promises concerning the bestowal
of divine grace.[40] This single point, it may be emphasised, pertains to
humanity's perception of God, rather than to the divine relationship with
or attitude towards humans. Christ represents God to humans, and not
humans to God.

These insights were developed by Gotthilf Samuel Steinbart in his
strongly moralist *Glückseligkeitslehre* (1778). For Steinbart, the divine dispensation towards humankind was totally concerned with the promotion
of 'a supremely excellent and complete morality',[41] which finds its per-
sonification in Jesus Christ. God demands nothing of humans that is not
directly and totally beneficial to them. Steinbart thus insists that God asks
nothing of his children other than that which leads immediately to their
increased happiness and perfection.[42] Steinbart's tendency to employ
the term *Besserung* where *Heiligung* had traditionally been used serves to
emphasise the moral cast of his theology.[43] The essential simplicity of this
moral gospel has, however, become obscured, according to Steinbart, by
the intrusion of 'arbitrary hypotheses', of which the most significant are
the following:[44]

1. The Augustinian doctrine of original sin.
2. The Augustinian doctrine of predestination.
3. The Anselmian doctrine of the satisfaction of Christ.
4. The Protestant doctrine of the imputation of the righteousness of
   Christ.

It will be evident that all these 'arbitrary hypotheses' are of direct relevance
to our study. On the basis of extensive historical arguments,[45] Steinbart
concludes that the origins of these concepts are such as to call their continued use into question. Thus Augustine's doctrines of original sin and
predestination represent vestiges of his Manichaeism, which should be

---

[40] See his important essay 'Alle Erklärungsarten vom versöhnenden Tode Christi laufen
auf Eins heraus', in *Theologische Untersuchungen* 2.316–35.
[41] *Glückseligkeitslehre*, 78.   [42] *Glückseligkeitslehre*, 73.
[43] *Glückseligkeitslehre*, 93–162.   [44] *Glückseligkeitslehre*, 83.
[45] It is worth recalling Loofs's famous remark here: 'Die Dogmengeschichte ist ein Kind
der deutschen Aufklärungszeit' (F. Loofs, *Leitfaden zum Studium der Dogmengeschichte*,
4th edn, Halle: Niemeyer, 1904, 1). The original purpose of *Dogmengeschichte* was
the *criticism* of dogma through a historical investigation of its origins, rather than a mere
scientific documentation of its historical forms. This point is of particular importance in
relation to our study, in that the early studies of the development of the doctrine of justification (such as those of F. C. Baur and A. B. Ritschl) were undertaken for polemical,
rather than purely scholarly, motives.

eliminated in order that the teaching of the Greek fathers and Pelagius might be recognised as the older and authentic Christian teaching on the matter. Similarly, Steinbart argues, Anselm's concept of vicarious satisfaction represents a further distortion, based upon Augustinian presuppositions, of the original moral interpretation of Christ's death. The concept arises through the union of the Manichaean good and evil principles in one God, so that they constitute a permanent and internally irreconcilable tension which must be resolved from outside the Godhead.[46] No such tension may be found in the teaching of Jesus.[47] Furthermore, Steinbart appeals to Töllner's critique of the *obedientia Christi activa* as a devastating theological critique of a concept already virtually discredited on the grounds of its questionable historical origins.[48]

What, then, does Steinbart understand to be the objective grounds of the justification of humankind? According to Steinbart, Christ redeemed humanity from false understandings of God – such as the idea of God as wrathful, as a tyrant, or as one who imposed arbitrary penalties or conditions upon his creation.[49] Following the view – ultimately due to Hobbes – which we noted above, Steinbart insists that the only penalties due to humans are those which are the immediate natural consequences of their sins, or which are necessary to reform them, in order that they may avoid such natural penalties in future. Steinbart dismisses questions such as the necessity and significance of Christ's passion and death as beyond meaningful discussion,[50] and irrelevant to human happiness and moral perfection. The concept of vicarious satisfaction is both impossible theologically and unnecessary practically.[51]

It will be clear that the general position of the *Aufklärung* in relation to the objective grounds of justification leads to the total disintegration of the orthodox doctrine of reconciliation. The emphasis upon the intellectual and moral autonomy of humans, particularly evident in the writings of Töllner,[52] calls into question the crucial orthodox assertion that humankind was *naturally* alienated from God. For the *Aufklärer*, humans are not naturally alienated from God, although they may impose such an alienation upon themselves by their acts of sin. These acts of sin, however, are conceived dysteleologically – in other words, they work against

---

[46] *Glückseligkeitslehre*, 146. Note also his criticism of the Christological application of the concept of 'sacrifice': *Glückseligkeitslehre*, 288.
[47] *Glückseligkeitslehre*, 149.   [48] *Glückseligkeitslehre*, 130.
[49] *Glückseligkeitslehre*, 161–2.   [50] *Glückseligkeitslehre*, 162.
[51] *Glückseligkeitslehre*, 180: 'Gott fordert so wenig, als irgends ein menschlicher Vater von schwachen unmündigen Kindern mehr als aufrichtigen Willen und treuen Gebrauch der vorhandnen Kräfte.'
[52] See Baur, *Salus Christiana*, 134–8.

humanity's own interests, defined in terms of happiness and moral perfection. Sin is defined with reference to the injury it causes to humans:
God is affected by sin only indirectly, in so far as he is concerned with
the destiny of humanity. Sin is most emphatically *not* understood as an
offence against God, for which an appropriate satisfaction is required. If
Christ's death has any significance for humanity, this significance is to be
located in the effect that it has on the individuals themselves.

This important conclusion finds its expression in the 'moral' or 'exemplarist' interpretation of the death of Christ,[53] characteristic of the theologians of the later Enlightenment. Christ's death is understood to serve as a
supreme example or inspiration to humans, motivating and encouraging
them to emulate the outstanding moral character of Christ, in order that
they may become morally outstanding individuals.[54] The strong moralism and naturalism of the *Aufklärung* are evident in this moralist reduction of the Christian understanding of the nature of salvation, and in
the manner in which it is related to the death of Christ. If Christ may
be said to redeem humanity, it is in the restricted sense of 'redeeming
humankind from false concepts of God'. Thus Steinbart declares that
Christ has redeemed people from the *idea* of God as a tyrant, and from
the *idea* of Satan, illustrating with some clarity the notion of 'redemption' as 'intellectual liberation' so characteristic of the rationalism of the
movement.

By the year 1780, therefore, the foundations of the Christian doctrine of justification had been subjected to such destructive criticism by
the Enlightenment in England, France and Germany that it appeared
impossible that they could ever be restored. In fact, however, the period
which lay ahead saw the Enlightenment criticism of orthodoxy itself subjected to destructive criticism, with significant results for the development
of the doctrine. We thus turn to consider the distinctive contributions
of Kant and Schleiermacher to the re-establishment of the doctrine of
reconciliation.

5.2   The moral critique of the Enlightenment: I. Kant

The soteriologies of the later Enlightenment can be characterised in terms
of their rationalism, moralism and naturalism. Religion was regarded as
essentially ethical in character, expressing general universal moral truths
in a particular (though not necessarily the most appropriate) manner.
Whatever conditions might be conceded as being attached to humanity's

---

[53] See McGrath, 'The Moral Theory of the Atonement'.
[54] See Teller, *Religion der Vollkommnern*, 9–12, especially 12.

justification were regarded as essentially moral in character. Fundamental to such soteriologies was the axiom of the soteriological autonomy of the individual: all individuals must be regarded as possessing whatever soteriological resources were necessary for their justification.

In the present section, we are concerned with two critiques of the Enlightenment soteriology to emerge in the period 1790–1830. Both involved the relation between religion and morality, Kant arguing that the traditional Enlightenment account of this relationship was inadequate, and Schleiermacher developing a purely religious account of the Christian faith, thus severing this relationship altogether.

The modern era in European thought, particularly in epistemology, is frequently regarded as having been initiated by Kant. Kant has rightly been compared with Copernicus in the scale of the ideological revolution which he occasioned, especially in relation to his concept of the synthetic *a priori* judgement. Although the Kantian proclamation of the inalienable subjectivity of judgements has important consequences for Christian theology, it must be emphasised that Kant's significance in connection with the development of the doctrine of justification lies elsewhere – above all, in his insistence upon the autonomy and absoluteness of the moral consciousness, which has profound implications for the doctrine of reconciliation. Indeed, Kant's significance for the development of the doctrine lies in his analysis of the presuppositions of the concept of reconciliation which lies in the consciousness of moral freedom and moral guilt,[55] which led him to criticise the moral and exemplarist soteriologies of the Enlightenment.

Although Kant's exposition of the relationship between morality and religion is to be found in his *Critique of Pure Reason*, his most lucid and sustained discussion of the matter may be encountered in the important essay of 1793, *Religion within the Limits of Reason Alone*, which appeared some eleven years later.

The cornerstone of Kant's theology is the priority of the apprehension of moral obligation over anything else. For Kant, it is a fundamental axiom of theology, that everything humans believe themselves to be capable of doing to please God, apart from a moral way of life, is mere 'religious delusion' (*Religionswahn*) and 'pseudo-worship' (*Afterdienst*) of God.[56] Kant's emphasis upon the moral basis of the Christian religion, and his rejection of the idea of 'arbitrary demands' made by God of humanity, clearly parallel that of earlier Enlightenment writers. However, Kant diverges from

---

[55] See Ritschl's careful analysis of Kant's significance in this respect: *A Critical History of the Christian Doctrine of Justification and Reconciliation*, 320–86.

[56] *Schriften* 6.170.15–19.

the movement at two significant points. First, the essentially utilitarian or eudaemonistic approach to morality is replaced with an emphasis upon the concept of moral obligation as an end in itself (rather than as a means towards the end of human perfection or happiness), expressed in terms of the concept of the 'highest good'.[57] Second, Kant argues that to base morality upon the known commands of God would be to concede the heteronomous character of ethics; rather, morality must be held to be based upon the self-imposed 'categorical (or unconditional) imperative' (*unbedingte Forderung*) of the autonomous human will. The human sense of moral obligation (*das Sollen*) is prior to the correlation of virtue and happiness.

Furthermore, Kant insists that the apprehension of the categorical imperative is quite independent of the idea of 'another Being above humans' (in other words, God); however, Kant allows that the *idea* of such a Being may subsequently arise, through an act of faith which correlates the apprehension of *das Sollen* with the existence of God as a 'moral legislator apart from humanity'. Religiously disposed individuals will interpret *das Sollen* as an expression of divine obligations laid upon them, an interpretation which Kant's critical philosophy places beyond the scope of pure reason, even if it does not involve conceding that religion is essentially a postulate of practical reason.

Kant notes that the belief that the duty of humans is to pursue the highest good has as its necessary presupposition the possibility of moral perfection. For Kant, the denial of the possibility of moral perfection has as its corollary the denial of the possibility of the highest good, in that the former is the unconditioned component of the latter. Therefore the rejection of the possibility of the highest good entails the rejection of the moral law, which Kant dismisses as an *absurdum practicum*. For Kant, the apprehension of *das Sollen* has as its fundamental and necessary presupposition the possibility of moral perfection. It is of the utmost importance to appreciate that this presupposition forces him to break with the *Aufklärung* on several crucial points. The reasons for this will become clear when his concept of 'radical evil' is considered.[58]

It is to Kant's credit that he recognised that humans are free creatures, with an ability to misuse precisely that freedom. His account of moral obligation is able to take account of the possibility that people will ignore their apprehension of *das Sollen*. (It may be noted that he excludes the

---

[57] See the classic study of A. Döring, 'Kants Lehre vom höchsten Gut', *Kantstudien* 4 (1898), 94–101. The more recent studies of J. R. Silber should be noted, especially his essay 'The Importance of the Highest Good in Kant's Ethics', *Ethics* 73 (1963), 179–97.

[58] For a useful introduction to this concept, see G. E. Michalson, *Fallen Freedom: Kant on Radical Evil and Moral Regeneration*, Cambridge: Cambridge University Press, 1990.

suggestion that an individual may deliberately choose to do evil, knowing it to be evil.) The moral qualities of the will, both good and evil, are the consequences of human freedom. Individuals themselves must determine whether they are morally good or evil; if they do not, or are unable to do so, they cannot be held responsible for their moral condition, and thus cannot be considered to be good or evil *morally*. The consciousness of moral obligation leads Kant to conclude that humans must be free to exercise or to decide to exercise that obligation – otherwise the concept of 'obligation' becomes evacuated of its moral content. For Kant, as for the *Aufklärung* as a whole, the notion of original sin is to be rejected – and hence the origin of human evil is to be sought within the human will. But why should the human will choose evil? If there is no evil within humans until they themselves cause it, how does the will come to be corrupted in such a manner?

Kant answers this crucial question by developing the concept of the dispositional aspect of the human will (*Willkür*) to account for this fundamental ambivalence within human volition. While he defines evil in terms of a lesser good, so that evil persons are those who subordinate the demands of *das Sollen* to the demands of their sensible nature, it is clear that even this approach to the existence of evil calls into question the possibility of moral perfection. The thesis of 'radical evil' excludes the essential presupposition upon which Kant's ethics are based, in that it indicates that the most which can realistically be expected is progress towards, rather than attainment of, the end of moral perfection. Kant thus (re)defines moral perfection in terms of a 'disposition' (*Gesinnung*) towards this (unattainable) objective, which is now recognised as an *Urbild*, which humans recognise as good, and towards which they actively work.

Having defined a 'good disposition' as the intention to work towards the *Urbild* of moral perfection, Kant takes the noteworthy step of asserting that God treats those who possess an *intention* to work towards moral perfection *as if they were already in full possession of that perfection*. Although he concedes that humans have no right to expect God to treat them in this remarkable manner, he insists that God gratuitously (*aus Gnaden*) reckons the *Gesinnung* as the *Urbild*.[59] This striking reappearance of an *als-ob-Theologie*, or 'legal fiction', so vigorously rejected by Pietism and the *Aufklärung*, is of considerable importance. As we noted earlier, the later Enlightenment had stressed that the bestowal of grace or divine

---

[59] *Schriften* 6.75.1 – 76.6 (our italics). For the background to this remarkable statement, see 6.62.14 – 66.18. Elsewhere in this work, Kant asserts that a lenient judge who relaxes the moral law represents a contradiction in terms; 6.141.9 – 142.3. The apparent discrepancy between such statements is not discussed.

acceptation was contingent upon moral improvement; for Kant, grace seems to be implicated at the earliest phase of justification. The 'person who is pleasing to God' (*der wohlgefällige Mensch*) is 'pleasing' only on the basis of a gratuitous act by which God overlooks his or her deficiencies. As Kant puts this elsewhere, individuals who attempt to be pleasing to God 'in so far as it lies within their ability' (*so viel in seinem Vermögen ist*) may rely upon God to 'supplement' (*ergänzen*) their deficiencies.[60]

The parallels between Kant and the *via moderna* at this point will be evident, particularly in their shared presupposition that those who do their best (*quod in se est – so viel in seinem Vermögen ist*) will become pleasing to, or accepted by, God *as an act of grace, rather than of strict justice*.

The divergence between Kant and the general consensus of the Enlightenment becomes increasingly clear in Kant's discussion of how God may justify an individual who leads an immoral life but subsequently decides to repent. Kant insists that this is a *real* possibility – as, indeed, it must be, if the practical possibility of the unconditioned component of the highest good is to be maintained, even in the weakest of senses. However, Kant notes three difficulties raised by this possibility, of which the third is of particular significance.[61] Individuals who alter their evil disposition to the good are nevertheless the same individuals who formerly committed evil acts, and as a result are burdened with the guilt associated with that evil. How can God justify such individuals? Kant actually merely demonstrates that it is acceptable for God to permit guilt to go unpunished, and defers his solution to the problem of how such an individual may be justified (in the strict sense) until a later section of the work. This solution is, however, of enormous significance.

Kant's solution to this difficulty is, in fact, apparently irreconcilable with the general principles upon which his moral philosophy is based, particularly the axiom that individuals are responsible for *their own* moral actions. No individual can be good on behalf of another, nor can the goodness of a morally outstanding individual be permitted to remove the guilt of another. The basis of Kant's rejection of the concept of vicarious satisfaction (*stellvertretende Genugthuung*) is the principle that guilt, like merit, is strictly non-transferable. It is therefore remarkable that Kant's solution to the difficulty noted above is based upon the assertion that the individual who turns away from his or her evil disposition to adopt a good

---

[60] *Schriften* 6.120.10–16.
[61] The first difficulty concerns the relationship between moral acts and the moral disposition, and forces Kant to discuss how God can accept a good moral disposition as equivalent to perfectly good moral acts: *Schriften* 6.66.21 – 67.16. The second difficulty concerns how individuals may know with certainty that their new disposition is, in fact, good; *Schriften* 6.67.17 – 71.20.1.

disposition may be regarded as having become a different person: the old disposition *ist moralisch ein anderer* from the new. The discontinuity between the old and the new disposition is such that Kant denies that they may be predicated of the same moral individual. This conclusion appears to rest upon the assumption that the disposition itself is the only acceptable basis of establishing the identity of the moral agent.

Having established this point, Kant takes the remarkable step of asserting that the new disposition 'takes the place' (*vertritt*) of the old in respect of the guilt which is rightly attached to the latter disposition. It is on account of the new disposition that the former guilt of humans is cancelled, and that they are justified before God. On the basis of these assumptions, Kant asserts that those who attempt to be pleasing to God may rest assured of the truth expressed by the doctrine of reconciliation, which represents their former sins as abolished (*abgetan*).[62] Kant thus interprets the doctrine of reconciliation to mean that individuals who determine to keep the moral law, whatever their previous history may have been, have the right to hope that their moral past may be abolished, and present moral deficiencies supplemented, through divine grace.

The significance of Kant's *Religion* lies in the recognition of the necessity of divine grace *as a postulate of practical reason*. The deep pessimism of his doctrine of 'radical evil' is counteracted by his optimism concerning the role of divine grace in the supplementation of a good disposition, and the abolition of the moral guilt of a prior evil disposition (by a process of vicarious satisfaction). Although Kant cannot be said to have advanced the orthodox doctrine of reconciliation (or, indeed, to have intended to do so), it may be argued that his analysis of practical reason suggested that the doctrines of justification and reconciliation had a proper and necessary place within moral philosophy, even if they were stated in forms quite distinct from their orthodox equivalents.

5.3   The religious critique of the Enlightenment: F. D. E. Schleiermacher

In the closing decade of the eighteenth century, more and more misgivings came to be expressed concerning the arid quality and severe spiritual limitations of Enlightenment rationalism. Reason, once seen as a liberator, came increasingly to be regarded as spiritually enslaving. These anxieties were expressed not so much within university faculties of philosophy as within literary and artistic circles, particularly in Berlin, where the Schlegel brothers – August Wilhelm (1767–1845) and Friedrich

---

[62] *Schriften* 6.183.37 – 184.3.

(1772–1829) – became particularly influential. The movement widely known as 'Romanticism' is notoriously difficult to define, and is perhaps best seen as a reaction against certain of the central themes of the Enlightenment, most notably the claim that reality can be known to the human reason.

Where the Enlightenment appealed to the human reason, Romanticism made an appeal to the human imagination, which it believed to be capable of recognising the profound sense of mystery arising from the realisation that the human mind cannot comprehend even the finite world, let alone the infinity beyond this. A strong sense of standing upon the borderlands of some greater reality, which the Romantics held to be both unknown and unknowable to pure reason, pervades the movement, and proved to be enormously attractive to an age which had become increasingly bored or frustrated with the banalities of rationalism.[63]

Although Schleiermacher is not best regarded as a Romantic, it is clear that the new significance attached to human 'feeling' (*Gefühl*) allowed him to develop an account of Christian faith which dissociated it from the hitherto prevailing rationalist reductions of the concept.[64] The fundamental fact (*Grundtatsache*) of Christian dogmatics is the existence of the individual's faith or 'piety' (*Frömmigkeit*), and it is the task of Christian dogmatics to give an account of the content of this *datum*, rather than to establish it in the first place.[65] The essence of 'piety', which Schleiermacher holds to be the irreducible element in every religion, is not some rational or moral principle, but 'feeling' (*Gefühl*), the immediate self-consciousness.[66] Thus Christian doctrines are, in essence, individually accounts of Christian religious feelings.[67] Schleiermacher constructs

---

[63] See, for example, M. H. Abrams, *Natural Supernaturalism: Tradition and Revolution in Romantic Literature*, New York: Norton, 1973. On the general question of the relation of Christianity and Romanticism, see R. E. Brantley, 'Christianity and Romanticism: A Dialectical Review', *Christianity and Literature* 48 (1999), 349–66.

[64] On the general background, see R. Eldridge, 'Kant, Hölderlin, and the Experience of Longing', in *The Persistence of Romanticism: Essays in Philosophy and Literature*, Cambridge: Cambridge University Press, 2001, 31–51. On the role of *Gefühl* in Schleiermacher's theology, see W. Schutz, 'Schleiermachers Theorie des Gefühls und ihre religiöse Bedeutung', *ZThK* (1956), 75–103; F. W. Graf, 'Ursprüngliches Gefühl unmittelbarer Koinzidenz des Differenten: Zur Modifikation des Religionsbegriffs in der verschiedenen Auflagen von Schleiermachers "Reden über Religion"', *ZThK* 75 (1978), 147–86.

[65] See J. Forstman, *A Romantic Triangle: Schleiermacher and Early German Romanticism*, Missoula: American Academy of Religion, 1977.

[66] *Der christliche Glaube*, §3, 2–4; 1.7–13.

[67] *Der christliche Glaube*, §15, 1; 1.99–100. Schleiermacher emphasises the communal dimension of such experience, and does not lapse into a form of solipsism; Christian faith is essentially and primarily faith in Christ as grounded in the community of faith. See further D. Offermann, *Schleiermachers Einleitung in die Glaubenslehre*, Berlin: de Gruyter, 1969, 293–321.

his dogmatics upon the basis of the fact of redemption in Christ, and thence upon the antithesis of sin and grace. In the first part of *Der christliche Glaube*, Schleiermacher discussed the human religious consciousness (*Bewußtsein*) in isolation from this antithesis. Although this consciousness is presupposed by Christian piety, the specifically Christian consciousness is to be distinguished from it, in that it is the 'feeling of absolute dependence' (*das Gefühl schlechthinniger Abhängigkeit*), which faith interprets as a consciousness of God.[68]

Having established Christian piety, and particularly the 'feeling of absolute dependence', as the starting point for Christian theology, Schleiermacher argues that the origins of this piety are to be explained soteriologically in terms of the perceived effects of Christ upon the collective consciousness of the Christian community. It must be emphasised that this represents a purely *religious* approach to the matter, which sharply distinguishes it from the moralism of the *Aufklärung*. Schleiermacher attributes to Christ an 'absolutely powerful God-consciousness' (*schlechthin kräftiges Gottesbewußtsein*), charged with such assimilative power that it is able to effect the redemption of humankind.[69] The essence of redemption is that the God-consciousness already present in human nature, although feeble and repressed, becomes stimulated and elevated through the 'entrance of the living influence of Christ'.[70] As the redeemer (*Erlöser*), Christ is distinguished from all other humans both in degree and in kind by the uninterrupted power of his God-consciousness. The redemptive activity of Christ consists in his assuming individuals into the power of his God-consciousness. On the basis of this presupposition, Schleiermacher criticises the soteriologies of both the *Aufklärung* and Protestant orthodoxy.

For Schleiermacher, the *Aufklärer* treated Christ solely as a prophet, regarding him primarily as the teacher of an *idea* of God, or the exemplar of a religious or moral principle. This view – which Schleiermacher designates the 'empirical' understanding of the work of Christ – 'attributes a redemptive activity on the part of Christ, but one which is held to consist only in bringing about an increasing perfection in us, and which cannot take place other than by teaching and example'.[71] If this account of the significance of Christ is correct, Schleiermacher argues that belief in redemption *im eigentlichen Sinne* becomes an impossibility. The orthodox

---

[68] *Der christliche Glaube*, §4, 4; 1.20–2. Cf. F. Beisser, *Schleiermachers Lehre von Gott*, Göttingen: Vandenhoeck & Ruprecht, 1970, 57–68; Offermann, *Schleiermachers Einleitung*, 47–65.

[69] *Der christliche Glaube*, §94, 1–3; 2.40–5. On the use of the term *Urbild*, see P. Seifert, *Die Theologie des jungen Schleiermacher*, Gütersloh: Gütersloher Verlagshaus, 1960, 141–2.

[70] *Der christliche Glaube*, §106, 1; 2.162.   [71] *Der christliche Glaube*, §100, 3; 2.101.

understanding of the work of Christ – which Schleiermacher designates as 'magical' – attributes to Christ a purely objective transaction which is 'not mediated by anything natural'. This approach, which Schleierma-cher considers to approximate to Docetism, is incapable of doing justice to the historical figure of Jesus of Nazareth; if Christ were able to exert his influence in this supernaturalist manner, it would have been possi-ble for him to work in precisely the same way at any time, so that his personal appearance in history would have been superfluous.[72] Under-lying this observation is Schleiermacher's conviction that the supranat-uralist approach involves a non-natural concept of divine causality. For Schleiermacher, divine causality operates through natural means – and at this point, his affinity with the *Aufklärung* is evident. The assimilative power of Christ's dominant God-consciousness is mediated to humanity through natural channels.

Having discussed how the individual believer enters into fellowship with Christ, Schleiermacher moves on to consider how this expresses itself in the life of the believer.[73] At this point, a significant theological continuity can be seen between Schleiermacher and Pietism, in that both hold that justification is contingent upon a real change in humans.

Justification presupposes something in respect of which a person is justified; and since no error is possible for the Supreme Being, it must be assumed that some-thing has happened to an individual between the former and present state, by which the divine displeasure has been removed and without which the individual could not have become the object of divine favour.[74]

That same theme passed into the Enlightenment; divine acceptation – in whatever form rationalism was prepared to accept – depended upon human transformation. Like Töllner, Steinbart and Teller, Schleierma-cher insists that justification is contingent upon a prior alteration within humans. Schleiermacher diverges from the Enlightenment in his under-standing of the nature of the alteration. For the Enlightenment, the alter-ation was to be conceived morally (note the tendency to refer to the condi-tion as *Besserung*, rather than *Heiligung*). For Schleiermacher, the critical alteration on which divine acceptance was dependent was to be conceived *religiously* as 'laying hold of Christ in a believing manner' (*Christum gläubig ergreifen*).[75] Although conceding that this might appear to suggest that humans are capable of justifying themselves, Schleiermacher states that

---

[72] *Der christliche Glaube*, §100, 3; 2.101.
[73] See H. Pieter, *Theologische Ideologiekritik: Die praktische Konsequenzen der Rechtferti-gungslehre bei Schleiermacher*, Göttingen: Vandenhoeck & Ruprecht, 1977.
[74] *Der christliche Glaube*, §107, 2; 2.167–8.
[75] *Der christliche Glaube*, §109, 4; 2.201. But note the emphatic rejection of the suggestion that faith is the instrumental cause of justification: §109,4; 2.202.

justification actually derives from the assumption of humans into fellowship with Christ,[76] and adopts an understanding of the role of humans in justification which is sharply distinguished from that of the *Aufklärung*.

Schleiermacher, developing the Kantian concept of radical evil, argues that humans are unable to attain a dominant God-consciousness unaided. There is an inherent disposition within humans towards sin, understood as a 'total incapacity for the good',[77] which leads them to recognise their need for external divine assistance.

This point is also developed in Schleiermacher's important discussion of the four 'natural heresies' of Christianity – the Docetic and Ebionite interpretations of the person of Christ, and the Pelagian and Manichaean interpretations of their soteriological resources.[78] As Schleiermacher observes, the understanding of human soteriological resources must be such that it can account for the necessity of redemption from outside humanity itself – in other words, that it can explain why all humans cannot be redeemers. The understanding of the object of redemption – humanity – must be such that it can accommodate the two presuppositions fundamental to Schleiermacher's soteriology: that humans require redemption from outside humanity, and that they are capable of receiving or accepting that redemption, once it is offered to them. If humans' need for redemption is conceded, and yet their impotence to provide such redemption is denied, the conclusion must be drawn that humans themselves could be the agent of their own redemption. Redemption could then be effected, either by the soteriologically sufficient individual, or by one individual for another; and if not by all people, then at least by some, to varying degrees. If the impotence of humans to redeem themselves is conceded, and yet their ability to appropriate that redemption, once offered, is denied, it will be clear that redemption is an impossibility. Broadly speaking, these two positions correspond to the Pelagian and Manichaean heresies, although the specific historical forms taken by these heresies differ somewhat from Schleiermacher's characterisations of them.

The importance of this discussion relates to Schleiermacher's definition of the distinctive feature of Christianity as the principle that 'all religious emotions are related to redemption in Christ'.[79] The Enlightenment axiom of the soteriological autonomy of humans eliminated this

---

[76] *Der christliche Glaube*, §107, 1; 2.165–7.

[77] *Der christliche Glaube*, §70; 1.376 '[eine] aufzuhebende vollkommne Unfähigkeit zum Guten'.

[78] *Der christliche Glaube*, §22, 1–3; 1.124–9. See further K.-M. Beckmann, *Der Begriff der Häresie bei Schleiermacher*, Munich: Kaiser Verlag, 1959, 36–62. For consideration of the four heresies in more detail, see 85–114.

[79] *Der christliche Glaube*, §22, 2; 1.125.

distinctive element of an Augustinian understanding of redemption, in that the principle of redemption from outside humanity was regarded as violating human autonomy. Schleiermacher's careful statement of the heteronomous character of human soteriological resources must be seen as an important attempt to recapture this traditional aspect of Protestant doctrines of justification at this point.

A further point at which Schleiermacher criticises the soteriologies of the *Aufklärung* relates to the concept of sin. Schleiermacher, as is well known, subordinates sin to the divine purpose of redemption, regarding human's recognition of sin as the necessary prelude to their redemption. The first consciousness of the actuality of sin is effectively the first presentiment of the possibility of redemption. Schleiermacher rejects the *Aufklärung* axiom of the reformatory character of punishment, as well as the distinction between natural and arbitrary punishments.[80] For him, a positive correlation is established by the divine righteousness between sin and penalty for sin *as a means of generating the consciousness of redemption*.[81]

The Enlightenment view that the divine righteousness recognises a positive correlation between human good (such as moral action) and divine reward (such as justification) is thus rejected. Defining the 'righteousness of God' as 'the divine causality by which a connection is established between evil and actual sin in the state of universal sinfulness', Schleiermacher concedes that this represents a considerable restriction upon the term, in that no correlation between good and reward is recognised.[82] However, he defends this restriction by observing that the Christian consciousness acknowledges no such positive correlation between human good and divine reward, save in the specific and unique case of Christ.[83] Consciousness of the divine righteousness is thus consciousness of the divine punitive justice (*strafende Gerechtigkeit*) alone, thus leading to the realisation of the possibility of redemption. It is therefore evident that Schleiermacher has replaced the moral understandings of divine punishment and the divine righteousness, characteristic of the *Aufklärung*, with *religious* understandings of the concepts, and that these are subordinated to a fundamentally *religious* concept of salvation.

5.4   The reappropriation of the concept of justification: A. B. Ritschl

Although Schleiermacher's soteriology was subjected to considerable criticism from both more radical and conservative theological traditions

---

[80] *Der christliche Glaube*, §84, 3; 1.470–1.   [81] *Der christliche Glaube*, §84, 3; 1.471–3.
[82] *Der christliche Glaube*, §84, 1; 1.465–6.   [83] *Der christliche Glaube*, §84, 1; 1.466–7.

during the period 1820–70, it is clear that it made a permanent impact upon the German theological consciousness. A purely rationalist or moralist account of the justification of humanity before God was increasingly seen to be religiously deficient. Yet Schleiermacher's critique of the Enlightenment did not include the reintroduction of an objective dimension to the doctrine of justification. Justification was still seen essentially in terms of human transformation.

In his influential study of the development of the doctrine of reconciliation, published in 1838, Ferdinand Christian Baur asserted, on the basis of a Hegelian understanding of the nature of historical development,[84] that an element of this doctrine, once eliminated, could no longer be restored. Baur's Hegelianism led him to suggest that objective soteriological concepts had been permanently eliminated from the doctrine of reconciliation. The use of Hegelian speculative categories was widespread within theological circles, and is particularly evident in the first work of one of Baur's most promising pupils: Albrecht Ritschl's *Die Entstehung des altkatholischen Kirche* (1850). As most of Baur's contemporaries were sympathetic to his Hegelian presuppositions, and thus to his views on the development of the doctrine of reconciliation, it was far from clear how this consolidation might take place, in that the objective elements of the doctrine rejected by the *Aufklärung* were generally regarded as irretrievably lost.

The sudden collapse of Hegelianism in the fifth decade of the nineteenth century led to a general rejection of the Hegelian understanding of the nature of historical development. The consequences of this are immediately apparent from the second edition of Ritschl's *Entstehung* (1857), in which a break with both Baur and Hegelianism is evident. More significant, from the standpoint of the present study, was Ritschl's decision to reinvestigate the development of the Christian doctrine of justification without the restrictions of the Hegelian interpretative framework imposed upon it by Baur.

After a series of preparatory articles in *Jahrbuch für deutsche Theologie*, the first volume of his *Christliche Lehre von der Rechtfertigung und Versöhnung* was published in 1870. The full importance of this historical analysis in consolidating the doctrine of justification has not been fully appreciated. In this work, Ritschl was able to demonstrate that, contrary to Baur's axiom, elements eliminated from the doctrine of reconciliation by one generation had subsequently been reappropriated by

---

[84] Baur, *Die christliche Lehre von der Versöhnung*, 748. It may be noted that Baur minimised the distinction between the soteriologies of the *Aufklärung* and both Kant and Schleiermacher, presumably to achieve consistency with his Hegelian theory of historical development.

another. Having shown that Baur's *a priori* imposition of the speculative and unempirical categories of Hegel's philosophy of history was incapable of accounting for the objectively given historical data pertaining to the progression of the doctrine of reconciliation, Ritschl was able to move towards the positive restatement of the doctrine through the reappropriation of *objective* soteriological concepts (such as sin) without being impeded by the constraints imposed upon such a restatement by Baur's understanding of the nature of historical development. It is this positive restatement which forms the subject of the third volume of his *Christliche Lehre von der Rechtfertigung und Versöhnung*.

For Ritschl, all religion is exclusively soteriological in character, seeking a resolution of the contradiction in which humans find themselves, in that they are at one and the same time a part of the world of nature, dependent upon and confined to the natural order, and yet also spiritual entities motivated by their determination to maintain their independence of nature.[85] Religion is therefore essentially an interpretation of the relation of humans to God and the world, based upon the belief that God may effect the redemption of humanity. Ritschl's theology in its entirety is based upon the centrality of God's redemptive action in history, with its associated (and subsequent) human response and obligations. In the second edition of *Die Entstehung der altkatholischen Kirche*, Ritschl drew an important, and highly influential, distinction between early authentic Christianity, and its later unauthentic form, which resulted from the intrusion of elements essentially alien to the gospel itself.

According to Ritschl, Christianity is essentially soteriologically orientated, but became corrupted through the intrusion of Hellenistic metaphysics into a Christologically centred religion. Ritschl's intense suspicion of the role of metaphysics in theology reflects his fundamental conviction that humanity has no true knowledge of God outside the sphere of his redemptive activity, and that, even then, this knowledge takes the form of 'value-judgements' (*Werthurtheile*), which cannot be allowed to be equivalent to disinterested and impartial knowledge.

In his polemic against the claims of idealistic rationalism, Ritschl argues that the specifically Christian knowledge of God takes the form of value-judgements evoked by divine revelation.[86] For him, we know the nature of

---

[85] *Die christliche Lehre von der Rechtfertigung und Versöhnung*, §27; 189–90. The third edition of this work (1888) has been used in the present study; for the differences between the various editions, see C. Fabricius, *Die Entwicklung in Albrecht Ritschls Theologie von 1874 bis 1889 nach der verschiedene Auflagen seiner Hauptwerke dargestellt und beurteilt*, Tübingen: Osiander, 1909.

[86] *Die christliche Lehre von der Rechtfertigung und Versöhnung*, §28; 195–200.

God and Christ only in terms of their perceived significance for us. Thus he makes frequent approving reference to Melanchthon's celebrated dictum that knowing Christ is about knowing his benefits: *Hoc est Christum cognoscere, beneficia eius cognoscere.*[87] Ritschl's theological method is based upon the assumption that faith is grounded in the saving revelation of God in Christ, so that the actual justification of humankind is defined as the point of departure for all Christian statements concerning God. All the statements of believers concerning God and Christ reflect the importance that they personally attach to them, and cannot be divorced from their faith. Thus, for Ritschl, the question 'Who is Christ?' must reduce to the more pertinent and radical question 'Who is Christ *for me*?' The theological question of the identity of Christ is thus fundamentally a *Werthurtheil*, which cannot be separated from the *Ding-an-sich*.

This point is made with particular clarity in the first edition of Ritschl's major work, which explores the Christological consequences of the phenomenalist thesis that *Dinge-an-sich* escape our perception altogether (except in the form in which they are perceived and evaluated).[88] Ritschl thus argues that our knowledge of the *person* of Christ, in so far as this represents a genuine possibility, derives from our knowledge of the *work* of Christ – in other words, that soteriology is prior to Christology in the theological *ordo cognoscendi*.

Ritschl regards the justification of humanity as the fundamental datum from which all theological discussion must proceed, and upon which it is ultimately grounded.[89] This conviction expresses itself in the manner in which Ritschl's systematic exposition of Christian theology proceeds. An initial examination of the concept of justification (§§5–26) is followed by an analysis of the presuppositions of human justification, such as the doctrines of sin and the work and person of Christ (§§27–50). After a discussion of the difficulties which might be thought to arise from the doctrine (§§51–61), the work ends with an analysis of the consequences of the justification of humanity (§§62–8).

---

[87] *Loci communes* (1521), preface. It should, of course, be noted that Melanchthon was not defining the basis of a theological programme with this statement, but merely explaining the omission of a locus regarding Christology from this work, which was primarily concerned with soteriology. Melanchthon's theological criticisms were directed against the medieval soteriologies, not the Christologies of the period. In subsequent editions, in which a Christological locus is included, this famous dictum is omitted.

[88] *Die christliche Lehre von der Rechtfertigung und Versöhnung*, Bonn: Marcus, 1874, §44; 343: 'Wir erkennen nämlich die Art und die Eigenschaften, d.h. die Bestimmtheit des Seins, nur an dem Wirken eines Dinges auf uns, und wir denken die Art und den Umfang seines Wirkens auf uns als sein Wesen.'

[89] See H. Timm, *Theorie und Praxis in der Theologie Albrecht Ritschls und Wilhelm Herrmanns*, Gütersloh: Mohn, 1967; J. Richmond, *Ritschl: A Reappraisal*, London: Collins, 1978, 124–67.

Ritschl's initial definition of justification is of immediate significance, in that it represents the reintroduction of objective concepts into the systematic discussion of the doctrine. 'Justification, or the forgiveness of sins (as the religious operation of God upon people, fundamental within Christianity), is the acceptance of sinners into that fellowship with God within which their salvation will be effected and developed into eternal life.'[90] Ritschl's explicit identification of justification and the remission of sins indicates his concern to emphasise the objective dimension of justification, and represents a reappropriation of certain aspects of the concept associated with the Reformation in general, and Luther in particular.[91] For Ritschl, sin separates humans from God, effecting the withdrawal of God's presence from the sinner; justification is therefore the divine operation through which the sinner is restored to fellowship with God. The objective dimension of justification is therefore prior to, although inseparable from, the subjective consciousness of this forgiveness.[92]

Ritschl thus criticises an earlier generation of Lutheran theologians for their excessive objectivism, which led to justification becoming divorced from personal experience and practice.[93] Of considerably greater importance, however, is Ritschl's critique of the axiom of the *Aufklärung* – that God enters into no real relationship with humanity, unless the individual in question is morally regenerate. This principle amounts to the destruction of the central and fundamental presupposition of Christianity which, according to Ritschl, is that God justifies *sinners*. Ritschl stresses that justification necessarily finds its expression in the lifestyle of the individual; justification (*Rechtfertigung*), which is concerned with the restoration of humanity's fellowship with God, necessarily finds its concrete expression in reconciliation (*Versöhnung*), the lifestyle of the reconciled community. In so far as the moral implications of justification and reconciliation derive from and are grounded in the new relationship of humankind to God, established in justification, it may be said that reconciliation is the ethical complement of justification – in other words, that the *moral* aspects of this fellowship with God are secondary to its specifically *religious* character.

It will be evident that Ritschl has significantly reinterpreted the concept of 'reconciliation' (*Versöhnung*). For orthodoxy, 'reconciliation' referred to the objective basis of justification, especially the historical work of

---

[90] *Die christliche Lehre von der Rechtfertigung und Versöhnung*, §16; 83. The other two definitions of justification offered by Ritschl represent an extension of this basic definition.
[91] See Schäfer, 'Rechtfertigungslehre bei Ritschl und Kähler', 69–70.
[92] *Die christliche Lehre von der Rechtfertigung und Versöhnung*, §31; 58–9.
[93] *Die christliche Lehre von der Rechtfertigung und Versöhnung*, §15; 72.

Christ. Ritschl inverted the traditional frame of reference, so that God is now understood as the *subject*, rather than the *object*, of reconciliation.[94] Indeed, Ritschl appears to regard the terms *Rechtfertigung* and *Versöhnung* as being essentially synonymous, their difference lying in the aspects of the God–human relationship to which they referred. *Rechtfertigung* refers to the divine judgement, understood as an unconditional act of will, independent of whether an individual or a community appropriates it. *Versöhnung* refers to the same basic concept of a synthetic divine judgement, as it is appropriated by an individual or community. In other words, *Versöhnung* expresses as an actual result the effect which is intended in *Rechtfertigung* – that the individual or community who is justified actually enters into the intended relationship.

For Ritschl, God's gracious gift of justification is inextricably and irrevocably linked with the ethical consequences of this divine act: 'Christianity, so to speak, resembles not a circle described from a single centre, but an ellipse which is determined by two *foci*.'[95] The first *focus* is 'redemption through Christ', and the second 'the ethical interpretation of Christianity through the idea of the kingdom of God'. His conviction that Lutheran orthodoxy had tended to concentrate upon redemption without correlating it with Christian existence led to his insistence upon the necessity of correlating the divine and human elements in justification and reconciliation.

Ritschl's statement that justification involves a *synthetic* judgement on the part of God represents a decisive break with the soteriologies of the Enlightenment and their immediate precursors within Pietism which even Schleiermacher had not felt able to make. In taking this step, Ritschl clearly considers himself to be reappropriating a vital element of the Reformation and orthodox soteriologies rejected by the 'Age of Reason'. If, on the one hand, justification involves an *analytic* judgement on the part of God, God is understood to 'analyse' the righteousness which is already present in an individual, and, on the basis of this analysis, to pronounce the sentence of justification. This pronouncement is thus based upon a quality already present within humans, prior to their justification, which God recognises and proclaims in the subsequent verdict of justification.

---

[94] See U. Barth, 'Das gebrochene Verhältnis zur Reformation: Beobachtungen zum Protestantismusverständnis Albrecht Ritschls', in M. Berger and M. Murrmann-Kahl (eds.), *Transformationsprozesse des Protestantismus: Zur Selbstreflexion einer christlichen Konfession an der Jahrtausendwende*, Gütersloh: Mohn, 1999, 80–99. See also W. von Loewenich, *Luther und der Neuprotestantismus*, Witten: Luther Verlag, 1963, 105; Schäfer, 'Rechtfertigungslehre bei Ritschl und Kähler', 73–4.
[95] *Die christliche Lehre von der Rechtfertigung und Versohnung*, §I; 11. For a helpful analysis of this structure, see G. Hok, *Die elliptische Theologie Albrecht Ritschls nach Ursprung und innerem Zusammenhang*, Uppsala: Uppsala Universitets, 1941.

'Righteousness' is already predicated of humanity – the function of the pronouncement of justification is simply to endorse its present status *coram Deo*. It will be evident that this corresponds to the moralist soteriology of the *Aufklärung*.

If, on the other hand, justification involves a *synthetic* judgement, God is understood to act in a creative manner, adding something to humanity which it did not previously possess. God 'synthesises' the righteousness upon the basis of which the divine verdict of justification proceeds. In justification, a predicate is added to humanity which is not already included in the notion of 'sinner'.[96] Ritschl declares his intention to break free from the moralism of Catholicism and the *Aufklärung* (which he considers to be fundamentally Socinian in character) by affirming that justification is a creative act of the divine will which, in declaring the sinner to be righteous, *effects* rather than *endorses* the righteousness of individual humans. Ritschl's insistence upon the synthetic character of the divine judgement of justification eliminates any claim by the morally renewed person to be justified on that account.[97] Ritschl thus argues that Pietism (and, by inference, the *Aufklärung*) represent an 'inversion of the Reformation point of view'.

Fundamental to Ritschl's critique of an analytic understanding of the divine judgement of justification is the question of the positive laws or principles by which such a judgement may be undertaken. 'Every judicial judgement is an analytic judgement of knowledge. The subsequent decree of punishment or acquittal is also an analytic judgement, in that it is a conclusion based upon the prohibitive or permissive law and the knowledge of the guilt or innocence of the person involved.'[98] If God's justifying verdict is based upon *law*, the question of God's status in regard to that law must be positively established. This question is, of course, particularly associated with the Arminian theologian Hugo Grotius, and Ritschl may be regarded as extending the critique of the orthodox doctrine of justification associated with this Arminian divine to exclude totally a judicial interpretation of justification.

'The attribute of God on the basis of which the older theology attempts to understand justification is that of lawgiver (*Gesetzgeber*) and judge (*Richter*).'[99] By these terms, Ritschl intends to convey the quite distinct

---

[96] *Die christliche Lehre von der Rechtfertigung und Versöhnung*, §16; 78: 'ein Prädicat gesetzt wird, welches nicht schon in dem Begriffe des Sünders eingeschlossen ist'.

[97] *Die christliche Lehre von der Rechtfertigung und Versöhnung*, §16; 77–83, especially 82–3. Note particularly Ritschl's criticism of Pietism, which would be developed in his *Geschichte des Pietismus*, 3 vols., Bonn: Marcus, 1880–6.

[98] *Die christliche Lehre von der Rechtfertigung und Versöhnung*, §17; 90.

[99] *Die christliche Lehre von der Rechtfertigung und Versöhnung*, §17; 84.

concepts of God as *rector* and *iudex* (underlying Grotius' critique of orthodox theologies of justification). Ritschl points out how the divine pardon of the sinner in justification was generally treated by orthodoxy as analogous to the bestowal of pardon upon a guilty individual by a head of state. On the basis of this analogy, it was argued that justification could be interpreted as a judicial act of God, by which the individual was found guilty of sin, and yet pardoned through precisely the same legal process. Any apparent contradiction between the divine justice and the divine grace could be resolved by developing a theory of penal substitution, so that any hint of injustice in relation to the pardoning of the guilty individual could be remedied.

Ritschl, however, argued that the exercise of the head of state's right to pardon is not comparable to the divine justification of the sinner. The head of state is obliged to act in accord with the best interests of the individual members of the state, and the established law is merely a means towards that end. As such, the law is subordinate to the greater good of the state:

> The right of granting pardon (*Begnadigung*) . . . follows from the fact that the legal order is merely a means to the moral ends of the people, and that consequences of legal action are conceivable, which are incongruous with the respect which is due to public morality, as well as to the moral position of guilty persons.[100]

The ability of the head of state to take certain moral liberties with the established law is a direct consequence of the fact that the moral good of the people is to be considered as being of greater importance than the strict observance of the law, which is merely a means to that end. As such, the question whether a guilty individual should be pardoned is not one of *law*, but one of *public moral interests*. The state may thus relax a law with this end in view, without its action being deemed to be improper.[101] The reason why the state is able to take such liberties with the established law is that it maintains two potentially conflicting principles at one and the same time – the need to obey the law, and the need to act towards the greatest good of the people.

Although these principles are usually reconcilable, situations inevitably must arise when they cannot be maintained simultaneously – and Ritschl argues that, on such occasions, it is the latter that must be upheld. It is therefore, according to Ritschl, impossible to model God upon the institution of the state and to assert that his action in justification is *judicial*, in that it is clearly *extrajudicial*. Ritschl thus notes with approval Tieftrunk's

---

[100] *Die christliche Lehre von der Rechtfertigung und Versöhnung*, §17; 86.
[101] *Die christliche Lehre von der Rechtfertigung und Versöhnung*, §17; 87–9.

emphasis upon the subordination of God's role as lawgiver to his role of public benefactor.[102] It is clear that Ritschl regards this extrajudicial approach to justification as avoiding the impasse of the orthodox doctrine of God as the righteous God who justifies humans, despite their being sinners, in order to develop an understanding of justification based upon a teleological principle paralleling that of the state as public benefactor.

Ritschl locates this teleological element of Christianity in the concept of the 'kingdom of God' (*Reich Gottes*). In adopting this position, Ritschl was following a general trend among the theologians of his time.[103] Ritschl's innovation lay in the significance he attached to the concept in connection with his doctrines of justification and reconciliation. His biblical investigations had led him to the conclusion that the concept of the kingdom of God was both the key to the preaching of Jesus and the unifying principle of the Old and New Testaments.[104] Ritschl thus rejects the 'Scotist' principle of God as *dominium absolutum* and the juristic concept of God, modelled upon the state, in favour of the concept of God as the originator and ground of the teleological principle of the kingdom of God. All else in Christian theology is to be regarded as subordinated to this goal. This general principle is of particular importance in connection with Ritschl's discussion of the divine attributes. Thus God's eternity may be taken to refer to the fact that God 'remains the same, and maintains the same purpose and plan by which he creates and directs the world'. Similarly, the divine attribute of 'righteousness' (*Gerechtigkeit*) is defined teleologically, in terms of the kingdom of God:

Omnipotence receives the particular character of *righteousness* in the particular revelation of the old and new covenants. By 'righteousness', the Old Testament signifies the consistency of the divine direction towards salvation (*die Folgerichtigkeit der göttlichen Leitung zum Heil*) . . . In so far as the righteousness of God achieves his dominion in accordance with its dominant purpose of salvation . . . it is *faithfulness*. Thus in the New Testament the righteousness of God is also recognised as the criterion of the special actions by which the community of Christ is brought into existence and led on to perfection. Such righteousness therefore cannot be distinguished from the grace of God.[105]

Ritschl regards this deobjectified teleological understanding of the 'righteousness of God' as having circumvented the difficulties of the orthodox concept, and to amount to a recovery of the teaching of the Old and New

---

[102] *Die christliche Lehre von der Rechtfertigung und Versöhnung*, §17; 89–90.
[103] See C. Walther, 'Der Reich-Gottes-Begriff in der Theologie Richard Rothes und Albrecht Ritschls', *KuD* 2 (1956), 115–38; R. Schäfer, 'Das Reich Gottes bei Albrecht Ritschl und Johannes Weiß', *ZThK* (1964), 68–88.
[104] Schäfer, 'Das Reich Gottes', 82–5.
[105] A. Ritschl, *Unterricht in der christlichen Religion*, Bonn: Marcus, 1875, §16.

390 The modern period

Testaments.[106] The concept clearly marks a break with the concept of *iustitia distributiva* (whether in the form associated with orthodoxy, with Pietism or with the *Aufklärung*), and permits Ritschl to avoid discussion of the question of how God *can* justify sinful humans (in that his understanding of the divine righteousness relates solely to the manner in which God *does* justify sinners).

On the basis of this teleological understanding of the economy of salvation, Ritschl mounts a sustained critique of the soteriology of Lutheran orthodoxy. He characterises the orthodox approach to the dogmatic analysis of the doctrine of justification as follows:[107]

1. A doctrine of original sin is developed on the basis of texts such as Romans 5:12, by which original sin is deduced from the actual sin of Adam and Eve.

2. The fact of this universally inherited sin of the human race is then used as the basis of the demonstration of the necessity of redemption. The mode of this redemption is determined by comparing sin with the divine attribute of retributive righteousness, following the general method of Anselm of Canterbury.

3. From this, the doctrine of the person and work of Christ is deduced, as is its application to the individual and the community of believers.

Ritschl argues that this approach is based upon purely rational ideas of God, sin and redemption, and is quite unsuited either to the positive exposition of the doctrine or to its defence against its rationalist critics. In particular, Ritschl objects to the Augustinian doctrine of original sin as implying a false hypostatisation of humankind over and against the individuals who are its members, and as failing to account for the fact that all humans are sinful to different degrees. Ritschl is at his closest to the soteriologies of the *Aufklärung* at this point.

It will, however, be clear that Ritschl's exposition of the doctrine of justification represents a significant consolidation of the doctrine in the face of earlier rationalist criticism. Three points may be singled out as being of particular importance:

1. The demonstration, on the basis of a historical analysis of the development of the doctrine of justification, that elements of the doctrine rejected in one cultural situation might subsequently be reappropriated in another. Thus the Enlightenment critique of the orthodox

---

[106] Particular attention should be paid to §§14 and 15 of the second volume of *Der christliche Lehre von der Rechtfertigung und Versöhnung*, Bonn: Marcus, 1874. Note particularly the reference to the study of L. Diestel, 'Die Idee der Gerechtigkeit, vorzüglich im Alten Testament, biblisch-theologisch dargestellt', *Jahrbuch für deutsche Theologie* 5 (1860), 173–204: *Die christliche Lehre von der Rechtfertigung und Versöhnung* §14; 102 n. 1.

[107] *Die christliche Lehre von der Rechtfertigung und Versöhnung*, §1; 5.

doctrine, and particularly its elimination of any objective dimension to justification, were not of permanent significance. It is difficult for modern readers to appreciate the full force of this point, in that they are unlikely to share the Hegelian framework within which theologians such as F. C. Baur constructed their thesis of the irreversibility of theological development.

2. The reappropriation of objective elements in the discussion of justification. Schleiermacher, although providing a strongly anti- rationalist foundation for his soteriology, had not taken this crucial step in re-establishing the traditional framework of the doctrine of justification.

3. The explicit statement that justification involves a *synthetic*, rather than an *analytic* judgement, which eliminated the theological foundation of the moral soteriologies of the *Aufklärung*.

It is also clear that Ritschl's analysis of the distinction between *rector* and *judex* has considerable implications for certain Enlightenment soteriologies; indeed, it is significant that the *Aufklärer* (Tieftrunk) singled out by Ritschl for approval in his exposition of this matter was one of the few who had responded to the Kantian critique of the moralism of the Enlightenment.

Nevertheless, a strong degree of affinity may still be detected between the *Aufklärung*, Schleiermacher and Ritschl in relation to their discussion of the work of Christ. The subjectivism of the earlier period is still evident in Ritschl's exposition of the work of Christ. Christ is the revealer of certain significant (and not necessarily rational) insights concerning an unchangeable situation between God and humanity, rather than the founder of a new relationship between them.[108] For Martin Kähler, there remained an essential continuity between Ritschl and the *Aufklärung* at precisely this point. According to Kähler, such a subjective approach to the meaning of the death of Christ represented a radical devaluation of its significance (*eine Entwertung des Werkes Christi*), in that Christ tends to be reduced to a mere symbol of the grace of God, without having any essential connection with that grace. It is this point which underlies his criticism of Ritschl's interpretation of the concepts of *Rechtfertigung* and *Versöhnung*; for Kähler, the latter corresponds to the objectively altered situation between God and humanity, arising through the historic work of Christ, while *Rechtfertigung* refers to a specific aspect of this situation – the individual's appropriation of this reconciliation through faith. The objective reality of reconciliation is necessarily prior to the subjective consciousness of this reconciliation.

---

[108] Note the question raised by M. Kähler, *Zur Lehre von der Versöhnung*, Leipzig: Deichert, 1898, 337: 'Hat Christus bloß irrige Ansichten über eine unwandelbare Sachlage berichtigt, oder ist er der Begründer einer veränderten Sachlage?'

Despite Kähler's strictures, the period 1880–1914 was characterised by the emergence of a significant degree of broad consensus relating to the question of justification. Drawing heavily upon the theme of the 'religious personality' of the historical Jesus, it was generally assumed that the justification of humanity came about through the influence of this supremely powerful religious personality as it impinged upon its existence.

5.5   The dialectical approach to justification: K. Barth

The outbreak of the First World War ushered in a new period in European theology, as the bourgeois optimism of the dawn of the century gave way to the sombre realism of the immediate post-war period. The impact of the war upon German theology, and particularly upon preaching, was momentous. The link between Christianity and culture, one of the most significant achievements of Ritschl's theological synthesis, was widely regarded as discredited through the Kaiser's war policies.

A growing sense of the 'otherness' of God from culture is reflected in many developments of the period, particularly in Karl Holl's famous lecture of 31 October 1917, delivered before the University of Berlin, which inaugurated the Luther renaissance by demonstrating how radically Luther's concept of God differed from the somewhat emasculated deity of liberal Protestantism.[109] Such radical developments in the world of religious ideas could not fail to have an impact upon the doctrine of justification.

To illustrate this impact, we turn to consider Karl Barth's lecture of 16 January 1916 in the Aarau Stadtkirche, on the theme of 'the righteousness of God'.[110] Even today, the rhetorical power of this lecture may still be felt, and the passage of time has done nothing to diminish the force of Barth's sustained critique of humanity's self-assertion in the face of God, which he links with the question of the true meaning of the 'righteousness of God'. For Barth, the 'deepest, inmost and most certain fact of life, is that "God is righteous"'.[111]

This fact is brought home to humans by their consciences, which affirm the existence of a righteous God in the midst of human unrighteousness, to be seen in the forces of capitalism as much as in the war which was raging over the face of Europe at that moment.[112] Deep within the inmost being of humans lies the desire for the righteousness of God – and yet paradoxically, just when this divine righteousness appears to be

---

[109] Karl Holl, 'Was verstand Luther unter Religion?', in *Gesammelte Aufsätze zur Kirchengeschichte*, 1.1–110.
[110] 'Die Gerechtigkeit Gottes', in *Das Wort Gottes und die Theologie*, 5–17.
[111] 'Die Gerechtigkeit Gottes', 5.   [112] 'Die Gerechtigkeit Gottes', 7.

on the verge of altering their nature and conduct, humans assert their own self-righteousness. They are unable to contemplate the concept of a 'righteousness' that lies beyond their own control. Humans welcome the intervention of divine righteousness if it puts an end to wars or general strikes – but feel threatened by it when they realise that behind the *results* of human unrighteousness lies the unfathomable reality of *human righteousness* itself. The abolition of the consequences of human unrighteousness necessarily entails the abolition of human unrighteousness itself, and hence an entirely new existence. Unable to accept this, people deform the 'righteousness of God' into various forms of human righteousness, of which Barth singles out three types for particular criticism.[113]

1. Moral righteousness. Barth rejects those spheres of human existence within which *Kulturprotestantismus* had located the locus of human morality (such as the family, or the state), on the grounds that, by restricting moral action to these spheres, humans are simply ignoring the obvious fact that their action is immoral in others. For Barth, the existence of the capitalist system and the war demonstrated the invalidity of this thesis, as *both* were perpetrated in the name of morality.

2. Legal righteousness (*die Gerechtigkeit des Staates una der Juristen*). Barth emphasises (prophetically, as the Third Reich was to demonstrate)[114] that human law is essentially orientated towards the ends specified by the state itself. At best, law could be regarded as an attempt to restrict the effect of human unrighteousness; at worst, it resulted in the establishment and perpetuation of human unrighteousness by the agencies of the state itself. Once more, Barth cites the war as exemplifying the defection of human ideas of 'righteousness' from those which conscience dictated should be recognised as divine.

3. Religious righteousness. Foreshadowing his mature critique of religion,[115] Barth argues that human religion, and indeed morality, constitute a tower of Babel, erected by humans in the face, and in defiance, of what their conscience tells them to be right.

In these three ways, Barth argues that humans are failing to take the 'righteousness of God' seriously, lest it overwhelm and transform them. They prefer to deal with shadows, and avoid the reality.[116]

---

[113] 'Die Gerechtigkeit Gottes', 10–12.
[114] For some useful reflections upon the impact of the *Rechtswillkür* of the Third Reich upon Protestant understandings of the theological significance of law, see Ernst Wolf, 'Zum protestantischen Rechtsdenken', in *Peregrinatio* II: *Studien zur reformatorischen Theologie, zum Kirchenrecht und zur Sozialethik*, Munich: Kaiser Verlag, 1965, 191–206.
[115] See J. A. Veitch, 'Revelation and Religion in the Thought of Karl Barth', *SJTh* 24 (1971), 1–22.
[116] 'Die Gerechtigkeit Gottes', 12–13.

For Barth, the First World War both questions and demonstrates the righteousness of God. It *questions* that righteousness, in that people are unable to understand how a 'righteous' God could permit such an outrage; it *demonstrates* that same righteousness, in that it shows up human caricatures of divine righteousness for what they really are. Humans have made their own concepts of righteousness into a God, so that God is simply the 'great personal or impersonal, mystical, philosophical or naive Profundity and patron saint of our human righteousness, morality, state, civilisation, or religion'.[117] For Barth, the war has destroyed this image of God for ever, exposing it as an idol. By asserting its own concept of righteousness in the face of God, humanity constructed a 'righteous' God who was the first and least mourned casualty of the war.[118] The 'death' of this God has forced people to recognise that the 'righteousness of God' is qualitatively different from, and stands over and against, human concepts of righteousness.

This lecture is of considerable significance in a number of respects. Of particular importance is the dialectic between human and divine righteousness, which marks an unequivocal break with the 'liberal' understanding of the nature of history, progress and civilisation. 'God's will is not a superior projection of our own will: it stands in opposition to our will as one that is totally distinct (*als ein gänzlich anderer*).'[119] It is this infinite qualitative distinction between human and divine righteousness which forms the basis of Barth's repeated assertion that God is, and must be recognised as, God.

The radical emphasis upon the 'otherness' of God so evident in Barth's programmatic critique of concepts of the 'righteousness of God' clearly parallels the theological concerns of the young Luther.[120] It might therefore be thought that Barth's early dialectical theology, or mature 'theology of the Word of God', might represent a recovery of the Reformer's insights into the significance of the *articulus iustificationis*. In fact, this is not the case. Paradoxically, to some, Barth actually appears to remain and operate within the conceptual framework established by the Enlightenment, Schleiermacher and Ritschl for the discussion of the justification of humans before God.

Barth's mature theology may be regarded as extended reflection upon the fact that God has spoken to humankind – *Deus dixit* – abrogating the epistemological chasm separating them in doing so. God has spoken,

---

[117] 'Die Gerechtigkeit Gottes', 13.
[118] 'Die Gerechtigkeit Gottes', 14.
[119] 'Die Gerechtigkeit Gottes', 15.
[120] See Althaus, 'Gottes Gottheit als Sinn der Rechtfertigungslehre Luthers'.

in the fullness of time, and it is this event – or these events – which stand at the heart of Barth's theological concerns. It is the task of any authentic and responsible *Christian* theology to attempt to unfold the nature and identity of the God who had spoken to sinners in the human-ward movement envisaged in the *Deus dixit*. The structures and the inner nexus of relationships presupposed by the fact – not the *idea* – of the *Deus dixit* determine what Christian theology has to say concerning the God who thus speaks.

Barth's theological system can be regarded, in essence, as the unfolding of the inner structures and relationships which characterise the *fact* that God has spoken. The theological enterprise could thus be portrayed as an exercise in *Nach-Denken*, following out the order of revelation in the human-ward movement of God in history. God has spoken to humans across the epistemological chasm which separates them, and, by so speaking to them, discloses both the reality of that separation and also the possibility of its abrogation. Barth confronts us with the paradox that the inability of humans to hear the Word of God is disclosed to them by that very Word. It is the reality of this divine abrogation of this epistemological chasm between God and humanity, and hence of the axiom *homo peccator non capax verbi Dei*, which stands at the heart of Barth's theological system.

Whereas, for Luther, the gospel was primarily concerned with the promise of the forgiveness of sins to sinful humanity, for Barth it is primarily concerned with the possibility of the right knowledge of God.[121] Barth has thus placed the *divine revelation to sinful humanity* at the point where Luther placed the *divine justification of sinful humanity*. Although there are clearly points of contact between Luther and Barth, it is equally clear that Barth cannot share Luther's high estimation of the *articulus iustificationis*. In what follows, we propose to explore why this might be the case.

In the course of his exposition of the doctrine of justification, Barth finds himself obliged to disagree with Ernst Wolf's analysis of the significance of the *articulus iustificationis* for the Reformers in general, and for Luther in particular.[122] Wolf locates the significance of the *articulus iustificationis* in terms of its function, which he conveniently finds expressed in the celebrated dictum of Luther: 'The article of justification is the master

---

[121] For an excellent analysis, see G. Ebeling, 'Karl Barths Ringen mit Luther', in *Lutherstudien III*, Tübingen: Mohr, 1985, 428–573.

[122] *Kirchliche Dogmatik*, IV/1 §61, 1; 581. On Barth's doctrine of justification, see Jüngel, *Das Evangelium von der Rechtfertigung*. The older study of H. Küng, *Rechtfertigung*, should also be consulted.

and prince, lord, ruler and judge of all kinds of doctrines, protecting and governing all church doctrine and directing our conscience towards God.' Wolf summarises Luther's understanding of the function of the *articulus iustificationis* in terms of its defining the 'centre and limits of Reformation theology'.

Wolf illustrates this interpretation of the function of the *articulus iustificationis* with reference to Luther's anthropology and ecclesiology – with convincing results – and argues for two important theses relating to its function. First, the *articulus iustificationis* is established as the leading principle of Luther's theology, as is the priority of soteriological considerations within the same context. Second, the *subjectum theologiae* is defined as God's salvific activity towards sinful humans.[123] The modesty of Barth's soteriological interests is emphasised when compared with Luther's insistence upon their dominating role in positive theological speculation. Furthermore, the secondary and derivative role of revelation within the context of Luther's theology will be evident,[124] although Barth does not seem to appreciate this point.

Barth is thus clearly obliged to dispute Wolf's analysis,[125] which he does in an important discussion of the *temporary* significance of the *articulus iustificationis*. He acknowledges the peculiar importance which Luther and his age attached to the doctrine, and further concedes that Luther did not regard the *articulus iustificationis* as the *primus et principalis articulus* merely in the polemic against Rome, but also against all form of sectarianism. However, he notes that no evangelical theologian – with the possible exception of Martin Kähler – ever dared to construct a dogmatics with the doctrine of justification at its centre.

This observation leads Barth to his critique of such a procedure. Conceding that the *articulus iustificationis* has been regarded as being *the* Word of the gospel on several occasions in the history of the church, he points out that these occasions represented instances where the gospel, understood as the free grace of God, was under threat – such as in the Pelagian controversy. Barth then argues that it is necessary to free the theological enterprise from the contingencies of such controversies.[126] He goes

---

[123] Wolf, 'Die Rechtfertigungslehre als Mitte und Grenze reformatorischer Theologie', 14. The reference to the *subjectum theologiae* derives from WA 40/II.328.17–21: 'Theologiae proprium subiectum est homo peccati reus ac perditus et Deus iustificans ac salvator hominis peccatoris. Quicquid extra hoc subiectum in theologia queritur aut disputatur, est error et venenum.'

[124] Thus Luther's celebrated distinction between *Deus absconditus* and *Deus revelatus* arises within the context of his soteriology; see H. Bandt, *Luthers Lehre vom verborgenen Gott: Eine Untersuchung zu dem offenbarungsgeschichtlichen Ansatz seiner Theologie*, Berlin: Evangelische Verlagsanstalt, 1958. Note the reference to Barth in the preface.

[125] *Kirchliche Dogmatik*, IV/1 §61, 1; 581.   [126] *Kirchliche Dogmatik*, IV/1 §61, 1; 583.

on to assert that the *articulus iustificationis* is not central to the Christian proclamation:[127] 'In the church of Jesus Christ, his doctrine has not always been *the* word of the gospel, and it would be an altogether restrictive and improperly exclusive act to treat it as such.'

In one sense, this is clearly correct; as a matter of history, it is true that the *articulus iustificationis* has not always been regarded as the centre of theological speculation. However, in that the *lex orandi* continually proclaims the centrality of the soteriological dimension of Christianity to Christian prayer, adoration and worship, and in that the community of faith is understood to be based upon a soteriological foundation, it is possible that Barth has not represented the situation accurately. Furthermore, the fundamentally soteriological orientation of the central patristic dogmatic debates leads to the conclusion that the Trinitarian and Christological dogmas are ultimately an expression of the soteriological convictions of the early church, whatever reinterpretation Barth may choose to place upon them. If the *articulus iustificationis* is taken to represent an assertion of the priority of soteriological considerations within the sphere of the church, Barth's statement must be regarded as seriously misleading.

It is, however clear that Barth's chief reason for relegating the *articulus iustificationis* to a secondary position is that it poses a serious and comprehensive threat to his own theological method. Luther's emphasis upon justification as the *articulus stantis et cadentis ecclesiae* is potentially subversive to Barth's theological undertaking. It is for this reason that Barth singles out Wolf's study of the function of the *articulus iustificationis* within the theology of the early Reformers for particular criticism. He therefore argues that the *articulus stantis et cadentis ecclesiae*, properly understood, is not the doctrine of justification as such, but its 'basis and culmination' in the 'confession of Jesus Christ'. This point is, however, hardly disputed, and is made by Wolf himself. The *articulus iustificationis* is merely a convenient statement of the salvific activity of God towards humanity, concentrated in Jesus Christ.

While Barth is prepared to retain the traditional designation of the *articulus iustificationis* as the *articulus stantis et cadentis ecclesiae*, it is only on account of the community of faith's need to know of the objective basis of its existence: 'without the truth of the doctrine of justification, there was and is no true Christian church'.[128] Nevertheless, so long as the essential truth of this article is not denied, Barth argues that it may withdraw into the background:

---

[127] *Kirchliche Dogmatik*, IV/1 §61, 1; 583.
[128] *Kirchliche Dogmatik*, IV/1 §61, 1; 583. Cf. *Kirchliche Dogmatik*, IV/1 §61, 1; 578.

It is precisely the justification of humanity itself, and our confidence in the objective truth of the doctrine of justiufication, which forbids us to postulate that its theological outworking in the true church must *semper, ubique et ab omnibus* be regarded and treated as the *unum necessarium*, as the centre or pinnacle of Christian proclamation and doctrine.[129]

Barth's criticism of those who see in the *articulus iustificationis* the centre of the Christian faith is thus a direct consequence of his theological method. Soteriology is necessarily secondary to the fact of revelation, *Deus dixit.* Barth's own theology may be regarded, at least in part, as a reaction against the anthropocentricity of the liberal school – a reaction particularly evident in his inversion of the liberal understanding of God and humanity as epistemic object and subject respectively. Yet Barth has essentially inverted the liberal theology without fundamentally altering its frame of reference. As such, he may be regarded as indirectly – perhaps even unintentionally – perpetuating the theological interests and concerns of the liberal school, particularly the question of how God may be known.

Most liberal Protestant theologians were not concerned with the question of 'guilt' or of 'righteousness *coram Deo*', in that they had no sense of human bondage or slavery to sin. Thus Albrecht Ritschl regarded Luther's *De servo arbitrio* (1525), which develops the notion of human bondage to sin in some depth, as 'an unfortunate botch' (*unglückliches Machwerk*) – even though it was precisely this work which Rudolf Otto singled out as the 'psychological key' to understanding Luther. Similarly, Karl Holl's celebrated 1917 lecture on Luther was primarily concerned with the correct *knowledge* of God, rather than with the soteriological dimension of his thought. It is significant that the Luther renaissance initially served to emphasise the Reformer's emphasis upon the deity and 'otherness' of God, rather than the importance of the *articulus iustificationis* within the context of his theology.[130] Dialectical theology was initially passionately concerned with the question of the right knowledge of God, inspired by a conviction of human ignorance of God and the impossibility of any theologically significant natural knowledge of God. There is no means by which the yawning chasm (which Barth designates a 'crevasse') between God and humanity may be bridged from humanity's side – hence the news that God has bridged this chasm from his side must be taken with the utmost seriousness.

---

[129] *Kirchliche Dogmatik*, IV/1 §61, 1; 584. Note also Barth's suggestion that a preoccupation with the question of how a gracious God may be found leads to a 'certain narcissism': *Kirchliche Dogmatik*, IV/1 §61, 1; 588.

[130] Holl, 'Was verstand Luther unter Religion?' Holl appears to treat Luther's doctrine of justification as an aspect of his *Gewissensreligion*.

Early dialectical theology thus took up one aspect of Luther's theology (the 'otherness' of God) and marginalised the other (human bondage to sin). Hence, for the young Barth, as we have seen, the significance of the 'righteousness of God' lay in the fact that it was diametrically opposed to human concepts of righteousness. The lack of interest in human bondage to sin, so characteristic of the liberal school and nineteenth-century theology in general, thus passed into the dialectical theology of the early twentieth century. The theological drama which constitutes the Christian faith is thus held to concern humans and their knowledge of God, rather than the salvation of sinful humans, caught up in the cosmic conflict between God and sin, the world and the devil.[131] Such a conflict is an impossibility within the context of Barth's theology, in that Barth shares with Hegel the difficulty of accommodating sin within an essentially monistic system. Barth has simply no concept of a divine engagement with the forces of sin or evil (unless these are understood in the epistemically reduced sense of 'ignorance' or 'misunderstanding'); instead, we find only talk about God making himself *known* to humanity. Barth even reduces the cross – traditionally the locus of precisely such a conflict – into a monologue between God the Father and God the Son.[132] The impartation of knowledge is no substitute for a direct confrontation with sin, death and evil.

The most significant aspect of Barth's criticism of the role allocated by Wolf to the *articulus iustificationis* lies in the different theological methods which they presuppose. For the later Barth, the concept of 'Christomonism' (Althaus) or 'Christological concentration' (von Balthasar) becomes of increasing importance. This Christological concentration finds its expression not in the history of Jesus of Nazareth in general, or even in the crucifixion or resurrection in particular, but in the pre-existence of Christ, before all eternity.[133] The reason for this lies in Barth's understanding of the divine freedom to reveal or not to reveal himself, and is particularly well expressed in his critique of Hegel.[134] The antecedence of the doctrine of the eternal generation of the Son preserves the divine freedom in revelation.

---

[131] On this theme in Luther's theology, see G. Aulén, 'Die drei Haupttypen des christlichen Versöhnungslehre', *ZSTh* 7 (1930), 301–38; M. Leinhard, *Luther témoin de Jésus Christ*, Paris: Editions du Cerf, 1968.

[132] A monologue which von Balthasar playfully derides as 'ein gespenstischer Spuk ohne Wirklichkeit': H. U. von Balthasar, *Karl Barth: Darstellung und Deutung seiner Theologie*, Cologne: Hegner, 1951, 225–6, 380.

[133] See J. de Senarclens, 'La Concentration christologique', in E. Wolff, C. von Kirschbaum and R. Frey (eds.), *Antwort: Karl Barth zum 70. Geburtstag*, Zürich: Evangelischer Verlag, 1956, 190–207.

[134] Karl Barth, *Die protestantische Theologie im 19. Jahrhundert*, Zürich: Evangelischer Verlag, 1952, 375–7.

As a result, Barth now finds himself obliged to assert that Christ is equally present at every stage of the history of salvation. That redemption presupposes sin is a difficulty which cannot really be accommodated within Barth's essentially supralapsarian understanding of the Fall. It is simply impossible to accommodate the existence of sin and evil in a convincing manner within the context of a theology which presupposes that the historical process is absolutely determined by what is already perfected at the beginning of time. For Paul, sin 'entered into the world'; Barth cannot convincingly speak of sin 'entering into' such a Christologically determined historical process.[135]

Setting aside for a moment Barth's general lack of interest in soteriology, it will be clear that his emphasis upon what has been Christologically determined from all eternity leads to a certain lack of interest in what pertains here and now. The *articulus iustificationis* deals with the predicament of humans here and now, as they are enslaved by sin and unable to redeem themselves. Barth's interests clearly lie elsewhere than with sinful humans, even if it is possible to argue that his theology ultimately represents the outcome of anthropological and epistemological considerations.

A further point of importance relates to theological method in general. If the starting point for theological speculation is defined as being the *articulus iustificationis*, an analytic and inductive method must be followed, arguing from the particular event of the divine justification of the sinner to the context in which it is set (such as the decrees of election). It can be shown that this methodology characterised the first period of Reformed theology, and is also characteristic of Arminius. However, the onset of Reformed orthodoxy saw the starting point for theological speculation shifted from the concrete event of the justification of the sinner in Christ to the divine decrees of election and reprobation. Instead of an analytic and inductive method, a synthetic and deductive method was employed, involving the appeal from general principles (such as the divine decree to elect) to particular events (such as the justification of the elect in Christ). As a result, justification is accorded a place of low priority in the *ordo salutis*, in that it is merely the concrete actualisation of the prior divine decision of election.

Barth approximates more closely to the theological method of Reformed orthodoxy than to that of Calvin. The synthetic and deductive approach necessitated by his insistence upon the antecedence of the doctrine of the eternal generation of the Son leads to the placing

---

[135] On this, and especially on Barth's concept of *das Nichtige*, see W. Krötke, *Sünde und Nichtiges bei Karl Barth*, Neukirchen-Vluyn: Neukirchener Verlag, 1983.

of the incarnation, death and resurrection of Christ low in the order of priorities within the context of his theological method. In that it is the application of a synthetic and deductive theological method by the theologians of Reformed orthodoxy (such as Beza) which leads to the abstract *decretum absolutum*, so heavily criticised by Barth, it is somewhat ironical that his own theological method approximates so closely to this method.

Barth's modest soteriological concerns also express themselves in his doctrine of the work of Christ, in which a remarkable degree of continuity is evident with the *Aufklärung*, Schleiermacher and Ritschl,[136] demonstrating once more Barth's close affinity with the theological framework of the liberal school, despite differences in substance. At first glance, Barth's theology of the work of Christ appears to be irreconcilably opposed to that of the *Aufklärung*. In his study of Protestant theology in the eighteenth and nineteenth centuries, Barth frequently displays his dislike of the theology of the Enlightenment.[137] Yet, as an analysis of the relation of his doctrine of the work of Christ, the passive nature of justifying faith and the related doctrine of the *servum arbitrium*, and the doctrine of election makes clear, Barth reproduces the main features of the *Aufklärung* soteriology. To make this point, we must begin with an analysis of Barth's Christological concentration of human knowledge of God.

For Barth, theology is essentially an exposition of the identity and significance of Jesus Christ.[138] In effect, Barth turns the whole of theology into Christology, in that the doctrines of creation, election and redemption are discussed in so far as they are determined by Christological considerations. Thus, in the exposition of his doctrine of election, Barth insists that the concept must not be regarded as a theological abstraction which bears witness to the divine omnipotence. He consciously distances himself from the pronouncements of the Synod of Dort by reinterpreting Calvin's concept of the *speculum electionis* to mean that Jesus Christ is at one and the same time the electing God and the elected human. If Christ were not the former, it would be necessary to look for the basis of election outside of Christ, and one would thus be driven to the doctrine of the *decretum absolutum* – which Barth considers unthinkable. Furthermore, in Jesus Christ the divine decision to become human is expressed

---

[136] See McGrath, 'Karl Barth als Aufklärer?'
[137] Barth, *Die protestantische Theologie*, 16–21.
[138] *Kirchliche Dogmatik*, IV/1 §57, 1; 16. See further H. J. Iwand, 'Vom Primat der Christologie', in Wolff, Kirschbaum and Frey (eds.), *Antwort*, 172–89; S. W. Sykes, 'Barth on the Centre of Theology', in *Karl Barth: Studies of his Theological Method*, Oxford: Oxford University Press, 1979, 17–54.

tangibly. As there is a duality in this election, Barth feels himself able to retain the term *praedestinatio gemina*, while totally altering its traditional meaning.[139]

Whereas Reformed orthodoxy had interpreted the term to mean that God irresistibly wills some to eternal life and others to eternal death, Barth argues that it refers to the divine decision to will *humanity* to election, salvation and life, and *God himself* to reprobation, perdition and death.[140] It is God himself who is condemned and rejected by his own judgement, and not those whom he elected in Christ. God thus chose as his own portion the negative element of the divine predestination, so that the positive element alone might be humanity's; in so far as predestination involves a negative verdict, that verdict is not pronounced against humans.[141] In other words, although Barth concedes that predestination includes a negative element, this is no longer directed at humanity.[142]

It is clear that God has elected humans unilaterally (*einseitig*) and autocratically (*selbstherrlich*), without any co-operation upon their part.[143] Christ took the place of humans as their federal representative and substitute, so that whatever needed to be done for our salvation has been done, without human consent or co-operation. Indeed, Barth insists upon the total inability of humans to justify themselves, or to co-operate in a significant manner with God in bringing about their salvation. For Barth, it is necessary to take a positive stand against the delusion (*Wahn*) of humanity's *liberum arbitrium* and co-operation with God, and to recognise that the Word of God includes a 'knowledge of the *servum arbitrium*, and the inability of humans to give God his due and thus justify themselves'.[144]

If humans are to have any say in their own justification – as the Catholic tradition within western Christianity has insisted is the case – they must have the freedom to respond to divine grace. Barth follows the 1525 Luther and Calvin in asserting that we possess no such freedom.[145] The freedom of human will is totally and irreparably compromised by sin. Barth's insistence upon the bondage of the human will, and his evident agreement with Calvin that faith is *res mere passiva*, serve to emphasise further that humanity is absolutely and totally unable to make any response whatsoever to the divine initiative in justification.[146] When his doctrine of

[139] See K. Stock, *Anthropologie der Verheißung: Karl Barths Lehre vom Menschen als dogmatisches Problem*, Munich: Kaiser Verlag, 1980, 65–72.
[140] *Kirchliche Dogmatik*, ii/2 §33, 2; 176–8.   [141] *Kirchliche Dogmatik*, ii/2 §33, 2; 181.
[142] *Kirchliche Dogmatik*, ii/2 §33, 2; 183.
[143] *Kirchliche Dogmatik*, iv/1 §57, 3; 72–3; §59, 2; 252.
[144] *Kirchliche Dogmatik*, iv/1 §60, 1; 458.   [145] *Kirchliche Dogmatik*, iii/2 §43, 2; 43.
[146] *Kirchliche Dogmatik*, iv/1 §61, 4; 679–718, especially 701.

the soteriological impotence of humans is related with Barth's theology of election, an astonishing situation results.

For Barth, it is impossible for God to select humanity to reprobation, as we have noted above. God has already elected this element of *praedestinatio gemina* for himself. In so far as predestination includes a 'No!', this 'No!' is not spoken against humanity.[147] Humans are totally unable to reject whatever God may have elected for them. This point is made by Barth repeatedly, as he emphasises the ultimate impotence of unbelief in the face of divine grace. Unbelief does not cancel God's decision to elect humans. God's judgement has been executed against Christ, and will never be executed against humanity itself, in whose place Christ stood. Humans may believe, or they may not believe – but whether they believe or not is quite irrelevant to their election. It may seem impossible for humans to be elected, on account of their sin and unbelief – but in fact, precisely the opposite is the case. It is impossible for them not to be elected. This aspect of Barth's theology has been criticised for its apocatastasian tendencies. His doctrine of election, when linked with his understanding of the capacities of fallen humanity, necessarily leads to a doctrine of universal restoration: all are saved, whether they know it or not, and whether they care for it or not.

With this point in mind, it will be clear that the crucial question now concerns human knowledge of this election. Barth frequently emphasises that Christ is the locus of human self-knowledge as a theological entity. Thus people know themselves to be sinners, and what this implies for their theological existence and status, only in the light of Jesus Christ.[148] Similarly, Barth insists that the election of humans is disclosed to them through the *speculum electionis*, Jesus Christ. In his discussion of both the positive and negative dimensions of the death and resurrection of Christ, Barth reveals an overriding concern for the *knowledge* which results:

In the mirror of Jesus Christ, who was offered up for us, and who was obedient in this offering, it is revealed (*wird offenbar*) who we ourselves are, that is, the ones for whom he was offered up, for whom he obediently offered himself up. In the light of the humility in demonstration of which he acted as true God for us, we are exposed, made known and have to acknowledge ourselves (*durchschaut, erkannt und haben wir uns selbst zu erkennen*) as the proud creatures who ourselves want to be God and Lord and redeemer and helper, and have, as such, turned away from God.[149]

---

[147] *Kirchliche Dogmatik*, II/2 §33, 2; 183: 'und heißt Prädestination Nicht-Verwerfung des Menschen'.
[148] *Kirchliche Dogmatik*, IV/1 §60, 1; 410.   [149] *Kirchliche Dogmatik*, IV/1 §61, 1; 574–5.

The frequent references to *Erkenntnis* and its cognates, where one might expect to find reference to *Heil* or *Versöhnung*, is one of the more remarkable aspects of Barth's discussion of human justification *coram Deo*, suggesting that Barth regards human knowledge and insight, rather than God's activity, as forming the centre of theological reflection. Barth's entire discussion of the justification of humanity appears to refer to the epistemic situation of humankind – in other words, to their *Christologically disclosed knowledge of the Christologically determined situation.*

Barth's frequently observed emphasis upon salvation as *Erkenntnis* is easily understood; given that all people will be saved eventually – which is the inevitable conclusion which must be drawn from his doctrines of election and *servum arbitrium* – the *present knowledge* of this situation is clearly of enormous importance. As all will be saved, it becomes of some importance that this salvation be actualised in the present – for such is the basic presupposition of Christian dogmatics and ethics alike. Both these disciplines are totally and absolutely dependent upon the presupposition that *humans know that they are saved.* Furthermore, in that dogmatics is a discipline which is carried out within the community of faith, it must reflect the basic presupposition upon which that community is grounded – in other words, the knowledge of its present salvation. Barth's repeated emphasis upon the cognitive character of salvation is perfectly consistent with this theology of election, in that, whatever salvation may be ultimately, it is certainly a deliverance from false thinking at present. Humankind may feel that all is lost, that there is no hope of salvation in a world permeated by sin and unbelief – and yet precisely the opposite is, in fact, the case.

As Brunner pointed out,[150] Barth's doctrine of election may be compared to a group of people who think that they are about to drown in a stormy sea, whereas the water is actually so shallow that there is no possibility whatsoever of drowning. This knowledge has, however, been withheld from them. What is necessary is that they be informed of the *true* situation which underlies the *apparent* situation. Thus Barth's doctrine of faith permits the believer to see beyond the sinful world of unbelief to the triumph of divine grace which lies behind it, and is disclosed in Christ, the *speculum electionis.* As all people will be saved eventually, apparently quite independently of their inclinations or interest, it is quite natural that Barth's attention should be concentrated upon the resolution of the epistemological confusion with which the believer is faced. Christ is thus

---

[150] E. Brunner, *Dogmatik* I: *Die christliche Lehre von Gott*, Zürich: Theologischer Verlag, 1946, 375–9.

the mirror, or locus, in which the Christologically determined situation is disclosed to humans.

With this point in mind, let us return to Martin Kähler's criticism of the soteriologies of the *Aufklärung*, Schleiermacher and the liberal school. For Kähler, a theology of the work of Christ could be classified under one of two types: the first, which corresponds to that of the *Aufklärung*, understands Christ to have communicated certain significant insights concerning an unchangeable situation; the second, which corresponds to his own view, understands Christ to be the founder of an altered situation.[151] Kähler's distinction allows two quite different approaches to the death of Christ to be identified:

1. Those which regard humanity's predicament as being *ignorance of the true situation*. Humans *are* saved, but do not realise it; upon being informed of the true situation, they are enabled to act upon the basis of this knowledge, and to adjust and reorientate their existence to what they now realise to be the true state of affairs. In so far as any alteration takes place in the situation, it is in the subjective awareness of humans; indeed, one could argue that the true situation is irrelevant, unless people recognise it as such – thus emphasising the necessity of being informed of it.

2. Those which regard the predicament of humanity as being *bondage to sin or evil*. Humans are enslaved, and may not realise it; upon being informed of the true situation, they still require liberation. The knowledge of their bondage may well lead to a recognition of the possibility of liberation, and hence to the search for the means of that liberation – but such liberation is not identical with, or given simultaneously with, or even a necessary consequence of, the knowledge of humanity's true situation. A victory of good over evil, of grace over sin, is required, which humans may appropriate and make their own, if they are to break free from the hegemony of sin – and precisely such a victory is to be had in the death of Christ upon the cross.

It is clear that Barth's understanding of the work of Christ falls into the first of these categories. For Barth and the *Aufklärer*, Christ is supremely the revealer of the knowledge of the true situation of humankind, by which humans are liberated from false understandings of their situation. For Barth, the death of Christ does not in any sense change the soteriological situation, in that this has been determined from all eternity – rather, he discloses the Christologically determined situation to humans. The dilemma of humanity concerns its knowledge of God, rather than its

---

[151] Kähler, *Zur Lehre von der Versöhnung*, 337.

bondage to sin or evil (unless these are understood in the epistemically reduced sense of 'ignorance' or 'confusion').[152] It will therefore be clear that Barth does not consider his emphasis upon the theocentricity of theology, and particularly his recognition of the divinity of God, as being associated with a revival in interest in the *articulus iustificationis*. Indeed, Barth operates within the same theological framework as the *Aufklärer*, Schleiermacher and the liberal school at this point, despite their evident differences at others.

Barth's disinclination to forge a link between his proposal for a revival of Christian dogmatics grounded in the priority of the revelation of God and the traditional framework of justification can be seen to mirror a general trend within twentieth-century theology, especially after the Second World War – a development which we may consider in more detail in the concluding section of this work.

5.6   The eclipse of justification, 1950–2000

Since the Second World War, Christian dogmatics has tended to marginalise the concept of justification. There are, of course, important exceptions to this generalisation, most notably within the Lutheran tradition.[153] Yet my own reading of works of systematic theology published since 1945 from a variety of traditions – Catholic, Anglican, Lutheran, Reformed and Baptist – does not suggest that there is any emerging consensus that the language and conceptual framework of the doctrine of justification is about to be recovered within mainline Christian theology. In fact, the only consensus that I can discern is a growing sense that these belong to the past, and that Christian dogmatics must therefore either focus on other traditional means of conceptualising the gospel proclamation of forgiveness and transformation through Christ, or forge new ones.

Some representative English-language writers, both reflecting and developing this trend, may be noted here. In his Gifford Lectures of 1956 and 1957, Leonard Hodgson declared that 'the phrase "justification by faith" has outlived its usefulness'.[154] In his view, the concept 'had better be dropped from our theological vocabulary'. A similar judgement

---

[152] For further discussion, see McGrath, 'Karl Barth als Aufklärer?', 280–3.

[153] The American dogmatician Robert Jenson (b. 1930) may be noted here; see Jenson, 'Justification as a Triune Event'; idem, 'Rechtfertigung und Ekklesiologie'. His more recent *Systematic Theology* (2 vols., New York: Oxford University Press, 1997–9) does not develop these themes to any significant extent.

[154] Leonard Hodgson, *For Faith and Freedom*, 2 vols., Oxford: Blackwell, 1956, 1.108, 110.

may be found in John Macquarrie, who suggested that the traditional Protestant emphasis on justification was 'vastly exaggerated'. Far from being the linchpin of the Christian faith, it was 'neither indispensable nor specially illuminating', being only 'one element in the Christian experience of reconciliation'.[155] Justification is to be seen as merely one way of conceptualising the Christian understanding of salvation by grace; earlier generations may have found it helpful or necessary on account of their historical or cultural situations – but this is no longer the case today.

Earlier (3.2), I noted how Luther's reforming agenda brought about a significant lexical development within western Christianity, in which the phraseology of 'justification by faith' displaced that of 'salvation by grace'. Both, of course, are equally Pauline. That development now appears to be in the process of reversal. In the case of Catholicism – Christianity's most theologically active constituency – this process of retrieval of the language of 'salvation by grace' was well under way by the seventeenth century, and was consolidated during the twentieth, as the minimal reference to 'justification by faith' in the *Catechism of the Catholic Church* indicates. Yet even in Protestantism, this process of conceptual eclipse and terminological marginalisation was well under way by 1950, and now appears to have become dominant. Why?

A number of factors may be noted, and will be explored in this concluding section. Perhaps the most obvious is the tendency, especially evident in ecumenical discussions about the doctrine of justification, to regard it as an essentially historically conditioned expression of faith, characteristic of the sixteenth century. Luther's emphasis upon the doctrine, while generally being treated with respect, is increasingly regarded as an idiosyncratic manner of expressing central Christian insights, which can be stated more satisfactorily using other conceptualities.

A second factor is the new climate of New Testament studies since the Second World War, which has expressed increasing concern about the reliability of certain traditional dogmatic interpretations of Paul's writings. Those concerns are often focussed on the issue of justification by faith, and especially on certain understandings of Paul's attitude to the law. The rise of increasingly sophisticated methods of biblical criticism led to the suggestion, especially during the later nineteenth century, that there existed a radical disjuncture between the preaching of Jesus and that of Paul, so that the doctrine of justification represented a gross distortion of the essentially simple message of Jesus.

New Testament scholarship began to question the assumption that Paul's gospel was focussed on the notion of justification, increasingly

---

[155] John Macquarrie, *Principles of Christian Theology*, London: SCM Press, 1966, 304.

regarding this as a theological idiosyncrasy due to Luther's dispropor-
tionate influence over western Protestantism.[156] In the late nineteenth
century, liberal theologians such as Schweitzer, Wernle and Wrede argued
that the Pauline doctrine of justification by faith was of purely historical
interest, being an aspect of Paul's anti-Jewish polemic rather than the
positive proclamation of a universal theology of redemption.[157] It was
at best a subsidiary aspect of Paul's conception of the transformation
of the human situation through Christ, not its core. By the late 1950s,
German-language New Testament scholarship was openly speaking of
the 'de-Lutheranization of Paul' (die Entlutherisierung Pauli).[158] This perception became increasingly influential in English-language scholarship
with the rise of the 'new perspective' on Paul.

A third factor relates to the rise of European secularism in the aftermath of the First World War, which led to increased scepticism concerning the relevance of God to 'modern emancipated humanity',[159] with a
consequent decline in the perceived significance of Luther's celebrated
question concerning the quest for a gracious God.[160] Whereas earlier generations of theologians were primarily concerned with the exposition and
analysis of the church's proclamation of the divine justification of sinful
humans, western theologians of recent decades have found themselves
increasingly obliged to defend its relevance and legitimacy in the face
of fundamental challenges to both. It is no longer humanity that needs
to be justified in the face of God, but God who needs to be justified in
the face of an increasingly sceptical humanity,[161] troubled as it is by the
violence and suffering of the world and the manifest failings of institutional religion. This has forced dogmaticians to reinterpret justification in
existential rather than traditional forensic categories, reinforcing the perception that the doctrine is increasingly out of place in western culture.

---

[156] For an excellent discussion, see Westerholm, *Perspectives Old and New on Paul*.
[157] In part, this reflected the views of the *Religionsgeschichte* school, such as W. Bousset's
    *Kyrios Christos: Die Geschichte des Christusglaubens von den Anfängen des Christentums
    bis Irenaeus*, Göttingen: Vandenhoeck & Ruprecht, 1913. See further P. Wernle, *Die
    Anfänge unserer Religion*, Tübingen, 1904, 222–3; A. Schweizer, *Geschichte der paulin-
    ischen Forschung von der Reformation bis auf die Gegenwart*, 2nd edn, Tübingen, 1933,
    132.
[158] For the phrase, see H. J. Schoeps, *Die Theologie des Apostels im Lichte der jüdischen
    Religionsgeschichte*, Tübingen: Mohr, 1959, 207.
[159] See Subila, *La giustificazione per fede*, 343–51; J. Moltmann, 'Justification and New
    Creation', in *The Future of Creation*, London: SCM Press, 1979, 149–71, especially
    151–2, 157–64.
[160] See Walter Kern, 'Atheismus – Christentum – emanzipierte Gesellschaft', *ZKTh* 91
    (1969), 289–321. Cf. C. Villa-Vicencio, 'Protestantism, Modernity and Justification
    by Faith', *SJTh* 38 (1985), 369–82.
[161] Subilia, *La giustificazione per fede*, 343–51.

We shall explore this further in what follows, before turning to examine further the two factors noted earlier.

5.6.1   Reinterpretation: justification as an existential category

The twentieth century witnessed a growing theological tendency to relate the doctrine of justification to the question of the meaning of human existence, rather than restricting it to the justification of humanity *coram Deo*.[162] The concept was seen to be in urgent need of translation out of the legal and forensic language of the sixteenth century into the *lingua franca* of modern western culture. In effect, a process of 'demythologisation' (in the strict sense of the term, as used by R. Bultmann) began,[163] by which the concept was transferred from the conceptual horizons of the sixteenth century to those of the twentieth. It is this trend which underlies the existentialist reinterpretation of the doctrine, associated with Bultmann, Tillich and Ebeling, to which we now turn. To understand the existentialisation of the doctrine, we need to consider the work of Martin Heidegger, widely credited with laying the conceptual foundations for this line of exploration and reinterpretation.

In his highly influential *Sein und Zeit* (1927), Martin Heidegger employed the phenomenological method of Husserl to develop an existential understanding of the structures of human existence. Arguing that the basic meaning of the word 'existence' derives from *ex-sistere*, 'to stand outside', Heidegger characterised the existence of humans in terms of their ability to stand outside the world of things. What is it that distinguishes the existence of people from that of inanimate objects? Heidegger argues that there are three fundamental senses in which humanity's peculiar way of being (*Dasein*) may be distinguished from that of things (*Vorhandenheit*).[164]

1. Humans transcend the subject–object relationship, in that they are at one and the same time both subject and object to themselves. They have the unique ability to reflect upon their nature, to understand themselves, and to be open to themselves in their being. They may properly be said to be at one with themselves, or at war with themselves, in that their relation to *Dasein* is open and alterable.

2. Human existence must be regarded as open-ended, in that humans are never fixed or complete in their being. In other words, it is to be understood in terms of possibility, rather than of actuality.

[162] Leppin, 'Luthers Frage nach dem gnädigen Gott – heute'.
[163] F. Gogarten, *Entmythologisierung und Kirche*, Stuttgart: Vorwerk-Verlag, 1953.
[164] Heidegger, *Sein und Zeit*, Halle: Niemeyer, 1927, 41–2. See further P. Bourdieu, *L'Ontologie politique de Martin Heidegger*, Paris: Editions de Minuit, 1988.

3. Human existence must be regarded as individual. Heidegger lays emphasis upon the 'individuality' (*Jemeinigkeit*) of existence, which cannot be separated from the individual in question.

Although it is clear that Heidegger's analysis of human existence in general is of considerable potential theological significance,[165] the aspect of his analysis which is of particular relevance to our study is his distinction between authentic (*eigentlich*) and unauthentic (*ineigentlich*) existence.[166] Humans exist in the world, which defines the arena within which they are confronted with the various possibilities open to them. People are in the world, and are bound up with its existence, even though they are quite distinct from its way of being. The possibility that humans will be overwhelmed by the way of being which the world represents, and thus 'fall' from an authentic to an unauthentic mode of existence, is an essential element of Heidegger's analysis of existence. Humans may fall away (*abfallen*) from themselves, obliterating their awareness of the essential distinction from the world by becoming absorbed in it, and thus becoming 'uprooted' (*entwurzelt*) from their proper way of being. Humans thus become alienated from their true existence through their fall into the world. Although it is tempting to equate Heidegger's concept of *Verfallenheit* directly with the theological concept of original sin, it is clear that Heidegger maintains that fallenness and alienation are merely existential *possibilities open to humanity*, rather than a normative definition of human existence.

The relevance of this existential analysis of human existence to the Christian theology of justification was indicated by Heidegger himself, who pointed out that Luther's doctrine of justification, especially when considered in relation to the question of the assurance of salvation, could be interpreted in existentialist categories.[167] Although critics have subsequently pointed out that Luther is primarily concerned with the justification of humans *coram Deo*, rather than with their self-justification in their particular existential situation,[168] it is this understanding of the significance of the doctrine of justification which achieved considerable influence through the works of Bultmann and Tillich.

For Bultmann, the New Testament is concerned with the fundamental question of the nature of human existence. The Christian kerygma,

---

[165] See J. Beaufret, 'Heidegger et la théologie', in R. Kearny and J. S. O'Leary (eds), *Heidegger et la question de Dieu*, Paris: Grasset, 1980, 19–36.

[166] J. A. Macquarrie, *An Existentialist Theology*, London: Collins, 1973, 29–105, 127–49.

[167] R. Lorenz, *Die unvollendete Befreiung vom Nominalismus: Martin Luther und die Grenzen hermeneutischer Theologie bei Gerhard Ebeling*, Gütersloh: Mohn, 1973, 131–44.

[168] See G. Ebeling, 'Gewißheit und Zweifel: Die Situation des Glaubens im Zeitalter nach Luther und Descartes', *ZThK* 64 (1967), 282–324.

expressed in mythical form in the New Testament, is a divine word addressed directly to humans, revealing that their present state of existence is unauthentic, and making known the possibility of authentic existence through the Christ-event, upon condition of the decision (*Entscheidung*) of faith – an issue which Bultmann holds to be directly addressed in Paul's doctrine of justification by faith.[169] Humanity is a 'potentiality to be' (*ein Sein-Können*), whose innate potentiality for authentic existence is exposed and developed by the kerygma. The Pauline concept of justification by faith thus concerns a fundamental aspect of human existence. In coming to their decision of faith, in response to the kerygma, individuals attain their authentic self (*sein eigentliches Sein*). Although Bultmann was criticised for his use of Heidegger's analysis of human existence, in that it appeared to reduce the gospel to an analysis of the condition of natural humanity,[170] Bultmann argued that the specifically Christian answer to the question of how authentic existence might be attained served to distinguish the gospel from secular understandings of human existence.[171]

A similar existential interpretation of the doctrine of justification is associated with Paul Tillich. In an important essay of 1924, Tillich noted that the doctrine of justification applied, not merely to the religious aspects of moral life, but also to the intellectual life of religion, in that it is not merely the *sinner*, but also the *doubter*, who is justified by faith.[172] Tillich thus extends the scope of the doctrine to the universal human situation of despair and doubt concerning the meaning of existence. Consequently, he argues that the doctrine of justification, when rightly understood, lies at the heart of the Christian faith.[173] While, in the nineteenth century, humans were characterised by their idealism, their twentieth-century counterparts are characterised by existential despair and anxiety – and it is to this latter humanity that the Christian message must be made relevant. Tillich attempts this task by the 'method of correlation', by which the Christian proclamation is 'correlated' with

---

[169] J. M. Millás, 'Justicia de Dios: Rudolf Bultmann intérprete de la teología paulina de la justificación', *Gregorianum* 71 (1990), 259–291.

[170] G. Kuhlmann, 'Zum theologischen Problem der Existenz: Fragen an Rudolf Bultmann', *ZThK* 10 (1929), 28–57.

[171] R. Bultmann, 'Die Geschichtlichkeit des Daseins und der Glaube: Antwort an Gerhardt Kuhlmann', *ZThK* 11 (1930), 339–64.

[172] The original essay, 'Rechtfertigung und Zweifel', was published in the 1924 *Vorträge der theologischen Konferenz zu Gießen*. Cf. P. Tillich, *The Protestant Era*, London: Nisbet, 1951, xxix.

[173] For what follows, see 'The Protestant Message and the Man of Today', in *The Protestant Era*, 189–204.

the existential questions arising from human existence. For Tillich, the doctrine of justification addresses a genuine human need; humans must learn to accept that they are accepted, despite being unacceptable.[174]

Similarly, Gerhard Ebeling argues that the concept of 'justification' is as strange to modern humanity 'as an Egyptian sphinx', and argues that the concept must be demythologised and interpreted in order that it may be shown to have an essential connection with human existence and its problems.[175] For Ebeling, in the event of justification, a fundamental change in the situation of humans takes place, by which they are transferred from the state of non-existence (*Nichtsein*) to that of authentic existence (*Sein*).[176]

Although Ebeling's approach to the doctrine may appear to parallel that of Bultmann or Tillich, Ebeling has gone far beyond them in drawing attention to the hermeneutical insights which lay at the basis of Luther's doctrine of justification *sola fide*, thus clarifying the nature of the doctrine as a critical principle in judging thought and practice. According to Ebeling, the central point of the Christian faith is that the proclamation of the grace of God in word and sacrament is itself the saving event, in that it proclaims the death and resurrection of Christ, and thence effects what it proclaims.

On the basis of this analysis, it will be clear that there has been a growing tendency to treat the doctrine of justification as a hermeneutical principle for interpreting, and subsequently transforming, human existence. As a result, there has been a corresponding increased emphasis upon the subjective or anthropological dimension of the doctrine, as well as upon the proclamation which brings about this existential transformation of the human situation.[177] This increased emphasis upon the role of the kerygma, or the Word of God, evidently raises the question of the legitimation of the kerygma – in other words, whether the soteriological or existential interpretation placed upon the history of Jesus of Nazareth by the Christian church, and expressed in the doctrine of justification, is justifiable. Lying behind the kerygma of the justification of the ungodly is the problem of the justification of the kerygma itself.

[174] See Tillich, 'You are Accepted', in *The Shaking of the Foundations*, London: SCM Press, 153–63.
[175] Ebeling, *Dogmatik des christlichen Glaubens*. 3 vols: Tübingen: Mohr, 1979, 3.20–6, 218. On the concept of 'relational ontology' which underlies Ebeling's statements, see Miikka Ruokanen, *Hermeneutics as an Ecumenical Method in the Theology of Gerhard Ebeling*, Helsinki: Agricola Society, 1982, 72–100.
[176] *Dogmatik des christlichen Glaubens*, 3.195–200.
[177] For the relation of anthropology, the Word of God and justification according to Eberhard Jüngel, see J. B. Webster, *Eberhard Jüngel: An Introduction to His Theology*, Cambridge: Cambridge University Press, 1986, 93–103.

This problem is particularly linked with the question of the relation between the preaching of Jesus and the proclamation of Paul – in other words, the question of how a legitimate and theologically coherent account may be given of the transition from the preaching *of* Jesus to the proclamation *about* Jesus. Enlightenment thinkers argued that the Pauline interpretation of Jesus (expressed in the doctrine of justification) was an improper and unnecessary dogmatic transformation of what was originally an essentially ethical proclamation. While the twentieth century did not witness a general abandonment of the doctrine of justification, it did give rise to an often critical discussion of aspects of the doctrine which were taken for granted by earlier generations. The difficulties which contemporary western theologians have been obliged to consider were not envisaged to any significant extent in the pre-modern period. Although the church continues to proclaim the justification of humankind through the free grace of God, and although this message continues to find a response in those to whom it is addressed, there has been growing recognition of the need to establish and defend the relevance and legitimacy of this proclamation in the first place.

5.6.2   Marginalisation: justification as an ecumenical problem

It will be clear from the analysis set out earlier in this volume that the doctrine of justification is of major importance in creating the fissures which opened up within the western church during the sixteenth century, and in maintaining that division subsequently. One of the sociological functions of doctrinal statements is to divide – whether to distinguish the church from the world, or one denomination from another.[178] But what if Christian groups wish to work more closely together, stressing what they hold in common, and marginalising what separates them?

The question whether the historical divisions which are associated with the doctrine can be overcome is of more than theoretical importance, and has come to the fore in the last few decades. One of the most important developments within Christianity since the Second World War has been the rise of the ecumenical movement, with its willingness to discuss past divisions with a view to overcoming them, to whatever extent this may be possible. The new, open relationship between the Roman Catholic and Protestant churches may partly be explained on the basis of the progressive attitudes adopted at the Second Vatican Council (1962–5), although it is likely that the social factors which lessened the tension between the

---

[178] See the analysis in A. E. McGrath, *A Scientific Theology*, III: *Theory*. Grand Rapids, MI: Eerdmans, 2003, 66–76.

churches in western liberal democracies must be taken into consideration in this matter as well.

The new willingness on the part of Roman Catholic theologians to discuss the controverted issue of justification is widely thought to have been stimulated by an early work of the Swiss theologian Hans Küng. In his major study *Justification* (German edition, 1957; English translation, 1964), Küng compared the views of Karl Barth with those of the Council of Trent, and argued that there was fundamental agreement between the position of Barth and that of the Roman Catholic church, seen in its totality.[179] This conclusion was the cause of some surprise at the time (1957), as well as of a certain degree of uncritical optimism concerning its significance. A more reliable judgement of the importance of Küng's work would be that he demonstrates that, if the Council of Trent is interpreted in a Thomist sense (rather than a Franciscan sense), and if certain aspects of Barth's doctrine of justification are overlooked, a significant degree of convergence between Trent and Barth emerges.[180]

Küng's work is open to criticism on a number of points. For example, Küng is perhaps somewhat unduly selective in those aspects of Barth's theology of justification which he chooses to expound. The obvious differences between Barth and Trent on the question of the freedom of the will and the nature of election are not touched upon by Küng, whereas they clearly require attention. Furthermore, Küng does not interpret the Tridentine decree on justification in terms of its historical context, and thus presents one interpretation of Trent – as it happens, that approximating most closely to the views of Barth – as *the* Tridentine doctrine of justification. This point is of particular importance in relation to Trent's teaching on merit, as we noted earlier. Küng represents Trent as teaching 'no merit whatsoever prior to justification', which is questionable (in that it overlooks the role played by the concept of congruous merit). Additionally, Küng fails to consider the implications of the post-Tridentine debates on justification for a contemporary Roman Catholic understanding of justification.

Despite such criticisms, Küng's book may be regarded as having initiated the ecumenical discussion of justification, indicating that at least some degree of agreement on the doctrine of justification could be reached between Roman Catholics and Protestants. It is, of course, true that Küng deals primarily with sixteenth-century *misunderstandings* rather than with sixteenth-century *disagreements*, with the result that he

[179] Küng, *Rechtfertigung*. See also his earlier article 'Ist in der Rechtfertigungslehre eine Einigung möglich?'
[180] See McGrath, 'Justification: Barth, Trent and Küng'.

does little more than demonstrate that Roman Catholics and Protestants share a common Christocentric anti-Pelagian theology of justification; this achievement, however, did much to highlight the misconceptions which abounded on both the Protestant and the Roman Catholic sides concerning the other's teachings on the matter, and pointed ahead to the possibility of a sustained discussion of the doctrine by ecumenical commissions.

It is no exaggeration to suggest that Küng's book marked the dawn of a new era of positive ecumenical discussion of a doctrine which had hitherto been seen largely as an insuperable obstacle to such dialogue.[181] In a period of two decades (1970–89), a significant number of such dialogues took place, of which we shall note two: the dialogue between Roman Catholics and Lutherans on the one hand, and that between Roman Catholics and Anglicans on the other. These adopt significantly different approaches to the contemporary role of the doctrine, one attempting to confront the theological difficulties head-on, the other marginalising the concept of justification in order to secure ecumenical agreement on other grounds.

In 1972 the Joint Study Commission of the Lutheran World Federation and the Vatican Secretariat for Promoting Christian Unity published the document now generally known as the 'Malta Report'.[182] This commission noted a developing ecumenical consensus on the doctrine of justification. This development underlies the important discussion, begun in 1978, between Lutheran and Roman Catholic theologians in the United States, which led to the publication of the most significant ecumenical document to date on the doctrine of justification.

On 30 September 1983, the US Lutheran–Roman Catholic dialogue group released a 24,000-word document which represented the fruit of six years of discussions on the doctrine of justification. This document, entitled *Justification by Faith*,[183] is among the most important ecumenical documents to deal with the theme of justification to date, and represents a landmark in ecumenical discussions. All who wish to deal with the dialogue between Protestant and Roman Catholic theologians on justification will have to make this document their point of departure. The document consists of a thorough analysis of the historical development of the doctrine, along with a careful assessment of the nature and significance of the controverted issues between Lutherans and Roman Catholics.

---

[181] For documentation and evaluation, see Lane, *Justification by Faith in Catholic–Protestant Dialogue*.

[182] 'The Gospel and the Church', published jointly in *Lutheran World* 19 (1972), 259–73, and *Worship* 46 (1972), 326–51.

[183] 'Justification by Faith', *Origins: NC Documentary Service*, 6 October 1983, 277–304.

The document begins by dealing with the history of the question. A careful study of the development of the doctrine prior to the sixteenth century allows the most recent scholarly insights into crucial historico-theological questions (such as the nature of the Pelagian controversy) to be brought to bear on their discussions. This is followed by a particularly comprehensive, competent and insightful account of the sixteenth-century debates on justification, in which the points at issue between Lutheranism and the Council of Trent are identified and analysed. 'Lutheranism' tends to be defined with reference to the Formula of Concord, facilitating the harmonisation of Lutheran and Tridentine views; Luther was perhaps too close to Calvin and Reformed orthodoxy in his teaching on justification to function as a basis of such harmonisation. Nevertheless, the document's treatment of Luther is fair, in relation both to his thought and to the historical context in which his reforming programme was set.

This is followed by an analysis of developments after the sixteenth century, including excellent summaries of the relevance of Jansenism, Baianism, Pietism, Vatican II, and the particularly important discussions of the Helsinki Assembly of the Lutheran World Federation (1963). By the end of this historical analysis, critical readers will almost certainly be persuaded that the contributors to this document are competent and informed, so that it is with some confidence that they will turn to the crucial section dealing with theological reflections and interpretation, in which the contemporary relevance of the historical course of the great Reformation controversies is evaluated. This is a particularly fine attempt to come to terms with the historical memories of these two great traditions, and, indeed, ought to serve as a model for contemporary ecumenical theological reflection on past differences.

Six areas of *convergence* (note the decision not to use the term 'agreement') are then noted, concerning the forensic nature of justification, the sinfulness of the justified, the sufficiency of faith, the concepts of merit and of satisfaction, and criteria of authenticity. In these areas, the dialogue group notes that, despite differing theological perspectives and structures of thought, similar concerns and foundational beliefs can be discerned as lying beneath the specific doctrinal formulations of each church. The final section of the document then considers perspectives for reconstruction. It affirms a 'fundamental consensus on the gospel', which is reached through extensive engagement with the appropriate texts in the light of the best New Testament scholarship, both Lutheran and Roman Catholic – and the convergences which have become evident in this scholarship of late are thus harnessed to considerable ecumenical advantage.

The fact that there are 'remaining differences' between the two churches on a number of important aspects of the doctrine is explicitly acknowledged; these are interpreted, however, in terms of *complementary* rather than *contradictory* approaches to the doctrine. In this way, the document recognises the quite distinct approaches to the doctrine associated with each of the two churches, arguing that they are complementary and convergent, rather than contradictory and divergent. The document thus affirms that the quite distinct ideas of forensic justification and justification by inherent righteousness are two ways of conceptualising essentially the same theological principle:

> It must be emphasised that our common affirmation that it is God in Christ alone whom believers ultimately trust does not necessitate any one particular way of conceptualising or picturing God's saving work. That work can be expressed in the imagery of God as judge who pronounces sinners innocent and righteous . . . and also in a transformist view which emphasises the change wrought in sinners by infused grace.[184]

The crucial question of the formal cause of justification – the *real* crux of division in the sixteenth century – is thus resolved by suggesting that both positions (justification by an alien righteousness and justification by an intrinsic righteousness) are appropriate (but not *identical*) ways of conceptualising the ultimate foundation of our justification in the action of God in Jesus Christ. The document recognises that this is no mere difference of words – it amounts to quite distinct theological frameworks, vocabularies, hermeneutics, emphases and manners of conceptualising the divine action. The fundamental point which the document wishes to affirm is that both positions are legitimate ways of attempting to safeguard the same crucial insight.

A quite different approach, reflecting a somewhat more pragmatic attitude to the matter, is found in the report of the Second Anglican–Roman Catholic International Commission (ARCIC II), *Salvation and the Church* (1987).[185] This document appears somewhat reluctant to address the disagreements which classical Anglican theologians of the late sixteenth and early seventeenth centuries perceived to exist between themselves and Rome, such as the Caroline emphasis upon the formal cause of justification as the central issue, even the 'grand question which hangeth yet in controversy' (R. Hooker), between Rome and the Church of England.

The commission is evidently aware of the difficulties raised by this difference, but chooses to address it rather circumspectly. It is far from clear whether we are to regard the question of the formal cause of justification as having been *resolved*, or as having been declared to be *irrelevant*. The

---

[184] 'Justification by Faith', §158; 298.
[185] *Salvation and the Church: An Agreed Statement by the Second Anglican–Roman Catholic International Commission*, London: Church House Publishing, 1987.

impression gained is that it is quietly being marginalised. The document concedes the forensic nature of justification, but argues that this image must be complemented by 'other biblical ideas and images of salvation', so that other dimensions of salvation (such as renewal, sanctification, and so forth) might be included.

Even the evasion of the term 'justification' in the title is significant, in that it points to the pursuit of ecumenical agreement by focussing on other, more malleable soteriological issues without problematic historical associations. 'Justification' is too heavily freighted, rhetorically and theologically, to be the basis of ecumenical reconciliation; the simplest procedure is to marginalise it, and to concentrate on other ways of speaking about the reconciliation of God to humanity. This is not to condone this process of theological sleight of hand; it is, however, to note that the late twentieth century's ecumenical interests led to perceiving the doctrine of justification as problematic to the unity of the church, rather than as foundational to the identity of the church. It is an important contributing factor to the quiet marginalisation of the doctrine in Christian theology at the opening of the twenty-first century.

Our attention now turns to the development of the 'new perspective on Paul', which has called into question some traditional notions concerning justification, especially those inherited from the Lutheran wing of the Reformation.

5.6.3   Criticism: the 'new perspective' on Paul

Late nineteenth-century German New Testament scholarship regarded the Lutheran reading of Paul as highly questionable, not least in the light of growing interest in the *religionsgeschichtlich* approach to the interpretation of the New Testament.[186] This led to an explosion of interest in exploring the shaping of Paul's thought against its background in Judaism and Hellenistic culture. Although many of the conclusions reached were more provisional than some realised, an emerging consensus can be discerned on two points: first, that a 'Lutheran' reading of Paul was increasingly problematic in the light of an increased understanding of the intellectual and cultural background to the New Testament; second, that justification could no longer be considered as constituting or determining the centre of Paul's theology, let alone of the Christian gospel itself.

---

[186] For the debate, see J. Gottschick, 'Paulinismus und Reformation', *ZThK* 7 (1897), 398–460; E. Vischer, 'Jesus und Paulus', *Theologische Rundschau* 8 (1905), 129–43, 173–88; W. Heitmüller, 'Zum Problem Paulus und Jesus', *ZNW* 13 (1912), 320–37; W. Michaelis, 'Rechtfertigung aus Glauben bei Paulus', in K. L. Schmidt (ed.), *Festgabe für Adolf Deißmann zum 60. Geburtstag*, Tübingen: Mohr, 1927, 117–158.

This process of critiquing the 'Lutheran' perspective on Paul has since proceeded apace, often, it must be said, with surprisingly little reference to Luther. In 1964, R. N. Longenecker argued that Judaism could not be regarded as 'legalist' in any meaningful sense of the term; it should rather be regarded as 'nomist'.[187] The appearance of E. P. Sanders' works in the 1970s catalysed this mood of suspicion over Pauline interpretative schemas inherited from the period of the Reformation, which were increasingly held to have been determined by the ecclesiastical polemics and cultural presuppositions of the period.

To put it crudely, the nub of the criticism is that westerners tended to read Paul in the light of the deeply ingrained assumptions of modern individualism, failing to appreciate that Paul inhabited a significantly different world.[188] Western concerns were thus read into, rather than out of, the Pauline texts. In contrast to Luther, Paul was not interested in the question 'How can the individual be righteous in God's sight?', but in the very different question, 'On what grounds can Gentiles participate in the people of God in the last days?'[189]

J. D. G. Dunn argued that the doctrine of justification as rediscovered by Luther, and as subsequently expounded within Protestantism, has neglected important aspects particularly of Paul's original formulation of that doctrine in the context of his mission.[190] While Dunn does not criticise the Protestant doctrine of justification as such, he speaks of 'a significant misunderstanding of Paul' – such as the assumption that Paul affirmed his doctrine against a degenerate Jewish legalism, typical of Judaism as a whole.[191] Dunn affirms that Paul's teaching on justification is an expression of his mission to the Gentiles, and that it embodies a protest against national or ethnic presumption and disdain for the Gentiles. The gospel is thus for all who believe, Jew first but also Gentile. Whereas Luther interpreted the phrase 'the works of the law' to refer to human moral self-righteousness in general, Dunn argues that an integral aspect of 'the works of the law' was a concern to maintain Israel's distinctiveness and separateness from the Gentiles, and that this aspect of the idea has been neglected in attempts to clarify Paul's key theological formulation, which affirms that we are 'justified by faith apart from works of the law' (Romans 3:28).

Of the various criticisms directed against Luther by the 'new perspective' on Paul, two are of especial importance to this study, in that they

---

[187] R. N. Longenecker, *Paul: Apostle of Liberty*, New York: Harper & Row, 1964, 65–85.
[188] See Stendahl, 'Paul and the Introspective Conscience of the West'; S. Stowers, *A Re-Reading of Romans*, New Haven: Yale University Press, 1994, 6.
[189] E. P. Sanders, *Paul*, Oxford: Oxford University Press, 1991, 50. For an excellent survey of Sanders' approach, see Westerholm, *Israel's Law and the Church's Faith*, 46–51.
[190] Dunn, 'The Justice of God'.   [191] Dunn, 'The Justice of God', 5–8.

relate directly to the theological place and contents of the doctrine of justification.

1. Justification cannot be regarded as the centre of Paul's thought, nor of Christianity. Any suggestion that the doctrine of justification is the 'article by which the church stands or falls' is without adequate biblical warrant.

2. The situation envisaged by Paul in formulating his doctrine of justification by faith is not a universal human self-righteousness which makes Pelagian claims on God's favour, but a specifically Jewish concern about the covenantal limits of the people of God. If this is so, the traditional interpretation of the Pauline doctrine of justification, from Augustine through Luther and beyond, requires revision.

The debate is far from over. The huge literature it has spawned has noted that there are genuine difficulties with the 'new perspective' on Paul, and that traditional readings of Paul may have more in their favour than has been generally appreciated.[192] Nevertheless, the debate continues to overshadow contemporary theological reflection on the doctrine of justification, and on its place within a Christian dogmatics.

Perhaps more seriously, the debate has opened up concerns about whether systematic theologians and New Testament scholars talk to each other, or read each other's works. The 'new perspective on Paul' has reinforced a growing perception that systematic theology has lost its moorings in the Bible, and prefers to conduct its disputes with reference to systematic theologians of the past, rather than by direct engagement with biblical texts.

The question of the future of the concept of justification thus remains open. Will the twenty-first century witness a renewed conviction of the importance of the doctrine? Or will it see the further consolidation of the later twentieth-century marginalisation of the concept within both biblical studies and Christian dogmatics?

5.7   Conclusion

It is customary for volumes which have surveyed the history of a specific Christian teaching to conclude by propounding the author's views on how the doctrine should be restated or redeveloped in the situation faced by the churches today. The history of the doctrine thus forms merely the prolegomenon to the real purpose of the work, and is often subservient

---

[192] See, for example, F. Thielman, *The Law and the New Testament*, New York: Herder & Herder, 1999; D. A. Carson et al. (eds.), *Justification and Variegated Nomism: A Fresh Appraisal of Paul and Second Temple Judaism*, Tübingen: Mohr Siebeck, 2001; and especially Westerholm, *Perspectives Old and New on Paul*.

to that end. No such intention underlies this work. The history of the development of the Christian doctrine of justification is here traced and documented as an enormously interesting and complex subject, worthy of careful consideration. There is no doubt that the material set out in this work will be of major interest to all concerned with ecumenical discussions, with the history of the theology of the Protestant and Catholic Reformations, and with the development of Christian doctrine, to name but three obvious categories of readers.

But the real joy of this volume, if I dare mention it, has been to allow its author to spend twenty-five years of his professional career as a historical theologian to read the works of a vast number of theologians and biblical scholars, and to attempt to analyse, correlate and summarise what I have found. If this work encourages others to do the same, it will have served a useful purpose.

Glossary of medieval soteriological terms

acceptatio divina The divine act by which God grants humanity eternal life. In later medieval theology, the term is used to emphasise the fact that the salvation of humans is ultimately dependent upon the divine decision to accept them, rather than upon any quality (such as a created habit) which individuals may themselves possess. It should be stressed that *acceptatio divina* must not be confused with *acceptio personarum*; this latter term is used by Julian of Eclanum and others to refer to the idea of divine favouritism, which is rejected in favour of the divine *aequitas*.

amor amicitiae The pure love of another for the sake of love itself, without any ulterior motive. The term is frequently employed by the theologians of the *via moderna* in discussing the preconditions of justification.

attritio An imperfect natural form of repentance for sin, which arises out of fear of divine punishment, to be distinguished from *contritio*.

concursus generalis The natural influence of God upon the creation, also referred to as the *influentia generalis*. The concept is usually discussed in terms of Aristotelian physics, where the general *concursus* of the first cause (i.e., God) is understood to be essential if the potentiality of second causes is to be actualised.

contritio A perfect form of repentance for sin arising out of love for God (*amor amicitiae*), to be distinguished from *attritio*. *Contritio* is usually regarded as being possible only with the assistance of divine grace.

ex natura rei – ex pacto divino Two fundamentally different concepts of causality underlying the medieval discussion of justification. Ontological, or *ex natura rei*, causality is based upon the presupposition that an inherent connection exists between the related entities or processes, which necessitates their causal relationship; covenantal, or *ex pacto divino*, causality is based upon the presupposition that whatever connection exists between the causally related entities or processes exists solely on account of a divine ordination that such a relationship shall exist.

ex puris naturalibus   The abilities of humans in their purely natural state, without any special assistance of God, except the *concursus generalis*. This should not be confused with the concept of *natura pura* introduced later by Cajetan.

facere quod in se est   The requirement laid upon people by God if they are to dispose themselves towards the reception of the gift of grace.

gratia gratis data   A transitory gift of grace to the *viator* which may coexist with a state of sin.

gratia gratum faciens   A habitual gift of grace which renders the *viator* acceptable to God, and which may not coexist with a state of mortal sin.

habitus   A permanent state or disposition within the *viator*, to be distinguished from a transitory act. The habit of grace is understood to be a created form within the soul of the *viator*, intermediate between the divine and human natures, through whose influence the *viator* is changed to become more like God. The *habitus gratiae* is often referred to as *gratia creata*, to distinguish it from the uncreated grace (*gratia increata*) of the Holy Spirit himself.

meritum de condigno   Merit in the strict sense of the term – that is, a moral act performed in a state of grace, and worthy of divine acceptation on that account.

meritum de congruo   Merit in a weak sense of the term – that is, a moral act performed outside a state of grace which, although not meritorious in the strict sense of the term, is considered an 'appropriate' ground for the infusion of justifying grace (*gratia prima*). The concept is generally discussed in relation to the axiom *facienti quod in se est Deus non denegat gratiam*.

pactum   The 'covenant' between God and humankind which governs the theology of the *via moderna*.

potentia Dei absoluta   The absolute power of God – that is, the possibilities open to God before God entered into any decisions concerning a course of action which led to the establishment of the ordained order through creation and subsequently redemption. It refers primarily to God's ability to do anything, subject solely to the condition that the outcome should not involve logical contradiction.

potentia Dei ordinata   The ordained power of God – that is, the established order of salvation, which, although contingent, is totally reliable. The dialectic between the absolute and ordained powers of God was used by the theologians of the later Franciscan school, the *via moderna* and the *schola Augustiniana moderna* to demonstrate the contingency of the involvement of created habits of grace in justification.

viator   Literally, 'wayfarer' or 'pilgrim'. The traditional medieval term used to refer to a believer on his or her way to the heavenly Jerusalem.

Bibliography

1 PRIMARY LITERATURE

1.1 COLLECTED WORKS

Die Bekenntnisschriften der evangelisch-lutherischen Kirche. 2nd edn. Göttingen: Vandenhoeck & Ruprecht, 1952.

Die Bekenntnisschriften der reformierten Kirche, ed. E. F. K. Müller. Leipzig: Deichert, 1903.

Concilium Tridentinum diarorum, actorum, epistularum, tractatuum nova collectio. Freiburg: Societas Goersiana, 1901–50.

Corpus Christianorum Series Latina. Turnholt: Brepols, 1953– .

Corpus Scriptorum Ecclesiasticorum Latinorum. Vienna: Verlag der österreichischen Akademie der Wissenschaften, 1886– .

Denzinger, H., *Enchiridion Symbolorum Definitionum et Declarationum de Rebus Fidei et Morum,* 39th edn. Freiburg: Herder, 2001.

Hardwick, C., *A History of the Articles of Religion,* 3rd edn. London: Bell, 1890.

Lloyd, C., *Formularies of Faith put forth by Authority during the Reign of Henry VIII.* Oxford: Oxford University Press, 1825.

Migne, J. P., *Patrologia cursus completus series Graeca.* 162 vols. Paris: Migne, 1857–66.

Patrologia cursus completus series Latina. 221 vols. Paris: Migne, 1844–64.

1.2 BIBLICAL

Biblia Hebraica, ed. R. Kittel. 17th edn. Stuttgart: Württembergische Bibelanstalt, 1972.

Biblia Sacra iuxta Vulgatam versionem. Stuttgart: Württembergische Bibelanstalt, 1975.

Septuaginta, ed. A. Rahlfs. 9th edn. Stuttgart: Württembergische Bibelanstalt, 1975.

1.3 PRIMARY SOURCES

Aegidius Romanus, *Commentarius in secundum librum sententiarum.* 2 vols. Venice, 1581.

Albertus Magnus, *Opera omnia,* ed. S. C. A. Borgnet. 38 vols. Paris: Vives, 1890–9.

Alexander of Hales, *Glossa in IV. libros sententiarum.* 4 vols. Quaracchi: Typographia Collegii S. Bonaventurae, 1951–7.
   Quaestiones disputatae antequam esset frater. 3 vols. Quaracchi: Typographia Collegii S. Bonaventurae, 1960.
Alexander of Hales (attributed), *Summa theologica.* 4 vols. Quaracchi: Typographia Collegii S. Bonaventurae, 1924–48.
Alsted, Johann Heinrich, *Theologia scholastica didactica.* Hanover, 1618.
Andrewes, Launcelot, *Works.* 11 vols. London, 1841–52.
Anselm of Canterbury, *Opera omnia,* ed. F. S. Schmitt. 6 vols. Stuttgart: Frommann, 1968.
Anselm of Laon, *Anselms von Laon systematische Sentenzen,* ed. F. P. Bliemetzrieder. Münster: Aschendorff, 1919.
Arminius, Jakobus, *Works.* 3 vols. London: Thomas Baker, 1825–75.
Baius, Michel, *Opera.* Cologne, 1696.
Barlow, Thomas, *Two Letters written by the Rt Rev. Thomas Barlow.* London, 1701.
Barrow, Isaac, *Theological Works,* ed. A. Napier. 9 vols. Cambridge, 1859.
Barth, Karl, *Das Wort Gottes und die Theologie.* Munich: Kaiser, 1925.
   Kirchliche Dogmatik. 13 vols. Zurich: Evangelischer Verlag, 1932–68.
Baxter, Richard, *Aphorisms on Justification.* London, 1649.
   A Treatise of Justifying Righteousness. London, 1676.
[Benedetto da Mantova, Dom?], *Il beneficio di Cristo con le versioni del secolo XVI.,* ed. Salvatore Caponetto. Florence: Salvatori, 1972.
Beveridge, William, *Theological Works.* 12 vols. Oxford, 1844–8.
Beza, Theodore, *Tractationes theologicae.* 2nd edn. Geneva, 1632.
Biel, Gabriel, *Canonis missae expositio,* ed. H. A. Oberman and W. J. Courtenay. 4 vols. Wiesbaden: Steiner, 1963–67.
   Collectorium circa quattuor libros sententiarum, ed. W. Werbeck and U. Hoffmann. 4 vols. Tübingen: Mohr, 1973–84.
   Sermones dominicales de tempore. Hagenau, 1510.
Bonaventure, *Opera omnia.* 10 vols. Quaracchi: Typographia Collegii S. Bonaventurae, 1882–1902.
Bradwardine, Thomas, *De causa Dei contra Pelagium.* London, 1618.
Bramhall, John, *Works.* 5 vols. Oxford, 1842–5.
Brochmand, Jesper Rasmussen, *Universae theologiae systema.* Ulm, 1638.
Bucanus, Guillaume, *Institutiones theologicae.* N.p., 1604.
Bucer, Martin, *Praelectiones in epistolam ad Ephesios.* Basel, 1561.
   Metaphrasis et enarratio in epistolam ad Romanos. Basel, 1562.
Budde, Johann Franz, *Institutiones theologiae dogmaticae.* Jena, 1723.
Bull, George, *Harmonia apostolica.* London, 1842.
Bullinger, Heinrich, *Sermonum decades quinque.* Zurich, 1552.
   De gratia Dei iustificante. Zurich, 1554.
Burmann, Franz, *Synopsis theologiae.* Amsterdam, 1699.
Calov, Abraham, *Systema locorum theologicorum.* Wittenberg, 1655.
Calvin, John, *Opera omnia quae supersunt.* 59 vols. Brunswick, 1863–1900.
   Opera selecta, ed. P. Barth and W. Niesel. 5 vols. Munich: Kaiser, 1922–36.
Chemnitz, Martin, *Loci theologici.* 3 vols. Frankfurt, 1599.
   Examinis Concilii Tridentini. Frankfurt, 1646.

Clarke, Samuel, *The Saints Nosegay, or, 741 Spiritual Flowers*. London, 1642.

Cocceius, Johannes, *Summa theologiae*. Amsterdam, 1665.

Opera. 8 vols. Amsterdam, 1673–5.

Contarini, Gasparo, *Regesten und Briefe*, ed. F. Dittrich. Braunsberg: Emil Bender, 1881.

Gegenreformatorische Schriften 1530–42. Münster: Aschendorf, 1923.

Cosin, John, *Works*. 5 vols. Oxford, 1843–55.

Cotton, John, *Christ the Fountaine of Life*. London, 1651.

Gods Mercie mixed with his Iustice. London, 1641.

A Treatise of the Covenant of Grace. London, 1659.

Cranmer, Thomas, *Works*. 2 vols. Cambridge, 1844–6.

Dante Alighieri, *La divina commedia*, ed. D. Mattalia. 3 vols. Milan: Rizzoli, 1975.

Davenant, John, *A Treatise on Justification, or the 'Disputatio de Iustitia Habituali et Actuali'*. London, 1844.

Downham, George, *A Treatise of Justification*. London, 1639.

Duns Scotus, *Commentaria Oxoniensia*. 2 vols. Quaracchi: Typographia Collegii S. Bonaventurae, 1912–14.

Opera omnia, ed. C. Balic. Rome: Typis Polyglottis Vaticanis, 1950– .

Durandus of St Pourçain, *In Petri Lombardi sententias theologicas commentariorum*. 2 vols. Venice, 1571.

Eck, Johannes, *Chrysospassus praedestinationis*. Augsburg, 1514.

In primum librum sententiarum annotatiunculae, ed. L. Moore. Leiden: Brill, 1976.

Edwards, Jonathan, *Five Discourses on Justification by Faith*. Boston, 1738.

Works, ed. E. Hickman. 2 vols. London, 1834.

Erasmus, Desiderius, *Novum instrumentum omne*. Basel, 1516.

Opera omnia, ed. J. Clericus. 10 vols. Leiden, 1703–6.

Fisher, John, *English Works*, ed. J. E. B. Mayor. EETS extra series 27. London, 1876.

Opera. Würzburg, 1597.

Forbes, William, *Considerationes modestae et pacificae*. 2 vols. London, 1850–6.

Frith, John, *Whole Workes*. London, 1573.

Gerhard, Johann, *Loci communes*, ed. Cotta. 10 vols. Tübingen, 1768.

Godescalc of Orbais, *Oeuvres théologiques et grammaticales*, ed. C. Lambot. Louvain: Spicilegium Sacrum Lovaniense, 1945.

Goodwin, John, *Imputatio fidei; or A Treatise of Justification*. London, 1615.

Gregory of Rimini, *Lectura super primum et secundum sententiarum*, ed. A. D. Trapp. 6 vols. Berlin/New York: de Gruyter, 1979–84.

Gropper, Johann, *Enchiridion Christianae institutiones*. Cologne, 1536.

Hafenreffer, Matthias, *Loci theologici*. Tübingen, 1603.

Hall, Joseph, *Works*. 12 vols. Oxford, 1837–9.

Hammond, Henry, *A Practical Catechism*. London, 1847.

Heidegger, Johann Heinrich, *Medulla theologiae Christianae*. Zurich, 1616.

Henke, Heinrich Philipp Konrad, *Lineamenta institutionum fidei Christianae*. Helmstedt, 1793.

Hincmar of Reims, 'Zwei Schriften des Erzbischofs Hinkmar von Reims', ed. W. Gundlach. *ZKG* 10 (1889), 92–145, 258–310.

Holcot, Robert, *Opus super sapientiam Salomonis*. Hagenau, 1494.

Quaestiones super IV libros sententiarum. Leiden, 1497.

Hooker, Richard, *Works*, ed. J. Keble. 3rd edn. 3 vols. Oxford, 1845.

Hooker, Thomas, *The Soules Humiliation*. London, 1638.

The Soules Preparation for Christ. London, 1632.

The Unbeleevers Preparing for Christ. London, 1638.

Thomas Hooker: Writings in England and Holland 1626–33. Cambridge, MA: Harvard University Press, 1975.

Huss, John, *Opera omnia*, ed. V. Flajshans. 3 vols. Prague, 1903–8.

Hutter, Leonhard, *Compendium locorum theologicorum*. Wittenberg, 1652.

Jackson, Thomas, *Works*. 12 vols. Oxford, 1844.

Jansenius, Cornelius, *Augustinus*. Paris, 1641.

John of La Rochelle, *Die neuen Quästionen der Gnadentheologie des Johannes von Rupella*, ed. L. Hodl. Munich: Hueber, 1964.

Kant, Immanuel, *Gesammelte Schriften*. 22 vols. Berlin: de Gruyter, 1902–42.

Knewstub, John, *Lectures upon the Twentieth Chapter of Exodus*. London, 1577.

Knox, Alexander, *Remains*, ed. J. H. Newman. 2nd edn. 4 vols. London, 1836–7.

Koenig, Johann Friedrich, *Theologia positiva acroamatica*. 11th edn. Rostok/Leipzig, 1703.

Locke, John, *Essay concerning Human Understanding*, ed. P. H. Nidditch. Oxford: Oxford University Press, 1975.

The Reasonableness of Christianity, in *Works*, VII, London, 1823, 1–159.

Löscher, V. E., *Vollständiger Timotheus Verinus oder Darlegung der Wahrheit und des Friedens in denen bisherigen Pietistischen Streitigkeiten*. 2 vols. Wittenberg, 1718–21.

Luther, Martin, *Kritische Gesamtausgabe*. Weimar: Böhlau, 1883– .

Maresius, Samuel, *Collegium theologicum*. Geneva, 1662.

Mastricht, Peter van, *Theoretico-practica theologia*. Amsterdam, 1725.

Matthew of Aquasparta, *Quaestiones disputatae de gratia*, ed. V. Doucet. Quaracchi: Typographia Collegii S. Bonaventurae, 1935.

Melanchthon, Philip, *Opera omnia quae supersunt*. 28 vols. Brunswick, 1834–60.

Werke in Auswahl, ed. R. Stupperich. 8 vols. Gütersloh: Bertelsmann, 1951– .

Molina, Luis de, *Concordia liberii arbitrii cum gratiae donis*. Lisbon, 1588.

Morgan, Thomas, *The Moral Philosopher*. 3 vols. London, 1738–40.

Mosheim, Lorenz vom, *Elementa theologiae dogmaticae*. Nuremburg, 1758.

Mosse, Miles, *Iustifying and Saving Faith distinguished from the Faith of the Devils*. Cambridge, 1614.

Musculus, Wolfgang, *Loci communes sacrae theologiae*. Basel, 1561.

Newman, John Henry, *Lectures on the Doctrine of Justification*. 3rd edn. London/Cambridge, 1874.

Remarks on Certain Passages in the Thirty-Nine Articles. Tract 90. Oxford, 1841.

Odo Rigaldi, *In II Sent. dist. xxvi–xxix*, ed. J. Bouvy, in 'Les Questions sur la grâce dans le Commentaire des Sentences d'Odon Rigaud'. *RThAM* 27 (1960), 305–43; 'La Nécessité de la grâce dans le Commentaire des Sentences d'Odon Rigaud'. *RThAM* 28 (1961), 69–96.

Owen, John, *Works*, ed. T. Russell. 21 vols. London, 1826.

Perkins, William, *Workes*. 3 vols. Cambridge, 1608–9.

Petavius, Dionysius, *Opus de theologicus dogmatibus*. 3 vols. Antwerp, 1700.

Peter Aureoli, *Commentarorium in primum librum sententiarum*. Rome, 1596.

Peter of Bergamo, *Summa aurea*. Venice, 1593.

Peter Cantor, *Summa de sacramentis et animae consiliis*, ed. J.-A. Dugauquier. 5 vols. Louvain: Nauwelaerts, 1954–67.

Peter Lombard, *Libri IV Sententiarum*. 2nd edn. 2 vols. Quaracchi: Typographia Collegii S. Bonaventurae, 1916.

Peter of Tarantaise, *In IV libros sententiarum commentaria*. 4 vols. Toulouse, 1649–52.

Pfaff, Christoph Matthaeus, *Institutiones theologiae dogmaticae et moralis*. Tübingen, 1720.

Polanus a Polansdorf, Amandus, *Syntagma theologiae Christianae*. Geneva, 1612.

Quenstedt, Johannes Andreas, *Theologia didactico-polemica*. Wittenberg, 1685.

Richard of Middleton, *Supra quattuor libros sententiarum*. 4 vols. Brescia, 1591.

Rijssen, Leonhard van, *Compendium theologiae didactico elencticae*. Amsterdam, 1695.

Ritschl, A. B., *Die christliche Lehre von der Rechtfertigung und Versöhnung*. III. *Die positive Entwickelung der Lehre*. 3rd edn. Bonn: Marcus, 1888.

Robert of Melun, *Questiones theologice de epistolis Pauli*, ed. R. M. Martin. Louvain: Spicilegium Sacrum Lovaniense, 1938.

Roger of Marston, *Quaestiones disputatae de statu naturae lapsae*. Quaracchi: Typographia Collegii S. Bonaventurae, 1932.

Roland of Cremona, *Summae magistri Rolandi Cremonensis*, ed. A. Cortesi. Bergamo: Edizioni Monumenta Bergomensia, 1962.

Sanderson, Robert, *Sermons*, ed. P. Montgomery. 2 vols. London, 1841.

Scherzer, J. A., *Breviculus theologicus*. 3rd edn. Leipzig, 1680.

Schleiermacher, F. D. E., *Der christliche Glaube*. 4th edn. 2 vols. Berlin, 1842–3.

Simon of Tournai, *Les disputationes de Simon de Tournai*, ed. J. Warichez. Louvain: Spicilegium Sacrum Lovaniense, 1932.

Soto, Domingo de, *De natura et gratia*. Paris, 1549.

In epistolam ad Romanos commentarii. Antwerp, 1550.

Stapleton, Thomas, *Opera*. 4 vols. Paris, 1620.

Steinbach, Wendelin, *Opera exegetica quae supersunt omnia*, ed. H. Feld. Wiesbaden: Steiner, 1976.

Steinbart, Gotthilf Samuel, *System der reinen Philosophie oder Glückseligkeitslehre des Christenthums*. Zullichau, 1778.

Suárez, Francisco de, *Opera omnia*. 28 vols. Paris Vives, 1856–78.

Taylor, Jeremy, *Works*, ed. C. P. Eden. 10 vols. London, 1847–54.

Teller, Wilhelm Abraham, *Die Religion der Vollkommnern*. Berlin, 1792.

Thomas Aquinas, *Opera omnia*. 31 vols. Rome: Typis Polyglottis Vaticanis, 1882–1947.

Scriptum super libros sententiarum Magistri Petri Lombardi, ed. P. Mandonnet and F. Moos. 4 vols. Paris: Lethielleux, 1929–47.

Thomas of Strasbourg, *Commentaria in IIII libros sententiarum*. Venice, 1564.

Tindal, Matthew, *Christianity as Old as the Creation*, ed. G. Gawlick. Stuttgart: Frommann-Holzboog, 1968.

Toland, John, *Christianity not Mysterious*, ed. G. Gawlick. Stuttgart: Frommann, 1964.

Töllner, Johann Gottlieb, *Der thätige Gehorsam Christi untersucht*. Breslau, 1768.

Theologische Untersuchungen. 2 vols. Riga, 1772–4.

Turrettini, Franciscus, *Institutio theologiae elencticae*. Geneva, 1688.

Tyndale, William, *Works*. 3 vols. Cambridge, 1848.

Ussher, James, *Whole Works*, ed. C. R Elrington and J. H. Todd. 17 vols. Dublin/London, 1847–64.

Valdés, Juan de, *Las ciento diez divinas consideraciones*, ed. J. I. T. Idigoras. Salamanca: Centro de Estudios Orientales y Ecuménicos, 1975.

Diálogo de doctrina cristiana, ed. B. F. Stockwell. Mexico: Mexico City, 1946.

Vega, Andrés de. *De iustificatione doctrina universa*. Cologne, 1572.

Opusculum de iustificatione. Venice, 1546.

Walker, George. *A Defence of the True Sense and Meaning of the Words of the Holy Apostle: Rom. 4 ver. 3.5.9*. London, 1641.

Wendelin, Friedrich. *Christianae theologiae*. Amsterdam, 1646.

Wesley, John, *Standard Sermons*. 2 vols. London: Epworth Press, 1921.

Works. 14 vols. London, 1829–31.

William of Auvergne, *Opera omnia*. 2 vols. Paris. 1674.

William of Auxerre, *Summa aurea in quattuor libros sententiarum*. Paris, 1500.

William of Ockham, *Commentaria in quattuor libros sententiarum*. Leiden, 1495.

Opera philosophica et theologica. 9 vols. New York: Franciscan Institute, 1966– .

Tractatus de praedestinatione et de praescientia Dei et de futuris contingentibus, ed. P. Boehmer. New York: Franciscan Institute, 1945.

Wollebius, Johannes, *Christianae theologiae compendium*. Amsterdam, 1637.

Zwingli, Huldrych, *Sämtliche Werke*. 4 vols. Zurich: Theologischer Verlag, 1905– .

2 SECONDARY STUDIES

Abercrombie, N., *The Origins of Jansenism*. Oxford: Oxford University Press, 1936.

Alfaro, J., 'Sobrenatural y pecado original en Bayo'. *RET* 12 (1952), 3–76.

Althaus, P., 'Gottes Gottheit als Sinn der Rechtfertigungslehre Luthers'. *Luther Jahrbuch* 13 (1931), 1–28.

Alzeghy, S., *Nova creatura: la nozione della grazia nei commentari medievali di S. Paolo*. Rome: Pontificia Università Gregoriana, 1956.

Amand de Mendieta, D., *Fatalisme et liberté dans l'antiquité grecque*. Louvain: Bibliothèque de l'université, 1945.

Anciaux, P., *La Théologie du sacrament du pénance au XIIe siècle*. Louvain: Bibliothèque de l'université, 1949.

Armstrong, B. G., *Calvinism and the Amyraut Heresy: Protestant Scholasticism and Humanism in Seventeenth-Century France*. Madison: University of Wisconsin Press, 1969.

Auer, J., *Die Entwicklung der Gnadenlehre in der Hochscholastik*. 2 vols. Freiburg: Herder, 1942–51.

Die menschliche Willensfreiheit im Lehrsystem des Thomas von Aquin und Johannes Duns Skotus. Munich: Hueber, 1938.

Avemarie, F., *Tora und Leben: Untersuchungen zur Heilsbedeutung der Tora in der frühen rabbinischen Literatur*. Tübingen: Mohr, 1996.

Bakhuizen van den Brink, J. N., 'Mereo(r) and meritum in Some Latin Fathers'. *Studia Patristica* 3 (Berlin: de Gruyter, 1961), 333–40.

Ball, D., 'Les Développements de la doctrine de la liberté chez Saint Augustin'. *AThA* 7 (1946), 400–30.

'Libre arbitre et liberté dans Saint Augustin'. *AThA* 6 (1945), 368–82.

Bannach, K., *Die Lehre von der doppelten Macht Gottes bei Wilhelm von Ockham*. Wiesbaden: Steiner, 1975.

Bauke-Ruegg, J., 'Die Frage nach dem gnädigen Gott: Erinnerungen an einige Implikationen der reformatorischen Rechtfertigungslehre'. *EvTh* 57 (1997), 474–95.

Baur, J., *Salus Christiana: Die Rechtfertigungslehre in der Geschichte des christlichen Heilsverständnisses*. Gütersloh: Mohn, 1968.

Bavaud, G., 'La Doctrine de la justification d'après Calvin et le Concile de Trent'. *VCaro* 22 (1968), 83–92.

'La Doctrine de la justification d'après Saint Augustin et la Réforme'. *REAug* 5 (1959), 21–32.

Beachy, A. J., *The Concept of Grace in the Radical Reformation*. Nieuwkoop: De Graaf, 1977.

Beck, H., *Vorsehung und Vorherbestimmung in der theologischen Literatur der Byzantiner*. Rome: Institutum orientalium studiorum, 1937.

Becker, K. J., *Die Rechtfertigungslehre nach Domingo de Soto: Das Denken eines Konzilsteilnehmers vor, in und nach Trient*. Rome: Gregorian University Press, 1967.

Beltrán de Heredia, V., 'Controversia de certitudine gratiae entre Domingo de Soto y Ambrosio Catarino'. *Ciencia Tomista* 62 (1941), 33–62.

Betz, O., 'Rechtfertigung in Qumran', in O. Betz (ed.), *Jesus: Der Messias Israels: Aufsätze zur biblischen Theologie*. Tübingen: Mohr, 1976, 39–58.

Beumer, J., 'Gratia supponit naturam: Zur Geschichte eines theologischen Prinzips'. *Gregorianum* 20 (1939), 381–406, 535–52.

Bizer, E., *Fides ex auditu: Eine Untersuchung über die Entdeckung der Gerechtigkeit Gottes durch Martin Luther*. 3rd edn. Neukirchen: Neukirchener Verlag, 1966.

Theologie der Verheissung: Studien zur theologische Entwicklung des jungen Melanchthon 1519–1524. Neukirchen: Neukirchener Verlag, 1964.

Blomme, R., *La Doctrine de la péché dans les écoles théologiques de la première moitié du XIIe siècle*. Louvain: Publications universitaires de Louvain, 1958.

Boisset, J., 'Justification et sanctification chez Calvin', in W. H. Neusner (ed.), *Calvinus Theologus: Die Referate des Congrès Européen de recherches Calviniennes*. Neukirchen: Neukirchener Verlag, 1976, 131–48.

Bornkamm, H., 'Zur Frage der Iustitia Dei beim jungen Luther'. *ARG* 52 (1961), 16–29; 53 (1962), 1–60.

Bouillard, H., *Conversion et grâce chez S. Thomas d'Aquin*. Paris: Aubier Editions Montaigne, 1944.

Braunisch, R., *Die Theologie der Rechtfertigung im 'Enchiridion' (1538) des Johannes Gropper: Sein kritischer Dialog mit Philipp Melanchthon*. Münster: Aschendorff, 1974.

Bruch, R, 'Die Urgerechtigkeit als Rechtheit des Willens nach der Lehre des hl. Bonaventuras'. *FS* 33 (1951), 180–206.

Brunner, P., 'Die Rechtfertigungslehre des Konzils von Trient', in *Pro veritate: Eine theologischer Dialog*. Münster/Kassel, 1963, 59–96.

Burger, C. P., 'Das auxilium speciale Dei in der Gnadenlehre Gregors von Rimini', in H. A. Oberman (ed.), *Gregor von Rimini: Werk und Wirkung bis zur Reformation*. Berlin: de Gruyter, 1981, 195–240.

Burnaby, J., *Amor Dei: A Study of the Religion of St. Augustine*. London: Hodder & Stoughton, 1947.

Buuck, F., 'Zum Rechtfertigungsdekret', in G. Schreiber (ed.), *Das Weltkonzil von Trient: Sein Werden und Wirken*. 2 vols. Freiburg: Herder, 1951, 117–43.

Capánaga, V., 'La deificación en la soteriología agustiniana', in *Augustinus Magister*. 3 vols. Paris: Etudes Augustiniennes, 1954, 2.745–54.

Chéné, J., 'Que significiaient "initium fidei" et "affectus credulitatis" pour les sémipélagiens?' *RSR* 35 (1948), 566–88.

'Le Sémipélagianisme du Midi et de la Gaule d'après les lettres de Prosper d'Aquitaine et d'Hilaire à Saint Augustin', *RSR* 43 (1955), 321–41.

Cosgrove, C. H., 'Justification in Paul: A Linguistic and Theological Reflection'. *JBL* 106 (1987), 653–70.

Courtenay W. J., *Adam Wodeham: An Introduction to his Life and Writings*. Leiden: Brill, 1978.

'Covenant and Causality in Pierre d'Ailly'. *Speculum* 46 (1971), 94–119.

'The King and the Leaden Coin: The Economic Background of Sine Qua Non Causality'. *Traditio* 28 (1972), 185–209.

Courtney, F., *Cardinal Robert Pullen: An English Theologian of the Twelfth Century*. Rome: Pontificia Università Gregoriana, 1954.

Dalmau, J. M., 'La teología de la disposición a la justificación en visperas de la revolución protestante'. *RET* 6 (1946), 249–75.

Davids, E. A., *Das Bild vom neuen Menschen: Ein Beitrag zum Verständnis des Corpus Macarianum*. Salzburg/Munich: Pustet, 1968.

Davies, W. D., *Paul and Rabbinic Judaism: Some Rabbinic Elements in Pauline Theology*. 4th edn. Philadelphia: Fortress Press, 1980.

Dettloff, W., 'Die antipelagianische Grundstruktur des scotischen Rechtfertigungslehre'. *FS* 48 (1966), 267–70.

Die Entwicklung der Akzeptations- und Verdienstlehre von Duns Scotus bis Luther mit besonderer Berücksichtigung der Franziskanertheologen. Münster: Aschendorff, 1963.

Die Lehre von der acceptatio divina bei Johannes Duns Scotus mit besonderer Berücksichtigung der Rechtfertigungslehre. Werl: Dietrich Coelde Verlag, 1954.

Dhont, R.-C., *Le Problème de la préparation à la grâce: débuts de l'école franciscaine*. Paris: Editions Franciscaines, 1946.

Doms, H., *Die Gnadenlehre des sel. Albertus Magnus*. Breslau: Müller & Seiffert, 1929.

Donfried, K. 'Justification and Last Judgement in Paul'. *ZNW* 67 (1976), 90–110.

Douglass, E. J. D., *Justification in Late Medieval Preaching: A Study of John Geiler of Strassburg*. Leiden: Brill, 1966.

Dunn, J. D. G., 'The Justice of God: A Renewed Perspective on Justification by Faith'. *JThS* 43 (1992), 1–22.

'The New Perspective on Paul'. *BJRL* 65 (1983), 95–122.

Ehrle, F., *Der Sentenzenkommentar Peters von Candia des Pisanerpapstes Alexander V.* Münster: Aschendorff, 1925.

Eno, R. B., 'Some Patristic Views on the Relationship of Faith and Works in Justification'. *RechAug* 19 (1984), 3–27.

Ernst, W., *Gott und Mensch am Vorabend der Reformation: Eine Untersuchung zur Moralphilosophie und -theologie bei Gabriel Biel.* Leipzig: St Benno-Verlag, 1972.

Feckes, C., *Die Rechtfertigungslehre des Gabriel Biel und ihre Stellung innerhalb der nominalistischen Schule.* Münster: Aschendorff, 1925.

Flick, M., *L'attimo della giustificazione secondo S. Tomasso.* Rome: Pontificia Università Gregoriana, 1947.

Fock, O., *Der Socianismus nach seiner Stellung.* Kiel, 1847.

Gibbs, Lee W., 'Richard Hooker's Via Media Doctrine of Justification'. *HThR* 74 (1991), 211–20.

Gillon, B., 'La grâce incréée chez quelques théologiens du XIVe siècle'. *Divinitas* 11 (1967), 671–80.

Göhler, A., *Calvins Lehre von der Heiligung dargestellt auf Grund der Institutio, exegetischer und homiletischer Schriften.* Munich: Kaiser Verlag, 1934.

Gonzáles Rivas, S., 'Los teólogos salmantinos y el decreto de la justificación'. *EE* 21 (1947), 147–70.

Grabmann, M., *Die Geschichte der scholastischen Methode.* 2 vols. Berlin: Akademie Verlag, 1957.

Mittelalterliches Geistesleben: Abhandlungen zur Geschichte der Scholastik und Mystik. 3 vols. Munich: Hueber, 1926–56.

Grane, L., 'Augustins "Expositio quarumdam propositionum ex Epistola ad Romanos" in Luthers Römerbriefvorlesung'. *ZThK* 69 (1972), 304–30.

Contra Gabrielem: Luthers Auseinandersetzung mit Gabriel Biel in der Disputatio contra scholasticam theologiam 1517. Copenhagen: Gyldendal, 1962.

'Gregor von Rimini und Luthers Leipziger Disputation'. *StTh* 22 (1968), 29–49.

Grass, H., 'Die durch Jesum von Nazareth vollbrachte Erlösung: Ein Beitrag zur Erlösungslehre Schleiermachers', in O. Kaiser (ed.), *Denkender Glaube: Festschrift für Carl Heinz Ratschow.* Berlin/New York: de Gruyter, 1976, 152–69.

Greschat, M., *Melanchthon neben Luther: Studien zur Gestalt der Rechtfertigungslehre zwischen 1528 und 1537.* Witten: Luther-Verlag, 1965.

Gross, J., *La Divinisation du chrétien d'après les pères grecs.* Paris: Gabalda, 1938.

Guerard des Lauriers, M. L., 'Saint Augustin et la question de la certitude de la grâce au Concile de Trente', in *Augustinus Magister* (congrès international augustinien). 3 vols. Paris: Etudes augustiniennes, 1954, 2.1057–69.

Gundry, R. H., 'Grace, Works and Staying Saved in Paul'. *Biblia* 60 (1985), 1–38.

Gyllenkrok, A., *Rechtfertigung und Heiligung in der frühen evangelischen Theologie Luthers.* Uppsala: Lundequistska bokhandeln, 1952.

Hahn, F., 'Gibt es eine Entwicklung in den Aussagen über die Rechtfertigung bei Paulus?' *EvTh* 53 (1993), 342–66.

Hamm, B., *Promissio, pactum, ordinatio: Freiheit und Selbstbindung Gottes in der scholastischen Gnadenlehre*. Tübingen: Mohr, 1977.

Häring, N., *Die Theologie der Erfurter Augustiner-Eremiten Bartholomäus Arnoldi von Usingen*. Limburg: Pallottiner Verlag, 1939.

Härle, W., 'Analytische und synthetische Urteile in der Rechtfertigungslehre'. *NZSTh* 6 (1974), 17–34.

'Zur Gegenwartsbedeutung der "Rechtfertigungs"-Lehre. Eine Problemskizze'. *ZThK* 10 (1998), 101–39.

Harnack, A., *History of Dogma*. 7 vols. Edinburgh: Williams & Norgate, 1894–9.

Hauke, R., *Gott-Haben, um Gottes Willen: Andreas Osianders Theosisgedanke und die Diskussion um die Grundlagen der evangelisch verstandenen Rechtfertigung*. Frankfurt am Main: Peter Lang, 1999.

Hefner, J., *Die Entstehungsgeschichte des Trienter Rechtfertigungsdekretes: Ein Beitrag zur Geschichte des Reformationszeitalters*. Paderborn: Verlag Bonifacius-Druckerei, 1939.

Heil, J. P., 'Christ, the Termination of the Law (Romans 9:30 – 10:8)'. *CBQ* 63 (2001), 484–98.

Hermann, R., *Luthers These 'Gerecht und Sünder zugleich': Eine systematische Untersuchung*. Darmstadt: Wissenschaftliche Buchgesellschaft, 1960.

Hernández, M. O., 'La certeza del estado de gracia según Andrés de Vega: Oportación cientifica al decreto de la justificatión del concilio de Trento'. *VyV* 3 (1945), 46–98, 325–56, 502–43.

Heynck, V., 'Die aktuelle Gnade bei Richard von Mediavilla'. *FS* 22 (1935), 297–325.

'Der Anteil des Konzilstheologen Andreas de Vega O.F.M. an dem ersten amtlichen Entwurf des Trienter Rechtfertigungsdekretes'. *FS* 33 (1951), 49–81.

'Die Bedeutung von "mereri" und "promereri" bei dem Konzilstheologen Andreas de Vega O.F.M.'. *FS* 50 (1968), 224–38.

'A Controversy at the Council of Trent concerning the Doctrine of Duns Scotus'. *FrS* 9 (1949), 181–258.

'Untersuchungen uber die Reuelehre der tridentinischen Zeit'. *FS* 29 (1942), 25–44, 120–50; 30 (1943), 53–73.

'Zum Problem der unvollkommenen Reue auf dem Konzil von Trient', in G. Schreiber (ed.), *Das Weltkonzil von Trient: Sein Werden und Wirken*. 2 vols. Freiburg: Herder, 1951, 231–80.

'Zur Kontroverse uber die Gnadengewissheit auf dem Konzil von Trient'. *FS* 37 (1955), 1–17, 161–88.

Hinlicky, P. R., 'Theological Anthropology: Toward Integrating Theosis and Justification by Faith'. *Journal of Ecumenical Studies* 34 (1997), 38–73.

Hirsch, E., *Die Theologie des Andreas Osiander und ihre geschichtlichen Voraussetzungen*. Göttingen: Mohn, 1919.

Hocedez, E., *Richard de Middleton: sa vie, ses oeuvres, sa doctrine*. Louvain: Spicilegium Sacrum Lovaniense, 1925.

Hochstetter, E., 'Nominalismus?' *FrS* 9 (1949), 370–403.

Hohenberger, T., *Lutherische Rechtfertigungslehre in den reformatorischen Flugschriften der Jahre 1521–2.* Tübingen: Mohr, 1996.

Holfelder, H. H., *Solus Christus: Die Ausbildung von Bugenhagens Rechtfertigungslehre in der Paulusauslegung (1524/25) und ihre Bedeutung für die theologische Argumentation im Sendbrief 'Von dem christlichen Glauben'.* Tübingen: Mohr, 1981.

Tentatio et consolatio: Studien zu Bugenhagens Interpretatio in librum psalmorum. Berlin/New York: de Gruyter, 1974.

Holl, K., *Gesammelte Aufsätze zur Kirchengeschichte.* 3 vols. Tübingen: Mohr, 1928.

'Die justitia Dei in der vorlutherischen Bibelauslegung des Abendlandes', in *Gesammelte Aufsätze zur Kirchengeschichte.* 3 vols. Tübingen: Mohr, 1928, 3.171–88.

Horn, S., *Glaube und Rechtfertigung nach dem Konzilstheologer Andres de Vega.* Paderborn: Verlag Bonifacius-Druckerei, 1972.

Hövelmann, H., 'Die ökumenische Vereinbarung zur Rechtfertigungslehre im Diskurs der Lutherforscher'. *Luther* 71 (2000), 143–50.

Hultgren, A. J., *Paul's Gospel and Mission.* Philadelphia: Fortress Press, 1985.

Hünermann, F., *Wesen und Notwendigkeit der aktuellen Gnade nach dem Konzil von Trient.* Paderborn: Verlag Bonifacius-Druckerei, 1926.

Huthmacher, H., 'La Certitude de la grâce au Concile de Trente'. *NRTh* 60 (1933), 213–26.

Iserloh, E., *Gnade und Eucharistie in der philosophischen Theologie des Wilhelm von Ockham: Ihre Bedeutung für die Ursachen der Reformation.* Wiesbaden: Steiner, 1956.

Jansen, F.-X., *Baius et la Baianisme.* Louvain: Editions du Muséum Lessianum, 1927.

Janz, D., 'A Reinterpretation of Gabriel Biel on Nature and Grace'. *SCJ* 8 (*1977*), 104–8.

Jedin, H., *Geschichte des Konzils von Trient.* 4 vols: Freiburg: Herder, 1951–75.

Kardinal Contarini als Kontroverstheologe. Münster: Aschendorff, 1949.

Jenson, R., 'Justification as a Triune Event'. *MoTh* 11 (1995), 421–7.

'Rechtfertigung und Ekklesiologie'. *KuD* 42 (1996), 202–17.

Joest, W., *Gesetz und Freiheit: Das Problem des tertius usus legis bei Luther und die neutestamentliche Parainese.* Göttingen: Vandenhoeck & Ruprecht, 1956.

'Die tridentinische Rechtfertigungslehre', *KuD* 9 (1963), 41–59.

Jorissen, H., 'Einig in der Rechtfertigungslehre: Das Verständnis der Rechtfertigung im Konzil von Trient und bei Martin Luther', in M. Beintker (ed.), *Rechtfertigung und Erfahrung.* Gütersloh: Gütersloher Verlagshaus, 1995, 81–103.

Jüngel, E., *Das Evangelium von der Rechtfertigung des Gottlosen als Zentrum des christlichen Glaubens: Eine theologische Studie in ökumenischer Absicht.* Tübingen: Mohr Siebeck, 1999.

Kähler, E., *Karlstadt und Augustin: Der Kommentar des Andreas Bodenstein von Karlstadt zu Augustins Schrift De spiritu et litera.* Halle: Niemeyer, 1952.

Kaiser, A., *Natur und Gnade im Urstand: Eine Untersuchung der Kontroverse zwischen Michael Baius und Johannes Martinez de Ripaldi.* Munich: Hueber, 1965.

Käsemann, E., *Commentary on Romans*. Grand Rapids: Eerdmans, 1980.

New Testament Questions of Today. London: SCM Press, 1969.

Kaup, J., 'Zum Begriff der iustitia originalis in der älteren Franziskanerschule', *FS* 29 (1942), 44–55.

Kertelge, K. *'Rechtfertigung' bei Paulus: Studien zur Struktur und zum Bedeutungsgehalt des paulinischen Rechtfertigungsbegriffs*. Münster: Aschendorff, 1971.

Knox, D. B., *The Doctrine of Faith in the Reign of Henry VIII*. London: James Clarke, 1961.

Kolb, R., *Nikolaus von Amsdorf: Popular Polemics in the Preservation of Luther's Legacy*. Nieuwkoop: De Graaf, 1978.

Kooij, A. van der, 'Zur Theologie des Jesajabuches in der Septuaginta', in H. Reventloh (ed.), *Theologische Probleme der Septuaginta und der Hellenistischen Hermeneutik*. Gütersloh: Kaiser Verlag, 1997, 9–25.

Kriechbaum, F., *Grundzüge der Theologie Karlstadts: Eine systematische Studie zur Erhellung der Theologie Andreas von Karlstadts*. Hamburg: Reich, 1967.

Kroeger, M., *Rechtfertigung und Gesetz: Studien zur Entwicklung der Rechtfertigungslehre beim jungen Luther*. Göttingen: Vandenhoeck & Ruprecht, 1968.

Kruger, F., *Bucer und Erasmus: Eine Untersuchung zum Einfluss des Erasmus auf die Theologie Martin Bucers*. Wiesbaden: Steiner, 1970.

Küng, H., 'Ist in der Rechtfertigungslehre eine Einigung möglich?' *Una Sancta* 12 (1957), 116–21.

Rechtfertigung: Die Lehre Karl Barths und eine katholische Besinnung. Einsiedeln: Johannes Verlag, 1957.

Kuula, K., *The Law, the Covenant, and God's Plan: Paul's Polemical Treatment of the Law in Galatians*. Göttingen: Vandenhoeck & Ruprecht, 1999.

Landgraf, A. M., *Dogmengeschichte der Frühscholastik*. 8 vols. Regensburg: Verlag Friedrich Pustet, 1952–6.

Einführung in die Geschichte der theologischen Literatur der Frühscholastik. Regensburg: Verlag Friedrich Pustet, 1948.

'Mitteilungen zur Schule Gilberts de la Porrée'. *CFr* 3 (1933), 185–208.

'Neue Funde zur Porretanerschule'. *CFr* 6 (1936), 354–63.

'Der Porretanismus der Homilien des Radulphus Ardens'. *ZKTh* 64 (1940), 132–48.

'Untersuchungen zu den Eigenlehren Gilberts de la Porrée'. *ZKTh* 54 (1930), 180–213.

Lane, A. N. S., 'Cardinal Contarini and Article 5 of the Regensburg Colloquy (1541)', in O. Meuffels and J. Bründl (eds.), *Grenzgänge der Theologie: Alexandre Ganoczy zum 75. Geburtstag*. Münster: LIT Verlag, 2004, 163–90.

Justification by Faith in Catholic–Protestant Dialogue: An Evangelical Assessment. London: T. & T. Clark, 2002.

Laplanche, F., *Orthodoxie et prédication: l'œuvre d'Amyraut et la querelle de la grâce universelle*. Paris: Presses universitaires de France, 1965.

Laun, J. F., 'Die Prädestination bei Wiclif und Bradwardin', in H. Bornkamm (ed.), *Imago Dei: Festschrift für G. Kruger*. Giessen: Topelmann, 1932, 63–84.

Leff, G., *William of Ockham: The Metamorphosis of Scholastic Discourse*. Manchester: Manchester University Press, 1975.

Lennerz, H., 'De historia applicationis principii "omnis ordinate volens prius vult finem quam ea quae sunt ad finem" ad probandam gratuitatem praedestinationis ad gloriam'. *Gregorianum* 10 (1929), 238–66.

Lennerz, J., 'Voten auf dem Trienter Konzil über die Rechtfertigung'. *Gregorianum* 15 (1934), 577–88.

Lexutt, A., *Rechtfertigung im Gespräch: Das Rechtfertigungsverständnis in den Religionsprächen von Hagenau, Worms und Regensburg, 1540/41*. Göttingen: Vandenhoeck & Ruprecht, 1996.

Lindbeck, G., 'Nominalism and the Problem of Meaning as Illustrated by Pierre d'Ailly on Predestination and Justification'. *HThR* 52 (1959), 43–60.

Loewenich, W. von, *Duplex Iustitia: Luthers Stellung zu einer Unionsformel des 16. Jahrhunderts*. Wiesbaden: Steiner, 1972.

Von Augustin zu Luther. Witten: Luther-Verlag, 1959.

Logan, E. M. T., 'Grace and Justification: Some Italian Views on the 16th and Early 17th centuries'. *JEH* 20 (1969), 67–78.

Lonergan, B. J. F., *Grace and Reason: Operative Grace in the Thought of St. Thomas Aquinas*. London: Darton, Longman & Todd, 1971.

Loofs, F., 'Der articulus stantis et cadentis ecclesiae'. *ThStKr* 90 (1917), 323–400.

Leitfaden zum Studien der Dogmengeschichte. 4th edn. Halle: Niemeyer, 1906.

Lottin, O., 'Le Concept de justice chez les théologiens du moyen âge avant l'introduction d'Aristôte'. *RThom* 44 (1938), 511–21.

Psychologie et morale aux XIIe et XIIIe siècles. 8 vols. Gembloux: Duculot, 1942–60.

McGrath, A. E., 'The Anti-Pelagian Structure of "Nominalist" Doctrines of Justification'. *EThL* 57 (1981), 107–19.

'"Augustinianism?" A Critical Assessment of the So-Called "Medieval Augustinian Tradition" on Justification'. *Augustiniana* 31 (1981), 247–67.

'Divine Justice and Divine Equity in the Controversy between Augustine and Julian of Eclanum'. *DR* 101 (1983), 312–19.

'Forerunners of the Reformation? A Critical Examination of the Evidence for Precursors of the Reformation Doctrines of Justification'. *HThR* 75 (1982), 219–42.

'Humanist Elements in the Early Reformed Doctrine of Justification'. *ARG* 73 (1982) 5–30.

'The Influence of Aristotelian Physics upon St Thomas Aquinas' Discussion of the "Processus Iustificationis"'. *RThAM* 51 (1984), 223–9.

The Intellectual Origins of the European Reformation. 2nd edn. Oxford: Blackwell, 2003.

'John Calvin and Late Medieval Thought: A Study in Late Medieval Influences upon Calvin's Theological Thought'. *ARG* 77 (1986), 58–78.

'Justice and Justification: Semantic and Juristic Aspects of the Christian Doctrine of Justification'. *SJTh* 35 (1982), 403–18.

'Justification: Barth, Trent and Küng'. *SJTh* 34 (1981), 517–29.

'Justification and the Reformation: The Significance of the Doctrine of Justification by Faith to Sixteenth Century Urban Communities'. *ARG* 81 (1990), 5–19.

'Karl Barth and the Articulus Iustificationis: The Significance of His Critique of Ernst Wolf within the Context of His Theological Method'. *ThZ* 39 (1983), 349–61.

'Karl Barth als Aufklärer? Der Zusammenhang seiner Lehre vom Werke Christi mit der Erwählungslehre'. *KuD* 30 (1984), 273–83.

Luther's Theology of the Cross: Martin Luther's Theological Breakthrough. Oxford: Blackwell, 1985.

'Mira et nova diffinitio iustitiae: Luther and Scholastic Doctrines of Justification'. *ARG* 74 (1983), 37–60.

'The Moral Theory of the Atonement: An Historical and Theological Critique'. *SJTh* 38 (1985), 205–20.

'Rectitude: The Moral Foundations of Anselm of Canterbury's Soteriology'. *DR* 99 (1981), 201–13.

'"The Righteousness of God" from Augustine to Luther'. *StTh* 36 (1982), 63–78.

MacQueen, D. J., 'John Cassian on Grace and Free Will, with Particular Reference to Institutio XII and Collatio XII'. *RThAM* 44 (1977), 5–28.

McSorley, H. J., *Luther – Right or Wrong? An Ecumenical-Theological Study of Luther's Major Work, The Bondage of the Will*. Minneapolis: Augsburg Publishing House, 1969.

Martin, R. M., *La Controverse sur le péché originel au début du XIVe siècle*. Louvain: Spicilegium Sacrum Lovaniense, 1930.

Mitzka, F., 'Die Anfänge der Konkurslehre im 13. Jahrhundert'. *ZKTh* 54 (1930), 161–79.

'Die Lehre des hl. Bonaventura von der Vorbereitung auf die heiligmachende Gnade'. *ZKTh* 50 (1926), 27–72, 220–52.

Modalsi, O., *Das Gericht nach den Werken: Ein Beitrag zu Luthers Lehre vom Gesetz*. Göttingen: Vandenhoeck & Ruprecht, 1963.

Molteni, P., *Roberto Holcot O.P. Dottrina della grazia e della giustificazione*. Pinerolo: Editrice Alzani, 1968.

Moltmann, G., 'Prädestination und Heilsgeschichte bei Moyse Amyraut'. *ZKG* 65 (1954), 270–303.

Müller, O., *Die Rechtfertigungslehre nominalistischer Reformationsgegner, Bartholomäus Arnoldi von Usingen und Kaspar Schatzgeyer, über Erbsünde, erste Rechtfertigung und Taufe*. Breslau: Müller & Seiffert, 1940.

Neuser, W. H., 'Calvins Urteil über den Rechtfertigungsartikel des Regensburger Buches', in M. Greschat and J. F. G. Goeters (eds.), *Reformation und Humanismus; Robert Stupperich zum 65. Geburtstag*. Witten: Luther Verlag, 1969, 176–94.

Niesel, W., 'Calvin wider Osianders Rechtfertigungslehre'. *ZKG* 46 (1982), 410–30.

Nygren, A., 'Simul iustus et peccator bei Augustin und Luther'. *ZSTh* 16 (1940), 364–79.

Nygren, G., *Das Prädestinationsproblem an der Theologie Augustins*. Göttingen: Vandenhoeck & Ruprecht, 1956.

Oakley, F., 'Pierre d' Ailly and the Absolute Power of God: Another Note on the Theology of Nominalism'. *HThR* 56 (1963), 59–73.

Oberman, H. A., *Archbishop Thomas Bradwardine: A Fourteenth Century Augustinian*. Utrecht: Kemink & Zoon, 1957.

'Facientibus quod in se est Deus non denegat gratiam: Robert Holcot O.P. and the Beginnings of Luther's Theology'. *HThR* 55 (1962), 317–42.

Forerunners of the Reformation: The Shape of Late Medieval Thought. New York: Holt, Rinehart & Winston, 1966.

The Harvest of Medieval Theology: Gabriel Biel and Late Medieval Nominalism. Cambridge, MA: Harvard University Press, 1963.

'Headwaters of the Reformation: Initia Lutheri – Initia Reformationis', in H. A. Oberman (ed.), *Luther and the Dawn of the Modern Era*. Leiden: Brill, 1974, 40–88.

'"Iustitia Christi" and "Iustitia Dei": Luther and the Scholastic Doctrines of Justification'. *HThR* 59 (1966), 1–26.

'Das tridentinische Rechtfertigungsdekret im Lichte spätmittelalterlicher Theologie'. *ZThK* 61 (1964), 251–82.

Werden und Wertung der Reformation: Vom Wegestreit zum Glaubenskampf. Tübingen: Mohr, 1977.

'Wir sind pettler. Hoc est verum: Bund und Gnade in der Theologie des Mittelalters und der Reformation'. *ZKG* 78 (1967), 232–52.

Olazarán, J.,'La controversia Soto–Caterino–Vega sobre la certeza de la gracia', *EE* 19 (1942), 145–83.

Documentos inéditos tridentinos sobre la justificación. Madrid: Ediciones Fax, 1957.

Olley, J. W. 'The Translator of the Septuagint of Isaiah and "Righteousness"'. *BIOSCS* 13 (1980), 58–74.

Pannenberg, W., *Die Prädestinationslehre des Duns Skotus in Zusammenhang der scholastischen Lehrentwicklung*. Göttingen: Vandenhoeck & Ruprecht, 1954.

'Die Rechtfertigungslehre im ökumenische Gespräch'. *ZThK* 88 (1991), 232–46.

'Das Verhältnis zwischen der Akzeptationslehre des Duns Skotus und der reformatorischen Rechtfertigungslehre', in C. Bérubé (ed.), *Regnum hominis et regnum Dei: Acti quarti congressus Scotistici Internationalis*. Rome: Societas Internationalis Scotistica, 1978, 213–18.

Pas, P., 'La Doctrine de la double justice au Concile de Trente'. *EThL* 30 (1954), 5–53.

Peñamaria de Llano, A., *La salvación por la fe: La noción 'fides' in Hilario de Poitiers: Estudio filológico-teológico*. Burgos: Aldecoa, 1981.

Pesch, O. H., *Die Theologie der Rechtfertigung bei Martin Luther und Thomas von Aquin*. Mainz: Grünewald, 1967.

Peters, A., *Glaube und Werk: Luthers Rechtfertigungslehre im Lichte der heiligen Schrift*. 2nd edn. Berlin/Hamburg: Lutherisches Verlagshaus, 1967.

Pfnür, V., *Einig in der Rechtfertigungslehre? Die Rechtfertigungslehre der Confessio Augustana (1530) und die Stellungsnahme der katholischen Kontroverstheologie zwischen 1530 und 1535*. Wiesbaden: Steiner, 1970.

Philips, G., 'La Justification luthérienne et la Concile de Trente'. *EThL* 47 (1971), 340–58.

'La Théologie de la grâce chez les préscholastiques'. *EThL* 48 (1972), 479–508.

'La Théologie de la grâce dans la "Summa Fratris Alexandris"'. *EThL* 49 (1973), 100–23.

L'Union personnelle avec le Dieu vivant: essai sur l'origine et le sens de la grâce créée. Gembloux: Duculot, 1974.

Rich, A., *Die Anfänge der Theologie Huldrych Zwinglis.* Zurich: Zwingli-Verlag, 1949.

Ritschl, A. B., *A Critical History of the Christian Doctrine of Justification and Reconciliation.* Edinburgh: Edmonston & Douglas, 1871.

Ritter, G. *Studien zur Spätscholastik* I: *Marsilius von Inghen und die okkamistische Schule in Deutschland.* Heidelberg: Carl Winters Universitätsbuchhandlung, 1921.

Studien zur Spätscholastik II: *Via Antiqua und Via Moderna auf den deutschen Universtitäten des XV Jahrhunderts.* Heidelberg: Carl Winters Universitätsbuchhandlung, 1922.

Rivière, J., 'Le Dogme de la rédemption au XIIe siècle d'après les dernières publications'. *RMAL* 2 (1946), 101–12.

Le Dogme de la rédemption au début du moyen âge. Paris: Vrin, 1934.

Roo, J. C. R. de, 'The Concept of "Works of the Law" in Jewish and Christian Literature', in S. E. Potter and B. W. R. Pearson (eds.), *Christian–Jewish Relations through the Centuries.* Sheffield: Sheffield Academic Press, 2000, 116–47.

Rückert, H., 'Promereri: Eine Studie zum tridentinischen Rechtfertigungsdekret als Antwort an H. A. Oberman'. *ZThK* 68 (1971), 162–94.

Die Rechtfertigungslehre auf dem Tridentinischen Konzil. Bonn: Marcus & Weber, 1925.

Rupp, E. G., *The Righteousness of God: Luther Studies.* London: Hodder & Stoughton, 1953.

Studies in the Making of the English Protestant Tradition. Cambridge: Cambridge University Press, 1966.

Sagués, J., 'Un libro pretridentino de Andrés de Vega sobre la justificación'. *EE* 20 (1946), 175–209.

Salguiero, T., *La Doctrine de Saint Augustin sur la grâce d'après le traité à Simplicien.* Porto: Faculdade de Letras de Coimbra, 1925.

Sanders, E. P., *Paul, the Law, and the Jewish People.* London: SCM Press, 1983.

Paul and Palestinian Judaism. London: SCM Press, 1977.

Santoro, S., 'La giustificazione in Giovanni Antonio Delfini, teologo del Concilio di Trento'. *MF* 40 (1940), 1–27.

Schäfer, R., 'Die Rechtfertigungslehre bei Ritschl und Kähler'. *ZThK* 62 (1965), 66–85.

Schelkle, K. H., *Paulus Lehrer der Väter: Die altkirchliche Auslegung von Römer 9–11* Düsseldorf: Patmos, 1959.

Schierse, F. J., 'Das Trienterkonzil und die Frage nach der christliche Gewissheit', in G. Schreiber (ed.), *Das Weltkonzil von Trient: Sein Werden und Werken.* 2 vols. Freiburg: Herder, 1951, 145–67.

Schreiber, G. (ed.), *Das Weltkonzil von Trient: Sein Werden und Wirken.* 2 vols. Freiburg: Herder, 1951.

Schreiner, T. R., *The Law and Its Fulfillment: A Pauline Theology of Law*. Grand Rapids: Baker, 1998.

Schrenk, G., *Gottesreich und Bund im alteren Protestantismus*. Darmstadt: Wissenschaftliche Buchgesellschaft, 1967.

Schupp, J., *Die Gnadenlehre des Petrus Lombardus*. Freiburg: Herder, 1932.

Schwan, R., *Fides, spes und caritas beim jungen Luther, unter besonderer Berücksichtigung der mittelälterlichen Tradition*. Berlin: de Gruyter, 1962.

Schwarz, R., 'Luthers Rechtfertigungslehre als Eckstein der christlichen Theologie und Kirche'. *ZThK* 10 (1998), 14–46.

Seifrid, M. A., *Justification by Faith: The Origin and Development of a Central Pauline Theme*. Leiden: Brill, 1992.

Serry, J. H., *Historia congregationis de auxiliis*. Louvain, 1700.

Seybold, M., *Glaube und Rechtfertigung bei Thomas Stapleton*. Paderborn: Bonifacius-Druckerei, 1967.

Sheridan, T. L., *Newman on Justification: A Theological Biography*. Staten Island, NY: Alba House, 1967.

Sider, R. J., *Andreas Bodenstein von Karlstadt: The Development of His Thought 1517–1525*. Leiden: Brill, 1974.

Siewerth, G., *Thomas von Aquin: Die menschliche Willensfreiheit*. Düsseldorf: Patmos, 1954.

Söding, T., 'Der Skopos der paulinischen Rechtfertigungslehre: Exegetische Interpretationen in ökumenische Absicht'. *ZThK* 97 (2000), 404–33.

Stadtland, T., *Rechtfertigung und Heiligung bei Calvin*. Neukirchen: Neukirchener Verlag, 1972.

Staedtke, J., *Die Theologie des jungen Bullinger*. Zurich: Zwingli-Verlag, 1962.

Stakemeier, A., *Das Konzil von Trient über die Heilsgewissheit*. Heidelberg: Kerle, 1949.

Stakemeier, E., *Der Kampf um Augustin: Augustinus und die Augustiner auf dem Tridentinum*. Paderborn: Bonicacius-Druckerei, 1937.

'Die theologischen Schulen auf dem Trienter Konzil während der Rechtfertigungsverhandlung'. *ThQ* 117 (1936), 188–207, 322–50, 446–504.

Stegmüller, F., *Francisco de Vitoria y la doctrina de gracia en la escuela salmantina*. Barcelona: Librería Cervantes, 1934.

'Zur Gnadenlehre des spanischen Konzilstheologen Domingo de Soto', in G. Schreiber (ed.), *Das Weltkonzil von Trient*. Freiburg: Herder, 1951, 169–230.

Steinmetz, D. C., *Misericordia Dei: The Theology of Johannes von Staupitz in its Late Medieval Setting*. Leiden: Brill, 1968.

Stendahl, K., 'The Apostle Paul and the Introspective Conscience of the West'. *HThR* 56 (1963), 199–215.

Stoeckle, B., *'Gratia supponit naturam': Geschichte und Analyse eines theologischen Axioms*. Rome: Pontificia Università Gregoriana, 1962.

Studer, B., 'Jesucristo, nuestra justicia, según san Augustin'. *Augustinus* 26 (1981) 253–82.

Stufler, J., 'Die entfernte Vorbereitung auf die Rechtfertigung nach dem hl. Thomas'. *ZKTh* 47 (1923), 1–23, 161–83.

'Der hl. Thomas und das Axiom omne quod movetur ab alio movetur'. *ZKTh* 47 (1923), 369–90.

Stuhlmacher, P., *Gerechtigkeit Gottes bei Paulus*. Göttingen: Vandenhoeck & Ruprecht, 1966.

Stupperich, R., 'Der Ursprung des Regensburger Buches von 1541 und seine Rechtfertigungslehre'. *ARG* 36 (1939), 88–116.

Subilia, V., *La giustificazione per fede*. Brescia: Paideia Editrice, 1976.

Tellechea, I., 'El articulus de iustificatione de Fray Bartolomeo de Carranza'. *RET* 15 (1955), 563–635.

Toner, N., 'The Doctrine of Justification according to Augustine of Rome (Favaroni)'. *Augustiniana* 8 (1958), 164–89, 229–327, 497–515.

Trape, A., *Il concorso divino nel pensiero di Egidio Romano*. Tolentino: Tipografia S. Nicola, 1942.

Trapp, D., 'Augustinian Theology of the Fourteenth Century'. *Augustiniana* 6 (1956), 146–274.

Vanneste, A., 'Nature et grâce dans la théologie du XIIe siècle'. *EThL* 50 (1974), 181–214.

'Nature et grâce dans la théologie de Saint Augustin'. *RechAug* 10 (1975), 143–69.

Van't Spijker, W., 'Prädestination bei Bucer und Calvin', in W. Neusner (ed.), *Calvinus Theologus*. Neukirchen: Neukirchener Verlag, 1976, 85–111.

Vignaux, P., *Justification et prédestination au XIVe siècle*. Paris: Vrin, 1934.

Luther, Commentateur des Sentences (livre I, distinction XVII). Paris: Vrin, 1935.

'Sur Luther et Ockham'. *FS* 32 (1950), 21–30.

Villalmonte, A. de, 'Andrés de Vega y el proceso de la justificación según el Concilio Tridentina'. *RET* 5 (1945), 311–74.

Vogelsang, E., *Die Anfänge von Luthers Christologie nach der ersten Psalmenvorlesung*. Berlin/Leipzig: de Gruyter, 1929.

Walz, A., 'La giustificazione tridentina'. *Angelicum* 28 (1951), 97–138.

Watson, N. M., 'Justified by Faith, Judged by Works: An Antimony?' *NTS* 29 (1983), 209–21.

Weingart, R. E., *The Logic of Divine Love: A Critical Analysis of the Soteriology of Peter Abailard*. Oxford: Oxford University Press, 1990.

Weisweiler, H., 'L'Ecole de Laon et de Guillaume de Champeaux'. *RThAM* 4 (1932), 237–69, 371–91.

Werbeck, W., *Jacobus Perez von Valencia: Untersuchungen zu seiner Psalmenkommentar*. Tübingen: Mohr, 1959.

Werbick, J., 'Rechtfertigung des Sünders – Rechtfertigung Gottes: Thesen zur ökumenischen Diskussion um die Rechtfertigungslehre'. *KuD* 27 (1981), 45–57.

Westerholm, S., *Israel's Law and the Church's Faith: Paul and His Recent Interpreters*. Grand Rapids: Eerdmans, 1988.

Perspectives Old and New on Paul: The 'Lutheran' Paul and His Critics. Grand Rapids: Eerdmans, 2004.

Wolf, E., 'Die Rechtfertigungslehre als Mitte und Grenze reformatorischer Theologie', in *Peregrinatio* II: *Studien zur reformatorischen Theologie, zum Kirchenrecht und zur Sozialethik*. Munich: Kaiser Verlag, 1965, 11–21.

Wörter, F., *Die christliche Lehre über das Verhältnis von Gnade und Freiheit von den apostolischen Zeiten bis zu Augustinus*. 2 vols. Freiburg: Herder, 1855–60.

Wright, N. T., *The Climax of the Covenant: Christ and the Law in Pauline Theology*. Edinburgh: T. & T. Clark, 1991.

Xiberta, B., 'La causa meritoria de la justificación en las controversias pretridentinas'. *RET* 5 (1945), 87–106.

Yarnold, E. J., '*Duplex iustitia*: The Sixteenth Century and the Twentieth', in G. R. Evans (ed.), *Christian Authority*. Oxford: Oxford University Press, 1988, 204–23.

Yinger, K. L., *Paul, Judaism and Judgment according to Deeds*. Cambridge: Cambridge University Press, 1999.

Zahl, P. F. M., *Die Rechtfertigungslehre Ernst Käsemanns*. Stuttgart: Calwer Verlag, 1996.

Zimmermann, G., 'Calvins Auseinandersetzung mit Osianders Rechtfertigungslehre'. *KuD* 35 (1989), 236–56.

Zumkeller, A., 'Der Augustiner Angelus Dobelinus, erster Theologieprofessor der Erfurter Universität, über Gnade, Rechtfertigung und Verdienst'. *AnAug* 44 (1981), 69–147.

'Der Augustinertheologe Johannes Hiltalingen von Basel über Erbsünde, Gnade und Verdienst'. *AnAug* 43 (1980), 57–162.

Dionysius de Montina: Ein neuentdeckter Augustinentheologe des Spätmittelalters. Würzburg: Augustinus Verlag, 1948.

'Erbsünde, Gnade und Rechtfertigung im Verständnis der Erfurter Augustinertheologen des Spätmittelalters'. *ZKG* 92 (1981), 39–59.

'Hugolin von Orvieto über Prädestination, Rechtfertigung und Verdienst'. *Augustiniana* 4 (1954), 109–56; 5 (1955), 5–51.

'Hugolin von Orvieto über Urstand und Erbsünde'. *Augustiniana* 3 (1953), 35–62, 165–93; 4 (1954), 25–46.

'Johannes Klenkok O.S.A. im Kampf gegen den "Pelagianismus" seiner Zeit: Seine Lehre über Gnade, Rechtfertigung und Verdienst'. *RechAug* 13 (1978), 231–333.

'Die Lehre des Erfurter Augustinertheologen Johannes von Dorsten über Gnade, Rechtfertigung und Verdienst'. *ThPh* 53 (1978), 7–64, 127–219.

'Der Wiener Theologieprofessor Johannes von Retz und seine Lehre von Urstand, Erbsünde, Gnade und Verdienst'. *Augustiniana* 22 (1972), 118–84; 540–82.

Index